World Trade Organization
Dispute Settlement Decisions

Bernan's Annotated Reporter

Volume 2
Decisions Reported
February 26, 1997 – May 31, 1997

World Trade Organization
Dispute Settlement Decisions

Bernan's Annotated Reporter

Bernan Press
Lanham, Maryland, USA

Published 1998

Printed in the United States of America

Bernan Press
4611-F Assembly Drive
Lanham, MD 20706-4391
(800) 274-4447 (301) 459-2255
email: info@bernan.com

ISBN: 0-89059-105-9

PREFACE

The WORLD TRADE ORGANIZATION DISPUTE SETTLEMENT DECISIONS: BERNAN'S ANNOTATED REPORTER series is intended to provide the user with comprehensive and efficient access to the Decisions of the World Trade Organization's Dispute Settlement Body. Provided herein are the full text cases of all WTO Panels and of the Appellate Body.

Cases are set forth in chronological order, based on date of the decision being reported. They are reproduced in full text with footnotes from the original opinion. Reproductions are verbatim, with only minor formatting adjustments. References to the disputes may be limited to the common name (i.e. *Japan – Alcohol)*, or the Dispute Settlement reference (i.e. WT/DS8/R). Please note that endnotes in the original decisions have been converted to footnotes for easier reference. Additionally, the editor has added paragraph numbers (like those used in Panel Reports) to the Appellate Body decisions. Before each opinion, several additional features are offered. Each case has a front section which includes:

i) Title of case
ii) Parties
iii) Procedural history
iv) Summary of conclusions
v) Annotations
vi) Table of contents

The annotations recite significant legal determinations made by the Panel (or Appellate Body) in the course of its ruling. Each such annotation includes a paragraph reference, a principle, and a World Trade Organization source document. An example follows:

7.70 – 7.72 **Allocation of quotas** [GATT, Article XIII.2(d)]

On paragraphs 7.70 – 7.72 the user will find a ruling by the Panel (or Appellate Body) on quota allocation as regulated under the terms of GATT General Agreement, Article XIII.2(d). The principles used in reference to General Agreement provisions are based on the *GATT Guide to Law and Practice,* co-published by the World Trade Organization and Bernan Press.

Four tables follow the reported cases.

I. Overview of Dispute Settlement Activity
II. Countries Involved in Disputes
III. Treaty Provisions Interpreted
IV. BISD and Dispute References

The first two of these relate to dispute settlement activity generally under the Dispute Settlement Body. Table I provides an update of disputes which have been acted upon during the time period covered within this volume. Noted are requests for consultations, panel requests, establishment of panels, reports issued by the Panels and Appellate Body, adoption of those reports, and appeal of reports. Also noted are connections between complaints, where the same laws, regulations or government practices are being disputed by more than one Member. Table II shows the distribution of dispute activity to date by country.

The third and fourth tables refer to the cases reported in this volume. Table III indicates which World Trade Organization agreements have been interpreted by the Panels and Appellate Body in the cases within this volume. Paragraph references are again provided, with the number indicating the beginning of the analysis of the given provision. Table IV is a table of references within the reports to other WTO and GATT materials, particularly decisions, protocols, announcements and reports published in the Basic Instruments and Selected Documents (BISD), and dispute settlement references. Dispute settlement references include the WTO Dispute Settlement Decisions (WTO DSD) and other unadopted or unpublished reports noted within.

Lastly, each volume includes a topical index. The index also provides reference to the cases by paragraph number.

* * * * *

The goal of producing this series is to increase access to the World Trade Organization's Dispute Settlement System through the conveyance of its decisions in a comprehensive and accessible manner. Please submit any questions or remarks to the address on page iv, or by email to jpatton@bernan.com.

James J. Patton
Managing Editor
Bernan Press

TABLE OF CONTENTS

UNITED STATES – MEASURE AFFECTING IMPORTS OF WOVEN WOOL SHIRTS AND BLOUSES FROM INDIA

REPORT OF THE APPELLATE BODY
WT/DS33/AB/R

Appellant: India

Appellee: United States

Third Parties: None

Decided: April 25, 1997
Adopted: May 23, 1997

Procedural History

December 30, 1994 the United States requested consultations with India under paragraphs 19 and 20 of the Multifibre Arrangement (MFA).

April 18, 1995 the United States withdrew its previous request for consultations and requested consultations under Article 6 of the Agreement on Textiles and Clothing (ATC).

July 14, 1995 the United States notified India and the Textiles Monitoring Body (TMB) that a restraint would be applied.

September 15, 1995 the TMB completed its examination and found that actual threat of serious damage to the United States' domestic industry had been demonstrated (G/TMB/R/3).

October 16, 1995 India notified the TMB of its inability to conform with the recommendations of the TMB.

November 17, 1995 the TMB notified India that no additional recommendations could be offered (G/TMB/R/6).

March 14, 1996 India requested a panel under the Dispute Settlement Understanding (DSU).

April 18, 1996 the Dispute Settlement Body established a panel in WT/DS33.

February 24, 1997 India appealed.

Conclusions

- The Appellate Body upholds the legal findings and conclusions of the Panel brought on appeal by India as to burden of proof, scope of the TMB's review, and judicial economy.

Annotations

4.13 **Burden of proof** [ATC Agreement, Art. 6]

The Panel did not err in requiring the complainant, India, to put forward evidence and legal argument sufficient to demonstrate the transitional safeguard measure is inconsistent with Articles 2 and 6 of the ATC. The transitional safeguard mechanism established in Article 6 is a fundamental right of the signatories concerning textiles and clothing products during the transitional period.

6.3, 6.7 **Function of panels** [Dispute Settlement Understanding, Art. 11]

A Panel need only address those claims that must be addressed in order to resolve the matter at issue in a given dispute. Nothing in Article 11 of the DSU or in previous GATT practice requires a panel to examine all legal claims made by the complaining party. The Panel's decision not to review certain of India's legal bases having established that the measure in dispute was inconsistent with WTO obligations did not deny India any rights under the DSU.

UNITED STATES MEASURE AFFECTING IMPORTS OF WOVEN WOOL SHIRTS AND BLOUSES FROM INDIA

REPORT OF THE APPELLATE BODY
WT/DS33/AB/R

TABLE OF CONTENTS

I. INTRODUCTION

1.1 India appeals from certain issues of law and legal interpretations in the Panel Report, *United States - Measure Affecting Imports of Woven Wool Shirts and Blouses from India*, WT/DS33/R (the "Panel Report"). That Panel was established on 17 April 1996 to consider a complaint by India against the United States relating to a transitional safeguard restraint imposed on imports of woven wool shirts and blouses (category 440) from India.

1.2 The measure was imposed by the United States on 14 July 1995 after bilateral consultations with India in April and June 1995 did not result in a mutually-agreed solution. The restraint was effective as from 18 April 1995 for one year and was later extended through 17 April 1997. The United States took this transitional safeguard action pursuant to Article 6 of the *Agreement on Textiles and Clothing* (the "ATC"). As required by Article 6.10 of the ATC, the United States referred the matter to the Textiles Monitoring Body (the "TMB"), which concluded – and confirmed upon review – that the transitional safeguard action in this case was imposed in accordance with the requirements of the ATC. The TMB found that "actual threat of serious damage had been demonstrated" and that "this actual threat could be attributed to the sharp and substantial increase in imports from India."[1] At India's request, the Dispute Settlement Body (the "DSB") established a panel (the "Panel") to examine the legality of the United States' transitional safeguard measure.

1.3 After the release of the interim report of the Panel, the United States announced that it would withdraw the transitional safeguard measure, effective as of 22 November 1996, due to a steady decline in imports of woven wool shirts and blouses from India and the adjustment of the industry. Nevertheless, India requested that the Panel continue its work and produce a comprehensive report on the dispute. The Panel Report in *United States - Measure Affecting Imports of Woven Wool Shirts and Blouses from India* was circulated to the Members of the World Trade Organization (the "WTO") on 6 January 1997. The Panel Report contains the following conclusions and recommendations:

> 8.1 We conclude that the US restraint applied as of 18 April 1995 on imports of woven wool shirts and blouses, category 440, from India and its extensions violated the provisions of Articles 2 and 6 of the ATC. Since Article 3.8 of the DSU provides that "In cases where there is an infringement of the obligations assumed under a covered agreement, the action is considered *prima facie* to constitute a case of nullification and impairment", we conclude that the said US measure nullified and impaired the benefits of India under the WTO Agreement, in particular under the ATC. The Panel recommends that the Dispute Settlement Body make such a ruling.

1.4 On 24 February 1997, India notified the DSB[2] of its decision to appeal certain issues of law covered in the Panel Report and certain legal interpretations developed by the Panel, pursuant to Article 16.4 of the *Understanding on Rules and Procedures Governing the Settlement of Disputes* (the "DSU"), and filed a notice of appeal with the Appellate Body pursuant to Rule 20 of the *Working Procedures for Appellate Review* (the "Working Procedures"). Pursuant to Rule 21 of the Working Procedures, India filed an appellant's submission on 6 March 1997. At the request of the United States, pursuant to Rule 16(2) of the Working Procedures, the Appellate Body extended the time for the United States to file its appellee's submission to 24 March 1997. On that date, the United States filed its submission pursuant to Rule 22 of the Working Procedures.

1.5 The oral hearing provided for in Rule 27 of the Working Procedures was held on 7 April 1997. The participants presented their arguments and answered questions from the Division of the Appellate Body hearing the appeal.

---

[1] G/TMB/R/3, confirmed in G/TMB/R/6.

[2] WT/DS33/3, 24 February 1997.

II. ARGUMENTS OF THE PARTICIPANTS

A. India

2.1 India agrees with the overall conclusions of the Panel Report, but alleges that the Panel erred in law when making its findings on the burden of proof, on the TMB and on the issue of judicial economy.

1. *Burden of proof*

2.2 India notes that the Panel made statements on the burden of proof in its findings in paragraph 7.12 of the Panel Report as well as in its comments on the interim review in paragraph 6.7 of the Panel Report. India argues that both statements are incorrect, and furthermore, are contradictory. India asserts that the specific interim review comments at issue are part of the findings to be reviewed by the Appellate Body.

2.3 India asserts that the fact that India had initiated dispute settlement proceedings did not impose upon India the obligation to establish that the United States had violated Article 6 of the ATC, as the Panel stated in paragraph 7.12, nor the obligation to present a *prima facie* case to that effect, as the Panel stated in paragraph 6.7. According to India, the issue of the burden of proof is an issue of substantive law and must be answered solely on the basis of the substantive law of the WTO in the light of the customary rules of interpretation of public international law. India maintains that the question of whether it is up to a particular Member to demonstrate an inconsistency with the *Marrakesh Agreement Establishing the World Trade Organization*[3] (the "WTO Agreement") does not depend on whether the Member is a complaining or a respondent party in the proceedings in which the inconsistency is at issue, but rather on the nature of the provision invoked. In India's view, the rules on the burden of proof determine which party in the dispute must make a legal claim and supply the evidence; the function of the rules is to ensure that a dispute can be settled even if the legal claims and factual information before the panel are incomplete. As India reads it, according to the Panel's comments on the interim review, both parties bear a burden of proof of different degrees.

2.4 Moreover, India argues that the Panel's finding on the distribution of the burden of proof is inconsistent with the finding on the same issue by the concurrent WTO panel in *United States - Restrictions on Imports of Cotton and Man-made Fibre Underwear*.[4] India points to that panel's statement that the principle that the party invoking the exception carries the burden of proof is well-established in the GATT 1947 practice.[5] Thus, India argues that in making its finding on burden of proof in this case, the Panel failed to take into account the customary practice of the CONTRACTING PARTIES under the GATT 1947. India maintains that the ATC is an exception to the GATT 1994 because it authorizes the temporary maintenance of measures inconsistent with Articles XI and XIII of the GATT 1994. India argues that within that temporary and exceptional regime deviating from basic GATT principles, Article 6 of the ATC establishes an exception from the general principles of trade in textiles and clothing that are set out in Article 2.4 of the ATC by authorizing the introduction of new and discriminatory quantitative restraints within the framework of what Article 6.1 of the ATC describes as "a specific transitional safeguard mechanism" that "should be applied as sparingly as possible." India concludes that the principles applied to the exceptions in the GATT 1994, therefore, apply with even greater force to Article 6 of the ATC. In India's view, the Panel's finding on burden of proof changes the operation of the substantive requirements under Article 6 of the ATC, upsetting the negotiated balance of interests between importing and exporting Members under the ATC.

---

[3] Done at Marrakesh, Morocco, 15 April 1994.

[4] Adopted 25 February 1997, WT/DS24/R, para. 7.16.

[5] India cites seven GATT 1947 panel reports to demonstrate that there has been a consistently applied and well-established practice that the party invoking an exception bears the burden of proof.

2. *The TMB*

2.5 India asserts that the Panel's finding in paragraph 7.20 of the Panel Report that the TMB, when examining a transitional safeguard measure in accordance with Article 6.10 of the ATC, "is not limited to the initial information submitted by the importing Member as parties may submit additional and other information in support of their positions, which, we understand, may relate to subsequent events,"[6] was requested neither by India nor by the United States. India contends that this finding attributes to the TMB discretionary powers that neither of the parties to the dispute suggested the TMB had.

2.6 India argues that the ATC and the DSU accord exporting Members three important procedural rights: (i) the right to hold consultations on the proposed transitional safeguard action on the basis of specific and factual information; (ii) the right to a review of a transitional safeguard action by the TMB; and (iii) the right to refer the matter to the DSB for examination by a panel. In India's view, the Panel's finding denies Members the benefit of the first two of these three rights.

2.7 India submits that the Panel bases its finding on the erroneous notion that the ATC and the DSU establish a "two-track process" for the review of transitional safeguard actions, and that therefore the matter on which the TMB makes a recommendation and the matter submitted to the DSB can be different. In India's view, the ATC and the DSU establish a two-stage procedure under which the same measure is first submitted to the TMB and, if its recommendations are not acceptable, to the DSB. India stresses that the TMB review is a substitute for consultations normally held before the request for the establishment of a panel, and India argues that information that was not available at the time when the safeguard determination was made is not information that is "relevant" in the TMB's review of that determination under Article 6.10 of the ATC.

2.8 India further asserts that the task of the TMB is to deal with disputes arising from measures actually taken and to carry out those functions that are specifically assigned to it by the ATC. According to India, the expression of views on transitional safeguard actions that have not yet been taken is not part of this task. India maintains that by attributing to the TMB this additional competence, even when the Members did not agree to seek views on that matter, the Panel attributed to the TMB the authority to conciliate without the consent of the Members concerned, which is not consistent with the DSU.

2.9 Finally, India asserts that a comparison of the provisions of the ATC on the TMB and the provisions of the Multi-Fibre Arrangement (the "MFA") on the Textiles Surveillance Body (the "TSB"), reveals that the TMB, in contrast to the TSB under the MFA, has a well-defined, limited function of a legal nature.

2.10 In response to the argument by the United States that the Panel's statement on the role of the TMB is merely *obiter dicta* on which the Appellate Body need not rule, India argues that Articles 17.6, 17.12 and 17.13 of the DSU do not distinguish between *dicta* and findings. According to India, the right to appellate review would be seriously impaired if panels could express legal opinions on any point other than the issues involved in the case before them and Members of the WTO could not seek an appellate review of those opinions.

3. *Judicial economy*

2.11 India points out that the Panel did not make findings on two of the four issues India submitted to the Panel for examination: namely, whether the United States' failure to specify in its request for consultations whether the proposed transitional safeguard action related to serious damage or the actual threat of serious damage was consistent with Article 6 of the ATC; and whether the retroactive application by the United States of its transitional safeguard action was consistent with Article 2 of the ATC.

---

[6] Panel Report, para. 7.20.

2.12 India argues that, within the framework of the ATC, the determination, the request for consultations on a proposed transitional safeguard action and the actual application of the transitional safeguard action must be regarded as distinct measures that can be contested separately. India states that it contested these measures separately not for the purpose of making the panel address theoretical issues, but rather out of a practical concern relating to the implementation of the Panel's recommendations by the United States. India argues that by defining the three factually and legally distinct measures as a single, "contested measure", the Panel denied India the right to an objective assessment of the request for consultations and the application of the transitional safeguard action in accordance with Article 11 of the DSU.[7] India insists that it is not arguing that panels have to address in all instances all legal claims made by the parties. India acknowledges that there are many instances in which a finding on one matter resolves the dispute on another matter. In the present case, however, India maintains that the Panel's findings did not resolve the dispute on the two matters referred to above.

2.13 India asserts that the Panel failed to distinguish the contested "measure" from the matter to be examined. India explains that any dispute brought by a WTO Member under Article XXIII:1(a) of the GATT 1994 concerns an act or omission of another Member, that is a "measure". India notes that the dispute settlement procedures of the WTO begin with consultations on a specific measure and end with a recommendation on that measure. However, India maintains that the matter the panel must examine in accordance with Articles 6, 7 and 11 of the DSU is not the measure by itself, but rather the legal claims which the parties to the dispute make in connection with the measure. India concludes that the function assigned to a panel under Article 11 of the DSU is, thus, to examine all legal claims made relating to all measures at issue. India concludes that by defining its task solely in terms of the measure to be brought into conformity with the ATC, the Panel curtailed India's right to an objective assessment of all the legal claims it had made in its request for a panel. India also observes that while a panel must examine all claims made by the parties to the dispute and cannot go beyond these claims, it need not examine all arguments of the parties and can develop its own arguments.

2.14 India asserts that the panels established under the GATT 1947 did not apply the concept of judicial economy as suggested by the Panel in the Panel Report. India contends that those previous panels did not systematically end their legal analysis as soon as they had found the contested measure to be inconsistent with the GATT 1947, but instead determined the scope of their examination in the light of the objectives and legal interests of the parties to the dispute. India argues that had the Panel in this case been guided by the customary practice of the CONTRACTING PARTIES to the GATT 1947, it would have determined the scope of its examination in the light of India's expressed legal interest in findings on which the Panel failed to rule. Because the Panel in this case was not guided by this customary practice, India argues that matters that could be resolved in one proceeding will have to be resolved instead in multiple proceedings if future panels apply this Panel's concept of judicial economy.

2.15 Therefore, India submits that the Panel's application of the notion of judicial economy undermines the objectives of the DSU, which are described in Article 3.2 of the DSU and in India's view, include both dispute resolution as well as dispute prevention. India maintains that these objectives can only be achieved if panels resolve both the dispute over the particular contested measure and the issues of interpretation arising from all legal claims made in connection with that measure.

B. United States

2.16 With respect to each of the three issues raised in this appeal, the United States argues that the Panel acted correctly. The United States asks the Appellate Body to affirm the Panel Report.

---

[7] India also asserts that the question of what constitutes the "measure" that may be maintained in accordance with Article 6.12 of the ATC for a period of up to three years and the question of what constitutes "the specific measures at issue" within the meaning of Article 6 of the DSU are obviously completely different issues.

1. Burden of proof

2.17 The United States argues that the Panel properly addressed the issue of burden of proof in paragraphs 6.7 and 7.12 of the Panel Report. Unlike India, the United States does not see any contradiction between the Panel's statements in paragraphs 6.7 and 7.12 of the Panel Report, and considers paragraph 6.7 to be the final interpretative word on this issue by the Panel. As the United States sees it, the Panel found, consistently with the DSU, that both India and the United States had differing burdens to present factual and legal arguments: first, as the complaining party, India had the initial burden of establishing "a *prima facie* case of violation of the ATC, namely, that the restrictions imposed by the United States did not respect the provisions of Article 2.4 and 6 of the ATC;" then, after India had established a *prima facie* case, the United States had the burden "to convince the Panel that, at the time of its determination, it had respected the requirements of Article 6 of the ATC."

2.18 The United States argues that the Panel did not assign any burden of proof, in the sense of burden of persuasion, to either India or the United States. The United States contends that India distorts the findings of the Panel when it claims that the Panel held that India had the ultimate burden of persuasion. According to the United States, the Panel merely required India to meet the burden of going forward with the evidence. The United States argues that it is clear from the ordinary meaning of Articles 3.8, 6.2 and paragraph 5 of the working procedures for panels in Appendix 3 of the DSU that India had the obligation to initiate and commence the legal and factual issues, not only at the stage of a request for a panel, but also at the first substantive meeting of the parties. In other words, India had to make a *prima facie* demonstration that the United States' measure violated provisions of the ATC. The United States stresses that, in fact, India did so successfully in the present case.

2.19 The United States argues that India incorrectly asserts that there is a "consistently applied" and "well-established" GATT practice that the party invoking an exception carries the burden of proof of justifying the use of the exception. According to the United States, the panel reports cited by India in its appellant's submission do not reflect GATT practice justifying India's arguments that: (1) everything other than India's "core rules" are exceptions; (2) all "exceptions" are required to be construed narrowly; and (3) the complaining party has no burden to demonstrate that a so-called "exception" was improperly invoked. The United States maintains that the reports cited are either distinguishable, irrelevant, or contradicted by other reports, and that only in a few special situations involving the general exceptions of the GATT 1994 and other isolated exceptions of the GATT 1994 have panels consistently assigned the ultimate burden of persuasion to a particular party.

2.20 According to the United States, in disputes involving the vast majority of GATT provisions, it is well-established practice that the complaining party has the burden of making a *prima facie* case. Furthermore, the United States argues that India's legal taxonomy is overly simplistic in that it treats all so-called "exceptions" identically and fails to consider the reasons why such so-called "exceptions" exist. The United States argues that India also ignores the fact that, in addition to "obligations", WTO Member also have "rights", and that many, if not most, of what would be considered "exceptions" under India's taxonomy are more properly viewed as "rights". The United States argues that India's approach results in a "crude" method of treaty interpretation that is at odds with what the Appellate Body said in *United States - Standards for Reformulated and Conventional Gasoline*, in the sense that India's treatment of so-called "exceptions" is not case-by-case, but instead is a simplistic, "one-size-fits-all" mechanical approach to treaty interpretation.[8]

---

[8] Referring to the Appellate Body Report in *United States - Standards for Reformulated and Conventional Gasoline*, AB-1996-1, adopted 20 May 1996, WT/DS2/9, p. 19, the United States argues that India's approach ignores the "object and purpose" of provisions, it provides for no "scrutiny of the factual and legal context in a given dispute" and it disregards "the words actually used by WTO Members themselves to express their intent and purpose."

2.21 Finally, the United States argues that India's theory, if accepted, would alter significantly the rights and obligations of WTO Members with respect to a multitude of provisions of the GATT 1994 and other WTO agreements.[9]

2.22 Assuming *arguendo* that India correctly asserts that there is a "consistently applied" and "well-established" GATT practice that the party invoking an exception carries the burden of proof, the United States argues that Article 6 of the ATC is not such an exception. The non-exceptional nature of Article 6 is reflected in Article 2.4 of the ATC, which states two very general rules, namely, that textile restrictions existing before the ATC came into force would be grandfathered, and that new restrictions may be introduced only in accordance with the provisions of the ATC and other relevant provisions of the GATT 1994. The United States contends that the term "except" used in Article 2.4 of the ATC is in this context a synonym for "only", "provided that", or "unless" and cannot be read as an indication that Article 6 of the ATC is an exception. The United States adds as well that the text, context and object of Article 6 of the ATC support the conclusion that Article 6 is not a provision that compels a shifting of the burden of proof. The United States argues that for importing countries, Article 6 constituted a critical *quid pro quo* for the acceptance of the ATC's phase-out of pre-existing quotas and integration of textiles and clothing trade into the multilateral trading system. The United States asserts that as an integral ATC provision, the transitional safeguard mechanism is on an equal footing with the other provisions of the ATC, such as the integration schedule of Article 2. Therefore, the United States concludes, the phrase "should be applied as sparingly as possible" in Article 6.1 of the ATC does not provide support for the notion that Article 6 is an exceptional provision; rather, that phrase merely reminds Members not to abuse their right to use temporary, transitional safeguard measures.[10] The United States asserts that the treatment of Article 6 of the ATC as an exception would upset the carefully negotiated balance of rights and obligations of Article 6.[11]

2. *The TMB*

2.23 The United States argues that the Panel's discussion of the TMB was mere *obiter dicta* which had no effect on the outcome of the case, and that it is difficult to see how India's procedural rights under the ATC have been denied in any way by this *dicta*. The United States considers that the appropriate manner of "addressing" this Panel's *dicta* on an issue raised by neither of the parties would be for the Appellate Body simply to declare this aspect of the report to be *dicta* and not to offer any additional *dicta* of its own with respect to the role of the TMB.

2.24 Furthermore, the United States observes that nothing in the text of the ATC supports India's assertion that the information considered by the TMB in its examination of the transitional safeguard action must be limited to the information used by the importing Member in making its determination to take the transitional safeguard action. According to the United States, Article 6.10 of the ATC, and in particular the phrase, "any other relevant information", clearly contemplates the consideration of information that is not the same as that used by the importing Member at the time of the determination to take the action. The United States also argues that nothing in the ATC supports India's assertion that the TMB, in contrast to the TSB, has a well-defined, limited function of a legal nature.

---

[9] The United asserted that under India's theory, all of the WTO provisions providing special and differential treatment for developing countries would be labelled as exceptions and that, therefore, the burden of persuasion would be on the developing country seeking to rely on one of these provisions.

[10] The United States notes that the Appellate Body in *United States - Restrictions on Imports of Cotton and Man-made Fibre Underwear*, AB-1996-3, adopted 25 February 1997, WT/DS24/AB/R, p. 15, did not interpret Article 6 of the ATC either narrowly or broadly and indicated that the "as sparingly as possible" language could not be examined in isolation.

[11] The United States notes that the Appellate Body in *United States - Restrictions on Imports of Cotton and Man-made Fibre Underwear*, did not "loosen up the carefully negotiated language of Article 6.10, which reflect an equally carefully drawn balance of rights and obligations of Members ...".

3. *Judicial economy*

2.25 The United States argues that the Panel did not err by declining to rule on all claims made by India. According to the United States, nothing in the DSU or elsewhere in the WTO Agreement requires a panel to rule on every claim raised by a party. The United States argues that the text of Article 11 of the DSU does not impose such obligation. The United States cites Article 3.7 of the DSU for the proposition that the primary function of the dispute settlement system is to resolve disputes by achieving the withdrawal of WTO-inconsistent measures, not to render interpretations or to generate opinions on any issue. The United States notes that Article IX of the WTO Agreement provides a mechanism for obtaining authoritative interpretations, as recognized in Article 3.9 of the DSU.[12] The United States does not accept India's argument that WTO dispute settlement has the "twin objective" of "dispute resolution" and "dispute prevention". According to the United States, this argument is at odds with Articles 3.7 and 3.9 of the DSU. The United States maintains that "dispute prevention" is, at most, a subsidiary function under the DSU, and one which does not translate into a legal requirement that a panel address every claim raised by a party.

2.26 With respect to India's argument that there are three "measures", rather than one, at issue in this case,[13] the United States observes that it is clear from Article 6.12 of the ATC that the "measure" is in fact the transitional safeguard action, not the procedures leading up to the imposition of the transitional safeguard action. In the opinion of the United States, India's interpretation of "measure" constitutes the sort of arbitrary subdivision of a measure that the Appellate Body criticized in *United States - Standards for Reformulated and Conventional Gasoline*. The United States also argues that India's belated identification of three measures, rather than one measure, is nothing more than a *post hoc* argument presented for the first time in this appeal.

2.27 The United States points out that in addition to being consistent with the text of the DSU, the Panel's decision to refrain from ruling on certain issues raised by India was consistent with the well-established practice of the GATT 1947 panels, which frequently declined to address claims in situations where the resolution of a claim was unnecessary for the purpose of resolving a dispute. The United States asserts that this practice has been continued under the DSU and the WTO Agreement by both WTO panels and the Appellate Body.

2.28 The United States also suggests that, as an alternative to finding that the Panel did not err when it declined to make findings on certain issues, the Appellate Body, as it did in *Brazil - Measures Affecting Desiccated Coconut*, could simply address the issue by deciding that it is unnecessary to resolve the procedural issue raised by India since it will have absolutely no effect on the previous conclusion by the Panel that the transitional safeguard measure imposed by the United States was inconsistent with the ATC.

2.29 Finally, the United States observes that the practice of panels and the Appellate Body in refraining from making findings that are unnecessary to the resolution of disputes has been described as being based on concerns of judicial economy. The United States argues that to the extent such concerns were valid under the pre-WTO regime, they are, in view of the number of matters now referred to the DSB, even more valid today. In order to preserve the integrity of the WTO system in general, and the dispute settlement mechanism in particular, the United States argues that both panels and the Appellate Body should focus only on those claims that must be addressed to resolve a dispute.

---

[12] The United States refers in this context to the Appellate Body Report in *Japan - Taxes on Alcoholic Beverages*, AB-1996-2, adopted 1 November 1996, WT/DS8/AB/R, WT/DS10/AB/R, WT/DS11/AB/R, pp. 13-15.

[13] India argues that not only the United States' determination, but also the United States' request for consultations and the backdating of the United States' restraint each constitute a distinct "measure" that can be contested separately.

III. ISSUES RAISED IN THIS APPEAL

3.1 This appeal raises the following legal issues:

(a) Whether a party claiming that a transitional safeguard action violates Article 6 of the ATC has the burden of demonstrating that there has been an infringement of the obligations assumed under the ATC;

(b) Whether the TMB is limited in its examination of a transitional safeguard action pursuant to Article 6.10 of the ATC to the evidence used by the importing Member in making its determination to take such action, or may also consider developments and information subsequent to that determination; and

(c) Whether, under Article 11 of the DSU, a complaining party is entitled to a finding on all of the legal claims it makes to a panel relating to the measure in dispute.

IV. BURDEN OF PROOF

4.1 On the issue of burden of proof, the Panel concluded the following at paragraph 7.12 of the "Findings" section of the Panel Report:

> The parties seem to have addressed two different aspects of what one might call the "burden of proof" issue. We believe that a distinction should be made. First, we consider the question of which party bears the burden of proof before the Panel. Since India is the party that initiated the dispute settlement proceedings, we consider that it is for India to put forward factual and legal arguments in order to establish that the US restriction was inconsistent with Article 2 of the ATC and that the US determination for a safeguard action was inconsistent with the provisions of Article 6 of the ATC. Second, we consider the question of what the importing Member must demonstrate at the time of its determination. Concerning the substantive obligations under Article 6 of the ATC, it is clear from the wording of Article 6.2 and 6.3 of the ATC that, in its determination of the need for the proposed restraint, the United States had the obligation to demonstrate that it had complied with the relevant conditions of application of Article 6.2 and 6.3 of the ATC.

4.2 The Panel illuminated this finding at paragraph 6.7 in the "Interim Review" section of the Panel Report:

> Concerning India's comment about burden of proof, it was for India to submit a *prima facie* case of violation of the ATC, namely, that the restriction imposed by the United States did not respect the provisions of Articles 2.4 and 6 of the ATC. It was then for the United States to convince the Panel that, at the time of its determination, it had respected the requirements of Article 6 of the ATC.

4.3 Although the Panel's finding at paragraph 7.12 and comments on interim review at paragraph 6.7 of the Panel Report are not a model of clarity, we do not believe the Panel erred in law. We agree with the Panel that it was up to India to present evidence and argument sufficient to establish a presumption that the transitional safeguard determination made by the United States was inconsistent with its obligations under Article 6 of the ATC. With this presumption thus established, it was then up to the United States to bring evidence and argument to rebut the presumption.

4.4 The foundation of dispute settlement under Article XXIII of the GATT 1994 is the assurance to Members of the benefits accruing directly or indirectly to them under the GATT 1994. This was true as well of dispute settlement under the GATT 1947. If any Member should consider that its benefits are nullified or impaired as the result of circumstances set out in Article XXIII, then dispute settlement is available. With respect to complaints of violation of obligations pursuant to Article XXIII:1(a) of the GATT 1994, Article 3.8 of the DSU codifies previous GATT 1947 practice:

> In cases where there is an infringement of the obligations assumed under a covered agreement, the action is considered *prima facie* to constitute a case of nullification or impairment. This means that there is normally a presumption that a breach of the rules has an adverse impact on other Members parties to that covered agreement, and in such cases, it shall be up to the Member against whom the complaint has been brought to rebut the charge.

4.5 Article 3.8 of the DSU provides that in cases where there is an infringement of the obligations assumed under a covered agreement – that is, in cases where a violation is established – there is a presumption of nullification or impairment. Article 3.8 then goes on to explain that "the Member against whom the complaint has been brought" must rebut this presumption. However, the issue in this case is not what happens after a violation is established; the issue in this case is which party must first show that there is, or is not, a violation. More specifically, the issue in this case is which party has the burden of demonstrating that there has, or has not been, an infringement of the obligations assumed under Article 6 of the ATC.[14]

4.6 In addressing this issue, we find it difficult, indeed, to see how any system of judicial settlement could work if it incorporated the proposition that the mere assertion of a claim might amount to proof. It is, thus, hardly surprising that various international tribunals, including the International Court of Justice, have generally and consistently accepted and applied the rule that the party who asserts a fact, whether the claimant or the respondent, is responsible for providing proof thereof.[15] Also, it is a generally-accepted canon of evidence in civil law, common law and, in fact, most jurisdictions, that the burden of proof rests upon the party, whether complaining or defending, who asserts the affirmative of a particular claim or defence. If that party adduces evidence sufficient to raise a presumption that what is claimed is true, the burden then shifts to the other party, who will fail unless it adduces sufficient evidence to rebut the presumption.[16]

4.7 In the context of the GATT 1994 and the WTO Agreement, precisely how much and precisely what kind of evidence will be required to establish such a presumption will necessarily vary from measure to measure, provision to provision, and case to case.

4.8 A number of GATT 1947 panel reports contain language supporting the proposition that the burden of establishing a violation under Article XXIII:1(a) of the GATT 1947 was on the complaining party. As early as 1952, in *Treatment by Germany of Imports of Sardines*, concerning a complaint by Norway, the panel clearly put

[14] Article 8.10, last sentence, of the ATC, allows a Member to invoke Article XXIII of the GATT 1994.

[15] M. Kazazi, *Burden of Proof and Related Issues: A Study on Evidence Before International Tribunals* (Kluwer Law International, 1996), p. 117.

[16] See M.N. Howard, P. Crane and D.A. Hochberg, *Phipson on Evidence*, 14th ed. (Sweet & Maxwell, 1990), p. 52: "The burden of proof rests upon the party, whether plaintiff or defendant, who substantially asserts the affirmative of the issue." See also L. Rutherford and S. Bone (eds.), *Osborne's Concise Law Dictionary*, 8th ed. (Sweet & Maxwell, 1993), p. 266; Earl Jowitt and C. Walsh, *Jowitt's Dictionary of English Law*, 2nd ed. by J. Burke (Sweet & Maxwell, 1977), Vol. 1, p. 263; L.B. Curzon, *A Directory of Law*, 2nd ed. (Macdonald and Evans, 1983), p. 47; Art. 9, Nouveau Code de Procédure Civile; J. Carbonnier, *Droit Civil*, Introduction, 20th ed. (Presses Universitaires de France, 1991), p. 320; J. Chevalier and L. Bach, *Droit Civil*, 12th ed. (Sirey, 1995), Vol. 1, p. 101; R. Guillien and J. Vincent, *Termes juridiques*, 10th ed. (Dalloz, 1995), p. 384; O. Samyn, P. Simonetta and C. Sogno, *Dictionnaire des Termes Juridiques* (Editions de Vecchi, 1986), p. 250; J. González Pérez, *Manual de Derecho Procesal Administrativo*, 2nd ed. (Editorial Civitas, 1992), p. 311; C.M. Bianca, S. Patti and G. Patti, *Lessico di Diritto Civile* (Giuffré Editore, 1991), p. 550; F. Galgano, *Diritto Privato*, 8th ed. (Casa Editrice Dott. Antonio Milani, 1994), p. 873; and A. Trabucchi, *Istituzioni di Diritto Civile* (Casa Editrice Dott. Antonio Milani, 1991), p. 210.

the burden of establishing a violation of the GATT 1947 obligations at issue on the complaining party, when it concluded:

> The examination of the evidence submitted led the Panel to the conclusion that no sufficient evidence had been presented to show that the German Government had failed to carry out its obligations under Article I:1 and Article XIII:1.[17]

4.9 In 1978, in *EEC - Measures on Animal Feed Proteins*, concerning a complaint by the United States, the panel made it equally clear that the burden of proof in that case was on the complaining party. In the final paragraph of that panel report, the panel stated:

> Having heard no evidence that either the purchasing obligation, the security deposit or the protein certificate discriminated against imports of "like products" from any contracting party, the Panel concluded that the EEC measures were not inconsistent with the EEC obligations under Article I:1.[18]

4.10 Two recent panel reports under the GATT 1947 which follow this approach are the 1992 report in *Canada - Import, Distribution and Sale of Certain Alcoholic Drinks by Provincial Marketing Agencies*[19] and the 1994 report in *United States - Measures Affecting the Importation, Internal Sale and Use of Tobacco*.[20] In the first case, the United States claimed that Canada had not fully eliminated the listing and delisting practices that a prior GATT panel report had found to be inconsistent with Article XI of the GATT 1947. The panel concluded, however, that with the exception of the listing and delisting practices of the province of Ontario, the United States had not substantiated its claim that Canada still maintained listing and delisting practices inconsistent with Article XI of the GATT 1947. In the second case, the complainants claimed, *inter alia*, that the penalty provisions of the Domestic Marketing Assessment legislation enacted by the United States were separate taxes or charges within the meaning of Article III:2 of the GATT 1947, and that Section 1106(c) of the 1993 Budget Act of the United States, mandated action inconsistent with Article VIII:1(a) of the GATT 1947. With regard to both claims, the panel concluded that the evidence submitted to it did not support the complainants' claims of inconsistency with the GATT 1947 obligations involved.

4.11 India has argued that it is "customary GATT practice" that the party invoking a provision which is identified as an exception must offer proof that the conditions set out in that provision are met. We acknowledge that several GATT 1947 and WTO panels have required such proof of a party invoking a defence, such as those found in Article XX[21] or Article XI:2(c)(i)[22], to a claim of violation of a GATT obligation, such as those found in Articles I:1, II:1, III or XI:1. Articles XX and XI:(2)(c)(i) are limited exceptions from obligations under certain other provisions of the GATT 1994, not positive rules establishing obligations in themselves. They are in the

---

[17] Adopted 31 October 1952, BISD 1S/53, para. 15. See also the report of the Working Party in *The Australian Subsidy on Ammonium Sulphate*, adopted 3 April 1950, BISD Vol. II/188, para. 11.

[18] Adopted 14 March 1978, BISD 25S/49, para. 4.21. See also *European Communities - Refunds on Exports of Sugar, Complaint by Brazil*, adopted 10 November 1980, BISD 27S/69, para. (e) of the Conclusions; *Canada, Administration of the Foreign Investment Review Act*, adopted 7 February 1984, BISD 30S/140, para. 5.13; and *Japan - Tariff on Import of Spruce, Pine, Fir (SPF) Dimension Lumber*, adopted 19 July 1989, BISD 36S/167, para. 10.

[19] Adopted 18 February 1992, BISD 39S/27, paras. 5.2-5.3.

[20] Adopted 4 October 1994, DS44/R, paras. 82 and 124.

[21] *Canada - Administration of Foreign Investment Review Act*, adopted 7 February 1984, BISD 30S/140, para. 5.20; *United States - Section 337 of the Tariff Act of 1930*, adopted 7 November 1989, BISD 36S/345, para. 5.27; *United States - Measures Affecting Alcoholic and Malt Beverages*, adopted 19 June 1992, BISD 39S/206, paras. 5.43 and 5.52; and Panel Report, *United States - Standards for Reformulated and Conventional Gasoline*, as modified by the Appellate Body Report, AB-1996-1, adopted 20 May 1996, WT/DS2/9, para. 6.20.

[22] *Japan - Restrictions on Imports of Certain Agricultural Products*, adopted 22 March 1988, BISD 35S/163, para. 5.1.3.7; *EEC - Restrictions on Imports of Dessert Apples*, Complaint by Chile, adopted 22 June 1989, BISD 36S/93, para. 12:3; and *Canada - Import Restrictions on Ice Cream and Yoghurt*, adopted 5 December 1989, BISD 36S/68, para. 59.

nature of affirmative defences. It is only reasonable that the burden of establishing such a defence should rest on the party asserting it.[23]

4.12 We do not believe that these particular previous GATT 1947 panel reports are relevant in this case. This case concerns Article 6 of the ATC. The ATC is a transitional arrangement that, by its own terms, will terminate when trade in textiles and clothing is fully integrated into the multilateral trading system. Article 6 of the ATC is an integral part of the transitional arrangement manifested in the ATC and should be interpreted accordingly. As the Appellate Body observed in *United States - Restrictions on Imports of Cotton and Man-made Fibre Underwear* with respect to Article 6.10 of the ATC, we believe Article 6 is "carefully negotiated language ... which reflects an equally carefully drawn balance of rights and obligations of Members ... ."[24] That balance must be respected.

4.13 The transitional safeguard mechanism provided in Article 6 of the ATC is a fundamental part of the rights and obligations of WTO Members concerning non-integrated textile and clothing products covered by the ATC during the transitional period. Consequently, a party claiming a violation of a provision of the WTO Agreement by another Member must assert and prove its claim. In this case, India claimed a violation by the United States of Article 6 of the ATC. We agree with the Panel that it, therefore, was up to India to put forward evidence and legal argument sufficient to demonstrate that the transitional safeguard action by the United States was inconsistent with the obligations assumed by the United States under Articles 2 and 6 of the ATC. India did so in this case. And, with India having done so, the onus then shifted to the United States to bring forward evidence and argument to disprove the claim. This, the United States was not able to do and, therefore, the Panel found that the transitional safeguard action by the United States "violated the provisions of Articles 2 and 6 of the ATC."[25]

4.14 In our view, the Panel did not err on this issue in this case.

V. THE TMB

5.1 India appealed the following statement relating to Article 6.10 of the ATC at paragraph 7.20 of the Panel Report:

> During the review process, the TMB is not limited to the initial information submitted by the importing Member as parties may submit additional and other information in support of their positions, which, *we understand*, may relate to subsequent events. (emphasis added)

5.2 In our view, this statement by the Panel is purely a descriptive and gratuitous comment providing background concerning the Panel's understanding of how the TMB functions. We do not consider this comment by the Panel to be "a legal finding or conclusion" which the Appellate Body "may uphold, modify or reverse."[26]

---

[23] Furthermore, there are a few cases that are similar in that the defending party invoked, as a defence, certain provisions and the panel explicitly required the defending party to demonstrate the applicability of the provision it was asserting. See, for example, *United States - Customs User Fee*, adopted 2 February 1988, BISD 35S/245, para. 98, concerning Article II:2 of the GATT 1947; *Canada - Import, Distribution and Sale of Certain Alcoholic Drinks by Provincial Marketing Agencies*, adopted 22 March 1988, BISD 35S/37, para 4.34, concerning Article XXIV:12 of the GATT 1947; and *United States - Measures Affecting Alcoholic and Malt Beverages*, adopted 19 June 1992, BISD 39S/206, para. 5.44, concerning the Protocol of Provisional Application.

[24] AB-1996-3, adopted 25 February 1997, WT/DS24/AB/R, p. 15.

[25] Panel Report, para. 8.1.

[26] Within the meaning of Article 17.13 of the DSU.

VI. JUDICIAL ECONOMY

6.1 With respect to the issue of whether Article 11 of the DSU entitles a complaining party to a finding on each of the legal claims it makes to a panel, the Panel stated in paragraph 6.6 of the Panel Report:

> Concerning India's argument that Article 11 of the DSU entitles India to a finding on each of the issues it raised, we disagree and refer to the consistent GATT panel practice of judicial economy. India is entitled to have the dispute over the contested "measure" resolved by the Panel, and if we judge that the specific matter in dispute can be resolved by addressing only some of the arguments raised by the complaining party, we can do so. We, therefore, decide to address only the legal issues we think are needed in order to make such findings as will assist the DSB in making recommendations or in giving rulings in respect of this dispute.

6.2 The function of panels is expressly defined in Article 11 of the DSU, which reads as follows:

> The function of panels is to assist the DSB in discharging its responsibilities under this Understanding and the covered agreements. Accordingly, a panel should make an objective assessment of the matter before it, including an objective assessment of the facts of the case and the applicability of and conformity with the relevant covered agreements, and *make such other findings as will assist the DSB* in making the recommendations or in giving the rulings provided for in the covered agreements ... (emphasis added).

6.3 Nothing in this provision or in previous GATT practice requires a panel to examine all legal claims made by the complaining party. Previous GATT 1947 and WTO panels have frequently addressed only those issues that such panels considered necessary for the resolution of the matter between the parties, and have declined to decide other issues. Thus, if a panel found that a measure was inconsistent with a particular provision of the GATT 1947, it generally did not go on to examine whether the measure was also inconsistent with other GATT provisions that a complaining party may have argued were violated.[27] In recent WTO practice, panels likewise have refrained from examining each and every claim made by the complaining party and have made findings only on those claims that such panels concluded were necessary to resolve the particular matter.[28]

6.4 Although a few GATT 1947 and WTO panels did make broader rulings, by considering and deciding issues that were not absolutely necessary to dispose of the particular dispute, there is nothing anywhere in the DSU that requires panels to do so.[29]

---

[27] See, for example, *EEC - Quantitative Restrictions Against Imports of Certain Products from Hong Kong*, adopted 12 July 1983, BISD 30S/129, para. 33; *Canada - Administration of the Foreign Investment Review Act*, adopted 7 February 1984, BISD 30S/140, para. 5.16; *United States - Imports of Sugar from Nicaragua*, adopted 13 March 1984, BISD 31S/67, paras. 4.5-4.6; *United States - Manufacturing Clause*, adopted 15/16 May 1984, BISD 31S/74, para. 40; *Japan - Measures on Imports of Leather*, adopted 15/16 May 1984, BISD 31S/94, para. 57; *Japan - Trade in Semi-Conductors*, adopted 4 May 1988, BISD 35S/116, para. 122; *Japan - Restrictions on Imports of Certain Agricultural Products*, adopted 22 March 1988, BISD 35S/163, para. 5.4.2; *EEC - Regulations on Imports of Parts and Components*, adopted 16 May 1990, BISD 37S/132, paras. 5.10, 5.22, and 5.27; *Canada - Import, Distribution and Sale of Certain Alcoholic Drinks by Provincial Marketing Agencies*, adopted 22 March 1988, BISD 35S/37, para. 5.6; and *United States - Denial of Most-Favoured-Nation Treatment as to Non-Rubber Footwear from Brazil*, adopted 19 June 1992, BISD 39S/128, para. 6.18.

[28] See, for example, Panel Report, *Brazil - Measures Affecting Desiccated Coconut*, adopted 20 March 1997, WT/DS22/R, para. 293; and Panel Report, *United States - Standards for Reformulated and Conventional Gasoline*, as modified by the Appellate Body Report, AB-1996-1, adopted 20 May 1996, WT/DS2/9, para. 6.43.

[29] See, for example, *EEC - Restrictions on Imports of Dessert Apples*, Complaint by Chile, adopted 22 June 1989, BISD 36S/93, para.12.20, where the panel explicitly stated that given its finding that the EEC measures were in violation of Article XI:1 of the GATT 1947 and were not justified by Article XI:2(c)(i) or (ii) of the GATT 1947, no further examination of the administration of the measures would normally be required. In that case, the panel nonetheless considered it "appropriate" to examine the administration of the EEC measures in respect of Article XIII of the GATT 1947 in view of the questions of great practical interest raised by both parties.

6.5 Furthermore, such a requirement is not consistent with the aim of the WTO dispute settlement system. Article 3.7 of the DSU explicitly states:

> The aim of the dispute settlement mechanism is to secure a positive solution to a dispute. A solution mutually acceptable to the parties to a dispute and consistent with the covered agreements is clearly to be preferred.

6.6 Thus, the basic aim of dispute settlement in the WTO is to settle disputes. This basic aim is affirmed elsewhere in the DSU. Article 3.4, for example, stipulates:

> Recommendations or rulings made by the DSB shall be aimed at achieving a satisfactory settlement of the matter in accordance with the rights and obligations under this Understanding and under the covered agreements.

6.7 As India emphasizes, Article 3.2 of the DSU states that the Members of the WTO "recognize" that the dispute settlement system "serves to preserve the rights and obligations of Members under the covered agreements, and *to clarify the existing provisions of those agreements* in accordance with customary rules of interpretation of public international law" (emphasis added). Given the explicit aim of dispute settlement that permeates the DSU, we do not consider that Article 3.2 of the DSU is meant to encourage either panels or the Appellate Body to "make law" by clarifying existing provisions of the WTO Agreement outside the context of resolving a particular dispute. A panel need only address those claims which must be addressed in order to resolve the matter in issue in the dispute.[30]

6.8 We note, furthermore, that Article IX of the WTO Agreement provides that the Ministerial Conference and the General Council have the "exclusive authority" to adopt interpretations of the WTO Agreement and the Multilateral Trade Agreements.[31] This is explicitly recognized in Article 3.9 of the DSU, which provides:

> The provisions of this Understanding are without prejudice to the rights of Members to seek authoritative interpretation of provisions of a covered agreement through decision-making under the WTO Agreement or a covered agreement which is a Plurilateral Trade Agreement.

6.9 In the light of the above, we believe that the Panel's finding in paragraph 7.20 of the Panel Report is consistent with the DSU as well as with practice under the GATT 1947 and the WTO Agreement.

VII. FINDINGS AND CONCLUSIONS

7.1 For the reasons set out in this Report, the Appellate Body upholds the legal findings and conclusions of the Panel.

7.2 The Appellate Body *recommends* that the Dispute Settlement Body make a ruling consistent with the legal findings and conclusions in the Panel Report and this Report.

---

[30] The "matter in issue" is the "matter referred to the DSB" pursuant to Article 7 of the DSU.

[31] *Japan - Taxes on Alcoholic Beverages*, AB-1996-2, adopted 1 November 1996, WT/DS8/AB/R, WT/DS10/AB/R, WT/DS11/AB/R, p. 13.

CANADA – CERTAIN MEASURES CONCERNING PERIODICALS

REPORT OF THE PANEL
WT/DS31/R

Complainant: United States

Respondent: Canada

Third Parties: None

Decided: March 14, 1997

Procedural History

March 11, 1996 the United States requested consultations with Canada pursuant to Article 4 of the DSU and Article XXIII of the GATT.

May 24, 1996 the United States requested establishment of a panel.

June 19, 1996 the Dispute Settlement Body established a panel in accordance with Article 6 of the DSU.

Conclusions

- The Panel concludes that Tariff Code 9958 is inconsistent with Article XI.1 of the General Agreement.
- Tariff Code 9958 can not be justified under Article XX(d) of the General Agreement.
- Part V.1 of the Excise Tax Act is inconsistent with Article III.2, first sentence, of the General Agreement.
- The application by Canada Post of lower "commercial Canadian" postal rates to domestically produced periodicals than to imported periodicals, including additional discount options available only to domestic periodicals, is inconsistent with Article III.4 of the General Agreement.
- Maintenance of the "funded" rate scheme is justified under Article III.8(b) of the General Agreement.

Annotations

5.5 **"Prohibitions or restrictions other than duties, taxes or other charges"** [GATT, Article XI.1]

Since the importation of certain foreign periodicals into Canada is completely denied under Tariff Code 9958, this provision is inconsistent with Article XI.1 of the General Agreement on its own terms.

5.8 **Mandate of Panel** [DSU, Article 7.2]

The United States is not challenging the GATT consistency of Section 19 of Canada's Income Tax Act in this proceeding. Therefore, the GATT consistency of the underlying law or regulation, as required by Article XX(d), is not before the Panel.

5.9, 5.10 **"Secure compliance"** [GATT, Article XX(d)]

For Tariff Code 9958 to be justified as an exception under Article XX(d), it must be found a measure "to secure compliance" with Section 19 of the Income Tax Act. The interpretation by the GATT panel in *European Economic Community – Regulations on Imports of Parts and Components* that to secure compliance means to enforce obligations imposed under other laws or regulations (not to ensure attainment of objectives of those laws and regulations) is found applicable in the present case. Such an interpretation is appropriate despite Canada's argument that Section 19 and Tariff Code 9958 are economic incentives. Under such an interpretation, Tariff Code 9958 can not be found a measure to secure compliance with Section 19 of the Income Tax Act.

5.13 - 5.19 **Scope of Article III** [GATT, Article III]

Article III of the General Agreement is applicable to the Excise Tax Act. Regulations regarding taxation of advertising services provided within periodicals should comply with both the GATT and the General Agreement on Trade in Services (GATS). Furthermore, Canada's not having undertaken sector-specific commitments under GATS does not immunize provisions regarding mixed services and goods from review under the GATT.

5.26 - 5.30 **"Like products"** [GATT, Article III.2]

Imported split-run periodicals and domestic periodicals that are not split-run are found to be like products under Article III.2 of the General Agreement. Also, the taxation of advertisements in certain foreign periodicals on a per issue basis permits the finding that taxes imposed under the Excise Tax Act are indirectly imposed on imported goods. Therefore, the Excise Tax Act is in violation of Article III.2, first sentence.

5.36 **"Governmental"** [GATT, Article III.4]

Canada Post's pricing policy for periodicals, distinguishing between international, Canadian commercial, and funded rates, is found to be a governmental measure. Despite Canada Post being an allegedly private Crown corporation, the Canadian government exercises substantial control over Canada Post's pricing policies, including those applicable to commercial periodicals. As such, the pricing policies are inconsistent with Article III.4 of the General Agreement.

5.41 – 5.44 **"Subsidies to domestic producers"** [GATT, Article III.8(b)]

Payment of subsidies from the Department of Canadian Heritage to Canada Post, when fully transferred to domestic producers of periodicals qualify as a permitted subsidy under Article III.8(b) of the General Agreement. Therefore Canada Post's "funded" rates are permissible under Article III.

CANADA – CERTAIN MEASURES CONCERNING PERIODICALS

REPORT OF THE PANEL
WT/DS31/R

TABLE OF CONTENTS

I. INTRODUCTION

1.1 On 11 March 1996, the United States requested Canada to hold consultations pursuant to Article 4 of the Understanding on Rules and Procedures Governing the Settlement of Disputes (DSU) and Article XXIII of the General Agreement on Tariffs and Trade 1994 (GATT 1994) on certain measures maintained by Canada, namely, measures prohibiting or restricting the importation into Canada of certain periodicals; tax treatment of so-called "split-run" periodicals; and the application of favourable postage rates to certain Canadian periodicals (WT/DS31/1). These consultations were held on 10 April 1996. As they did not result in a satisfactory adjustment of the matter, the United States, in a communication dated 24 May 1996, requested the Dispute Settlement Body (DSB) to establish a panel to examine the matter (WT/DS31/2).

1.2 The DSB, at its meeting on 19 June 1996, established a panel on the matter in accordance with Article 6 of the DSU. In document WT/DS31/3, the Secretariat reported that the Panel would have the following standard terms of reference and composition:

> To examine, in the light of the relevant provisions of the covered agreements cited by the United States in document WT/DS31/2, the matter referred to the DSB by the United States in that document and to make such findings as will assist the DSB in making the recommendations or in giving the rulings provided for in those agreements.

1.3 On 25 July 1996, the Panel was constituted with the following composition:

Chairman: Mr. Lars Anell

Panelists: Mr. Victor Luiz do Prado
Mr. Michael Reiterer

1.4 No Members reserved their rights to participate in the Panel proceedings as a third party.

1.5 The Panel met with the parties to the dispute on 11 October 1996 and 14-15 November 1996. The Panel submitted its report to the parties on 21 February 1997.

II. FACTUAL ASPECTS

2.1 This Panel concerns three Canadian measures: Tariff Code 9958 which prohibits the importation into Canada of certain periodicals; Part V.I of the Excise Tax Act, as enacted by Bill C-103 of 15 December 1995, which imposes an excise tax on certain "split-run" periodicals; and the application of certain postal rates to certain Canadian periodicals including through actions of Canada Post Corporation and the Department of Canadian Heritage.

A. Tariff Code 9958 - Import Prohibition

2.2 In 1965, the Canadian Government enacted Tariff Code 9958, in Schedule VII of the Customs Tariff. It is put into effect by Article 114 of the Customs Tariff which provides that "the importation into Canada of any goods enumerated or referred to in Schedule VII is prohibited."[1] Tariff Code 9958 applies if an issue of a periodical imported into Canada is a special edition, including a split-run or regional edition, that contains an advertisement that is primarily directed to a market in Canada and that does not appear in identical form in all editions of that issue of the periodical that were distributed in the periodical's country of origin. The Code defines an "issue" to include a special annual issue, and a "periodical" to mean a periodical, the issues of which other than the special annual issue, are published at regular intervals of more than six days and less than fifteen weeks and are distributed as issues of a distinct publication or as a supplement to more than one newspaper, but does not include a catalogue, a newspaper, or a periodical, the principal function of which is the encouragement, promotion or development of the fine arts, letters, scholarship or religion.

2.3 For the purposes of determining whether or not an advertisement is primarily directed at the Canadian market, a number of factors are taken into consideration such as whether there are enticements to the Canadian market, references to the goods and services tax, listing of Canadian addresses as opposed to foreign addresses, and specific invitations to Canadian consumers only.

2.4 The Code also applies where an issue of a periodical imported into Canada is an edition in which more than five per cent of the advertising content consists of advertisements directed to the Canadian market. Advertisements directed to the Canadian market include those that indicate specific sources of product or service availability in Canada or which include specific terms or conditions relating to the sale of goods or services in Canada.[2] The publisher of a periodical is notified by the Department of National Revenue for Customs and Excise when a periodical is found to be in contravention of Tariff Code 9958.[3]

2.5 In 1988, the Canadian Parliament enacted an exception to Tariff Code 9958 which allows Canadian publishers to have their periodicals, which must otherwise be Canadian issues of Canadian periodicals, typeset or printed wholly or partially in the United States.

B. Part V.I of the Excise Tax Act

2.6 In 1995, Bill C-103, which added Part V.I - Tax on Split-run Periodicals to the Excise Tax Act, became law.[4] The amendment calls for the imposition, levy and collection, in respect of each split-run edition of a periodical, a tax equal to 80 per cent of the value of all the advertisements contained in the split-run edition. The

---

[1] R.S.C. 1985, c. 41 (3rd Supp.) as amended to 30 April 1996, s.114, Sch. VII, Item 9958, (1996 Customs Tariff: Departmental Consolidation) Ottawa: Minister of Supply & Services Canada, 1996.

[2] The Department of National Revenue for Customs and Excise has adopted and published guidelines providing details relating to the application and administration of Code 9958 of the Customs Tariff (Revenue Canada Memorandum D9-1-10, 21 May 1993).

[3] The Importation of Periodicals Regulations (C.R.C., c. 533 as amended on 30 April 1996) describe the review process as carried out by an officer or the Deputy Minister of the Department of National Revenue for Customs and Excise.

[4] An Act to amend the Excise Tax Act and the Income Tax Act, S.C. 1995, c. 46.

tax is levied on a per issue basis. The value of all advertisements in a split-run edition of a periodical is the total of all the gross fees for all the advertisements contained in the edition.[5] The term "periodical" means printed material that is published in a series of issues that appear not less than twice a year and not more than once a week. Where an issue of a periodical is published in several versions, each version is an edition of the issue. Each edition of the issue must be considered separately when determining whether an edition is a split-run edition. The definition of "periodical" explicitly excludes a catalogue which is substantially made up of advertisements.[6]

2.7 The amendment defines a split-run edition as an edition of an issue of a periodical that:

(i) is distributed in Canada;
(ii) in which more than 20 per cent of the editorial material is the same or substantially the same as editorial material that appears in one or more excluded editions of one or more issues of one or more periodicals; and
(iii) contains an advertisement that does not appear in identical form in all the excluded editions.

There are two exclusionary provisions. Under the first, the particular edition is not a split-run edition if it is an edition that is primarily circulated outside Canada. In effect, this is an exemption for editions that are distributed in Canada, but are mainly distributed outside Canada. Under the second, a particular edition of an issue of a periodical that would otherwise be a split-run edition is not a split-run edition if all the advertisements in the particular edition appear in identical form in one or more editions of that issue that are primarily distributed outside Canada and that have a combined circulation outside Canada that is greater than the circulation in Canada of the particular edition. The purpose is to prevent a publisher from qualifying for this exemption by having all the advertisements in its Canadian split-run edition also appear in one of its excluded editions that has a very small circulation.[7]

2.8 Further, a grandfathering provision provides limited "grandfathering" treatment to certain existing periodicals that distributed Canadian split-run editions prior to 26 March 1993. A particular periodical is eligible for "grandfathering" treatment and therefore not subject to the tax on split-runs if the number of split-run editions per year does not exceed the number of split-run editions that were distributed during the 12-month period ending on 26 March 1993, provided that the periodicals continue to be similar in editorial content and direction to the split-run editions distributed before that date. If the number of split-run editions per year is increased, the tax applies to the additional split-run editions.[8]

2.9 Depending on the circumstances, the person responsible for paying the tax is the publisher, a person connected with the publisher, the distributor, the printer or the wholesaler of the split-run edition. (The Excise Tax Act stipulates that a person is considered to be connected to another person if one of them is controlled by the other or if both of them are controlled by the same person.[9] A corporation is controlled by a particular person if 50 per cent or more of its share of capital with voting rights belongs to that person or to persons with whom that person does not deal at arm's length. A partnership is controlled by a particular person if the person or persons with whom that person does not deal at arm's length is or are entitled to 50 per cent or more of the partnership's income.[10]) The responsible person is the first of these persons who resides in Canada.[11] The responsible person can be domestic- or foreign-owned or controlled. In order to ensure enforcement and collection of the tax, the tax is imposed on a person who resides in Canada. The persons connected with the responsible person are jointly and severally liable

[5] *Ibid.*, s. 38.
[6] *Ibid.*, ss.35(1) and 35(5).
[7] *Ibid.*, ss.35(5).
[8] *Ibid.*, s. 39.
[9] *Ibid.*, ss.35(2).
[10] *Ibid.*, ss.35(3).
[11] *Ibid.*, ss.35(1).

for payment of the tax.[12] As well, where the responsible person is a distributor, a printer or a wholesaler (and if there is more than one), they are jointly and severally liable for payment of the tax.[13] Where a person other than the publisher pays the excise tax in respect of a split-run edition, the person is deemed to have paid the tax on behalf of the publisher of the periodical. The legislation authorizes the person to recover the amount of the tax from the publisher in a court of competent jurisdiction or to deduct or withhold the amount from any amount payable by the person to the publisher or distributor of the periodical.[14]

C. Funded and Commercial Postal Rates

2.10 In 1981, the Canada Post Corporation (hereafter called Canada Post) was established by the Parliament of Canada as a Crown corporation pursuant to the Canada Post Corporation Act (CPC Act).[15] Crown corporations are created by one of three methods: an Act of Parliament; letters patent under the Canada Business Corporations Act; or Articles of Incorporation under the Canada Business Corporations Act. According to a treatise on Crown law cited by Canada, Crown corporations are created to separate the management of an activity from continuous partisan intervention and to provide independence from the close financial controls within the government departmental structure.[16] The Government of Canada gains control over, and accountability from, Crown corporations primarily through the Financial Administration Act (FA Act) and its Regulations. The FA Act endeavours to strike a balance between the desires for public accountability and for private industry independence. Parliament is required to approve the creation, mandate, and financing of new parent Crown corporations. Government approval is required for annual corporate plans operating and capital budgets, and major corporate acquisitions. The FA Act and the CPC Act define the responsibilities for the direction and daily operation of the corporations.

2.11 The Canada Post publication entitled *Publications Mail Postal Rates*, (effective 4 March 1996), describes the three categories of publications mail postal rates which are the subject of this dispute: the "funded" publications rates and the commercial "Canadian" and commercial "International" publications rates. The first two categories apply to periodicals published and printed in Canada. "Funded" rates are rates that are subsidized by the Canadian Government and commercial rates are for publications ineligible for "funded" rates. "Canadian" rates are commercial rates available to Canadian publications and "International" commercial rates apply to all foreign publications mailed in Canada.

1. "Funded" rates

2.12 Since its incorporation, the Government of Canada has provided funding to Canada Post to support special rates of postage for eligible publications through the Publications Distribution Assistance Program (hereafter called the Program). The Program, which was developed to promote Canadian culture, provided funding through Canada Post to eligible Canadian publications, including periodicals, mailed in Canada for delivery in Canada. "Funded" postal rates are available to Canadian-owned and -controlled paid circulation publications that are published and printed in Canada and meet certain editorial and advertising requirements. In January 1990, the Government announced plans to gradually phase out the Program and replace it with a system of direct funding to eligible publications. Since the announcement, funding available for the Program has been gradually reduced. On 30 April 1996, the current policy and funding agreement concerning the Program between

[12] *Ibid.*, s. 41.1.

[13] *Ibid.*, s. 41.2.

[14] *Ibid.*, ss.41.3(2).

[15] R.S.C. 1985, c. C-10.

[16] P. Lordon, Crown Law (Toronto: Butterworth's 1991) at 49, 57 and 58. The next five sentences are also from this source.

Canada Post and the Department of Canadian Heritage (hereafter called Canadian Heritage) was set to expire. At that time, available funding would have been directed to eligible publishers through a replacement program.[17]

2.13 The Program and its funding structure was extended for three years through a Memorandum of Agreement (MOA), signed in March 1996 and effective 1 May 1996, between the Department of Communications (now the Department of Canadian Heritage) and Canada Post.[18] This new agreement provides for payments of funds in quarterly instalments by Canadian Heritage to Canada Post "in exchange for providing prescribed postage rates for publications deemed eligible to the Publications Assistance Program", and the transfer of the program administration from Canada Post to Canadian Heritage.[19] Canadian Heritage had requested within the new agreement that Canada Post initiate the complete removal of funded publications mail from the regulations associated with the CPC Act, effective April 1996.[20] On 23 April 1996, Canada Gazette published a repeal of the Newspapers and Periodicals Regulations pursuant to Subsection 19(1) of the CPC Act. The revocation was intended to facilitate the transfer of eligibility assessment from Canada Post to Canadian Heritage, to reduce the Program's administrative costs while expediting and simplifying modifications to its policies[21], and to allow Canada Post and Canadian Heritage to respond more appropriately and more rapidly to Program and customer needs.

2.14 The amounts authorized by the MOA are CD$58 million for the period commencing 1 May 1996 and ending 31 March 1997; CD$57.9 million for the period 1 April 1997 to 31 March 1998; and CD$47.3 million for the period 1 April 1998 to 31 March 1999.

2.15 Canadian Heritage administers the eligibility requirements for the Program based on the criteria specified in Schedule A to the MOA. Canadian Heritage is responsible for the administration of the eligibility requirements for the Program, and Canada Post must accept for distribution all publications that are eligible under the Program once the publication is approved by Canadian Heritage. For eligible publications to receive funded rates, the publisher must first enter into a sales agreement with Canada Post prior to posting under the Program. Rates of postage for publications eligible under the Program are set out in Schedule C of the MOA and are as follows:

a) First 10,000 copies of an issue addressed to *Bona Fide* Subscribers and newsdealers in Canada:

per kg or fraction thereof: Year 1: $0.390
Year 2: $0.395
Year 3: $0.405

or, per individually addressed copy whichever is the greater:
Year 1: $0.078
Year 2: $0.079
Year 3: $0.081

---

[17] *Canada Gazette*, Part II, Vol 130, No. 10, Newspapers and Periodicals Regulations, repeal, SOR/96-209, 23 April 1996, Regulatory Impact Analysis Statement.

[18] Memorandum of Agreement (MOA) Concerning the Publications Assistance Program Between the Department of Communications and Canada Post Corporation.

[19] *Canada Gazette*, Part II, Vol 130, No. 10.

[20] *Ibid.*

[21] *Ibid.*

b) Copies exceeding the first 10,000 copies of an issue addressed to *Bona Fide* Subscribers and newsdealers in Canada:

per kg or fraction thereof: Year 1: $0.430
Year 2: $0.435
Year 3: $0.445

or, per individually addressed copy, whichever is the greater:
Year 1: $0.086
Year 2: $0.087
Year 3: $0.089

(Year 1: 1 May 1996 to 31 March 1997; Year 2: 1 April 1997 to 31 March 1998; Year 3: 1 April 1998 to 31 March 1999.)

2.16 In order to be eligible for funded rates, Canadian publications must generally meet the following criteria: (i) produced by a person or company whose primary business is publishing;[22] (ii) Canadian ownership and control; (iii) published, printed and mailed in Canada; (iv) edited in Canada;[23] (v) eligible editorial categories;[24] (vi) minimum paid circulation requirement;[25] (vii) maximum advertising allowance;[26] (viii) frequency;[27] and (ix) minimum price.[28]

2. *Commercial "Canadian" and commercial "international" rates*

2.17 Canada Post has authority to set its commercial rates outside of regulation, pursuant to subsections 16(1) and 21(a) of the CPC Act, for any person who has entered into an agreement with Canada Post for (a) the variation of rates of postage on the mailable matter of that person in consideration of his mailing in bulk, preparing the mailable matter in a manner that facilitates the processing thereof or receiving additional services in relation thereto;...."[29] In order to take advantage of this provision and receive commercial postal rates and service, a publisher must enter into an agreement with Canada Post. For a Canadian publication, this agreement is the "Publications Mail Product Service Agreement"[30], and for a foreign publication mailed in Canada, this agreement is the "International Publications Mail Product (Canadian Distribution) Sales Agreement."[31] These arrangements are intended to benefit Canadian and foreign publications and their subscribers by reducing mailing costs and improving delivery standards. Appendix A of each "Agreement" contains the commercial "Canadian" and commercial "International" rates. These rates are identical to those found in the *Publications Mail Postal Rates* (referred to in paragraph *2.11*) which divides commercial rates into those that apply for (i) mail service for Canadian publications that are ineligible for "funded" rates (Rate Code 5); and (ii) mail service for international publications (Rate Code 6 or what are called "International" rates in this dispute). Further, special agreements may

---

[22] Funded rates cannot be used to promote a specific business, service, fraternal, trade or professional organizations (MOA).

[23] An eligible publication must be edited by persons residing in Canada (editing encompasses the commissioning of editorial material and artwork, supervising writers, illustrators and photographers regarding the final format of the material, as well as laying out, copy editing and proofreading, and otherwise preparing the contents for printing) (MOA).

[24] Eligible publications must be published for the dissemination to the public consisting of either news, comment and analysis of news and articles on topics of current public interest; or articles on religion, the sciences, agriculture, forestry, the fisheries, social or literary criticism, reviews of literature or the arts, or be an academic or scholarly journal; or articles promoting public health and published by a non-profit organization administered on a national or provincial basis (MOA).

[25] No less than 50 per cent of an eligible publication's total circulation must be paid circulation (MOA).

[26] No more than 70 per cent of the space, including advertising inserts, in an eligible publication may be devoted to advertising (MOA).

[27] It must be published not less than twice a year and not more than 56 times a year (MOA).

[28] It must have a stated subscription price of $0.50 or more per copy and $6.00 or more per year.

[29] R.S.C. 1985, c.C-10, s. 21(a).

[30] Canadian Publications Mail Products Sales Agreement, 1 March 1995.

[31] International Publications Mail Product (Canadian Distribution) Sales Agreement, 1 March 1994.

be entered into for both Canadian and non-Canadian publications whereby terms and conditions (including rates of postage) may be established on a case-by-case basis.

2.18 Publications must meet the six criteria enumerated below in order for their publishers to enter into either a "Publications Mail Products Sales Agreement" or an "International Publications Mail Product Sales Agreement". Additionally for the former, the publication "must be a newspaper, newsletter or periodical, published, printed and mailed in Canada".[32] Additionally for the latter, the publications "must be a newspaper, newsletter or periodical printed outside of Canada or registered under Rate Code 5 prior to 1 March 1992."[33]

Six criteria:

(i) published for the purposes of disseminating to the public news, articles containing comments on or analysis of the news, and articles with respect to other topics currently of interest to the general public;
(ii) devoted primarily to one or more of religion, the sciences, agriculture, forestry, the fisheries, social or literary criticism or reviews of literature or the arts, or academic or scholarly writings;
(iii) published at a frequency of not less than four times a year;
(iv) addressed to a subscriber, non-subscriber, company or to a newsdealer in Canada;
(v) containing not more than 70 per cent of the space devoted to advertising in more than 50 per cent of the issues published during any twelve month period; and
(vi) published by or at the direction of a person whose principal business is publishing.

2.19 The rates for the commercial "Canadian" and commercial "International" publications mail service are summarized as follows:

Commercial "Canadian" rates:

Minimum postage per addressed copy (100g or less)	Price per copy
Local rural rates	$0.103
Local urban rates	$0.231
Regional rates	$0.184
National rates	$0.378

Commercial "International" rates:

Minimum postage per addressed copy (100g or less)	Price per copy
Rates for foreign magazines, newspapers or newsletters mailed in Canada (inbound)	$0.436

Two sub-categories include discounts for palletization and by-pass. Non-subsidized Canadian publications can receive discounts of $0.01 to $0.02 per copy if palletized, and discounts ranging from $150.00 to $200.00 per truck load for a by-pass or downstream entry. These discounts are not available generally to foreign publications mailed in Canada. Further, the commercial "Canadian" and commercial "International" categories have not been subject to regulation since 1994 and 1992, respectively.[34]

[32] Canadian Publications Mail Products Sales Agreement, para. 5.1.

[33] International Publications Mail Product (Canadian Distribution) Sales Agreement, para. 4.1.

[34] SOR/94-210, 24 February 1994 and SOR/91-641, 7 November 1991.

III. MAIN ARGUMENTS

3.1 The United States asked the Panel to find that:

(a) Tariff Code 9958 is inconsistent with Article XI of GATT 1994;

(b) Part V.I of the Excise Tax Act is inconsistent with Article III:2 of GATT 1994, or in the alternative, Article III:4 of GATT 1994; and

(c) The application by Canada Post of lower postal rates to domestically-produced periodicals under the "funded" and "commercial" rate systems is inconsistent with Article III:4 of GATT 1994, and is not a domestic subsidy within the meaning of Article III:8 of GATT 1994.

3.2 Canada asked the Panel to find that:

(a) Tariff Code 9958 is justifiable under Article XX(d) of the GATT 1994;

(b) Article III of GATT 1994 does not apply to Part V.I of the Excise Tax Act, and if the Panel decides that it does apply, Part V.I is consistent with Article III of GATT 1994;

(c) Article III:4 of GATT 1994 does not apply to the commercial rates charged by Canada Post, and the funds paid by the Department of Canadian Heritage to Canada Post for the "funded" rates are allowable subsidies pursuant to Article III:8(b) of GATT 1994.

A. Tariff Code 9958 - Import Prohibition

1. *Article XI:1*

3.3 The United States argued that the Canadian import prohibition on the products listed in Tariff Code 9958 is a violation of Article XI:1 of GATT 1994, which prohibits quantitative restrictions on imports. By its terms, Tariff Code 9958 applies both to special Canadian editions of magazines that are also published in versions targeted at readers in other countries (i.e. split-runs) and to magazines produced solely for the Canadian market. In either case, the import ban applies if the periodical contains even a small amount of advertising directed primarily at Canadian readers – single advertisement in the case of split-runs and five per cent or more of the advertising space in the case of magazines generally. The ban eliminates these magazines from the Canadian magazine market, and ensures that only Canadian magazines can compete for domestically-oriented advertising. Canada did so for the specific purpose of ensuring that Canadian magazines can enjoy a monopoly on the sale of magazines containing such advertisements. Advertising is an important source of revenue for magazine publishers. Thus, granting domestic magazines a monopoly on local advertising provides them a competitive advantage over foreign-produced magazines that are denied the right to carry such advertisements.

3.4 Canada argued that the United States claim that the Canadian legislation creates a "monopoly" for Canadian publishers of advertisements directed at the Canadian market is inconceivable in the North American environment. The existence of "spill-over" advertising, whereby advertisements for generally-available products in wide-circulation US magazines automatically reach the Canadian public, with very significant consequences for the competitiveness of the Canadian industry, is sufficient by itself to prevent the creation of any true monopoly. The "monopoly" effect complained of by the United States has nothing to do with the first part of the Code, dealing with split-runs, or with the Excise Tax Act. It is true that the second part of the Tariff Code prevents the entry of foreign magazines with substantial amounts of advertising directed specifically at Canadian, as a means of preventing an easy way to get around the split-run prohibition. However, the 5 per cent rule applies only to a limited type of advertising with Canadian addresses and phone numbers, and this aspect of the policy has not been carried forward to the excise tax provisions, which are strictly limited to the split-run phenomenon.

2. Article XX(d)

3.5 Canada added that Tariff Code 9958 is a measure intended to secure the attainment of the objectives of Section 19 of the Income Tax Act. The issue is whether Tariff Code 9958 can be justified as a necessary measure within the meaning of Article XX(d). Because it forms an integral part of a package of measures with a single objective, it can be so justified on a natural and reasonable reading of the treaty language. Canadian public policy for the magazine industry is designed to provide Canadians with a distinctive vehicle for the expression of their own ideas and interests. Such a vehicle faces enormous competition from foreign magazines for both advertising and readership. Public policy measures aim to balance the need to establish and maintain a place for Canadian periodicals in their own domestic market while at the same time ensuring that Canadians have unrestricted access to foreign periodicals. To achieve this long-standing policy objective, government policy has focused on two areas: advertising and distribution. The Government of Canada has introduced a series of measures to ensure that magazines with editorial content developed for the Canadian market can compete for the limited advertising revenues. These measures include Tariff Code 9958, Sections 35-41 of the Excise Tax Act and Section 19 of the Income Tax Act. Section 19 of the Income Tax Act allows a deduction for advertising directed at the Canadian market. Tariff Code 9958 restricts the importation into Canada of periodicals whose advertising has been purchased especially to reach a Canadian audience. The general objective of these measures is to help the Canadian periodical industry raise advertising revenues. Tariff Code 9958 ensures the achievement of this goal, with Section 19 of the Income Tax Act.

a) "Secure compliance"

3.6 The United States referred to the panel on *United States - Standards for Reformulated and Conventional Gasoline ("US - Standards for Gasoline")* which states that a party invoking an exception under Article XX(d) has to demonstrate the following elements:

> (1) that the measures for which the exception are being invoked - that is, the particular trade measures inconsistent with the General Agreement - *secure compliance* with laws or regulations themselves not inconsistent with the General Agreement;
>
> (2) that the inconsistent measures for which the exception is being invoked are *necessary* to secure compliance with those laws or regulations; and
>
> (3) that the measures are applied in conformity with the requirements of the *introductory clause* of Article XX.

In order to justify the application of Article XX(d), all the above elements have to be satisfied".[35]

3.7 Canada's import prohibition fails to meet *any* of these requirements. With respect to the first requirement, Canada has failed to demonstrate that its import ban secures compliance with Section 19 of the Income Tax Act. Canada has not claimed that the import ban is meant to enforce the income tax provisions, only that the import ban and the income tax measures advance the same objective (through different means), which is to channel all domestic advertising to domestic magazines.

---

[35] Panel Report on *United States - Standards for Reformulated and Conventional Gasoline*, adopted on 20 May 1996, WT/DS2/R, para. 6.31 (emphasis in original).

3.8 Canada noted that the conformity of the Income Tax Act with GATT 1994 is not being challenged. Tariff Code 9958 and Section 19 of the Income Tax Act are conceived to deal with the problem of split-runs with inserted Canadian advertising. The idea is that the income tax provision would cover magazines printed in Canada and the border measure would cover magazines printed outside the country. The effectiveness of the non-deductibility provision standing by itself would obviously be very limited. The problem is that of foreign companies that sold into the Canadian market but are not subject to Canadian income tax. This would be more than a loophole, given the open nature of the Canadian economy and the degree of import penetration. It would largely destroy the effectiveness of the income tax measures.

3.9 Canada drew the Panel's attention to the panel report on *EEC - Regulations on Parts and Components*[36] ("*EEC - Parts and Components*") which introduces a very stringent test for the application of Article XX(d), under which the non-conforming measures have to be necessary for the enforcement of another law, and not merely in order to ensure that the objectives of that law be fulfilled. This test is entirely appropriate where the issue is the enforcement of regulatory statutes and ordinary fiscal measures designed to raise revenue, where compliance with the statute is virtually synonymous with the attainment of its objectives. If, for example, an environmental measure is complied with, its objective is *ipso facto* attained.

3.10 The *EEC - Parts and Components* panel interpreted Article XX(d) in terms of enforceability as opposed to measures designed to ensure that the objectives of another measure are not undermined. Canada is not challenging that decision or its reasoning. It makes sense in the context of regulatory statutes with prohibitions or even tax statutes that are designed to raise revenue and prevent tax evasion. It is doubtful, on the other hand, that an enforceability test is meaningful in the case of a fiscal or other economic incentive where formal compliance is not the real object, and *substantial* compliance can not be separated from the underlying social and economic objectives the measure is designed to secure. In the case of a fiscal incentive whose sole purpose is to influence business decisions in a certain direction, compliance has to be judged in terms of effectiveness. Canada suggests, therefore, that the application of the exception in Article XX(d) should take account of the nature of the measures under consideration, and that the test in the *EEC - Parts and Components* panel decision should not be rigidly applied without taking account of these circumstances.

3.11 Further, the US consideration that compliance is always a matter of enforceability, no more no less, may be a valid proposition, as held in *EEC - Parts and Components*, for mandatory legislation based on prohibitions or exactions. Compliance and effectiveness are synonymous in the case of the vast majority of legislative measures. But Section 19 is not an ordinary tax measure, designed to raise revenue for the public purse or prevent tax evasion. In the case of a fiscal or other economic incentive whose sole purpose is to influence business decisions in a certain direction, compliance has to be judged in terms of effectiveness as well as enforceability. The distinction is between formal compliance and real or substantial compliance, which in this case has nothing to do with whether deductions are properly claimed but with the policy behind this entire set of measures.

3.12 The United States argued that the panel on *EEC - Parts and Components* dismisses the argument that Article XX(d) permits governments to maintain GATT-inconsistent measures to "ensure the attainment of the *objectives* of [GATT-consistent] laws and regulations" rather than to prevent violations of the GATT-consistent laws or regulations.[37] That panel stated that the interpretation it rejects would make the function of Article XX(d) "substantially broader" and would not be consistent with the fact that Article XX(d) applies only in the specific circumstances set out in that paragraph – namely, to secure compliance with GATT-consistent laws or regulations.

3.13 Canada's claim that the import ban does not seek "formal compliance" with Section 19 of the Income Tax Act, but rather "real or substantial compliance", which Canada admits "has nothing to do with whether deductions are properly claimed," is simply another way of stating that the import ban helps advance the same overall

---

[36] Panel Report on *European Economic Community - Regulations on Parts and Components,* adopted on 16 May 1990, BISD 37S/132.

[37] Ibid., para. 5.17 (emphasis added).

(protectionist) aim as Section 19. However, the import ban does not "secure compliance" with Section 19, and thus does not fall within the purview of Article XX(d). If accepted, Canada's view of Article XX(d) would allow WTO Members to adopt all manner of GATT-inconsistent measures on the ground that they further the same objectives as other protectionist legislation. As the *EEC - Parts and Components* panel makes clear, the phrase "secure compliance" does not reach measures that merely help ensure that domestic policy goals are realized.

b) "Necessary"

3.14 The United States noted that the panel report on *United States - Section 337 of the Tariff Act of 1930* ("*US - Section 337*") observed that :

> [A] contracting party cannot justify a measure inconsistent with another GATT provision as 'necessary' in terms of Article XX(d) if an alternative measure which it could reasonably be expected to employ and which is not inconsistent with other GATT provisions is available to it.[38]

The normal way for tax authorities to enforce income tax provisions is to audit the relevant tax returns, and to make adjustments to those returns where necessary to secure compliance. Tax, civil, or criminal penalties may be imposed where warranted in individual cases. Such measures would normally be entirely consistent with GATT and in any event would be applied to particular taxpayers, not to imports. It is extraordinary for income tax enforcement measures to take the form of restrictions on trade in goods. Canada has demonstrated no basis for why, of all possible measures, it is necessary to impose a blatantly GATT-inconsistent *import ban* to secure compliance with Section 19 of the Income Tax Act nor why normal tax enforcement procedures were insufficient.

3.15 Canada stated that the panel in *US Section 337*[39] held that the term "necessary" required the use of the least trade-restrictive measure available. Canada submits that there are no other measures, less restrictive or otherwise, that would accomplish the objective. If split-runs could be imported, with Canadian advertisements often placed by businesses for which Canadian tax liability is irrelevant, the program would simply no longer work.

3.16 Canada therefore reiterates its suggestion that the application of the exception in Article XX(d) should take account of the nature of the measures under consideration, and that the test in the *EEC -Parts and Components* and the *US - Section 337* panel decisions should not be rigidly applied without taking account of these circumstances. The Panel should recall that Code 9958 and the income tax provision have always been considered part of a single, indivisible package of complementary, indivisible measures and should be treated as such for the purposes of Article XX(d).

3.17 The United States stated that even if one were to credit Canada's argument that Article XX(d) covers measures necessary to secure the attainment of the domestic policy goals embedded in other laws, the import ban would still not be "necessary" for such a purpose. The objective of Section 19 is to support Canada's magazine industry. Canada has not shown why GATT-consistent measures (such as subsidies paid directly to producers) would not reasonably be available to it for advancing this objective.

3. Chapeau to Article XX

3.18 Canada noted that each term of Article XX(d), including its Preamble, should be given consideration when examining whether Tariff Code 9958 could be justified as a necessary measure within the meaning of the treaty. Since Tariff Code 9958 is a "measure" directed against imports from all foreign countries and not only the United States, it is "not applied in a manner which would constitute a means of arbitrary or unjustifiable

---

[38] Panel Report on *United States - Section 337 of the Tariff Act of 1930*, adopted on 7 November 1989, BISD 36S/345, para. 5.26.

[39] *Ibid.*, at 392, paras. 5.25-5.27.

discrimination between countries where the same conditions prevail," as stated in the preamble to Article XX. Similarly, having regard to the application of Tariff Code 9958 since its adoption, it could not be claimed that it has been "applied in a manner which would constitute ... a disguised restriction on international trade". Tariff Code 9958 is not applied in such a way as to constitute a restriction on international trade, as the evidence so strongly demonstrates, nor does it prohibit the importation of foreign periodicals into Canada or threaten their dominant position in the English-Canadian market place.

3.19 The United States considered that because the import ban does not satisfy the terms of paragraph (d) of Article XX, the Panel does not need to ascertain whether or not it is in conformity with the introductory clause of Article XX. However, were the Panel to reach this issue, it should find that Canada's import ban does not meet the requirements of the introductory clause, because the import ban constitutes "a means of arbitrary and unjustifiable discrimination between countries where the same conditions prevail," and is also "a disguised restriction on international trade." In the *US - Standards for Gasoline* case, the Appellate Body states that whatever else the term "disguised restriction on international trade" means, it could be read to encompass any "... restrictions amounting to arbitrary or unjustifiable discrimination in international trade taken under the guise of a measure formally within the terms of an exception listed in Article XX".[40] The import ban's "arbitrary" and "unjustifiable" nature is apparent from the very structure of Tariff Code 9958. Application of the import ban depends on advertising content and on sales in more than one country - factors that are relevant only for purposes of distinguishing between those categories of foreign-produced magazines that compete with Canadian magazines for Canadian advertising revenues and those that do not. The import ban therefore constitutes a "disguised restriction on international trade."

3.20 Moreover, the expression "between countries" in the chapeau to Article XX includes a comparison between Canada and other countries as well as between countries other than Canada. The import prohibition bars only magazines produced outside Canada, thus discriminating in favour of magazines produced in Canada. There are no relevant conditions prevailing in Canada or elsewhere that would justify the discrimination imposed on foreign-produced split-runs. Thus, for the reasons discussed above, the import ban constitutes "arbitrary or unjustifiable discrimination between countries where the same conditions prevail."

3.21 Canada considered that the United States argued that the prohibition on arbitrary or unjustifiable discrimination requires a comparison between other countries and Canada, and not just between countries other than Canada. This, in effect turns this Article into a national treatment proviso. An import prohibition or restriction could never meet this test. The effect would be to remove Article XI almost completely from the range of measures that can potentially be subject to Article XX derogations. The interpretation suggested here is novel. It does not correspond to the way the chapeau to Article XX has been interpreted in the past, as shown by the 1982 decision on *United States - Prohibition on Imports of Tuna and Tuna Products from Canada*,[41] and the 1983 decision on *United States - Imports of Certain Automotive Spring Assemblies*.[42] In both those decisions, a US import prohibition was held not to be discriminatory within the meaning of the chapeau to Article XX, because it applied equally to all foreign countries exporting to the United States.

B. Part V.I of the Excise Tax Act

3.22 The United States argued that the excise tax was designed specifically to shore up Canada's GATT-inconsistent import prohibition. Canada did not deny that this is so, or that the tax was designed to eliminate the competition between split-run magazines and domestically produced magazines. The purpose of the tax is

---

[40] Appellate Body Report on *United States - Standards for Reformulated and Conventional Gasoline*, adopted on 20 May 1996, WT/DS2/AB/R at 25.

[41] Panel Report on *United States - Prohibition on Imports of Tuna and Tuna Products from Canada*, adopted on 22 February 1982, BISD 29S/91 .

[42] Panel Report on *United States - Imports of Certain Automotive Spring Assemblies*, adopted 26 May 1993, BISD 30S/107.

protectionist - namely, to ensure that only Canadian magazine producers capture all of the revenues associated with advertisements directed specifically at Canadian readers. The Canadian magazine tax is designed to ensure that foreign-based publishers forego the commercially attractive option of publishing a split-run edition of an existing magazine for the Canadian market. Any such edition will be hit with a prohibitive 80 per cent excise tax. This means that foreign magazine producers contemplating sales in the Canadian market can not make use of the economies of scale that split-run editions provide. Split-run editions drive down per unit production costs by spreading the expense of producing articles and photographs over a greater number of magazines. The Canadian tax ensures that no foreign-based publisher can take advantage of those lower costs to compete in the Canadian market against wholly Canadian-produced magazines.

3.23 Canada's policy of protecting its domestic publishing industry from import competition is long-standing. Since the early 1900s, Canada has provided subsidized, lower postal rates exclusively to Canadian-produced magazines.[43] More recently, Canada sought to protect its industry by targeting imported periodicals sold into Canada as "split-run" or "regional" editions. A publisher produces a "split-run" edition of a single issue of a magazine by separating ("splitting") the editorial content (articles, photographs, artwork, etc.) and the advertising content of the magazine. The publisher then produces two or more separate regional editions of the issue of the magazine. Each edition shares some or all of the editorial content, but the advertising content in each edition may differ, because each edition is distributed in a different geographic market and the advertising is directed at that specific market.

3.24 Concerned that imported split-run editions of magazines would divert advertising revenues from domestic competitors, Canada enacted Tariff Code 9958 in 1965 specifically to prohibit the importation of split-run editions as well as any other magazine containing a more than a *de minimis* amount of advertising directed at the Canadian public, and in 1976 prohibited income tax deductions for advertisements placed in foreign-owned publications. Within a matter of a few decades, however, technological advances made it practical for foreign-based publishers to transmit editorial material electronically across the border into Canada and to publish split-run editions in Canada, thus avoiding the application of Tariff Code 9958. To plug this perceived loophole - and ensure that split-run editions could not compete in the domestic marketplace - Canada enacted a punitive excise tax on split-run editions in December 1995.

3.25 In an opinion dated 15 August 1990, Investment Canada advised Time Canada Ltd., a company controlled by Time Warner, Inc. of New York, N.Y., that its proposal to publish a Canadian edition of *Sports Illustrated* was not inconsistent with Section 15 of the Investment Canada Act. Based on that opinion, on 11 January 1993, Time-Warner announced plans to publish in Canada a special Canadian edition of *Sports Illustrated* magazine. Recognizing that Tariff Code 9958 could not be relied upon to keep a Canadian-produced version of *Sports Illustrated* or other foreign-based magazines out of the Canadian market, the Canadian Government responded to Time's announcement on 26 March 1993, by establishing a Task Force on the Canadian Magazine Industry whose mandate was "to recommend ways in which the current measures [supporting the Canadian magazine industry] could be brought up-to-date."[44]

3.26 The Task Force concluded that it in the absence of additional legislation it was highly likely that a significant number of US split-runs would be sold in Canada. The Task Force estimated that there were 53 potential US consumer magazine entrants into the Canadian market, and 70 potential US business and trade magazine entrants, and that the majority of these would actually enter the Canadian market.[45] In December 1994, the Canadian Government announced its intention to implement the Task Force's recommendation to implement a new excise tax on all split-run magazines that contain ads directed at Canadians.[46] On 25 September 1995, the Government formally introduced Bill C-103, the excise tax bill, in the Canadian House of Commons. In

---

[43] *A Question of Balance, Report of the Task Force on the Canadian Magazine Industry*, 1994 ("*Task Force Report*") at 72.

[44] Task Force Report at iii.

[45] Task Force Report at 50-52.

[46] News Release, Canadian Heritage, December 22, 1994 at 1.

introducing Bill C-103, Minister of Canadian Heritage Dupuy stated: "*Sports Illustrated Canada* managed to get around custom tariff 9958, because most of its content was sent electronically from the United States. It was simply a loophole in the tariff laws since electronic transmission made it possible to avoid tariff regulations. . . . Task Force members explored several avenues and finally concluded that the proposed excise tax was the best solution. It could be designed and implemented in order to avoid split-run editions."[47] In the Parliamentary debate, one Member described the bill in the following terms:

> [I]t is important to be very clear about the nature of the bill. In essence it is designed to kill international competition between magazines, more specifically magazines which come into Canada. The killing of that competition kills a lot of good things which flow from competition.[48]

3.27 Canada argued that the excise tax measure is designed to prevent the diversion of advertising to low-cost publications reproducing recycled editorial content, at the expense of publications created for Canadians. The Excise Tax Act is carefully designed to deal with a particular combination of circumstances. What it targets is the combination of recycled editorial content plus Canadian advertisements. Magazines derive their revenues predominantly from the sale of advertising space and from the circulation of the magazine. Advertising revenue is by far the most important revenue stream for Canadian magazines, accounting for 60 per cent of total revenue. Circulation revenue accounts for 33 per cent of total revenue, or $287 million. Advertising revenue is crucial for the Canadian magazine industry, allowing the publisher to provide the magazine at an affordable cost or, in some cases, free of charge.

3.28 Canada explained that there is a direct correlation between circulation, advertising revenue and editorial content. The larger the circulation, the more advertising a magazine can attract. With greater advertising revenue, a publisher can afford more to spend on editorial content. The more a publisher spends, the more attractive the magazine is likely to be to its readers, resulting in circulation growth. Similarly, a loss of advertising revenue will produce a "downward spiral". Less advertising entails less editorial, a reduction in readership and circulation and a diminished ability to attract advertising. Magazines can be sold on news-stands, or through subscriptions, or distributed at no cost to selected consumers. The Canadian market is not large, particularly when compared to the US market. It is also highly fragmented from a language perspective. There are two official languages in Canada as well as a number of other languages. Canadian English-language publications face tough competition on news-stands; they account for only 18.5 per cent of English-language periodicals distributed on news-stands, where space is dominated by foreign publications. Subscriptions are the main source of circulation revenue for most Canadian magazines.

3.29 The constraints imposed by the demographics of the Canadian market have a significant impact on the ability of a magazine primarily addressed to Canadian interests to obtain the broad base of circulation that is necessary to achieve economic viability. Canadian magazine publishers compete with other media for the same limited amount of advertising dollars in the Canadian market. Magazines have been losing market share to other media forms such as direct mail and television. It is unlikely that the share held by magazines will increase. The amount of money spent by advertisers to reach Canadian consumers is also not likely to grow. In addition, "spill-over" advertising (the ability of advertisers of internationally distributed products to reach Canadian consumers through US magazines) is a further limitation on the competitive position of the Canadian industry. Canadian periodical publishers face a major competitive challenge in their business environment that is not common to their counterparts in countries with a larger population to serve. The pivotal fact is the penetration of the Canadian market by foreign magazines. Canadian readers have unrestricted access to imported magazines. At the same time, Canadian readers have demonstrated that they value magazines that address their distinct interests and perspectives. However, foreign magazines dominate the Canadian market. They account for 81.4 per cent of all

---

[47] *Commons Debates* at 14790-1 (Sept. 25, 1995).

[48] *Commons Debates* at 14795 (statement of Mr. Monte Solberg).

news-stand circulation and slightly more than half (50.4 per cent) of the entire circulation of English-language magazines destined for the general public in Canada.

3.30 Magazines are a particularly good medium for advertisers wishing to reach a specific market defined by regional location. Both Canadian and foreign magazines currently have regional editions in their respective home markets. Publishers and advertisers recognize the importance of regional editions as an advertising vehicle. The marketing strategy behind regional editions is that they allow publishers to offer very specific advertising vehicles for advertisers interested in targeting a particular audience, hence they maximize advertising revenues. Some foreign publishers view Canada as a separate "region" within their own national market. The "Canadian" regional edition produced by such publishers generally contains the same editorial content as the other editions but different advertising content, reflecting the addition of advertisements from Canadian advertisers. The term "split-run" is used in Canada to refer to such a Canadian regional edition. For a foreign publisher, the incentive to produce a Canadian regional edition of its magazine containing advertising directed at Canadians is, of course, profit. A profit for the foreign publisher only requires that the incremental revenue from advertising in the regional edition exceeds the costs of producing the split-run. Since its fixed costs have already been recovered in the larger home market, this offers an inviting prospect for a foreign magazine.

3.31 The Task Force on the Canadian Magazine Industry was established as a result of the anticipated publication of *Sports Illustrated Canada. Sports Illustrated Canada* was a split-run edition that was printed in Canada using text that was electronically transmitted from the United States. The editorial content of *Sports Illustrated Canada* was largely the same as the content in the American editions of *Sports Illustrated* but it contained advertisements that had been specifically purchased to reach a Canadian audience. Tariff Code 9958 was not applicable to *Sports Illustrated Canada* because it was printed in Canada rather than being imported. The emergence of *Sports Illustrated Canada* as a new split-run edition revealed the limitations of Canada's existing policy instruments. Accordingly, the Task Force was created to recommend ways to bring these policy instruments up to date. The Task Force's main recommendation was that an excise tax be imposed on advertising contained in split-run editions of periodicals that are distributed in Canada. The object of the excise tax is not to discourage readership of foreign magazines, but to maintain an environment in which Canadian magazines can exist in Canada alongside with imported magazines. It is also intended to foster conditions in which indigenous magazines can be published, distributed and sold in Canada on a commercial basis. The tax is consistent with the broad principles of the cultural and media policies of successive federal governments.

1. *Article III:2 versus coverage under the General Agreement on Trade in Services (GATS)*

a) Applicability of Article III of GATT 1994

3.32 The United States argued that Canada's 80 per cent excise tax on split-run editions is inconsistent with Article III:2, first sentence, of GATT 1994 because it creates an artificial distinction between "split-run" magazines and all other types of magazines and applies the 80 per cent tax solely to split-runs. It therefore applies a higher tax to certain types of imported magazines than to "like" domestic magazines.

3.33 Canada argued that this dispute concerns the provision of advertising services to Canadian advertisers and that Part V.I of the Excise Tax Act was a measure pertaining to advertising services. A magazine publisher derives revenue from both the sale of the magazine to consumers and from the sale of advertising space to advertisers. The sale of the right to advertise to a magazine's audience is an advertising service. As the tax imposed by the Excise Tax Act is imposed on the revenues earned through the provision of advertising services by a magazine publisher, it is a tax in respect of the provision of an advertising service. Multilateral trade disciplines on advertising services fall within GATS and not GATT 1994; Article III of GATT 1994 does not apply to Part V.I of the Excise Tax Act. However, the terms of reference direct the Panel to examine only trade matters within the purview of GATT 1994. Thus, the examination of Part V.I of the Excise Tax Act in light of GATS is not covered by the terms of reference. The first distinctive aspect of a magazine is its character as a public good which is largely defined by its content. The second distinctive feature is the magazine's dual nature in that it is both a consumer good and an advertising service with two distinct revenue streams. The two separate revenue streams are circulation revenue, which is derived from the sale of a good, and advertising revenue, which is derived from the sale of a service. The two consumers are readers and advertisers. All magazines exhibit this essential duality, which represents two distinct economic outputs.

3.34 GATT 1994 establishes the standards that govern international trade in goods. The central obligations of GATT 1994 are the tariff concessions by which WTO Members commit themselves (in Article II and the Schedules) to limit the level of tariffs they will impose on imports from other Members. A second obligation is that of the most-favoured-nation ("MFN") obligation in Article I. Articles III through XVII comprise most of the other substantive obligations of GATT 1994. These obligations apply to goods only. Article III of GATT 1994 sets out the national treatment obligation pertaining to treatment of imported goods. The Uruguay Round has produced a similar framework for trade in services. Specific commitments are recorded in national schedules that are attached to, and form an integral part of, the GATS. Every undertaking contained in a schedule to GATS is a binding commitment to allow the supply of the service in question on the terms and conditions specified and to not impose any new measures that would restrict entry into the market or the operation of the service. In the absence of any scheduled commitments, there are no disciplines on the introduction or the maintenance of measures of any type, even those that may be inconsistent with market access or national treatment commitments. Advertising services appear on the Services Sectoral Classification List of the Secretariat under the business sector.[49] The provision of advertising services is consequently a GATS matter, not a GATT matter.[50] Canada has not undertaken any commitments in respect of the provision of advertising services in its Schedule of Specific Commitments. In the absence of any scheduled commitments, there are *no* restrictions on Canada in respect of the introduction of measures concerning the provision of advertising services. In particular, Canada is not bound, nor in any way obliged, to provide national treatment to Members of the WTO in respect of the provision of advertising services in the Canadian market.

3.35 This challenge in respect of the Excise Tax Act measures is an indirect attempt by the United States to obtain trading benefits that it has been unable to obtain directly. In the guise of a GATT goods argument, the United States now attempts to persuade the Panel to allow it to have access to a service sector to which, in full accordance with the terms of international trade law, it is presently not entitled. Should the Panel agree that a Member can obtain benefits under a covered agreement that have been expressly precluded under another covered agreement, the Panel risks introducing uncertainty into the relationship between GATS and GATT disciplines.

3.36 The United States argued that the Canadian argument was baseless because: (1) nothing in GATS purports to reduce or eliminate the obligations that GATT has imposed since 1947; (2) GATS does not have primacy over GATT with respect to measures affecting trade in goods; and (3) Canada can observe its obligations under GATT Article III consistently with the provisions of GATS. There is no indication in the Agreement Establishing the WTO, GATT, or GATS, that adoption of GATS was intended as a limitation on the scope of GATT 1994. Had the negotiators intended to adopt a principle as fundamental as the one Canada now puts forward, they certainly would have provided for it in the text of GATT, GATS or WTO Agreement. In the absence of such an indication, or an irreconcilable conflict - neither of which Canada can point to here - GATT and GATS

---

[49] Canada notes that there are three Articles in Part III of the GATS on Specific Commitments, entitled Market Access, National Treatment, and Additional Commitments (Articles XVI, XVII and XVIII respectively). In general, the classification of sectors in national schedules is based on the Secretariat's Services Sectoral Classification List. This reference list of the Secretariat is based on the Central Product Classification (CPC) of the United Nations. See *Services Sectoral Classification List: Note by the Secretariat,* MTN.GNS/W/120 (10 July 1991). See also *Scheduling of Initial Commitments in Trade in Services: Explanatory Note,* MTN.GNS/W/164 (3 September 1993).

[50] Canada cites United Nations, Dept. of International Economic and Social Affairs, Statistical Office of the United Nations, *Provisional Central Product Classification*, Statistical Papers, Series M No. 77, U.N. Doc. ST/ESA/STAT/SER.M/77 (New York: United Nations, 1991) at 147-148, 173. Item 8711 states: sale or leasing services of advertising space or time. Services provided in soliciting advertising space or time for newspapers, other periodicals, and television stations. Item 8712 states: planning, creating and placement services of advertising. Planning, creating and placement services of advertisements to be displayed through the advertising media. Item 8719 states: other advertising services. Other advertising services not elsewhere classified, including outdoor and aerial advertising services and delivery services of samples and other advertising material.

must be applied according to their terms. (It is theoretically possible that the same measure may be covered by, and may even violate, both agreements. Indeed, a measure may violate more than one goods agreement as well, provided the measure is within the scope of each agreement and is inconsistent with the provisions of each.) By contrast, the negotiators of the WTO did establish a rule for addressing conflicts between GATT 1994 and the multilateral agreements on trade in goods in Annex 1A to the WTO Agreement.[51] By their terms, GATT Article III:2 covers taxes applied to products "directly or indirectly", and GATT Article III:4 applies even to measures affecting *services* connected to goods, such as "distribution" and "transportation".

3.37 Canada's decision not to inscribe relevant commitments on advertising services in its GATS schedule of specific commitments means that Canada is not assuming certain GATS obligations as to those services. Canada does not thereby insulate all measures having any connection to advertising from review under any other WTO agreement. Such a result would improperly exalt GATS over GATT and other WTO agreements. Canada's view would open a huge hole in GATT because there is no shortage of "service-related" measures that could be used to discriminate against imported goods. Under Canada's interpretation, a Member could, consistently with GATT: tax the rental of foreign cars, place a prohibitive surcharge on telecommunication services that are carried out using imported equipment, or impose a room tax on persons staying at hotels that were built using imported construction materials. Although each of these measures relates to the provision or consumption of a service, each also obviously imposes a competitive disadvantage on imported products and provides protection to domestic production, and each would be within the scope of GATT Article III. It is irrelevant whether or not the excise tax could be a measure affecting trade in advertising services. The excise tax is a direct or indirect tax on a product, split-run magazine editions, within the meaning of Article III:2.

3.38 Canada noted that it does not claim that there is a conflict between GATT 1994 and GATS in this case. The two treaties may very well apply in their own respective jurisdiction. GATS does not have as its object, and does not result in, the carving out of part of the jurisdiction of GATT 1994. The negotiators of GATS have merely developed new rules for a sector of international trade to which the existing rules did not apply. They have not, in doing so, redefined the scope of Article III of GATT 1994. The interpretation suggested by Canada of the area of application of Article III with respect to the provisions relating to services would have been the same in 1993 before the GATS treaty came into force. The interpretation is autonomous and based on specific terms of Article III:2 as well as on its intent and its original scope. The issue of overlapping obligations or conflicts arises because of the existence of two treaties, GATT 1994 and GATS, which contain different sanctions with respect to the provisions relating to services. Because of the existence of these two treaties which may apply to a given measure, it is necessary to interpret the scope of application of each such as to avoid any overlap. Such overlaps between the areas of GATT 1994 and GATS could lead to conflicts in the application of the treaties which should be resolved on the basis of the rules of interpretation of public international law.

3.39 The Canadian interpretation of the scope of Article III:2 of GATT 1994 and Article I:1 of GATS avoids such overlaps, respects the autonomy of each treaty and ensures the harmonious application thereof. It is not necessary in the instant case to determine the primacy of one treaty over the other. The Panel does not have to decide this question since there is no conflict. What must be decided is the individual scope of Article III:2 of GATT 1994 and Article I:1 of GATS. Part V.1 of the Excise Tax Act is a measure regarding the provision of services which is dealt with by Article I:1 of GATS. It is on the basis of an interpretation of the specific terms of Article III:2 of GATT 1994 and of Article I:1 of GATS, made in accordance with Article 31 of the Vienna Convention on the Law of Treaties, that the scope of application of each of the two treaties must be determined. The analysis of the measure which is the subject of the dispute leads to the determination of which of the two treaties apply. Canada does not rely on the rules of conflict to resolve the question of the applicability of Article III:2 of GATT to Part V.I of the Act. It is the interpretation of the word "indirectly" in Article III:2 which enables Canada to conclude that the Article does not apply to this measure.

[51] See General interpretive note to Annex 1A.

3.40 To determine which disciplines apply to a given measure, one must examine not only the object of the tax and the fiscal mechanism used, but most of all one must examine the effects of the tax, by distinguishing between principal and incidental effects. Some relevant factors for such a determination are: the nature of the economic activity covered by the measure, the structure and effects of the measure and the intention of the measure. A measure may have different aspects and may, as a result, attract different disciplines under different agreements, but no single aspect of a measure should be subject to both disciplines at the same time. In any case at the margins of the two disciplines, Canada suggests that the dominant or essential characteristics of the economic activity at issue should control the determination of whether GATT or GATS is applicable. In the case of the excise tax on split-run periodicals, the principal effect is to restrict the access of foreign publishers to the Canadian advertising market since, in principle the periodical could very well be sold on the Canadian market with advertising not specifically addressed to Canada. This is evidenced by the fact that plans for prospective split-runs for the Canadian market are based on actual sales in Canada of the original version of the magazine which does not contain specific advertising for that market.

3.41 The tax is intended to prevent the penetration of the Canadian advertising market by publishers who sell their advertising services in association with split-run magazines. It is clear that the measure pertains to the supply of a service and as such is a measure that WTO Members intended to be disciplined under GATS. This was recognized by the United States Trade Representative, in the *1995 National Trade Estimate Report on Foreign Trade Barriers* (NTE), where Canada's practices with respect to split-run advertising were listed and described under the heading Services Barriers.[52]

3.42 The United States responded that Canada's suggestion that GATT or GATS should apply based on the "dominant or essential characteristics of the economic activity at issue" was simply a test Canada had invented. Like Canada's other assertions relating to the GATS, it found no support in any of the WTO Agreements or their negotiating history. Adoption of such a test would alter the rights and obligations of WTO Members, in violation of Article 3.2 of the DSU. The United States submitted that whereas Canada referred to the need to avoid conflicts between GATT and GATS, it had failed to identify exactly what those conflicts were. A true "conflict" between two agreements arose only where compliance with one agreement necessarily resulted in non-compliance with the other. This simply was not the case with respect to the excise tax. Applying taxes to imported split-run magazines in a GATT-consistent manner (i.e., at a rate no higher for split-run than for non-split-run magazines) in no way requires Canada to breach its GATS obligations with regard to advertising services or any other service sector. Moreover, there is nothing that is even "inconsistent" about the obligations that the two agreements impose on Canada. The United States also asserted that, although USTR's *1995 NTE Report* listed the excise tax and other similar Canadian barriers under the heading of "services barriers", the report noted that these practices "restrict US access to the Canadian market for *publications and* media advertising" (emphasis added). In the *1996 NTE* report, the United States discussed Canadian restriction on US publications under the heading "Import Policies", not "Services Barriers".

b) *"Taxes applied directly or indirectly to products"*

3.43 The United States further argued that the tax is covered by Article III because it is imposed on the split-run edition which, like all magazines, are "products" for purposes of GATT. Magazines are physical goods that are manufactured, traded, and in the absence of a ban such as Canada's, imported. While the amount of the tax is *measured* in terms of "the value of all advertising in the edition," the tax is *applied* to each split-run edition. By its terms the tax is applied "in respect of each split-run edition of a periodical". Moreover, the tax is applied on a "per issue" basis. In addition, the obligation to pay the tax is imposed on those who produce or trade in the magazine as a final product, such as the publisher, distributor, printer or wholesaler, *as opposed to those who design or purchase advertising*. Finally, even the method of calculating the tax is based on revenues derived from an integral

[52] See *1995 National Trade Estimate Report on Foreign Trade Barriers* (Washington, D.C.: United States Trade Representative, 1995) at 38.

element of the physical magazine itself – the printed advertisements. Thus, the excise tax is applied directly on split run editions themselves, not on a service offered in connection with such editions.

3.44 Canada argued that the tax is not applied directly to a split-run magazine and in particular it is not based on, or applied to, the price of a split-run magazine. The tax is applied to the value of advertising carried by each issue of a split-run magazine and is assessed against the publisher of the split-run magazine, as the seller of the advertising service. The expression "in respect of each edition" serves as a basis for determining and calculating liability that relates to advertising revenue as the subject matter of the tax. The significant point, which decisively identifies the subject matter of the tax, is that the tax is measured not in terms of the price of the magazine but in terms of the advertising revenues it generates.

3.45 The tax is imposed on the publisher in the publisher's capacity as a provider of advertising services. The tax is tied to the service provided rather than the good. The publisher is the person responsible for the payment of the tax. The distributor, the printer and the wholesaler have been identified as potentially liable where it would be impossible to collect the tax in Canada from the publisher. In such cases, the Act grants those persons a right of recovery against the publisher.[53] Accordingly, there is no doubt that the ultimate liability falls on the publisher, and because the *ad valorem* basis of the tax is advertising, this liability arises directly out of the services dimension of the publisher's business. The collection mechanism is designed to ensure that there is always a person in Canada from whom the tax can be collected. It is doubtful whether collection machinery should ever be used as a basis for characterizing the nature of a tax, and in the particular circumstances of this case it would be entirely inappropriate.

3.46 The United States responded that Canada's allegation that the excise tax is collected from the publisher in connection with its provision of advertising services ignored that the publisher was the producer of the magazine as a product. With regard to imported magazines, Canada admitted that it is the *distributor* "who has to pay the tax." A magazine's distributor had absolutely no connection to the provision of any "advertising services". Moreover, if the foreign publisher of the imported magazine did not have a sufficient business presence in Canada, the magazine's distributor who paid the tax would be unlikely to obtain indemnification from the publisher at all. Indeed, the excise tax on split-run magazines was collected in a fashion similar to other excise taxes on products, such as the excise taxes in the *Japan - Alcoholic Beverages* case, and the federal excise taxes in the *US - Malt Beverages* case. Like the split-run tax, in those cases the excise taxes with respect to domestic products were collected from the producer, and the excise taxes with respect to imported products were collected from the importer, who was essentially a type of distributor.

3.47 Article III:2, first sentence, governs taxes applied directly or indirectly to products. Canada's argument that the tax is actually on advertising services confuses how the tax is *measured* (i.e., in terms of advertising fees) with what the tax *applies* to (i.e., split-run editions). There is ample additional evidence that the excise tax is a tax applied to split-run magazines as a product:

> - The Task Force's recommendation – which the Canadian Government adopted and which the Canadian Parliament enacted – describes the tax as a tax "*imposed on a magazine or periodical.*"[54]
>
> - In introducing the bill to enact the excise tax, Minister of Canadian Heritage Dupuy stated that the excise tax "would *apply to all periodicals* distributed in Canada and containing more than 20 per cent of reused editorial material as well as one or more advertisements aimed at Canadians", and that "[t]he publisher, the distributor, the printer or the wholesaler of *any magazine subject to the tax* would be responsible for paying the tax."[55]

---

[53] *Excise Tax Act*, R.S.C. 1985, c. E-15 as amended by S.C. 1995, c. 46, s. 41.3(2).

[54] *Task Force Report* at vi, 64 .

[55] *Commons Debates* at 14790, Sept. 25, 1995 (emphasis added).

- Following House of Commons passage of the excise tax bill, Canadian Heritage issued a press release describing the tax as follows: "The amendment to the Excise Tax Act will *place an excise tax on split-run magazines* distributed in Canada that contain more than 20 per cent recycled material . . . and one or more advertisements aimed at Canadians."[56]

Thus, during the time the excise tax was being formulated and enacted, Canadian officials had considered the tax to be a tax imposed on split-run magazines. It is only in the context of this panel proceeding, and in the light of US claims that the tax is inconsistent with Article III of GATT 1994, that Canada has advanced the argument that the tax is really a tax on advertising services and not a tax on split-run magazines. Indeed, given the statements of Canadian Government officials that the excise tax was designed to eliminate split-runs from its market, Canada's argument that split-run magazines are neither directly nor indirectly subject to the excise tax is not credible.

3.48 Even if the tax is not applied *directly* to split-runs, it is at a minimum applied *indirectly* to them because it is based on one of the two key uses to which magazines are put – in this case, the placement of advertisements. Moreover, it is impossible to separate the advertising that goes into a magazine from the magazine itself. Advertising is a significant component of commercial magazines, typically accounting for half or more of total pages. A magazine's advertisements can significantly affect its appeal and usefulness to readers. In addition to virtually eliminating their use as advertising vehicles – thus drastically reducing the revenues available to market such magazines – the tax reduces the appeal of such magazines to Canadian readers by effectively eliminating advertisements of interest to them.

3.49 Canada argued that the excise tax does not apply "indirectly" to a good within the meaning of Article III:2. In discussions at the London session of the Preparatory Committee, it was suggested that the word "indirectly" covers a tax not on a product as such but on the processing of the product".[57] The panel report in *Japan - Customs Duties, Taxes and Labelling Practices on Imported Wines and Alcoholic Beverages*[58] gave an interpretation of the term "indirectly" that was consistent with this reading:

> The Panel...found that the wording "directly or indirectly" and "internal taxes... of any kind" implied that, in assessing whether there is tax discrimination, account is to be taken not only of the rate of the applicable internal tax but also of the taxation methods (e.g. different kinds of internal taxes, direct taxation of the finished product or indirect taxation by taxing the raw materials used in the product during the various stages of its production) and of the rules for the tax collection (e.g. basis of assessment).

The concept of "indirectly" in Article III:2 does not capture measures that are disciplined under GATS. It is intended to capture taxes that apply to "inputs" that contribute to the production of a good raw materials, service inputs, intermediate inputs, etc. The question of whether the excise tax is covered by Article III:2 of GATT 1994 by reason of the expression "indirectly" must be examined in light of the relationship between GATS and GATT 1994.

3.50 Article III:2, to the extent that it allows a challenge of measures relating to services that "indirectly" impact on trade in goods, covers only measures concerning inputs such as raw material or services inputs that are directly involved in the production of a good. Taxes on such production inputs are properly subject to Article III:2 because they affect the costs and prices, and therefore the competitive position of goods that are subject to Article III:2. It is important, however, for the Panel to distinguish service inputs that are directly involved in the

---

[56] *House of Commons Passes Bill C-103, News Release,* Department of Canadian Heritage, Nov. 3, 1995 at 2 (emphasis added).

[57] EPCT/A/PV/9 at 19; and EPCT/W/181 at 3.

[58] Panel Report on *Japan - Customs Duties, Taxes and Labelling Practices on Imported Wines and Alcoholic Beverages,* adopted on 10 November 1987, BISD 34S/83 at 118, para. 5.8.

production of a good and services that are "end-products" in their own right. The publishers' advertising services, although closely associated with the magazines, are separate products. They are not involved in the production process of the magazines. The advertising services of the publisher are not, like labour in the production of a car, an input in the production of a good.

3.51 In order for a measure with respect to services to fall "indirectly" under Article III:2 of the GATT 1994, it has to affect the competitive situation of the importer on the market. In other words, the provision of the service has to be ancillary to the provision of the good in that market. The situation is reversed where the good produced by the exporter is used to gain access to a service market. In such an instance, the provision of the good becomes ancillary to the provision of the service which has the effect of transferring jurisdiction from GATT 1994 to GATS. Consequently, the argument on Article III:2 (and Article III:4) does not hold. Otherwise, such a restrictive interpretation could considerably diminish the scope of GATS and could lead to absurd situations such as those provided as examples by the United States. For example, irrespective of a Member's right not to make commitments with respect to foreign legal services, it would be impossible to maintain measures that restrict access when provided in a printed format. If allowed, the US interpretation of the expression "indirectly" would force Canada to accord national treatment to foreign publishers with respect to advertising services when it did not make any commitments in that respect in GATS. Such an interpretation would create an imbalance in carefully negotiated concessions on services sectors made by WTO Members during the last round of Multilateral Trade Negotiations. It would also void GATS of its effectiveness as it concerns Canada's right not to make commitments on advertising services.

3.52 If the United States is successful in persuading the WTO to condemn Canada's measures as inconsistent with GATT, the United States will be able to obtain direct access to a market from which it is otherwise properly precluded under international law. The measures in question are designed to protect access to Canada's advertising services market and they are effective in doing so. If the measures are struck down under the guise of GATT inconsistency, the WTO will have facilitated an unnegotiated concession on the part of Canada. The consequences of such an effect are far reaching. If the WTO is in any doubt about the nature of the dispute, it must simply look at what the United States will gain if successful. The United States will not gain greater access for its magazines. These magazines in exactly the same form as they are distributed in the United States already enter unimpeded. It will gain access to Canada's advertising market and the revenues to be had in that market.

3.53 The periodical publication industry is one which combines two commercial activities which are economically linked, the production of periodicals and the sale of advertising services. It cannot be denied that the autonomous economic activity which is the sale of advertising services significantly contributes to the financial viability of the publishing industry. However, this has nothing to do with the designation of two separate activities of an industry for the purposes of the application of GATT 1994 and GATS. The fact that an integrated industry uses some of its commercial activities and revenues so generated in order to facilitate the marketing of some of its other activities should not influence the characterization of the activities for the purposes of determining which sections of the WTO apply to them. The key element in the application of Article III:2, when considering whether a tax applies indirectly to a good, is whether this tax affects indirectly the global income generated by the industry under consideration. Hence the distinction made by Canada between a service as an input in the production of a good, which is within the scope of Article III:2, and a service which is a product of an independent activity such as the advertising services of a publisher, which are within the scope of Article I:1 of GATS. Canada also raised the further distinction which must be made between the services that are within the scope of GATT 1994 and GATS on the basis of the accessory or principal nature of the service. A service, as an input in the production of a good, is an accessory in the production of a good. However, the advertising services of a publisher are the principal product for which a periodical is the accessory.

3.54 A large number of services result in the production of a good. The fact that the result of the provision of the service is physically incorporated in the production of a good is not in itself a key factor in the characterization of the measure which relates to such a service. It is because of the economic integration of the two activities which form the periodical publication industry that advertising, in its physical form, is incorporated into periodicals. It is because a periodical is the accessory of the advertising service, its vehicle, that advertising in its physical form is incorporated into a periodical. It is not because advertising is physically "necessary" to the material production of a periodical as an editorial vehicle. Unlike printing services (the work of the printers), the advertising services of the publisher have nothing to do with the physical production of periodicals. Those services only relate to the financial viability of the integrated activities of the periodical publishing industry. This has nothing to do with the protection found in Article III:2 of GATT 1994. To extend the scope of Article III:2 and of the phrase "indirectly" would result in en extension beyond natural and reasonable meaning in the circumstances. The level of integration of an industry cannot be a factor in the characterization of a measure which relates to one of its activities for the purposes of determining which WTO treaties applies thereto. The only factors applicable are the nature of the measure and the scope of application of each of the two treaties.

3.55 There are no contradictions in the Canadian approach. Canada provided a general description of the periodical publishing industry and pointed out the integration of advertising and publishing activities. This explains the close relationship of these activities as far as overall income for the industry is concerned as well as the accessory nature of periodicals for the advertising services of publishers. Canada's main position is very clear. There is no doubt that the advertising services of publishers are services that are not accessory services or inputs in the production of periodicals. The fact that these services are part of the integrated activities of a publisher and that the income which results from them contributes to the overall financial viability of the industry does not affect the characterization of the activity for the purposes of the applicability of Article III:2. The latter does not apply to measures relating to the ability of a publisher to market its advertising services. Part V.1 of the Excise Tax Act is beyond the scope of Article III:2 of GATT 1994.

3.56 The United States asserted that neither the plain meaning of the term "indirectly" in Article III:2, nor the limited negotiating history concerning it, supports a restrictive meaning of that term. Rather, the negotiating history reveals that a tax with respect to the processing of a product was one example, but not necessarily the only example, of an "indirect" tax on a product. Advertisements are a substantial feature or component of a magazine as a product, accounting for half or more of the pages of a typical magazine sold in Canada. It is not logical to say, as Canada does, that a tax with respect to inputs - that is to say, things that are consumed in making a product - is a tax directly or indirectly on a product, but a tax that concerns a major feature or component of that actual product is not. If anything, the latter is more directly a tax applied to the product itself. Advertisements affect a magazine's price, cost, and competitive position as much as any input consumed in the production of a product. The carrying of advertisements is, moreover, a major use to which magazines are put. A tax with respect to a substantial use of a product can be viewed as a tax, directly or indirectly, applied to the product.

2. *Conformity of Part V.I with Article III of GATT 1994*

3.57 Canada observed that there is an artificial quality to any attempt to assess how Article III applies to a tax that has never been applied to a foreign product. It has been assumed that the tax does not apply to imported products in view of the maintenance of Tariff Code 9958. Article III:2 requires a comparison of an imported and a domestic product, a comparison that has to remain purely hypothetical in this case. Subject to this observation, Canada provides an alternative argument to be considered in the event the Panel is of the view that Part V.I is a taxation measure that applies to magazines as "goods" and that an examination of the application of Article III of GATT 1994 has to be conducted.

3.58 The United States remarked that, by Canada's own admission, the excise tax applies to imported (as well as domestically produced) magazines. To the extent that the tax had not actually been *levied* on imported split-runs, it is because those imports had been completely banned by Canada. It is entirely possible that even if there were no import ban the excise tax would still not be levied because the tax is set at such a high level that it would likely discourage producers from marketing imported split-runs in the first place. It is well-settled in GATT that the level of actual imports is not the basis for assessing whether a violation of GATT Article III exists. The 1949

Working Party on *Brazilian Internal Taxes* stated that the obligations of Article III "were equally applicable whether imports from other contracting parties were substantial, small or non-existent."[59] This is because the purpose of Article III is not to protect expectations on trade volumes, but rather "expectations on the competitive relationship between imported and domestic products."[60]

3.59 Thus, the plain fact that the excise tax is mandatory legislation that applies by its terms to imported magazines brings it within the purview of Article III. The principle that actual imports are not required is especially appropriate in this case because Canada has banned the relevant imports to which the tax would otherwise apply. A WTO Member cannot use a GATT-inconsistent import prohibition to shield its discriminatory domestic regulations from scrutiny. In the absence of the import prohibition, the excise tax would immediately affect imported split-run magazines. By making imported split-runs prohibitively expensive to sell in Canada, the tax would accomplish what the import ban now does: the absence of imported split-runs in the Canadian market. The effect of this scheme is that dozens of US split-runs would be sold in Canada but for barriers Canada has erected to their sale. This case is not based on Canada's treatment of US publishers' split-run magazines produced *in Canada*. Such magazines are not imported products within the scope of GATT Article III.

a) *Article III:2, first sentence*
   (i) *like product issue*

3.60 The United States argued that the Canadian excise tax created an artificial distinction between otherwise entirely like products - split run and non-split run magazine editions - based on the extent to which the same or a similar version of the product was sold abroad. The excise tax defines a split-run magazine entirely in terms of its relationship to another magazine sold outside Canada. It is, therefore, impossible to determine whether a magazine is a split-run based simply upon an examination of its physical form, its editorial content, or its advertising content. The fact that a similar edition of a magazine is sold in a country other than Canada does not differentiate the magazine from another magazine in terms of physical characteristics, end-uses, content, advertising, or any other attribute. In fact, the defining characteristic of a split-run magazine under the excise tax - the existence of another magazine sold outside Canada – is an extraneous factor having nothing to do with the character of the split-run itself.

3.61 Canada argued that periodicals with editorial content developed for the Canadian market and split-runs substantially reproducing foreign editorial content are not "like products" within the meaning of Article III:2 and are distinguishable on the basis of their content, the essential characteristic of any magazine. Magazines are distinct from ordinary articles of trade. Magazines are intended, by their very nature, for intellectual consumption as opposed to physical use (like a bicycle) or physical consumption (like food). It follows that the intellectual content of a cultural good such as a magazine must be considered its prime characteristic. Consequently, the "like product" analysis of whether imported split-run magazines share the same characteristics as domestic magazines with editorial content developed for the Canadian market must be approached in terms of intellectual content as opposed to the traditional approach of examining material or physical characteristics. The periodical industry is keenly aware of the importance of editorial content. It is editorial content and its ability to attract readers that determine the ability of a periodical to attract advertising revenues to securing its financial viability.

3.62 Periodicals with editorial content developed for the Canadian market and split-run periodicals envisaged by the legislation are distinct products on the basis of their editorial content. The definition of "split-run edition" reflects this distinction. Editorial material developed for the Canadian market reflects a Canadian perspective and contains specific information of interest to Canadians. The content is qualitatively different from editorial material copied from foreign publications.

---

[59] The 1949 Working Party on *Brazilian Internal Taxes,* adopted on 31 June 1949, BISD II/181, 185, para. 16 .

[60] Panel Report on *United States - Taxes on Petroleum and Certain Imported Substances*, adopted on 17 June 1987, BISD 34S/136, 158, para. 5.1.9.

3.63 What has been said of the essential properties of magazines is equally applicable to their end-use. The end-use of a magazine is not simply reading; it is the transmission and acquisition of specific information. The information in, for example, a sports magazine, cannot be considered essentially the same as that in a philosophical journal. Any attempt to characterize the "end-use" of products so broadly that they all end up in the same category would deprive this consideration of any real meaning and would run afoul of the principle that the expression "like" in this context is to be narrowly construed.[61]

3.64 The United States argued that a distinction of the type Canada had drawn in its excise tax should be inherently suspect under Article III because it is founded on distinctions other than differences between the products being sold in the importing country. In *US - Standards for Gasoline,* the panel rejected an argument that the US "Gasoline Rule" did not provide less favourable treatment to imported products as compared to like domestic products because it treated similarly situated parties similarly noting that

> in the *Malt Beverages* case, a tax regulation according less favourable treatment to beer on the basis of the size of the producer was rejected.

and observing that, under the US argument in that case

> *Imported goods would be exposed to a highly subjective and variable treatment according to extraneous factors. This would thereby create great instability and uncertainty in the conditions of competition as between domestic and imported goods in a manner fundamentally inconsistent with the object and purpose of Article III.* [62]

3.65 The same concerns about "highly subjective and variable treatment according to extraneous factors" that the panel identified also apply in this case. The "extraneous factors" on which application of Canada's excise tax depends are the existence or non-existence of a product sold in a country other than Canada, and the extent of that product's similarities to, and differences from, the product sold in Canada. The United States described examples that it considered showed how Canada's distinction between split-runs and other magazines produced odd and arbitrary results based on sales of products outside Canada.

3.66 Canada argued that the point is not whether originality could be perceived as such, but whether there was a difference between the two products at issue - the split-run replicating a foreign magazine, on the one hand, and the domestic magazine with original content, on the other. This had nothing to do with "subjective and variable treatment according to extraneous factors" as identified in the panel on *US - Standards for Gasoline.* It made no difference in terms of product characteristics whether the gasoline was handled by refiners, blenders, or producers. Gasoline was gasoline, but any careful examination would show that content differences between split-runs and original Canadian magazines were characteristics of the products themselves. A recurring theme of the United States argument is that the Canadian legislation is not based upon objective product differences; that it is based on a distinction unrelated to product characteristics. This is said to be the result of a definition that depends entirely on the existence of a foreign companion edition with sales outside Canada. In the words of the United States, this is an extraneous factor that has nothing to do with the character of the split run itself. On the contrary, it has everything to do with the character of the split-run itself. The legislation does not focus on the existence of a so-called companion edition as a factor unrelated to the characteristics of a split-run marketed in Canada. It focuses on the fact that the split-run marketed in Canada is to a substantial degree no more than a reproduction of a

---

[61] Appellate Body Report on *Japan - Taxes on Alcoholic Beverages*, adopted 11 July 1996, WT/DS8/R, WT/DS10/R and WT/DS11/R .

[62] *United States - Standards for Reformulated and Conventional Gasoline, op. cit.*, paras. 6.11-6.12 (emphasis added). The United States added that in *United States - Taxes on Automobiles*, DS31/R (29 Sept. 1994, unadopted), the panel (para. 5.55) found that "Article III:4 does not permit treatment of an imported product less favourable than that accorded to a like domestic product, based on factors *not directly relating to the product as such.* The Panel found therefore that, to the extent that treatment under the CAFE measure was based on factors relating to the control or ownership of producers/importers, it could not in accordance with Article III:4 be applied in a manner that also accorded less favourable treatment to products of foreign origin" (emphasis added).

foreign edition, with the content characteristics invariably associated with such material. It is not the existence of a foreign companion edition, or sales of that edition outside Canada, that counts. It is the reproduction in the Canadian split-run of content that originated in that foreign edition. Contrary to the United States argument, this is a product characteristic of the split-run magazine. The replication of foreign content is not only an attribute of the split-run a defining attribute, in fact it is readily discernible from an examination of the product itself.

3.67 Canada further considered that the United States' approach to like products is *necessarily* over-broad because it ignores the only basis on which one magazine can be distinguished from another – the content. If magazines are treated as ordinary articles of manufacture, defined only by the fact that they are physically made up of printed paper and staples, then it would obviously have to follow that all magazines are exactly the same. The United States submission even implies when it refers to Canada's tariff item 49.02, that newspapers, journals and periodicals are like goods. This leads to the second basic principle Canada referred to in this connection: that "like product" determinations under Article III.2 are to be made on a case-by-case basis. The reason for proceeding case-by-case is obvious: to avoid over-generalization and a mechanical or automatic transfer of criteria that are suitable in one context to another context where they no longer properly apply. A case-by-case approach is one that takes account of the particular circumstances. It cannot be denied that cultural products are different, that they have their own distinguishing characteristics. By treating them as if they were ordinary items of merchandise trade, the United States has ignored the entire rationale of the case-by-case approach.

3.68 The chief and for all practical purposes the *only* distinguishing characteristic of a magazine is its content. Content plays a role in the case of cultural products that is analogous to physical properties in the case of ordinary items of trade. Content is what the reader is looking for – the message and not the medium. The end-use of a magazine is the transmission of specific information. A magazine has a utilitarian function – it may be to keep up on current events; to acquire information about specific topics like computers or investments; in some cases, to provide entertainment but in every case, the function and value of the magazine to the reader is inseparably linked to its specific content or subject matter. The United States' emphasis on physical properties leads inevitably to a lumping together of all magazines as indistinguishable commodities, contrary to the principle of narrow construction and the case-by-case approach. The approach that Canada advocates, giving content the decisive role, does not lead to the opposite extreme. Magazines can easily be classified by type, either broadly or narrowly, on the basis of content. Exactly where the lines are to be drawn can be a matter of judgment, but no more so than in the case of any other like product determination.

3.69 The legislation uses the concept of original material as the defining element – material that is not, to quote the statute, "the same or materially the same as editorial material" in editions that circulate primarily in foreign markets. This criterion of original versus replicated material might seem abstract at first, but in its practical effect it refers to a dividing line that is very easily recognized. Original material means content developed for and aimed at the Canadian market – this means Canadian content in terms of subject matter as opposed to authorship or production. The idea that Canadian content is the same as foreign content is simply not tenable. The events, topics and people covered will be Canadian. They may not be exclusively Canadian, but the balance will be recognizably and even dramatically different than in a replicated foreign publication, where articles on Canada are close to non-existent. Foreign magazines are almost devoid of content dealing with Canada, and what little there is quite logically fails to reflect a Canadian perspective. Even where the topics covered are the same, the perspective will be different. Some of these qualities like "perspective" are admittedly somewhat intangible; but where cultural products are at issue, these assessments cannot be avoided. And they fall well within the legitimate range of the kind of "discretionary judgment" the Appellate Body has identified as inherent in like products determinations for the purposes of Article III – discretionary but not arbitrary. It is the prevailing characteristics of each category that we should look at in determining whether or not publications created for Canada are the same as publications replicated from foreign editions. There may be individual articles that might conceivably have appeared in either type of magazine. Some issues might be more different or less different than others. But the prevailing pattern is what counts. Canadian content and foreign content are significantly different. Local publications deal with local topics. People are preoccupied with their own affairs and communities. Periodicals are the mirror image of those communities. The content of a periodical created for one community will necessarily differ from what is created for another community.

3.70 Further, the only actual magazines the United States has chosen to exhibit in this case are *Pulp & Paper*,[63] which is not a split-run and has no relevance to the Excise Tax Act, *Paris Match* and *The Economist*. *Paris Match* is an imported non-split-run and *The Economist* is an imported split-run that is exempt from the tax as a North American edition without advertising specifically directed at the Canadian market. *None* of these magazines is relevant to the comparison between domestic and imported products that has to be made under Article III:2, first sentence. But the evidence is readily available, because there are grand-fathered split-runs in Canada that can be compared with other domestic Canadian magazines. This evidence has been filed by Canada, although Canada does not bear the burden of proof. The evidence consists of *Time US*, *Time Canada* and *Maclean's* – what the United States would call a foreign companion magazine, a split-run that would be taxable without the grandfathering provision, and an original domestic magazine. And the issue, in a nutshell, is whether the last two – *Time Canada* and Maclean's – are "like" products, having regard to the narrow construction and the case-by-case approach mandated by the *Japan - Alcoholic Beverage* Appellate ruling.

3.71 Canada's evidence in the form of actual magazines provides typical examples of a split-run in the form of *Time Canada*, the parent edition in the form of *Time US*, and a domestic magazine in the form of *Maclean's*. The proper basis of comparison is of course *Maclean's* and *Time Canada*. Almost every article in *Maclean's* deals with Canada. This is true of the editorial, the letters, the business news, the entertainment coverage, the arts, crime, people, the law, much of the news – everything in fact but the lead international stories covering about 8 out of 88 pages. Next, a comparative look at *Time Canada* shows that it has practically *no* reference to Canada or Canadian subject. There are two out of 21 letters from Canadian sources. There is a travel advisory on Montreal, but it turns out to be about an exhibit dedicated to an American landscape architect. The difference between *Time Canada* and *Maclean's* is striking. It would escape no reader and no consumer. This is about as typical an example as one could find. These are mainstream, mass circulation magazines. Canada suggests that there is a significant, objective, discernible difference between a split-run and a magazine created with original content for the Canadian market.

3.72 The United States contested Canada's argument that imported split-runs were not like or directly competitive or substitutable with non-split runs because non-split-runs contain original content that is from a Canadian perspective. An examination of the structure of the tax showed this to be false. Moreover, even if this assertion were true it would not form a legitimate basis for distinguishing between otherwise like products. First, by its terms the tax applied or did not apply, to particular magazines irrespective of their editorial "perspective". For example, a magazine published solely for the Canadian market, or that contained no advertising specifically directed at Canadians, automatically avoided the tax regardless of how "foreign" its contents might be. However, the very same magazine became subject to the tax if it had a somewhat different foreign companion edition. Second, the editorial content need not be "original" at all. Rather, a magazine could avoid the tax, but still be identical to what is sold abroad, as long as the publisher did not advertise to Canadians. This suggested that the real basis for the distinction is simply whether the magazine might compete for advertising revenues with purely domestically produced Canadian magazines. That, indeed, is a purpose that Canada did not hide. Finally, even if one could somehow credit Canada's argument that it is seeking through the excise tax to ensure "original content" in magazines sold in Canada this purpose would be equally illegitimate. If GATT permitted governments to require that imported goods be designed exclusively or primarily for their markets, they could easily insulate their markets from the comparative economic advantages of other WTO Members. Such a result would undermine the foundations of international trade.

[63] Referred to in paragraph 3.91.

3.73 The recent Appellate Body report in *Japan - Alcoholic Beverages* shares the focus of the *US - Standards for Gasoline* panel report on objective *product* differences in judging product likeness. There the Appellate Body observed:

"The Report of the Working Party on *Border Tax Adjustments*, adopted by the CONTRACTING PARTIES in 1970, set out the basic approach for interpreting 'like or similar products' generally in the various provisions of GATT 1947:

> ...The interpretation of the term should be examined on a case-by-case basis. This would allow a fair assessment in each case of the different elements that constitute a "similar" product. Some criteria were suggested for determining, on a case-by-case basis, whether a product is "similar"; the product's end-uses in a given market; consumers' tastes and habits, which change from country-to-country; the product properties, nature and quality.
>
> This approach was followed in almost all adopted panel reports after *Border Tax Adjustments*".[64]

The Appellate Body found that the term "like product" in Article III:2, first sentence must be "construed narrowly" in light of the existence of the second sentence of Article III:2 which covered "directly competitive or substitutable" products, and that distinguishing between "like products" and "directly competitive or substitutable" products "is a discretionary decision that must be made [by panels] in considering the various characteristics of the *products* in individual cases".[65]

3.74 Thus the Appellate Body in *Japan - Alcoholic Beverages*, like the *US - Standards for Gasoline* decision, endorsed a case-by-case approach that focused on differences in *products,* rather than on distinctions based on extraneous factors such as the production method. The illustrative list of like-product factors cited by the Appellate Body – end-uses, the product's properties, and so forth – are identical for a magazine sold only in Canada and a magazine for which a companion edition is sold abroad. While "like product" in Article III:2, first sentence, must be interpreted narrowly, it cannot be interpreted so narrowly as to permit less favourable treatment based on distinctions between literally identical products depending on whether a companion product is sold in another market. This interpretation would be so narrow as to eliminate "like product" altogether from Article III:2, first sentence.

3.75 Canada considered that the US arguments on the like product issue failed to present any positive evidence that an imported split-run had enough in common with original-content Canadian magazines to allow them to be considered like products. The absence of such evidence is fatal because the United States had the burden of proof. Canada was not suggesting that a magazine had only one attribute. Nor did it back away from the proposition that the assessment had to take into account all the relevant circumstances. But the circumstances had to be weighed and balanced according to their importance, and editorial content was the most important distinguishing feature and was the chief and for all practical purposes the *only* distinguishing characteristic of a magazine. A magazine is nothing without its content which was what defined the end-use and the value of a magazine to its readers. Treating content as "one attribute among many" as the United States would say, would tend to sweep all or at least very broad classes of magazines into the same category. This would disregard the narrow characterization of like products required by the Appellate Body in *Japan - Alcoholic Beverages.*

3.76 As the complainant, the United States bears the burden of proving that Canada acted inconsistently with its obligations under Article III:2, first sentence. This is a principle of long standing in GATT jurisprudence. To date the United States has made no effort to discharge this burden. Instead, it has relied upon general allegations and assertions such as the following: "there is no identifiable difference between split-run magazines, on the one

---

[64] Appellate Body Report on *Japan - Taxes on Alcoholic Beverages, op. cit.*,at 20.

[65] *Ibid.*, at 21 (emphasis added).

hand, and magazines without a companion edition, on the other hand, in terms of their physical characteristics, appearance, uses, tariff classifications, or even editorial content". Such statements do not constitute the empirical evidence required to both substantiate the claim made by the United States that all magazines are the same or that magazines based on local content are the same as magazines replicating foreign content; and to fulfil the burden of proof borne by the United States.

3.77 While Canada also recognized the definition of what constitutes a "like product" by the Working Party on Border Tax Adjustments, it considered that the "like products" test requires a much more sophisticated analysis than that suggested by the United States. The Working Party had concluded that the determination of what constitutes "like products" must be made on a case-by-case basis in order to allow for the consideration of the specific circumstances of each case. In that context the Working Party suggested some criteria: "... the product's end-uses in a given market; consumers' tastes and habits, which change from country to country; the product's properties, nature and quality."[66] This line of thinking evolved into an established GATT practice and was recently reaffirmed by the panel in *US - Standards for Gasoline*.

3.78 The United States considered that with Canada's argument - that the US like product analysis is incomplete because it relies solely on the physical characteristics of magazines, and ignores their editorial content - Canada appears to concede that there is no other basis to consider split-run magazines and other magazines to be "unlike" based on the specific criteria established by the Appellate Body in *Japan - Alcoholic Beverages.* By focusing solely on "editorial content," Canada ignores the Appellate Body's instruction that the analysis of "like product" must take into account "the *various* characteristics of products in individual cases."[67] Editorial content is only one attribute of a magazine, among many. The type, texture, colour, thickness, and even the perfume, of the paper can be important factors to market appeal. The dimensions of the magazine, the manner in which its pages are bound, the typesetting, and the appearance of the ink, can also be significant. The type, appearance, and frequency of advertisements may be a factor in a consumer's purchasing decision as well. Readers may purchase a magazine in part for the information its advertisements contain about where and how to purchase products or services locally. All of these attributes – including editorial content – combine to form an *overall package* that a consumer may or may not be attracted to. For the Canadian and US magazine industries, editorial content generally represents substantially less than 20 per cent of the cost of producing a consumer magazine.

3.79 Even if one were to examine editorial content in isolation, Canada's argument that magazines can be differentiated solely according to the percentage of "original" versus "non-original" editorial content they contain is untenable. There simply is no readily identifiable difference in actual editorial content between what the excise tax deems to be "original" and "non-original" content. That is because the distinction drawn by the excise tax is not based on the specific contents of magazines distributed in Canada but simply on whether those contents are used in magazines distributed abroad. A magazine reader in Canada cannot discern whether a magazine is "original" or not based on an examination of the magazine's contents, and thus could not be expected to consider "non-original" magazines to be any different from "original" magazines. For purposes of consumer use – as well as use by advertisers – magazines are judged by what they themselves offer, not by what a companion edition may contain.

3.80 In fact, Canada's "original content" requirement is not really meant to ensure that magazines sold in Canada have any particular type of content. Rather, it is meant to ensure that one type of production method – regional or split-runs – cannot be employed for magazines sold in the Canadian market. A distinction drawn to favour one type of production method has obvious protectionist implications and is not one that GATT should countenance for distinguishing between otherwise-like products.

---

[66] *Border Tax Adjustments* (Report of the Working Party adopted on 2 December 1970), BISD 18S/97.

[67] Appellate Body Report on *Japan - Taxes on Alcoholic Beverages, op. cit.*, at 21 (emphasis added).

3.81 Further, Canada's argument that split-runs usually differ from magazines sold only in Canada with respect to the perspective and orientation of their editorial content is legally irrelevant. A panel must assess the distinction that a measure *actually draws*, not a distinction a measure might have drawn but does not. In this case, to the extent the excise tax concerns content, it differentiates between magazines whose content is contained in a product sold in another country and magazines whose content is sold only in Canada. Thus, the excise tax simply does not differentiate between content based on its Canadian focus or perspective. Application of the excise tax does not turn merely on a magazine's "originality". A magazine distributed both inside and outside Canada becomes subject to the tax based solely on the inclusion of a single advertisement that is not identical in both editions. The very same magazine whose several editions do *not* differ in advertising is not taxed. Canada has advanced no basis for distinguishing between magazines based on the type of advertisements they contain.

3.82 For example, a science magazine escapes from the tax even if it contains absolutely no articles about Canadian scientists or Canadian scientific research so long as it is not sold outside Canada. The very same magazine would be subject to the tax if it is sold both in Canada and abroad and contained an advertisement that differed between the version sold in Canada and the version sold abroad. Yet the same magazine would not be subject to the tax if it is sold both inside and outside Canada but did not contain such an advertisement. Thus, the excise tax does not, in fact, distinguish between magazines based on their editorial content, let alone based on the orientation of the content. Rather, it applies based on factors related to whether a magazine was produced for more than one market, and advertising content. Article III:2 does not permit governments to distinguish between otherwise like products based on such business and trade factors.

3.83 With regard to the Canadian assertion that the US analysis of like product with respect to the excise tax is unacceptably general and would necessarily lead to the conclusion that *all* magazines are the same like product, regardless of content, the Appellate Body made clear in *Japan - Alcoholic Beverages* that product likeness for purposes of Article III must be addressed on a case-by-case basis and in the light of all relevant circumstances. Thus, no sweeping once-and-for-all product likeness determinations are appropriate for magazines or other products. The distinction between "original" and "non-original" content was not based on objective content differences, or any differences at all, based on a comparison of products sold in Canada. Whether or not distinctions may ever properly be drawn between magazines based on their editorial content is not an issue that is before this Panel. The excise tax distinguishes between products based on whether a similar product is sold abroad, not on objective content differences between products being sold in Canada.

3.84 Canada argues that because magazines contain intellectual or cultural content, they should receive unique treatment under GATT. Many products, as diverse as works of art, designer clothing, phonograph records and cinematographic films contain intellectual or cultural content. Like magazines, these products were in widespread use prior to the adoption of GATT 1947. But of these products, only cinematographic films were accorded special treatment in GATT 1947. Had the drafters of GATT 1947 sought to treat other intellectual or cultural products differently from products in general, they would have done so.

3.85 Canada argued that the United States insists that it is impossible to determine whether a magazine is a split-run simply upon an examination of its physical form, its editorial content, or its advertising. This simply misses the point. A casual reader might not in fact know whether a magazine is a split-run or simply an imported foreign magazine. There might be practically no difference between the two. *Time US* and *Time Canada* are very close. But that basis of comparison is irrelevant, because the comparison is not between imported magazines and imported magazines. The comparison is between imported split-run with the domestic magazine – *Time Canada* and *MacLean's*. And here the reader would have no difficulty in seeing that the two are very different products, offering completely different benefits to the prospective reader. The point, in sum, is not whether a split-run can be identified as such by the consumer. It is whether it can be identified as a significantly different product when compared to a domestic magazine that is not a split-run.

3.86 The United States makes the same point when it says a magazine reader in Canada cannot discern whether a magazine is original or not, based on an examination of the magazine's contents, and thus could not be expected to consider non-original magazines to be any different from original magazines. This is based on the same misperception. The point is not whether originality can be perceived as such, but whether there is a difference between the two products at issue – the split-run replicating a foreign magazine, on the one hand, and the domestic magazine with original content, on the other. And nothing the United States has said casts any doubt on the proposition that difference would be obvious to any reader. This has nothing to do with subjective and variable treatment according to extraneous factors, as identified in the panel report on *US - Standards for Gasoline*. That situation obviously had nothing to do with objective product differences. It makes no difference in terms of product characteristics whether the gasoline is handled by refiners, blenders, or producers, or what data these various companies are likely to hold. Gasoline is gasoline, but any careful examination will show that content differences between split-runs and original Canadian magazines are characteristics of the products themselves.

3.87 At some points the United States refers to split-runs as a production method. In fact it is not a production method, it is a specific type of magazine. The United States says that a distinction drawn to favour one production method over another has protectionist implications that GATT should not countenance. This reflects a passage of the *United States - Measures Affecting Alcoholic and Malt Beverages* ("*US - Malt Beverages*") decision that was specifically overruled in *Japan - Alcoholic Beverages*.[68] In any event, it mis-characterizes the legislation, which distinguishes not on the basis of production method but of product content. The United States argument on like products is based on a highly abstract reading of the Canadian legislation taken out of its real-world context. It is based in fact on a refusal to take account of the effect of the distinction between original and reproduced content on which the legislation is based. But it is only on the basis of the effect of the distinction that one can determine whether in fact the legislation has the effect of taxing imported products in excess of like domestic products.

3.88 Canada noted the United States' contention that Canadian content or Canadian perspective are legally irrelevant, and that a panel must assess the distinction a measure actually draws, not a distinction it might have drawn but does not. In fact, the point is to assess what the legislation actually does – not simply what it says but what it does. It is obvious that the basis of the legislation – content reproduced from foreign sources – has concrete effects. These are effects that any reader can see – from the stories, the people, the subjects and, indeed, the perspective. They determine the character and the subject matter of the publication. The suggestion that these are not objective, visible product differences makes no sense. When the United States says that the nature of the content is irrelevant because that is not the distinction the legislation actually draws, they are asking the Panel simply to close its eyes to the actual operation and effect of the legislation in a real-world context. The implication is that one should look at the form, not the substance; that the assessment should be in the abstract and that the concrete effect should be ignored. None of this makes sense in the context of Article III:2, first sentence, which requires a finding of excess taxation in fact. One of the reasons why Canadian magazines do not sell well in the US market is precisely that they have a different content, content designed for Canadians. The American public is not attracted to this content. If American consumers can recognize the difference between an American and a Canadian magazine, surely Canadians can recognize it just as easily.

3.89 The United States asserted that the terms of the excise tax itself define the distinction Canada has drawn and this is what is at issue in this case. An analysis of the way the tax is structured shows the two to be like products. Canada's claim that the United States had failed to produce evidence of imported split-runs ignores the fact that Canada has banned imported split-runs. Canada could not, on the one hand, ban the relevant imported product, then argue on the other hand that there are no "real-life" examples of how that (banned) product is actually similar to domestic products, or actually competes. In fact, Canada's own example – *Time Canada* and *Maclean's* – does not involve an imported split-run magazine. Moreover, one simply could not say that the concrete effects of the terms of the excise tax are to separate out imported split-runs (of which there are none) that have no Canadian content from domestic non-split-runs that do.

---

[68] Panel Report on *United States - Measures Affecting Alcoholic and Malt Beverages*, adopted on 19 June 1992, BISD 39S/274, para. 5.25.

3.90 In the *US - Section 337* panel report, the panel stated that it "had to assess whether or not Section 337 *may* lead to the application to imported products of treatment less favourable than that accorded to products of the United States [i.e. domestic] origin. It noted that this approach is in accordance with previous practice of the Contracting Parties in applying Article III, which has been to base their decisions on *the distinctions made by the laws, regulations or requirements themselves* and on their potential impact, rather than on the actual consequences for specific imported products" (emphasis added). In this case, the excise tax law *itself* did not distinguish between editorial content that is about Canada and editorial content that is not, but is instead based on the existence or non-existence of a similar product in a foreign country, and on advertising.

3.91 The United States questioned the necessity for specific product examples in light of this analysis of the *US - Section 337* panel report and Canada's longstanding import ban. The United States argued that while there were no specific examples of imported split-runs because none exist; should the Panel find specific examples relevant, a useful comparison to demonstrate the "likeness" of imported and Canadian-produced magazines exists between a US (*non*-split-run) magazine, *Pulp & Paper*, and *Pulp & Paper Canada*, a Canadian magazine unconnected to *Pulp & Paper* (US). The two publications have substantially similar editorial content and subject matter - pulp and paper technology, products, processes and marketing. Both contain a number of technical reports on various paper and pulp subjects that have little, if any, connection with particular paper and pulp operations in either Canada or the United States. Both contain information about paper and pulp operations and statistics in both Canada and the United States. Both contain a wide variety of advertisements from suppliers of products and services directly related to the pulp and paper products. Both contain classified advertising sections, and both contain an advertisers' index. Only a handful of pages out of the 78 pages in *Pulp & Paper Canada* were devoted to exclusively Canadian pulp and paper, and the vast majority of the publication consists of advertisements and feature articles that did not focus specifically on Canadian production or issues. Moreover, a Canadian paper industry publication reader study conducted by an independent advertising agency indicated that the two magazines have comparable readership and that readers use these magazines for the same purposes such as product information and mill news. Based on these and other similarities, the United States argued there can be no doubt that *Pulp & Paper Canada* is "like" *Pulp & Paper* (US). The United States further argued that these examples also show the importance of advertisements to the usefulness and appeal of magazines as products. The ads in the pulp and paper magazines are so obviously highly useful to those in the pulp and paper business. Both the Canadian and the US publications go so far as to contain an advertisement directory so that readers can more readily access pertinent advertisements.

3.92 In response to Canada's reliance on the editorial content of the *Time Canada* and *Maclean's,* the United States argued that this editorial content does not show that split-run and non-split-run magazines are not like products. First, one example out of over 1,000 magazines sold in Canada hardly proves the point. The fact is that, under the terms of the excise tax, a non-split-run magazine need not contain any "Canadian" editorial content, as long as the content is not sold outside Canada, or the advertisements in the Canadian and foreign editions are identical. Second, even as to these two magazines, Canada ignores the similarities between the two products, in terms of all factors other than Canadian focus. Indeed, the similarities are so great - including with respect to subject matter - that the two magazines were recognized to be direct competitors by industry witnesses in testimony before a Canadian Senate committee.[69]

3.93 The United States considered that Canada sought to minimize the significance of the fact that its WTO tariff commitments did not distinguish between split-runs and non-split runs. Canada's relevant tariff binding also includes newspapers, which are obviously not like products. However, the fact that Canada's tariff binding reflects the single Harmonized System (HS) heading for all magazines *does* provide support for a finding that split-runs and non-split-runs are the same like product. The Appellate Body in *Japan - Alcoholic Beverages* stated that,

[69] See, e.g. Senate of Canada, Proceedings of the Standing Senate Committee on Banking, Trade and Commerce, Issue no. 49 (30 November 1995) at 57, 64 (testimony of officials of Canadian Magazine Publishers Association).

while broad GATT tariff bindings that cut across HS headings may not be useful to determine product likeness, GATT 1947 practice has looked to similar categorization in the *HS itself* in determining like product:

> Uniform classification in tariff nomenclatures based on the Harmonized System (the 'HS') was recognized in GATT 1947 practice as providing a useful basis for confirming 'likeness' in products. However, there is a major difference between tariff classification nomenclature and tariff bindings or concessions made by Members of the WTO under Article II of GATT 1994. There are risks in using tariff bindings that are too broad as a measure of product 'likeness'.... Many of [the] least-developed countries, as well as other developing countries, have bindings in their schedules which include broad ranges of products that cut across several different HS tariff headings . . ..[70]

3.94 Thus, the Appellate Body distinguished between the situation in which products fell within common HS categories, and the situation in which a Member made broad tariff bindings that cut across multiple HS categories. In this case, all periodicals, whether split-run or not, and whether or not they contain advertising, are included within the same HS category: HS 49.02. The fact that the distinction Canada is drawing in this case is not one reflected in the HS supports our claim that split-runs and non-split-runs are the same like product.

3.95 With regard to the Canadian argument that implementation of its import ban through a provision in its tariff code is proof that there *are* differences in tariff classification between split-runs and non-split-runs, the Appellate Body in *Japan - Alcoholic Beverages* referred to universally-accepted HS nomenclature, not to one Member's protectionist restrictions that happen to find themselves in that Member's "Customs Tariff". The reason why it was practice under GATT 1947 to look to HS nomenclature is because it generally reflects an objective assessment of the intrinsic similarity of products. As far as the United States knew, Canada is unique in drawing lines (in a "tariff-related" provision or elsewhere) based on an artificial distinction such as "split-run" versus "non-split-run". Thus, the Panel should reject Canada's effort to be rewarded for its import ban, and find that the common HS classification of split-runs and non-split-runs provides additional support for a finding that split-runs and non-split-runs are the same like product.

3.96 Canada considered that the US reference to the Canadian tariff classification in heading 49.02 had the effect of sweeping not only all periodicals, but newspapers as well into a single very comprehensive classification. The inappropriateness of this kind of result was pointed out by the Appellate Body in its recent decision on *Japan - Alcoholic Beverages*, when it said that "tariff bindings that include a wide range of products are not a reliable criterion for determining or confirming product "likeness" under Article III:2".[71] The use of tariff classifications in this case is especially inappropriate. The categories of products listed under tariff item 49.02 are as diverse as periodicals and newspapers. Where the policy framework relates to periodicals and their intellectual *content*, the argument that the two media are "like" would be difficult to sustain. Tariff Code 9958 has effectively carved split-runs out of the general tariff classification; it has been in effect for over 30 years, through several GATT rounds, including the most recent Uruguay Round. The *de facto* exclusion of split-runs from the general tariff classification means at the very least that the US position can derive no support from tariff classification.

3.97 With respect to the support the United States seeks in the HS category, the fact is that this classification is far too broad to serve as a basis for identifying like products. Surely the fundamental point in the Appellate Body decision is that *any* very broad tariff classification is inappropriate, whether it is based on the HS or on tariff bindings. The short answer to the United States argument based on the common HS classification is that, at least in the case of this category, it is far too broad. It puts all magazines and all newspapers into a single global grouping. It also has the practical effect of making editorial content irrelevant. In the circumstances of this case, the use of

---

[70] Appellate Body Report on *Japan - Taxes on Alcoholic Beverages, op. cit.*, at 22.

[71] *Ibid.* at 22.

tariff classifications is inconsistent with the requirement stipulated by the Appellate Body that "like products" under Article III:2, first sentence, should be narrowly construed.

(ii) discrimination

3.98 Canada considered that the first sentence of Article III:2 speaks of products "imported *into the* territory" of a contracting party, and it deals with tax discrimination *against* imported products. There is no such discrimination on the facts of this case. To get around this difficulty, the United States has introduced the notion of "foreign-based" split-runs meaning periodicals produced in Canada but replicating foreign editorial content. This is a concept that simply has no legal meaning in the context of Article III:2. If the product is domestically produced, and is not physically moved across the border, it is not an imported product. And if there is no imported product, then there is nothing to which Article III can apply. But even if there were imported split-runs on the Canadian market, the absence of discrimination would be clear. Some imported magazines might attract the tax, but not to any greater extent than the domestically produced split-runs which were and remain the primary object of the legislation. For this reason, the measure is consistent with Article III:2 on its face and in its operation and practical effect. There is no reason why a measure that is non-discriminatory in both form and effect – *de jure* and *de facto* – should be considered inconsistent with Article III:2.

3.99 As the Appellate Body has observed in *US - Standards for Gasoline* in connection with Article III:4 that where there is "identity of treatment – constituting real, not merely formal, equality of treatment ... it is difficult to see how inconsistency would have arisen in the first place". The same conclusion is equally valid here. That the tax is free from any taint of overt discrimination is clear from the terms of the legislation, which make no distinction between domestic and imported products. Canada provided an example of the Canadian-owned magazine, *Harrowsmith Country Life*. Before the adoption of Part V.1, this magazine had two editions - a Canadian edition and a US edition. The Canadian and the US editions had different advertisements and a certain amount of common editorial content. Because more than 20 per cent of the editorial content in the Canadian edition was the same as that in the US edition, the tax would have applied to the Canadian edition (even if the editorial content was entirely produced in Canada). As a result of the excise tax, *Harrowsmith Country Life* stopped publishing its US edition. It could hardly be suggested that the tax is discriminatory in its practical operation, since it was designed to prevent the production in Canada of split-runs.

3.100 The Appellate Body on *Japan - Alcoholic Beverages*[72] held that where imported products are taxed in excess of "like domestic products," the general principle set out in Article III:1 may be assumed to have been violated. There is consequently no need to apply that principle as a "separate test" in order to find an inconsistency with Article III:2, first sentence. The Appellate Body has thus established a balance in the interpretation of Article III:2. The concept of "like products" is to be very narrowly construed, on a case-by-case basis in a way that requires "discretionary judgment;" but once the determination is made, excess taxation of imported products entails a violation without any need to conduct a further inquiry under paragraph 1. The essential elements of the interpretation of this provision have thus been authoritatively identified.

3.101 One question, however, was not addressed in the recent decision: whether taxation of imported products "in excess of" like products is to be determined in terms of classes of products, or whether any single instance of differential taxation creates an automatic *per se* violation even when it results from fiscal classifications that are not themselves discriminatory in form or in fact. The answer is clear both from the wording of Article III:2, first sentence, and from the object and purpose of Article III as a whole, which is the prevention of discrimination against imported products. The use of the plural in referring to "imported products" and "like domestic products" indicates clearly that the concern is with classes of products, not with the isolated instances of differential taxation that necessarily result when product "A" is taxed at a different rate than product "B" because it happens to fall into a different, but non-discriminatory, fiscal classification.

---

[72] *Ibid.*

3.102 This interpretation also seems necessary to create a workable rule. Article III:2 is not intended to impose fiscal harmonization in rates, methods or classifications. It therefore remains not only possible but inevitable that domestic fiscal classifications may in certain instances have the effect of subdividing or straddling "like product" categories, or otherwise crossing "like product" category lines. Since fiscal classifications have no other purpose than to allow differences in tax treatment, any such classifications that failed to correspond precisely to "like product" categories under Article III:2, first sentence, would automatically lead to a violation. Quite apart from imposing a degree of harmonization that goes beyond the language or the purpose of this provision, such an interpretation would lead to an intolerable unpredictability so long as "like product" determinations are to be made on a case-by-case basis, as the recent decision has reaffirmed.

3.103 It could also lead, paradoxically, to results that would make nonsense of the Appellate Body's assumption that excess taxation under Article III:2 automatically entails a departure from the general principles in Article III:1; and that would in fact make nonsense of the underlying purpose of Article III. It could lead to situations where fiscal classifications decisively *favouring* imported products would be considered inconsistent with the first sentence of Article III:2, so long as the tax classification attracting the higher rate contained at least *some* imported products. It makes no sense to say that Article III is automatically violated in any case where tax differences result from domestic classifications that are "origin-neutral" in form and that might even favour imported products in effect as might well be true of the tax at issue here. A particular instance of differential taxation in such circumstances should not create a *per se* violation, absent a discriminatory effect or cause to believe such an effect to be probable.

3.104 The United States considered that the Canadian argument that under Article III:2, first sentence, a "single" or "particular" instance of higher taxation of a certain subset of a broader category of imported like products "should not create a *per se* violation, absent a discriminatory effect or cause to believe such an effect to be probable", meritless for a number of reasons. First, the United States is not confronted with a mere "single" or "particular" instance of higher taxation of imported products than domestic like products in this case. Rather, a broad group of imported products – split-run magazines – is taxed at higher, not lower, rates than a broad group of like Canadian products - non-split run magazines. Canada has neither defined nor identified what it considers to be a "single instance" of discriminatory treatment in the context of this case.

3.105 In addition, Canada claims that the Appellate Body in the *Japan - Alcoholic Beverages* decision somehow left the door open to allow for discriminatory higher taxes applied to certain imported products within a category of like products. The Appellate Body left no such opening. It made it clear at page 19 that "[i]f the imported and domestic products are 'like products', and if the taxes applied to the imported products are 'in excess of' those applied to the like domestic products, then the measure is inconsistent with Article III:2, first sentence." No further test of "discriminatory effect" or discriminatory aim, is warranted. Canada's proposed "discriminatory effect" test based on "classes" of products if flatly inconsistent with the recent panel and Appellate Body decision in *Japan - Alcoholic Beverages*. In that case, once the panel found vodka and shochu to be like products, the taxation of imported vodka at a higher rate than domestic shochu (even though the tax was facially neutral) was found to be a violation of Article III:2, first sentence. This finding was affirmed by the Appellate Body.

3.106 The United States considered that Canada's argument that, in the absence of such a "discriminatory effect" test, a scheme that, overall, favoured imports over domestic products, might be found to violate Article III:2, first sentence, suggested that less favourable treatment of certain imported products could be counterbalanced by more favourable treatment of others. The *US - Section 337* panel decisively rejected any such "balancing" of less-favourable and more-favourable treatment, observing that "such an interpretation would lead to great uncertainty about the conditions of competition between imported and domestic products and thus defeat the purpose of Article III."[73] Similarly, in the panel report on *US - Malt Beverages* report, the panel observed that "Article III...requires treatment of imported products no less favourable than that accorded to the most-favoured

[73] Panel Report on *United States - Section 337 of the Tariff Act of 1930, op. cit.,* at para. 5.14.

domestic products."[74] Thus, the fact that imported and domestic split-run magazines receive the same tax treatment is irrelevant. Rather, the fact that imported split run magazines are taxed more heavily than like domestic non-split-run magazines establishes the requisite higher taxation under Article III:2, first sentence.

3.107 According to the United States, the fact that Article III:2 is phrased in terms of "products" does not mean that tax discrimination with respect to *one* product is outside the scope of Article III:2, or that such discrimination would be GATT-consistent as long as it is restricted to *one* product. In this case the drafters clearly intended non difference between the treatment of the plural and the treatment of the singular. This fact is confirmed by the drafting of the Note *Ad* Article III (which refers to the "like domestic product" and the "imported product") and Article III:3, a special case of application of Article III:2 which refers to the "taxed product". The 1970 Working Party report on Border Tax Adjustments, which is often referred to in this connection, uses the singular and plural forms in free variation. It is not necessary to demonstrate that all imported magazines are taxed more heavily than all domestic like magazines, or even that the average tax on all imported magazines is higher than the average tax on all like domestic magazines.

3.108 Finally, Canada's proposed "discriminatory effect" test appears to be based on predictions of the level of future trade flows. It is well-established that Article III is not designed to protect expectations of relative trade flows, but rather to ensure equal competitive conditions for imported products. Moreover, in this case, the type of effects analysis Canada suggests would be impossible. There is no basis for judging future levels of split-run magazine imports because Canada has completely eliminated them from its market for the last 30 years. Given its GATT-inconsistent ban, Canada should not be permitted to defend the excise tax on grounds that a small volume of imports would be subject to it.

3.109 Canada responded that its interpretation of discrimination under Article III:2 would not require any overall balancing test as the United States stated. It would not require prediction of trade flows and is not an aim-and-effect test in another guise. It says only that if the fiscal categories of a contracting party are origin-neutral and exhibit no inherent bias against imported products, then the mere existence of such categories, with differential rates of taxation, does not violate Article III:2. A simplified example illustrates this point. Suppose raspberries are taxed higher than strawberries, and that all red berries are determined to be like products. Under the Canadian view, there is no violation if the two categories apply to both imported and domestic products and there is no inherent bias against imported products. The United States would say there is a violation because a box of imported raspberries is taxed higher than a box of domestic strawberries. This is accurate only if a single instance of differential taxation creates a violation. Canada submits that there is no violation because imported products as a class are not being subjected to excess taxation over domestic products. The US interpretation leads to results that are close to absurd and would not reflect the language of Article III:2, first sentence, in particular the use of the plural, nor its object and purpose which is non-discrimination or more specifically to protect expectations of the competitive relationship between imported and domestic products. Further, in the *Japan - Alcoholic Beverages* case, it is clear from paragraph *5.19* of the report that the panel based its findings on the assumption that shochu was largely a domestic product.

3.110 The United States responded that Canada's attempt to distinguish this case from the *Japan -Alcoholic Beverages* case based on the fact that most shochu was produced domestically in Japan, while in this case one could not show that split-run magazines have a comparable import focus, is inappropriate. Canada has *banned* the relevant imports. Of course there is no preponderance of imported split-run magazines over domestic split-runs. There is also no basis for judging future levels of split-run magazine imports because Canada has completely eliminated them from its market for the last 30 years. Given its GATT-inconsistent ban, Canada should not be permitted to defend the excise tax on grounds that a small amount of imports would be subject to it, or that a small percentage of split-run magazines would be imported. Moreover, the United States contested Canada's claims that the US argument would prevent differential taxation of strawberries and raspberries, if the two fruits were found to

[74] Panel Report on *United States - Measures Affecting Alcoholic and Malt Beverages, op. cit.*, para. 5.17.

be like products. In fact, the distinction the excise tax draws is not analogous to distinguishing between raspberries and strawberries (which are different fruits), but is instead analogous to distinguishing between raspberries and *raspberries*. Specifically, it is analogous to distinguishing between raspberries produced in fields whose harvest is sold only in one country, and raspberries produced in fields whose harvest is sold in multiple countries.

b. *Article III:2, second sentence*
(i) *directly competitive or substitutable*

3.111 The United States argued that in the event the Panel does not find split-runs and non-split-runs to be "like products" for purposes of Article III:2, first sentence, it should find them to be "directly competitive or substitutable" products within the meaning of Article III:2, second sentence, of GATT 1994. The Appellate Body in *Japan - Alcoholic Beverages* provided that, in assessing an allegation of a violation of Article III:2, second sentence, one must examine whether:

> (1) the imported products and the domestic products are "directly competitive or substitutable products" which are in competition with each other;
> (2) the directly competitive or substitutable imported and domestic products *are "not similarly taxed"*; and
> (3) the dissimilar taxation of the directly competitive or substitutable imported [and] domestic products *is "applied . . . so as to afford protection to domestic production.*[75]

Canada has not challenged the fact that split-runs and non-split runs are "not similarly taxed". The 80 per cent tax applies solely to split-runs. Split-runs and non-split runs are "directly competitive or substitutable", and the excise tax is "applied so as to afford protection to domestic production". Thus, the excise tax violates Article III:2, second sentence.

3.112 The Appellate Body in *Japan - Alcoholic Beverages* indicated that "directly competitive or substitutable" products was a "broader category" of products than "like products" in Article III:2.[76] The Appellate Body observed that it was appropriate to examine such factors as physical characteristics, common end-uses, tariff classifications, and the "market place", but that the "decisive criterion" in determining whether products were directly competitive or substitutable was "common end-uses".[77] Split-runs and non-split runs compete in the Canadian market and have common end-uses. Magazines covering the same general subject matter – e.g., current events magazines, hobby magazines, technical journals – compete with each other whether or not they are split-runs. Whether a magazine is split-run or not cannot be determined simply by examining the magazine, but is based, instead, on how similar the magazine is to a magazine sold outside Canada in another country. Split-runs, as defined by the excise tax, do not differ from other magazines in any way related to their ability to compete with other magazines. Indeed, the excise tax is applied precisely, and solely, because split-runs compete with wholly domestically produced magazines for readers and advertising. As discussed above with respect to the issue of like product, the distinction between split-runs and other magazines is not based on content. Even if one could somehow credit Canada's assertion that the content of non-split-runs has more of a "Canadian perspective" than split-runs, this distinction could not possibly be considered a different "end-use".

3.113 Canada argued that split-run edition periodicals are not "directly competitive with or substitutable for" periodicals with editorial content developed for the Canadian market. Although they may be substitutable *advertising* vehicles, they are not competitive or substitutable information vehicles. Moreover, as mentioned above, the excise tax on advertising contained in split-run editions was not introduced so as to protect the Canadian production of periodicals and it does not have this effect. Rather, it was adopted to prevent an unfair practice in the

---

[75] Appellate Body Report on *Japan - Taxes on Alcoholic Beverages, op. cit.*, at 24 (emphasis in original).
[76] *Ibid.*, at 25.
[77] *Ibid.* (emphasis added).

advertising service sector. Under the second sentence of Article III:2 and the *Ad* Article III, Paragraph 2, the complaining party must demonstrate that a tax is being applied to imported products or domestic products that are "directly competitive or substitutable" and that the tax is being applied "in such a way as to protect domestic production". The complainant bears the burden of proof. The United States must therefore demonstrate that split-run edition periodicals and periodicals with editorial content developed for the Canadian market are competitive or substitutable products, and that the Parliament of Canada imposed the 80 per cent tax on split-run edition periodicals in order to protect Canadian production of periodicals which are not split-run editions.

3.114 The interpretation of this phrase shares many characteristics with the interpretation of "like products". A case-by-case approach is required here as well – in other words, an interpretation that takes account of all the relevant circumstances, and in particular the unique characteristics of cultural products. It's also a multi-factorial analysis, as it is for like products as well – no single test is decisive. To a significant extent, one takes account of all the factors that go into a like products determination, including properties and end-uses. Because of this common ground, many of the points Canada has made in the context of like products, and how the concept has to be adapted to reflect the special nature of cultural products, are also relevant here.

3.115 Canada noted the United States' unsubstantiated assertion that split-runs and other magazines clearly compete with each other. They do of course compete for the advertising dollar because a split-run recycling foreign content offers a far cheaper vehicle. But competition for advertising is not the issue and is not subject to GATT 1994 disciplines. The only legitimate focus is competition in the consumer marketplace. And the United States has not demonstrated, as it is required to do, that the products at issue are competitive or substitutable, or that they meet the threshold test implied by the word "directly". Substitution implies interchangeability. Once content is accepted as relevant it seems obvious that magazines created for different markets are not interchangeable. They are not substitutes, and certainly not direct substitutes. They serve different end-uses. Canadian periodical consumers have a demand for periodicals containing information that specifically addresses their interests. Canadian magazines contain information developed for and directed to the interests of Canadian consumers over a broad range of genres. Split-runs and magazines with editorial material developed for the Canadian market cannot be considered direct substitutes as information vehicles; and for the same reason they are not in *direct* competition. Ultimately, of course, there may be some degree of competition for disposable income between all cultural products and all luxury products – for everything beyond the necessities of life – but this is far too remote. It is not *direct* competition and it does not therefore fall within the rule. There would not be 1440 different magazine titles produced in Canada alone if the products were directly substitutable, or directly competitive, in the sense contemplated by the *Ad* Article to Article III:2.

3.116 Without embarking on an exercise in economic analysis, there are important respects in which price and demand comparisons are more complicated in the case of magazines and other cultural products than in the case of ordinary commodities. It is not the same as comparing consumer behaviour in response to price changes on a bottle of shochu and a bottle of vodka. There are too many qualitative differences in the case of magazines. To give one example, if the ratio of editorial content to advertisements decreases this can be the same as a price increase. That is a fairly objective, measurable variation, but other qualitative differences of equal importance can also have an effect tantamount to a price change – the quality of the content, the attractiveness of the graphics, the intrinsic interest of the articles.

3.117 The United States considered that the very existence of the tax was itself proof of competition of split-runs and non-split-runs in the market. Canada would not have gone to such extraordinary lengths to keep split-runs out of its market if they did not compete with other magazines in the Canadian market. As Canada itself has acknowledged, split-runs compete with wholly, domestically produced magazines for advertising revenue, which demonstrates that they compete for the same readers. The only reason firms place advertisements in magazines is to reach readers. A firm would consider split-runs to be an acceptable advertising alternative to non-split-runs only if that firm had some reason to believe that the split-run products themselves would be an acceptable alternative to non-split-runs in the eyes of readers. According to the United States, Canada acknowledges that "[r]eaders attract advertisers," and that: "The Canadian publishers are ready to compete with magazines published all over the world in order to keep their readers, but the competition is fierce."

3.118 The Report of the Task Force on the Canadian Magazine Industry provides further acknowledgment of the substitutability of magazines produced for the Canadian market and other magazines:

> [Canadian publishers'] English-language consumer magazines face significant competition for sales from imported consumer magazines. In large measure, this is because the majority of the magazines are from the United States and *are a close substitute.* ...It is reasonable to expect that the content of American magazines will be of interest to Canadians....

This report also observes that "there is considerable price competition" on news-stands between domestic and imported magazines",[78] and that:

> the initial effect of the entry of Canadian regional editions of foreign magazines into the Canadian advertising market would be a loss of advertising pages in Canadian publications offering advertisers a readership with similar demographics.[79]

Minister of Canadian Heritage the Honourable Michel Dupuy described the situation as follows:

> Canadians are much more interested in American daily life, be it political or sports life or any other kind, than vice versa. Therefore, the reality of the situation is that we must protect ourselves against split-runs coming from foreign countries and, in particular, from the United States.[80]

Canadian Government officials have repeatedly acknowledged outside this proceeding the close substitutability and competitiveness of split-run and non-split-run magazines. Canada affirmed this fact where it refers to domestic and imported magazines competing for readers. Furthermore, Canada admits that split-run and non-split-run magazines compete for advertising; this itself demonstrates that the two are directly competitive and substitutable, since carrying advertising is a principal to which magazines are put.

3.119 Canada argued that the US reference to the Task Force in the preceding paragraph does not look into the supporting evidence. The evidence before the Task Force, on which its conclusions were at least partially based, was a study by the economist Leigh Anderson[81] which states:

> US magazines can probably provide a reasonable substitute for Canadian magazines in their capacity as an advertising medium, although some advertisers may be better served by a Canadian vehicle. In many instances however, they would provide a very poor substitute as an entertainment and communication medium.

The report went on to characterize the relationship as one of "imperfect substitutability" – far from the direct substitutability required by this provision. The market share of imported and domestic magazines in Canada has remained remarkably constant over the 30-plus years between the O'Leary Report and the Task Force. If competitive forces had been in play to the degree necessary to meet the standard of "directly competitive" goods,

---

[78] *Task Force Report* at 40 and 42.

[79] *Ibid.*, at 53.

[80] Statement of Minister of Canadian Heritage Michel Dupuy before Canada's Standing Senate Committee on Banking, Trade and Commerce, 5 December 1995, Issue No. 50 at 14.

[81] Anderson, Leigh, An Analysis of Advertising Revenues to the Canadian Magazine Industry: the effect of foreign split-run magazines (19 January 1994). Prepared by Leigh Anderson for the Task Force on the Canadian Magazine Industry.

one would have expected some variations. All this casts serious doubt on whether the competition or substitutability is sufficiently "direct" to meet the standard of Ad Article III.

(ii) so as to afford protection to domestic production

3.120 The United States argued that the excise tax is applied so as to afford protection to Canadian magazine publishers. In *Japan - Alcoholic Beverages*, the Appellate Body indicated that proof of protective *intent* is not required in order to establish a violation of the second sentence of Article III:2, and that the issue is "how the measure in question is *applied*":

> Although it is true that the aim of a measure may not be easily discerned, nevertheless its protective application can most often be discerned from the design, the architecture, and the revealing structure of a measure. The very magnitude of the dissimilar taxation in a particular case may be evidence of such a protective application, as the panel rightly concluded in this case. Most often, there will be other factors to be considered as well ....[82]

3.121 The Canadian excise tax clearly affords protection to domestic production of magazines directed at the Canadian market. It applies in a manner that effectively eliminates from the Canadian market split-run magazines, which compete directly with and are close substitutes for magazines produced solely for the Canadian market. The "very magnitude of the dissimilar taxation" – an 80 per cent tax on the former and no tax on the latter – is proof of the protective application of the Canadian excise tax, as it applies *only* to split-runs and is set at a prohibitive level. The structure and design of the excise tax are clear: the tax makes it uneconomical to sell any magazines that advertise to Canadians and that are produced for another market or for both Canada and another market. The measure thereby insulates the domestic Canadian magazine industry from competition from imported split-runs. The terms of the tax were crafted deliberately to target *Sports Illustrated* magazine, to direct advertising revenues solely to domestically-produced magazines, and to eliminate the competitive advantages conferred on split-runs by virtue of their economies of scale. *Sports Illustrated* Canada ceased publication in Canada with the issue dated 12 December 1995. Time Warner continues to sell subscriptions of the US national edition of *Sports Illustrated* in Canada and also sells the US edition of *Sports Illustrated* on the news-stands in Canada. These copies are printed in the United States and exported to Canada.

3.122 Canada argued that it is not applying the excise tax to imported periodicals so as to afford protection to the Canadian production of periodicals. Part V.I of the Excise Tax Act has no effect on the ability of foreign periodicals to enter Canada and to hold a very large share of the Canadian market. The Excise Tax Act applies to all split-run periodicals – wherever produced – in the same way. Contrary to the US contention, the purpose of Part V.I of the Excise Tax Act is not to protect the production of periodicals in Canada, but to prevent the diversion of advertising revenues to magazines based on content produced for foreign markets, and thus to ensure the production of editorial content for Canadians.

3.123 The purpose of Article III is to protect the competitive relationship between domestic and imported goods. As stated in the report on *United States - Taxes on Petroleum and Certain Imported Substances*:

> ... The general prohibition of quantitative restrictions under Article XI ... and the national treatment obligation of Article III ... have essentially the same rationale, namely to protect expectations of the contracting parties as to the competitive relationship between their products and those of the other contracting parties.[83]

---

[82] Appellate Body Report on *Japan - Taxes on Alcoholic Beverages, op. cit.*, at 28, 29.

[83] Panel Report on *United States - Taxes on Petroleum and Certain Imported Substances, op. cit.*, at 160, para. 5.2.2.

Therefore, when Article III:1 specifies that a contracting party must not adopt measures "so as to afford protection to domestic production", the object is to prevent the adoption or maintenance of measures that protect domestic products to the disadvantage of products imported from the territory of another party.

3.124 Part V.I of the Excise Tax Act is not a protectionist measure adopted "so as to afford protection to domestic production" for the following reasons:

(a) It does not affect the competitive relationship between imported and domestically-produced periodicals;

(b) it is not based on the physical origin of periodicals, which is what is contemplated by the reference to "domestic production"; and

(c) far from having a protectionist aim, it is a legitimate response to an anti-competitive abuse in the advertising field, with the ultimate object of ensuring the survival of a distinct Canadian culture.

3.125 Because GATT 1994, including Article III, applies to trade in goods, the expression "domestic production" must refer to the physical production of the good. This refers to its manufacturing, cultivation, extraction, etc. Article III of GATT 1994 cannot address the competitive relationship between service-providers such as the authors and artists contributing to the intellectual material contained in periodicals. Nor does it protect the competitive relationship between publishers in their capacity as sellers of advertising space. In terms of physical production, the sole perspective that is relevant to Article III, Part V.I of the Excise Tax Act is entirely neutral. It does not have the effect of protecting the production of periodicals in Canada; indeed its principal target was the production *in Canada* of split-run magazines as defined in the Act.

3.126 The measure has valid policy objectives that fit within what the *US - Malt Beverages* decision called a "public policy purpose" that is consistent with Article III. The immediate objective of Parliament was directed against the aggressive marketing of advertising services in Canada by publishers who were recycling in Canada editorial material whose production costs had already been covered in a larger market. The net result of this practice was to cut into the small share of the advertising market available to Canadian publishers, who were producing editorial content specific to Canadians. Part V.I of the Excise Tax Act was drafted in such a way as to curtail this advertising practice and not so as to prevent the entry into Canada of foreign periodicals or in such a way as to disadvantage foreign periodicals in the Canadian market.

3.127 Canada noted that it had never intended to decrease the level of competition between imported and domestic magazines. On the contrary, the members of the Task Force on the Canadian Magazine Industry wrote: "We are convinced that what is being proposed interferes as little as possible with freedom of expression or choice. Indeed, in the final analysis, we are seeking to expand choice by ensuring the continued availability of magazines with original content."[84] These measures did not prevent and were not intended to prevent foreign periodicals from competing in the Canadian market on an equal footing with Canadian periodicals.

3.128 Further, the United States has completely misrepresented the true trade position. There is an enormous penetration of American magazines in Canada, and nothing in the Canadian tax measure would change this or is designed to change this. Nor are there any significant trade effects to the measure. This tax concerns a very narrow segment of the total number of American periodicals streaming across the border daily. This very narrow segment was affected in the same way that a narrow segment of Canadian periodicals was affected. And this narrow segment of both the Canadian and the US industry was affected because the Parliament of Canada believed that a certain practice, a services practice, had to be discouraged.

---

[84] *Task Force Report* at 64.

3.129 Protectionism means protection against imported products. There is no protectionist application to be found in a measure that is not aimed at imported products as such, and that does not in fact have a disproportionate impact on imported products. The excise tax is not aimed at imported split-runs and, more important, it has (or would have) no greater effect on imported split-runs than it does on domestically produced magazines of the same kind. There is no doubt that the tax insulates Canadian magazines from a certain form of competition in the advertising sector. It does not, however, insulate Canadian producers from competition resulting specifically from *imported* split-runs. The United States has fundamentally mischaracterized the situation when it says "the measure...insulates the domestic Canadian magazine industry from competition from imported split-runs". This is not the effect of the tax. It affects split-runs in general, not just imported products. It is wrong to think of split-runs as an inherently or a presumptively imported product. The actual effect of the tax in practice has so far been very clear. It caused *Sports Illustrated* to move its production for the Canadian market *out* of Canada and back to the United States. The effect was to substitute imported products for domestic products. This is exactly the opposite of what is understood by protectionism. Even apart from what happened in the case of *Sports Illustrated*, the local production of a split-run – a regional edition – makes eminent business sense.

3.130 The United States considered the protectionist nature of the tax is evident from its confiscatory character, the statements of the Canadian Government regarding the tax both before and after its enactment, and from the manner in which it applies. The effective date of the tax was deliberately set to eliminate the split-run edition of *Sports Illustrated* magazine. The tax applies only to those split-runs that began publication after 26 March 1993, a few weeks before *Sports Illustrated* launched its Canadian split-run edition, but more than *two years* prior to enactment of the tax. The excise tax applies in a manner that inherently favours Canadian-based producers, who are much more likely than foreign producers to publish magazines directed solely at Canadian readers. Foreign-based producers who wish to expand operations by entering the Canadian market must create a new magazine for distribution exclusively in Canada (or sell their foreign editions in identical form in Canada). The Canadian magazine tax is designed to ensure that foreign-based publishers forego the commercially attractive option of publishing a split-run edition of an existing magazine for the Canadian market. In introducing the excise tax bill to the House of Commons, Minister of Canadian Heritage Michel Dupuy asked, "Why is this tax necessary?", and answered: "Canadian publishers would be at a grave disadvantage if they were forced to compete for advertising revenues with magazines that have recovered their editorial costs in markets which are much larger than the Canadian market."

3.131 Mr. Dupuy's reference to "markets which are much larger than the Canadian market" was undoubtedly a reference to the United States, whose production of Canadian-edition split-runs was significant prior to the 1965 import ban, and whose potential for re-establishing split-run editions in the Canadian market was the basis for the imposition of the excise tax in 1995. The 1961 O'Leary Report, which preceded the import ban, noted that there were 76 US magazines offering split run or regional editions in Canada.[85] In 1994 the Government-appointed Task Force on the Canadian Magazine Industry concluded that it in the absence of additional legislation it was highly likely that a significant number of US split-runs would be sold in Canada. The Task Force estimated that there were 53 potential US consumer magazine entrants into the Canadian market, and 70 potential US business and trade magazine entrants, and that the majority of these would actually enter the Canadian market.[86] (By contrast, although the Task Force report describes in some detail the structure of the Canadian magazine industry, it makes no mention of the existence of split-run editions of *Canadian* publications.) The effect of the 80 percent excise tax is to keep the potential US entrants out of the Canadian market, whether they choose to transmit their magazines electronically for printing in Canada or - should Canada's GATT-illegal import prohibition be removed - to import them. By its terms, the tax applies to all split-runs, whether imported or domestically-produced. The tax makes it unprofitable for split-runs to be sold in Canada. Indeed, this is the whole – and the stated – purpose of the tax. As Minister Dupuy stated: "[The tax] could be designed and implemented in order to avoid split run editions."[87]

---

[85] Report, Royal Commission on Publications, May 1961 ("OLeary Report") at 36.

[86] *Task Force Report* at 50-52.

[87] *Commons Debates* at 14790

3.132 The Canadian argument that the tax is not applied so as to afford protection because it is reasonable to assume that, in the absence of the import ban, split-runs would be published in Canada as much as in the United States was dubious as a factual matter. More importantly, it is legally irrelevant because the tax protects domestic *non*-split-runs from competition from imported split-runs. The appropriate comparison is between the treatment of imported split-runs and domestic *non*-split-runs, not between domestic and imported split-runs. "Article III...requires treatment of imported products no less favourable than that accorded to the *most*-favoured domestic products"[88], not the *least*-favoured. Further, regardless of what Canada's legislators may have intended, the tax does apply, by its terms, to imported split-run magazines. If the import ban were lifted, it would have an immediate and exclusionary effect on imported split-runs.

3.133 In its argument that its excise tax on split-run magazines is meant to address an "anti-competitive abuse in the advertising field", Canada has completely failed to indicate in what way split-run magazines constitute such an abuse, why it has concluded that all, as opposed to some such magazines represent such an abuse, and why its has chosen to apply a tax measure to address such abuses. It is apparent that the "anti-competitive abuse" Canada is concerned about in connection with split-run magazines is competition itself. Canada's real quarrel with split-runs is that they are produced in a manner that takes advantage of economies of scale, in which costs are spread out over a greater number of units produced. This means simply that split-run producers may have a lower cost structure than other producers, which may put them at a competitive advantage.

3.134 Competitive advantage is not competitive abuse, however. Canada has well-developed competition laws to address any such abuses. If Canada were truly interested in remedying competitive abuses, it would have employed those laws. Those laws do not permit application of remedies in a vacuum, however. They require a detailed analysis of the conduct of particular actors and their position in the market, and do not have as their goal the removal of entire product categories from the market. Indeed, it would be difficult to imagine a less pro-competitive remedy than one that effectively removes competing products from the marketplace.

3.135 Further, Canada's claim that marketing split-runs in Canada is akin to dumping is equally untenable. Dumping is generally understood to mean pricing products in a foreign market below the sales price in the home market, or selling products below cost. Canada has not alleged either such practice in this case. There are well-developed WTO procedures for conducting anti-dumping investigations and for determining dumping margins. These procedures do not allow for imposition of duties in arbitrary amounts (e.g., 80 per cent) across the entire range of imported products on the basis of legislative fiat.

3.136 Canada argued that protection is afforded to domestic production for the purpose of Article III:2, second sentence, if there is a "discriminatory or protective effect against imported products". "Imported products" means products physically transported into the territory of a Member. The United States concedes that the *Sports Illustrated* innovation that led to the legislation involved a domestic product, where the only thing "imported" was the electronically-transmitted foreign content. The United States has thus conceded, in the case of *Sports Illustrated Canada*, that there was no discrimination or protective effect against imported products. It follows that "foreign based" split-runs are not imported products if they are printed and published in Canada.

3.137 The Excise Tax Act thus applies to domestic and imported products without distinction, and it is primarily aimed at a form of domestic product. While the tax secures advertising revenues for Canadian publishers, protection in the sense of Article III:1 as read into III:2 means protection against *imported products*. As the preceding paragraph has shown, split-runs are not intrinsically imported products. Even if there were no import prohibition, given the economies of local production and distribution and the ease of electronic transmission, it is likely that most split-runs would be locally produced. It is highly significant, moreover, that, as the United States noted in response to a question at the hearing, the effect of the tax was to induce *Sports Illustrated* to cease its Canadian production and to resume direct imports from the United States. The substitution of imports for domestic

[88] Panel Report on *United States - Measures Affecting Alcoholic and Malt Beverages, op. cit.* para. 5.17 (emphasis added).

products, as the result of a public policy measure, is the direct opposite of what almost everyone understands by protectionism. It suffices by itself to refute the contention that the Excise Tax Act operates to "afford protection to domestic production."

3.138 The excise tax measure is designed to prevent the diversion of advertising to low-cost publications reproducing recycled editorial content, at the expense of publications created for Canadians. It does not guarantee the survival of Canadian magazines that the public does not want. What it targets, very simply put, is the combination of recycled editorial content plus Canadian advertisements. This combination, because the crucial input of content comes with minimal cost, is destructive of fair competition in the market place and consumer choice. It eliminates any possibility of a "level playing field". It would lead ultimately to a reduction of material dealing with the Canadian scene and in turn to a Canadian public that is less well-informed on Canadian affairs. These are not only legitimate legislative concerns; they are far removed from the idea of protecting domestic production which is referred to in Article III. Ultimately, of course, the concern behind this legislation is with the preservation of Canadian culture in the face of an extraordinary challenge from across the border. It is not Canadian public policy to restrict the importation or circulation of imported magazines. It does, however, reinforce the validity of the distinction Canada makes between original content and domestic production as one that is based upon a public policy purpose that has nothing to do with trade protectionism. Split-run editions of magazines compete unfairly for advertising revenues with regular magazines, since their editorial costs are largely paid for in their original market.

3.139 As to the United States' inquiry why Canada failed to apply the WTO dumping procedures, those procedures, and the Canadian domestic legislation that implements them, have never been applied, and would probably not even be applicable, to advertising as a service sector not covered by GATT. The United States also asks, in effect, why Canada has not used the Canadian Competition Act. There is no reason why specially-tailored measures cannot be adopted for specific sectors of the economy that have their own unique characteristics. Competition issues in Canada have never been reserved exclusively to the Competition Act. They are addressed, in the context of specific sectors, through a variety of regulatory statutes. Split-runs and the magazine advertising market are unique. There is no reason why their problems should not be addressed through special legislation. And there is no reason why that legislation should not take the form of a tax. Fiscal incentives and disincentives that have little or nothing to do with raising revenue – ranging from child tax credits to super-depletion allowances – are familiar techniques in Canadian legislative practice.

3.140 The United States asserted that, in addition to characterizations by Canadian officials, Canada's submissions to the Panel themselves confirm that the excise tax was structured to protect domestic production. A statement in Canada's submission is instructive:

> The object of the excise tax is not to discourage readership of foreign magazines, but to *maintain an environment in which Canadian magazines can exist in Canada alongside with imported magazines. It is also intended to foster conditions in which indigenous magazines can be published, distributed and sold in Canada on a commercial basis*..."(emphasis added).

Although couched in the best possible light, this statement does not disguise the fact that the purpose of the excise tax is to protect Canadian magazines from import competition. It appeared to be Canada's position that because it does not *completely* restrict imports of magazines, it should be free to impose *certain* import barriers to benefit its domestic industry. There is absolutely no basis in GATT for this position. Canada's contractual obligations under GATT Article III are not limited to affording a certain amount of national treatment to imports; Canada must provide full national treatment, comparative trade advantages (i.e. to protect domestic producers from legitimate import competition). Tariffs (within bound rates) and certain types of domestic subsidies are among the permitted measures. Internal taxes imposed at rates higher for imported products than domestic like products are not. Moreover, Canada's submissions consistently imply an import penetration much higher than it actually is.

Canada's Task Force Report states that , in reality, "Canadian publications account for 67.6 per cent of the magazines sold in Canada in a year."

3.141 Canada asserts repeatedly that the excise tax is designed to encourage "original content", as though such a purpose would justify imposition of a discriminatory excise tax. In fact, the whole notion of "original content" is protectionist in nature. Permitting a Member to require that a product be sold in its territory be a *different* product than that sold abroad would open up the WTO system to serious abuses. For example, a Member concerned about the ability of a local industry to compete with foreign manufacturers of the same product (automobiles, footwear, jewellery, etc.) could impose a prohibitive tax - on the pretext of ensuring that local consumers can purchase products designed exclusively for them – on "non-original" product designs, in order to keep foreign producers from exporting their best-selling products to the Member's market. In order to sell into such a market, the foreign manufacturer would be required to design products and set up new production lines exclusively for that market. That would erase any scale efficiencies the foreign manufacturer might otherwise have gained from sales in its domestic market and to other countries.

3.142 Canada considered that the US reliance on the concept of economies of scale is misplaced. The concept is normally associated with large production runs, typically for an international market. A local production run for a single regional market is by definition a relatively low volume production run that does not fit the definition. What the legislation is against is not economies of scale but the clearly unfair competitive advantage that comes from prepaid costs, providing what amounts to a free ride in the Canadian advertising market. The US industry gets tremendous economies of scale through its ordinary operations of publishing large runs in the United States for the international export market. The US publisher is free to produce and then to promote and sell as many copies of the magazine in Canada as possible. None of this is touched by the legislation. The tax does not insulate the domestic Canadian magazine industry from competition for readers. *Harper's*, *Sports Illustrated*, and *Vanity Fair* can all benefit fully from economies of scale of which a Canadian publisher, and in fact most publishers outside the United States, could never dream.

3.143 The United States submits further that the "whole notion of original content" is protectionist in nature, and that the policy has the same protectionist characteristics as if local product designs were to be required. The argument is revealing, because it amounts to a blanket denial that cultural products have any specificity that distinguishes them from ordinary items of trade. Content distinguishes one magazine from another. Original content created for a specific national community differentiates magazines in a way that product design seldom if ever does. The United States has raised a spectre that is not only far-fetched; it is based on a false analogy, and a failure to recognize the distinctive characteristics of cultural products, and of magazines above all. "Original content" does not have to be domestically-produced. Canadian content, in terms of subject matter, does not have to be content produced by Canadians or in Canada. Most often it will, but the assertion that "original content" is inherently protectionist is incorrect.

c. *Article III:4*

3.144 The United States argued that if the Panel decides that the excise tax does not fall within the scope of Article III:2, the tax should then be viewed as a measure affecting the sale or use of split-run magazines within the meaning of GATT Article III:4. The excise tax provides less favourable treatment to imported split-runs than to like domestic non-split-runs and therefore violates Article III:4. The excise tax clearly affects the *sale* of split-run magazines. In fact, it is set at a level so high as to prevent any sales of split-runs in the Canadian market. Indeed, Canadian officials have repeatedly stated that to be the purpose of the tax. An 80 per cent excise tax is obviously not intended to generate tax revenue. The excise tax also affects the *use* of split-run magazines, by applying a prohibitive tax whenever they are used to convey advertising to the Canadian public. Moreover split-run magazines and non-split-run magazines are "like products" for purposes of Article III:2 and should thus be considered "like products" for purposes of Article III:4 as well. The panel in *US - Standards for Gasoline* considered that similar factors were relevant to like product analyses under paragraphs III:2 and III:4.[89]

3.145 Finally, the excise tax accords less favourable treatment to imported split-run magazines than to other domestically-produced magazines. As discussed above, by its terms the tax applies to imported split-runs. The excise tax treats imported split-runs less favourably than other purely domestic magazines because it effectively prevents split-runs from being sold profitably in the Canadian magazine market, and makes it effectively impossible for split-runs to be used to carry domestic advertising. Thus, if the excise tax is not covered by Article III:2, it falls within the scope of, and is inconsistent with, Article III:4.

C. Funded and Commercial Postal Rates

1. Article III:4

a) "Regulations and requirements affecting the internal sale, offering for sale, purchase, transportation, distribution or use"

3.146 The United States argued that Canada's postal rates for magazines are openly discriminatory and in contravention of III:4 of GATT 1994. Canada Post is a Canadian Government entity that charges domestic magazines lower rates (either "commercial" or "funded" depending on the magazine) than it charges imported magazines that are mailed in Canada. Canada Post also offers certain discounts (such as for "palletization" and "pre-sort") only to domestic magazines. These measures amount to "regulations" or "requirements" that affect the internal sale, transportation, or distribution of magazines in Canada, and provide less favourable treatment to imported magazines than to like domestic magazines, in violation of GATT Article III:4.

3.147 In the report on *EEC - Parts and Components*, the panel recognized that requirements that an enterprise voluntarily accepts to gain government-provided advantages are nonetheless "requirements":

> The Panel noted that Article III:4 refers to "all laws, regulations or requirements affecting (the) internal sale, offering for sale, purchase, transportation, distribution or use". The Panel considered that the comprehensive coverage of "*all* laws, regulations or requirements *affecting*" the internal sale, etc. of imported products suggests that not only requirements which an enterprise is legally bound to carry out, . . . but also those which an enterprise voluntarily accepts in order to obtain an advantage from the government constitute "requirements" within the meaning of that provision. . . .[90]

Magazine publishers that sought to make use of the Canadian mails have to agree to pay the postal fees charged by Canada Post. Those charges are requirements, or regulations, within the meaning of Article III:4.

3.148 Canada Post's postal rates also clearly "affect" the sale, transportation and distribution of imported magazines, because they specify the cost of using the services of Canada Post to transport or distribute magazines to subscribers in Canada. A publisher seeking to have Canada Post transport and distribute its magazines to subscribers in Canada – and virtually all subscription magazines sold in Canada were distributed in this manner – would have to pay the postal fees prescribed by Canada Post. The postal fees directly affected the competitive conditions under which the product is transported, distributed, and sold to subscribers. These rates therefore "affect" the sale, transportation, and distribution of magazines in Canada.[91]

[89] Panel Report on *United States - Standards for Reformulated and Conventional Gasoline, op.cit.*, para. 6.8.
[90] Panel Report on *European Economic Community - Regulations on Parts and Components, op.cit.*, at 132, 197, para. 5.21, Italics in original. *See also, Canada - Administration of the Foreign Investment Review Act*, adopted on 7 February 1984, BISD 30S/140, 158 para. 5.4.
[91] Panel Report on *Italian Discrimination Against Agricultural Machinery*, adopted on 23 October 1958, BISD 7S/64 para. 12.

3.149 Canada's discriminatory postal rates have a particular impact on the transportation of magazines in Canada. The drafters of GATT clearly intended to include the rates charged for government-provided transportation services under the disciplines of Article III. Canada Post's divergent postal rates are not based on neutral economic considerations, but explicitly discriminatory criteria – namely, whether the magazine is Canadian or foreign in origin.[92]

3.150 Canada underscored the importance of the distinction between the subsidized rates, those rates available as a result of a subsidy granted exclusively to domestic publishers by Canadian Heritage, and commercial publications rates, those rates available to all publishers (Canadian or otherwise) that do not qualify for the subsidy granted by Canadian Heritage. Whereas the subsidized rates are the result of an expressed intention on the part of the Government to assist domestic publishers (as specifically permitted by GATT Article III:8(b)), the commercial publications rates are the result of generally accepted commercial and marketing practices and are not influenced by government policy. Unfortunately, the United States has failed to make this important distinction.

3.151 Canada Post is a corporation in its own right, with a legal personality distinct from that of the Government, and considerable autonomy in the conduct of its operation; far more than would ever be accorded to a government department. Canada Post is a Crown corporation and its objectives are set out in the CPC Act. In addition, under the FA Act, as a Schedule III, Part II Crown Corporation, Canada Post is expected to: operate in a competitive environment; earn a return on equity; not depend on government appropriation; and finally, provide a reasonable expectation that it would pay dividends. Both the CPC Act and the FA Act essentially establish a commercial mandate for Canada Post comparable to a private sector interest.

3.152 This legislative framework provides Canada Post with the legal and operational flexibility to implement its commercially-oriented mandate. With respect to publications, i.e., newspapers and periodicals, Canada Post is not a government monopoly and does not have the exclusive right of delivery. Canada Post does not have the power of a monopoly when it sets commercial rates for the delivery of publications.[93] It competes in an open competitive market for its share of the publications delivery market. Any publisher, foreign or domestic, is free to arrange for the delivery of his newspaper or periodical via Canada Post or with any other distributor. Section 14(2) of the CPC Act states that "[n]othing in this Act shall be construed as requiring any person to transmit by post any newspaper, magazine, book, catalogue or goods". Pursuant to Section 2 of the Act,"post" means to leave in a post office or with a person authorized by the Corporation to receive mailable matter. Foreign publishers have the additional option of mailing their copies addressed to Canadian addresses with their own postal administration at the applicable international printed matter rates.

3.153 The principle of national treatment of Article III:4 of GATT 1994 does not apply to the commercial postal rates charged by Canada Post. The United States contends that commercial rates set by Canada Post are "regulations" or "requirements" affecting the internal sale of imported publications. The term "regulation" in the context of GATT 1994 means the rules or orders having the force of law that are issued by executive or administrative authorities of government. The rates for the delivery of letters in Canada are set by regulations.[94] However, the commercial rates for publications are set by market forces and fluctuate with commercial imperatives – not to mention that in many cases they are the result of negotiations with both domestic and international large volume customers pursuant to specific agreements. The responsibility for setting those rates rests exclusively with senior management of the Corporation who exercise their discretion based on commercial principles without government intervention.

---

[92] The United States recommended the Panel to see also, *U.S. - Malt Beverages* (panel found that restrictions on private delivery of imported, but not domestic beer, was inconsistent with Article III:4).

[93] Canada added that Canada Post does have a limited exclusive privilege with respect to the collection, transmission and delivery of "letters" in Canada, including addressed advertising mail. This exclusive privilege represents in aggregate approximately 50 per cent of total corporate revenues. Canada Post has no statutory protection for the remainder of its business and must compete with existing or potential competitors, as the case may be. The Corporation's exclusive privilege is defined in Section 14 and 15 of the *Canada Post Corporation Act*.

[94] *Letter Mail Regulations*, SOR/88-430 as amended to April 30, 1996.

3.154 The term "requirement" in the context of GATT also implies a demand or direction proclaimed by an authority within government. Again, commercial imperatives and market forces dictate the commercial rates for publications charged by the Corporation to its customers. The government has never issued a directive to the Corporation regarding publications mail. The Corporation's prices are set to meet market demands and opportunities (as in the case of any private sector company), and are clearly not the product of "laws, regulations or requirements" of Canada. It is incorrect to suggest, as does the United States, that the differential between the commercial rate provided to Canadian publishers and the commercial rate provided to non-Canadian publishers is calculated to place non-Canadian publishers at a competitive disadvantage. Canada Post has no policy of giving a competitive advantage to one segment of its customers over another, and has no interest in pursuing any such practice. For their part, customers have access to competing delivery channels and, as in all open markets, have the ability to negotiate rates in a manner reflecting their purchasing power.

3.155 The international commercial rates reflect the reality that suppliers in any competitive market would attempt to obtain the best possible price. Pricing is set to maximize contribution while remaining competitive. Factors such as the availability and cost to customers of competing distribution channels, currency exchange rates, service standards, etc., are all taken into consideration by Canada Post (as would any company in a competitive market) when setting its pricing. As a Crown corporation with a commercial mandate, Canada Post operates on the same basis as a private sector interest. The commercial postage rate applicable to non-Canadian publications is set on the basis of the commercial business reality that the next-best option faced by mailers of publications that are printed outside Canada is the much higher international rate charged by the postal administration in the country of publication. In the case of publications from the United States, this means a rate for deposit in Canada with Canada Post that is about half of what they would have to pay the United States Postal Service (USPS) for delivery of the same items to Canada. The commercial mandate given to Canada Post requires it to obtain the best possible rate in order to maximize its returns.

3.156 Almost half the direct-deposit foreign periodicals business Canada Post receives is contracted through specific agreements, negotiated on a case-by-case basis subject to customer- and market-specific needs and opportunities as opposed to generic pricing policies. Canada Post's commercial pricing policies are determined by the demands of the markets in which it operates and not by governmental directives or public policy considerations. In the case of commercial publications, there is no direction, instruction or any other obligation to provide this service or to provide this service at certain rates. This means that the management of Canada Post is free to establish commercial services and rates for publications purely on commercial principles and market realities so as to maximize the financial advantage to Canada Post providing such commercial publication services. The decision to maintain a separate, higher rate for international as opposed to Canadian commercial publications is made purely by Canada Post management for commercial reasons and in no way reflects any explicit or implicit request by government that Canada Post use its rate structure to disadvantage foreign commercial publications relative to Canadian commercial publications. The Canadian Government could express its views on commercial and international rates much in the same way it might choose to comment on pricing of a private sector firm. However, to compel change, the Government would have to instruct Canada Post under the directive power in Section 22 of the CPC Act. Indeed, Canada Post has received no instruction or advice, implicit or explicit, to set international commercial rates in excess of domestic commercial rates for periodicals. This action is of Canada Post's own creation based on its perception of market opportunity.

3.157 The United States argued that the Government of Canada is responsible for Canada Post's activities, including its so-called commercial postal rates. Canada's argument implicitly concedes that Canada Post is a governmental entity, and exercises a governmental function, when it applies "funded" (subsidized) postal rates to, and provides for the delivery of, certain domestically produced magazines. Canada seeks to convince the Panel that Canada Post sheds its governmental character when it applies its so-called "commercial" rates and provides for the delivery of magazines subject to those rates.

3.158 Canada Post is a wholly, government-owned, government-created chartered body, subject to the control of a board of directors appointed by the Minister responsible for Canada Post. (The existence of a Government Minister responsible for Canada Post is further proof that Canada Post is an arm of the Canadian Federal Government.) The Chairman of the Board and the President of Canada Post are both appointed by the Governor-in-Council. Section 5(2)(e) of the CPC Act provides explicitly that Canada Post is "an institution of the Government of Canada". The Canadian Parliament created Canada Post and fixed its operating mandate. Moreover, Canada Post's mandate to operate, in part, on a "commercial" basis is itself set by the Government. An important oversight role is played by the Minister responsible for Canada Post. In "The Mandate of Canada Post Corporation and its Development", Canada acknowledged that: "Section 22 of the CPC Act provides that Canada Post is required to comply with directions issued by the Minister responsible for the corporation. This gives the Minister powers analogous to those exercisable by shareholders of other privately held corporations through unanimous shareholders agreements."[95] Thus, Canada Post is entirely a creature of the Canadian Government, subject to its direct supervision and control.

3.159 Recent events confirm that the Canadian Government considers Canada Post to be a government entity fully subject to Canadian Government direction, and a vehicle for the expression of Government policy - including through Canada Post's "commercial" operations. On 8 October 1996, Diane Marleau, the Minister responsible for Canada Post Corporation, presented the Canadian Government's reaction to a report issued by an independent task force chaired by Mr. George Radwanski (the "Radwanski Report"). The report addressed financial and policy issues related to the future of Canada Post.

3.160 The Radwanski Report was highly critical of Canada Post and, *inter alia,* charged Canada Post with engaging in unfair competition with its private sector competitors in the delivery of commercial services, such as courier and advertising mail services.[96] In her press conference responding to the report, Ms. Marleau stated:

> I want to emphasize that *the government regards Canada Post as a significant federal institution, and that it sees Canada Post continuing to carry out a public policy role* based on the provision of mail to all Canadians, no matter where they live...The federal government is expected to embody certain values and principles in how it carries out its affairs, in particular: fairness, transparency, openness and accountability. *Canada Post is part of the federal government and must live up to these standards.* As *Minister Responsible for Canada Post,* I expect immediate corrective action wherever these values and principles have been compromised. To this end, I have asked Mr. Ouellet, as Chair of Canada Post Corporation, to develop an action plan for improving the transparency of Canada Post's activities, and addressing these issues...The government will consider the rest of the recommendations of the report of the Mandate Review, recognizing that there are certain basic principles which must guide our deliberations:...
>
> - *Canada Post is a valuable federal institution.* Canadians have invested in it, and the government must protect this value.
> - Canada Post will remain a Crown corporation and not be privatized, *as long as it continues to fulfil a public policy role.*"...[97]

---

[95] "The Mandate of Canada Post Corporation and its Development".

[96] The report did not specifically discuss Canada Post's publications mail activities.

[97] *Speaking Notes for the Honourable Diane Marleau, Minister Responsible for Canada Post Corporation, Release of the Canada Post Mandate Review Report*, 8 October 1996, at 1-3 (emphasis added).

3.161 With respect to Canada Post's commercial courier service activities, Minister Marleau stated that:

> [A]s long as Canada Post remains in this line of business, it must compete on a level playing field. As I noted earlier, Canada Post's operations must be conducted under the tenets of fairness, transparency, openness, and accountability.[98]

These excerpts confirm that the Canadian Government considers Canada Post to be a Canadian federal government institution and that the Government is fully responsible for Canada Post's activities – even those carried out in commercial sectors.

3.162 Canada Post's so-called "commercial" (non-subsidized) postage rates reflect an overlay of Canadian government policy having nothing to do with marketplace considerations. Notwithstanding Canada's statement that commercial publications rates "are available to all publishers (Canadian or otherwise) that do not qualify for the subsidy granted by Canadian Heritage," in fact only certain types of publications qualify for commercial mail rates. Among the eligibility criteria are: the content of the publication (e.g., devoted to religion, the sciences, social or literary criticism), the amount of space it devoted to advertising, and whether the publisher is a person whose principal business is publishing. These criteria are all irrelevant as commercial considerations, but are indicative of types of publications which a government might wish to support as a matter of public policy. This suggests that Canada Post continues to operate as an instrument of the Canadian Government in its commercial mail operations and does not operate according to purely commercial considerations.

3.163 Finally, the United States considered that Canada's claim that the disparity in "commercial" rates between imports and domestic magazines reflects the lack of commercially feasible alternative delivery options for imports as compared to domestic magazines is dubious as a factual matter. Also, Canada's explanation that the disparity in rates does not reflect Government policy is suspect in light of the existence of a whole set of Canadian Government policy measures whose explicit goal is to benefit domestic magazines. Even if true, Canada's explanation would not remove this measure from the scope of Article III:4. Article III:4 is precise - a Member must accord "treatment no less favourable" to imports as compared to domestic products - regardless of whether imports have fewer commercial alternatives as compared with domestic magazines. It is in the nature of imported products that they often are in an inferior economic and political bargaining position. Article III was included in the GATT because imports are vulnerable to discrimination.

3.164 Canada argued that government ownership is not in itself sufficient to qualify the practices of an enterprise as regulations for the purposes of Article III:4 of GATT 1994. The independent nature of Canada Post's commercial operations for the distribution of publications and the competitive environment within which it operates and sets its rates removes such rates from the provisions of Article III:4. Although at one time the Post Office was an integral part of the Government of Canada and its rates were set by statute and regulation, that relationship was changed in a fundamental way in 1981. Concerned with issues relating to service, management, labour relations and the financial performance of the Post Office Department, the Government decided to turn over the postal administration to a Crown corporation with a commercial orientation and an independent management charged with attaining financial self-sufficiency. The CPC Act gave the Corporation the powers of a natural person, an attribute more typical of a private sector corporation than of traditional Crown corporations. The FA Act later confirmed the Corporation's status as an entity expected to operate in a competitive environment, not to be dependent on appropriations, earn a return on equity and pay dividends to its shareholder.

3.165 At the time of the creation of Canada Post, there were those who suggested that it should remain under the direct control of the Government. It was proposed that its activities be overseen by the Postmaster General assisted by a Secretariat. However, what had happened was that supervision of the Corporation had been entrusted to a board of directors composed of independent outside directors and officers of the Corporation (none of whom are

[98] *Ibid.*, at 3.

civil servants). The Board, like traditional private sector boards of directors, is empowered to establish the general policy of the Corporation, including the making of decisions concerning finance, personnel management and commercial orientation, without the restrictions inherent in government departments. The Board has, since incorporation, pursued the goal of financial self-sufficiency by allowing management the latitude, in commercial operations, to generate revenues through rate and product management and to manage the Corporation's expenditures in a manner consistent with any competitive enterprise, essentially free of government intervention.

3.166 Crown corporations are distinct legal entities wholly owned by the Crown with boards of directors that oversee the management of the corporation and hold management accountable for the company's performance. The board of directors, through the chair, is accountable to the responsible minister and the responsible minister functions as the link between the corporation and both the Cabinet and Parliament. It is the duty of the board of directors to oversee the management of their Crown corporation with a view to the best interests of both the corporation and the long-term interests of the shareholder. This concept is similar to that of private sector corporations. Boards of directors of Crown corporations are expected to exercise judgement in the broad areas of: the establishment of a corporation's strategic direction; the safeguarding of the corporation's resources; the monitoring of corporate performance; and reporting to the Crown. Each Crown corporation is accountable to Parliament for the conduct of its affairs through a minister who represents the Crown. It is through the minister that the Crown corporation reports on its plans and its performance to the Government and to Parliament.

3.167 Canadian and international commercial categories of rates had been set by Canada Post outside of the regulations since March 1994 and March 1992, respectively. Non-subsidized publications formerly subjected to the rates set out in the *Newspapers and Periodicals Regulations* are now subject to commercial Canadian Publications Mail and International Publications Mail rates, respectively, which are established and approved by Canada Post senior management. They are not established by Canadian Government regulations.

3.168 Canada Post is a corporation with a distinct legal personality. It can contract separately from the Government. It contracts with the Government for the supply of postal and other services. The Corporation is obligated to pay corporate income tax to the Government on its revenues.[99] Contrary to US assertions, employees of the Corporation are not employees of the Government. Indeed, Section 12 of the CPC Act authorizes Canada Post to hire employees, fix the terms and conditions of their employment and pay them their remuneration. The statutory regime[100] applicable to employees of the Government does not apply to employees of Canada Post, whose employment conditions and labour relations are governed by the same provisions of the Canada Labour Code that apply to the federal private sector.[101] Furthermore, if Canada Post employees had government employee status, there would have been no need to include a special "deeming" provision in the Act in order to preserve employees' pension rights at the time of the creation of Canada Post. The above attributes are certainly not those of a corporation over which the Canadian Government maintains a "hands-on level of administrative control" as the United States would like the Panel to believe.

3.169 The degree of control that the Government exercises over Canada Post's commercial operations is one dictated by the Government shareholder's interests. The Government requires sound financial administration of the Corporation's business and a fair return on its equity investments. To achieve this goal, the Corporation must offer satisfactory services to customers at a competitive price that will maximize profits. In a competitive environment, pricing policies of Canada Post must take into account basic economic principles of supply and demand. It must consequently consider the effects that its commercial postal rates will have on current or potential competition.

---

[99] *Income Tax Regulations, amendment*, SOR/94-405.

[100] Canada states that employees of the Government are appointed by the Public Service Commission under the unique provisions of the *Public Service Employment Act.* Employment conditions and labour relations are governed by the *Public Service Staff Relations Act and the Public Service Employment Act*.

[101] Canada notes that the federal private sector includes such industries as banks, interprovincial trucking, radio, television, railways, ports and the aeronautics industry.

3.170 Canada Post does not have a monopoly with respect to the delivery of publications (newspapers and periodicals) in Canada. Canada Post, through the CPC Act, does have a limited exclusive privilege with respect to the collection, transmission and delivery of "letters" in Canada including addressed advertising mail, but the Corporation has no statutory protection for the remainder of its business and has to compete with existing or potential competition, as the case may be.

3.171 Almost 50 per cent of foreign publications mailed in Canada are accorded special rates negotiated by major foreign publishers pursuant to long-term agreements with Canada Post. Those rates are substantially less than the commercial International Publications Mail rate and relatively close to the commercial Canadian Publications Mail rate.[102] The willingness of the Corporation to enter into such special-rate agreements reflects the reality that large foreign publishers have the resources and purchasing power to credibly threaten full or partial delivery in Canada via current and potential private distributors. Smaller foreign publishers have neither the volume nor the density of mailings to warrant their effort to access private distribution (often organised on a city by city basis) in Canada. Canadian commercial publishers have credibly threatened to move to private distribution in the past.[103] This motivated the Corporation to develop commercial Publications Mail rates that are financially attractive when compared to that of current or potential private distributors.

3.172 Canada Post currently faces competition for delivery of addressed publications.[104] The principal form of competition for the delivery of addressed subscriber copies of daily and weekly newspapers (those not eligible for subsidized postal rates) is delivery by the publishers themselves. In general, almost all such newspapers choose to deliver their own publications wherever volume densities warrant, with the residual volumes being mailed to subscribers via Canada Post's commercial Publications Mail rates. There is somewhat less competition for the delivery of addressed periodicals, where competition exists mainly in the dense urban areas. Competition for the delivery of addressed periodicals is limited because commercial publications rates are designed to attract the delivery of addressed periodicals not eligible for subsidized rates. It is also limited due to Canada Post's successful bid to Canadian Heritage for the delivery of publications eligible for funded rates. Canada Post's competitors cannot enter into the same arrangement with Canadian Heritage because all available program dollars have been committed to the arrangement signed with Canada Post.

3.173 Canadian Heritage agreed to a fixed price contract with Canada Post, taking into account the fact that this would be an exclusive contract for the delivery of eligible publishers' publications at subsidized rates, and therefore committing all of its funding available for distribution assistance of these publications. Obviously, this precludes any alternative supplier of delivery services from signing a similar agreement with Canadian Heritage during the three-year term of the current agreement. However, Canada Post won the exclusive three-year arrangement in the context of a real possibility of a direct-to-publishers funding program without exclusive suppliers. Such an option or an option of awarding an exclusive supply contract to a supplier or suppliers other than Canada Post is again a possibility at the expiry of the current three-year contract. It should be noted that Canada Post is obliged under the current agreement to provide service without limitation at the agreed funded rates to all existing and new publications that are deemed by Canadian Heritage to meet the agreed eligibility conditions. If the publisher of an eligible publication chooses to deliver the publication via another carrier, the publisher would not have access to special rates given that Canadian Heritage has chosen to negotiate an exclusive supplier contract with Canada Post for the term of the contract.

---

[102] Canada asserts that contrary to what the United States contends, several large foreign publishers enjoy discounts, pursuant to long-term agreements, similar to the mail preparation discounts offered to Canadian publishers.

[103] Canada notes that those threats are substantiated by certain factors such as the proximity of the Canadian publications to their markets, generally greater density of those markets (typically commercial trade publications oriented towards businesses in urban areas) and concentration of ownership in the industry.

[104] Examples of such competitors are Globe and Mail Distribution Services Ltd., A1Tours Ltd. (bundle distribution of magazines to business/professional offices), C.D. Woods Ltd., (Vancouver B.C.), Roltek Ltd., Insurance Courier Services Ltd. and an emerging co-operative delivery venture of Canadian trade publications.

3.174 With respect to the use of the Radwanski Report by the United States, the mandate review was partially a review of the appropriateness of the monopoly that the Government has granted to Canada Post on letter delivery. The Report recommends, among other things: (1) that providing universality of service and uniformity of price for letter mail be regarded as integral elements of the mandate of Canada Post; and (2) that the exclusive privilege of Canada Post with regard to letter mail be maintained in its current form. Secondly, the mandate review was a review by the shareholder of the validity of the strategic, operational and financial direction of Canada Post and in this regard the mandate review is similar in nature to periodic reviews conducted in the private sector by shareholders of both publicly and privately held corporations. The recommendations contained in the Report, in whole or in part, are not government policy but rather recommendations to the government for consideration. The government has rejected certain of the recommendations, adopted others and taken the balance under advisement. The Radwanski Report did not address Canada Post's distribution services for publications.

3.175 The United States asserted that the fact that the Government has to date not intervened to put a stop to Canada Post's discriminatory postal rates does not mean that it is not responsible for them. A WTO Member cannot create a government institution, allow it to take actions inconsistent with the Member's WTO obligations, and then claim it has no responsibility for the actions of the institution. The market access concessions that WTO Members have negotiated over the years would not be secure if governments could escape their obligation to provide national treatment to imported products by creating government corporations and then claiming that they are not responsible for the discrimination imposed by the entities they themselves created. Intervention by the Government to ensure that Canada Post complies with Canada's international obligations under the GATT is within the power of the Canadian Government. It is especially important that the Canadian Government take remedial action because publishers of imported magazines have only limited alternatives to using Canada Post's services for delivery and transportation of magazines to Canadian subscribers. Indeed, Canada Post itself boasts that, "*We are the only national distribution service that reaches every single address in Canada.* No one does this – no other competitor comes close."[105] Canada acknowledges that Canada Post faces only limited competition for the delivery of addressed magazines. Magazines seeking to reach destinations other than business addresses in major cities have no practical alternative to using the delivery services of Canada Post.

3.176 Because of Canada Post's status as a Canadian Government institution that delivers and transports magazines and other mail, its actions – including the rates it applies – in respect of these activities are necessarily regulations or requirements affecting the internal sale, distribution or transportation of magazines within the meaning of Article III:4. If the Canadian Government told private Canadian delivery services to charge more for delivering imported goods than for delivering domestic goods, it would be in clear violation of Article III:4. If the Canadian Government accomplishes this same result through rate discrimination in its own delivery services, Article III:4 should apply with equal force. With respect to Canada's arguments concerning the Radwanski report, the United States responded that although that report did not refer to publications mail, it was primarily concerned with advertising mail and courier services, which are both commercial services. Thus, the statements made by Minister Marleau with respect to these services as commercial services are equally applicable to publications mail.

b) Like product issue

3.177 The United States argued that imported magazines are "like" domestic magazines for the purposes of Article III:4. Canada Post's rates distinguish between magazines based on whether they are imported or produced in Canada. In particular, Canada established two rate classes for magazines that are printed and published in Canada (the "commercial" and "funded" rates) and a third rate class for imported magazines (the "international" rate). Magazines eligible for "funded" rates are not only printed and published in Canada, but have to meet other requirements, namely: (a) the periodical must be typeset and edited in Canada; (b) the exclusive right to produce and publish the periodical must be held by a Canadian citizen, or a corporation controlled by Canadian citizens;

[105] Canada Post, Publications Mail, Product Guide at B-1 (bold in original).

and (c) the issue can not be published under license from a foreign publisher, or contain editorial content substantially the same as an issue printed outside Canada that was not first edited in Canada.[106]

3.178 However, all of these categories of magazines are "like products" for purposes of Article III:4 and the distinction that Canada has drawn between them is solely, indeed openly, intended to favour domestic production. Domestic and imported magazines share the same physical characteristics and commercial uses. Neither the location of production, nor the ownership of the right to publish, nor whether editorial content appeared in an issue printed outside Canada, make imported magazines unlike domestically-produced magazines in terms of physical characteristics or end uses. The rates established by Canada Post for imported and domestically-produced magazines draw an impermissible distinction based on the origin of the magazine, a distinction that, on its face, is applied "so as to afford protection to domestic production".

c) *Treatment of imported and domestic magazines*

3.179 The United States stated that the rates established by Canada Post discriminate against imported magazines. Canada Post charges rates for domestically-produced magazines that are either 10 or 80 per cent lower on average than the rates applicable to imported magazines. These rates accord manifestly less favourable treatment to imported magazines by comparison to their domestically-produced counterparts. Moreover, Canada Post routinely makes discounts (such as "palletization" and "bypass" options) available to domestic magazines but not to imported magazines that increase the degree of discrimination still further. The higher postal rates for imported magazines are calculated to place them at a competitive disadvantage by comparison to competing domestically-produced magazines by creating a disparity between the distribution and transportation costs for imported and domestic magazines. Article III:4, second sentence, confirms that discrimination with respect to transportation based on the "nationality of a product" is not consistent with Article III:4. Canada has made no secret of the fact that the explicit purpose for its varying postal rates is to protect the Canadian publishing industry from import competition. Canada's discriminatory magazine postal rates represent precisely the kind of protectionist regulatory measure that GATT Article III:4 condemns.

3.180 It is no answer for Canada to assert that Canada Post enters into special lower-rate arrangements with certain larger foreign magazines. Canada Post's standard commercial rates for imported magazines are higher than for domestic magazines. Smaller foreign publishers, who cannot enter into special arrangements, are subject to the standard discriminatory rates. Moreover, negotiations for special rates between Canada Post and larger publishers (both foreign and domestic) presumably use the standard discriminatory commercial rates as the starting point. Thus, the resulting negotiated rates are in all likelihood discriminatory as well. Indeed, Canada states that the negotiated rates offered to large foreign publishers are only "relatively" close to the *standard* commercial rates are offered to Canadian publishers.

3.181 Canada argued that the economic factors applicable to foreign and domestic periodicals are not the same which is why their respective rates are different. Those rates are a reflection of competitive situations, not the result of discriminatory practices as was argued by the United States. Canada Post has no policy of giving a competitive advantage to one segment of its customers over another, and would have no interest in pursuing any such practice. Given appropriate competitive factors, it might very well be that certain foreign periodicals would enjoy better rates than non-subsidized Canadian magazines. This is exactly the type of scenario that Article III of GATT 1994 is intended to preserve. If foreign magazines are in better competitive situations, they should be able to take advantage of it. If on the contrary, they are not in such a position, Article III should not be there to grant them advantages that market forces do not provide. In the commercial and competitive environment in which Canada Post operates, it is under no obligation by virtue of Article III:4 to subsidize US publications by setting a better postal rate then what their specific market conditions require.

---

[106] *Regulations Respecting Newspapers and Periodicals*, Section 3(2) (definition of "Canadian Periodical"), S.O.R./91-179, 28 February, 1991.

2. *Article III:8(b)*

3.182 The United States argued that Canada Post's discriminatory postal rates do not constitute the payment of subsidies exclusively to domestic producers within the meaning of Article III:8(b), because domestic producers receive no subsidy payments. Under their 1 May 1996 Agreement, Canadian Heritage provides Canada Post with fixed annual payments to support Canada Post's below-cost "funded" postal rates for certain magazines produced in Canada. Those payments are not distributed to domestic magazine producers; instead Canada Post uses the funds to underwrite the lower postage rates it charges domestically-produced magazines. Thus, Canada's discriminatory postal rates are not direct payments to Canadian producers; rather, they modify the conditions of competition between domestic and imported products in contravention of Article III:4.

3.183 A series of GATT 1947 panel reports had interpreted Article III:8(b) very narrowly to hold that the only subsidies subject to exclusion from the national treatment provisions of Article III are those subsidies that are paid *directly* to domestic producers. So, for example, credit facilities provided to purchasers, and not producers,[107] and payments whose benefits could be partially retained by processors,[108] have been found not to qualify under Article III:8(b). Nor does the annual payment that Canadian Heritage makes to Canada Post constitute a subsidy to domestic producers under Article III:8(b). Canadian Heritage does not provide its funds to domestic producers. The low-priced "funded" postal rate that Canada applies to certain favoured periodicals produced in Canada do not fall within the terms of Article III:8(b). Rather, these rates, together with the "commercial" rate and various discounts applicable only to Canadian-produced magazines, are part of an overtly discriminatory postal rate scheme designed to create further protection for Canada's domestic magazine industry.

3.184 Canada argued that the funds paid by Canadian Heritage to Canada Post to enable it to grant Canadian publishers of publications reduced postal rates are allowable subsidies under GATT Article III:8(b), which explicitly recognizes that subsidies to domestic producers are not subject to the national treatment rules of Article III. Paragraph 8(b) applies with respect to all provisions of Article III, including Article III:4. Public policy has been developed to ensure that Canadians, regardless of where they live, have access on a reasonable basis to periodicals. Subsidized postal rates are provided to maximize the opportunity for distribution, particularly in light of Canada's relatively small and widely dispersed population. This measure is critical, since Canadian magazines have only limited access to news-stands and rely mainly on paid subscriptions for circulation. Subsidized postal rates have enabled Canadian magazines to reach a widely dispersed readership. The provision of reduced postal rates is a way of paying subsidies that is compatible with GATT 1994. These payments are made to Canada Post four times a year in return for its undertaking to deliver eligible publications at the agreed reduced rates. The benefit of the subsidies flows directly to eligible Canadian magazine publishers. The Canadian publication industry is the exclusive beneficiary of these subsidies and has to qualify for these subsidized rates in accordance with criteria set by Canadian Heritage before being found to be eligible.

3.185 The decision of the panel in *US - Malt Beverages* lends no support to the US position. This panel held that the expression "payment of subsidies" applies only to direct subsidies and not to other kinds of subsidies such as tax credits or tax abatements.[109] The panel was concerned solely with the distinction between subsidies, tax remissions and differential taxation rates, because a failure to make that distinction would destroy the effect of Article III:2. The formal distinction between taxation measures – benefits not involving direct expenditures by government – and subsidies is vital to the operation of the Article as a whole. Canada's postal subsidy meets the requirement of directness, in the sense in which that concept is used in the *US - Malt Beverages* decision, because a payment by government for the exclusive benefit of the producers is being made. It is only the mechanics of payment that were indirect.

---

[107] Panel Report on *Italian Discrimination Against Agricultural Machinery, op. cit.*, at 60, 64, para. 14.

[108] Panel Report on *European Economic Community - Payments and Subsidies Paid to Processors and Producers of Oilseeds and Related Animal-Feed Proteins*, adopted on 25 January 1990, 37S/86, 124, para 137.

[109] Panel Report on *United States - Measures Affecting Alcoholic and Malt Beverages, op. cit.*

3.186 The position held by the United States is therefore based on a difference of form, not substance. The specific form in which the subsidy is paid is irrelevant to the operation of Article III:8(b), provided that a payment is made by the government for the exclusive benefit of domestic producers.[110] Before being granted the privilege of posting using funded postal rates, a publisher has to sign a service agreement with Canada Post. This simple fact is evidence that publishers are direct beneficiaries. Canada Post is an intermediary, not the beneficiary. Whether the subsidy is paid to Canada Post or paid directly to the publishers, the economic effect is the same, namely that the eligible publishers are the beneficiaries of the subsidy.

3.187 In practical terms, payments to individual publishers would be a cumbersome and ineffective method of delivering this subsidy. The administrative and financial burden of such a process would erode the benefits of the program. If an eligible Canadian publisher of a monthly magazine were to receive the payment, the advantages this publisher enjoys relative to foreign competition would be essentially unchanged. Canadian publishers would find themselves in the same position as they are in now, namely with an advantage over their foreign competitors. Therefore, Canadian Heritage provides Canada Post with an agreed-upon payment on a quarterly basis. The current process is far more efficient in minimizing the administrative overhead related to the program.

3.188 Based on the panel report on the *EEC – Payments and Subsidies Paid to Processors and Producers of Oilseeds and Related Animal-feed Proteins*[111] ("*EEC - Oilseeds*"), the United States argued that subsidies not paid directly to producers are not paid to them "exclusively" within the meaning of Article III:8(b). The word "exclusively" as used in this provision is concerned with the distinction between "domestic" as opposed to "non-domestic" producers, not whether third parties benefit from the subsidies. Whether an incidental benefit might be conferred upon Canada Post from the subsidy payment is irrelevant. Under the interpretation of this clause suggested by the United States, virtually any subsidy payment that would confer a third party benefit, however minimal, would be non-compliant. This is surely not the intended application of the exemption. Subsidies have an economic impact on third parties in almost all circumstances. The definition of the term "exclusive" proposed by the United States would lead, in practical terms, to the nullification of the Article III:8(b) exemption.

3.189 The United States argued that were Canada to provide payments directly (and exclusively) to domestic producers of magazines, the United States agreed that such payments would be protected by Article III:8(b). Under Canada's postal rate scheme for periodicals, however, domestic magazine producers receive *no* government payments. The only "payments" are made from one government entity (Canadian Heritage) to another (Canada Post).[112] Thus Canada's postal scheme simply does not comply with the requirement of Article III:8(b) that there be "payment . . . to domestic producers".

3.190 With regard to Canada's argument that its funded-rates system satisfied Article III:8(b) because it includes "payments" (to Canada Post), and because the resulting lower postal rates on domestic magazines have the same "economic effect" on domestic producers as payments made directly to them, the United States stated that the mere existence of "payments" (from one government entity to another, in this case) is not enough. The payments have to go to domestic producers. Under Canada's postal rate scheme, domestic *periodicals* are provided lower postal rates than imported magazines; domestic periodical *producers* receive no payments. Instead, so-called "funded publications" are charged lower postal rates. Because imported magazines do not qualify for these rates, they are placed at a commercial disadvantage in terms of the transportation and delivery of their magazines in Canada. This is precisely the type of discrimination that Article III:4 is meant to prohibit. Canada Post's discriminatory postal rates clearly confer an economic benefit on domestic *products*, but a benefit of that sort is not within the scope of

---

[110] Canada noted that the *US-Malt Beverages* panel read subparagraph 8(b) having regard to the context of the whole of Article III but, except in the context of taxation measures, it was never stated that for every subsidy to qualify, the payment must be made directly to domestic producers. The panel simply said that the words "payment of subsidies" refer only to direct subsidies involving a payment, not to other subsidies such as tax credits or tax reductions (*ibid.* at 271, para. 5.8).

[111] Panel Report on *European Economic Community - Payments and Subsidies Paid to Processors and Producers of Oilseeds and Related Animal-Feed Proteins, op. cit.*, at 124-125, paras. 137-141.

[112] Memorandum of Agreement.

Article III:8(b). That Article applies only to "the payment of subsidies exclusively to domestic *producers*" (emphasis added).

3.191 GATT panels have consistently applied Article III:8(b) strictly according to its terms. They have rejected appeals to ignore its actual language in favour of what Canada claims to be "an economic perspective". They have uniformly denied the protection of Article III:8(b) to measures that provided no direct payments to domestic producers, including measures that may have conferred economic benefits indirectly on domestic producers by favouring the purchase or use of domestic products. Indeed, the "economic benefits" argument was explicitly rejected by the panel on *United States - Measures Affecting the Importation, Internal Sale and Use of Tobacco* ("*US - Tobacco*").[113]

3.192 If Canada's view - that Article III:8(b) encompasses the indirect provision of economic benefits to domestic producers through government advantages conferred on their goods - is accepted, it would dramatically expand the types of measures exempted from discipline under Article III. That is because virtually *any* form of more-favourable treatment accorded by a government to domestic products could be characterized as providing economic benefits similar to the payment of subsidies to domestic producers. Past panels have uniformly interpreted Article III:8(b) to require actual payments to domestic producers. In the panel on *Italian Discrimination Against Agricultural Machinery*, that panel

> agreed with the contention of the United Kingdom delegation that in any case the provisions of paragraph 8(b) would not be applicable to this particular case since the credit facilities provided under the Law were granted to the purchasers or agricultural machinery and could not be considered as subsidies accorded to the producers of agricultural machinery.[114]

3.193 In that case it could have been argued that even though a subsidy was granted to purchasers of agricultural machinery, economic benefits also flowed directly or indirectly to the domestic producer of the machinery, since the availability of inexpensive credit limited to the purchase of domestic goods would stimulate the sales of such goods. However, the panel had correctly interpreted the words "exclusively to domestic producers" according to their plain meaning and found that the Italian credit scheme did not qualify for the Article III:8(b) exemption.

3.194 The panel report on *US - Malt Beverages*, cited by Canada in its submissions, does not deal with the issue of payments to third parties. The panel rejected a US argument that tax credits for small domestic producers of beer and wine constituted a domestic subsidy permitted under Article III:8(b), and holding that

> Article III:8(b) . . . clarifies that the product-related rules in paragraphs 1 through 7 of Article III "shall not prevent the payment of subsidies exclusively to domestic producers" (emphasis added [in original text]). The words 'payment of subsidies' refer only to direct subsidies involving a payment. . .[115]

The panel thus continued the practice of past panels of invoking a narrow and literal interpretation of that provision. In this case, the only "payment" goes from Canadian Heritage to Canada Post, not to magazine producers. In fact, this "payment" is more akin to an internal transfer of government funds than a true economic "payment" to an unrelated entity.

[113] Panel report on *United States - Measures Affecting the Importation, Internal Sale and Use of Tobacco*, adopted 4 October 1994, DS44/R.

[114] Panel Report on *Italian Discrimination Against Agricultural Machinery, op. cit.*para. 14.

[115] Panel Report on *United States - Measures Affecting Alcoholic and Malt Beverages, op. cit.*

3.195 In *US - Tobacco*,[116] the panel found that price support payments made to domestic tobacco farmers out of the proceeds of the No Net Cost Assessment ("NNCA") were within the scope of Article III:8(b). The panel rejected an interpretation of Article III:8(b) based on a measure's economic impact:

> The Panel was cognizant of the fact that a remission of a tax on a product and the payment of a producer subsidy out of the proceeds of such a tax could have the *same economic effects. However, the panel noted that the distinction in Article III:8(b) is a formal one, not related to the economic impact of a measure.* Thus, in view of the explicit language of Article III:8(b), which recognizes that the product-related rules of Article III "shall not prevent the payment of subsidies exclusively to domestic producers," the Panel did not consider, as argued by the complainants, that the payment of a subsidy to tobacco producers out of the proceeds of the NNCA resulted in a form of tax remission inconsistent with Article III:2.[117]

3.196 Finally, the *EEC - Oilseeds*[118] panel examined EEC legislation that, like the payments by the Department of Canadian Heritage to Canada Post, included government payments to a middleman rather than to the domestic producer itself, on the theory that the payments would induce the middleman to provide preferential treatment to the domestic producer. The EEC legislation provided for the payment of subsidies to processors of oilseeds whenever they established by documentary evidence that they had transformed oilseeds of Community origin. In that decision:

> The Panel noted that Article III:8(b) applies only to payments made *exclusively* to domestic producers and considered that *it can reasonably be assumed that a payment not made directly to producers is not made "exclusively" to them.* It noted moreover that if the economic benefits generated by the payments granted by the Community can at least partly be retained by the processors of Community oilseeds, the payments generate a benefit conditional upon the purchase of oilseeds of domestic origin inconsistently with Article III:4. Under these circumstances Article III:8(b) would not be applicable because in that case *the payments would not be made exclusively to domestic producers but to processors as well.*[119]

3.197 Canada mischaracterizes the *EEC - Oilseeds* decision as standing for the proposition that the phrase "exclusively to domestic producer," as used in Article III:8(b), is intended only to distinguish between "domestic" as opposed to "non-domestic" producers. The emphasized language makes it clear that the distinction is between "direct payments to producers" and "payments to ... processors" (who might in turn provide an indirect benefit to producers). So, too, in this case, the only "payments" are to an entity other than the domestic producers (and this "payment" is an internal transfer of government funds).

3.198 Canada considered it paradoxical if not contradictory for the United States to challenge Canada Post's international commercial rates on the grounds that Canada Post and the Government are one and the same, and to object to subsidized rates on the grounds that the same Corporation is obtaining, as a third party, a share of the benefits which the postal subsidy extends to Canadian periodical publishers. The argument that the Corporation is obtaining a benefit presupposes that it is an entirely separate entity from the Government: were it an organ of the Government, it would make little difference if it benefitted in any way from the payments, for in this case it would not be a government subsidy but simply a transfer of funds. The United States cannot maintain that the commercial rates and subsidized rates are discriminatory because Canada Post is part of the Government in the first case but not part of the Government in the second case. This is a clear contradiction.

---

[116] Panel Report on *United States - Measures Affecting the Importation, Internal Sale and Use of Tobacco, op. cit.*

[117] *Ibid.*, para. 109 (emphasis added).

[118] Panel Report on *European Economic Community - Payments and Subsidies Paid to Processors and Producers of Oilseeds and Related Animal-Feed Proteins, op. cit.*,, para. 137.

[119] *Ibid.*, para. 137 (emphasis added).

3.199 The United States concedes that the protection provided by Article III:8(b) would extend to direct payments made exclusively to domestic periodical producers. At the same time, the United States takes a highly formalistic approach based on a very narrow interpretation of Article III:8(b). However, the formalism which the United States is asking the Panel to enshrine is supported neither by the text of Article III:8(b) nor by GATT practice. The method of subsidy payment is not in and of itself conclusive in determining whether Article III:8(b) applies. The essential factor is that the payment be made by the government for the benefit of domestic producers.

3.200 The panel reports quoted by the United States do not support the conclusion that the subsidy must always be paid directly and exclusively to domestic producers. For example, it cannot seriously be argued that the panel on *Italian Discrimination against Agricultural Machinery* determined that the subsidy had to be paid to domestic producers through actual payments. The panel found that Article III:8(b) did not apply in that case because the credit facilities provided by the legislation were extended to the purchasers of agricultural machinery and could not be considered to be subsidies paid to the producers of agricultural machinery. In the case of the Italian legislation, government support in the form of credit facilities for the purchase of Italian agricultural machinery was granted to the purchasers of agricultural machinery, and in the view of the panel the provisions of Article III:8(b) do not apply in these circumstances. The postal subsidy program involves no similar circumstances, since the Canadian Government's assistance in the form of reduced postal rates does not go to Canada Post Corporation.

3.201 It would appear that the formalism advocated by the United States stems from the report of the *US – Malt Beverages* panel, which dealt with a lower excise tax levied on domestic beer than on imported beer. The United States argued that the clear purpose of the lower tax was to subsidize small producers, and that reducing the excise tax was a way of granting such a subsidy which was compatible with the GATT. The panel concluded that "the words `payment of subsidies' refer only to direct subsidies involving a payment, not to other subsidies such as tax credits or tax reductions." In the opinion of the panel, the prohibition on discriminatory internal taxes in Article III:2 would be rendered inoperative were it possible to offer a general justification for such taxes on imported goods on the grounds that these were subsidies paid to competing domestic producers in accordance with Article III:8(b).

3.202 The *US – Malt Beverages* report must be read and understood within the full context of Article III:2 and with consideration to tax credits and reductions. In that specific case, the tax reductions and exemptions could not be deemed equivalent to the subsidies provided for by Article III:8(b). The panel did not make a determination on all other forms of subsidies. The Canadian postal subsidy, which has nothing in common with a tax abatement, exemption, credit or reduction, is consistent with the provisions of Article III:8(b) and is in no way incompatible with the *US - Malt Beverages* decision. In the present case, payments are made four times a year for the exclusive benefit of periodical producers. Only the mechanics of payment are indirect.

3.203 This interpretation is supported by the *US – Tobacco* report, which the United States quotes and to which it attributes an unwarranted scope in light of Article III:8(b). Without entering into the details, the issue in this case was whether the net self-financing levy on imported tobacco was higher than the self-financing levy on domestic tobacco, since the latter received a *de facto* tax remission by virtue of the operation of the tobacco price support program. The panel did not consider that the payment of a subsidy to tobacco producers out of the proceeds of the self-financing levy resulted in a form of tax remission inconsistent with Article III:2. The panel noted the formal distinction between a tax remission on the one hand and the payment of a subsidy on the other, even if they could have the same economic effect. The economic impact in the case of tax remission is irrelevant to the application of Article III:8(b). The formal distinction between taxation measures and subsidies is vital to the operation of Article III:2. It cannot be concluded from this panel report, as the United States did, that in the case of a producer subsidy, the examination of the measure's economic impact is irrelevant to determine whether the measure is consistent with the provisions of Article III:8(b).

3.204 Lastly, the United States suggests that Article III:8(b) is inapplicable in light of the *EEC – Oilseeds* report, in which the panel provides an unusual interpretation of the word "exclusively". Contrary to the US contention,

Canada has not misinterpreted this report. It simply supports a more common interpretation of the word "exclusively". The general thrust of Article III is against discrimination between imported and domestic products. In this context, granting a government subsidy "exclusively" to domestic producers can only mean granting a subsidy only to the producers of domestic products, in the sense that it is paid to them alone and not to foreign producers.

3.205 In the case under study, the payments to processors were an incentive for them to buy oilseeds of EEC origin instead of imported oilseeds. The incentive derived from the fact that the payments made to processors could be greater than the difference between the price processors actually paid to EEC producers and the price that processors would have had to pay for imported oilseeds. This excess compensation created an incentive to buy products of EEC origin instead of imports. It is for this reason that Article III:8(b) was not applicable, for in this case the payments were not made to domestic EEC producers exclusively, but to processors as well.

3.206 The panel demonstrated that the payments could constitute benefits granted to EEC processors if the latter purchased EEC products. There is no parallel between the postal subsidy and the flaws in the EEC system. The United States has failed to demonstrate such a parallel. Moreover, the United States claim that the panel developed a general principle of interpretation by which Article III:8(b) does not apply if there is an intermediary between the government and the beneficiary is groundless. The panel would not have taken the trouble to perform such a complex analysis of the various prices (in paragraphs 136 through 141) were it only a matter of putting forward a general principle. The United States has not presented any analysis comparable to the one performed by the panel.

3.207 Moreover, there is no parallel with the postal subsidy because Canada Post does not receive "bonus payments" for handling and distributing periodicals from Canadian publishers rather than from foreign publishers. The Corporation receives an amount that is stipulated in a memorandum of understanding or contract in exchange for the provision of reduced postal rates. This amount is based on estimates of expected eligible Canadian periodical volumes at the negotiated reduced rates, which estimates are developed independently by each of Canada Post and Canadian Heritage in the course of negotiating the contract. There is no incentive to handle the periodicals of Canadian publishers rather than those of foreign publishers, since delivering a larger number of Canadian magazines than that originally estimated by Canada Post would not increase the Corporation's net income. The postal subsidy does not grant the Corporation any particular benefit. The EEC system provided incentives favouring EEC processors whereas there are no such measures favouring Canada Post in the memorandum of understanding with Canadian Heritage.

3.208 The agreement between Canadian Heritage and Canada Post expressly stipulates the rates paid by eligible Canadian periodical publishers. The terms of the agreement ensure that the payments to the Corporation secure the price it must charge publishers who mail their periodicals at subsidized rates. The contract for the provision of delivery services for eligible publications is at a fixed rate. Canada Post receives a lump sum in exchange for providing delivery services at the reduced rate. It should be noted that the predetermined annual payment to Canada Post from Canadian Heritage is a negotiated value for service in the spirit of any fixed price contract; that is, Canada Post must provide delivery at the agreed reduced rates to all eligible publications in return for the fixed amount. Both parties are aware that variances up or down in a given year relative to each's view of expected volume are to be expected. However, it is each party's studied view that in spite of these risks, it has an equal chance to gain or lose relative to those expectations of volumes. In view of the fixed price nature of the agreement, there is no relevance to arguments of payments in excess of value of service provided. The value provided is by definition exactly what was contracted to be provided in return for the pre-determined fixed payment.

3.209 The United States has conceded that were the payments made directly and exclusively to Canadian periodical publishers, these payments would qualify for protection under Article III:8(b). The question the Panel must consider is whether such a change in the method of subsidy payment would place foreign periodical publishers in a more favourable competitive position in relation to Canadian publishers in respect of the postal subsidy. There is no reason to believe that this would be the case. The method of payment is merely the subsidy's technical, administrative aspect. It does not reveal who benefits from the subsidy. If payments were made directly to publishers, Canada Post would increase its rates for the delivery and distribution of the magazines that had previously enjoyed reduced rates, in accordance with its practice for commercial services and its profit maximization objectives. Eligible Canadian publishers would continue to buy periodical delivery services from the Corporation at a cost "lower" than the commercial rate, in view of the compensatory payments they would receive. As for foreign publishers, they would continue to buy periodical delivery and distribution services from Canada Post at the same rates as before.

3.210 If the subsidy were paid directly to publishers rather than to Canada Post, the effects would be the same. Eligible publishers would be the beneficiaries of the subsidy. Only administrative costs would increase substantially. There is no valid reason in this case, such as for example a concern that provisions of the 1994 GATT would be rendered inoperative, which demand that the Panel uphold an interpretation which would have the effect of replacing the relatively simple and economical existing system with a costly and complicated system. Lastly, there are no grounds for claiming, as the United States has done, that our interpretation of Article III:8(b) would have the effect of encouraging the governments of member states to introduce a host of discriminatory measures in favour of domestic goods for the sole reason that these would economically benefit domestic producers. Canada is not proposing the abolition of the disciplines in the 1994 GATT but only a reading of Article III:8(b) that respects its terms.

3.211 The United States concluded that over the years GATT panels had been very careful to apply the precise language of Article III:8(b) and to avoid expanding the scope of that Article to encompass measures other than the direct payment of subsidies that convey economic benefits on the domestic producers. This caution was completely justified because the liberal reading Canada suggests for Article III:8(b) would permit governments to employ a wide variety of discriminatory measures in favour of domestic products that could be justified on the ground of conferring economic benefits on domestic producers. Such a result could dramatically alter the competitive environment in the markets of Members around the world. Canada's "funded" postage rate scheme for domestically-produced periodicals was a very good example of a product transportation and distribution regime that may well confer economic benefits on domestic producers but that plainly altered the competitive relationship between imported and domestic products.[120]

IV. INTERIM REVIEW

4.1 On 23 January 1997, the United States requested the Panel to review, in accordance with Article 15.2 of the DSU, precise aspects of the interim report that had been issued to the parties on 16 January 1997. Canada did not request a review, but wished to reserve its right to respond to the US comments. The Panel ruled that, given the circumstances in this particular case, Canada could submit its response by 31 January 1997. Canada submitted its response to the US comments on 31 January 1997, urging the Panel to disregard a large part of the US comments. Neither the United States nor Canada requested the Panel to hold a meeting. The Panel reviewed the entire range of arguments presented by the parties in their written submissions, and finalized its findings as in Section V below, taking into account the specific aspects it considered to be relevant.

4.2 Regarding Tariff Code 9958, the interim report had focused on the "split-run" rule, which the Panel found to be the principal issue, and had not mentioned the second part of the Code, namely the five-per-cent rule. The

---

[120] The United States argued that even if it were concluded that the payments made by Canadian Heritage to Canada Post to support the "funded" postal rates somehow gave rise to payments to domestic producers within the meaning of Article III:8(b), because domestic producers ultimately received an economic benefit, such a benefit would not be provided "exclusively" to domestic producers. Canada Post itself might well be a beneficiary. This is because Canada Post's pre-determined annual payment from Canadian Heritage might exceed Canada Post's cost of delivering all eligible periodicals in a given year. Moreover, Canada Post could further benefit economically from having a captive set of customers who must use its services in order to obtain the "funded" rates. For these reasons, according to the United States, it cannot be said that the benefits of Canada's Publications Assistance Program are provided "exclusively to domestic producers".

United States requested the inclusion of this part in the findings. Canada did not object to this request. The Panel agreed to the inclusion and introduced some drafting modifications in the final report at paragraphs *5.1* and *5.4*.

4.3 The interim report had, in a part corresponding to paragraph *5.24* of the final report, stated that the definition of a "split-run" edition relied *solely* on factors external to the Canadian market. The United States suggested that the Panel change this word to *decisively*. Canada objected to this change. However, the Panel considered the US suggestion to be a useful one to improve the accuracy of the findings, and accordingly modified the expression in the way it now appears in paragraph *5.24*.

4.4 Regarding paragraph *5.25* of the final report, the United States suggested that the Panel add that "(1) any number of additional hypothetical examples could be devised that would further show that split-run and non-split-run periodicals need not be any different, and that (2) this is to be expected because the definition of split-run periodicals provides that two virtually identical products can be taxed differently depending on whether or not a similar product is sold outside Canada". While the Panel did not disagree with this observation, it was not persuaded that such an addition would enhance the clarity of the logic in the final report. The Panel therefore decided not to introduce the suggested change.

4.5 Regarding the directness of the taxation (paragraphs *5.28* and *5.29* of the final report), the United States argued that this was a case of direct taxation because the excise tax was focused on a particular type of good. The Panel rejected this argument. However, in this connection, the United States pointed out that a certain citation of past cases in the interim report could be somewhat misleading. The Panel accepted this point, and modified the paragraphs accordingly.

4.6 Regarding the differences between "commercial Canadian" and "international" rates applied by Canada Post to periodicals, the United States commented that the interim report failed to mention certain additional discount options which were available only to Canadian periodicals. The Panel accepted this comment and introduced some drafting modifications in the final report at paragraphs *5.1*, *5.39* and *6.1*. The United States further requested that the final report refer to the long-term discount contracts between Canada Post and large-circulation magazine publishers (see paragraph *3.171*). Canada objected to this request on the grounds that these agreements or contracts had "never been one of the objects of this dispute". The Panel considered that this particular issue was not presented by the United States in a coherent manner during the proceedings, and that it was too late for the United States to raise this issue as an additional claim at the interim review stage. Accordingly, the Panel did not accept the US request on this point.

4.7 The United States suggested that the Panel restructure paragraph *5.36* of the final report as an alternative argument because, according to the United States, the fact that Canada Post is an entity of the Canadian Government was a sufficient reason to find a violation of Article III:4 of GATT 1994 in this instance. However, the Panel considered such a change unnecessary. In the Panel's view, it was clear that the *Semi-Conductor* case was cited here as supporting evidence, not as decisive reason for finding the violation.

4.8 The United States questioned the appropriateness of paragraphs *5.37* and *5.38* of the final report, suggesting that the examination of Article III:1 of GATT 1994 was unnecessary in this case. Canada did not object to this comment. However, in the Panel's view, the Appellate Body Report on *Japan - Taxes on Alcoholic Beverages* clearly mandates it to engage in such an examination. The Panel therefore decided to retain these paragraphs unchanged from the way in which they appeared in the interim report.

4.9 Regarding paragraphs *5.42* to *5.44* of the final report, the United States considered that the Panel erroneously concluded that the "funded" rate scheme constituted a payment of subsidies permitted by Article III:8 of GATT 1994. The Panel disagreed for reasons elaborated in its final report. The Panel accordingly did not introduce modifications to the final report in this respect.

4.10 The United States also made other drafting suggestions concerning the descriptive part, some of which the Panel accepted and introduced in its final report.

V. FINDINGS

A. Introduction

5.1 This dispute essentially arises from the following facts: *(a)* Canada prohibits imports of "split-run" periodicals (periodicals with the same or similar editorial content as those published in foreign countries, which contain an advertisement directed to the Canadian market) through Tariff Code 9958. Tariff Code 9958 further prohibits imports of periodicals in which more than five per cent of the advertising content consists of advertisements directed to the Canadian market, whether or not an edition with similar editorial content is sold outside Canada; *(b)* Canada, through Part V.1 of the Excise Tax Act, imposes an excise tax of 80 per cent on the value of advertisements in "split-run" periodicals distributed in Canada on a per issue basis; and *(c)* Canada Post Corporation ("Canada Post") applies reduced ("funded") postal rates, funded by the Department of Canadian Heritage ("Canadian Heritage"), to certain periodicals published in Canada. Postal rates applied to Canadian periodicals not eligible for the "funded" rates ("commercial Canadian" rates) are lower than those applied to imported periodicals ("international" rates). Certain additional discount options (such as for "palletization" and "pre-sort") are available to Canadian periodicals but are not generally available to imported periodicals.

5.2 The United States claims that *(a)* Tariff Code 9958 is inconsistent with Article XI of the General Agreement on Tariffs and Trade 1994 ("GATT 1994"); *(b)* Part V.1 of the Excise Tax Act is inconsistent with Article III:2 of GATT 1994, or in the alternative, is inconsistent with Article III:4 of GATT 1994; and *(c)* the application by Canada Post of lower postal rates to domestically-produced periodicals than to imported periodicals is inconsistent with Article III:4 of GATT 1994, and the "funded" rate scheme is not a domestic subsidy within the meaning of Article III:8 of GATT 1994. The United States requests that the Panel recommend that Canada bring its measures into conformity with its obligations under GATT 1994.

5.3 Canada requests the Panel to dismiss the US claims on the grounds that *(a)* Tariff Code 9958 is justifiable under Article XX(d) of GATT 1994; *(b)* Article III of GATT 1994 does not apply to Part V.1 of the Excise Tax Act; even if the Panel decides that Article III of GATT 1994 applies to these provisions, they do not violate Article III of the GATT 1994; and *(c)* Article III:4 of GATT 1994 does not apply to the "commercial" rates charged by Canada Post because they are the result of a commercial and marketing policy and not influenced by government policy and the "funded" rate scheme is a payment of subsidies allowable under Article III:8(b) of GATT 1994.

B. Tariff Code 9958

5.4 Tariff Code 9958 prohibits the importation into Canada of the following:

> 1. Issues of a periodical, one of the four immediately preceding issues of which has, under regulations that the Governor in Council may make, been found to be an issue of special edition, including a split-run or a regional edition, that contained an advertisement that was primarily directed to a market in Canada, and that did not appear in identical form in all editions of that issue of that periodical that were distributed in the country of origin.
>
> 2. Issues of a periodical, one of the four immediately preceding issues of which has, under regulations that the Governor in Council may make, been found to be an issue of more than five per cent of the advertising space in which consisted of space used for advertisements that indicated specific sources of availability in Canada, or specific terms or conditions relating to the sale of provision in Canada, of any goods or services except where the

> indication of such sources of availability or such terms or conditions was primarily directed at persons outside Canada.[121]

5.5 Since the importation of certain foreign products into Canada is completely denied under Tariff Code 9958, it appears that this provision by its terms is inconsistent with Article XI:1 of GATT 1994. Article XI:1 reads in relevant part as follows:

"No prohibitions or restrictions other than duties, taxes or other charges ... shall be instituted or maintained by any [Member] on the importation of any product of the territory of any other [Member] ...".

5.6 The question presented here is whether the import prohibition under Tariff Code 9958 may be justified under other provisions of the WTO Agreement. Canada claims that the measure is justified under Article XX(d) of GATT 1994. The relevant part of Article XX of GATT 1994 reads as follows:

> Subject to the requirement that such measures are not applied in a manner which would constitute a means of arbitrary or unjustifiable discrimination between countries where the same conditions prevail, or a disguised restriction on international trade, nothing in this Agreement shall be construed to prevent the adoption or enforcement by any [Member] of measures: ... (d) necessary to secure compliance with laws or regulations which are not inconsistent with the provisions of this Agreement, including those relating to customs enforcement, the enforcement of monopolies operated under paragraph 4 of Article II and Article XVII, the protection of patents, trade marks and copyrights, and the prevention of deceptive practices; ....

5.7 The panel on *United States - Standards for Reformulated and Conventional Gasoline* approached this provision in the following fashion. Having stated that the party invoking an exception under Article XX bore the burden of proving that the inconsistent measures came within its scope, the panel observed that the complainant had to demonstrate the following elements:

> (1) that the measures for which the exception were being invoked - that is, the particular trade measures inconsistent with the General Agreement – *secure compliance* with laws or regulations themselves not inconsistent with the General Agreement;
>
> (2) that the inconsistent measures for which the exception was being invoked were *necessary* to secure compliance with those laws or regulations; and
>
> (3) that the measures were applied in conformity with the requirements of the *introductory clause* of Article XX.[122]

In order to justify the application of Article XX(d), according to the panel, all the above elements had to be satisfied. We will follow the same approach in the present case.[123]

5.8 First, as to whether the import prohibition under Tariff Code 9958 secures compliance with a law or regulation not inconsistent with GATT 1994, Canada argues that Tariff Code 9958 is a measure intended to secure the attainment of the objectives of Section 19 of the Income Tax Act, which allows for the deduction of expenses

---

[121] Paragraphs 2.2-2.3 *supra*.

[122] Panel Report on *United States - Standards for Reformulated and Conventional Gasoline*, adopted on 20 May 1996, WT/DS2/R, para. 6.31 (emphasis in original). The relevant part of the panel report was not modified by the Appellate Body.

[123] We note that the Appellate Body in a recent report stated as follows: "[Adopted panel reports] create legitimate expectations among WTO Members, and, therefore, should be taken into account where they are relevant to any dispute". Appellate Body Report on *Japan - Taxes on Alcoholic Beverages*, WT/DS8/AB/R, WT/DS10/AB/R and WT/DS11/AB/R, p. 14.

for advertising directed to the Canadian market on condition that the advertisements appear in Canadian editions of Canadian periodicals. Since the United States is not challenging the GATT consistency of Section 19 of the Income Tax Act in this proceeding, the issue of GATT consistency is not before the Panel. However, the United States claims that Tariff Code 9958 is not a measure to "secure compliance" with the Income Tax Act.

5.9 The interpretative issue here is what is meant by "to secure compliance with laws and regulations" in Article XX(d) of GATT 1994. In this connection, the panel on *European Economic Community - Regulations on Imports of Parts and Components* found this phrase to mean "to enforce obligations under laws and obligations", not "to ensure the attainment of the objectives of the laws and regulations".[124] Canada suggests that this precedent should not be rigidly followed in the case of fiscal or economic incentives in general, and particularly in the present case, because Tariff Code 9958 and the income tax provision have always been considered part of a single, indivisible package. We are not persuaded by this argument. Canada's view will inherently lead to a situation where "[w]henever the objective of a law consistent with the General Agreement cannot be attained by enforcing the obligations under that law, the imposition of further obligations inconsistent with the General Agreement could then be justified under Article XX(d) on the grounds that this secures compliance with the objectives of that law", as was pointed out by the aforementioned panel.[125] We fail to see any differences that would obviate this problem in the case of fiscal or economic incentives. It should be noted, however, that we are neither examining nor passing judgment on the policy objectives of the Canadian measure regarding periodicals; we are nevertheless called upon to examine the ***instruments*** chosen by the Canadian Government for the attainment of such policy objectives.

5.10 Tariff Code 9958 cannot be regarded as an enforcement measure for Section 19 of the Income Tax Act. It is true that if a government bans imports of foreign periodicals with advertisements directed at the domestic market, as does Canada in the present case, the possibility of non-compliance with a tax provision granting tax deductions for expenses incurred for advertisements in domestic periodicals will be greatly reduced. It would seem almost impossible for an enterprise to place an advertisement in a foreign periodical because there would be virtually no foreign periodical available in which to place it. Thus, there would be no way for the enterprise legally to claim a tax deduction therefor. However, that is an incidental effect of a separate measure distinct (even though it may share the same policy objective) from the tax provision which is designed to give an incentive for placing advertisements in Canadian, as opposed to foreign, periodicals.[126] We thus find that Tariff Code 9958 does not "secure compliance" with Section 19 of the Income Tax Act.

5.11 In view of the above finding that Tariff Code 9958 does not secure compliance with Section 19 of the Income Tax Act, we need not consider whether the import prohibition under the Code is "necessary" to secure compliance with the tax provision or whether the measure meets the conditions in the introductory clause (or "chapeau") to Article XX. Canada has failed to satisfy at least one of the conditions identified in paragraph *5.7* above. Thus we conclude that Tariff Code 9958 is inconsistent with Article XI:1 of GATT 1994 and cannot be justified under Article XX(d).

C. The Excise Tax Act

5.12 We now turn to the examination of whether the 80 per cent excise tax on advertisements in split-run periodicals under Part V.1 of the Excise Tax Act is compatible with Canada's obligations under Article III of

---

[124] Panel Report on *European Economic Community - Regulations on Imports of Parts and Components*, adopted on 16 May 1990, BISD 37S/132, paras. 5.14-5.18.

[125] *Ibid.*, para. 5.17.

[126] An import ban under these circumstances is rather likely to be an enforcement measure in respect of a ban on possession or sale of a product. An import ban on alcoholic beverages might share the same objective as a criminal statute against drunk driving, but if alcoholic drinks are not banned or their sale prohibited domestically, the import ban could not be considered as an enforcement measure of the criminal statute.

GATT 1994. The United States claims that Part V.1 of the Excise Tax Act is inconsistent with Article III:2 of GATT 1994, or in the alternative, is inconsistent with Article III:4.

1. Applicability of GATT 1994

5.13 Since Canada challenges the applicability of GATT 1994 to this part of the Excise Tax Act, we address this issue first. Canada claims that Article III of GATT 1994 does not apply to Part V.1 of the Excise Tax Act because the latter is a measure pertaining to advertising services, which is within the purview of the General Agreement on Trade in Services ("GATS"). Canada further claims that the examination of Part V.1 of the Excise Tax Act in light of GATS is not covered by the terms of reference of this Panel.

5.14 Canada's argument is essentially that since Canada has made no specific commitments for advertising services under GATS, the United States should not be allowed to "obtain benefits under a covered agreement that have been expressly precluded under another covered agreement".[127] Put another way, Canada seems to argue that if a Member has not undertaken market-access commitments in a specific service sector, that non-commitment should preclude all the obligations or commitments undertaken in the goods sector to the extent that there is an overlap between the non-commitment in services and the obligations or commitments in the goods sector. Canada claims that because of the existence of the two instruments – GATT 1994 and GATS – both of which may apply to a given measure, "it is necessary to interpret the scope of application of each such as to avoid any overlap."[128]

5.15 We are not fully convinced by Canada's characterization of the Excise Tax as a measure intended to regulate trade in advertising services, in view of the fact that there is no comparable regulation on advertisements through other media and the fact that the tax is imposed on a "per issue" basis. However, assuming that Canada intended to carve out Part V.1 of the Excise Tax Act from the coverage of its GATS commitments by not inscribing advertising services in its Schedule[129], does that exonerate Canada from the Panel's scrutiny regarding the alleged violation of its obligations and commitments under GATT 1994?

5.16 In order to answer this question, we need to examine the structure of the WTO Agreement including its annexes. Article II:2 of the WTO Agreement is the relevant provision, which reads as follows:

> The agreements and associated legal instruments included in Annexes 1, 2 and 3 ... are integral parts of this Agreement, binding on all Members.[130]

5.17 According to Article 31(1) of the 1969 Vienna Convention on the Law of Treaties ("Vienna Convention"), a treaty must be interpreted in good faith in accordance with the ordinary meaning to be given to the terms of the treaty in their context and in the light of its object and purpose. Furthermore, as the Appellate Body has repeatedly pointed out, "one of the corollaries of the 'general rule of interpretation' in the Vienna Convention is that interpretation must give meaning and effect to all the terms of the treaty. An interpreter is not free to adopt a reading that would result in reducing whole clauses or paragraphs of a treaty to redundancy or inutility."[131] The ordinary meaning of the texts of GATT 1994 and GATS as well as Article II:2 of the WTO Agreement, taken together, indicates that obligations under GATT 1994 and GATS can co-exist and that one does not override the other. If the consequences suggested by Canada were intended, there would have been provisions similar to Article XVI:3 of the WTO Agreement or the General Interpretative Note to Annex 1A in order to establish hierarchical order between GATT 1994 and GATS. The absence of such provisions between the two instruments

---

[127] Paragraph 3.35 *supra*.

[128] Paragraph 3.38 *supra*.

[129] We note in this connection that Part V.1 of the Excise Tax Act was enacted in 1995, after Canada's acceptance of the WTO Agreement.

[130] GATT 1994 is included in Annex 1A. GATS is included in Annex 1B.

[131] Appellate Body Report on *United States - Standards for Reformulated and Conventional Gasoline*, adopted on 20 May 1996, WT/DS2/AB/R, p. 23. Also cited in the Appellate Body Report on *Japan - Taxes on Alcoholic Beverages*, *op. cit.*, p.12.

implies that GATT 1994 and GATS are standing on the same plain in the WTO Agreement, without any hierarchical order between the two.

5.18 In this connection, Canada also argues that overlaps between GATT 1994 and GATS should be avoided.[132] We disagree. Overlaps between the subject matter of disciplines in GATT 1994 and in GATS are inevitable, and will further increase with the progress of technology and the globalization of economic activities. We do not consider that such overlaps will undermine the coherence of the WTO system. In fact, certain types of services such as transportation and distribution are recognized as a subject-matter of disciplines under Article III:4 of GATT 1994. It is also noteworthy in this respect that advertising services have long been associated with the disciplines under GATT Article III. As early as 1970, the Working Party on Border Tax Adjustment made the following observation:

> The Working Party noted that there was a divergence of views with regard to the eligibility for adjustment of certain categories of tax and that these could be sub-divided into
>
> (a) "Taxes *occultes*" which the OECD defined as consumption taxes on capital equipment, auxiliary materials and *services* used in the transportation and production of other taxable goods. Taxes on *advertising*, energy, machinery and transport were among the more important taxes which might be involved. ... ;
>
> (b) Certain other taxes, ...".[133]

We also note that there are several adopted panel reports that examined the issue of services in the context of GATT Article III. For instance, the panel on *Canada - Import, Distribution and Sale of Certain Alcoholic Drinks by Provincial Marketing Agencies* addressed the issues of access to points of sale and restrictions on private delivery of beer.[134] The panel on *United States - Measures Affecting Alcoholic and Malt Beverages* also dealt with the issues of distribution of wine and beer.[135] More to the point, the panel on *Thailand - Restrictions on Importation of and Internal Taxes on Cigarettes* specifically addressed the question of advertising.[136]

5.19 In any event, since Canada admits that in the present case there is no conflict between its obligations under GATS and under GATT 1994[137], there is no reason why both GATT and GATS obligations should not apply to the Excise Tax Act. Thus, we conclude that Article III of GATT 1994 is applicable to Part V.1 of the Excise Tax Act.

2. *GATT Article III:2*

5.20 The next issue to be examined is whether there is a violation of Article III. The principal claim of the United States is that Part V.1 of the Excise Tax is inconsistent with Article III:2 of GATT 1994. The relevant parts of Article III read as follows:

> 1. The [Members] recognize that internal taxes and other internal charges, and laws, regulations and requirements affecting the internal sale, offering for sale, purchase,

---

132 Paragraphs 3.38 and 5.14 *supra*.

133 "Border Tax Adjustments", Report of the Working Party adopted on 2 December 1970 (L/3464), BISD 18S/97, para. 15 (emphasis added).

134 Panel Report on *Canada - Import, Distribution and Sale of Certain Alcoholic Drinks by Provincial Marketing Agencies*, adopted on 18 February 1992, BISD 39S/27.

135 Panel Report on *United States - Measures Affecting Alcoholic and Malt Beverages*, adopted on 19 June 1992, BISD 39S/206.

136 Panel Report on *Thailand - Restrictions on Importation of and Internal Taxes on Cigarettes*, adopted on 7 November 1990, BISD 37S/200, para. 78.

137 Paragraph 3.38 *supra*.

transportation, distribution or use of products, and internal quantitative regulations requiring the mixture, processing or use of products in specified amounts or proportions, should not be applied to imported or domestic products so as to afford protection to domestic production.

2. The products of the territory of any [Member] imported into the territory of any other [Member] shall not be subject, directly or indirectly, to internal taxes or other internal charges of any kind in excess of those applied, directly or indirectly, to like domestic products. Moreover, no [Member] shall otherwise apply internal taxes or other internal charges to imported or domestic products in a manner contrary to the principles set forth in paragraph 1.

Furthermore, the Interpretative Note *ad* Article III reads in part as follows:

> A tax conforming to the requirements of the first sentence of paragraph 2 would be considered to be inconsistent with the provisions of the second sentence only in cases where competition was involved between, on the one hand, the taxed product and, on the other hand, a directly competitive or substitutable product which was not similarly taxed.

5.21 In the present case, the following two questions need to be answered to determine whether there is a violation of Article III:2 of GATT 1994: *(a)* Are imported "split-run" periodicals and domestic non "split-run" periodicals like products?; and *(b)* Are imported "split-run" periodicals subject to an internal tax in excess of that applied to domestic non "split-run" periodicals? If the answers to both questions are affirmative, there is a violation of Article III:2, first sentence.[138] If the answer to the first question is negative, we need to examine further whether there is a violation of Article III:2, second sentence.

3. *Like product issue*

5.22 As the Appellate Body confirmed in its report on *Japan - Taxes on Alcoholic Beverages*, the definition of "like products" in Article III:2, first sentence, should be construed narrowly, on a case-by-case basis, in light of such factors as the product's end uses in a given market, consumer's tastes and habits, and the product's properties, nature and quality.[139] In applying these criteria to the present case, it should be noted that our mandate under the terms of reference of this Panel is not to discuss the likeness of periodicals in general. The question before us, as presented by the United States in its request for the establishment of a panel (WT/DS31/2) and subsequently elaborated,[140] is a comparison between imported "split-run" periodicals and domestic non "split-run" periodicals.

5.23 This comparison, at first glance, might seem impossible in view of the fact that there are no imported "split-run" periodicals marketed in Canada due to the import prohibition under Tariff Code 9958. However, as the panel on "United States - Taxes on Petroleum and Certain Imported Substances" observed, the rationale for the national treatment obligation of Article III is to protect expectations of the Members as to the competitive relationship between their products and those of other Members.[141] In so far as imported "split-run" periodicals are

---

[138] In this context, we need not examine the applicability of Article III:1 separately, because, as the Appellate Body noted in its recent report, the first sentence of Article III:2 ***is***, in effect, an application of the general principle embodied in Article III:1. Therefore, if the imported and domestic products are "like products", and if the taxes applied to the imported products are "in excess of" those applied to the like domestic products, then the measure is inconsistent with Article III:2, first sentence. Appellate Body Report on *Japan - Taxes on Alcoholic Beverages*, *op. cit.*, pp. 18-9.

[139] *Ibid.*, p.20. According to the Appellate Body, the narrow construction of the term was necessary in Article III:2, first sentence, "so as not to condemn measures that its strict terms are not meant to condemn".

[140] See paragraphs 3.104-3.108 *supra*.

[141] Panel Report on *United States - Taxes on Petroleum and Certain Imported Substances*, adopted on 17 June 1987, BISD 34S/136, para. 5.2.2. See also the Panel Reports on *Italian Discrimination against Imported Agricultural Machinery*, adopted on 23 October 1958, BISD 7S/60, para. 18, and on *United States - Section 337 of the Tariff Act of 1930*, adopted on 7 November 1989, BISD 36S/345, para. 5.13.

subject to the relevant provisions of the Excise Tax Act (as Canada admits to be the case),[142] the comparison can be made on the basis of a hypothetical import.

5.24 We note in this regard that the Excise Tax Act defines a "split-run" edition of a periodical in terms of its editorial content (whether more than 20 per cent of the editorial material is the same or substantially the same as editorial material that appears in editions that are primarily distributed outside Canada) and advertising content (whether it contains an advertisement that does not appear in identical form in other editions distributed outside Canada). Despite the Canadian claim that the purpose of the legislation is to promote publications of original Canadian content, this definition essentially relies on factors external to the Canadian market – whether the same editorial content is included in a foreign edition and whether the periodical carries different advertisements in foreign editions.

5.25 Putting these external factors aside, imported "split-run" periodicals and domestic non "split-run" periodicals can be extremely similar. In the course of the Panel process, Canada made the following statement:

> *Harrowsmith Country Life* is a Canadian-owned magazine. Before the adoption of Part V.1 of the Excise Tax Act, *Harrowsmith Country Life* had two editions - A Canadian edition and a US edition. The Canadian and the US editions had different advertisements and a certain amount of common editorial content. Because more than 20 per cent of the editorial content in the Canadian edition was the same as that in the US edition, the tax would have applied to the Canadian edition (even if the editorial content was entirely produced in Canada). As a result of the excise tax, *Harrowsmith Country Life* stopped publishing its US edition.[143]

In the case of this particular periodical, if all the volumes of *Harrowsmith Country Life* had been printed in the United States (including its Canadian edition) and the Canadian edition had been exported to Canada because they were somehow exempted from the coverage of Tariff Code 9958, and if the publisher decided to publish the final issue of the US edition after the introduction of the excise tax, the publisher would have been subject to the tax for the imported Canadian edition. If this publisher thereafter discontinued the publication of the US edition, it would no longer be subject to the excise tax. Now, let us compare the two issues of this hypothetical *Harrowsmith Country Life* (Canadian edition) before and after the discontinuation of the US edition. These two editions would have common end uses, very similar physical properties, nature and qualities. It is most likely that the two volumes would have been designed for the same readership with the same tastes and habits. In all respects, these two volumes are "like", and yet one is subject to the Excise Tax, while the other is not.

5.26 Thus, we conclude that imported "split-run" periodicals and domestic non "split-run" periodicals can be like products within the meaning of Article III:2 of GATT 1994. In our view, this provides sufficient grounds to answer in the affirmative the question as to whether the two products at issue are like because, as stated earlier, the purpose of Article III is to protect expectations of the Members as to the competitive relationship between their products and those of other Members, not to protect actual trade volumes. If Tariff Code 9958 were lifted, a wide variety of "split-run" periodicals ranging from general news magazines to specialty journals dedicated to specific areas of business or profession could be imported into Canada. This situation can hardly be called an "isolated instance of differential taxation" as Canada describes.[144]

5.27 Having found that imported "split-run" periodicals and domestic non "split-run" periodicals are like products, we need not consider the second sentence of Article III:2. The only remaining question is whether imported "split-run" periodicals are subject to an internal tax in excess of that applied to domestic non "split-run" periodicals.

---

[142] Paragraphs 3.58 and 3.98 *supra*.

[143] See paragraph 3.99 *supra*.

[144] Paragraph 3.101 *supra*.

4. *Taxation in excess: "directly or indirectly"*

5.28 In light of the fact that the excise tax is applied only with respect to "split-run" periodicals, it would seem evident that imported "split-run" periodicals are subject to an internal tax in excess of one that is applied to domestic non "split-run" periodicals. However, Canada argues that the excise tax does not apply "indirectly" to a good within the meaning of Article III:2. According to Canada, the drafting history of this paragraph suggests that the expression "indirectly" was intended to capture taxes that apply to inputs that contribute to the production of a good, and not to end products in their own right. Canada also claims that the panel on *Japan - Customs Duties, Taxes and Labelling Practices on Imported Wines and Alcoholic Beverages* interpreted the term in a manner consistent with Canada's position.[145]

5.29 We note that the excise tax is not "directly" applied to periodicals in that it is levied on the value of advertisements, not on the value of periodicals *per se*. However, it is clear that the tax is applied in respect of each split-run edition of a periodical on a "per issue" basis. Therefore, the tax is applied "indirectly" to periodicals within the ordinary meaning of the terms of Article III:2. Canada's narrow reading of the term "indirectly" is supported only by Canada's own interpretation of the drafting history, which is contested by the United States.[146] Since, according to Article 32 of the Vienna Convention, the preparatory work of a treaty is merely a supplementary means of interpretation to be relied upon in cases where the terms of the treaty, taken in their context and in light of its object and purpose, are ambiguous or obscure, or lead to a manifestly absurd or unreasonable result, we need not take the drafting history into account on this particular point. Furthermore, the panel report cited by Canada in support of its argument referred to taxation on raw materials by way of example. It did not conclude that the scope of the term "indirectly" is limited to taxation on inputs.[147] We thus conclude that imported "split-run" periodicals are subject to an internal tax in excess of that applied to domestic non "split-run" periodicals.

5.30 Having found that Part V.1 of the Excise Tax Act to be in violation of Article III:2, first sentence, we need not examine whether it is inconsistent with Article III:2, second sentence or with Article III:4.

D. Postal Rates

5.31 Now we proceed to examine whether the postal rates scheme applied by Canada Post discriminates against foreign periodicals in contravention of Article III of GATT 1994, as argued by the United States. There are two separate issues involved here: *(a)* whether the fact that Canada Post applies the "commercial Canadian" rates or the "funded" rates to Canadian periodicals, which are lower than the "international" rates applied to imported periodicals, constitute a violation of Article III:4;[148] and *(b)* whether the "funded" rate scheme for certain periodicals is allowed as a subsidy within the meaning of Article III:8(b).

---

[145] Paragraph 3.49 *supra*.

[146] Paragraph 3.56 *supra*.

[147] Paragraph 3.49 *supra*.

[148] We are aware that "international" rates applied to foreign periodicals belong to a subcategory of the "commercial" rate scheme in a broader sense. See paragraphs 2.17-2.19 *supra*. However, in so far as different rates are applied between "international" periodicals and "commercial Canadian" periodicals, it is necessary to draw the distinction. We are also aware, as described in paragraph 5.1, that there are additional discounts for Canadian periodicals which are not generally available to imported periodicals. In our view, these additional discounts constitute part of the "commercial Canadian" rate scheme.

1. "International" versus "commercial Canadian" and "funded" rates

5.32 The United States claims that Canada Post's practice of charging domestic periodicals lower postal rates than imported periodicals is in violation of Article III:4 of GATT 1994. The relevant part of the Article reads as follows:

> 4. The products of the territory of any [Member] imported into the territory of any other [Member] shall be accorded treatment no less favourable than that accorded to like products of national origin in respect of all laws, regulations and requirements affecting their internal sale, offering for sale, purchase, transportation, distribution or use. The provisions of this paragraph shall not prevent the application of differential internal transportation charges which are based exclusively on the economic operation of the means of transport and not on the nationality of the product.

In examining the relevance of this provision in the present dispute, we also need take into account the first paragraph of Article III, which reads:

> 1. The [Members] recognize that internal taxes and other internal charges, and laws, regulations and requirements affecting the internal sale, offering for sale, purchase, transportation, distribution or use of products, and internal quantitative regulations requiring the mixture, processing or use of products in specified amounts or proportions, should not be applied to imported or domestic products so as to afford protection to domestic production.

5.33 There is no disagreement between the parties to the dispute that, in respect of this issue, domestic and imported periodicals are like products. We, too, so find. Nor does Canada contest the fact that Canada Post applies higher postal rates to imported periodicals than to domestic periodicals, which clearly affects the sale, transportation and distribution of imported periodicals. Canada's argument is essentially that since Canada Post is a privatized agency (a Crown corporation) with a legal personality distinct from the Canadian Government, the "commercial Canadian" or "international" rates it charges for the delivery of periodicals are out of the Government's control and do not qualify as "regulations" or "requirements" within the meaning of Article III:4.

5.34 The United States argues that Canada Post is a government entity fully subject to Canadian Government direction because it is a wholly-government-owned, government-created chartered body, managed by a board of directors appointed by the Canadian Government. Canada argues that the different rates charged by Canada Post are a reflection of competitive situations and that the degree of control the Government exercises over Canada Post's commercial operations (including delivery of periodicals) is one dictated by the Government shareholder's interests. In other words, Canada argues here that Canada Post's pricing policy is not a governmental measure subject to Article III:4. The essential question then is whether Canada Post is implementing Canadian Government policy in such a manner that its postal rates on periodicals may be viewed as governmental regulations or requirements for the purposes of Article III:4.

5.35 First, it is clear that Canada Post generally operates under governmental instructions. Canada Post has a mandate to operate on a "commercial" basis in this particular sector of periodical delivery: a mandate that was set by the Canadian Government.[149] Second, Canada admits that if the Canadian Government considers Canada Post's pricing policy to be inappropriate, it can instruct Canada Post to change the rates under its directive power based on

[149] From the entirety of Canada's submissions, we take it that the Canadian Government considers Canada Post's pricing policy on periodicals to be driven by "commercial" considerations, although we fail to understand why any document delivery operation aiming at profit maximization would want to make artificial distinctions based on the origin of documents.

Section 22 of the Canada Post Corporation Act.[150] Thus, the Canadian Government can effectively regulate the rates charged on the delivery of periodicals.

5.36 This analysis is unaffected by the fact that Canada Post has a legal personality distinct from the Canadian Government. The panel on *Japan - Trade in Semi-Conductors* faced a similar question with respect to the interpretation of the status of "administrative guidance" given to private-sector entities in interpreting the term "measures" in Article XI:1. The panel stated as follows:

> In order to determine [whether the measures taken in this case would be such as to constitute a contravention of Article XI], the Panel considered that it needed to be satisfied on two essential criteria. First, there were reasonable grounds to believe that sufficient incentives or disincentives existed for non-mandatory measures to take effect. Second, the operation of the measures ... was essentially dependent on Government action or intervention. The Panel considered each of these two criteria in turn. The Panel considered that if these two criteria were met, the measures would be operating in a manner equivalent to mandatory requirements such that the difference between the measures and mandatory requirements was only one of form and not of substance, and that there could be therefore no doubt that they fell within the range of measures covered by Article XI:1.[151]

Applying this two-pronged test, *mutatis mutandis*, to the present case, we conclude that the pricing policy of Canada Post is a governmental measure. First, in view of the control exercised by the Canadian Government on "non-commercial" activities of Canada Post, we can reasonably assume that sufficient incentives exist for Canada Post to maintain the existing pricing policy on periodicals. Second, as analyzed in the previous paragraph, Canada Post's operation is generally dependent on Government action. This leads us to the conclusion that Canada Post's pricing policy on periodicals can be regarded as governmental regulations or requirements within the meaning of Article III:4 of GATT 1994.

5.37 Given that imported and domestic periodicals are like products and that Canada Post charges lower rates on domestic periodicals than imported ones, this conclusion might seem sufficient to determine that a less favourable treatment is accorded to imported products in violation of Article III:4. However, before reaching that determination, as the Appellate Body has stated, we need to turn to Article III:1 as a general principle that informs the rest of Article III.[152] Article III:1 constitutes part of the context of Article III:4, which is to be taken into account in our interpretation of the latter, under Article 31(1) of the Vienna Convention.

5.38 Article III:1 articulates a general principle that internal measures should not be applied so as to afford protection to domestic production.[153] The protective application of a measure can most often be discerned from the design, the architecture, and the revealing structure of the measure.[154] We find that the design, architecture and structure of Canada Post's different pricing policy on domestic and imported periodicals all point to the effect that the measure is applied so as to afford protection to the domestic production of periodicals. In the case of "funded" rates, the scheme is clearly designed to promote domestic production of periodicals with Canadian content under the supervision of Canadian Heritage. In the case of "commercial Canadian" rates, the very fact that they are lower

---

[150] Paragraph 3.156 *supra*.

[151] Panel Report on *Japan - Trade in Semi-Conductors*, adopted on 4 May 1988, BISD 35S/116, para. 109.

[152] Appellate Body Report on *Japan - Taxes on Alcoholic Beverages*, *op. cit.*, p. 18. The Report states: "The purpose of Article III:1 is to establish this general principle as a guide to understanding and interpreting the specific obligations contained in Article III:2 and in the other paragraphs of Article III, while respecting, and not diminishing in any way, the meaning of words actually used in the texts of those other paragraphs".

[153] *Ibid.*, p. 18.

[154] *Ibid.*, p. 29.

than "international" rates which are applied to imported products strongly suggests that the scheme is operated so as to afford protection to domestic production.

5.39 In light of the above, we find that Canada Post's application of the "commercial Canadian" and "funded" rates to Canadian periodicals, which are lower than the "international" rates applied to imported periodicals (including the availability of additional discounts only to Canadian periodicals), is inconsistent with Article III:4 of GATT 1994.

2. *Applicability of Article III:8(b) to the "funded" rate scheme*

5.40 Having found that the "funded" rate scheme violates Article III:4 of GATT 1994, we next examine whether this scheme is justified under Article III:8(b) of GATT 1994, as argued by Canada. The relevant part of Article III:8 reads as follows:

> (b) The provisions of this Article shall not prevent the payment of subsidies exclusively to domestic producers, including payments to domestic producers derived from the proceeds of internal taxes or charges applied consistently with the provisions of this Article and subsidies effected through governmental purchases of domestic products.

5.41 The United States claims that this provision is not applicable in the present case because the payment of subsidies by Canadian Heritage is not made directly to Canadian publishers, but rather to Canada Post. The United States argues that past panels have interpreted the term "exclusively" narrowly, to mean only direct payments to domestic producers.[155] To support its argument, the United States quotes the following paragraph from the panel report on *European Economic Community - Payments and Subsidies Paid to Processors and Producers of Oilseeds and Related Animal-Feed Proteins* (the "*Oilseeds*" case):

> The Panel noted that Article III:8(b) applies only to payments made *exclusively* to domestic producers and considered that it can reasonably be assumed that a payment not made directly to producers is not made "exclusively" to them. It noted moreover that, if the economic benefits generated by the payments granted by the Community can at least partly be retained by the processors of Community oilseeds, the payments generate a benefit conditional upon the purchase of oilseeds of domestic origin inconsistently with Article III:4. Under these circumstances Article III:8(b) would not be applicable because in that case the payments would not be made exclusively to domestic producers but to processors as well.[156]

5.42 We do not disagree with this panel report. However, the United States has failed to show that the factual situation in the present case is similar to that in the *Oilseeds* case. Particularly, the United States has not submitted any evidence to indicate that the economic benefits are partly retained by Canada Post. Furthermore, this argument by the United States is inconsistent with its position regarding Article III:4, where it maintains that Canada Post is a government agency. If Canada Post is a government agency, the payment of funds from Canadian Heritage to Canada Post is merely an internal transfer of resources, and the payment of the subsidy is made directly to Canadian publishers.

5.43 Canada, on the other hand, explains that the payment of the funds from Canadian Heritage to Canada Post is made based on negotiations between the two agencies, taking into account the fact that Canada Post gets an exclusive contract for the delivery of periodicals at subsidized rates.[157] Following the logic of the *Oilseeds* panel

---

[155] Paragraphs 3.191-3.197 *supra*.

[156] Panel Report on *European Economic Community - Payments and Subsidies Paid to Processors and Producers of Oilseeds and Related Animal-Feed Proteins*, adopted on 25 January 1990, BISD 37S/86, para. 137 (emphasis in original).

[157] Paragraph 3.173 *supra*.

cited above, one could argue that there is a reasonable assumption that the "funded" rate scheme is not an exclusive payment of subsidies because the payment is not made directly to the beneficiary. However, in our view, Canada has presented an effective rebuttal to this assumption.

5.44 Thus, we do not find that Canada Post retains any economic benefits from the "funded" rate scheme it applies to certain Canadian periodicals. The payment of the subsidy is made "exclusively" to Canadian publishers that qualify for the scheme. Since Article III:8(b) explicitly recognizes that subsidies exclusively paid to domestic producers are not subject to the national treatment rules of Article III, including those under Article III:4, we find that Canada's "funded" rate scheme on periodicals can be justified under this provision.

E. Concluding Remarks

5.45 Before concluding, in order to avoid any misunderstandings as to the scope and implications of the findings above, we would like to stress that the ability of any Member to take measures to protect its cultural identity was not at issue in the present case. The only task entrusted to this Panel was to examine whether the treatment accorded to imported periodicals under specific measures identified in the complainant's claim is compatible with the rules of GATT 1994.

VI. CONCLUSIONS

6.1 On the basis of the findings set out in paragraphs *5.1* to *5.44* above, the Panel concludes that *(a)* Tariff Code 9958 is inconsistent with Article XI:1 of GATT 1994 and cannot be justified under Article XX(d) of GATT 1994; *(b)* Part V.1 of the Excise Tax Act is inconsistent with Article III:2, first sentence, of GATT 1994; *(c)* the application by Canada Post of lower "commercial Canadian" postal rates to domestically-produced periodicals than to imported periodicals, including additional discount options available only to domestic periodicals, is inconsistent with Article III:4 of GATT 1994; but *(d)* the maintenance of the "funded" rate scheme is justified under Article III:8(b) of GATT 1994.

6.2 The Panel recommends that the Dispute Settlement Body request Canada to bring the measures that are found to be inconsistent with GATT 1994 into conformity with its obligations thereunder.

EUROPEAN COMMUNITIES – REGIME FOR THE IMPORTATION, SALE AND DISTRIBUTION OF BANANAS

REPORT OF THE PANEL
WT/DS/27/R

Complainants: Ecuador
Guatemala
Honduras
Mexico
United States

Respondent: European Communities

Third Parties: Belize
Canada
Costa Rica
Dominica
Ghana
India
Japan
The Philippines
Saint Vincent and the Grenadines
Suriname
Cameroon
Columbia
Côte d'Ivoire
The Dominican Republic
Grenada
Jamaica
Nicaragua
Saint Lucia
Senegal
Venezuela

Procedural History

February 5, 1996 Ecuador, Guatemala, Honduras, Mexico and the United States requested consultations with the European Communities.

March 14 and 15, 1996 consultations between the parties were held.

April 11, 1996 Ecuador, Guatemala, Honduras, Mexico and the United States requested the establishment of a panel.

May 8, 1996 the Dispute Settlement Body established a panel.

Conclusions

- The European Communities' argument for dismissal of this case on the grounds that consultations held concerning this dispute did not perform their minimum function of affording a possibility for arriving at a mutually satisfactory solution and a clear setting out of the different claims of which a dispute consists.

- The Panel request made by the Complainants was sufficient to meet the requirements of Article 6.2 of the DSU to the extent that it alleged inconsistencies with the requirements of specific provisions of specific WTO agreements. Since the invocation of the Agreement on Agriculture in the panel request did not indicate a specific provision thereof which was in dispute, the Panel will not consider the claims raised by Ecuador in its first written submission under that Agreement. The Panel will also not consider the claims raised by Ecuador, Guatemala, Honduras and the United States in their first written submissions under Article 5 of the TRIM's Agreement since the panel request referred only to Article 2 of the TRIM's Agreement.

- The United States, having a potential interest in trade in bananas and an interest in determining its rights and obligations under the WTO Agreement, has a right to advance the claims that it has raised in this case.

- Under Article 9 of the DSU, the European Community is entitled to individual reports for each of the four first submissions originating the complaints [Guatemala and Honduras filed a joint first submission]. As a number of the proceedings were conducted jointly, it is decided that he description of the Panel's proceedings, the factual aspects and the parties' arguments should be identical in each of the four reports. In the findings section, however, the reports will differ to the extent that the Complainant's initial written submissions to the Panel differ in respect of alleging inconsistencies with the requirements of specific provisions of specific agreements.

- Bananas are like products, for purposes of Articles I, III, X and XIII of the General Agreement, irrespective of whether they originate in the EC, in ACP countries, in BFA countries or in other countries.

- The European Communities' allocation of tariff quota shares by agreement and by assignment to some Members not having a substantial interest in supplying bananas to the EC but not to other Members is inconsistent with the requirements of Article XIII.1.

- The tariff quota reallocation rules of the BFA as established by the EC are inconsistent with Article XIII.1.

- Ecuador is not required to accept the validity of the BFA as contained in the EC's Schedule of Commitments, nor is it pre-empted from invoking Articles XIII.2 or XIII.4 by its not having addressed banana-related issues in its Protocol of Accession.

- To the extent that the EC has acted inconsistently with its obligations under Article XIII.1, the Lomé waiver waives that inconsistency to the extent necessary to permit the EC to allocate shares of its banana tariff quota to specific traditional ACP banana supplying countries in an amount <u>not exceeding</u> their pre-1991 best-ever exports to the EC.

- Neither the negotiation of the BFA and its inclusion in the EC's Schedule of Commitments nor the Agreement on Agriculture permit the EC to act inconsistently with Article XIII of the General Agreement.

- The inconsistency under General Agreement Article I.1 of the EC's preferential tariff treatment of non-traditional ACP bananas is permitted by the Lomé waiver.

- The Licensing Agreement applies to licensing procedures for tariff quotas.

- The EC's licensing procedures for traditional ACP bananas and third-country and non-traditional ACP bananas should be examined as one and not two licensing regimes.

- The allocation under the EC's licensing procedures to Category B operators of a 30% share of the licenses allowing the importation of third-country and non-traditional ACP bananas at in-quota tariff rates is inconsistent with the treatment no less favorable requirements of Article III.4 of the General Agreement.

- The application in general of operator category rules to third country and non-traditional ACP bananas at in-quota tariff rates, and particular the category B operator allocation (above), in the absence of such rules being applied to traditional ACP bananas, is inconsistent with the most-favored nation requirement of Article I.1. Furthermore, the Lomé waiver does not eliminate the EC's obligations under Article I.1 in respect of licensing procedures applied to non-traditional ACP and third country imports, including those related to operator category rules.

- The application of activity function rules in respect of the importation of third-country and non-traditional ACP bananas at in-quota tariff rates, in the absence of the application of such rules to traditional ACP banana imports, is inconsistent with the most-favored nation requirement of Article I.1.

- The EC import licensing procedures are subject to the requirements of Article X of the General Agreement.

- The application of activity function rules in respect of the importation of third-country and non-traditional ACP bananas, in the absence of such rules on traditional ACP banana imports, is inconsistent with the requirements of Article X.3 of the General Agreement.

- The requirement to match EC import licenses with BFA export certificates is inconsistent with the EC's Article I.1 obligations.

- To the extent that the EC licensing procedures are inconsistent with Articles I, III, and X of the General Agreement, such licensing procedures are also inconsistent with Article 1.2 of the Licensing Agreement.

- There is no legal basis for an *a priori* exclusion of measures within the EC banana import licensing regime from the scope of the GATS.

- The distribution of bananas, regardless of whether they are green or ripened, falls within the scope of category CPC 622 "wholesale trade services" as inscribed in the EC's GATS Schedule of Commitments so long as it involves the sale of bananas to retailers, to industrial, commercial, institutional or other professional business users, or other wholesalers.

- The EC's obligations under Article II of GATS and commitments under Article XVII of GATS cover the treatment of suppliers of wholesale trade services within the jurisdiction of the EC.

- The obligation contained in Article II:1 of GATS to extend "treatment no less favourable" should be interpreted *in casu* to require providing no less favourable conditions of competition.

- The EC has undertaken a full commitment on national treatment in the sector of "Wholesale Trade Services" with respect to supply through commercial presence.

- The allocation to Category B operators of 30 per cent of the licences allowing the importation of third-country and non-traditional ACP bananas at in-quota tariff rates creates less favourable conditions of competition for like service suppliers of Complainants' origin and is therefore inconsistent with the requirements of Article XVII of GATS.

- The allocation to Category B operators of 30 per cent of the licences allowing the importation of third-country and non-traditional ACP bananas at in-quota tariff rates creates less favourable conditions of competition for like service suppliers of Complainants' origin and is therefore inconsistent with the requirements of Article II of GATS.
- The allocation to ripeners of 28 per cent of the Category A and B licences allowing the importation of third-country and non-traditional ACP bananas at in-quota tariff rates creates less favourable conditions of competition for like service suppliers of Complainants' origin and is therefore inconsistent with the requirements of Article XVII of GATS.
- The exemption of Category B operators of EC origin from the requirement to match EC import licences with BFA export certificates creates less favourable conditions of competition for like service suppliers of Complainants' origin and is therefore inconsistent with the requirements of Article XVII of GATS.
- The exemption of Category B operators of ACP origin from the requirement to match EC import licences with BFA export certificates creates less favourable conditions of competition for like service suppliers of Complainants' origin and is therefore inconsistent with the requirements of Article II of GATS.
- The allocation of hurricane licences exclusively to operators who include or directly represent EC producers creates less favourable conditions of competition for like service suppliers of Complainants' origin and is therefore inconsistent with the requirements of Article XVII of GATS.
- The allocation of hurricane licences exclusively to operators who include or directly represent ACP producers creates less favourable conditions of competition for like service suppliers of Complainants' origin and is therefore inconsistent with the requirements of Article II of GATS.

Annotations

7.8 **Third parties** [DSU, Article 10]

Members of governments of third parties are permitted in this case to observe the second substantive meeting of the Panel with the Parties. Third party observers will also have the opportunity to make a brief statement during the second meeting, but will not submit written materials to the Panel during this meeting beyond responses to the questions already posed during the first meeting.

7.9 **Third parties** [DSU, Article 10]

Third parties will not be permitted to participate beyond the second substantive meeting, including during the interim review.

7.11 **Private lawyers** [DSU, Appendix 3, Working Procedures; Sections 2 and 3]

Only members of governments may attend Panel meetings. Private counsel may be consulted by third parties or participants before and after the meetings but private counsel is not permitted to be present at any of the sessions with the Panel.

7.19 - 7.21 **Adequacy of consultations** [DSU, Article 4]

While a mutually agreed upon solution is to be preferred, in some cases such agreement is not possible. The function of the Panel is only to ascertain that consultations were held or at least requested. Consultations also need not lead to an adequate explanation of the Complainants' case. The only prerequisite for requesting a panel is that the consultations have failed to settle a dispute within 60 days of receipt of the request for such consultations.

7.31, 7.45 - 7.46 **Specificity of panel request** [DSU, Article 6.2]

The DSU Article 6.2 requirement that "specific measures at issue [be] identified" and that "a brief legal summary of the legal basis of the complaint sufficient to present the problem clearly" has been met by the Complainants to the extent that their panel request alleged inconsistencies with the requirements of specific provisions of specific WTO Agreements. All legal bases for claims raised in the first submissions of the Complainants were sufficiently specific to permit review by the Panel except for the claim raised by Ecuador as to the Agreement on Agriculture. Such claim will, therefore, not be considered by this Panel. Additionally, claims raised by Ecuador, Guatemala, Honduras and the United States in their first written submission regarding Article 5 of the TRIM's Agreement will not be considered, as the only reference to the TRIM's Agreement in the Panel request related to Article 2.

7.50, 7.52 **Legal interest, "standing"** [DSU, Article 3.3, 3.7, 3.8]

A Member's potential interest in trade in goods or services and its interest in a determination of rights and obligations under the WTO Agreement are each sufficient to establish a right to pursue a WTO dispute settlement proceeding. Thus, the United States has a right to advance the claims it has raised in this case.

7.58 **Procedures for multiple complainants** [DSU, Article 9]

Under Article 9 of the DSU, the European Community is entitled to individual reports for each of the four first submissions originating the complaints [Guatemala and Honduras filed a joint first submission]. As a number of the proceedings were conducted jointly, it is decided that he description of the Panel's proceedings, the factual aspects and the parties' arguments should be identical in each of the four reports. In the findings section, however, the reports will differ to the extent that the Complainant's initial written submissions to the Panel differ in respect of alleging inconsistencies with the requirements of specific provisions of specific agreements.

7.62, 7.63 **Like products** [GATT, Articles I, III, X and XIII]

Bananas are like products, for purposes of Articles I, III, X and XIII of the General Agreement, irrespective of whether they originate in the EC, in ACP countries, in BFA countries or in other countries, and in spite of any differences in size, quality or taste that may exist.

7.70 - 7.72 **Allocation of quotas** [GATT, Article XIII.2(d)]

GATT Article XIII.2(d) allows for allocation of tariff quota shares to particular supplying countries, either by way of agreement with Members having a substantial interest in supplying the product concerned or by allotting shares in accordance with the requirements of Article XIII.2(d), second sentence. The combined use of agreements and unilateral assignment of shares to Members with substantial interests is prohibited by Article XIII.2(d).

7.73 - 7.75 **"Similarly prohibited or restricted"** [GATT, Article XIII.1]
"Aim at distribution of trade" [GATT, Article XIII.2(d)]

The Article XIII.1 requirement that quantitative restrictions including tariff quotas be non-discriminatory, coupled with the Article XIII.2(d) requirement that quantitative restrictions including tariff quota regimes be as non-trade distorting as possible effectively requires use of a general "others" category for all Members not having a substantial interest in supplying the product in question.

7.78 - 7.82 **Tariff quota regimes** [GATT, Article XIII.5]

The EC allocated tariff quota quantities to traditional ACP suppliers of bananas. In addition, the EC reached an agreement on shares in its bound tariff quota for bananas with the Framework Agreement on Bananas (BFA) countries. The EC allocated shares of that tariff quota in respect of non traditional African Caribbean and Pacific (ACP) bananas, and created an "others" category in that tariff quota for other Members and non-Members. Such a division of tariff quota methods does not support the EC's argument that it has established two separate quota regimes for the importation of bananas.

7.85, 7.89 - 7.90 **All third countries** [GATT, Article XIII.1]

The tariff quota reallocation rules of the BFA are inconsistent with Article XIII.1

7.89, 7.90 **"Similarly prohibited or restricted"** [GATT, Article XIII.1]

The EC's allocation of tariff quota shares by agreement and by assignment to some Members not having a substantial interest in supplying bananas to the EC (including Nicaragua, Venezuela and certain ACP countries) but not to other members (such as Guatemala) is inconsistent with the requirements of Article XIII.1

7.91 - 7.93 **New Members** [GATT, Article XIII.4]

Ecuador is not required to accept the validity of the BFA as contained in the EC's Schedule of Commitments, nor is it pre-empted from invoking Articles XIII.2 or XIII.4 by its not having addressed banana-related issues in its Protocol of Accession.

7.103, 7.110 **Allocation of tariff quota shares to ACP countries** [The Lomé Convention and waiver]

To the extent that the EC has acted inconsistently with its obligations under Article XIII.1, the Lomé waiver waives that inconsistency to the extent necessary to permit the EC to allocate shares of its banana tariff quota to specific traditional ACP banana supplying countries in an amount not exceeding their pre-1991 best-ever exports to the EC.

7.118, 7.127 **Article II schedules of concessions' priority as compared to other GATT obligations** [GATT, Article II]

Article II permits a Member country to incorporate into its schedules of concessions acts yielding rights under the General Agreement, but not acts diminishing obligations under that Agreement. Therefore, the inclusion of the BFA tariff quota shares in the EC's Schedule does not permit it to act inconsistently with the requirements of Article XIII of the General Agreement.

7.120 - 7.127 **Priority of Agreement on Agriculture** [Agreement on Agriculture, Article 4 and 21]

General Agreement rules apply subject to the various provisions in the Agreement on Agriculture, including Article 4 relating to market access. This priority does not, however, preempt application of General Agreement requirements on all agricultural product market access agreements without express mention of such in the Agreement on Agriculture. As long as application of Article XIII does not conflict with rights provided in the Agreement on Agriculture, requirements thereby generated are enforceable. In the present case, the EC is not entitled to act inconsistently with General Agreement Article XIII merely because there is a provision in the Agreement on Agriculture pertaining to market access agreements, when such provision has no bearing on the matter in question.

7.131 - 7.136 **Tariff issues and the Lomé waiver** [The Lomé Convention and waiver]

As the Members did not limit the extent to which the EC could provide preferential tariff treatment to ACP countries under GATT Article I.1 by way of the Lomé waiver, the EC is not in violation of its Article I.1 obligations in providing "non-traditional ACP bananas" (bananas from ACP countries that have not traditionally supplied the EC with bananas and bananas in excess of traditional supplies from countries who historically supply the EC with bananas) preferential tariff treatment.

7.154 - 7.156 **Scope of the Licensing Agreement** [Agreement on Import Licensing Procedures, in general]

The licensing procedures used for the implementation of measures other than quantitative restrictions, including tariff quotas, are subject to the disciplines of the Licensing Agreement.

7.180 - 7.182 **Treatment no less favorable** [GATT, Article III.4]

This Panel adopts the findings of the second *Banana* panel report as to unfavorable treatment under Article III.4 imposed by the EC's allocation of licenses to different operator categories.

7.193 - 7.195, 7.202 - 7.204 **Any advantage, favor, privilege or immunity** [GATT, Article I.1]

The procedural and administrative requirements for imports of third-country and non-traditional ACP bananas arising from the application of the operator category rules differ from, and go significantly beyond those required in respect of traditional ACP bananas. Such treatment, particularly the 30% allocation of licenses to category B operators from non-traditional ACP and third-country imports, thereby provides an advantage to traditional ACP banana importers, in violation of Article I.1 Also, such measures are not required by the Lomé Convention and therefore not permitted under a Lomé waiver.

7.220 - 7.223 **Any advantage, favor, privilege or immunity** [GATT, Article I.1]

Application of activity function rules to non-traditional ACP and third-country imports in the absence of such rules being applied to traditional ACP imports imposes a disadvantage on such imports, and thereby violates Article I.1.

7.240 **Any advantage, favor, privilege or immunity** [GATT, Article I.1]

The requirement to match BFA export certificates with EC import licenses in connection with the country-specific allocation of tariff quota shares under the BFA is an advantage or privilege in the terms of Article I.1 in respect of rules and formalities in connection with importation. Since the EC accords this advantage to a product originating in Colombia, Costa Rica and Nicaragua while denying the same advantage to a like product originating in the territories of the Complainants, the requirement to match EC import licenses with BFA export certificates as provided in Article 3 of Regulation 478/95 is inconsistent with Article I.1.

7.283, 7.286 **Scope of GATS** [GATS, in general]

The claim by the EC that the scope of the GATS and GATT cannot overlap has no legal basis. Therefore, there is no legal basis for an *a priori* exclusion of measures within the EC banana import licensing regime from the scope of the GATS.

7.296 **Scope of GATS** [GATS, in general]

With respect to situations of supply through commercial presence, Members' obligations under the GATS cover the treatment of services and service suppliers.

7.301 - 7.304 **Treatment no less favorable** [GATS, Article II.1]

GATS Article II.1 requires treatment no less favorable, regardless of whether that is achieved through the application of formally identical measures. The obligation of treatment no less favorable should be interpreted *in casu*.

7.338 - 7.341, 7.351 - 7.353 **Treatment no less favorable** [GATS, Article II]
National treatment [GATS, Article XVII]

Although operator category rules arguable apply on a formally identical basis regardless of the origin of the service or service supplier concerned, allocation of a 30% share of licenses required for in-quota imports of third-country and non-traditional ACP country imports to Category B operators results in less favorable competition from suppliers other than those from traditional ACP importers.

7.366, 7.368, 7.369 - 7.372 **Treatment no less favorable** [GATS, Article II]
National treatment [GATS, Article XVII]

Allocation of fixed percentages of licenses according to activity functions performed by operators, despite arguably applying on a formally identical basis to regardless of origin, nationality, ownership or control, modifies the conditions of competition where the EC has provided advantage to those activity functions predominantly performed by companies of European origin.

7.378 - 7.380, 7.384 - 7.385 **Treatment no less favorable** [GATS, Article II]
National treatment [GATS, Article XVII]

The requirement to match export certificates and import licenses based solely on operator category conveys an advantage or privilege in violation of Article XVII.3 of GATS where operators in categories excluded from this obligation are predominate in the country (EC) issuing the regulation and operators and operators regulated by this requirement are predominantly foreign companies.

7.392 – 7.398 **Treatment no less favorable** [GATS, Article II]
National treatment [GATS, Article XVII]

Assignment of "hurricane licenses" to import in compensation for national disasters affecting producer regions for EC producers and based on operator categories are likewise discriminatory when operator categories favor traditional ACP importers and EC companies.

EUROPEAN COMMUNITIES – REGIME FOR THE IMPORTATION, SALE AND DISTRIBUTION OF BANANAS

REPORT OF THE PANEL
WT/DS27/R

TABLE OF CONTENTS

Editor's Note: The reports of each of the Complainants, combined herein, have identical paragraph and footnote numbering. In the FINDINGS section of the report, notations are made above sections where the opinion pertains only to certain Complainants.

I. INTRODUCTION

1.1 On 5 February 1996, Ecuador, Guatemala, Honduras, Mexico and the United States acting jointly and severally, requested consultations with the European Communities ("the Community" or the "EC") pursuant to Article 4 of the Understanding on Rules and Procedures governing the Settlement of Disputes ("DSU"), Article XXIII of the General Agreement on Tariffs and Trade 1994 ("GATT"), Article 6 of the Agreement on Import Licensing Procedures (to the extent that it related to Article XXIII of GATT), Article XXIII of the General Agreement on Trade in Services, Article 19 of the Agreement on Agriculture (to the extent that it related to Article XXIII of GATT), and Article 8 of the Agreement on Trade-Related Investment Measures (to the extent that it related to Article XXIII of GATT) regarding the EC regime for the importation, sale and distribution of bananas established by Council Regulation (EEC) 404/93[1], and the subsequent EC legislation, regulations and administrative measures, including those reflecting the provisions of the Framework Agreement on Bananas, which implemented, supplemented and amended that regime (WT/DS27/1).

1.2 Consultations were held on 14 and 15 March 1996. As they did not result in a mutually satisfactory solution of the matter, Ecuador, Guatemala, Honduras, Mexico and the United States, in a communication dated 11 April 1996, requested the establishment of a panel to examine this matter in light of the GATT, the Agreement on Import Licensing Procedures, the Agreement on Agriculture, the General Agreement on Trade in Services ("GATS") and the Agreement on Trade-Related Investment Measures (WT/DS27/6).

1.3 The Dispute Settlement Body ("DSB"), at its meeting on 8 May 1996, established a panel with standard terms of reference in accordance with Article 6 of the DSU (WT/DS27/7). Belize, Canada, Cameroon, Colombia, Costa Rica, Côte d'Ivoire, Dominica, Dominican Republic, Ghana, Grenada, India, Jamaica, Japan, Nicaragua, the Philippines, Saint Vincent and the Grenadines, Saint Lucia, Senegal, Suriname, Thailand and Venezuela reserved their third party rights to make a submission and to be heard by the Panel in accordance with Article 10 of the DSU. Several of these countries also requested additional rights (see paragraph *7.4*). Thailand subsequently renounced its third party rights.

A. Terms of Reference

1.4 The following standard terms of reference applied to the work of the Panel:

> To examine, in the light of the relevant provisions of the covered agreements cited by Ecuador, Guatemala, Honduras, Mexico and the United States in document WT/DS27/6, the matter referred to the DSB by Ecuador, Guatemala, Honduras, Mexico and the United States in that document and to make such findings as will assist the DSB in making the recommendations or in giving the rulings provided for in those agreements.

B. Panel Composition

1.5 On 29 May 1996, the Director-General was requested by Ecuador, Guatemala, Honduras, Mexico and the United States to compose the Panel by virtue of paragraph 7 of Article 8 of the DSU.

1.6 On 7 June 1996 the Director-General announced the composition of the Panel as follows:

Chairman: Mr. Stuart Harbinson

Members: Mr. Kym Anderson
Mr. Christian Häberli

[1] Official Journal of the European Communities No. L 47 of 25 February 1993, pp.1-11.

1.7 The Panel submitted its interim report to the parties to the dispute on 18 March 1997 and the final report on 29 April 1997.

II. PROCEDURAL ISSUES

2.1 In this section, the parties' arguments are set out with respect to three procedural issues: (i) the adequacy of the consultations and the specificity of the request for panel establishment; (ii) the requirement of legal interest; and (iii) multiple panel reports. The organizational matter with respect to the participation of third parties in these proceedings and presence of private lawyers in meetings of the Panel is addressed in the "Findings" section of this report. Arguments presented by third parties on their participation in these proceedings are summarized in Section V.

A. Adequacy of the Consultations and Specificity of the Request for Panel Establishment

2.2 The EC noted that consultations on the EC banana regime were held in the autumn of 1995 between the EC, a number of banana producing countries, parties to the Lomé Convention, Guatemala, Honduras, Mexico and the United States. These consultations were inconclusive and were terminated when a new round of consultations started. After Ecuador had become a WTO Member on 26 January 1996, Ecuador as well as Guatemala, Honduras, Mexico and the United States requested consultations with the EC on its banana regime by letter dated 5 February 1996 and circulated to Members as document WT/DS27/1 on 12 February 1996. It contained, in the view of the EC, only the barest outline of the complaints against the EC banana regime. Bilateral consultations were held with each of the Complaining parties on 14 and 15 March 1996 in Geneva.

2.3 The EC, being of the view that consultations were intended not only to "give sympathetic consideration" to the considerations and the questions of the Complaining parties, but also to enable the responding party to obtain a clear view of the case held against it, prepared a large number of questions in an attempt to better understand the complaints of Ecuador, Guatemala, Honduras, Mexico and the United States. These questions were transmitted on 3 April 1996. In the meantime, the EC was preparing its answers to the numerous questions posed by the Complaining parties. On 11 April 1996, however, Ecuador, Guatemala, Honduras, Mexico and the United States submitted a request for the establishment of a panel to the Chairman of the DSB (WT/DS27/6). Under these circumstances, the EC, concluding that the Complaining parties were of the view that the consultation phase was over, decided not to submit its answers to these questions nor received any answers to its own questions.

2.4 The EC considered that, although the parties to the earlier consultations did exchange questions and answers in writing, these documents could not, in the opinion of the EC, be relied upon in the present procedure. During the consultations both sides agreed that the parties would re-exchange these questions and answers from the earlier consultation so as to include them in the record of the present consultations. This would also have enabled Ecuador to obtain this material since, as a non-participant in the earlier consultations, it had no access to it. Such re-exchange of questions and answers did not take place, however, and hence these questions and answers were not part of the consultation and did not form a basis for the present dispute settlement procedure.

2.5 In the opinion of the EC, the consultation stage preceding a possible panel procedure should serve to afford the possibility to come to a mutually satisfactory solution as foreseen in Article 4.3 of the DSU. The obligation to seek such a solution could not be fulfilled unless the individual claims, of which a matter or a problem brought to dispute settlement was composed, were set out in the consultation phase of the procedure.[2] The EC noted that the parties had exchanged a considerable number of questions and answers and that the oral

[2] "United States - Imposition of Anti-Dumping Duties on Imports of Fresh and Chilled Atlantic Salmon from Norway", ADP/87 para. 335. Confirmed by the (unadopted) panel report on "Japan-Audiocassettes", ADP/136, para. 295 ff.

consultations within two half-days could not possibly cover all questions and in reality were highly perfunctory, the largest part of the consultations being spent by the Complaining parties reading out identical statements. It was evident, therefore, in the view of the EC, that these consultations had not fulfilled their minimum function of affording a possibility for arriving at a mutually satisfactory solution and for a clear setting out of the different claims of which the dispute consisted.

2.6 In the view of the EC, the request for the establishment of a panel was intended to be the culmination of the preparatory stage of the dispute settlement procedure. This was not the case in this dispute. The request for the establishment of a panel was in several respects a step backward from the somewhat greater clarity provided during the consultations (a point illustrated by the EC with examples). The EC asserted that, in the case of several claims, it was not in a position to know whether the claims advanced during the consultations were maintained, altered, refined or dropped.

2.7 The EC noted that, after the request for a panel had been discussed for the second time by the DSB at its meeting on 8 May 1996, the DSB decided to establish the Panel under standard terms of reference (WT/DS27/7) which implied that the matter at issue was entirely defined in the document requesting the establishment of a panel (WT/DS27/6).

2.8 The EC claimed that this request was unacceptably vague in the light of Article 6.2 of the DSU and past practice from earlier panels. Article 6.2 of the DSU prescribed, *inter alia*, that the request for the establishment of a panel:

> shall ... identify the specific measures at issue and provide a summary of the legal basis of the complaint sufficient to present the problem clearly.

In the opinion of the EC, these two functions could be properly fulfilled only if the request for the establishment of a panel did not merely restate the matter at issue in its broadest terms, as did the request by the Complaining parties, but contained a list of concrete claims, i.e. brief statements which linked a specific measure (and not the whole banana regime) with the infringement of a specific rule or obligation under the WTO (and not just a whole list of provisions).

2.9 The request for the establishment of a panel thus clearly infringed, in the opinion of the EC, the terms of Article 6.2 of the DSU. It did not identify specific measures at issue – it merely cited "the regime". And it did not relate the specific measures to the alleged infringement of a specific obligation – it merely cited a list of Articles. It was therefore impossible to know which Article might be related to which specific measure and, thus, which claim was being made against the EC. The EC was of the view that the consultations in the present case had not been able to fulfil their function because the Complaining parties were not prepared to wait for a further exchange of questions and answers as agreed during the oral consultations on 14 and 15 March 1996. Hence the request was a nullity and, at the very least, the consultations should be restarted and lead to a proper request for a panel responding to the requirements of Article 6.2. The EC therefore requested the Panel to decide this issue prior to any examination of the substance of the case and prescribe any remedial action deemed necessary *in limine litis*. The EC argued that at the stage of the first submission procedural illegalities could still be "healed" without much damage. If, at the last stage of the proceeding before this Panel, or before the Appellate Body, the request for the establishment of a panel were ruled to be contrary to Article 6.2 of the DSU, in the view of the EC, the complications would be considerable.

2.10 The EC considered that it was time to impose discipline where it concerned the formulation of the request for the establishment of a panel. Although there were large variations in practice, such requests sometimes clearly fell below the minimum standard necessary to inform both the defending party and possibly interested third parties of the scope of the case. In the present case, Complaining parties had clearly not met the minimum requirements of Article 6.2 of the DSU and of the *Salmon Panel.*[3]

2.11 The Complaining parties responded that the EC's claims were without basis in the DSU. Referring to the text of Article 4.2 of the DSU, the Complaining parties argued that the EC was obliged to accord the Complaining parties sympathetic consideration and afford adequate opportunity for consultation regarding representations made by the Complainants. This obligation was not reciprocal. Article 4.5 of the DSU stated that Members "should attempt" to obtain a satisfactory adjustment of the matter in consultations, but it referred to "attempt" and did not require that Members succeed in settling matters bilaterally. Article 4.7 of the DSU was unconditional in providing for the establishment of a panel upon request of the Complaining party or parties after the expiration of the 60-day consultation period.[4]

2.12 The Complaining parties considered that they had provided the EC with ample notice and explanation of their concerns during the consultation phase going beyond any DSU requirement by providing a detailed seven-page joint statement and a hundred questions detailing the many aspects of the EC banana regime about which they had concerns. The statement and the appended "Non-Exhaustive List of Questions" identified specific measures at issue and various legal bases for concern with a degree of specificity well beyond what was normally provided in any stage before the panel procedure. The EC's current insistence that the consultations had to permit the EC to identify each and every legal argument that would be presented in the panel proceeding was, in the view of the Complaining parties, without basis in the DSU. The banana regime in the EC had in any event been the subject of exhaustive and repeated consultations, negotiations, and GATT dispute settlement procedures even before 1991. There was nowhere in the WTO agreements any requirement that the consultations be a dress rehearsal for a panel proceeding.

2.13 With reference to the EC's arguments concerning the nullity of the request for establishment of a panel, the Complaining parties argued that Article 6.2 of the DSU required all panel requests to contain two elements. First, the request should "identify the specific measures at issue". Second, it should "provide a brief summary of the legal basis of the complaint sufficient to present the problem clearly". Contrary to the EC claim, the primary qualifying emphasis of this provision was, in the opinion of the Complaining parties, brevity, continuing the prior GATT emphasis on brevity enunciated in the Montreal Rules.[5] Nowhere did Article 6.2 require a detailed exposition tying each specific measure to each provision of law to be claimed by the Complaining parties. This was what submissions to the panel had to do to enable the panel to perform the task of examining particular measures in the light of the covered agreements. The Complaining parties considered that their request of 11 April 1996 complied fully with the requirement of Article 6.2. The request identified the specific measures at issue by citation to the "basic" enabling regulation and all laws, regulations and administrative measures that implemented, supplemented or amended that regulation (which numbered in the hundreds), including specifically those reflecting the BFA. The request then provided a "brief summary of the legal basis of the complaint", with a listing of the specific agreements and particular Articles implicated by the regime. All of the claims made by the Complaining parties in this dispute were covered by this request. None of the claims related to aspects of the regime that were not identified as problems in the consultations.

---

[3] "US-Norway Salmon Panel" ("United States - Imposition of Anti-Dumping Duties on Imports of Fresh and Chilled Atlantic Salmon from Norway") ADP/87, paras. 335-336; see also the panel report on "Japan-Audiocassettes", ADP/136, para. 295 ff.

[4] The Complaining parties noted that even under earlier GATT practice, it was clear that it was not necessary for both parties to agree before a panel could be established; such a condition would mean that one party could indefinitely block the procedures simply by saying that bilateral consultations had not yet been terminated. See Statement of Legal Adviser to the Director-General in relation to Japan's attempt in 1986 to block establishment of a panel on Japan's taxes on alcoholic beverages, C/M/205 p.10, cited in WTO "Analytical Index" (1995 ed.), p.673.

[5] "Improvements to the GATT Dispute Settlement Rules and Procedures", Decision of 12 April 1989, BISD 36S/61, para. F(a) ("The request for a panel ... shall indicate whether consultations were held, and provide a brief summary of the factual and legal basis of the complaint sufficient to present the problem clearly.").

2.14 The Complaining parties submitted several examples of panel requests filed since 1 January 1995 that in their view reflected a level of "specificity" comparable to the request in this dispute. If any requests for establishment of a panel filed since 1 January 1995 did provide more detail, it was, in the opinion of the Complaining parties, not detail compelled by Article 6.2. If some Members saw fit to provide a more detailed exposition of the problems than that contained in the Complaining parties' request, they were free to do so, but their providing such detail did not amount to "practice" under the DSU that would dictate how Article 6.2 should be interpreted. The arguments with respect to the panel report on *United States - Imposition of Anti-Dumping Duties on Imports of Fresh and Chilled Atlantic Salmon from Norway* (*Salmon Panel*), adopted on 30 November 1992 (ADP/87), were misplaced in the view of the Complaining parties. To the extent the *Salmon Panel* declined to examine claims raised in that action, it did so for two reasons that were inapplicable in the current case. The first was that certain claims were outside the panel's terms of reference. The other was that various claims were not the subject of consultations and conciliation in accordance with Article 15.3 of the Agreement on Implementation of Article VI of GATT. Neither finding had any bearing on the claim that "a lack of specificity" in the request failed to meet the requirements of an entirely different agreement, the DSU.

2.15 The Complaining parties had requested the establishment of a panel at two meetings of the DSB: on 24 April and on 8 May 1996. At neither one of those meetings did the EC or any other Member complain that the request was too vague to "present the problem clearly." On these occasions, the EC representative mentioned numerous other issues, including its reservation of rights under Article 9.2 of the DSU, but did not request any further explanation of the request. The number of third parties participating in this proceeding further illustrated that other Members certainly understood the "problem" sufficiently to gauge their respective national interests in this proceeding.

2.16 The Complaining parties further argued that, as a legal matter, the EC was asking the Panel to take an action outside its terms of reference. The Panel was bound to complete its task of examining the EC measures in light of the covered agreements, as specified in those terms of reference. Those terms of reference did not permit the Panel to "dissolve itself": the DSU was not one of the agreements covered by the Panel's terms of reference. The EC argument that it needed an early decision on this issue to avoid "prejudice" was, in the Complaining parties' view, without basis. The EC had had more than adequate notice of the aspects of the regime that were of concern to the Complaining parties. If anything, the Complaining parties had only narrowed their focus since the consultations which amounted to a windfall, not prejudice, to the EC. The further contention that participating in the second meeting with the Panel and further proceedings constituted prejudice was equally misguided. Indeed, it misapprehended entirely the nature of dispute settlement proceedings under the DSU. Article *3.10* reflected the Members' understanding that:

> the use of dispute settlement procedures should not be intended or considered as contentious acts and that, if a dispute arises, all Members will engage in these procedures in good faith in an effort to resolve the dispute.

The DSU thus considered participation in dispute settlement proceedings an obligation of membership that improved trade relations, not a prejudicial process in itself. The remedy sought by the EC - additional time to defend itself - was only further proof of the opportunistic nature of this "procedural" claim. It was not likely that additional time would have changed the EC's presentation of its defence, as the first meeting of the Panel confirmed. The EC's claim of harm resulting from alleged lack of specificity should therefore be rejected.

2.17 The EC responded that the Complaining parties mischaracterized its position on this point. The EC's position was very simple: the request for the establishment did not satisfy the requirements of Article 6.2 of the DSU because of (i) lack of identification of specific measures at issue (i.e. the regime); and (ii) lack of a brief summary of the legal basis of the complaint sufficient to present the problem clearly (i.e. a list of Articles). Therefore, the request for the establishment of the Panel was null and void.

2.18 On 21 January 1996, the EC continued, Ecuador became a Member of the WTO; by 5 February 1996, the other Complaining parties had convinced Ecuador to join them and start new consultations which they requested on that day. Because of problems concerning the modalities of consultations and scheduling problems, these consultations took place only on 14-15 March 1996. Mutual promises were made to reply to long questionnaires, but before the process had run its course a request for a panel was filed. In the view of the EC, undue haste had resulted in the panel request being too brief a summary to present the problem clearly, in particular in a case where a new agreement, i.e. the GATS, was brought up for the first time in a panel procedure. As a separate identification was not made and the list of relevant Articles was so long, it was not even possible for the reader of the request to create his own link between the specific issues and the alleged infringement of a specific provision. This was at least possible in some earlier requests for establishment of panels which were at the border line of what could be deemed acceptable under Article 6.2 of the DSU.

2.19 The EC explained that in not mentioning the issue of the too summarized character of the request at the DSB meeting, the EC followed the by then well-established line that the respect for the basic procedural rules of the dispute settlement system was a task for the panels. Given that this was a well-established practice, raising the matter in the DSB and trying to prevent the DSB from establishing the panel for that reason would have been seen as a stalling tactic and onslaught on the "right to a panel" recently confirmed in the Marrakesh Agreement. Seen in this light, the argument advanced by the Complaining parties that the Panel, by ruling on Article 6.2, would be transgressing its terms of reference, was somewhat disturbing. This amounted to saying that the terms of reference prevailed over the DSU. If the Panel were not bound by what was in effect the constitution of the dispute settlement system and would not be held to apply the rules of the DSU, Members might just as well not have negotiated the DSU in the Uruguay Round. The Complaining parties had finally asserted that Article 6.2 should not be upheld because the EC had suffered no prejudice as a consequence. This position was misconceived in fact and in law. In fact, the EC had suffered a prejudice, i.e. the lack of minimal clarity handicapped the EC in the preparation of its defence, which was not unimportant given that the respondent normally had less time than the complaining Member to make its written submission. In law, procedural rules, and in particular the rule that the respondent must have a clear view of the case held against it, had a certain value in themselves. And that value should be defended by the Panel. As the "healing" measures suggested at the stage of the EC's first submission were no longer feasible at the stage of the rebuttal submissions, there was no alternative for the Panel but to draw the consequences of the serious defects inherent in this important document: nullity of this procedure.

2.20 In response to a question by the Panel, the EC analyzed, in light of Article 6.2 of the DSU, eight panel requests that were brought to the WTO (some of which with multiple Complaining parties). As a preliminary matter, the EC noted that it was puzzled as to how the WTO practice with respect to Article 6.2 could already have changed the interpretation to be given to this Article as it appeared from the (adopted) *Salmon Panel* report. Time had been too short and practice had been too inconsistent. In the view of the EC, several of the eight analyzed panel reports did not meet or barely met the requirements of Article 6.2 in the sense that there was a clear indication of the specific measure at issue, of the provision of the agreements allegedly infringed, and a link between the two. A considerable number of these requests, however, posed lesser problems in the light of Article 6.2 than the present panel request since they were concerned with one specific measure only or with a limited number of clearly defined measures which made it easier to link the measures to an alleged infringement if the number of provisions cited in the panel request was limited. In the present case, however, there was a total lack of specificity in the description of the measures, on the one hand, and an extremely long and unspecified list of the allegedly infringed WTO provisions, on the other hand. According to the EC, this was clearly contrary to Article 6.2 and did not fulfil the function of properly giving notice to the EC of the case held against it.

B. The Requirement of Legal Interest

2.21 The EC argued that in any system of law, including international law,[6] a claimant must have a legal right or interest in the claim he was pursuing. The rationale behind this rule was that courts existed to decide cases and not to reply to abstract legal questions; the court system (in the WTO context, the panel system) should not be burdened needlessly by cases without legal or practical consequences. Likewise, the respondent should not be forced to bear the costs and inconvenience of conducting a panel case, when the complaining Member had no legal right, or no legal or material interest in the outcome of the case. The EC submitted that in the present case the United States had no legal right or no legal or material interest in the case that it had brought under the GATT and the other Agreements contained in Annex 1A to the WTO Agreement since none of the remedies it could obtain would be of any avail to it: compensation or retaliation would not be due, since the United States had only a token production of bananas and had not traded in bananas with the EC, not even with those geographical sectors which under the old regime had maintained virtually free access or only a low tariff. Furthermore, the EC considered that a declaratory judgement would be of no interest since there was no serious indication that banana production in the United States could make exports feasible within the foreseeable future. The EC referred to the Working party report on *Brazilian Internal Taxes* (first report) which had made it clear, in the view of the EC, that a country must at least have potentialities as an exporter in order to be able to file a claim against another Member.[7] Moreover, under the GATT/WTO system the United States could not set itself up as private attorney-general and sue in the public interest and there were no indications that the GATT/WTO system accepted an *actio popularis* by all Members against any alleged infringement by any other Member. There were no indications so far in the GATT/WTO system that panels were willing to give declaratory rulings at the request of Members which had no legal right or interest in such a ruling, either in the form of a potential trading interest or in the form of a right to compensation or retaliation under Article XXIII of GATT (Article 22 of the DSU). The EC concluded that, on the issues raised under the GATT and other instruments of Annex 1A, the United States had no legal right or interest in obtaining a ruling from the Panel. Therefore, the EC requested that the Panel should decide, *in limine litis*, that it would not rule on the issues with respect to the United States.

2.22 It was obvious to the EC that the interest of companies, such as Chiquita and Dole Foods, was not the same as a legal interest of the United States in bringing a case under the GATT. The GATT was concerned with the treatment of products, not companies or their subsidiaries. In so far as the United States had a systemic interest in the case, where it professed to be concerned about the general law-abidingness of the EC, it advanced an interest as intervenor with a general interest in the interpretation of the GATT. If the Panel were to take position on the issue of the United States' legal interest in this matter, the United States might perhaps be admitted as intervenor, i.e. third party, in the GATT-related part of the case.

2.23 The United States responded that it had a significant commercial interest in seeing the EC comply with its GATT and other WTO obligations with respect to its banana regime. Two US fruit companies, Chiquita and Dole Foods, had played a major role over many decades in developing the European market for bananas. Although these bananas were mainly grown in Latin America, US companies were seriously affected by the manner in which the EC was distributing market share opportunities on a basis that was unrelated to past imports of third-country bananas or ability to import third-country bananas. The EC's measures had the effect of constraining US companies' import, delivery, and distribution flexibility and required them to expand substantial capital just to try to restore their former business. A regime violating GATT rules could be expected to adversely affect such major participants in the market. Both companies expressed concerns about the discrimination in the EC banana regime and sought an end to it.

---

[6] See the South-West Africa cases, 1966 ICJ Reports, pp.4 *et seq.*

[7] BISD Vol. II/181, para. 16. According to the EC, the panel's interpretation of GATT Article III:2 that it made no difference "whether imports from other contracting parties were substantial, small or non-existent" should be read in this light.

2.24 The United States further argued that the EC was well aware of the interests and concerns of the United States since they had been explained to the EC by diplomatic efforts that had begun over five years ago and that had intensified after two GATT panel proceedings had only resulted in additional GATT violations by the EC. The United States had reiterated its concerns during efforts to more formally negotiate a solution to these problems with the EC Commission. The EC's arguments with respect to US banana production had no bearing on this proceeding. However, the United States did produce bananas in both the state of Hawaii and in Puerto Rico, which was within the US customs territory. The Hawaiian producers had expressed their concerns that the EC banana regime was lowering the price of bananas in the free market, adversely affecting their ability to continue to produce and potentially export bananas. The United States considered that it was not for the EC to decide which producers in the world had an interest or potential to export.

2.25 As far as legal rights or interests were concerned, the United States was a Member of the WTO and a founding contracting party of the GATT. Article XXIII of GATT, as amplified in the DSU, permitted the initiation of dispute settlement proceedings when any Member was concerned about the inconsistency of another Member's measures. In fact, dispute settlement proceedings could be instituted to consider measures that were not even alleged to be inconsistent with any WTO agreement. The "interest" that a Member had to have in order to initiate proceedings was self-defined: a Member could initiate procedures whenever (in its judgement) it considered that benefits accruing to it, directly or indirectly, under the GATT were being nullified or impaired or whenever it considered, in its own judgement, that the attainment of any objective of GATT was being impeded or impaired as a result of another Member's failure to carry out its GATT obligations. This was the multilateral procedure under which governments had agreed to address such disputes.

2.26 Mexico considered that the view expressed by the EC that Mexico did not have a substantial interest in participating in this Panel as a Complaining party since its banana exports to the EC were minimal or non-existent was incorrect both from the point of view of Mexico's rights under the GATT and from the point of view of its interest in the international banana trade. It had been clearly established that it was not necessary to prove the existence of adverse effects for a panel to confirm the inconsistency of a particular measure with the provisions of the GATT. Mexico had therefore refrained from providing a more detailed explanation of the impact of the EC's regime on its banana sector. In the view of Mexico, the consistency of a measure with WTO obligations should be examined in legal terms and not in terms of its impact on the economies of other Members. Any other approach would imply, wrongly, that certain Members had more rights than others or that the interpretation of the WTO's provisions varied according to the characteristics of the countries involved in a dispute.

2.27 In order to avoid any misconception as to Mexico's interest in the international banana trade and ultimately in the EC market, Mexico made, however, the following points: (i) Mexico was currently the eighth largest banana producer in the world; (ii) total exports from Mexico exceeded 250,000 tonnes in 1992 and 1993, and fell to just under 200,000 tonnes in 1994; (iii) bananas occupied the fourth place in Mexico's fruit production in terms of area under crop, and the second after oranges in terms of both production volume and value; (iv) bananas now occupied the first place in Mexico's fruit exports; (v) an estimated 50,000 persons were directly employed in banana production in the tropical areas of Mexico, not to mention the persons indirectly employed in transport and marketing of bananas; (vi) the Soconusco region in the state of Chiapas was the most important banana exporting region of Mexico (it was well known that Chiapas was one of the poorest rural states in the country); (vii) bananas provided the only activity of the port Francisco I. Madero, the only port in Chiapas; and (viii) the international banana trade was of vital importance to the recovery of investment in the banana producing regions. With respect to services, Mexico argued that its legal interest in participating in the proceeding did not depend on the market share of its service suppliers, but that in any event, a major banana distribution company, Del Monte, remained in Mexican ownership.

2.28 The EC subsequently clarified its position regarding Mexico's legal interest in this dispute with the statement that, although Mexico had never exported bananas to the EC other than in symbolic quantities, the EC did not contest the legal interest of Mexico in this procedure under the GATT since it clearly was a potential exporter of bananas to the EC with a considerable capacity.

2.29 The Complaining parties considered that the manner in which the EC had continuously and increasingly defied the rules of the international trading system, affecting so many countries, impeded the objectives of the GATT, and of the WTO Agreement, to eliminate discrimination in international commerce.

2.30 With respect to this claim, the United States noted that with each GATT proceeding and each opportunity to reform its regime, the EC had only added new layers of discrimination against imports from third countries. In the view of the United States, this pattern was unprecedented in post-war international commerce.

2.31 The Complaining parties noted that the nature and scope of the Panel's inquiry was set by its terms of reference. All the Complaining parties' claims before the Panel fell within its terms of reference. Those terms did not provide authority to the Panel simply not to consider the Complaining parties claims. Moreover, the DSU had no *locus standi* limitation. The WTO agreements at issue in this dispute and the DSU set forth comprehensive, detailed rules and procedures governing WTO dispute settlement. Had the DSU drafters intended to institute a limitation of the sort being advanced by the EC, they would have done so. Instead, Article 3.7 of the DSU simply requested that:

> Before bringing a case, a Member shall exercise its judgement as to whether action under these procedures would be fruitful.

The DSU in effect already recognized that recourse to dispute settlement under the WTO agreements was self-limiting in that a Member would not initiate and pursue a resource-intensive proceeding unless it considered itself adversely affected; it respected each Member's determination in that regard.

2.32 The Complaining parties considered that the findings that would result from this proceeding were necessary to bring about a positive solution to the dispute. It was accordingly clear that all five Complaining parties were fully within their legal rights to assert all claims being advanced in this action with respect to both goods and services, and to benefit from the Panel's findings. The Complaining parties were not standing in the place of others, in *actio popularis*, as the EC suggested. The Complaining parties were raising issues in their capacity as Members of the WTO, and sought EC compliance with specific disciplines which the EC had, in the WTO agreements, agreed to submit to dispute settlement proceedings for interpretation in accordance with the DSU.

2.33 Where the DSU addressed nullification and impairment, it did not address rights to engage in dispute settlement, nor did it limit the panel's consideration of the extent to which the measures at issue violated the agreements. Referring to Article 3.8 of the DSU, the Complaining parties argued that this provision defined nullification and impairment quite broadly, to cover any "adverse impact" on a Member, presupposing a prior finding of an infringement. The kind of economic predictions that the EC would require to determine "trade potentiality" would, in the view of the Complaining parties, involve very difficult and speculative calculations of the type panels had wisely eschewed. From a global perspective, the EC approach would protect only current exporters or investors, at the expense of firms that might later invest in the country, or goods that might later be produced for export in the absence of trade or investment barriers. Such a rule could have a particularly adverse effect on developing countries. It was essential for emerging economies to guard future trade opportunities even before "potentialities" became apparent. Otherwise, opportunities to promote trade and development could be forever limited or foreclosed. Since one of the basic objectives of the GATT was to raise the standard of living and progressively develop the economies of all Members, particularly developing country Members,[8] governments had

[8] GATT, Part IV, Article XXXVI:1(a).

to have the opportunity to seek dispute settlement proceedings as they saw fit in order to preserve their potential interests.

2.34 The Complaining parties submitted that as recently as 1993, in the panel report on *United States - Restrictions on Imports of Tuna* (*Tuna Panel*),[9] the EC had argued that any time a country produced a product, even if the application of another country's measure to its exports was only hypothetical, the potential effect on price in its market gave rise to a "legal interest". The EC had stated that it was challenging US trade sanctions that were not applicable to the EC on the basis that:

> It is clear that such sanctions can have an enormous impact on third countries, especially when fish and fish products normally exported to the United States have to be sold on other markets. It is primarily for that reason that the EC has an interest in seeking the condemnation [by the panel].

The EC had later affirmed that its principal concern was with potential price depression in its own market resulting from global trade diversion. The EC also had gone so far as to say that even a tariff binding provided benefits to non-suppliers. At the first meeting with the panel in that dispute, the EC had acknowledged that the two measures it was challenging were "presently not applicable to the Community," but had admonished that:

> The GATT does not protect actual trade flows, but trading opportunities created by tariff bindings and other rules. Even though a contracting party is not a principal supplier at all (perhaps even a non-supplier), it profits from the tariff concessions concluded between principal suppliers.

The Complaining parties concluded that as a factual matter, by such a standard, the nullification and impairment issue would be conclusively resolved with respect to all the Complaining parties. With respect to goods, the United States produced more bananas than several of the EC's domestic and ACP supplying sources; with respect to services, all the Complaining parties had banana service suppliers within their own territories that were or would be affected by measures discriminating against foreign service suppliers in the EC. More to the point, however, the DSU and WTO agreements did not permit the EC or a panel to limit recourse to dispute settlement proceedings to only some Members whom the EC might consider to have "potential trade" or whatever other concepts the EC might wish to superimpose on the DSU on the basis of so-called "natural justice". Such an approach would fundamentally undercut the multilateral nature of these agreements.

2.35 The EC responded that it contested the legal (and material) interest of the United States in obtaining a panel ruling under the GATT. In turn, the United States had contested this but did so from the angle of formal requirements of standing or admissibility. This was perhaps understandable since in the common law countries the distinction between absence of the formal requirements for standing and the lack of legal interest to sue was often not sharply made. Both were called "standing". However, in the opinion of the EC, its reference to the maxim "point d'intérêt, point d'action" should have made things clear to the United States. In any case, the EC failed to see how affirmations of the United States fulfilling the formal requirements to appear before the Panel could detract from the EC's demonstration that the United States could not possibly derive any legal or material benefit from its case under the GATT (no compensation, no retaliation, whilst a declaratory judgement was of no interest to the United States either).

2.36 The EC noted that according to official US statistics, the United States for many years has not, and does not now, export bananas. The EC further noted that it did not contest the accuracy of these official US statistics. The EC argued that the United States had claimed that, although the United States had no information that would contradict US export figures (which were nil), import statistics were more reliable and these showed that the

[9] DS29/R, circulated 16 June 1994.

United States had exported over 1,000 tonnes of bananas annually to the EC since 1990. In the view of the EC, this was a misrepresentation of the facts. It was well-known and accepted that the United States did not export bananas and that the relevant US statistics were correct. Furthermore, EC import statistics did not show the origin of bananas, but their provenance. This meant that a shipload of bananas from Costa Rica, for example, which first might have headed for a US port and subsequently been bound for the EC would be registered as of US provenance. Or, as another example, intra-EC trade showed significant banana imports into France from the Benelux countries. This clearly proved that import statistics registered the countries of provenance, not of origin (since the Benelux countries did not produce any bananas). The EC noted that the United States had also submitted FAO data on production and exports, according to which the United States had produced between 5,126 and 6,210 tonnes annually between 1990 and 1995, but had exported between 337,365 tonnes and 383,216 tonnes annually in the same period. In the view of the EC, this again demonstrated how misleading statistics relying on aggregate imports from the rest of the world might be. According to the EC, any trade from Puerto Rico was obviously with the US mainland and other US territories, such as the Virgin Islands. Since this was a situation that had existed for many years, the EC was of the view that the United States was not a potential entrant in the banana trade, could not possibly suffer any nullification or impairment, did not even have an interest in a declaratory judgement because it could not take advantage of the possible competitive opportunities and, hence, had no legal interest in a ruling under the GATT.

2.37 The United States submitted that it had no basis for contradicting FAO figures that showed exports of bananas from Puerto Rico, and that it did not possess the administrative ability to ascertain its export quantities with the same precision that it had with respect to imports.

2.38 The EC argued that the question of legal or material interest in this case was a serious matter and deserved a serious answer. This was best demonstrated by the United States reverting to the *Tuna Panel*. The EC's approach in the *Tuna Panel* proceeding was entirely consistent with the EC's present approach. The EC had argued in its second submission in the *Tuna Panel* case: "... potential entrants into a trade have a legitimate interest in a breach of GATT provisions." In the present case, the EC considered that the United States had demonstrated over many years, by not entering the trade in bananas, that it was not a potential entrant as referred to in the *Tuna Panel*.

2.39 The United States observed with respect to the *Tuna Panel* proceeding that the EC had challenged three US measures, the third of which had no potential effect on any EC exports, and that the EC had explained its "legal interest" in that particular measure solely on the basis of collateral price effects on products sold in its own market.

2.40 The EC argued further that the Complaining parties were hiding behind a formalistic approach to nullification and impairment. In the view of the EC, it was logical to apply the rule of lack of legal interest, if one could already see at an early stage that nullification and impairment would not occur. It had demonstrated that there was no such interest, not even in terms of a declaratory judgement. Moreover, it was not necessary to engage in "difficult and speculative calculations" in order to see that the United States had no trade interest in the matter.

2.41 The EC argued that, even if the Panel were not to accept the Community's argument on the lack of a legal right or interest of the United States to pursue the case under the GATT, the United States had not suffered any nullification or impairment under Article XXIII of GATT. If in the present case an infringement of the GATT were to be found, it was, unlike in other cases, not difficult to rebut the presumption of nullification or impairment: the United States had never exported any bananas to the EC and it did not do so, not because it was blocked in any way by the Community's measures, but because it did not have the capacity to export and, through a combination of climatic and economic reasons, was unlikely to have such capacity in the near or medium term. Under these circumstances, the United States could not be considered to suffer nullification or impairment as a result of the Community's measures under the banana regime.

C. Multiple Panel Reports

2.42 The EC argued that the present procedure was a procedure with multiple Complaining parties and hence the EC had the right to request that the Panel organize its examination and present its findings to the DSB in such a manner that the rights, which the EC would have enjoyed had separate panels examined the complaints, were in no way impaired. In particular, the EC had a right to a separate report on each complaint, if it so requested (Article 9.2 of the DSU). The EC made such a request at the DSB meeting of 8 May 1996. In the course of this proceeding, the EC had reiterated this request and had asked the Panel to prepare four separate reports, with the reports for Guatemala and Honduras being joined, since they had filed a joint submission.

2.43 Referring to the text of Article 9.2 of the DSU, the Complaining parties conceded that the DSU appeared to require the Panel to accede to the EC's request, if the EC insisted on separate panel reports - in spite of the administrative burden on the Panel and the Secretariat, and the potential waste of resources. If the EC continued to insist on separate reports, the Complaining parties would assume that, in keeping with a general policy favouring uniformity of results, the Panel's four different reports would make the same findings and conclusions with respect to the same claims. Past panels had accomplished this with ease.[10] However, the Complaining parties believed that there were several reasons why the rights which the EC "would have enjoyed" in separate proceedings could be satisfied by a single report. As the Complaining parties' first submissions, their joint oral presentation of 10 September 1996, and the rebuttal submission made clear, with the exception of the tariff rates being challenged by Guatemala and Honduras, all the Complaining parties were challenging the same aspects of the EC banana regime. A single panel report could easily identify the separate claims,[11] if any, made by each country, since the claims all related to the same measures. Ecuador's separate legal claim under Article 4.2 of the Agreement on Agriculture was based on the same aspects of the EC's regime as the claims made by the other Complaining parties. Such an approach would preserve any rights the EC would have had with separate reports. The different "legal situations" of any of the Complaining parties were, in the opinion of the Complaining parties, irrelevant to the Panel's ability to carry out its task: to examine the measures identified by the Complaining parties in light of the covered agreements.

2.44 The EC replied that the Complaining parties had deliberately followed a course during this procedure of effacing the differences between them. In their second submission they presented, in a single submission, the claims made by different Complaining parties as if they had been made by all. There was thus a constant threat of confusion about which of the Complaining parties claimed what. It was very important to recall that different Complaining parties had made different claims (especially with regard to services) and that they were in different legal situations (especially with respect to legal interest). The common second submission even seemed to take the position that in situations, where there had been a claim only by one Complaining party, such claim was extended to all. This should be firmly rejected. According to the EC: (i) Ecuador had made claims with respect to both goods and services. These claims were contested by the EC on their merits. Ecuador was the one country making a claim under Article 4.2 of the Agreement on Agriculture; (ii) Guatemala and Honduras had made no claims on services; their claims in the first submission related only to goods. The EC contested the claims with respect to goods on their merits. Guatemala was the only country making a claim under Article II of GATT; (iii) Mexico had made claims on goods and services, but its claims on services in the first submission were extremely limited and totally unsubstantiated. The EC contested the claims in both domains on their merits; (iv) the United States

---

[10] See "Republic of Korea - Restrictions on Imports of Beef - Complaint by Australia", adopted 7 November 1989, BISD 36S/202; "Republic of Korea - Restrictions on Imports of Beef - Complaint by New Zealand", adopted 7 November 1989, BISD 36S/234; and "Republic of Korea -Restrictions on Imports of Beef - Complaint by the United States", adopted 7 November 1989, BISD 36S/268 (in which the findings were identical except where a unique claim was made by a complaining party). See also "EEC - Restrictions on Imports of Dessert Apples - Complaint by Chile", adopted 22 June 1989, BISD 36S/93 and "EEC - Restrictions on Imports of Apples - Complaint by the United States", adopted 22 June 1989, BISD 36S/135 (in which findings were largely identical except for arguments relating to Part IV and goods en route uniquely made by Chile).

[11] See "United States - Taxes on Petroleum and Certain Imported Substances", adopted 17 June 1987, BISD 34S/136.

had made claims on trade in goods and on trade in services. The EC contested the claims on trade in goods for reasons of lack of legal interest on the part of the United States. The United States claims on services were contested on their merits.

2.45 The EC further argued that the Complaining parties were in very diverse legal positions as demonstrated in the foregoing paragraph. If there was one situation in which the right to separate reports in the case of multiple complaining parties had a function, it was in the present case, as it was far from clear that the Panel could reach the same findings and conclusions with respect to the same claims for all Complaining parties. It was of great importance for the EC that it be clearly established at the end of this procedure which of the Complaining parties had seen which claims accepted by the Panel and which not. In these circumstances, the EC considered it only logical to invoke what was its perfect right under Article 9.2 of the DSU.

2.46 The Complaining parties considered that the EC had misstated the nature of their claims. All five were making all the claims made in their joint presentations, both with respect to goods and services. While some had made one or two additional claims in the goods area, these were minimal.

III. FACTUAL ASPECTS

3.1 The complaint examined by the Panel relates to the EC's common market organization for bananas introduced on 1 July 1993.

A. Banana Production and Trade

3.2 World production of bananas in 1995 is estimated at 54.5 million tonnes (FAO). The largest producer countries were India (9.5 million tonnes) and Brazil (5.7 million tonnes) followed by Ecuador (5.4 million tonnes), China (3.3 million tonnes) and the Philippines (3.2 million tonnes). Banana production of the Complaining parties, other than Ecuador, was as follows: Mexico 2.1 million tonnes, Honduras 0.8 million tonnes, Guatemala 0.5 million tonnes and the United States (including Puerto Rico) 54,500 tonnes.[12] In 1994 (the most recent year for which FAO data are available) the largest exporters were: Ecuador (2.35 million tonnes), Costa Rica (2 million tonnes), Colombia (1.7 million tonnes), the Philippines (1.2 million tonnes) and Panama (0.7 million tonnes). According to the same source, Honduras, Guatemala and the United States[13] each exported 0.4 million tonnes and Mexico 0.2 million tonnes.

3.3 In 1994, the EC was the world's second largest importer of bananas, after the United States (3.7 million tonnes) and followed by Japan (0.9 million tonnes).[14] According to data submitted by the EC, supplies of fresh bananas in the EC - 12 totalled approximately 3.5 million tonnes in 1994, 2.1 million tonnes of which originated in Latin American countries and 727,000 tonnes in African, Caribbean and Pacific (ACP) countries that are parties to the Lomé Convention. The leading suppliers of Latin American bananas to the EC were Costa Rica, Ecuador, Colombia, Panama and Honduras (in descending order).[15] The leading suppliers of ACP bananas to the EC were Cameroon, Côte d'Ivoire, St. Lucia, the Dominican Republic, Jamaica, Belize and Dominica (in descending order). For many ACP countries, banana exports to the EC represent a very high proportion of their total banana exports (see the Attachment to this report). Domestic EC producers supplied, according to the EC, approximately 645,000

---

[12] Source: FAO.

[13] In the case of the United States, the FAO export data are contested by the EC (see above in section II -procedural issues). It would appear that according to US export figures there are no, or only negligible, quantities of bananas exported.

[14] Eurostat and FAO.

[15] EC import statistics for 1989-95 are contained in the Attachment to this report, although it should be noted that some of these data, which were submitted by the EC, are contested by the Complaining parties.

tonnes of the bananas consumed in the EC, with the producing areas being the Canary Islands, Martinique, Guadeloupe, Madeira, the Azores and the Algarve, and Crete and Lakonia. The conditions of production differ among all countries and so do the costs of production.

B. The EC's Common Organization of the Banana Market

3.4 The common market organization for bananas, as established by Council Regulation (EEC) 404/93 ("Regulation 404/93"), replaced the various national banana import regimes previously in place in the EC's member States. Subsequent EC legislation, regulations and administrative measures implemented, supplemented and amended that regime.

3.5 Under the previous national import regimes, France, Greece, Italy, Portugal and the United Kingdom restricted imports of banana by means of various quantitative restrictions and licensing requirements. Spain maintained a de facto prohibition on imports of bananas.[16] The French market was supplied principally from the overseas departments of Guadeloupe and Martinique, with additional preferential access granted to the ACP States of Côte d'Ivoire and Cameroon. The United Kingdom granted preferential access to bananas from the ACP States of Jamaica, the Windward Islands (Dominica, Grenada, St. Lucia and St. Vincent and the Grenadines), Belize and Suriname. Bananas from ACP countries were permitted duty-free into all EC member States. The Spanish market was almost exclusively supplied by domestic production from the Canary Islands. A major part of Portuguese supply came from Madeira, the Azores and the Algarve, with additional volumes being imported from Cape Verde and any remaining requirements being imported from third countries. The Greek market was in part supplied by bananas from domestic sources (Crete and Lakonia) and in part by third countries. Italy offered preferential access to bananas from Somalia. Belgium, Denmark, Germany, Luxembourg, Ireland and the Netherlands did not apply quantitative restrictions and, except for Germany, used a 20 per cent tariff as the sole border measure. These countries almost exclusively imported bananas from Latin America. Germany had a special arrangement, set out in the banana protocol of the Treaty of Rome, permitting duty-free imports of third-country bananas reflecting the level of estimated consumption.

3.6 Regulation 404/93 consists of five separate titles. Titles I to III regulate the internal aspects of the common market organization. Title I provides that common quality and marketing standards for bananas are to be established in subsequent regulations. Title II contains rules concerning producers' organizations and "concentration mechanisms" to promote the establishment of organizations for the purposes of, *inter alia*, concentrating supply, regulating prices at the production stage, and improving EC production structures and quality. Title III establishes EC assistance for the domestic banana sector. Under this title, members of recognized EC producer organizations (and individual producers under certain circumstances) are eligible for compensation of any income loss resulting from the implementation of the EC banana regime, the maximum quantity for such compensation being fixed at 854,000 tonnes of bananas for the EC as a whole.

1. *Tariff treatment*

3.7 Title IV, which regulates trade with third countries, establishes three categories of imports: (i) traditional imports from twelve ACP countries;[17] (ii) non-traditional imports from ACP countries which are defined as both any quantities in excess of traditional quantities supplied by traditional ACP countries and any quantities supplied by ACP countries which are not traditional suppliers of the EC; and (iii) imports from third (non-ACP) countries. The EC applies the following tariffs to these banana imports:

---

[16] See "Panel on EEC - Import Regime for Bananas", DS38/R (not adopted), paras. 17 *et seq*.

[17] Belize, Cape Verde, Côte d'Ivoire, Cameroon, Dominica, Grenada, Jamaica, Madagascar, Suriname, Somalia, St. Lucia, and St. Vincent and the Grenadines (Article 15.1 of Council Regulation (EEC) 404/93 (as amended) and the Annex thereto).

EC tariff treatment of banana imports		
Category of banana imports	**Source/Definition**	**Tariffs applied**
Traditional ACP bananas	Bananas within country-specific quantitative limits totalling 857,700 tonnes established for each of 12 ACP countries.	Duty-free.
Non-traditional ACP bananas	Either ACP imports above the traditional allocations for traditional ACP countries or any quantities supplied by ACP countries which are non-traditional suppliers.	Duty-free up to 90,000 tonnes, divided into country-specific allocations and an "other ACP countries" category; ECU 693 per tonne for out-of-quota shipments in 1996/97.
Third-country bananas	Imports from any non-ACP source.	ECU 75 per tonne up to 2.11 million tonnes as provided in the EC Schedule. An additional 353,000 tonnes were made available in 1995 and 1996. Country-specific allocations were made for countries party to the Framework Agreement on Bananas (BFA), plus an "others" category;[18] ECU 793 per tonne for out-of-quota shipments in 1996/97.

2. *Quantitative aspects, including country allocations*

   a) *Traditional ACP imports*

3.8 Imports of bananas from the twelve traditional ACP countries enter duty-free up to the maximum quantity fixed for each ACP country (see table below which also includes allocations for non-traditional ACP countries).[19] These allocations collectively amount to 857,700 tonnes. These quantities are not bound in the EC Schedule. There is no provision in the EC regulations for an increase in the level of traditional ACP allocations.

---

[18] The EC has opened additional tariff quota access under hurricane licences (para. 0 below refers).

[19] Article 15.1 of Council Regulation (EEC) 404/93 (as amended) and the Annex thereto.

Allocations for duty-free banana imports from ACP countries		
Country	**Traditional quantities as set out in EC Regulation 404/93 (tonnes)**	**Non-traditional quantities as set out in EC Regulation 478/95 (tonnes)**
Belize	40,000	15,000
Cameroon	155,000	7,500
Cape Verde	4,800	
Côte d'Ivoire	155,000	7,500
Dominica	71,000	
Dominican Republic		55,000
Grenada	14,000	
Jamaica	105,000	
Madagascar	5,900	
Somalia	60,000	
St. Lucia	127,000	
St. Vincent and the Grenadines	82,000	
Suriname	38,000	
"Other"[20]		5,000
Total	**857,700**	**90,000**

b) Non-traditional ACP and third-country imports

3.9 Imports of non-traditional ACP bananas and bananas from third countries are subject to a tariff quota (also referred to by the EC as the "basic tariff quota") of, originally, 2 million tonnes (net weight). This tariff quota was increased to 2.1 million tonnes in 1994 and to 2.2 million tonnes as of 1 January 1995. These tariff quota quantities were bound in the EC Uruguay Round Schedule.[21] The tariff quota can be adjusted on the basis of a "supply balance" to be derived from production and consumption forecasts prepared in advance of each year.[22] In 1995 and 1996, a volume of 353,000 tonnes was added to the tariff quota as a result of "consumption and supply needs" resulting from the accession of three new EC member States, Austria, Finland and Sweden. This additional volume is not bound in the EC Schedule. In practice, however, the EC's tariff quota for non-traditional ACP and third-country banana imports was increased to 2.553 million tonnes.[23]

[20] E.g. Ghana and Kenya.

[21] Schedule LXXX - European Communities.

[22] Article 16 of Council Regulation (EEC) 404/93 (as amended).

[23] In addition, the EC issued hurricane licences, see para. *3.15* below.

3.10 Of the tariff quota referred to above, 90,000 tonnes are reserved for duty-free entries of non-traditional ACP bananas. This volume is bound in the EC Schedule as a result of the BFA. By regulation, the EC allocated this import volume largely among specific supplying countries.[24]

3.11 Under the terms of the BFA, the EC allocated in its Schedule specific shares of the bound tariff quota of 2.1 million tonnes in 1994 and 2.2 million tonnes in 1995, respectively, as follows.[25]

BFA allocations under the bound tariff quota for third-country and non-traditional ACP banana suppliers	
Country	**Share**
Costa Rica	23.40 %
Colombia	21.00 %
Nicaragua	3.00 %
Venezuela	2.00 %
Others	(1994) 46.32 % (1995) 46.51 %
Dominican Republic and other ACP countries concerning non-traditional quantities	90,000 tonnes

3.12 The BFA also provides that, "In case of *force majeure*, a country listed above, may, on the basis of an agreement notified in advance to the Commission, fulfil all or part of its quota with bananas originating in another country listed above. In this case, the deliveries from the two countries concerned shall be adjusted accordingly in the following year."[26]

3.13 Furthermore, "If a banana exporting country with a country quota informs the Community that it will be unable to deliver the quantity allocated to it, the short-fall shall be reallocated by the Community in accordance with the same percentage shares indicated (including 'others'). However, countries with country quotas may jointly request and the Commission shall agree to a different allocation amongst those countries."[27]

3.14 The EC also undertook to allocate any increase in the EC tariff quota in proportion to the shares set above, including to "others". However, according to the BFA, "... countries with country quotas may jointly request and the Commission shall agree to a different allocation amongst those countries."[28]

---

[24] Article 1 of Commission Regulation (EC) 478/95 (as amended) and Annex 1 thereto.

[25] "Framework Agreement on Bananas", Annex to Part I, Section I-B (tariff quotas) in Schedule LXXX - European Communities.

[26] Idem, para. 3.

[27] Idem, para. 4.

[28] Idem, para. 5.

c) *Hurricane licences*

3.15 From November 1994 to May 1996, the EC issued 281,605 tonnes of supplemental "hurricane licences". Hurricane import volumes enter in addition to the 2.553 million tonne tariff quota and are subject to the third-country (non-ACP) in-quota tariff (ECU 75 per tonne). Hurricane licences may be used to import bananas from any source.[29]

3. *Licensing requirements*

3.16 Imports of both traditional ACP and non-traditional ACP/third-country bananas are subject to licensing procedures.

3.17 According to Commission Regulation (EEC) 1442/93 ("Regulation 1442/93"), banana imports into the EC are managed on a quarterly basis. For each of the first three quarters in any year, "indicative quantities" are established based on past trade patterns, seasonal trends, and the supply and demand balance prevailing in the EC market. These indicative quantities determine the volumes of traditional ACP bananas and non-traditional ACP/third-country bananas, respectively, that are available for a given quarter for the purpose of issuing import licences.[30] The import volumes thus available are divided proportionally among origins in accordance with the allocations indicated in the tables above.[31] The licences available in the fourth quarter of any calendar year are determined by subtracting those issued in the first three quarters from the total quantity available for each origin. Import licence applications are to be lodged with the competent authority of a EC member State within a specified period of time for the purpose of obtaining a licence for the subsequent quarter.[32] In the case of "unused" quantities covered by licences, there is a procedure for reallocation to the same operators in any subsequent quarter.[33]

a) *Traditional ACP imports*

3.18 Licence applications for imports of traditional ACP bananas must state the quantity and origin from which operators intend to source their bananas. Applications are also required to be accompanied by an ACP certificate of origin testifying to the status as traditional ACP bananas.[34] When licence applications exceed the indicative quantities of traditional bananas fixed for a particular country of origin, a single reduction coefficient is applied to all applications (a reduction coefficient serves to reduce importers' licence applications proportionally to the available volume).[35]

3.19 Licences are issued by the competent member State authority no later than the 23rd day of the last month of the preceding quarter (where that day is not a working day, the licences are issued on the first subsequent working day). The validity of import licences expires on the seventh day following the end of the quarter in question.

---

[29] See e.g. Commission Regulation (EC) 2791/94.

[30] Article 16 of Council Regulation (EEC) 404/93 (as amended); Articles 9 and 14 Commission Regulation (EEC) 1442/93 (as amended).

[31] Article 14 Commission Regulation (EEC) 1442/93 (as amended); Article 1 of Commission Regulation (EC) 478/95 (as amended).

[32] Commission Regulation (EEC) 1442/93 (as amended), Articles 9 and 14.

[33] Idem, Articles 10 and 17.

[34] Idem, Articles 14.4 and 15.

[35] Idem, Article 16.2.

b) Non-traditional ACP and third-country imports

3.20 Import licences for third-country bananas and non-traditional ACP bananas are allocated on the basis of several cumulatively applicable procedures, including: (i) allocation of licences based on three operator categories; (ii) allocation of licences according to three activity functions; (iii) export certificate requirements for imports from Costa Rica, Colombia and Nicaragua; and (iv) a two-round quarterly procedure to administer licence applications.

3.21 *Operator categories*: Under the EC's operator category rules, import licences are distributed among three categories of operators based on quantities of bananas marketed during the latest three year period for which data are available (see table below).[36] As operators in Category C ("newcomers") do not have reference quantities based on past trade, their allocation is dependent on the volume of licence applications the newcomer portion of the tariff quota.[37] Category A and B licences are transferable (tradeable) among operators, including to operators in Category C. Category C licences are, however, not transferable to Categories A and B. Transferred licences are taken into account in establishing reference quantities.[38]

Operator categories under the tariff quota for third-country/non-traditional ACP imports		
Operator category definition[39]	**Allocation of import licences allowing the importation of bananas at in-quota rates**	**Basis of determining operator entitlement**
Category A: operators that have marketed third-country and/or non-traditional ACP bananas.	**66.5%**	Average quantities of third-country and/or non-traditional ACP bananas marketed in the three most recent years for which data are available.
Category B: operators that have marketed EC and/or traditional ACP bananas.	**30%**	Average quantities of traditional ACP and/or EC bananas marketed in the three most recent years for which data are available.
Category C: operators who started marketing bananas other than EC and/or traditional ACP bananas as from 1992 or thereafter ("newcomer category").	**3.5%**	Divided pro rata among applicants.

[36] Article 19 of Council Regulation (EEC) 404/93 (as amended).

[37] Commission Regulation (EEC) 1442/93 (as amended), Article 4.4 .

[38] Idem, Article 13.

[39] Article 19 of Council Regulation (EEC) 404/93 (as amended) and Article 2 of Commission Regulation (EEC) 1442/93 (as amended).

3.22 *Activity functions*: The operator Categories A and B are further subdivided into three types of qualifying entities ("activity functions"), as set forth in the table below. In order to qualify as Category A and/or B operators, economic agents must have performed at least one of these activities in "marketing"[40] bananas during the rolling three-year reference period (i.e. the period determining their reference quantities; for 1993, the years 1989-91). In addition, operators must be established in the EC and have traded a minimum of 250 tonnes of bananas in any one year of the reference period.[41]

Activity function system under the tariff quota for third-country/non-traditional ACP imports		
Activity functions	**Definitions**[42]	**Weighting coefficients**
Activity (a): "primary importer"	"the purchase of green third-country bananas and/or ACP bananas from the producers, or where applicable, the production, and their subsequent consignment to and sale of such products in the Community"	57 per cent
Activity (b): "secondary importer or customs clearer"	"as owners, the supply and release for free circulation of green bananas and sale with a view to their subsequent marketing in the Community; the risks of spoilage or loss of the product shall be equated with the risk taken on by the owner"	15 per cent
Activity (c): "ripener"	"as owners, the ripening of green bananas and their marketing within the Community"	28 per cent

3.23 The weighting coefficient assigned to each type of activity function multiplied by the average quantity of bananas marketed by each operator of Categories A and B in the three most recent years, determines the individual operator's reference quantity.[43] According to Regulation 1442/93, the weighting coefficients are designed to reflect the level of commercial risk borne by operators for each of the activities in the marketing chain for bananas.[44]

3.24 Operators are expected to identify the activity function or functions upon which they are making their claim of licence entitlement (operators may have performed more than one activity and thus obtain a weighting coefficient of up to one hundred per cent). The reference quantities are, after the application of a single provisional reduction coefficient for operator Categories A and B, respectively, used in calculating an individual operator's provisional annual entitlement to banana import licences.[45] These entitlements are normally determined a few months before the beginning of the applicable year, although they may be, and generally are, subject to changes throughout the year (including the application of a final reduction coefficient).[46] In practice, the total reference quantities established by the EC for each of the marketing years since the introduction of the common market

---

[40] According to Article 15.5 of Council Regulation (EEC) 404/93 (as amended), "'market' and 'marketing' mean placing on the market, not including making the product available to the final consumer". Furthermore, Article 3.2 of Commission Regulation (EEC) 1442/93 (as amended) provides that "wholesalers and retailers shall not be considered operators solely by virtue of such activities" (i.e. the activities as set out in the table below) but does not define these terms.

[41] Commission Regulation (EEC) 1442/93 (as amended), Article 3.

[42] Idem, Article 3.

[43] Idem, Article 5.

[44] Idem, Recitals.

[45] Idem, Article 6.

[46] E.g. Commission Regulation (EC) 2947/94.

organization for bananas have exceeded the volume of the tariff quota available for distribution amongst operators so that reduction coefficients were applied.

3.25 *Export certificates*: Pursuant to the BFA, supplying countries that have country allocations may deliver special export certificates for up to 70 per cent of their allocations. Colombia, Costa Rica and Nicaragua have chosen to issue such certificates. According to EC regulation, presentation of such certificates ("export licences") by Category A and Category C operators constitutes a prerequisite for the issuance, by the EC, of licences for the importation of bananas from these countries.[47]

3.26 *Two-round quarterly licence applications*: Regulation 478/95 (as amended) establishes two rounds of import licence applications within each quarter. In the first round, A and B operators can request licences up to their quarterly entitlements. Category C operators may apply for their full annual entitlement in any given quarter. In their applications, companies must designate the source from which they plan to import and the desired volumes. Category A and C operators importing from BFA countries other than Venezuela must attach special export certificates. All licence applications are transmitted by the competent authorities of the EC member States to the EC Commission which, if the applications for any country of origin exceed the indicative quantity available for that origin (in any given quarter), applies a country-specific reduction coefficient which reduces such applications proportionally. "First round" licences are to be issued by the competent authorities by the 23rd day of the month preceding the relevant quarter (where that day is not a working day, the licences are issued on the first subsequent working day).

3.27 After the first round, the EC publishes the sources and quantities that were not exhausted (so far, mainly quantities from BFA countries and certain non-traditional ACP countries[48]) for purposes of a second round allocation. Those operators whose initial licence applications are scaled back by a reduction coefficient have the option to participate in a second round of applications in respect of the difference between their original application and their allocation for one of the origins where the allocations are not exhausted.[49] After the EC publishes the first round reduction coefficients, by the 23rd day of the month prior to the beginning of the quarter, the operators have ten days to re-apply for the second round. On the basis of applications received, the EC Commission determines, if necessary, reduction coefficients and then publishes the quantities for which licences may be issued in the second round. In practice, publication of these quantities often occurred two weeks into the quarter for which the licences were issued.[50] Both "first" and "second" round licences are valid until the seventh day of the month following the end of the quarter.

c) Hurricane licences

3.28 Hurricane licences are granted, on an ad hoc basic, to operators who "include or directly represent" a producer adversely affected by a tropical storm and are thus unable to supply the EC market.[51] As noted above, hurricane licences may be used to import bananas from any source. Bananas imported with hurricane licences may be counted as reference quantities for future eligibility for Category B licences.

[47] Article 3.2 of Commission Regulation (EC) 478/95 (as amended).

[48] See e.g. Commission Regulations (EC) 704/95, 1387/95, 2234/95 (as amended) and 2913/95.

[49] Article 4 of Commission Regulation (EC) 478/95 (as amended).

[50] See Commission Regulations (EC) 2500/95, 45/96, 670/96, 1371/96, respectively.

[51] E.g. Article 2 of Commission Regulation (EC) 2791/94.

C. Trade Policy Developments Concerning Bananas

1. *Disputes relating to bananas under the GATT*

3.29 Elements of the present EC market organization for bananas were the subject of a complaint by Colombia, Costa Rica, Guatemala, Nicaragua and Venezuela in 1993. The panel which was established by the GATT CONTRACTING PARTIES to examine the matter submitted its report on 11 February 1994 (second *Banana* panel).[52] Prior to the establishment of the common market organization for bananas on 1 July 1993, the banana regimes of individual EC member States were the subject of a complaint by the same countries mentioned above. The resulting GATT panel (first *Banana* panel) issued its report on 3 June 1993.[53] Neither panel report was adopted by the GATT CONTRACTING PARTIES.

2. *Framework Agreement on Bananas (BFA)*

3.30 In 1994, the EC negotiated the BFA with Colombia, Costa Rica, Venezuela and Nicaragua. As described above, the BFA contains provisions concerning the size of the basic tariff quota, the in-quota tariff (ECU 75 per tonne), country-specific allocations and transferability of those allocations, the 90,000 tonne allocation for non-traditional ACP bananas, and export certificates. The four Latin American parties to the BFA agreed not to pursue the adoption of the report of the second *Banana* panel. Guatemala, the fifth complaining contracting party to the second *Banana* panel, is not a party to the BFA. The BFA was incorporated into the EC's Uruguay Round Schedule in March 1994.[54] The BFA came into force on 1 January 1995[55] and its functioning is scheduled to be reviewed "before the end of the third year" with full consultations with Member Latin American suppliers. The BFA is applicable until 31 December 2002.[56]

3. *Tariff changes*

3.31 From 1963, the EC had a consolidated tariff of 20 per cent ad valorem on bananas. Initial negotiating rights were held by Brazil. With the introduction of the common market organization for bananas on 1 July 1993, a tariff quota was established with an in-quota tariff of ECU 100 per tonne for third-country bananas and ECU 850 per tonne for out-of-quota imports. Out-of-quota imports of ACP bananas were subject to a tariff of ECU 750 per tonne. On 26 October 1993, the EC notified the CONTRACTING PARTIES of its intention to renegotiate the 1963 concession on bananas in accordance with the provisions of Article XXVIII:5 of GATT 1947. On 1 July 1995, the EC's Uruguay Round Schedule, including its tariff concession on bananas, became effective (see also above).[57]

3.32 In accordance with the EC reduction commitments as a result of the Uruguay Round, the level of the bound tariff was reduced on 1 July 1995 to ECU 822 per tonne and on 1 July 1996 to ECU 793 per tonne. The final bound MFN rate at the end of the six-year implementation period of the Uruguay Round results will be ECU 680 per tonne. In accordance with the BFA entered into by the EC with Colombia, Costa Rica, Nicaragua and Venezuela, the MFN in-quota tariff rate was reduced and bound at ECU 75 per tonne from 1 July 1995 (though it was applied from 1 January 1995).

---

[52] Panel on "EEC - Import Regime for Bananas", DS38/R (not adopted).

[53] Panel on "EEC - Member States' Import Regimes for Bananas", DS32/R (not adopted).

[54] Schedule LXXX - European Communities.

[55] Commission Regulation (EC) 3223/94 (as amended).

[56] Paragraph 9 of the Annex "Framework Agreement on Bananas" in Schedule LXXX - European Communities.

[57] In signing the Final Act, Guatemala submitted a letter stating that it was reserving "all GATT and WTO rights" relative to the EC's Schedule as regards bananas.

4. *Lomé waiver*

3.33 The Fourth Lomé Convention, signed on 15 December 1989 between the EC and 70 African, Caribbean and Pacific developing countries, many of which are Members of the WTO, contains a protocol concerning bananas, along with provisions applying to products more generally. Like its predecessors, the Fourth Lomé Convention was notified to the GATT and considered by a working party.

3.34 On 10 October 1994, the EC requested, together with the ACP contracting parties, a waiver from the EC's obligations under Article I:1 of GATT 1947.[58] The waiver was granted by the CONTRACTING PARTIES on 9 December 1994 and provides, in paragraph 1 of the waiver decision, as follows:

> [T]he provisions of paragraph 1 of Article I of the General Agreement shall be waived, until 29 February 2000, to the extent necessary to permit the European Communities to provide preferential treatment for products originating in ACP States as required by the relevant provisions of the Fourth Lomé Convention, without being required to extend the same preferential treatment to like products of any other contracting party.[59]

3.35 On 14 October 1996, the Lomé waiver as granted by decision of the GATT CONTRACTING PARTIES at its December 1994 session was extended until 29 February 2000 (in accordance with the procedures mentioned in paragraph 1 of the Understanding in respect of Waivers and those of Article IX of the WTO Agreement).[60]

5. *Accession of Austria, Finland and Sweden to the EC*

3.36 Following the accession of Austria, Finland and Sweden to the EC on 1 January 1995, the EC autonomously increased access under in-quota tariff conditions (ECU 75 per tonne) by 353,000 tonnes.[61] The administration of these additional quantities is subject to the same procedures as the bound tariff quota, although they have not been bound in the EC Schedule.

III. MAIN ARGUMENTS

A. General

4.1 In their request for the establishment of the Panel, Ecuador, Guatemala, Honduras, Mexico and the United States, acting jointly and severally, submitted that the EC maintained a regime for the importation, sale and distribution of bananas as established by Regulation 404/93 (O.J. L 47 of 25 February 1993, page 1), and subsequent EC legislation, regulations and administrative measures, including those reflecting the provisions of the Framework Agreement on Bananas. The Complaining parties considered that the regime and related measures were inconsistent with the following Agreements and provisions among others:

- Articles I, II, III, X, XI and XIII of the General Agreement on Tariffs and Trade 1994 ("GATT")
- Articles 1 and 3 of the Agreement on Import Licensing Procedures ("Licensing Agreement")
- the Agreement on Agriculture
- Articles II, XVI and XVII of the General Agreement on Trade in Services ("GATS")
- Article 2 of the Agreement on Trade-Related Investment Measures ("TRIM's Agreement")

---

[58] GATT document L/7539 of 10 October 1994 and L/7539/Corr.1.

[59] Para. 1 of GATT document L/7604 of 19 December 1994.

[60] WT/L/186 of 18 October 1996.

[61] According to data submitted by the EC, this volume corresponds to the average yearly consumption of bananas in these three countries in the period 1991-93.

In addition, they claimed that the measures also produced distortions which nullified or impaired benefits accruing to Ecuador, Guatemala, Honduras, Mexico and the United States, directly or indirectly, under the cited Agreements; and the measures impeded the objectives of the GATT and the other cited Agreements (WT/DS27/6).

4.2 Following the joint request for the establishment of the Panel, its composition and the establishment of terms of reference, Ecuador, Guatemala, Honduras, Mexico and the United States made submissions to the Panel. The first submissions were made by each Complaining party separately, with the exception of Guatemala and Honduras which made a joint submission. Aspects of the EC's measures applying to bananas were cited as being inconsistent with the following provisions and Agreements in those submissions:

Ecuador:

- concerning tariff issues: Article I:1 of GATT;
- concerning allocation issues: Article XIII of GATT; and
- concerning the import licensing regime: Articles I:1, III:4 and X of GATT; Articles 1.2, 1.3 and 3.2 of the Licensing Agreement; Articles 2 and 5 of the TRIM's Agreement; Article 4.2 of the Agreement on Agriculture; and Articles II and XVII of GATS.

Guatemala and Honduras:

- concerning tariff issues: Articles I:1 and II of GATT;
- concerning allocation issues: Articles I:1 and XIII of GATT; and
- concerning the import licensing regime: Articles I:1, III:4, X and XIII of GATT; Articles 1.3 and 3.2 of the Licensing Agreement; and Articles 2 and 5 of the TRIM's Agreement;

Mexico:

- concerning tariff issues: Article I:1 of GATT;
- concerning allocation issues: Article XIII of GATT; and
- concerning the import licensing regime: Articles I:1, III:4, X and XIII of GATT; Articles 1.2, 1.3, 3.2 and 3.5 of the Licensing Agreement; Article 2 of the TRIM's Agreement; and Articles II and XVII of GATS.

United States:

- concerning tariff issues: Article I:1 of GATT;
- concerning allocation issues: Article XIII of GATT; and
- concerning the import licensing regime: Articles I:1, III:4 and X of GATT; Articles 1.3, 3.2 and 3.5 of the Licensing Agreement; Articles 2 and 5 of the TRIM's Agreement; and Articles II and XVII of GATS.

4.3 Following the first submissions, the Complaining parties generally made joint statements and submissions to the Panel, including a joint rebuttal submission and joint responses to questions posed by the Panel. In their joint statements and submissions, they cited the following aspects of the EC's measures applying to bananas as being inconsistent with the following provisions and Agreements:

- concerning tariff issues: Article I:1 of the GATT;
- concerning allocation issues: Article XIII of the GATT; and
- concerning the import licensing regime: Articles I, III, X, XI and XIII of the GATT; Articles 1.3, 3.2 and 3.5 of the Licensing Agreement; Article 2 of the TRIM's Agreement; and Articles II and XVII of GATS.

4.4 The EC requested the Panel to find that the EC banana regime was not incompatible with the General Agreement on Tariffs and Trade and other instruments of Annex 1A of the WTO Agreement. In so far as the

Panel might arrive at the opposite conclusion, the EC submitted that the Panel should find that the EC banana regime was covered by the Lomé waiver. The EC further submitted that the EC banana regime was not incompatible with the General Agreement on Trade in Services.

B. Trade in Goods

4.5 This part begins with a general overview of the claims presented by the Complaining parties and the responses of the European Communities. It is not intended to be a detailed or exhaustive presentation, but to provide a clear picture of the structure of the arguments at a broad level. In this regard it highlights the three major areas focused on by the Complaining parties and includes a number of horizontal issues raised by the EC. In order to provide a format for the many detailed claims, a measure-by-measure approach has then been taken addressing the detailed arguments concerning trade in goods under three major headings: tariff issues, allocation issues and licensing issues. Within these general headings, arguments by the Complaining parties and the EC are broken down into more specific sub-headings with the appropriate references made to horizontal issues at each stage.

1. General overview of the case

a) Overview of the claims presented by the Complaining Parties

4.6 The Complaining parties presented their claims within three broad headings: (i) tariff issues; (ii) allocation issues; and (iii) import licensing issues. Additional specific claims were presented in all areas as set out in the section which follows the overview. The responses of the Complaining parties with respect to the more horizontal arguments submitted by the EC in reply to the Complaining parties initial claims are also given in the section dealing with the detailed arguments.

(i) tariff issues

4.7 With respect to issues concerning the tariffs applied to the importation of bananas by the EC, the Complaining parties submitted that the tariff quota's tariff structure was challengeable because it imposed differential rates as between third-country bananas on the one hand, and non-traditional ACP bananas on the other. The application of such differential customs duties on the basis of foreign source contradicted in a direct way the GATT's most fundamental guarantee of "non-discriminatory tariff treatment" set forth in Article I:1.

4.8 In addition, Guatemala and Honduras claimed that the rates applicable to third-country bananas breached the long-standing EC's GATT-bound tariff of 20 per cent ad valorem for the product, to which Guatemala continued to hold a claim.

(ii) allocation issues

4.9 The Complaining parties submitted that the EC had allocated shares to its market among supplying countries in a manner inconsistent with GATT Article XIII:2. It provided country-specific allocations to some countries (ACP and BFA signatories), while not providing them to others with similar or greater historical levels of trade. Furthermore, in their view most of the allocations provided to those favoured countries greatly exceeded the shares of trade they would be expected to obtain in the absence of restrictions as set out in the chapeau to Article XIII:2. The Complaining parties considered that the EC also disregarded the principles of Article XIII when it provided the BFA signatories the exclusive right to increase their access when other BFA countries experienced a shortfall in the quantity they could supply to the EC.

4.10 In addition, Guatemala and Honduras submitted that the banana regime's differential volume restrictions by source fell within the prohibition of Article XIII:1 of GATT and, in so far as the system conferred market advantages to some foreign sources over others, it was a violation of Article I:1. Mexico and Ecuador submitted that the differential treatment did not "similarly prohibit or restrict" imports of third-country bananas and therefore was not consistent with Article XIII:1.

(iii) import licensing issues

4.11 The Complaining parties argued that the EC regulations imposed on imports from Latin America, a licensing scheme that was highly complex. The system, both in its totality and in its individual elements, created highly unfavourable conditions of competition compared to the simple arrangements for traditional ACP bananas. Unnecessarily burdensome, discriminatory, trade-restrictive and trade-distortive, the licensing regime implicated both the basic provisions of the GATT and the newer Uruguay Round disciplines pertaining specifically to licensing procedures and trade-related investment measures, in the view of the Complaining parties. The implementation of the scheme, including the number of implementing regulations issued, administrative procedures such as the two-round procedure used to allocate licences, and the delays in the issuance of import licences, was not, in their view, consistent with the provisions of the GATT and certain aspects of the Licensing Agreement.

4.12 Within the import licensing system, the Complaining parties argued that the core of the import licensing system, i.e. the Category B operator criteria, was discriminatory under, *inter alia*, Articles I and III of GATT and also in conflict with the Agreement on Trade-Related Investment Measures. Thirty per cent of the in-quota quantity for the tariff quota was allocated to companies, known as Category B operators, on the basis of three previous years' marketings of EC bananas and imports of ACP bananas. The exemption from export certificate requirements and the exclusive receipt of hurricane licences provided additional advantages to Category B operators. Export certificates also constituted violations of non-discrimination and neutrality requirements in their own right.

4.13 Furthermore, the Complaining parties submitted that the activity function rule, under which 43 per cent of the licences were distributed to parties other than primary importers, and the manner in which the rule was administered, additionally burdened and discriminated against imports from Latin America. By its nature, it increased transaction costs because it distributed licences to parties that did not previously import and who did not have the capacity to do so. The actual importers (those who were engaged in procuring the bananas from overseas) had to link up with particular ripeners or customs clearers or even invest in ripening facilities, in order not to lose a portion of their entitlement to import in the following year.

4.14 In addition, Ecuador argued that the EC import licensing regime was inconsistent with Article 4.2 of the Agreement on Agriculture because various features of it involved discretionary import licensing which was not permitted by that Article.

b) Overview of the responses presented by the European Communities

4.15 In addition to responding to specific claims (often on a subsidiary basis), the EC responded with several broad arguments of principle, or horizontal arguments. These arguments covered, in most cases, a number of specific claims set out by the Complaining parties. The relevant arguments included: (i) the presence of two separate banana access regimes; (ii) GATT schedules and Articles I and XIII in the context of the Agreement on Agriculture; (iii) the non-applicability of the Agreement on Import Licensing Procedures to tariff quotas; and (iv) the non-applicability of Articles III:4 and X of GATT to border measures. In addition, in so far as the Panel found that any aspects of the EC banana regime were incompatible with GATT and other agreements specified by the Complaining parties, the EC argued the Panel should find that the banana regime was covered by the Lomé waiver. The details of these horizontal arguments, along with related arguments by the Complaining parties, are provided in the section containing detailed arguments which follows the overview.

(i) separate regimes

4.16 The EC argued that the external aspects of the EC common organization of the markets for bananas consisted of two distinct regimes:

(a) the regime for so-called traditional ACP bananas which should be treated in accordance with the Lomé Convention and be given preferential treatment. This regime was now covered by the waiver from the obligations of the European Communities under paragraph 1 of Article I of GATT with respect to the Fourth ACP - CEE Convention of Lomé; and

(b) a bound rate of duty for imports in excess of tariff quota quantities and a tariff quota allocation for all other bananas. This was, in the view of the EC, a normal tariff quota as exists for many agricultural products in many Members.

With respect to (b), non-traditional ACP bananas benefited from preferential treatment which, in the EC's view, was covered, as the traditional ACP regime, by the Lomé waiver.

4.17 Given the two separate external regimes for bananas, in the view of the EC no discrimination (and consequent violation) could be alleged against the country allocation within the tariff quota contained in the EC Schedule as compared to the traditional ACP allocation. Article XIII of GATT was relevant and applicable only in so far as one specific quota or tariff quota was considered, and specifically its administration. No argument could be made under Article XIII, in particular Article XIII:1, alleging discrimination in the administration of two different regimes, which were independent one from the other and each legally justified on a different basis. Likewise, any comparison between the licensing system for traditional ACP bananas and the tariff quota licensing system for all other bananas had no legal value and was not relevant. The EC argued that it was evident that the fact that the two separate and independent regimes had marginal differences in their respective licensing systems was not a violation of any GATT provision.

4.18 In the view of the EC, the conclusion that Article XIII could not be applied simultaneously to the two different and separate parts of the EC banana regime, was confirmed by the interpretation of the scope of Articles I and XIII of GATT 1994. While both Articles contained a general principle of non-discrimination with regards to the importation or the exportation of like products originating in all third countries, the evidence did not imply that the two provisions overlapped. Article XIII was concerned only with the administration of each of the parts of the regime, and, in particular, all the border measures related to the importation or exportation of the products subject to a specific quota. In the view of the EC, this implied that, in GATT terms, comparing, under the authority of Article XIII, the internal licensing requirements within the ACP traditional allocation to the requirements of the tariff quota bound in the EC Schedule was legally wrong.

(ii) GATT schedules and Articles I and XIII in the context of the Agreement on Agriculture

4.19 The EC submitted that as bananas were an agricultural product, the tariff and tariff quota on bananas were consolidations under the Agreement on Agriculture. Even though the old consolidated tariff of the EC for bananas was de-consolidated and negotiations begun under Article XXVIII of GATT 1947 with the countries which were (then) countries with initial negotiating rights or with a principal supplying interest, in the end the tariff and tariff quota were consolidated in the framework of the Uruguay Round. The EC argued that the consolidation and scheduling of concessions and commitments in the agricultural sector followed its own dynamic and its own rules during the Uruguay Round and this led, for instance, to the widespread recourse to tariff quotas in tariff scheduling; many of these tariff quotas being country-specific, i.e. they listed a limited number of countries to which they applied and for which certain quantities were reserved, while what was left was allocated to an "others" category.

4.20 In the EC view, the specificity of the agricultural market access concessions was implicitly recognized in Article 4 of the Agreement on Agriculture, where the existence of market access concessions in this economic sector was specifically recorded and a special reference was made in its paragraph 1 to schedules. This gave these schedules a particular status which was all the more important if one also drew Article 21 of the Agreement on Agriculture into the analysis which confirmed the "agricultural specificity" in its clearest form and demonstrated that the rules of the Agreement on Agriculture, including the Schedules specifically referred to in Article 4.1, superseded, if necessary, the provisions of GATT 1994 and any agreement in Annex IA of the WTO Agreement.

4.21 Moreover, the EC considered that, as Article II:7 of GATT 1994 clearly indicated, the EC banana concession was an integral part of Part I of the GATT and was, therefore, to be considered an integral part of Article I and Article II as appropriate. This was the acknowledgement of the fact that concessions were the result of multilateral negotiations after a sometimes long and difficult give-and-take process. The parties solemnly accepted, by explicit and binding agreement duly reflected by internal ratification or approval procedures, the content of the schedules mutually exchanged but only if and when they considered that, as a whole, the give-and-take process was satisfactory or, at least, acceptable for them. This entailed the consequence that any application of the MFN principle set out in Article I could not prevail *per se* on the terms and conditions of a concession since this would mean giving priority to one part of Article I on top of other parts of the same Article as supplemented by the concessions.

4.22 In the specific case of the EC banana concession, the EC argued that the CONTRACTING PARTIES had agreed for the first time at the end of the Uruguay Round to the EC new banana regime based on the establishment of the EC tariff quota after the de-consolidation of the old and obsolete 20 per cent ad valorem bound rate and the creation of the EC-wide internal banana market. All the parties had agreed explicitly, knowingly and deliberately to this new concession: nothing could subsequently justify any Member reopening the negotiations by contesting the internal balance of the negotiation that had recently ended. In the EC view, this would be violating the fundamental principle "*pacta servanda sunt*" as expressed in the Vienna Convention on the law of the Treaties and the customary international law.

4.23 The provision of Article I of GATT thus could not be considered applicable as such to the actual content of the EC banana tariff quota without taking into account the results of the Uruguay Round negotiations. Members had negotiated their commitments on bananas during the Uruguay Round in the framework of the agreed "agricultural specificity" and, therefore, no violation of Article XIII of GATT could be claimed with respect to the consolidated EC banana regime.

(iii) the non-applicability of the Agreement on Import Licensing Procedures to tariff quotas

4.24 The EC submitted the opinion that, as far the Agreement on Import Licensing Procedures (Licensing Agreement) was concerned, the text specified that its scope was to regulate all the procedures, others than customs operations, prior to the importation. The provisions of that agreement appeared then as further specifications of some of the rules contained in Article XIII of GATT in which, *inter alia*, explicit reference was made "to import licences issued in connection with import restrictions." However, nothing in the Licensing Agreement specified (like Article XIII:5 of GATT) that it applied also to cases, such as the banana tariff quota, where no import restriction was applied at the border. In the view of the EC, the Licensing Agreement could not, therefore, be deemed applicable to cases where no import restriction was applied at the border and, specifically, the banana tariff quota.

4.25 Furthermore, the EC argued that the existence of the licence could not be confused with the physical importation of bananas: the licences were only needed to benefit from a particular duty rate within the tariff quota, but not to physically import bananas, from any origin, into the EC customs territory. Licences were tradable, and traded, and were not a "prior condition" to any importation as referred to in Article 1.1 of the Licensing

Agreement; they were needed only for the application of a specific duty rate. The fact that no limitation in quantities existed under the GATT-bound commitments was of paramount importance and, in the view of the EC should be sufficient to dismiss the applicability of the Licensing Agreement to tariff quotas.

(iv) The non-applicability of Articles III:4 and X of GATT to border measures

4.26 The EC submitted that the banana tariff quota was a set of border measures ensuring the correct management of the regime, and not a set of rules applicable to bananas after they had cleared customs. In the view of the EC, practically all measures concerning the functioning and the administration of the tariff quota which concerned operators while importing bananas into the EC market were border measures and not internal rules applicable to all bananas after they had been introduced in the EC market. This simple and undisputable reality had an important legal implication when applying GATT: the internal sale and distribution system pertained to the internal rules applicable to that market and was relevant to the imported goods only if and when those goods had cleared customs.

4.27 On the contrary, provisions like Articles XI and XIII of GATT and the Licensing Agreement clearly applied only to border measures at the moment of the importation or the exportation of a product and did not concern any alleged discrimination in the application of internal measures after the product had been cleared through customs. Consequently, the EC argued, it was impossible to allege that a specific measure violated at the same time Articles III:4 and X of GATT and Article XIII of GATT and/or the Licensing Agreement.

(v) The Lomé waiver

4.28 On the basis of the responses outlined above and specific arguments made by the EC, the EC requested the Panel to find that the EC banana regime was not incompatible with GATT and other instruments of Annex 1A of the WTO Agreement. In so far as the Panel might arrive at the opposite conclusion, the EC argued that the Panel should find that the EC banana regime was covered by the Lomé waiver. The EC submitted that the Lomé Convention was one of the most important instruments of the EC's policy of development cooperation and as such was intended to "promote and expedite the economic, cultural and social development of the ACP States". The Convention covered various fields of cooperation, one of the most important being trade. Various provisions of the Convention dealt directly with trade and, all these provisions, aims and objectives applied equally to trade in bananas. Moreover, the Convention also included a Protocol which covered bananas specifically and stated, *inter alia,* that "no ACP State shall be placed, as regards access to its traditional markets and its advantages on those markets, in a less favourable situation than in the past or at present." On 19 December 1994, the GATT Council, at the request of the EC, decided that "Subject to the terms and conditions set out ..., the provisions of paragraph 1 of Article I of the General Agreement shall be waived, until 29 February 2000, to the extent necessary to permit the European Communities to provide preferential treatment for products originating in ACP States as required by the relevant provisions of the Fourth Lomé Convention, without being required to extend the same preferential treatment to like products of any other contracting party."

4.29 In the view of the EC, in analysing the waiver the following elements had to be taken into account:

(a) the Lomé waiver clearly stated that the provisions of paragraph 1 of Article I of GATT shall be waived to the extent necessary to permit the EC to provide preferential treatment for products originating in ACP States; and

(b) in the second part of paragraph 1 of the waiver, the GATT Council had indicated that the preferential treatment to be accorded by the EC was limited to what was required by the relevant provisions of the Fourth Lomé Convention.

The EC submitted that by the first part of paragraph 1 of the waiver, the CONTRACTING PARTIES had accepted the principle that the EC should be put in the position of fully respecting its obligations vis-à-vis ACP countries to provide the preferential treatment for products, including bananas, originating in those countries. According to the waiver, the preferential treatment was "designed to promote the expansion of trade and economic development of beneficiaries in a manner consistent with the objectives of the General Agreement and with the trade, financial and development needs of the beneficiaries" while not raising "undue barriers" or creating "undue difficulties for the trade of the other contracting parties." The EC argued that, as a consequence, any measure necessary to permit it to fulfil its obligations under the Lomé Convention to provide a preferential treatment to ACP countries for products originating in those countries was covered by the waiver.

4.30 Furthermore, the EC submitted that the parties to the Lomé Convention understood their agreement as implying that the EC was subject to the obligations of: (a) contributing to remedy the instability in the revenues flowing from the marketing of ACP agricultural products by promoting trade between those parties and by taking measures ensuring a treatment more favourable than the one accorded to other countries benefiting of the MFN treatment for the product concerned; and (b) ensuring that no ACP States shall be placed, as regards access to its traditional banana markets and its advantages on those markets, in a less favourable situation than in the past or at present. The Lomé waiver, therefore, covered any measure taken by the EC in order to fulfil its legal obligations as indicated under the Lomé Convention with regards to any product originating in ACP countries, including bananas. In the case of bananas, the legal obligations were fulfilled by the EC by: (a) creating a specific and separate regime for the importation to the EC market of the ACP traditional banana production; (b) by the allocation to ACP countries of a limited share of the bound tariff quota at a duty-free rate, that was lower that the MFN bound rate; (c) by a marginal reduction of the tariff rate applicable for the importation of bananas outside the tariff quota; and (d) by facilitating trade and commercial relations between the EC and the ACP countries through the creation of the so-called Category B operator licences to ensure that the quantities for which access opportunities were given could actually be sold and that the EC could thus fulfil its obligations to guarantee traditional ACP bananas their existing advantages, while not providing by this mean any incentive to purchase ACP bananas.

4.31 The EC also argued that the Panel was not empowered to give authoritative interpretation on any agreement other than those under the agreements covered by the Uruguay Round of multilateral trade negotiations as relevant for the settlement of the dispute within the terms of reference agreed by the DSB in its meeting of the 8 May 1996. In particular it could not interpret the extent of reciprocal obligations under an agreement especially any interpretation that contradicted the common understanding of the contracting parties to that agreement.

2. *Detailed arguments*

a) Tariff issues

4.32 This section outlines the case concerning issues involving tariff matters. After a presentation of the claims of the Complaining parties, the responses of the EC are outlined. As such, this section contains the major arguments, including background and general interpretative issues, of the EC and the Complaining parties surrounding the Lomé waiver, which was the main argument presented by the EC in response to the claims of the Complaining parties. Further arguments concerning the Lomé waiver also appear in the following sections: (b) allocation issues; and (c) import licensing issues, although in these cases, the basic arguments presented in this section are not repeated in detail.

4.33 The Complaining parties submitted that the tariff quota tariff structures arising out of Regulation 404/93 were challengeable in that those structures imposed differential rates as between third-country bananas, on the one hand, and non-traditional ACP bananas, on the other. In addition, Guatemala and Honduras submitted that the rates applicable to third-country bananas breached the long-standing 20 per cent ad valorem EC GATT-bound rate, to which Guatemala continued to hold a claim.

(i) tariff preferences for non-traditional ACP banana imports

(a) arguments of the Complaining Parties

4.34 The Complaining parties argued that the EC granted preferential treatment to so-called non-traditional ACP bananas, which designation had come to mean not only countries that had not been traditional suppliers, but amounts for traditional suppliers over and beyond the excessive quantities already allocated to them. Within the tariff quota for third countries, 90,000 tonnes of non-traditional ACP bananas entered duty free, while third-country bananas were dutied at the rate of ECU 75 per tonne. Over-quota, non-traditional ACP bananas received a ECU 100 per tonne reduction below the MFN rate applied to Latin American bananas. The Complaining parties considered that this differential treatment was a violation of the most-favoured-nation obligation treatment and therefore, in their opinion, was inconsistent with Article I of the GATT.

4.35 Guatemala and Honduras submitted that the preferential tariffs for non-traditional ACP bananas were not included in the EC's Uruguay Round Schedules or other parts of the Uruguay Round Agreements. The application of such differential customs duties on the basis of foreign source contradicted in a direct way the GATT's most fundamental guarantee of tariff non-discrimination set forth in Article I:1. Guatemala and Honduras argued that GATT panels had strictly construed this tariff non-discrimination requirement, disallowing exceptions to be read into it that were never negotiated or agreed to by the contracting parties. In *Spain - Tariff Treatment of Unroasted Coffee*, the panel ruled that differences in the entered product arising from geographical or other factors could not be considered a basis for avoiding Article I obligations.[62] In *EEC - Member States' Import Regimes for Bananas*, the panel further found that the trade impact of discriminatory tariff rates was irrelevant to an Article I:1 violation.[63] In both that banana case and the subsequent one involving bananas, the panels condemned preferential tariff rates accorded ACP bananas under Article I:1.[64] According to Guatemala and Honduras, the EC ignored that legal standard by conferring a trade advantage on non-traditional ACP bananas over third-country bananas "in order to ensure satisfactory marketing of bananas ... originating in the ACP States."[65] Admitted tariff discrimination had thus occurred, for which no legitimate WTO defence could be shown.

(b) arguments of the EC

4.36 The EC submitted it was clear that non-traditional ACP bananas had been allocated a consolidated share of the tariff quota up to 90,000 tonnes. However, non-traditional ACP bananas benefited from a preferential treatment which was covered, just as the ACP traditional allocation, by the Lomé waiver, consisting in duty-free importation for the quantities indicated in the tariff quota. Moreover, non-traditional ACP bananas benefited from a preferential treatment of ECU 100 per tonne reduction from the bound rate for imports outside the tariff quota. This preferential treatment was equally covered by the Lomé waiver.

---

[62] BISD 28S/102, para. 4.4 (adopted 11 June 1981); see also "EEC - Member States' Import Regimes for Bananas", DS32/R, paras. 211, 375 (issued May 1993).

[63] DS32/R, paras. 214, 364-375 (issued 3 June 1993) (wherein the panel gave no weight to Respondent's argument that the 20 per cent ad valorem tariff discrimination among suppliers could not be considered discriminatory because the rate had no trade effect). See also "United States - Taxes on Petroleum and Certain Imported Substances", BISD 34S/136 (adopted 17 June 1987) (wherein the panel rejected an analogous argument by the United States that its discriminatory taxes and tax differential were *de minimis*, and therefore did not nullify or impair benefits under the General Agreement).

[64] "EEC - Member States' Import Regimes for Bananas", DS32/R, para. 375 (issued 3 June 1993); "EEC - Import Regime for Bananas", DS38/R, para. 155 (issued 11 February 1994).

[65] Council Regulation (EEC) No. 404/93, recital fifteen.

(c) the Lomé waiver

- Background on the Convention

4.37 The EC submitted that the Lomé IV Convention was an extremely broad treaty between the EC and its member States on the one hand and 70 States of Africa, the Caribbean and the Pacific (ACP States) on the other hand. It was one of the most important instruments of the EC's policy of development co-operation and as such was intended to "promote and expedite the economic, cultural and social development of the ACP States" (Article 1 of the Convention). The Convention had existed in one form or another since the moment that many of these countries became independent from one of the member States of the Community in the early 1960s, and there was the need for the replacement of the Association regime for overseas territories as laid down in Article 131 of the EC Treaty. Originally called the Yaoundé Convention, the treaty had evolved through many versions following the latest insights of development policy into the present instrument for development cooperation, including provisions on free trade, accompanied by many variegated cooperation provisions, a stabilization system for agricultural commodities ("Stabex"[66]), a special financing system for countries which were very dependent on mining activities ("Sysmin"), as well as a development fund ("EDF") of considerable size.

4.38 Among the various fields covered by the Convention, the EC considered that trade was certainly among the most important. Especially with respect to the trade issues involved in the present case, the EC referred to the following provisions of the Convention:

> Article 15(a) of the Convention:
>
> trade development shall be aimed at developing, diversifying and increasing the ACP States' trade and improving their competitiveness.... The Contracting Parties undertake to use all the means available under this Convention, including trade cooperation, financial and technical cooperation for the achievement of this objective.

Title I on Trade Cooperation stated further in Article 167, which was one of the instruments of trade development:

> In the field of trade cooperation, the object of this Convention is to promote trade between the ACP States and the Community,

and continued with:

> In pursuit of this objective, particular regard shall be had to securing effective additional advantages for ACP States' trade with the Community, and to improving the conditions of access for their products to the market in order to accelerate the growth of their trade and, in particular, of the flow of exports to the Community.

All these provisions, aims and objectives applied equally to trade in bananas.

[66] Stabex could be applied for a shortfall in income from banana exports to the Community (Article 187). Because Stabex resources were finite and many products were covered by it, in reality it could not, and was not intended to, fully compensate for such shortfalls. It aimed at stabilization instead of compensation. It provided a temporary cushion in case shortfalls were very abrupt.

4.39 Moreover, attached to the Lomé Convention was Protocol 5 on bananas. Under this Protocol, the EC had made another undertaking (in Article 1) to ensure that:

> In respect of its banana exports to the Community markets, no ACP State shall be placed as regards access to its traditional markets and its advantages on those markets, in a less favourable situation than in the past or at present.

Similar preferential treatment was granted to ACP bananas under the earlier Lomé Conventions and under the two Yaoundé Conventions, all of which had been notified to the relevant GATT bodies and examined by working parties.[67]

4.40 The EC noted that originally the free trade provisions of the Yaoundé Conventions were reciprocal; later, at the insistence of the ACP States themselves, as well as some third states, including the United States, they were made unilateral in favour of the ACP States. This was presently the case and this system of free trade in favour of the ACP States, with the exception of some primarily agricultural products (for which favourable tariff quotas were opened) was laid down in Article 168 of the Lomé Convention. This Article also stipulated that even for those products which were not subject to full free trade treatment by the Community, *inter alia*, because after the entry into force of the Convention they had been made subject to a common organization of the market under the common agricultural policy, a preference should be given to the ACP countries (Article 168(2)(a)(ii) together with 168(2)(d)). This was the case for bananas.

4.41 During the negotiations of the Lomé Convention, the EC single market programme was already under way and it could be foreseen that this would have some repercussions on the way in which the Banana Protocol was going to be applied. Hence a Joint Declaration relating to Protocol 5 was agreed and included in Annex LXXIV to the Lomé Convention. According to this interpretative declaration, the Community was not prevented by Article 1 of Protocol 5 from establishing common rules for bananas, as long as no ACP State which was traditional supplier to the Community, was placed as regards access to and advantages in the Community, in a less favourable situation than in the past or at the time of conclusion of the Lomé Convention. This interpretative declaration, while leaving the liberty to the Community to unify the heterogeneous national rules which were in place at the time when the Lomé Convention was concluded, put an obligation on the Community to preserve the pre-existing situation as far as access to and advantages in the Community market for traditional ACP bananas were concerned.[68]

- <u>Background on the waiver</u>

4.42 The EC further noted that in the autumn of 1994 it took the initiative to obtain a waiver for the Fourth Lomé Convention. Although the Community disagreed thoroughly with the report of the so-called second *Banana* panel and could not accept that the Lomé Convention did not respond to the criteria of Article XXIV, it nevertheless availed itself the possibility to obtain such a waiver. This was in the interest of legal security both for the Community and for its partners in the Lomé Convention. The most important provision of the waiver (L/7604), point 1, was as follows:

> Subject to the terms and conditions set out hereunder, the provisions of paragraph 1 of Article I of the General Agreement shall be waived, until 29 February 2000, to the extent necessary to permit the European Communities to provide preferential treatment for products originating in ACP States as required by the relevant provisions of the Fourth Lomé Convention, without

---

[67] Yaoundé I: BISD 14S/22 and 100; Yaoundé II: BISD 18S/1333; Lomé I: BISD 23S/46; Lomé II: BISD 29S/119; Lomé III: BISD 35S/321.

[68] The Community made a declaration, contained in Annex LXXV to the Lomé IV Convention to the effect that the new ACP States party to the Convention (i.e. Haiti and the Dominican Republic) were not considered as traditional suppliers.

being required to extend the same preferential treatment to like products of any other contracting party.

4.43 The EC argued that the Lomé waiver was of great importance in permitting the Community to give preferential treatment pursuant to the provisions of the Convention, and the Banana Protocol in particular. In this way the partners to the Convention could pursue their development strategy with the minimum legal security and continuity that was absolutely required. There could be no doubt that for bananas the relevant provisions of the Lomé Convention were such Articles as 15a, 168 and the Banana Protocol as interpreted by the declaration contained in Annex LXXIV. The preferential treatment contained in these provisions was not merely restricted to simple tariff preferences, but extended to advantages on the market.

4.44 In reaching this position, the EC submitted that the following elements should be taken into account. Firstly, the Lomé waiver clearly stated that the provisions of paragraph 1 of Article I of GATT shall be waived to the extent necessary to permit the EC to provide preferential treatment for products originating in ACP States. By this first part of paragraph 1 of the waiver, the CONTRACTING PARTIES accepted the principle that the EC should be put in the position of fully respecting its obligations, vis-à-vis ACP countries, to provide the preferential treatment for products originating in those countries. Bananas were products originating in those countries. Further, the preferential treatment, waived from the application of Article I:1 of GATT, was "... designed to promote the expansion of trade and economic development of beneficiaries in a manner consistent with the objectives of the General Agreement and with the trade, financial and development needs of the beneficiaries..." while not raising "undue barriers" or creating "undue difficulties for the trade of the other contracting parties." Consequently, in the view of the EC, any measure necessary to permit it to fulfil its obligations under the Lomé Convention to provide preferential treatment to ACP countries for products originating in those countries was covered by the waiver.

4.45 The EC submitted that the second element to be taken into account related to the second part of paragraph 1 of the waiver. The GATT Council, had indicated that the preferential treatment to be accorded by the EC within the limits explained above was limited to what was required by the relevant provisions of the Lomé Convention. The relevant provisions of the Lomé Convention as regards bananas were, *inter alia*, Articles 15a, 24, 168 and Protocol 5.

4.46 Before the entry into force of the common organization of the markets (COM) for bananas, ACP bananas entered the Community duty free under Article 168(2)(a)(i) of the Lomé Convention. These traditional quantities were therefore to be marketed enjoying the same advantages on the Community market as "in the past or at present", as guaranteed in Protocol 5, they had to therefore, in the view of the EC, continue to enjoy duty-free access. As regards non-traditional quantities, the EC submitted that since the entry into force of the COM, these fell under the scope of Article 168(2)(a)(ii) which stated: "the Community shall take the necessary measures to ensure more favourable treatment than that granted to third countries benefiting from the most-favoured-nation clause for the same products". Moreover, Article 168(2)(d) first indent stated: "if during application of the Convention, the Community subjects one or more products to common organisation of the market, [which is the case for bananas] it shall reserve the right to adapt the import treatment for those products originating in the ACP States, following consultations within the Council of Ministers".

4.47 When the common organization of the markets for bananas was set up, the Council of Ministers, in accordance with the above provision, decided that non-traditional ACP quantities would enjoy duty-free access (Article 18.1 of Council Regulation 404/93) within the tariff quota, thus ensuring that they were treated more favourably than other third-country supplies which were subject to a duty of ECU 75 per tonne. Outside the tariff quota, more favourable treatment was also ensured as non-traditional ACP imports were subject, in 1995, to a duty rate of ECU 722 per tonne as opposed to ECU 822 per tonne for other third-country supplies.

4.48 In summary, the EC submitted that the Parties to the Lomé Convention understood their agreement as implying that the EC was subject to the obligations of: (a) contributing to remedy the instability in the revenues flowing from the marketing of ACP agricultural products by promoting trade between those parties and by taking measures ensuring a treatment more favourable than the one accorded to other countries benefiting of the MFN treatment for the product concerned; and (b) ensuring that no ACP States shall be placed, as regards access to its traditional banana markets and its advantages on those markets, in a less favourable situation than in the past or at present. The EC argued, therefore, that the Lomé waiver should be deemed to cover any measure taken by the EC in order to fulfil its legal obligations as indicated under the Lomé Convention with regards to any product originating in ACP countries, including bananas.

4.49 The EC argued that the legal obligations it set out were fulfilled by: (a) creating a specific and separate system for the importation in the EC market of the ACP traditional banana production; (b) by the allocation to ACP countries of a limited share of the bound tariff quota at a duty free rate, that is lower that the MFN bound rate; (c) by a marginal reduction of the tariff rate applicable for the importation of bananas outside the tariff quota; (d) by facilitating trade and commercial relations between the EC and the ACP countries through the creation of the so-called Category B operator licences so as to ensure that the quantities for which access opportunities were given could actually be sold and that the EC could thus fulfil its obligations to guarantee traditional ACP bananas their existing advantages, while not providing by this mean any incentive to purchase ACP bananas.

4.50 The EC went on to remind the Panel that the scope of the present procedure was to consider the extent of the reciprocal obligations for the Members, parties to this procedure, under the Agreements covered by the Uruguay Round of Multilateral Trade Negotiations as relevant for the settlement of the dispute within the terms of reference agreed by the DSB in its meeting of 8 May 1996. On the contrary, the Panel was not empowered, in the EC view, to give authoritative interpretation on any other agreement, in particular regarding the extent of the reciprocal obligations under an agreement for the contracting parties to that agreement, let alone any interpretation contradicting the common understanding of the contracting parties to that agreement of their own reciprocal obligations.

4.51 In the view of the Complaining parties, not one measure at issue in the action fell within the narrow parameters of the Lomé waiver. The Lomé waiver accordingly was not a defence for the measures that were the subject of this dispute that were inconsistent with Article I of GATT.

4.52 The Complaining parties argued that the waiver only applied to violations of Article I "to the extent necessary to permit the EC to provide preferential treatment" to ACP products "as required by the relevant provisions" of the Lomé Convention. The waiver did not apply to all measures that the EC might adopt under the Lomé Convention's objectives. In their view, the Lomé Convention left the EC with broad discretion permitting it to comply with its WTO obligations as it sought to develop common rules for bananas. In order to determine whether an EC measure which might violate Article I was covered by the waiver, the Panel had therefore to reach a conclusion that such a measure was "required" by the Lomé Convention.

4.53 The Complaining parties submitted that the EC had attempted to portray this dispute as being "all about" the EC's need to meet its obligations under the Lomé Convention. The EC was subject to numerous requirements under the Lomé Convention, many of which involved direct assistance and development.[69] However, the Convention did not, according to the Complaining parties, cover non-traditional ACP bananas at all, did not require the kind of licensing arrangements applied to Latin American bananas, did not "guarantee" any specific level of imports from ACP countries, and was therefore not covered by the GATT waiver obtained in 1994 for violations of GATT Article I "required" by the relevant provisions of the Convention. Moreover, the EC provided trade

[69] See Article 186, guaranteeing export earnings under Stabex and the Financial Protocol, which required specific amounts of EC aid to be earmarked for regional projects and emergency assistance.

preferences with respect to a broad variety of exports, but had not seen fit to impose the kinds of licensing requirements in its MFN trade with respect to those other products.

4.54 According to the Complaining parties, the EC had misidentified the provisions of the Lomé Convention that were covered by the waiver and ignored the long-standing GATT interpretive framework requiring the strict construction of waivers. Upon proper analysis, in the view of the Complaining parties, the Panel could only conclude that the EC's Lomé obligations with respect to trade in bananas did not require it to adopt the measures for banana imports that were the subject of this dispute. The Complaining parties submitted that GATT panels had consistently considered that waivers from GATT obligations were granted only in exceptional cases and should be construed narrowly within their explicit terms. In the *Sugar Headnote* case, for example, the panel noted that because waivers abrogated obligations under the basic rules of the GATT, they "are granted according to Article XXV:5 only in `exceptional circumstances'," and "their terms and conditions consequently have to be interpreted narrowly."[70] This approach was consistent with the approach of past panels in interpreting GATT exceptions.[71]

4.55 The Complaining parties further submitted that the Lomé waiver had been precisely and narrowly drawn up by the CONTRACTING PARTIES to waive only Article I:1[72], and only "to the extent necessary ... to provide preferential treatment for ... ACP States as required by the relevant provisions of the Fourth Lomé Convention."[73] In October 1994, the EC originally had requested a broader waiver, one that extended to "preferential treatment ... as foreseen by the relevant provisions of the Fourth Lomé Convention." The United States and Guatemala had insisted that the originally-proposed language be changed to "preferential treatment ... as required by the relevant provisions of the Fourth Lomé Convention."[74] The deletion of the term "foreseen" had clarified the intent to exclude from the Lomé waiver's coverage any measure based solely upon an "authorization" or "exhortation" in the Lomé Convention. The insertion of the term "as required" had further clarified that only those measures that were mandatory and legally binding under the Lomé Convention were to be protected by the waiver. This drafting correction, combined with the GATT principles of waiver interpretation, did not permit the Lomé waiver to cover EC legislation allegedly based on Lomé Convention objectives, authorizations and exhortations. These were not, in the opinion of the Complaining parties, "requirements" of the Lomé Convention. As also observed in the context of Article XIII of the GATT, the Lomé waiver's explicit application to Article I could not be read to extend directly or indirectly beyond Article I to include other GATT or WTO obligations. The waiver for the Lomé Convention was not drafted to take care of the banana problem; it applied to all products covered by the treaty. It could not be presumed, in disregard of its explicitly limited application to Article I, to legitimize all EC banana measures in force as of December 1994. This would be contrary to the drafting history of the Lomé waiver and GATT practice. As stated by the working party examining the United States *Section 22 waiver*:

> Since the [waiver] Decision refers to the provisions of Articles II and XI of the Agreement, it does not affect the obligations of the United States under any other provisions of the Agreement.

---

[70] See "United States - Restrictions on the Importation of Sugar and Sugar-Containing Products Applied under the 1955 Waiver and under the Headnote to the Schedule of Tariff Concessions", adopted 7 November 1990, BISD 37S/228, para. 5.9; see also, E/PC/T/C.V/PV/9, p.8.

[71] See "United States - Countervailing Duties on Fresh, Chilled and Frozen Pork from Canada", adopted 11 July 1991, BISD 38S/30, para. 4.4 (Article VI:3); "United States - Measures Affecting Alcoholic and Malt Beverages", adopted 19 June 1992, BISD 39S/206, para. *5.41* (Article XX(d)); "Canada - Import Restrictions on Ice Cream and Yoghurt", adopted 5 December 1989, BISD 36S/68, para. 59 (Article XI:2(c)).

[72] Working Parties have been careful in writing the text of waivers to ensure that the language covered only those measures for which the waiver was sought. See e.g. "United States - Caribbean Basin Economic Recovery Act", adopted 15 February 1985, BISD 31S/20, para. 1 (wherein the language of the waiver specifically limited it to duty-free treatment for products of Caribbean Basin countries benefiting from the CBI).

[73] Lomé waiver, para. 1.

[74] See Minutes of the CONTRACTING PARTIES, SR 50/1.

> In particular, as its obligations under Article XIII are not affected, the United States would acquire no right by virtue of this waiver to deviate from the rule of non-discrimination provided for in that Article.[75]

4.56 The Complaining parties were of the view that the deliberately chosen language of the Lomé waiver and established principles of waiver interpretation confirmed that the EC bore the full burden of demonstrating how its numerous discriminatory measures inconsistent with Article I:1 were legally "required" by the relevant provisions of the Lomé Convention. The Complaining parties considered that the EC had failed to meet that burden in all respects.

4.57 The EC reiterated that it requested the waiver on 10 October 1994 with the aim "to improve legal certainty for the trade of ACP countries." In response to a question by the Panel, the EC noted that while the word "foreseen" in the original request was replaced by "required", the change was not a substantial one since the word "foreseen" was supposed to describe exactly the same intention as "required". Both words covered the preferential treatment which had been mutually agreed between the parties to the Lomé Convention, ACP on the one side and EC on the other. Subject to minor modifications, the text approved by the CONTRACTING PARTIES corresponded to the one proposed by the EC. Indeed, during the procedure for approval under Article XXV, Guatemala asked for consultations in a letter dated 22 November 1994. Consultations were held the 30 November 1994 in the presence of a representative from Jamaica on behalf of the other ACP countries. During that meeting, Guatemala had asked for some amendments to the text, in particular: preferential treatment in paragraph 1 to be limited to "customs duties"; the word "unduly" in paragraph 3 to be deleted; and that the waiver not to cover fresh bananas. None of these suggestions were retained by the Contracting parties. In the EC view, this meant, *inter alia*, that no doubt whatsoever could be raised on the fact that the waiver covered preferential treatment resulting from measures taken by the EC other than customs duties and that it concerned fresh bananas.

4.58 In the EC view it was clear from the text of the waiver itself, that the Lomé waiver concerned "'preferential treatment' for products originating in ACP States as required by relevant provisions of the Fourth Lomé Convention...". The waiver did not refer to measures of any kind, let alone measures of mandatory nature which should be allegedly present in the Lomé Convention. As already stated, the EC and the ACP countries had undertaken a certain number of obligations. Among them, the EC considered it was bound: (i) to ensure that no ACP State shall be placed, as regards access to its traditional markets and its advantages on those markets, in a less favourable situation than in the past or at present (Protocol 5, Article 1); (ii) to ensure more favourable treatment than that granted to third countries benefiting from the most-favoured-nation clause for the same product (Article 168(2)(a)(ii)); (iii) to use all means available under the Convention, including trade cooperation and those on financial and technical cooperation, for the achievement of the objective of trade development aimed at developing, diversifying and increasing the ACP States' trade and improving their competitiveness (Article 15a); and (iv) to provide special arrangements for the EC import of certain ACP products in order to promote and diversify trade between the contracting parties (Article 24, second indent).

4.59 In the EC view, what the Lomé waiver was about was the possibility for the EC not to extend a particular preferential treatment, required by the Lomé Convention under the above mentioned provisions, to the other Members. What the Lomé waiver was not about was the examination of the possible violation of any WTO provision by the measures taken by the EC to fulfil its obligations under the Lomé Convention. There was therefore no reason why the Complaining parties (and the Panel) should examine the content of the single measures taken by the EC with respect to the waiver and Article I:1 of GATT 1994 and not their end result, the preferential treatment, which was the only matter that was covered by the waiver. Even less evident was the argument raised that the measures taken by the EC to fulfil its obligations under the Lomé Convention should be linked to any "mandate", "exhortation" or "authorization". The word "required" was grammatically and logically

[75]"Import Restrictions Imposed by the United States Under Section 22 of the United States Agricultural Adjustment Act", 5 March 1955, BISD 3S/141, para. 10.

linked to the words "to provide preferential treatment" in the Lomé waiver. The preferential treatment was therefore the central issue for the interpretation of the scope of the Lomé waiver: the Panel should verify if and when preferential treatment was required by the Lomé Convention and, according to this verification, if that preferential treatment should be extended on an MFN basis to the other Members in application of Article I:1 or be waived from this obligation. The means by which the preferential treatment was achieved was of no avail for Article I:1 and, accordingly, for the interpretation of the scope of the waiver. For this reason, any reference to EC secondary legislation was ill placed and not relevant in this context. The EC submitted that the Panel should consider only the treatment for ACP bananas which was the result of such legislation. Any different interpretation would radically change *a posteriori* the understanding among the CONTRACTING PARTIES on the scope of the waiver and undermine the legal certainty that was the paramount reason that convinced the EC to request it in the first place. The Lomé Convention allowed full discretion, therefore, as to which means (and specific measures) the EC used to fulfil its obligations, in order that the overall objectives were met.

4.60 Furthermore, the term "preferential treatment" were not a generic expression but the evidence of a specific will of the CONTRACTING PARTIES to waive that treatment from the obligations of Article I:1, irrespective of the measures taken by the EC to achieve it. Previous waivers of similar nature like *United States - Caribbean Basin Countries, United States - Andean Trade Preferences Act, United States - Imports of Automotive Products, Canada - Commonwealth Caribbean Countries* referred much more specifically to "... provide duty-free treatment" and not to "preferential treatment". The different wording underlined the extended scope of the waiver covering any preferential treatment required by the Lomé Convention. A precedent in the same line could be found in the waiver *United States - Former Trust Territory of the Pacific Islands*.

4.61 According to the EC, this interpretation was indisputable: the whole text of the waiver referred only to the preferential treatment. The EC referred in particular to the language in paragraph 5 where reference was made to a requirement for an "annual report on the implementation of the preferential treatment for products originating in ACP States", and paragraph 2 where an obligation was imposed upon the parties to the Lomé Convention to "promptly notify the contracting parties of any changes in the preferential treatment to products originating in ACP States". Thus, the object of the Panel's examination was, according to the EC, limited to the verification of two elements: (i) the existence of a provision in the Lomé Convention requiring that a preferential treatment be granted to bananas originating in ACP States; and (ii) that the preferential treatment accorded did not manifestly "raise undue barriers or create undue difficulties for the trade of other contracting parties" as indicated in the third considering clause of the preamble to the waiver.

4.62 The EC suggested that the Panel, having verified the existence of the obligations for the EC to grant a preferential treatment for the bananas originating in ACP countries, accept that treatment could not be extended to other Members unless evidence was submitted by the Complaining parties that undue barriers or undue trade difficulties were created for the bananas imported from those Complaining parties. According to the EC, this had never been shown by any of the Complaining parties. On the contrary, the legal and factual reality showed that while Latin American bananas entered the EC market making full use of the EC tariff quota - whose size was not affected at all by the existence of a completely separate regime for ACP traditional bananas - the ACP traditional bananas were not able to fill their quota under the ACP regime in spite of the preference granted to those countries by the EC.

4.63 The Complaining parties noted that past reports had considered that the party invoking an exception bore the burden of demonstrating that each measure inconsistent with the GATT met every condition of the exception.[76] Both the EC and the ACP countries had sought to avoid this rigorous examination by arguing that the Lomé

[76] "EEC - Restrictions on Imports of Dessert Apples - Complaint by Chile", adopted 22 June 1989, BISD 36S/93, and "EEC - Restrictions on Imports of Apples - Complaint by the United States", adopted 22 June 1989, BISD 36S/135, para. 12.3. See also "Canada - Administration of the Foreign Investment Review Act", para. *5.20*; "United States - Countervailing Duties on Fresh, Chilled and Frozen Pork from Canada", para. 4.4.

Convention could only be interpreted by its signatories. The second *Banana* panel had rejected a similar argument in the context of the Lomé Convention's consistency with GATT Article XXIV, finding that review of the Lomé Convention was required in order to determine the EC's obligations. The panel declared:

> If this view were endorsed, a mere communication of a contracting party invoking Article XXIV could deprive all other contracting parties of their procedural rights under Article XXIII:2, and therefore also of the effective protection of their substantive rights.[77]

4.64 The Complaining parties submitted that the DSB had conferred on this Panel broad terms of reference. Paragraph 6 of the Lomé waiver, read in combination with Article 3 of the *Understanding in Respect of Waivers of Obligations Under the General Agreement on Tariffs and Trade 1994*, further clarified that a Member could request a panel to review the consistency of any measure with the terms and conditions of the Lomé waiver. Article IX of the WTO Agreement further reflected the intent of the Members to limit the use of waivers by increasing the number of votes required to approve a waiver. Given the EC's claims that it was exempted from its Article I:1 obligations under the terms of the Lomé waiver for several measures at issue, the Panel had no choice but to review the conformity of all such measures in order to satisfy its terms of reference. Unless the Panel undertook such a review, only the parties to the Lomé Convention could determine the coverage of a WTO waiver, enabling them to deviate from general WTO rules and obligations as they saw fit and impinge on the procedural and substantive rights of other Members.

4.65 The Complaining parties thus contested the EC's right to preclude the Panel from deciding what was and what was not required or relevant under the Lomé Convention, by reserving for Lomé signatories an exclusive right to interpret the treaty. This view was plainly inconsistent with the nature of the Panel proceedings; if the waiver was conditioned on a particular application of the Lomé Convention's relevant provisions (and the waiver was clearly a relevant provision of the WTO), the Lomé Convention's relevant provisions effectively amended the EC's WTO obligations, and therefore, were obviously within the Panel's terms of reference. Just as domestic laws and regulations were routinely reviewed by GATT dispute settlement panels, the meaning of another agreement simply presented a question of fact for the Panel to determine. If the Panel were to accept the argument put forth by the EC, it would mean that the parties to the Lomé Convention could unilaterally determine the scope of coverage of a WTO waiver, while Members or any panel interpreting the WTO could not. This would be absurd in the Complaining parties view. The Complaining parties claimed that as an exception to the General Agreement, a waiver must be strictly construed and the party invoking the waiver bore the burden of showing that it applied. In this particular instance, the burden was heavy indeed, since the waiver was only for "required" violations. In the opinion of the Complaining parties, the waiver did not give the EC *carte blanche* to adopt any discriminatory banana measure that it considered consistent with the objectives of the Lomé Convention.

4.66 The EC returned to its opinion that the Panel was not empowered to provide an interpretation of an international agreement, on which it has no jurisdiction, which was different from the one upon which the parties to that international agreement agree. In the EC view, the situation was legally different from the one described by the Complaining parties. When Panels were requested to judge on an alleged violation of certain WTO rules by measures implemented by a Member which were adopted in application of domestic laws or regulations, those laws or regulations were an element of the violation itself and therefore should be taken into the picture. In the present case, on the contrary, the Lomé Convention was not an element of any alleged violation of any WTO provision. Moreover, with respect to the Complaining parties' argument, those laws or regulations concerned only one Member and not an agreed provision between two Members, or, between a Member and a non-member, as was also the case here. In the particular case, an agreed interpretation about the extent of reciprocal obligations - as the Vienna Convention stipulated in Article 31.3(a) and (b) and 31.4 - was an essential element of the correct interpretation (and implementation) of the content of the agreement. Contrary to the description provided by the Complaining parties, the Lomé waiver was concerned with preferential treatment accorded by the EC to products

[77] Second *Banana* panel, paras. 156-158.

originating in ACP countries. No measure was referred to in the waiver since no specific measure was actually "required" by the Lomé Convention.

4.67 What the Panel should therefore verify when examining the scope of the waiver and its application, was if a certain preferential treatment accorded by EC to ACP originating bananas was "required" by the Lomé Convention itself; that was if it was founded on an obligation flowing from that Treaty. The provisions quoted earlier were of plain and direct comprehension, the EC argued, and did not need any interpretative exercise so one might suggest that the Roman wisdom should be (easily) followed: "*in claris non fit interpretatio*". However, should any doubt concerning the interpretation of a specific provision be raised, then only the parties to the Lomé Convention should be the ultimate authorities for the authentic interpretation of that clause. This was even more necessary, in the EC view, considering that the other parties to the Lomé Convention - that is the ACP States -did not have the opportunity fully to defend their case in front of the Panel. It could not be admitted that a party to an international agreement should be bound to an interpretation of that agreement that the contracting parties might not share and against which they were not even allowed to exercise completely their right of defence.

4.68 In response to a question posed by the Panel, the EC further submitted that the last paragraph of the Lomé waiver meant that any Member could complain of a lack of observance of the terms or conditions of the waiver. If the terms and conditions of a waiver were not fulfilled, this constituted a breach of the waiver and a panel could make any rulings and recommendations pertaining to such waiver, just as it can make such rulings and recommendations in respect of a breach of the GATT and Annex IA Agreements. The EC was, however, firmly convinced that a panel could not rule on a non-violation complaint in respect of a waiver. Article 3(b) of the 1994 Understanding in Respect of Waivers was clearly decided in error, because it was incoherent with standing case law on non-violation complaints. Non-violation complaints could only be granted if the complaining party had reasonable expectations that certain benefits would accrue to it, but they had been nullified or impaired by an act which was lawful under the GATT.[78] In the case of bananas, such reasonable expectations had been entirely destroyed by the granting of the Lomé waiver as recently as 1994, when the banana regime was already in force. The only reasonable expectation that a Member could have, in the EC's view, was that the terms of the waiver would be respected and this could lead to a complaint concerning the violation of the waiver. In the case the question did not arise as the Complaining parties had never seriously advanced a non-violation claim, whether during consultations, in their request for the establishment of a panel, in their submissions, or during the first meeting with the panel. Moreover, the Complaining parties had failed to discharge their special burden of justification under Article 26(a) of the DSU. All this demonstrated, the EC argued, that the Panel should not entertain a non-violation claim.

4.69 The Complaining parties considered that the EC's assertion that the waiver covered any and all kinds of preferential treatment that the EC decided to attribute to its Lomé Convention obligations was alarming and without any basis. They asked how many measures, and with respect to how many products, the EC would attempt to slip under such a broad waiver. In the view of the Complaining parties, after having accepted a WTO waiver in terms of certain preferential treatment required by the Lomé Convention, the EC could not now demand that dispute settlement panels refrain from any examination of the relationship between the two sets of obligations, in particular what was "required by" the Convention. The EC's theory that the waiver covered ACP benefits negotiated between the parties to the Convention (allegedly pursuant to broad Convention objectives) provided no security to Members that had provided the waiver. Granting the EC the exclusive right to interpret the waiver would only encourage future violations of GATT Article I which would be inconsistent with WTO objectives and practice. This was wholly contrary to the purpose of WTO obligations; only the WTO could interpret the Lomé waiver, and in order to do so, the Panel was required to examine what was strictly required by the Lomé Convention.

[78] See "Treatment by Germany of Imports of Sardines", BISD 1S/58, para. 16 and "EEC - Payments and Subsidies Paid to Processors and Producers of Oilseeds", BISD 37S/86, paras. 128-129.

4.70 With respect to the specific provisions of the Lomé Convention, Guatemala and Honduras argued that both Protocol 5 and Annex LXXIV, the two Lomé Convention provisions that most directly addressed the treatment of ACP bananas, pointedly emphasized that Lomé Convention benefits extended only to traditional ACP suppliers. Article 1 of Protocol 5 contained the statement that:

> no ACP State shall be placed, as regards access to its traditional markets and its advantages on those markets, in a less favourable situation than in the past or at present.

Annex LXXIV, paragraph one, added emphasis to this traditional-supplier limitation:

> [t]he Contracting parties agree that Article 1 of Protocol 5 does not prevent the Community from establishing common rules for bananas, in full consultation with the ACP, as long as no ACP State, traditional supplier to the Community, is placed as regards access to, and advantages in, the Community, in a less favourable situation than in the past or at present.

In its *Report of the ACP-EEC Council of Ministers*, the EC further confirmed the narrow reach of the benefits promised to those traditional ACP banana suppliers by the Lomé Convention. The EC rejected in that Report the ACP claim that the Lomé Convention guaranteed them "quantities, market shares and prices ..."; explaining that:

> the banana protocol only guaranteed the full application of Article 2 Lomé [now Article 168] in case of the establishment of a common market organisation.[79]

Article 168 of the Lomé Convention, as delimited by Protocol 5 and Annex LXXIV, could only be interpreted to authorize tariff preferences and direct aid as a means of ensuring that no traditional ACP State received less favourable access and advantages than those previously received.

4.71 The Complaining parties argued that in the first instance, the EC had mis-identified the Lomé Convention's requirements pertaining to bananas. Its list of relevant provisions included articles that did not fall within the reach of the Lomé waiver and omitted key provisions that did. By any standard, Article 15(a) was not obligatory on the subject of bananas, but hortatory and non-specific. Indeed, to the extent the language therein provided interpretive guidance on the issue of Lomé Convention requirements, it cut directly against the claim that preferential ACP access had to be enhanced through discriminatory licensing procedures for Latin American imports. As acknowledged by the EC in its information memorandum regarding the signing in Mauritius of the Agreement Amending the Fourth ACP-EC Convention of Lomé:

> [a]ccording to this Article [15(a)], the main aim of trade development is to improve the ACP States' competitiveness rather than, as in the past, extract maximum value from preferential arrangements ... . The Preferential regime is just one amongst many ways of developing trade ....[80]

4.72 Article 24 of the Lomé Convention was, according to the Complaining parties, even more general than Article 15(a), providing no requirement with respect to ACP bananas:

> In order to promote and diversify trade between the Contracting Parties, the Community and the ACP States are agreed on: general trade provisions; special arrangements for Community

---

[79] See "Report of the ACP-EEC Council of Ministers", 1976-1980, Brussels, 1980, p.44. See also Manganza, G., "La Convention de Lomé", Collection Mégret-droit de la CEE, vol. 13, p.317.

[80] EC Information Memorandum "Signing in Mauritius of the Agreement Amending the Fourth ACP-EC Convention of Lomé (4 November 1995) - Results of the Mid-Term Review and Presentation of the Contents of the Agreement", para. 2.3.3, Brussels, 25 October 1995.

> import of certain ACP products; arrangements to promote the development of the ACP States' trade and services, including tourism; [and] a system of reciprocal information and consultation designed to help apply the trade cooperation provisions of this Convention effectively.

The European Court of Justice ("ECJ"), too, considered the EC's only Lomé Convention obligations in the area of bananas to be those laid down in Article 168(2)(a)(ii), as exclusively defined and qualified by Protocol 5 and Annexes LXXIV and LXXV.[81] The latter two "joint declarations" spoke directly to the issue of banana obligations, but were omitted from the EC's apparent list of "relevant provisions". Article 168 provided in the relevant part that for ACP products such as bananas that were subject to a common organization of the market or for which EC measures were in force relating to the imported product: "the Community shall take the necessary measures to ensure more favourable treatment than that granted to third countries benefiting from the most-favoured-nation clause for the same products."[82] Protocol 5 on bananas, annexed to the Convention, set forth specific provisions relevant to banana trade. These provisions clearly superseded the more general provisions in Article 168.[83] The protocol opened with a statement that:

> The Community and the ACP States agree to the objectives of improving the conditions under which the ACP States' bananas are produced and marketed and of continuing the advantages enjoyed by traditional suppliers in accordance with the undertakings of Article I of this protocol and agree that appropriate measures shall be taken for their implementation.

Article 1 of Protocol 5 provided:

> In respect of its banana exports to the Community markets, no ACP State shall be placed, as regards access to its traditional markets and its advantages on those markets in a less favourable situation than in the past or at present.

Annex LXXIV contained a joint declaration appended to the Protocol that permitted the EC to derogate from its obligations under the Lomé Convention in order to establish common rules for bananas, subject to one condition. The declaration stated:

> The Contracting Parties agree that Article 1 of Protocol 5 does not prevent the Community from establishing common rules for bananas, in full consultation with the ACP, as long as no ACP State, traditional supplier to the Community, is placed as regards access to, and advantages in, the Community, in a less favourable situation than in the past or at present.

4.73 The Complaining parties submitted that Annex LXXV explicitly clarified that Haiti and the Dominican Republic, because they "do not at present export to the Community", were "accordingly not considered as traditional suppliers", and therefore did not benefit from the Protocol or Joint Declaration. The EC therefore had no special obligations with respect to their exports of bananas. With respect to traditional suppliers, as set out in Annex LXXIV, the EC was free to establish those common rules for bananas it deemed appropriate (and presumably, consistent with its international obligations) so long as it safeguarded a certain "situation" as regards past or present advantages with respect to traditional suppliers. As noted above, the ECJ was asked to review Article 168 as it related to non-traditional bananas and found that the "more favourable treatment" language of Article 168 was delimited by Protocol 5, Annex LXXIV and Annex LXXV to cover only access and advantages

[81] "Federal Republic of Germany v. Council of the European Union", ECJ Case C-280/93, para. 101 (5 October 1994).

[82] Article 168(2)(a)(ii).

[83] According to the Complaining parties, even if they did not, Article 168 did not require duty-free treatment for non-traditional ACP exports.

accorded to traditional ACP banana suppliers.[84] The ECJ's narrow reliance on Protocol 5, Annex LXXIV and Annex LXXV to define the Lomé Convention's banana requirements was, according to the Complaining parties, entirely consistent with recent EC statements regarding the EC's Lomé Convention obligations on bananas.

4.74 The EC referred to the reference made by the Complaining parties to Annexes LXXIV and LXXV to the Lomé Convention, indicating that the EC had not listed them because, in the view of the EC, they did not add anything to the main provisions, i.e. Article 168(2)(a)(ii) and Protocol 5 of the Lomé Convention, which set out the fundamental obligations for the preferential treatment for ACP bananas. In particular, Annex LXXV did nothing more than what the EC had acknowledged from the very beginning of the procedure, that is that bananas from Haiti and the Dominican Republic should not be considered as traditional and should not be subject to the provisions of Protocol 5. They were nevertheless covered by the provisions of Article 168(2)(a)(ii). According to the EC, and as set out in Article 368 of the Lomé Convention, the Protocols to the Lomé Convention formed an integral part of the Convention. Therefore, they constituted provisions of identical legal value as the ones contained in the main body of the Agreement, with the same legal value meaning identical binding effect on the contracting parties. But identical did not mean more value or, worse, repealing force of one provision vis-à-vis another existing provision under the same Agreement. Moreover, according to the EC, the Panel did not even need to enter into the difficult subject of examining the relation between the two provisions since no conflict existed between them: Protocol 5 applied only to traditional ACP bananas, thus supplementing Article 168(2)(a)(ii) which, in turn, applied to ACP bananas in general and to non-traditional ACP bananas in particular. Contrary to what the Complaining parties affirmed, there was no contradiction between the position expressed by the Court of Justice of the European Communities in its judgement in the case Germany v. Council of the European Union, C-280/93, published in ECJ Reports, 1994, I-5071 and the arguments developed by the EC in this procedure. In that decision (paragraph 101, *ab initio*) the Court of Justice stated: "with respect to the establishment of a tariff quota, the import of bananas from ACP States falls under Article 168(2)(a)(ii) of the Lomé Convention." The Court then added: "In accordance to Protocol 5, the Community is obliged to permit the access, free of customs duty, only of the quantities of bananas actually imported "at zero duty" in the best year before 1991 from each ACP State which is a traditional supplier." The Court of Justice therefore clearly distinguished the two regimes, the first, under the tariff quota (of which a limited amount is allocated to non-traditional ACP bananas) and the second, under the traditional ACP allocation. The correct conclusion was, as the Court of Justice had clearly indicated, that both provisions were in force and applied.

4.75 The Complaining parties submitted that the combined effect of Article 1 of Protocol 5 and Annexes LXXIV and LXXV was that the EC's obligations were limited, first, to bananas from traditional suppliers on the traditional markets and, second, to providing only a rough approximation to each such ACP supplier of the "situation" "as regards" access and advantages that each supplier enjoyed in particular EC markets before 1991, an obligation that had also to be read in light of the EC's need to establish common rules for bananas. They contained no specific obligations with respect to quantities or prices for traditional suppliers, nor did they contain any obligations whatsoever with respect to non-traditional suppliers. In the opinion of the Complaining parties, nothing in Protocol 5 or other provisions of the Lomé Convention required the EC to import certain volumes of bananas, to maintain a certain free-on-board price, or to implement measures additional to tariff preferences. Moreover, the Lomé Convention did not require country-specific allocations or even a general tariff quota for ACP bananas. Furthermore, the Complaining parties submitted, the EC had no obligations whatsoever with respect to bananas from ACP States exceeding historical amounts or to non-traditional shippers. The requirement was a general one, relating only to the "situation" "as regards" access and advantages prevailing in particular markets before Regulation 404/93.

---

[84] "Federal Republic of Germany v. Council of the European Union", ECJ case c-280/93, para. 101. ("In accordance with Protocol 5, the Community is obliged to permit the access, free of customs duty, only of the quantities of bananas actually imported at zero duty in the best year before 1991 from each State which is a traditional supplier. Moreover, Annexes LXXIV and LXXV relating to that Protocol confirm that the Community's only obligation is to maintain the advantages, with respect to access of ACP bananas to the Community market, which the ACP States had before the Lomé Convention.")

4.76 The Complaining parties noted the EC had indeed admitted that it was not required to maintain any free-on-board price, nor any particular volume, an interpretation that was consistent with the view of EC ministers expressed to ACP ministers in 1980. The Complaining parties considered that the EC had conceded that its only obligation was to maintain conditions by which each traditional ACP State's bananas could be effectively sold on the EC market, and that it had admitted that "the means to achieve this are diverse, and are not necessarily limited to tariff changes". The EC had also by implication acknowledged that with respect to at least some traditional ACP exports, a mere tariff reduction from MFN rates would be sufficient to ensure that the EC had met its obligations to ensure a real and effective opportunity to import. According to the Complaining parties, if the EC's obligations with respect to an ACP State could be met by tariff preferences alone, then all the other measures were obviously not covered by the waiver.

4.77 This interpretation of Protocol 5 and Annex LXXIV was confirmed, in the view of the Complaining parties, by the very different language employed by other provisions of the Lomé Convention in which such guarantees were explicitly provided. For example, Article 213 contained special undertakings on sugar, and Protocol 8, containing the text of Protocol 3 on ACP sugar provided that:

> The Community undertakes for an indefinite period to purchase and import, at guaranteed prices, specific quantities of cane sugar, raw or white, which originate in the ACP States and which these states undertake to deliver to it.

Other Articles in the Protocol also set forth specific quantities that had to be guaranteed. In addition, Protocol 7 on beef and veal stated:

> The Community and the ACP States agree to take the special measures set out below to enable ACP States which are traditional exporters of beef and veal to maintain their position on the Community market, thus guaranteeing a certain level of income for their producers.

Thus, if the EC had wanted to "guarantee" a level of access or advantages, it would, in the opinion of the Complaining parties, have used the appropriate language to do so. Instead, the Banana Protocol only required the maintenance of a general "situation" as regards access and advantages with respect to each supplier. In the opinion of the Complaining parties, a "situation" meant a combination of factors contributing to a "snapshot" of the whole. The use of this term in the Lomé Convention implied that no single element of that situation was guaranteed.

4.78 To analyze what "advantages" were relevant to the pre-404 "situation" of "each ACP State", it was, according to the Complaining parties, necessary to identify precisely those advantages that existed for each particular state in the past and at the time Regulation 404/93 was promulgated. An examination of this issue revealed that the access and advantages being provided to each ACP State under the current regime substantially exceeded the access and advantages provided by European countries to any single ACP State under previous national regimes. Before the implementation of Regulation 404/93, ACP exports to all member States were duty free. In the Netherlands, Belgium, Luxembourg, Denmark, Ireland and (beginning in 1990) Greece, each ACP State had to compete solely on the basis of a tariff preference of 20 per cent. In Germany, there was no such tariff preference at all, and the import quantities permitted reflected German demand. Spain did not authorize access of ACP bananas, and Portugal subjected most ACP bananas to quantitative restrictions established to protect domestic production, with Latin American bananas supplying the bulk of imports under the quota. In Italy, the only ACP State with reserved access was Somalia. France and the United Kingdom, which normally did not allow significant imports from Latin America, were the only countries to which ACP suppliers on the whole had substantial access reserved for them. Even there, however, no ACP State had a country-specific allocation "reserved" for it. Indeed, traditionally established trading practices - such as Geest's domination of United Kingdom imports from the

Windward Islands, and France's division of its market into two-thirds for its domestic suppliers and one-third for its former colonies in West Africa - limited access for various ACP origins.[85]

4.79 As a legal matter, therefore, the Complaining parties submitted, with the exception of Somalia, each individual ACP State had received protection from competition in only one of two member States -the United Kingdom or France. In neither case did the ACP bananas in question have a guarantee that either output or past shipment levels would be admitted. In France, total imports were limited by government estimates of French consumption needs. The high price of bananas kept per capita consumption low - at one-half of Germany's level. The United Kingdom, which was supplied primarily by Jamaica and the Windward Islands, imported most of what these countries produced. Geest, the exclusive importer of Windward Island bananas, sold bananas on a consignment basis, did not invest in banana production and, therefore, was interested in shipping as many bananas as possible (with little regard to quality). In neither country was any individual ACP State protected against competition from other ACP bananas. While importers in these closed markets experienced little competition, ACP bananas had to compete with other ACP bananas to enter even these protected markets. For example, Jamaica, the Windward Islands, Belize and Suriname competed for the United Kingdom market. Cameroon, Madagascar and Côte d'Ivoire competed for one-third of the French market. ACP sales in both markets depended on an annual assessment of consumption needs and price conditions by the relevant competent authorities.

4.80 Moreover, the Complaining parties noted, none of the European regimes ever guaranteed that any ACP country could send their best shipments from 1962, 1972 or any other period of time. An examination of the dates for the ACP's so-called "best ever" exports demonstrated this point. If countries were guaranteed sales at such a level until 1993, why would their "best ever" levels of exports to the EC have occurred 20 to 30 years ago? For example, Jamaica stated that its "best ever" shipment (201,000 tonnes) to the EC took place in 1965; yet despite the EC's claims that Jamaica was guaranteed this best ever level from the mid-1970's onward, Jamaica chose to ship annual amounts that were usually one third, and often less that 10 per cent, of this "best ever" quantity.

4.81 In sum, the Complaining parties argued, the "situation" for ACP bananas before Regulation 404/93 was hardly as favourable as the situation created by Regulation 404/93. The excessive country-specific allocations provided by Regulation 404/93, the duty-free treatment for these amounts, the special provisions for so-called non-traditional ACP bananas, the Category B licence criteria, hurricane licences and the excessively burdensome import licensing system imposed on Latin American bananas provided ACP States with a competitive advantage they never previously enjoyed. The fact that the Lomé Convention did not provide any requirement to import certain volumes, to maintain a certain price or to implement any other measures to guarantee market presence was indirectly recognized by the ECJ in the case interpreting the EC's obligations. In distinguishing the EC's obligations with respect to non-traditional bananas, the ECJ noted that the EC was only required "to permit the access" free of duty with respect to historical quantities of bananas.[86] Even the ECJ, therefore, only considered Protocol 5 to apply to access opportunities, not sales guarantees. The Commission's 25-page interdepartmental options report prepared in 1992, *Setting Up the Internal Market in the Banana Sector*, reflected a broader variety of possible approaches. That report explored several single-market alternatives that the Commission deemed satisfied the EC's Lomé Convention commitments on bananas.[87] The alternatives included tariff preferences, a programme of financial and technical assistance, a compensation mechanism, a "flexible" dollar-zone quota wherein annual growth would be guaranteed and the possibility of safeguards, as well as a partnership arrangement through which traditional marketers of Latin American bananas would be provided licences on the basis of purchases of ACP and EC bananas. This report did not include the particular measures currently in force.

---

[85] First *Banana* panel, paras. 19-39.

[86] "Federal Republic of Germany v. Council of the European Union", para. 101.

[87] In describing those commitments, the report speaks only of Protocol 5. See, e.g. paras. 16 and 41.

4.82 The EC reiterated its view that Protocol 5, Article 1, was self explanatory in indicating clearly the obligations on the EC. As the EC had spelled out, the EC had fulfilled its obligations by: (i) creating a specific and separate system for the importation in the EC market of the ACP traditional banana production; and (ii) by facilitating trade and commercial relations between the EC and the ACP countries through the creation of the so-called Category B licences so as to ensure that the quantities for which access opportunities were given an effective and not only theoretical opportunity to be sold, thus guaranteeing traditional ACP bananas their existing advantages, while not providing by this mean any incentive to purchase ACP bananas. The EC was under a legal obligation under the Lomé Convention to ensure, for traditional quantities of ACP bananas, not just the opportunity of pre-existing access to the EC market, but also the existing advantages on the Community market at the level of their highest sendings in any one year up to and including 1990 (the year the Lomé Convention entered into force). This was certainly an obligation to ensure a real and effective opportunity to import but did not mean that the EC was obliged to effectively import certain volumes of bananas.

4.83 The EC reminded the Panel that the regime was a market organisation. It set out conditions governing the market, but it was not the Commission itself, or EC member States who did the importing. Thus the guarantee was not that certain volumes were imported, but that market access, in principle and in practice, was maintained, i.e. that the market organisation was structured in such a way that the traditional ACP suppliers were able to find outlets for their bananas. This was much more subtle, and in fact more difficult than simply agreeing to purchase their bananas, because it implied creating a commercial climate in which traditional ACP bananas were attractive to commercial companies. In the same line of reasoning, the EC noted that even if it was not obliged to maintain a certain free-on-board price, it was certainly obliged to maintain conditions by which the ACP bananas could effectively be sold on the EC market, thus guaranteeing the advantages on that market. The means to achieve this were diverse and were not necessarily limited to tariff changes. The so-called Category B licences were another means to guarantee the advantages on the EC market through the reinforced and effective opportunity to import ACP bananas. One point to be retained in any case was that ACP bananas were now exposed to more competition than they were before the entry into force of the EC wide banana market, not less.

4.84 In this light, the EC recalled the differences in conditions of production had been documented in a study on ACP banana production conducted by CIRAD.[88] This study found that for 1993, production costs averaged on a national basis, ranged from ECU 325 per tonne to ECU 440 per tonne ($381-$515 per tonne or $6.9-$9.4 per 40 lb. box (18.14 kg)) depending on the country. Consideration of f.o.b. prices showed that in 1995, Caribbean ACP countries received approximately $9 per box and African ACP countries approximately $8 per box (these figures had changed little since 1994). A corresponding examination of 1994 f.o.b. prices for Latin American bananas sent to Europe (source UNSO) ranges from $3.7 per box in Guatemala, through $3.8 per box in Honduras, $4.21 per box in Ecuador, $5.1 per box in Colombia to $5.2 per box in Costa Rica. The EC noted, therefore, that even the most competitive ACP countries had production costs well above the prices paid to even the most expensive Latin American suppliers, and that FOB prices for ACP bananas were approximately double those for Latin American sourced fruit; thus ACP countries required special preferential treatment to market their bananas. (Further arguments concerning, *inter alia*, ACP production costs are given below in section IV.B.2(c) - Import licensing issues.)

4.85 The EC submitted that the Complaining parties attempted to reduce the scope of Article 1 of Protocol 5 of the Lomé Convention by mainly two means: first of all by establishing comparisons between the provisions on bananas under the Convention and those concerning other agricultural products like sugar, beef or veal etc. This was an extraordinary way of interpreting an international agreement in the EC's view. Under Article 31, paragraphs 1 and 3, of the Vienna Convention on the Law of the Treaties, the need to depart from the text of the agreement in order to interpret its provisions was limited to a case where the text itself was unclear or ambiguous and when the parties could not agree on its interpretation. Article 1 of Protocol 5 was according to the EC, clear and unambiguous. Moreover, the contracting parties to the Lomé Convention agreed completely about how it

[88] Centre de Coopération Internationale en Recherche Agronomique pour le Développement, Montpellier.

should be interpreted. This interpretation was acknowledged by the parties to have been correctly reflected in the EC legislation providing for preferential treatment for the ACP traditional bananas. The second way of reducing the scope of Article 1 of Protocol 5 was to try to shift the interpretation to subtle, and rather arcane differences between a "guarantee of a level of access" and the "maintenance of a general situation as regards access and advantages with respect to each supplier." The attempt was so subtle that it tended to be invisible and one might find the end result surprisingly identical. In fact, the EC could agree that the text of Protocol 5 of the Lomé Convention referred to "situations". But this in a context of a negative phrase stating that "no ACP State shall be placed, as regard access to its traditional markets and its advantages on those markets, in a less favourable situation than in the past or at present." The contracting parties to the Lomé Convention agreed that this unambiguous text meant what it said: any aspect of the access to the EC market of ACP bananas and, moreover, any advantage on those markets should be maintained in a not less favourable situation than in the past (before the entry into force of the Lomé Convention) or at present (taking into account existing realities which were not present in the past but still affected the access of bananas to the EC market and their advantages on this market). A situation was a combination of circumstances at a given moment: this meant that the single elements might change through time while not affecting the compliance with Article 1 of Protocol 5 if the overall result, the situation of access to the EC market and of advantages on that market, was maintained. This was again something the EC had always indicated and that fundamentally contradicted and undermined the Complaining parties' suggestion that the waiver was concerned with "required" measures and not, more correctly as the EC had always maintained, with the end result of their application, the "preferential treatment". The EC's analysis showed beyond any doubt, in the view of the EC, that the reading the Complaining parties have made Article 1 of Protocol 5 was not only restricted but, more fundamentally, wrong.

4.86 The Complaining parties considered that the EC had admitted that its only real requirement under the Convention was to maintain "conditions of effective sale" for ACP bananas. Although the EC had conceded that this did not require guaranteed volumes, prices or market shares, it had shed no further light on this alleged requirement. Instead, it had asked Members to give it unlimited discretion to promote ACP interests as it saw fit, even if it meant choosing options that were most likely to create unnecessary barriers and burdens for other developing countries in the WTO - with respect not only to bananas but to the great number of other products covered by the Convention. The Complaining parties considered such a theory was inconsistent with what the WTO represented for developing countries. In particular, if the waiver was permitted to erect such non-tariff barriers against exports of non-ACP developing countries, the WTO could hardly meet its objective of ensuring that all developing countries secured a "share in the growth of international trade". The Complaining parties further stated that they did not seek the destruction of ACP banana production, but only asked that preferences be provided in accordance with the WTO. Furthermore, they did not see why the needs of ACP countries should be met at the expense of the most basic principle of international trade upon which all countries relied to develop, that of comparative advantage. Finally, the Complaining parties considered that if the EC were really interested in helping developing countries, it would adopt a system that encouraged banana consumption in the EC and permitted the market to grow at its previous rate. Such a course would create jobs in all banana exporting countries.

(d) Parties' subsequent arguments - non-traditional ACP tariff preferences

4.87 The EC referred to the horizontal issue of the Lomé waiver and noted it had shown that it covered not only traditional ACP tariff preferences, but also tariff preferences applied to non-traditional ACP banana imports. Specifically with respect to the Complaining parties argument that the EC preferential treatment to non-traditional ACP bananas was inconsistent with Article I of the GATT, the EC recalled that the preferential treatment accorded to ACP bananas within the tariff quota (duty free for 90,000 tonnes) and when applying duty beyond the tariff quota (ECU 100 per tonne less than the bound duty) was not part of the EC Schedule LXXX, since it flowed directly from the relevant obligations under the Lomé Convention and was therefore covered by the Lomé waiver. Although non-traditional ACP bananas were not covered by the obligations of the EC under Article 1 of Protocol 5, under Article 168(2)(a)(ii) the EC had undertaken to "take the necessary measures to ensure more favourable treatment than that granted to third countries benefiting from the most-favoured-nation clause for the same product". This provision did not exclude bananas. The complainants argument was thus based on the wrong assumption that the Lomé waiver covered only the preferential treatment accorded by the EC to ACP countries which was related to the sole obligations under Protocol 5 to the Lomé Convention, and, more particularly, to the sole Article 1 of that Protocol. The general interpretative arguments set out above showed, in the view of the EC why this understanding was wrong and did not correspond either to the will of the contracting parties to the Lomé convention or to the scope of the Lomé waiver itself.

4.88 A duty-free treatment was a more favourable treatment than a ECU 75 per tonne duty imposed as MFN treatment within the tariff quota. A reduction of ECU 100 per tonne was more favourable treatment than the MFN treatment for quantities imported outside the tariff quota. No extension of this treatment to any other Member under Article I:1 of GATT could be claimed in the light of the terms of the Lomé waiver. As far as the fact that a certain quantity of bananas of ACP origin were benefiting from this more favourable treatment (and not countries, as the complainants had phrased it), more favourable treatment included not only tariff preferences but any other preference which might be appropriate in the circumstances of the case to achieve the objectives under the Lomé Convention. While implementing this more favourable treatment obligation by according a duty free treatment to non-traditional ACP bananas, the EC had substantially limited that treatment to a capped quantity of bananas, thus striking a very difficult political balance between different interests on the market; it amounted to a concerted effort between the ACP and the EC to maintain a fair balance between their access to the EC market and the general MFN treatment. It was really paradoxical, in the opinion of the EC, that this limitation should be seen as a violation of WTO rules: this approach should be dismissed.

4.89 Moreover, the EC submitted, Article 168(2)(d), first indent, stated that:

> If during application of the Convention, the EC subjects one or more products to common organisation of the market..., it shall reserve the right to adapt the import treatment for those products originating in the ACP States, following consultations within the Council of Ministers.

Consequently, when the common organisation of the market for bananas was set up, the Council of Ministers decided that non-traditional ACP quantities of bananas should enjoy duty-free access (Article 18(1) of Regulation 404/93) within the EC tariff quota, thus ensuring that they were treated more favourably than other third-country suppliers who were subject to a duty of ECU 75 per tonne.

4.90 According to Guatemala and Honduras, they had shown that the Lomé Convention, as qualified by Protocol 5 and Annex LXXIV, solely required the provision of duty-free access and specified direct aid to traditional ACP banana suppliers. Since non-traditional banana preferences were not covered by the Lomé Convention, they could not be considered to be "required by the relevant provisions of the Fourth Lomé Convention" such that the Lomé waiver would apply.[89] The tariff discrimination at issue likewise found no support under the three limited exceptions to Article I:1 contained in Articles I:2, XX and XXIV of GATT.

4.91 The Complaining parties submitted that the EC had not denied that its application of preferential tariff rates to so-called non-traditional ACP bananas was inconsistent with Article I:1 of GATT. Rather, the EC had claimed that Article 168 of the Lomé Convention required it to provide this treatment and that, accordingly, the discrimination at issue was allowed by the Lomé waiver. The EC's claim contradicted, in the opinion of the Complaining parties, its statement in its *Report on the Operation of the Banana Regime* that "the Community's obligations to the ACP States as embodied by the Lomé Convention have to be honoured. On bananas, these are set out in Protocol 5 to the Convention."[90] The EC's claim also contradicted the understanding EC Commission officials had concerning EC obligations under the Lomé Convention in 1992 when making plans for a single

[89] Lomé waiver, para. 1.

[90] "Report on the Operation of the Banana Regime", Commission of the European Communities, SEC (95) 1565 final, p.2.

market. In considering various options, EC Commission officials did not consider that the Lomé Convention required the EC to provide anything more than most-favoured-nation treatment to non-traditional ACP bananas. For example, the Commission's May 1992 options paper stated that "bananas from the non-traditional ACP suppliers and non-traditional quantities from traditional ACP suppliers would be treated in the same way as bananas from the dollar zone."[91] A review of the relevant provisions of the Lomé Convention, confirmed that nothing required the EC to provide this preferential treatment to bananas from non-traditional ACP suppliers or with respect to quantities exceeding historical shipments of traditional ACP suppliers.

4.92 As discussed above, the Complaining parties argued that, Article 168 of the Lomé Convention was exclusively defined and qualified by Protocol 5 and Annexes LXXIV and LXXV. Since Protocol 5 and the two relevant Annexes spoke only of traditional suppliers and referenced the past or present "situation" (up to 1991), the "non-traditional" quantities receiving any preference under the regime could not possibly be considered required by the Lomé Convention. By definition, with respect to traditional suppliers, non-traditional bananas were those exceeding traditional amounts. Annex LXXV explicitly excluded the non-traditional suppliers from EC obligations. Moreover, the EC Commission recognized in its 1992 options report that preferential allocations or tariff treatment for "non-traditional" ACP bananas were not required by the Lomé Convention when it discussed what it deemed to be a Lomé Convention - consistent "partnership" option in which "non-traditional ACP suppliers and non-traditional quantities from traditional ACP suppliers [were to] be treated in the same way as bananas from the dollar zone."[92]

4.93 With respect to the duty-free treatment provided to non-traditional ACP bananas, the Complaining parties considered that one needed to look no further than to the EC's own highest legal authority for a contradiction of the EC's position in this case. In its Judgment of 5 October 1994, on the challenge brought by Germany against the EC Council (Case C-280-93), the EC Court of Justice interpreted Protocol 5 of the Lomé Convention as limiting the EC's obligations on bananas. The Court declared that the EC was obliged to permit the access, free of customs duty, only of the quantities of bananas actually imported at zero duty in the best year before 1991 from each traditional ACP State. The Court noted that Annexes LXXIV and LXXV "confirm that the EC's only obligation is to maintain the advantages, with respect to access of ACP bananas to the EC market, which the ACP States had before the Lomé Convention." In sum, this meant, according to the Complaining parties, that there was no requirement to provide duty-free treatment to suppliers such as the Dominican Republic, that had not been party to the earlier Lomé Conventions, and there was no access or advantage obligation whatever with respect to quantities that exceeded the so-called traditional amounts supplied by traditional suppliers such as the Côte d'Ivoire and Cameroon. Protocol 5, which was specifically applicable to bananas, superseded any more general obligations in the Lomé Convention. Therefore, since the discrimination was not required by the Lomé Convention, the EC was obliged, by Article I:1 of the GATT, to accord immediately and unconditionally to third countries the same treatment as it accorded to non-traditional ACP bananas.

4.94 With respect to the specific reference made by the Complaining parties to the Court of Justice of the European Communities in its judgement in the case Germany v. Council of the European Union. The EC submitted that there was no contradiction between the position expressed. In the decision the Court of Justice stated: "with respect to the establishment of a tariff quota, the import of bananas from ACP States falls under Article 168(2)(a)(ii) of the Lomé Convention". The Court then added: "In accordance to Protocol 5, the Community is obliged to permit the access, free of customs duty, only of the quantities of bananas actually imported "at zero duty" in the best year before 1991 from each ACP State which is a traditional supplier." The Court of Justice therefore clearly distinguished the two regimes. The correct conclusion was, as the Court of Justice had clearly indicated, that both provisions were in force and applied.

91 "Setting Up the Internal Market", para. 69.

92 Idem.

(ii) third-country tariff rates

4.95 Guatemala and Honduras submitted that prior to Regulation 404/93, the EC applied a 20 per cent ad valorem tariff rate to fresh bananas, a rate which had been bound in the GATT 1947 and in effect since 1963. The ad valorem bound rate for bananas was revoked by Regulation 404/93 *et seq.* and replaced with a two-tiered structure. This new tariff structure raised the bound rate in two ways. First, it introduced two rates of duty, where previously there was only one, the higher of which was set at a trade-prohibitive level to prevent over-quota shipments. Second, it changed the valuation method from ad valorem to specific, which conversion further increased the tariff liability and made that liability harder to predict. Well after the 20 per cent ad valorem binding had been withdrawn, the EC notified the GATT CONTRACTING PARTIES, on 19 October 1993, of its intention to renegotiate the 1963 binding pursuant to Article XXVIII:5 of the GATT 1947. For Costa Rica, Colombia, Nicaragua and Venezuela, those negotiations led to the BFA. For Guatemala, no re-negotiation of the binding occurred. When Guatemala signed the Marrakesh Agreement, its signature was accompanied by an express reservation of all past, present, and future trade rights relative to the EC's treatment of bananas. Guatemala accordingly reasserted the claim it had successfully put forward in the second *Banana* panel, but which continued to go unheeded by the EC, that the new tariff rates effectuated by Regulation 404/93 *et seq.* were inconsistent with enduring Article II rights arising from the EC's 20 per cent ad valorem tariff binding.

4.96 According to Guatemala and Honduras, Article II:1(a) of the GATT imposed on Members an absolute requirement to "accord to the commerce of the other contracting parties treatment no less favourable than that provided for in the appropriate Part of the appropriate Schedule annexed to this Agreement". GATT panels had rigorously applied this requirement, recognizing the "fundamental importance of the security and predictability of GATT tariff bindings, a principle which constitutes a central obligation in the system of the General Agreement."[93] To protect that security, even small changes to tariff bindings, including those that did not even increase the protective effect of the tariff in question, had been disallowed.[94] The second *Banana* panel remained faithful to that strict Article II construction, ruling that because the specific nature of the banana tariffs of Regulation 404/93 "led to the levying of a duty on imports of bananas whose ad valorem equivalent was, either actually or potentially, higher than 20 percent ad valorem", Article II had clearly been breached.[95] The panel stressed that, consistent with prior Article II interpretations, the mere possibility that the specific tariff rates applied to third-country bananas by the EC might be higher than the corresponding bound ad valorem rate rendered them inconsistent with Article II. Guatemala and Honduras submitted data showing the following three-month average ad valorem equivalencies: (a) based on 1993 data: (i) ECU 100 per tonne - 30.03 per cent; and (ii) ECU 75 per tonne - 22.6 per cent; and (b) based on 1995 data: (i) ECU 850 per tonne - 255.3 per cent; and (ii) ECU 822 per tonne - 247.3 per cent.[96] Since in the present action, all tariff quota third-country rates, past and present, had, according to Guatemala and Honduras, exceeded in actuality the 20 per cent rate, no different conclusion could be reached.

4.97 Guatemala and Honduras noted that the second *Banana* panel further observed that the Article II inconsistency arising out of Regulation 404/93 was in no way altered by the EC's Article XXVIII:5 notification regarding its intention to modify the 20 per cent tariff binding. That notification was of no legal consequence to the breach, the panel concluded, because the EC had improperly commenced Article XXVIII negotiations following the withdrawal of the concession, rather than prior to the withdrawal, as required by Article XXV3. Thus, the EC's selective undertaking of Article XXVIII negotiations with Costa Rica, Colombia, Nicaragua, and Venezuela should be considered to have had absolutely no impact on Guatemala's continuing Article II rights.

---

[93] "Panel on Newsprint", BISD 31S/114, para. 52 (adopted 20 November 1984).

[94] "Exports of Potatoes to Canada", BISD 11S/88, para. 18 (adopted 16 November 1962); "Increase in Import Duties on Products Included in Schedule XXV (Greece)", BISD 1S/51 (adopted 3 November 1952); "Panel on Newsprint", BISD 31S/114, paras. 50, 52 (adopted 20 November 1984).

[95] DS38/R, para. 134 (issued 11 February 1994).

[96] The ECU per tonne figures used by Guatemala and Honduras reflected the in-quota and out-of-quota tariffs applied to bananas in the periods concerned.

Those Article II rights also remained unaltered by Guatemala's accession to the WTO. Guatemala fully preserved its pre-WTO Article II claim by expressing a reserve during the Uruguay Round verification process and again by posting a formal reservation to the Marrakesh Agreement as to "all GATT and WTO rights relative to the EC's Schedule of concessions for agricultural products as regards bananas."[97] Moreover, even without that reservation, the panel on *United States - Restrictions on Imports of Sugar* found that countries would not be inferred to have accepted, or acquiesced to, terms contained within a schedule of concessions arising out of a multilateral negotiation if those terms were otherwise actionable under the GATT.[98] This point was confirmed in the first *Banana* panel case.[99] Similarly, in *EEC - Production Aids Granted on Canned Peaches, Canned Pears, Canned Fruit Cocktail and Dried Grapes*, that case's finding of tariff impairment was predicated on the principle that tariff binding rights were not extinguished by subsequent tariff negotiations.[100] Thus, here, where Guatemala had expressly dissented, not consented, to the EC's breach of the 20 per cent binding and had reserved all claims related to it, its rights also should be ruled to have carried through to the new WTO. The tariff structure accorded to third-country suppliers should consequently be deemed inconsistent with Article II and brought into full conformity with the relevant provisions of the GATT.

4.98 The EC submitted first of all, that it did not accept the calculations made. Second, and more importantly, in establishing the tariff quota the EC had violated no GATT rule including Article II. The EC noted the reference to the unadopted report of the second *Banana* panel. Without even the need of entering into the examination of that panel report - which, like every unadopted panel report, had no authority whatsoever since the GATT CONTRACTING PARTIES never accepted nor endorsed its conclusions - it would be sufficient to say that the panel worked on a factual situation totally different from the present one. At the time of the report, the Uruguay Round had not been completed and the tariff quota was not in force. The EC could not see how the report could be of any use or relevance under these circumstances.

4.99 Moreover, Members freely signed and ratified the Uruguay Round which included, *inter alia*, the EC Schedule LXXX which had been, therefore, unconditionally accepted by all. Any comparison with the past, in a situation where a new general negotiation had taken place, was not only unacceptable but deprived of any logical base unless the Members were ready to accept that the Uruguay Round negotiations were not over after all, and any new settlement under that Round was susceptible to be reopened at the good will of any of the contracting parties. There was no doubt that any guidelines that existed for scheduling in the agricultural sector were left out of the Agreement on Agriculture on purpose. It was the clear view of the participants in the negotiation that, after the verification process of early 1994, there would be no chance to second-guess the agricultural bindings agreed in the Uruguay Round.

4.100 The EC also submitted that none of the previous GATT litigations quoted were relevant to the present dispute: The panel report *United States - Restrictions on Imports of Sugar* indicated only that a schedule of concessions "cannot justify the maintenance of quantitative restrictions ... inconsistent with the application of Article XI:1". The issue solved by that panel was therefore related to the existence of any violation of a GATT provision (outside Part I of the General Agreement) that could not be justified by the contrary indications of the schedule. This was not relevant to the present case where the possibility of shaping differently the schedules (from an ad valorem duty to a tariff quota) was disputed. The unadopted second *Banana* panel report never addressed the issue claimed: the issue there was about the applicability of the well-known international law principle of the

[97] See letter dated 15 April 1994 to Mr. Peter Sutherland, GATT Director-General, from Mrs. M. Ruíz de Vielman, Guatemala's Minister of Foreign Affairs, notifying the GATT of Guatemala's reservations to the EC's Uruguay Round Schedule of Concessions relating to bananas.

[98] "United States - Restrictions on Imports of Sugar", BISD 36S/331, paras. 5.1-5.3 (adopted 22 June 1989).

[99] DS32/R, paras. 361-363 (issued 3 June 1993).

[100] L/5778, paras. 71 and 75 (issued 20 February 1985) (wherein the panel ruled that multilateral tariff negotiations in 1979 did not extinguish tariff binding rights on canned peaches accruing to the United States from tariff concessions granted in 1974 prior to the EC's introduction of processing aids on canned peaches).

"estoppel" and its consequences on that dispute. The unadopted panel report just underlined that the "mere fact that the EEC had notified [these] restrictions to the CONTRACTING PARTIES, and that such measures had not been acted upon until now had not changed the obligations under the General Agreement". The present situation was not one of "a mere" notification of a restriction to otherwise passive parties: a schedule was negotiated during an official Round and expressly accepted by the CONTRACTING PARTIES by their ratification and the "estoppel" principle was simply not an issue here. Lastly, the unadopted panel report *EEC - Production Aids Granted on Canned Peaches, Canned Pears, Canned Fruit Cocktail and Dried Grapes* dealt with a "non-violation" claim concerning the introduction of subsidies which could have impaired tariff concessions granted by the EC under the Schedule. The unilateral introduction of certain subsidies, while the EC Schedule concerning those products remained unmodified, set off the dispute. The EC argued here again that nothing in that procedure was relevant to the present situation which dealt with the explicitly accepted modification by the EC of one of its Schedules during an official Round of negotiations.

4.101 Guatemala argued that it had shown that the EC had only completed its 20 per cent tariff binding renegotiations with Costa Rica, Colombia, Nicaragua and Venezuela, but had yet to conclude those Article XXVIII renegotiations with all other Members that had a trade interest in that binding. Guatemala argued that it had likewise shown that the verification process with respect to the EC's tariffs on third-country bananas was not concluded prior to the Uruguay Round ratification. With these procedures unfinished, GATT law made clear that all rights and interests attaching to the EC's breach of its 20 per cent binding continued to be enforceable. The EC disagreed, according to Guatemala, arguing that all legal shortcomings relating to the binding were cured by Guatemala's signature in Marrakesh. According to the EC, underpinning that argument were the concepts of "acquiescence" and "estoppel". The first *Banana* panel report made clear, however, that "acquiescence" and "estoppel" were generally only relevant under GATT law in cases where contracting parties expressly had consented to forego their GATT rights.[101] Guatemala could not be said to have granted its consent, express or implied, to the tariff quota tariff rates. Other panel reports reinforced Guatemala's opinion that the EC's breach of binding was not cured by the EC's Uruguay Round Schedule. The *Sugar Panel* found that countries would not be inferred to have acquiesced to terms contained within a schedule if those terms were otherwise GATT-illegal.[102] The EC's attempt to narrow the reach of the sugar decision to GATT obligations outside of Part I was, in the opinion of Guatemala, not supported by that Panel's unqualified language that "[Article II] could not justify inconsistencies with any Article of the General Agreement".[103]

4.102 The EC's rejection of the ad valorem equivalency calculations presented by Guatemala was also without merit. If the EC wished to disprove the technical breach of the binding at issue, it should provide supporting details. No such supporting details existed. Calculations comparable to those supplied in the first submission of Guatemala and Honduras were also submitted in the second *Banana* panel, leading the panel to conclude that:

> The EEC had neither argued nor submitted evidence that this tariff could never exceed 20 per cent ad valorem ... . The Panel consequently found that the new specific tariffs led to the levying of a duty on imports of bananas whose ad valorem equivalent was, either actually or potentially, higher that 20 per cent ad valorem.[104]

4.103 Guatemala submitted that since that Article II finding had neither been redressed nor legally altered by subsequent events, it had to be reaffirmed in the present action. Although Guatemala alone had asserted the Article II claim, the Panel's ruling on this issue should have legal effect for all other Members that had a trade interest in

---

[101] First *Banana* panel, citing "Report of the Panel on Japan - Imports of Certain Agricultural Products", adopted 2 February 1988, 35S/163; and "United States - Measures Affecting Alcoholic and Malt Beverages", adopted 19 June 1992, DS23/R.

[102] 36S/331, paras. 5.1-5.3.

[103] 36S/331, para. 5.8.

[104] Second *Banana* panel, para. 134.

the 20 per cent EC binding. Their right to this Article II claim was confirmed by the first *Banana* panel report, which made clear that the mere failure of a country to make a claim was not an expression of that country's consent to release the EC from its GATT obligations relating to that measure.[105]

4.104 The EC replied that the legal situation was clear: the Marrakesh Protocol indicated that "The schedule annexed to this Protocol relating to a Member shall become a schedule to GATT 1994 relating to that Member on the day on which the WTO Agreement enters into force". By ratifying the Uruguay Round package, Guatemala had accepted the whole EC Schedule LXXX and the banana tariff quota that appeared in that Schedule. Guatemala then claimed it had "preserved" its rights under a declaration attached to the Marrakesh Agreement. If any effect was given to such a declaration, it would reduce the scope of Guatemala's ratification of the Marrakesh Protocol which was an integral part to GATT. A declaration with that purpose could not, according to the EC, be defined differently as a reservation.[106]

4.105 Furthermore, the EC submitted, Article XVI:5 of the WTO Agreement indicated that "no reservations may be made in respect of any provision of this Agreement. Reservations in respect of any of the provisions of the Multilateral Trade Agreements may only be made to the extent provided for in those Agreements". The GATT did not provide for any right to introduce a reservation. Thus, any declaration to that effect was inadmissible under the GATT and would be deemed as having no legal value. Consequently, all references to previous panels quoted by the Complaining parties were of no avail for the simple reason that those panels could not have taken into account, in their analysis, the existence of provisions like Article XVI of the WTO approved after the release of those reports.

4.106 Concerning the issue with respect to the non-verification of the EC Schedule as raised in a question by the Panel, the EC submitted that no evidence had been presented to substantiate this claim, as indeed none could be since the Chairman of the Trade Negotiations Committee did not mention the EC Schedule among the non-verified ones at that Committee's next-to-last meeting of 30 March 1994. Guatemala itself, which had reserved its position on the EC banana offer at the same meeting, did not see fit to pursue the matter at the following and last meeting of the Committee on 7 April 1994. The EC also referred to the note of the GATT Secretariat in document MTN.GNG/MA/W/25 in which the closing date for the verification period for schedules was indicated as 31 March 1994. The EC's corrigendum on its banana concession was dated 29 March 1994. Nevertheless, there was no legal effect on the binding nature of the EC Schedule even assuming that such lack of completion of (re)negotiation and verification was indeed the case. The Marrakesh Protocol to the GATT 1994 was extremely blunt in this respect:

> The schedule annexed to this Protocol relating to a Member shall become a Schedule to GATT 1994 relating to that Member on the day on which the WTO Agreement enters into force for that Member.

By ratifying the Uruguay Round package, including the schedules annexed to it, Members had accepted the schedules as binding on themselves and others. Even if irregularities had occurred during the procedures leading up to the establishment of these schedules (assuming that these procedures were subject to binding rules), the final ratification of the schedules and the impossibility to make any reservations to any provision (including the schedules) of the Agreement, unless such reservations were provided for in the Annex IA agreements (which was not the case in respect of the schedules), made it impossible to call into question the schedules as contained in the results of the Uruguay Round (Article XVI:5, WTO Agreement). The parties in this case had not alleged fraud, corruption or coercion (Articles 49-51 of the Vienna Convention of 1969) in order to invalidate the schedules. Hence the schedules, including the EC consolidated tariff on bananas and the tariff quota, were part of a duly ratified agreement and could not be called into question any more.

---

[105] First *Banana* panel, para. 363.

[106] Vienna Convention on the Law of the Treaties, Article 17, para. 1.

b) Allocation issues

4.107 This section outlines the case concerning allocation matters. It sets out first general allocation issues and then the issue of the reallocation of shortfalls in the context of the BFA.

(i) general allocations

4.108 The general arguments of the Complaining parties concerning the requirements of Article XIII:2 of GATT are set below, followed by the EC responses to the claims and subsequent arguments by the Complaining parties. The EC responses include the major horizontal issues raised by the EC: (i) the presence of two separate banana access regimes; and (ii) the Agreement on Agriculture and its relationship to Articles I and II of GATT. Following the Article XIII:2 arguments, parties' arguments in relation to Article XIII:1 and Article I:1 are covered. Finally, arguments concerning the application of the Lomé waiver to allocation issues are presented.

4.109 The Complaining parties submitted that the EC had allocated access to its market among supplying countries in a manner inconsistent with GATT Article XIII:2. Guatemala, Honduras, Ecuador and the United States argued that the EC provided country-specific allocations to some countries (ACP and BFA signatories), while not providing them to others with similar or greater levels of past trade. Furthermore, the Complaining parties submitted that most of the allocations provided to those favoured countries greatly exceeded the shares of trade they would be expected to obtain in the absence of restrictions. The Complaining parties considered that the EC also disregarded the principles of Article XIII entirely when it provided BFA signatories the exclusive right to increase their access when other BFA countries experienced a shortfall in the quantity they could supply to the EC. In addition, Guatemala, Honduras, Ecuador and Mexico considered these aspects of the EC allocations violated Article XIII:1, and Guatemala and Honduras considered that, in the alternative, they were inconsistent with Article I.

(a) Article XIII:2 of GATT

- arguments of the Complaining Parties

4.110 The Complaining parties submitted that the EC had not complied with Article XIII:2 of GATT, which sets out the general principle that governed the allocation of a market among various supplying countries. Under that provision, "In applying import restrictions to any product," Members "shall aim at a distribution of trade in such product approaching as closely as possible the shares which [third country Members] might be expected to obtain in the absence of such restrictions." Paragraph 5 of Article XIII confirmed that the provisions of Article XIII applied to any tariff quota instituted or maintained by any Member. Referring to the panel on *Dessert Apples*, Ecuador, Guatemala, Honduras and the United States considered that Article XIII was *lex specialis* with respect to the provision of country allocations[107].

4.111 The Complaining parties considered that Article XIII:2(d) set forth two ways in which a Member could divide up its market and be presumed to comply with the general principle. Either the EC could have allocated shares to all substantially interested parties (if it obtained the consent of each and every one), or, in the absence of such agreement, it could have provided shares according to historical shipments during a representative period (in other words, in the absence of restrictions). If, in addition, the EC had chosen to assign shares to parties that did not have substantial interests, it had, nonetheless, to abide by the general principle of Article XIII:2. The EC, according to the Complaining parties, had not complied with any of these requirements.

---

[107] Report of the Panel on "EEC - Restrictions on Imports of Dessert Apples - Complaint by Chile", adopted on 22 June 1989, BISD 36S/93 at 133.

4.112 The United States noted that part of the EC market was reserved for country-specific allocations (which were not bound in the EC Schedule) provided to traditional Lomé countries[108], including non-WTO Members, whereas access to the rest of the market was limited by the third-country tariff quota, divided among country-specific allocations for non-traditional Lomé bananas (bound only in their totality) and for bananas exported by Latin American countries that had signed the BFA, which were also bound in the EC's Schedule. The remainder of the third-country tariff quota was allocated to a residuary "other" category for countries not otherwise receiving country-specific allocations.

4.113 Ecuador noted that the EC had allocated country specific shares of the EC import market to traditional ACP countries, to Latin American countries which had signed the BFA, and to certain non-traditional ACP suppliers. The remaining portion of the import market had been allocated to a catch-all "others" category, which included all third countries not included in the first three categories. This allocation scheme violated, according to Ecuador, Article XIII of the GATT in two ways. First, the scheme provided country-specific allocations to certain countries while denying country-specific allocations to other countries such as Ecuador which had a substantial interest in exporting bananas to the EC. Second, the allocation of the shares between the various countries and groups of countries did not reflect commercial or historical trade patterns.

4.114 In both of the options set out in Article XIII:2, Ecuador considered, allocations had to be made to all countries having a "substantial interest." Under virtually any criteria, Ecuador had to be considered as having a substantial interest in exporting bananas to the EC. Ecuador was one of the largest suppliers of bananas to the EC market and the banana industry was the second largest sector of Ecuador's economy. Ecuador's interest in exporting bananas to the EC was clearly more substantial than that of other countries which were given country specific allocations under the tariff quota. ACP countries and certain of the BFA signatory countries which were given country-specific allocations historically accounted for only a very small portion of all exports to the EC. Many of these countries, such as Belize, Cape Verde, the Dominican Republic, Grenada, Haiti, Venezuela, and Madagascar, accounted for less than 1 per cent of all imports between 1989 and 1991. Other countries in this category, such as Cameroon, Côte d'Ivoire, Dominica, Jamaica, Nicaragua, Somalia, St. Lucia, St. Vincent and the Grenadines, and Suriname accounted for less than 5 per cent of all imports of bananas into the EC during this period. Despite the fact that Ecuador had a more substantial interest than any other country in exporting bananas to the EC, the EC had failed to agree upon a country-specific allocation with Ecuador. In the opinion of Ecuador, the EC regime was, therefore, inconsistent with Article XIII.

4.115 According to Guatemala and Honduras, the allocation discrimination found no support in the provisions of Article XIII:2(d) which allowed quota allocations among supplying countries under specially circumscribed conditions. Article XIII:2(d) required that the EC either obtain an agreement regarding allocations from all Members having a "substantial" supplying interest or, where that approach was "not reasonably practicable," accord allocations that corresponded to shares during an unrestricted representative period. Guatemala and Honduras noted that the term "substantial interest" was not defined in Article XIII and was elsewhere established as "not capable of a precise definition."[109] Nevertheless, the EC had not attempted to follow any discernable "substantial interest" analysis based on what "might be expected ... in the absence of such restrictions." The most that could be said about its volume methodology was that it drew from periods of time in which illegal EC national policies were in effect. Even within those periods, however, a "substantial interest" approach was not pursued. Some of the preferential allocations, as in the case of Cape Verde and Somalia, were conferred to countries that were not even signatories of the WTO. Guatemala and Honduras, on the other hand – both of which were Members and both of which had greater trade interests than some or all traditional ACP suppliers – were denied the benefit of equivalent agreements. While the EC provided specific allocations even to the smallest ACP supplying countries, the EC had not awarded allocations to many third countries, including Guatemala and Honduras, that historically shipped greater volumes to the EC. Thus, the EC quite clearly ignored the "substantial interest"

[108] Regulation 404/93, Annex.

[109] Interpretative Note Ad Art. XXVIII, para. 1, note 7.

standard of Article XIII:2(d). The EC likewise could not defend its discriminatory tariff quota allocations on the grounds that the Complaining parties had the opportunity to accept source-specific allocations, but declined to do so. The EC had made clear that allocations would not be accorded to the Complaining parties unless they acquiesced to all illegalities inherent in the regime. Such an "opportunity" could not be seen as a legitimate exercise of fair trading interests. Tariff quota allocations were accordingly inconsistent with Article XIII:1 and XIII:2, and should be eliminated from the regime. The irregular allocation of tariff quota market share also violated the established requirement of Article XIII:2 that Members accord a distribution of trade comparable to that which would occur under unrestricted circumstances. Here, shares were guaranteed for certain sources, but not for similarly-placed other sources, a phenomenon that obviously would not occur under unrestricted market circumstances.

4.116 Guatemala and Honduras submitted that when Regulation 478/95 incorporated the BFA into the tariff quota, effective March 1995, it included tariff quota source allocations which assured inflated country-specific shares or volumes to numerous countries based on shares that prevailed under the national regimes, while forcing a deflated single "basket" portion to all others. The inflation of shares for every one of the BFA beneficiaries, and the deflation of shares for all others, pointedly demonstrated that preferential allocations were not only accomplished, but intended, by this apportionment.

4.117 The United States was of the view that the EC's distribution of market access did not reflect an attempt at a distribution of trade approaching as closely as possible the shares which Members could have been expected to obtain in the absence of restrictions. With respect to countries with a "substantial interest," the distribution did not reflect either of the two prescribed methods dependent on proportions supplied during a representative period. Indeed, the EC did not appear to have used consistently any criterion or set of criteria in allocating access to its market. In the first instance, the EC did not even use as a criterion membership in the GATT or WTO. The EC had awarded allocations to Cape Verde and Somalia, neither of which was a signatory of the GATT or the WTO agreements, while not awarding allocations to long-standing larger banana suppliers that were signatories.

4.118 With respect to Members, the EC did not appear to have considered any particular historical period as being representative for purposes of allocating shares of its market. The period 1989-91, which the EC claimed to have used to determine the size of the initial third-country tariff quota and to allocate import licences among the various "operators" could hardly, in the opinion of the United States, be considered "representative" in any event, since GATT-inconsistent restrictions on non-ACP bananas were in force at the time in several EC member States. However, even in 1989-91, with discriminatory restrictions in place, Ecuador was one of the EC's largest suppliers, with *15.53* per cent of global (including ACP) imports into the EC-12 (18.65 per cent in 1990-92). Counting only Latin American and other third-country suppliers, Ecuador had supplied well over 20 per cent of the EC-12 market in the years before Regulation 404/93. Since Ecuador had not agreed to the EC shares, the EC had surely failed to allocate the tariff quota in accordance with either of the methods prescribed by Article XIII:2(d) with respect to substantially interested parties. In contrast, the United States argued, although none of the ACP nations achieved even a 5 per cent share during the 1989-91 period, the EC awarded them all specific shares of the EC market. Several ACP nations to which the EC had awarded allocations did not even supply 1 per cent of total EC imports during the 1989-91 period; Madagascar shipped as little as 23 tonnes. Likewise, the EC had allocated a specific share to a BFA signatory, Venezuela, which supplied only 90 tonnes during 1989-91. The United States presented the following table:

EC-12 Imports: 1989-91 and 1990-92 compared to country allocations			
Country	**Average imports 1989-91 (tonnes)**	**Average imports 1990-92 (tonnes)**	**EC allocation (tonnes)**
Belize*	23,412	24,050	55,000
Bolivia	6	6	None
Cameroon*	83,180	101,394	162,500
Cape Verde*	2,820	2,534	4,800
Côte d'Ivoire*	98,914	119,283	162,500
Dominica*	52,897	54,355	71,000
Dominican Republic*	4,994	17,539	55,000
Ecuador	408,937	543,324	None
El Salvador	31	29	None
Ghana*	817	730	5,000
Grenada*	8,214	7,463	14,000
Guatemala	28,128	19,988	None
Honduras	136,910	153,223	None
Jamaica*	57,505	69,374	105,000
Madagascar*	23	3	5,900
Nicaragua	47,292	46,457	66,000
Panama	470,845	496,916	None
Somalia*	41,783	22,048	60,000
St. Lucia*	115,387	117,816	127,000
St. Vincent and the Grenadines*	70,732	72,516	82,000
Suriname*	28,465	28,466	38,000
United States	1,975	2,135	None
Venezuela	90	45	44,000
All Other Imports	940,989	1,011,732	-

* ACP country

Further, the United States noted that Article XIII did not appear to bar a country from providing allocations to countries that did not meet the substantial interest criteria but, in the opinion of the United States, the EC had to do so consistently with the general principle in Article XIII:2. In the opinion of the United States, the EC's regime was not based on such considerations. As set out in the above table the EC had provided allocations to many very small suppliers, but had not awarded allocations to many other countries with greater or nearly equivalent historical shipments. For example, during the EC's claimed representative period (1989-91), EC figures showed that El Salvador shipped roughly the same very small level of exports to the EC as Venezuela, and the United States exported over 20 times the quantity as Venezuela. Yet the EC gave only Venezuela a specific allocation. Likewise, the EC had awarded Belize and Nicaragua specific allocations based on average exports of 23,412 tonnes and 47,292 tonnes, respectively, while not granting an allocation to either Guatemala or Honduras, which had average exports of 28,128 tonnes and 136,910 tonnes, respectively. Thus, whatever criteria the EC had employed in establishing allocations for some countries, those same criteria had not been applied to other countries supplying similar or greater proportions of EC trade. The first sentence of Article XIII:2 did not permit the EC to provide country-specific allocations to some countries, and not to others, with disregard for the similarity of the countries' historic shipments. If Cape Verde, Dominican Republic, Somalia and Suriname had sufficient trade to warrant specific allocations, then so did Guatemala, Honduras and the United States.

4.119 Moreover, the United States pointed out that the EC did not apply consistently its 1989-91 "representative period" or any other apparent economic criterion when determining the precise allocations for those nations to which it gave such allocations. For example, St. Lucia supplied an average of 115,387 tonnes during 1989-91 and received an allocation equal to about 4.15 per cent of the EC's market, while the Côte d'Ivoire shipped less than St. Lucia (an average of 98,914 tonnes) and received a greater allocation (*5.07* per cent). Likewise, Jamaica shipped an average of 57,505 tonnes and received an allocation equal to *3.43* per cent, and St. Vincent and the Grenadines supplied an average of 70,732 tonnes and received an allocation equal to 2.68 per cent. Similar inconsistencies would have prevailed if the EC had used a later representative period, such as 1990-92.

4.120 The United States further claimed that the EC market allocation did not reflect historical shares within the third-country tariff quota. For example, among those countries currently subject to the tariff quota, Colombia's 1990-92 share of the EC-15 market, was under 19 per cent, compared to its allocation of 21 per cent presently. Also, the EC had failed to obtain the agreement of Ecuador, one of its major, obviously substantial, suppliers, or to provide Ecuador with an appropriate allocation along historical patterns of trade, as required by Article XIII:2(d). Moreover, the arbitrary manner in which the EC had provided country-specific allocations, even assuming that the restrictive, discriminatory period of 1989-91 were representative, demonstrated the EC's failure with respect to even the smallest suppliers to allocate its market to approximate the shares that would prevail in the absence of restrictions, in accordance with the first sentence of Article XIII:2.

4.121 Ecuador argued that in addition to the portion of the EC import market allocated to traditional ACP suppliers, the EC had allocated additional shares to Costa Rica, Colombia, Nicaragua and Venezuela, and to certain non-traditional ACP sources. These allocations were created through the BFA and the regulations implementing this agreement. The EC, Colombia, Costa Rica, Venezuela and Nicaragua concluded the BFA as part of a settlement of an earlier GATT challenge to the EC banana regime brought by the four Latin American countries along with Guatemala. In 1994, Colombia, Nicaragua, Venezuela, Costa Rica, and Guatemala challenged the EC import regime before a GATT panel. Although the panel found that several aspects of the regime violated GATT, the EC blocked the adoption of the panel report. However, as a condition for dropping their case against the EC, four of the five complaining countries concluded the BFA with the EC. The BFA granted each of the Latin American signatories country-specific shares of the tariff quota and adopted various other preferential and discriminatory import procedures. The allocation of tariff quota shares to the signatory countries did not represent, according to Ecuador, any rational distribution based on historical or commercial factors. Rather, the allocation was the arbitrary result of a political compromise.

4.122 According to Ecuador, the BFA allocated the third-country tariff quota as follows:

Colombia	21%
Costa Rica	23.4%
Nicaragua	3%
Venezuela	2%
Dominican Republic and other ACP countries	90,000 tonnes
Other	46.51%

4.123 The category "other" listed in the table included all other third-country suppliers, including Ecuador. Ecuador considered that the country-specific allocations for BFA countries violated Article XIII since no similar allocation was made for third countries in the "other" category despite that many of these countries had a substantial interest in exporting bananas to the EC, including Ecuador. Regulation 478/95, the regulation which implemented the BFA, also included, in Annex I, a country-specific allocation for non-traditional ACP sources which was not part of the BFA itself:

Dominican Republic	55,000 tonnes
Belize	15,000 tonnes
Côte d'Ivoire	7,500 tonnes
Cameroon	7,500 tonnes
Other ACP countries	5,000 tonnes

In the opinion of Ecuador, the EC had not satisfactorily explained why these suppliers were given country-specific allocations. In fact, the Commission had not provided a satisfactory explanation for how it calculated any of the country-specific allocations set out in the BFA and Regulation 478/95.

4.124 The United States observed that the EC's allocation method had resulted in a substantial reduction of the combined shares of the largely Latin American suppliers that were not signatories to the BFA. During 1989-91, these non-BFA signatories supplied over 40 per cent of EC-12 imports; yet, on the basis of the EC's method of granting allocations, these non-BFA signatories were permitted, collectively, to supply the EC-12 with less than 34 per cent of total imports.

EC enlargement

4.125 Ecuador argued that the share allocated to third countries included in the "other" category was substantially lower than the share which these countries held prior to the imposition of the EC banana regime. The EC had failed, according to Ecuador, to provide a satisfactory explanation justifying the discriminatory treatment of third-country suppliers in the "other" category. The EC effectively reduced the market access of Latin American bananas even further when, on 1 January 1995, it adopted transitional measures permitting the importation of only 353,000 additional tonnes of bananas[110] under the third-country tariff quota to take account of the accession of Austria, Finland and Sweden to the EC. The European Commission explained that the additional volume represented "the average net imports of these countries during the 1991-1993 reference period."[111] However,

[110] See Commission Regulation (EC) No. 3303/94, 21 December 1994; Commission Regulation (EC) No. 479/95, 1 March 1995; Commission Regulation (EC) No. 702/95, 30 May 1995; Commission Regulation (EC) No. 1924/95, 3 August 1995; and Commission Regulation (EC) No. 2008/95, 18 August 1995.

[111] See "Report on the Operation of the Banana Regime", Commission of the European Communities, SEC (95) 1565 final, p.11.

Ecuador noted, Eurostat data indicated that these countries imported an average of 388,000 tonnes annually during this period, 99 per cent of which, was imported from Latin American countries. In fact, the volume of third-country banana imports into the three new member States in 1994 alone was 465,900 tonnes, or 32 per cent above the volume allowed under the transitional measures. The data thus once again demonstrated the arbitrariness of the tariff quota allocations, especially compared to the ACP allocations.

4.126 The United States remarked that the EC did nothing to alleviate the discrimination in its allocation method when Austria, Finland and Sweden joined its customs union in 1995. The EC Council had not approved an increase in the tariff quota to account for Latin American access to these three countries. In 1995, the United States said, the EC Commission expanded the tariff quota by 353,000 tonnes under its discretionary authority to ensure an adequate market supply. The EC Commission was expected to make this same ad hoc expansion of the tariff quota in the fourth quarter of 1996 to accommodate consumption needs. Before 1995, the three new EC members imported almost all of their bananas from Latin American sources. By not approving a permanent increase in the tariff quota corresponding to imports by the new member States, the EC was in effect allocating shares for the EC-15 in the same proportions as for the EC-12. Since the new member States had purchased almost no bananas from ACP nations, this approach further skewed the allocation of the tariff quota away from being based on a representative period and highlighted the arbitrary nature of the overall allocation.

4.127 Even assuming the EC were to approve an increase in the tariff quota to account for the three new member States, the United States considered that the market shares the EC awarded to countries would remain inequitable when compared to historical imports. The EC gave, as shown in the table below (provided by the United States), ACP countries access to 27.8 per cent of the EC-15 market, significantly more than their shares during either the 1989-91 period or the 1990-92 period. At the same time, the EC failed to provide access even close to the historical shares of countries which did not join the BFA.

EC-15 historical market shares for groups of countries compared to current allocations			
Group	**Share of imports 1989-91 (per cent)**	**Share of imports 1990-92 (per cent)**	**EC allocation (per cent)**
ACP countries	20.0	19.5	27.8
Framework Agreement countries	37.4	36.1	37.0
Non-Framework Agreement countries	42.6	44.4	35.2
Total	100.0	100.0	100.0

4.128 Mexico argued that the reduction in access to the EC market had been maintained and increased due to the lack of a definitive increase in the EC's tariff quota to take account of the accessions of Austria, Finland and Sweden to the EC, as from 1995. In this case, despite the fact that imports originating in non-ACP countries to those markets amounted to 465,700 metric tonnes, the EC regime only authorized, on a transitional basis (during

1995), an amount of 353,000 metric tonnes. In 1996, there was no definitive increase to take into account the accession of the three new member States, and therefore the total amount of the EC tariff quota was still below what should be applied in accordance with the GATT.

- arguments of the EC

4.129 The EC presented its main arguments concerning the claims of the Complaining parties on allocation issues under two main headings: (i) that the application of Article XIII of GATT was not legally correct if applied to the totality of the EC market which consisted of two separate regimes; and (ii) that the application of Article XIII was not appropriate given the nature of the tariff bindings for agricultural products such as bananas and the specificity of the Agreement on Agriculture with respect to those bindings. Details of these matters are set out below along with the arguments of the Complaining parties concerning them. The arguments concerning Article XIII issues that have not been covered elsewhere, for example those concerning a representative period for allocation, are then reported. The EC also reiterated its arguments concerning the Lomé waiver. In this light it noted that while Article XIII could not be applied to two separate regimes as set out above, the Complaining parties had raised issues concerning the allocations to ACP countries. This allocation was, in the EC view, also covered by the provisions of the Lomé waiver: arguments concerning this aspect of the Lomé waiver are set out at the end of the section on general allocation issues (see also paragraph *4.173* below).

- separate regimes

4.130 With respect to the allegations raised by the Complaining parties concerning allocation issues, the EC submitted that no confusion should be allowed to arise between the ACP traditional allocation and the tariff quota allocation bound under EC Schedule LXXX. Specifically, the EC noted that the external aspects of the COM for bananas consisted of two distinct regimes:

(a) the regime for traditional ACP bananas which must be treated in accordance with the Lomé Convention and must be given preferential treatment. This regime was now covered by the waiver from the obligations of the European Communities under paragraph 1 of Article I of GATT with respect to the Lomé Convention; and

(b) a bound rate of duty for banana imports in excess of a tariff quota and a tariff quota allocation for all other bananas. This was a normal tariff quota, as it existed for many agricultural products in many Members.

4.131 The EC noted that the regime for ACP bananas involved the allocation of traditional quantities to ACP States. The quantities traditionally supplied (according to the "best ever" criterion up to and including the year 1990) by various ACP States, added up to 857,700 tonnes altogether, and entered the EC, as before, at zero duty (see Article 15(1) and the Annex of Regulation 404/93). The total of 857,700 tonnes was arrived at by adding up the individual allocations based on the best ever exports of the traditional ACP exporters to the Community. "Best ever" exports were interpreted broadly in the 12th preambular paragraph of Regulation 404/93. The EC recalled that in its meeting of 14-17 December 1992, the EC Agriculture Council decided that:

> The Lomé commitments will be met by allowing tariff-free imports from each ACP State up to a traditional level reflecting its highest sendings in any one year up to and including 1990. In cases where it can be shown that investment has already been committed to a programme of expanding production, a higher figure may be set for that ACP State.

It was clear that reasons of rational development policy inspired this decision to give a broad interpretation to the notion of "best ever" export performance; otherwise considerable investments, including in infrastructural works and therefore of benefit to the structure of a larger part of the economy than the banana sector alone, might have been redundant. Some of these investments in the banana industry and the infrastructure surrounding it were even carried out with substantial funding from the EDF and other development funds. Some of these investments, notably those relating to adaptation to new means of transport were necessary to maintain exports at a viable level.

4.132 In particular when establishing the "best ever" performances of Jamaica, Côte d'Ivoire, Cameroon and Belize such committed investments were taken into account. Obviously estimating "best ever" export performance by taking into account committed investments in banana plantations and banana related infrastructure was not an exact science, but the results were not excessive or unreasonable. Côte d'Ivoire was a good example. It claimed its "best ever" export year was 1972 with 146,200 tonnes exported to the EC. The result of an inquiry into investments committed over 1989-1992 showed that more productive plant varieties were being used and that additional irrigation and drainage works were being planned which, it was claimed, would raise production to over 200,000 tonnes. In the end, an amount of 155,000 tonnes was put in the Annex to Regulation 404/93.

4.133 The EC continued that Jamaica was a special case because it was reinvesting after extensive damage suffered from the hurricane Gilbert in 1988 and even from the 1980 hurricane Allen which, between them, had virtually destroyed banana production. One of the projects taken into account by the EC in this case was the complete reconstruction of the banana part of Port Antonio with the help of considerable EC funds. Many new plantings were also necessary. The EC stated that it was estimated that this would lead to exports of 105,000 tonnes in 1994 and this was the figure included in the Annex to Regulation 404/93. In the case of Cameroon, special attention was paid to the fact that banana production had dropped considerably during the 1980s and that in reaction thereto, the Cameroon Development Corporation, together with the World Bank, had undertaken important rehabilitation and development projects of three large plantations, which were intended to meet the needs of larger vessels and higher freight costs. The projects included drainage, irrigation, palletisation and packing stations. Estimated exports were over 200,000 tonnes as a consequence of these projects; a figure of 155,000 tonnes was adopted.

4.134 Belize was highly dependent on agricultural exports, of which bananas formed an important part. The European Development Fund, the World Bank and the Commonwealth Development Corporation cooperated in a project that was comparable to that of Cameroon, aimed at adaptation to newer and bigger vessels, with resulting investment not only in the plantations themselves, but also in roads and a port. Estimated production as a result was 59,000 tonnes by 1994, rising to a yearly average of 100,000 tonnes by 1996; the amount accepted as "traditional exports" was 40,000 tonnes, the EC submitted.

4.135 The EC went on to show to the Panel that separate import licensing regimes were also applied to tradition ACP bananas - this aspect is taken up more fully in section IV.B.2(c), below.

4.136 With respect to other banana imports, the EC noted that it had originally set a tariff quota for bananas at 2 million tonnes on a yearly basis and no specific shares for the various exporting countries were foreseen. The amount of 2 million tonnes was based on the average yearly imports during the period 1989-1991, the last three years for which according to the EC complete statistics had been available. The EC provided the following data:

Imports of Latin American and non-traditional ACP bananas (tonnes)

Year	1989	1990	1991	Average: 1989-91
Imports	1,716,931	2,023,660	2,294,414	2,011,669

The EC went on to note that the table was of little further relevance, however, as the total amount of the tariff quota had been consolidated in the Uruguay Round.

4.137 The Uruguay Round, concluded in Marrakesh on 15 April 1994, resulted in the consolidation of which was now part of the Schedule of the EC. It applied to fresh bananas, other than plantains, which appeared in tariff item number 0803.00.12. The EC MFN bound rate of duty for bananas was set out in Part I - Most-Favoured-Nation tariff, Section I - Agricultural Products, Section I-A Tariffs. The initial bound rate was ECU 850 per tonne, with a final rate for 2000 of ECU 680 per tonne, implemented in six equal annual reduction instalments. The rate for 1996 was ECU 793 per tonne. In addition, the EC included the following market access commitment in Part I Most-Favoured-Nation tariff, Section I - Agricultural Products, Section I-B Tariff quotas: initial and final tariff quota quantity (2,200,000 tonnes) and an in-quota tariff rate (ECU 75 per tonne) subject to the terms and conditions indicated in the Annex to that part of the schedule.

4.138 The Annex specified the market access commitments made under the Agreement of Agriculture and included the allocation of the tariff quota between the parties having a substantial interest in supplying the product concerned. The total was thus allocated, according to the Schedule, among various banana producing countries. The allocation reflects the shares in quantities of bananas imported in the EC as determined on the basis of the most recent statistical data available at the time of the negotiation, concerning the latest three years' representative of normal trade flows of importation of bananas into the EC. The Annex included the results of the conclusion of the BFA which implemented the same rules.

4.139 The EC went on to observe that, as it appeared clearly from the EC Schedule LXXX, non-traditional ACP bananas were allocated a consolidated share of the tariff quota up to 90,000 tonnes. However, non-traditional ACP bananas benefited from a preferential treatment which was covered, just as the ACP traditional allocation, by the Lomé waiver consisting of duty-free importation for the quantities indicated in the tariff quota. Moreover, the non-traditional ACP bananas benefited from preferential treatment of ECU 100 per tonne from the bound rate for non-tariff quota imports. This preferential treatment was equally covered by the Lomé waiver, as explained elsewhere.

4.140 Ecuador recalled that the EC had allocated 857,700 tonnes of the import market among twelve traditional ACP countries. The EC had stated that this allocation was based on the "best ever" import levels for each of these suppliers up to and including 1990. However, in virtually every case, the amounts allocated to the traditional ACP countries exceeded those countries' "best ever" import levels. In fact, the data indicated that there was no historical or commercial basis whatsoever to justify the allocation of the market given to traditional ACP suppliers. Ecuador considered that the "best ever" import levels for each of the traditional ACP countries given a country-specific allocation were far below the shares of the tariff quota allocated to each of these countries under Regulation 404/93. In the aggregate, the traditional ACP volume was 25 per cent higher than the "best ever" import volumes for traditional ACP countries up to and including 1990.

4.141 The disparity between the traditional ACP countries' historical imports and their share of the total EC import market was even more acute, according to Ecuador, if one focused on these countries' trade levels in the few years immediately before the signing of the Lomé Convention. According to Eurostat statistics, ACP banana exports to the EC averaged roughly 471,200 tonnes from 1986 to 1989, or 17.6 per cent of the EC's total imports. However, Regulation 404/93 guaranteed duty-free treatment for traditional ACP bananas for almost twice this amount. The disparity between the ACP countries' "best ever" import levels and the shares of the EC import market which they had been allocated under the EC's current banana regime was exacerbated even further by the fact that part of the third-country tariff quota was allocated to non-traditional ACP sources, i.e. bananas from traditional ACP suppliers imported above the traditional ACP tariff quota levels or bananas originating in non-traditional ACP countries. In 1995, the EC allocated 90,000 tonnes of the third-country tariff quota to non-traditional ACP sources.[112] With this supplemental ACP share, ACP countries were allocated 947,700 tonnes.

[112] Commission Regulation (EC) No. 478/95, 1 March 1995, Annex 1.

4.142 The United States noted that when allocating shares to ACP countries, the EC claimed to have used the "best ever" shipments up to 1990, presumably beginning this exercise after the first Lomé Convention was signed in 1975. This approach was, in the view of the United States, inconsistent with Article XIII. It inherently discriminated against other Members, since by definition using "best ever" meant that the shares of any other country would be reduced below its historical percentage. Moreover, the EC allocations had exceeded even the "best ever" figures for several countries. For example, Cameroon's actual "best ever" shipment was 79,596 tonnes, but the EC gave it an allocation of 162,500 tonnes. Furthermore, the EC's method of allocating shares was even more discriminatory than if it had used the actual "best ever" data for each ACP country and a 1989-91 representative period for Latin America. Using such a "combined" method, the Côte d'Ivoire would have received an allocation of the EC-12 market of *3.96* per cent, instead of the actual *5.31* per cent. Since the very premise of using a 1989-91 base period was, in the opinion of the United States, already flawed, the inequity for most Latin American banana-producing countries was all the more striking.

4.143 Mexico argued that the EC regime granted ACP countries access above the access that they should have received if the EC had applied the same reference period that it imposed on the remaining contracting parties, instead of computing its allocations on the basis of the exports made by ACP countries in the best year available. This situation could have been compatible with the obligations of the EC in light of the waiver of 9 December 1994, if the increase/advantage in favour of ACP countries had been provided in addition to the tariff quota for non-ACP countries. However, as the EC preferred to take part of the tariff quota of non-ACP countries and give it to the ACP countries, this situation resulted in a violation of Article XIII because it was no longer a case of an advantage (giving more to ACP) but of discrimination against non-ACP countries (taking away from non-ACP and giving to ACP).

4.144 The Complaining parties referred to the EC's main contention with respect to the allocation of its market that it had created discrete, legally separate regimes for ACP countries, BFA signatories and non-BFA signatories. They submitted that the notion of a distinct traditional ACP "regime" independent of the tariff quota was contradicted by the language of Regulation 404/93 and by the EC's many references to a single "banana regime." The EC's internal decision to treat products of these countries differently did not relieve the EC of its international obligations to apportion access to its market in accordance with Article XIII. However, even if the EC considered that it had created several regimes, nothing in Article XIII's rules on country allocations limited its application to "one specific quota or tariff quota" without regard to how other imports were treated. Article XIII:2(d) applied to the allocation of shares of a market. To the extent a Member created different types of restrictions, the Member had acted inconsistently with Article XIII:1 which required that imports from all sources be similarly restricted. To permit Members to circumvent the central GATT obligation of non-discrimination by allocating country shares under separate discriminatory "regimes" according to source would eviscerate Article XIII. The EC attempt to distinguish the *Dessert Apples* report on the basis that the report was only "confronted with one system", as opposed to the two arrangements at issue here was not appropriate as the panel in that case found that because "like products of all third countries had not been similarly prohibited" in the administration of import licences, the EC had acted inconsistently with its Article XIII obligations.[113] The EC's claim that separate quota allocation schemes (one preferential system and another system notified in the schedules) routinely existed among Members only underscored the danger of this approach. The Complaining parties were unaware of any other Members that allocated their markets in the manner described by the EC. If the EC was routinely engaging in such practices, it was, according to the Complaining parties, routinely violating Article XIII.

4.145 The Complaining parties argued that even using the so-called "best ever" shipments by ACP countries discriminated against other Members. By definition, "best ever" for one or more countries meant that the shares of other Members would be reduced below their historical, representative percentages. According to the Complaining parties, the EC had admitted that it also went beyond even the "best ever" shipments of some ACP countries to

[113] Dessert Apples, para. 12.21.

take into account "investments" being contemplated. These allocations exceeded, in their view, any access opportunities provided by EC member States in previous years, which, in the case of France and the United Kingdom, were defined not on the basis of pending investments or individual historical shipments, but on annual consumption needs in those countries.

4.146 As to the concern that EC investments would have been wasted if the allocations had not been overstated, the same could just as easily be said of the national banana investments under way or planned in the Latin American supplying countries. Moreover, the World Bank and other economists had pointed out that relative to "waste" that might derive from uncounted ACP investments, an EC funding waste of immensely greater magnitude had resulted from this EC regime, which had cost consumers $13.25 to transfer only $1.00 of benefit to ACP banana suppliers.[114] More to the point, other Members should not have to pay for the EC's budget mistakes.

4.147 The EC reiterated that there should be no confusion as to the totally separate nature of the two banana regimes of the Community: the ACP traditional allocation; and the EC regime for all other bananas. This reality was a direct result of both the Uruguay Round negotiations and of the existence of the Lomé Convention(s): any suggestion that this was designed in order to avoid a comparison of treatment under Article XIII was, in the view of the EC, a legal and factual nonsense. The EC submitted that the allocation of the EC tariff quota and the access to the EC market were not at all the same thing. The EC undertook at the end of the Uruguay Round to allow the importation of bananas into its customs territory under the conditions contained in its Schedule LXXX. Those bound commitments were: (i) unrestricted access to the EC market under a duty rate for 1996 of ECU 793 per tonne and with a final rate of ECU 680 per tonne in the year 2000; (ii) a tariff quota of 2,200,000 tonnes subject to a duty rate of ECU 75 per tonne and the conditions and terms indicated in the Annex to the Schedule. In this specific context, the only sensible meaning of the word "allocation" (and the only appropriate legal use of that concept), according to the EC, was to refer to the internal distribution of the tariff quota. It was the limited possibility of benefiting from the ECU 75 per tonne rate - that is the normal and accepted consequence of any tariff quota - that imposed a sharing out of the tariff quota in accordance with the relevant provisions of the GATT and, subject to the resolution of the legal issue concerning the prevailing application of the Agreement on Agriculture to the agricultural section of the schedules, eventually of Article XIII:5 of GATT. Allocation was therefore not synonymous with market access. In the view of the EC, this legal evidence had enormous consequences on the arguments presented by the Complaining parties.

4.148 Firstly, the EC considered that they could not claim that after the Uruguay Round there was a restriction of access to the EC banana market: the only thing the EC had done was to articulate its tariff concessions in two sections without restrictions of any kind on volumes of importation. Any allocation was therefore relevant only with respect to a special tariff rate and not to a volume. The size of the tariff quota, i.e. the actual extent of the concession made and bound by the EC at the end of the Uruguay Round had been accepted by ratification by all Members and was not and could not be under review in a Dispute Settlement procedure. Secondly, the EC argued, irrespective of the outcome of the legal analysis of the issue concerning the Agreement on Agriculture, the Complaining parties could not claim that Article XIII was applicable to totally separate regimes like the traditional ACP and the MFN regime under the WTO. Article XIII was in the view of the EC only applicable to tariff quotas by virtue of Article XIII:5 which extended the "provisions of this Article ... to any tariff quota instituted or maintained by any contracting party". It was only when allocating the tariff quota that the Complaining parties might be justified to request the application of Article XIII, if appropriate, and in particular of Article XIII:2. This had nothing to do with the separate allocation of a preferential regime, like the traditional ACP, which was governed by its own rules and procedures. The EC further argued that confusing allocation and access led to the paradoxical suggestion that Article XIII:2(d) applied to "the allocation of shares of a market". According to the EC, the Complaining parties view would inevitably entail the merging of the EC tariff quota and the traditional ACP allocations which should be analyzed under that provision as one regime and not as two separate ones. The

[114] See "Beyond EU Bananarama" Annex (1) at 22; see also Brent Borrell, "EU Bananarama III", Policy Research Working Paper 1386, The World Bank (1994), Annex (2).

EC considered this to be legally wrong: if Article XIII was to be applied obligatorily to shares of a market, and not to share of one quota or of one tariff quota, the consequence would be that the entire access of bananas to the EC market would be distributed in accordance with Article XIII -inside and outside of the tariff quota - even if that market was not restricted in any way. The EC considered that the correct conclusion was the opposite: Article XIII:5 indicated that in this particular context the provisions concerning allocations might be relevant with respect to the EC tariff quota. On a completely separate ground, other provisions, not contained in the EC commitments under the GATT, governed the preferential treatment of the ACP traditional allocation.

- GATT schedules and Articles I and XIII in the context of the Agreement on Agriculture

4.149 The EC noted that bananas were an agricultural product and hence the tariff and tariff quota on bananas were consolidations under the Agreement on Agriculture. Even though the old consolidated tariff of the EC for bananas was de-consolidated and negotiations begun under Article XXVIII of GATT with the countries which were (then) countries with initial negotiating rights or with a principal supplying interest, in the end the tariff and tariff quota were consolidated in the framework of the Uruguay Round. Further, as well known to all Members, the consolidation and scheduling of concessions and commitments in the agricultural sector followed its own dynamic and its own rules during the Uruguay Round and led, for instance, to the widespread recourse to tariff quotas in tariff scheduling. Many of these tariff quotas, were country-specific, i.e. they listed a limited number of countries to which they applied and for which certain quantifies were reserved, while what was left of the tariff quota was allocated to "others".

4.150 The specificity of the agricultural market access concessions was implicitly recognized in Article 4 of the Agreement on Agriculture, the EC submitted, where the existence of market access concessions in this economic sector was specifically recorded and a special reference was made in paragraph 1 to "Schedules relating to bindings and reductions of tariffs ... as specified therein." This gave these schedules a particular status which was all the more important when Article 21 of the Agreement on Agriculture was drawn into the analysis: "The provisions of GATT 1994 and of other Multilateral Trade Agreements in Annex IA to the WTO Agreement shall apply subject to the provisions of this Agreement". This Article confirmed the "agricultural specificity" in its clearest form and demonstrated that the rules of the Agreement on Agriculture, including the schedules specifically referred to in Article 4, superseded, if necessary, the provisions of GATT and the other agreements in Annex IA of the WTO Agreement. The EC submitted that Members negotiated their commitments on bananas during the Round in the framework of this agreed "agricultural specificity" and, therefore, no violation of Article XIII of GATT could be claimed with respect to the EC banana regime consolidated in the GATT.

4.151 Moreover, the EC noted that the general most-favoured-nation treatment principle as expressed in Article I of GATT was part of Part I of the GATT and read as follows:

> With respect to customs duties and charges of any kind imposed on or in connection with importation or exportation or imposed on the international transfer of payments for imports or exports, and with respect to the method of levying such duties and charges, and with respect to all rules and formalities in connection with importation and exportation, and with respect to all matters referred to in paragraphs 2 and 4 of Article III, *any advantage, favour, privilege or immunity granted by any contracting party to any product originating in or destined for any other country shall be accorded immediately and unconditionally to the like product originating in or destined for the territories of all other contracting parties (emphasis added).

In addition Article II:1(a) and (b) read:

> (a) Each contracting party shall accord to the commerce of the other contracting parties treatment no less favourable than that provided for in the appropriate Part of the appropriate Schedule annexed to this Agreement.
>
> (b) The products described in Part I of the Schedule relating to any contracting party, which are the products of territories of other contracting parties, shall, on their importation into the territory to which the Schedule relates, and subject to the terms, conditions or qualifications set forth in that Schedule, be exempt from ordinary customs duties in excess of those set forth and provided therein. Such products shall also be exempt from all other duties or charges of any kind imposed on or in connection with the importation in excess of those imposed on the date of this Agreement or those directly and mandatorily required to be imposed thereafter by legislation in force in the importing territory on that date.

Furthermore, Article II:7 clarified that "the schedules annexed to this Agreement are hereby made an integral part of Part I of this Agreement".

4.152 As Article II:7 clearly indicated, the EC banana concession was an integral part of Part I of GATT and was, therefore, to be considered integral part of Article I and Article II as appropriate. The EC submitted that this entailed the consequence that any application of the MFN principle set out in Article I could not prevail *per se* on the terms and conditions of the concession, in the present case the EC banana concession, since this would mean giving priority to one part of Article I on top of other parts of the same Article, as supplemented by the concessions. There was no evidence in the GATT that the CONTRACTING PARTIES were not aware of the effects of Article II:7. On the contrary, numerous indications supported this interpretation and excluded that it could be considered as unwanted or unwished by the CONTRACTING PARTIES (a sort of "*lapsus calami*").

4.153 The EC submitted that the CONTRACTING PARTIES to the GATT 1947 explicitly recognized that concessions were made part of Part I of the Agreement. This was acknowledgement of the fact that concessions were the result of multilateral negotiations after a sometimes long and difficult give-and-take process. The parties then solemnly accepted, by explicit and binding agreement duly reflected by the internal ratification or approval procedures, the content of the schedules mutually exchanged but only if and when they considered that, as a whole, the give-and-take process was satisfactory or, at least, acceptable for them. Without prejudice to what had been argued with respect of agricultural products' commitments under the Uruguay Round, the other parts of the GATT were to be applied taking into account at the same time two elements: the content of the concessions and the MFN principle, as supplemented by the concessions.

4.154 In the specific case of the EC banana concession, the EC continued, the CONTRACTING PARTIES agreed for the first time at the end of the Uruguay Round to the EC new banana regime based on the establishment of the tariff quota after the de-consolidation of the old and obsolete 20 per cent ad valorem bound rate and the creation of the EC-wide internal banana market. All the parties agreed explicitly, knowingly and deliberately to this new concession: nothing could justify now any of the Members reopening surreptitiously the negotiations by contesting within the present Panel procedure the internal balance of the negotiation that had just ended, violating the fundamental principle "*pacta servanda sunt*" as expressed in the Vienna Convention on the law of Treaties and customary international law.

4.155 Furthermore, the panel procedure *Canada/Japan - Import of Spruce, Pine, Fir (SPF) Dimension Lumber* (adopted on 19 July 1989), examined Canada's claim that Japan's application of an 8 per cent tariff on SPF dimension lumber was inconsistent with Article I:1 because SPF dimension lumber and dimension lumber of other types, which benefited from a zero duty rate, were like products within the meaning of Article I:1. The panel found that:

> ... a tariff classification going beyond the harmonized system's structure is a legitimate means of adapting the tariff scheme to each contracting party's trade policy interests, comprising both its protection needs and its requirements for the purposes of tariff and trade negotiations... The Panel considered that the tariffs referred to in the General Agreement are quite evidently, those of the individual contracting parties. It followed that if a claim of likeness was raised by a contracting party in relation to the tariff treatment of the goods on importation by some other contracting parties, such claim should be based on the classification of the latter, i.e. the importing country's tariff.[115]

Evidently, the panel and the GATT Council which adopted the report retained the interpretation that Article I of GATT was to be read together with the individual concessions for the relevant product contained in the schedules that were an integral part of Part I of GATT. This interpretation was, therefore, totally consistent with the wording and the purpose of Article II:7 of GATT.

4.156 In concluding on these issues, the EC argued that the provisions of Article I of GATT could not be considered applicable as such to the actual content of the EC banana tariff quota without taking into account the results of the Uruguay Round negotiations.

4.157 The Complaining parties rejected the EC claim that its banana regime enjoyed immunity from general WTO obligations, including GATT Article I and Article XIII, to the extent that its regime was reflected in its Schedule's market access concessions, which were generally referenced in the Agriculture Agreement. The Complaining parties noted that only a few elements of the EC banana regime were specified in the EC Schedule and provided the following table:

EC Uruguay Round Schedule relating to bananas	
Specified	**Not mentioned**
ECU 75 and ECU 850 per tonne tariffs	"Non-traditional" ACP tariffs (0 and ECU 750 per tonne)
2,200,000 tonnes tariff quota access	"Traditional" ACP allocations
BFA, including country allocations for BFA signatories and 90,000 tonnes set aside for non-traditional ACP supplies	"Non-traditional" ACP country-specific allocations laid down in Regulation 478/95
	Licensing arrangements for all foreign sources, including incentives to purchase EC bananas

Thus, this EC "defence" was irrelevant to all legal claims regarding discrimination against Latin American bananas in favour of ACP (and EC) bananas, and irrelevant to the legal analysis of import licensing procedures for bananas.

4.158 The Complaining parties submitted that the EC's claim that its country allocations were immunized because of a supposed conflict with the Agreement on Agriculture was unsubstantiated. In the Complaining parties' opinion, no provision of the Agreement on Agriculture pertained to non-discriminatory administration of

[115] BISD 36S/167, paras. 5.9 and *5.13*.

quantitative limitations. Article 4 of the Agreement on Agriculture, the only provision that even related to market access concessions at all, simply reminded Members that "[m]arket access concessions contained in schedules relate to bindings and reductions of tariffs, and to other market access commitments as specified therein." According to the Complaining parties, no provision in the Agreement on Agriculture conflicted with the EC's obligations to allocate market access in accordance with Article XIII of GATT. The Agreement on Agriculture did not address the allocation of tariff quotas and was never intended to re-write long-standing GATT rules on how such allocations had to be made or to allow members to deviate in their schedules from fundamental GATT principles such as the non-discrimination principle underlying Article XIII. If the Panel were to accept such a result, it would fundamentally undermine the Agreement on Agriculture and the WTO itself. The purpose, as stated in the preamble, of the Agreement on Agriculture was to create, "strengthened and more operationally effective GATT rules and disciplines," rather than to weaken the protection against discriminatory allocations of the tariff quotas. As a practical matter, those countries among Members which had allocated their markets as part of the Uruguay Round considered themselves bound by Article XIII. It would be highly inequitable if the Panel were to allow the EC to escape these same disciplines.

4.159 The Complaining parties argued that the EC assertion concerning agricultural specificity was irrelevant to the analysis of whether the EC had violated Article XIII with respect to its ACP allocations, since the EC's Schedule did not reflect country-specific allocations for either traditional or non-traditional ACP bananas. Moreover, this argument was without basis in the texts of the WTO agreements. Not only was there no provision of the Agreement on Agriculture that conflicted with the EC's obligations under Article XIII, it was also well established that the market access concessions in the schedules could not diminish Members' obligations under GATT and other WTO agreements. Referring to paragraph 1 of the Marrakesh Protocol, the Complaining parties agreed that in turn, Article II:7 of GATT provided: "The Schedules annexed to this Agreement are hereby made an integral part of Part I of this Agreement." Thus, all market access concessions in agriculture were considered an integral part of the GATT, and not of the Agreement on Agriculture, and therefore they could not present a conflict between the Agreement on Agriculture and any other agreement. Article 4.1 of the Agreement on Agriculture was nothing more than a cross reference to market access concessions - a reminder to Members that the result of the third element of the agriculture negotiations was largely contained elsewhere. In contrast, Article 21.2 made the Annexes to the Agriculture Agreement "an integral part of this Agreement." Had the drafters intended to make the schedules an integral part of the Agreement on Agriculture, they could have done so.

4.160 The Complaining parties noted that Article 21.1 of the Agriculture Agreement stated that "the provisions of GATT 1994 and of other Multilateral Trade Agreements in Annex 1A to the WTO Agreement shall apply subject to the provisions of this Agreement." This statement, inserted in tandem with Article 13 of the Agreement on Agriculture, was intended to ensure that Article 13 would supersede the separate disciplines of the Agreement on Subsidies and Countervailing Measures. The EC argument that this Article exempted any aspects of its banana regime mentioned in its Schedule from GATT and other WTO obligations was unsupported by the text. Since the market access concessions in the schedules did not constitute a "provision" of the Agreement on Agriculture, and no other provision in that Agreement pertained to allocation of market shares or any of the other aspects of the regime that were inconsistent with the GATT, Article 21.1 provided no defence to the EC's violations of the GATT or any other WTO agreement.

4.161 The EC reiterated that the provision of Article I of GATT could not be considered applicable as such to the actual content of the EC banana tariff quota without taking into account the results of the Uruguay Round negotiations. Members had negotiated their commitments on bananas during that Round in the framework of the agreed "agricultural specificity", and therefore no violation of Article XIII of GATT could be claimed with respect to the EC banana regime consolidated in the GATT. As for the separate preferential regime with regard to traditional Lomé suppliers, the EC had never claimed that the Agreement on Agriculture applied to it, since it was not included in the agricultural section of its Schedule. It was a wholly separate regime which originated in a preferential agreement covered by a waiver granted by the GATT contracting parties.

4.162 In reply to a question by the Panel, the EC noted that according to the Marrakesh Protocol, the schedules as such were incorporated into the GATT and not directly to the Agreement on Agriculture. Nevertheless, this formal element was not, in the EC's opinion, at all decisive while addressing the issue concerning the specificity of agricultural market access concessions and the priority of the rules of the Agreement on Agriculture, including the schedules referred to in Article 4, on the provisions of the GATT and the other Agreements of Annex 1A. The EC argued on both formal, i.e. based on the letter of the WTO texts, and substantive, i.e. based on the will of the contracting parties and the logic of the whole Uruguay Round negotiating process, grounds. From the formal point of view, paragraph 1 of the Marrakesh Protocol stated that "the schedule annexed to this Protocol relating to a Member shall become a schedule to GATT 1994 relating to that Member ...". The Marrakesh Protocol in itself was part of the GATT (GATT 1994, paragraph 1(d)). That being said, Article 1(g) of the Agreement on Agriculture defined, according to the EC, market access concessions as "all market access commitments undertaken pursuant to this Agreement". "All" commitments included, according to the EC, commitments other than bindings and the reduction of tariffs (as made clear in Article 4.1 of the Agreement on Agriculture) - including market access allocations. Article 4.1 of the Agreement on Agriculture further specified the notion of market access concessions, clarifying that "market access concessions contained in schedules relate to bindings and reduction of tariffs, and to other market access commitments as specified therein". Therefore the concept of "commitments undertaken pursuant to this Agreement", under Article 1(g) of the Agreement on Agriculture was, the EC argued, further specified by two elements present in Article 4.1 of the Agreement on Agriculture, i.e. "contained in the schedules" and "specified therein" and it could consist of "bindings", "reduction of tariffs" and "other market access commitments as specified therein" (i.e. allocations).

4.163 The EC thus submitted, on the basis of Article 4.1 and Article 1(g), it could be affirmed that market access commitments (including allocations) contained in Part I, Section I - Agriculture tariff schedules were commitments undertaken pursuant to the Agreement on Agriculture. Therefore the provisions of the Agreement on Agriculture applied to them. According to Article 21, provisions of the GATT applied subject to the Agreement on Agriculture provisions. In conclusion, the question to be asked was not whether the schedules were "incorporated" into the Agreement on Agriculture, but rather whether the provisions of the Agreement on Agriculture applied to them. In the opinion of the EC, the Agreement on Agriculture provisions did indeed apply to Part I, Section I of the schedules. More specifically, the relevant provision was Article 4.1, read in conjunction with Article 1(g): market access commitments undertaken pursuant to the Agreement were those contained in the schedule. This provision thus prevailed on the GATT. Moreover, paragraph 3 of the Marrakesh Protocol indicated clearly that the implementation of the concessions and commitments contained in the schedules "... would be without prejudice to the rights and obligations of Members under Agreements in Annex 1A of the WTO Agreement". When raising the issue of the applicability of Article XIII or of other provisions under any Agreement in Annex 1A to the provisions contained in the agricultural schedules, the Complaining parties were, according to the EC, referring themselves to the administration of those concessions (heading of Article XIII of GATT itself). The same Protocol, however, clarified that any right accruing under those concessions was subject, in the implementation of the concession, to the provisions of the Agreements in Annex 1A. In the case of the Agreement on Agriculture, therefore, while implementing those concessions, the rights of the parties were limited to "bindings and reduction of tariffs and to the other market access commitments as specified therein" (Article 4.1 of the Agreement on Agriculture) and not more. And no other GATT provision was applicable (Article 21.1 of the Agreement on Agriculture).

4.164 The EC considered that the actual drafting of the Agreement on Agriculture was also justified by a number of substantive reasons. Market access concessions were the subject of Article 4 of the Agreement on Agriculture. This Article stated the obvious, according to the EC, namely that these concessions were contained in schedules, that they related to bindings and reductions of tariffs and to other market access commitments as specified, and that Members would not revert to the practices which they converted into tariffs during the Uruguay Round agricultural tariffication exercise. As the Article stated the obvious, the only function of the Article could be to create a special link between the agricultural schedules, which had been included with the other schedules into the Marrakesh Protocol to the GATT and the Agreement on Agriculture. Through this special link, the agricultural schedules profited from the agricultural specificity as laid down in Article 21 of the Agreement on Agriculture. It would be absurd to restrict the scope of Article 21 only to the provisions of the Agreement on Agriculture and not extend it to the results of agricultural tariffication, and of the results of the negotiations on commitments on export subsidization and internal support. The methods of this negotiation, the resulting rules and finally the concessions made and commitments taken were none of them fully orthodox under the rules of the GATT, the Agreement on Subsidies and Countervailing Measures or the Agreement on Safeguards, but they constituted a sufficient protection of an exceptional regime for agriculture for some and a sufficient step in the direction of ultimate coverage of agriculture by the general rules of GATT, to be acceptable to all.[116] On the other hand, it was generally recognized that so-called agricultural specificity under Article 21 was necessary in order to give legal protection to this step in the right direction. One part of the overall result, i.e. the result of the tariffication exercise, could not now be excluded from this agricultural specificity without unbalancing the overall result of the negotiations. The widespread use of tariff quotas which were allocated according to the same method as that used by the EC (i.e. some country-specific allocations and an "other" category) in the case of bananas, was a clear indication that this practice was considered acceptable under the Agreement on Agriculture.

4.165 For the above-mentioned reasons, the EC was of the view that Article 21 of the Agreement on Agriculture implied that schedules on market concessions might contain commitments which were inconsistent with the obligations of the GATT and other Agreements of Annex 1A. The EC stressed that paragraph 1 of the Marrakesh Protocol indicated that "the schedule annexed to this protocol relating to a Member shall become a schedule to GATT 1994 relating to that Member on the day on which the WTO Agreement enters into force for that Member". The EC considered thus that terms, conditions and qualifications contained in market access concessions enjoyed complete immunity from legal challenge on the basis of any of the agreements listed in Annex 1A.

4.166 The EC referred to the Complaining parties claim that Article 21 of the Agreement on Agriculture shall prevail with regard to provisions of GATT and of the other Agreements under Annex 1A and was only connected to Article 13 of the Agreement in order to ensure that the provisions of that Article would prevail on the Agreement on Subsidies. The EC responded that it was sufficient to look at the text of the Agreement to contradict such an interpretation. There was no indication in the text of the Agreement that Article 21 was limited in scope. On the contrary, the reader was immediately struck by the general coverage of Article 21, as compared to Article 13 itself, which specifically set out its prevalence with respect to the Subsidies Agreement. The text of the Agreement supported no other conclusion but the one that Article 21 concerned all provisions of the Agreement on Agriculture. Furthermore, referring to the Complaining parties' affirmation that schedules were not provisions of the Agreement on Agriculture and that therefore Article 21 provided no defence for the EC's violations, the EC maintained that this was not what Article 21 said. Article 21 stated that the provisions of the GATT shall apply subject to the provisions of the Agreement on Agriculture. Article 21 did not require schedules to be provisions of the Agreement: it regulated prevalence of application of such provisions. The EC was of the view that the provisions of the Agreement on Agriculture applied to the market access commitments of the agricultural schedule of the EC, and prevailed on GATT.

4.167 The Complaining parties maintained that the EC had simply disregarded the texts of the Agriculture Agreement in arguing that the incorporation of certain country-specific allocations in its Uruguay Round Schedule somehow relieved it from its Article XIII obligations. In their view, although the EC had now admitted that the schedules were not incorporated in the Agriculture Agreement, it had dismissed the legal effect of this point by characterizing the text as a mere "formality."

4.168 Furthermore, the Complaining parties rejected the EC claims that Article XIII requirements did not apply to its market allocations and specifically that no challenge could be brought because the allocations for Colombia,

---

[116] The EC pointed out, however, that there were also similarities between the Agreement on Agriculture and the GATT. Both laid down a number of provisions which could not just exist by themselves, but for their full effect were dependent on the commitments laid down in schedules.

Costa Rica, Nicaragua and Venezuela were located in the EC's Uruguay Round Schedule: while the Complaining parties understood that the EC had provided tariff bindings protected by Article II of GATT to four countries, these bindings, in their view, did not relieve the EC of its obligations under Article XIII or any other WTO disciplines. As concerns the EC's Article II:7 argument generally, the Complaining parties referred to the *Sugar Headnote* case[117] which was presented with the claim, in relation to a provision in the United States Schedule XX, that Article II:1(b) permitted a country to place conditions in its schedule that would override other obligations of the GATT. The *Sugar Headnote* panel rejected this claim after analysing the wording, purpose and drafting history of Article II and GATT practice. With respect to the wording, the panel considered that Article II:1(b) might permit parties to qualify the obligation to exempt products from customs duties in excess of the levels specified in the schedule, but not to qualify their obligations under other Articles of the GATT. The panel also noted that the title of Article II was "Schedule of Concessions" and that the ordinary meaning of "to concede" was "to grant, yield," which further suggested that Article II permitted countries to incorporate into their schedules acts yielding rights under the GATT, but not acts diminishing their obligations. The panel then confirmed this interpretation in light of the preamble to the GATT, which noted that the Agreement consisted of "mutually advantageous arrangements directed to the substantial reduction of tariffs and other barriers to trade," language that was repeated in the preamble to the WTO Agreement. The panel observed that where the GATT referred to specific types of negotiations, it referred to negotiations aimed at the reduction of barriers to trade (Articles IV(d), XVII:3 and XXVIII bis), which further supported the assumption that:

> Article II gives contracting parties the possibility to incorporate into the legal framework of the General Agreement commitments additional to those already contained in the General Agreement and to qualify such additional commitments, not however to reduce their commitments under other provisions of that Agreement.

The panel further considered that other parts of the GATT, notably Article XVII:3, supported the interpretation that GATT obligations could not be diminished through a negotiation and that past practice showed that contracting parties "did not envisage that qualifications in schedules established in accordance with Article II:1(b) could justify measures inconsistent with the other Articles of the General Agreement." Finally, the panel noted that the drafting history of Article II did not support a contrary interpretation.[118] In the opinion of the Complaining parties, the reasoning and conclusions of the *Sugar Headnote* panel were no less valid with respect to the EC's Uruguay Round Schedule. Arguments that this interpretation would destabilize the market access concessions agreed to in the Round were an exaggeration. The Uruguay Round market access negotiations, particularly those concerning agricultural trade, were concluded with the full knowledge of this report.

4.169 Referring to the Complaining parties reference to the *Sugar Headnote* panel, and notwithstanding the EC's conviction that no violation of GATT had been demonstrated with regard to the EC concession on bananas, the EC underlined that the panel predated the entry into force of the WTO and of the Multilateral Agreements on Trade in Goods as set out in Annex 1A of that Agreement. The EC considered that in light of the general interpretative note to Annex 1A,[119] the relationship between GATT and the agreements on trade in goods, and more specifically in light of Article 21 of the Agreement on Agriculture which reinforced, in a way, such a rule with respect to the Agreement on Agriculture, the *Sugar Headnote* ruling had to be reviewed to take account of the prevalence of the provisions of the other Agreements on GATT 1994. It could not in any case be transposed as such into the present case.

---

[117] Report of the panel on "United States - Restrictions on the Importation of Sugar and Sugar-containing Products applied under the 1955 Waiver and under the Head Note to the Schedule of Tariff Concessions", adopted 7 November 1990, BISD 37S/228.

[118] Sugar Headnote case, paras. 5.2-5.7.

[119] "In the event of a conflict between a provision of the GATT 1994 and a provision of another Agreement in Annex 1A ..., the provision of the other Agreement shall prevail to the extent of the conflict."

- Parties' arguments - interpretive issues

4.170 Specifically with respect to the Complaining parties claims concerning an alleged violation of Article XIII concerning the structure of the tariff quota, the EC recalled its remarks in which it clearly indicated that the tariff and tariff quota consolidations on bananas were current access consolidations under the Agreement on Agriculture. The consequence of that analysis was that Article 21 of the Agreement on Agriculture confirmed the "agricultural specificity" in its clearest form and demonstrated that the rules of the Agreement on Agriculture, including the schedules specifically referred to in Article 4, superseded, if necessary, the provisions of the GATT and the other Agreements of Annex IA. Therefore, the EC continued, provisions of Article XIII of GATT, in particular, could not be considered applicable to the actual content of the tariff quota and the EC was of the opinion that no violation of this Article could be claimed with respect to the EC banana regime consolidated after the Uruguay Round.

4.171 It was therefore solely on the subsidiary basis that the EC would examine the claims presented by the Complaining parties about the alleged violation of Article XIII by the structure of the bound tariff quota. In this narrow and specific context, the EC argued that a preliminary distinction had to be made between two series of allegations: (i) no claim of discrimination (and consequent violation of Article XIII) could be raised against the country allocation within the MFN tariff quota as compared to the allocation within the ACP traditional quota. The EC had already demonstrated that Article XIII related only to the non-discrimination in the administration of a quota or a tariff quota. Therefore Article XIII was relevant and applicable only in so far one specific quota or tariff quota was considered, and specifically its administration. No argument could on the contrary be made under Article XIII, in particular Article XIII:1, alleging discrimination in the administration of two different regimes, which are independent one from the other and each legally justified on a different basis; and (ii) no violation of Article XIII, and in particular paragraph 2, had occurred in the structuring of the EC MFN tariff quota.

4.172 As a practical matter, the EC, by means of a graph showing supply trends and, in particular, the increase in third-country imports into the EC after the fall of the Berlin Wall in 1989, argued that: in every year since the start of the regime, quantities significantly above the bound tariff quota had been imported from "others" alone, not counting any non-traditional ACP volumes; the level of the bound quota was significantly above any volumes which came into the EC-15 up until 1990; and the dramatic effect on banana imports of the fall of the Berlin Wall and the subsequent reunification of Germany. In this light, the EC continued, volumes rose sharply from the end of 1989 through 1990 and into 1991 (when the effects of speculation also began to push up volumes temporarily) as the market and distribution systems developed. The increase was the result of 16 million additional consumers being added to the EC, and was not due to any increase in individual propensity to consume bananas - it was a one-off increase and not evidence of a trend to increased consumption.

4.173 The EC continued that the graph showed that the policy had not led to dramatic increases in supply from either domestic sources or ACP countries, thus refuted the arguments that the EC banana policy represented such advantages for EC and ACP producers that these would become the preferred sources of supply and that traders would rush to import these bananas in preference to Latin American fruit. In the view of the EC the graph clearly demonstrated the emptiness of the Complaining parties' chief arguments in that: the creation of the EC single market for bananas had not had unduly restrictive effects on Latin American exporting countries; the volume of the tariff quota was justifiable and reasonable; the volume imported under the tariff quota had always been significantly above its bound level; the administrative procedures governing imports were clearly not acting as a deterrent to the utilization of the tariff quota; and there was no discernable shift in sources of supply from "others", which had remained remarkably constant throughout the three and a half year life of the EC banana policy at 63-64 per cent of total supply.

4.174 With respect to Article XIII:2, the EC argued firstly that in applying it, one should refer to the chapeau of the paragraph where it was indicated that:

> in applying import restrictions to any product, contracting parties shall aim at the distribution of trade in such a product approaching as closely as possible the shares which the various contracting parties might be expected to obtain in the absence of such restrictions and to this end shall observe the following provisions.

The last part of that chapeau made it clear that the principle stated in the first part of the chapeau was respected as soon as one of the alternative provisions in paragraph 2(a) to (d) was correctly observed. Consequently the fulfilment of the obligations of one of the alternative provisions listed in Article XIII:2(a) to (d) entailed automatically the fulfilment of the obligations of non-discrimination under the Article. Secondly, in allocating the tariff quota among supplying countries the EC followed the principle of Article XIII:2(d). Under Article XIII:2(d) two methods of possible allocation of the (tariff) quota were indicated: (i) through an agreement with respect to the allocation of shares in the quota with all other contracting parties having a substantial interest in supplying the product concerned; and (ii) when method (i) was "not reasonably practicable", through allocation to contracting parties having a substantial interest in supplying the product of shares based upon proportions, supplied by such contracting parties during a previous representative period, of the total quantity or value of imports of the product, due account being taken of any special factors which have affected or may be affecting the trade in the product. In a response to a question posed by the Panel, the EC submitted that under Article 31 of the Vienna Convention on the Law of the Treaties, "a treaty shall be interpreted in good faith in accordance with the ordinary meaning to be given to the terms of the treaty in their context and in the light of its object and purpose". The text of Article XIII:2(d) imposed a hierarchy of criteria: method (i) above was to be applied prior to method (ii) above, but nothing in that Article indicated that the first criteria was an absolute alternative to the second. That was to say that in cases when an agreement could be reached only with some of the parties which were Members having a substantial interest, while agreement could not be reached with other similar parties, then the two criteria could (and perhaps should) be combined.

4.175 In this light, after the de-consolidation of the obsolete 20 per cent ad valorem tariff rate, the EC negotiated, during the Uruguay Round, the creation of a tariff quota where the shares in importing quantities were allocated, in their major part, among parties having "a substantial interest in supplying the product concerned". The allocation among the countries signatories of the BFA was based on the statistical data of the reference period which was based on the latest three years of importation which could be considered representative of normal trade flows. The same treatment was offered to Guatemala with which the EC sought agreement in applying the tariff quota - indeed Guatemala, was offered, in 1993, 1.5 per cent of the tariff quota (compared to the average imports to the EC from Guatemala for the period 1989-91 of 1.56 per cent) while after its entry into force, Guatemala has continued to supply similar quantities (1.3 per cent in 1993 and 1.0 per cent in 1994 according to the latest official statistics). Even Ecuador, Honduras and Panama, while not contracting parties to the GATT, were offered a share in the allocation on the basis of the same objective statistical evidence. They all refused.

4.176 The EC submitted that it proceeded to distribute the quota according to the agreement reached with the BFA on one side and the "others" on the other side, while at same time it preserved entirely "the distribution of trade of bananas approaching as closely as possible the shares which the various contracting parties might be expected to obtain in the absence" of such tariff quota. As it had already been indicated, many of the tariff quotas consolidated in the Uruguay Round were country-specific, i.e. they listed a limited number of countries to which they applied and for which certain quantities were reserved, while what was left of the tariff quota was allocated to "others". In the EC view, it could not be held responsible for the lack of will and cooperation of a Complaining party under the Uruguay Round negotiations to achieve a different result.

4.177 Thirdly, the EC argued, the size of the tariff quota itself or the very existence of the tariff quota could not be disputed in this procedure. The establishment of a tariff quota was legally admissible under the GATT and was one of three possible tariff structures that could be conceded in the schedules in application of Article II, the others were a specific duty and an ad valorem duty. A combination of them was also possible and accepted. From the structure and the drafting history of the GATT it was clear that a contracting party, even in case of legally bound tariffs (which was the case of 99 per cent of the products imported to developed countries under the present conditions after the Uruguay Round) was entitled to bind them at a level that it considered appropriate and even subsequently modify them under certain conditions (Article XXVIII of GATT). A party was entitled to apply a tariff that could be, for instance, 100 per cent, 1000 per cent or 10,000 per cent of the value of a given product expressed in terms of specific amount or ad valorem. The same result could legally be achieved through the creation of a tariff quota which was neither prohibited nor impeded provided that Articles II and XIII were respected.[120] The banana tariff quota was bound under the Uruguay Round in EC Schedule LXXX, and respected the provisions of Articles II and XIII. The other parties signatories of the Marrakesh Protocol and the parties acceding later to the WTO explicitly accepted the multilateral result of these negotiations.

4.178 With respect to the specific arguments made by the Complaining parties concerning the enlargement of the EC, the EC replied that the accession of Austria, Finland and Sweden to the EC became effective on 1 January 1995. As was usual in such circumstances, the EC engaged in the procedure of Article XXIV:6 of GATT, i.e. the EC made itself available for negotiations under Article XXVIII with any Member having initial negotiating rights or having a substantial interest in the trade of specific products. Although considerable interest was expressed by various Members in the adjustment of agricultural tariff quotas subsequent to accession, in particular in the grains sector, none of the traditional trading partners of the EC in bananas manifested itself for adjustment of the tariff quota on bananas. In these circumstances, the EC Commission decided that the EC should act autonomously. It ensured that there was an increase in the tariff quota by 353,000 tonnes as from the date of accession. This amount corresponded to the average yearly consumption of bananas in these three countries over the period 1991-1993.[121] Although the increase was autonomous, it was not ad hoc, as was borne out by the table below provided by the EC. This additional quantity had become part of the overall system and was subject to the same rules as the rest of the tariff quota. The actual consolidation of the tariff quota in the Schedule of the EC-15, however, remained the same as it was under the EC-12, i.e. 2.2 million tonnes.

Net imports, in tonnes, of bananas by the three new member States during the period 1991-93				
	1991	**1992**	**1993**	**Average**
Austria	121,597	120,355	115,896	119,283
Finland	73,041	80,836	72,187	75,355
Sweden	159,449	161,725	152,342	157,839
Total	354,087	362,916	340,425	352,476

According to the EC, these were the statistics supplied by the relevant authorities in Austria, Finland and Sweden and used to establish the appropriate volume to be added to the tariff quota. The EC submitted, in an answer to a question by the Panel, a table that showed the volume of re-exports of bananas from the three new member States. In 1994, re-exports totalled 119,408 tonnes. The import figures supplied by the relevant authorities in Austria,

[120] "EEC - Import of Beef from Canada", BISD 28S/92, adopted 10 March 1981 - "Newsprint", BISD 31S/114, adopted 20 November 1984.

[121] The EC noted that a total of over 464,000 tonnes in 1994 had been mentioned as imports in the three new member States. This total was from a year which could not serve as reference year for the additional quantities. There was also serious doubt that this figure was a net figure, i.e. re-exports might not have been subtracted from it.

Finland and Sweden, which were used to calculate the appropriate volume of tariff quota (353,000 tonnes) were net of re-exports.

4.179 Guatemala and Honduras considered that the EC's summary assertion that during the enlargement of the EC, "none of the traditional trading partners of the Community manifested itself for negotiations under Article XXIV:6" ignored the accession circumstances surrounding the banana regime in 1995. When Austria, Finland and Sweden acceded to the EC, it remained unclear how those countries were to be integrated into Regulation 404/93 *et seq.* For the whole of 1995, banana imports into the EFTA-3 were governed by "transitional" measures. In 1996, when the EFTA-3 were brought under the regime created by Regulation 404/93, Guatemala and Honduras were already beginning to prepare for a comprehensive WTO challenge, in which all rights and interests were to be pursued. Even so, throughout the "transition" period, Guatemala and Honduras had made their concerns known to the EC that EFTA-3 accession would compound restrictions and distortions in EC banana trade. Their concerns in fact proved valid, as even today, more than a year and a half after the accession of the EFTA-3 to the EC, the Commission had not fully incorporated the EFTA-3 volumes into the banana regime. The July 1996 regulation increasing the tariff quota by 353,000 tonnes was "autonomously" implemented, meaning that the 1997 tariff quota would return to 2.2 million tonnes, unless changed by EC Council action or another autonomous increase.

4.180 More generally, the Complaining parties claimed that the requirements of Article XIII did not permit the EC to invite some Latin American countries to obtain a country-specific allocation under the terms of the BFA, and then, after they refused, proclaim that the EC could not be held responsible for the lack of will and cooperation of the other parties. The Complaining parties were of the opinion that the EC was "responsible" under Article XIII. If the EC could not reach agreements with substantially interested parties, then it had to divide its market on an historical basis, consistent with the aim of providing shares that would be expected to prevail in the absence of restrictions. It could not provide generous country-specific allocations to BFA signatories and ACP countries that discriminated against other Members which had decided not to waive their GATT and WTO rights. It was precisely this kind of conditionality that was barred by Article XIII's requirement that the EC obtain agreement of all substantially interested parties.

4.181 The Complaining parties argued that with respect to the meaning of Article XIII requirements, the EC had blurred the distinctions in paragraph 2(d) between the two methods for allocating quotas among suppliers. The Complaining parties considered that the text of Article XIII:2(d) was clear: the methods presented alternative options, either one of which must be satisfied in order to comply definitively with the general principle stated in the first sentence of paragraph 2. The use of the word "all" in the first sentence of paragraph 2(d) required, according to the Complaining parties, a country to obtain agreement with all countries with a substantial interest. It did not allow agreement to be reached with only some selected countries. The requirement that agreement be reached with all substantially interested countries was recognized by the panel in *Norway - Restrictions on Imports of Certain Textile Products,*[122] which concluded that an agreement reached with six out of seven substantial supplying countries was not sufficient to satisfy the first sentence of Article XIII:2(d).

4.182 Moreover, the word "method" in the second sentence of paragraph (d) further implied that the first sentence represented a single approach, not an example of a way to deal with one substantially interested trading partner and not others. It might well be that a country employing the second method could also have the agreement of some of the substantially interested parties, but this would not be legally required, nor would it amount to a "combined method." Article XIII:2(d)'s provision for alternative options was also confirmed by the drafting history of this provision relating to the two methods. The London Report of the Preparatory Committee for the Havana Conference listed a "desirable set of principles" in "applying the principle of non-discrimination to import restrictions," which included the following:

[122] "Norway - Restrictions on Import of Certain Textile Products", adopted 18 June 1980, BISD 27S/119, paras. 15-16.

> the restrictions might take the form of a quota allocated among the various sources of supply. In this case the general principle should be to allocate the quotas on commercial principles such as price, quality and customary sources of supply. These commercial principles might be applied in principle in either of two ways - firstly, agreement might be sought between the exporters who have a substantial interest in supplying the product, and secondly, where this course is not reasonably practicable, reference should be made to shares in a previous representative period. ...[123]

Although the "commercial considerations" principle was dropped in the Geneva conference in August 1947 because its application by government authorities might not always be practicable, the draft's reference to "either of two ways" of applying the overriding principle explicitly confirmed that the two methods should be read as alternatives.[124]

4.183 The EC reiterated that on 26 October 1993 it notified that it wanted to de-consolidate its tariff binding of 20 per cent for bananas and modify its Schedule on bananas under Article XXVIII of GATT 1947. Hence the EC sought negotiation with the "contracting parties primarily concerned", and with those having "a substantial interest" in the EC's banana concession. As had, in the EC's opinion, rightly been indicated by certain third parties, by a constant practise under GATT 1947 that had never been questioned after the Uruguay Round, the term "substantial interest" was meant to cover only those Members which had "a significant share in market", as it was confirmed by paragraph 7 of the note to paragraph 1 of Article XXVIII of GATT 1994. That was interpreted under GATT 1947 as referring to contracting parties that could account for at least 10 per cent of the market. Colombia and Costa Rica (which could both claim to have a "substantial interest" in the trade, each with a share of around 20-25 per cent) were included along with Brazil which had the initial negotiating right for the product. At that time, other countries exporting to the EC, such as Ecuador, Panama and Honduras, were not contracting parties to the GATT and, therefore, had no rights under the General Agreement. Honduras became a Member on 1 January 1995 and Ecuador on 26 January 1996. Panama was in the process of acceding to the WTO. They were nevertheless kept aware of the discussions. Also included in the discussions with the countries having a substantial interest in the EC's banana concession were other countries which had been involved as complaining parties in the second *Banana* panel. These were Venezuela, Nicaragua and Guatemala. The negotiations under Article XXVIII became bound up with the Uruguay Round negotiations and the scheduling exercise that was going on for agricultural products in general. Bananas being an agricultural product, their tariff re-consolidation had to respond to the criteria for scheduling in the agricultural sector, as a so-called current access commitment.[125] The consolidations of current access commitments led to the widespread use of tariff quotas. These negotiations and discussions resulted in the BFA which was integrated in the EC's final Uruguay Round Schedule.

4.184 Indeed the offer the EC made to its negotiating partners in the Uruguay Round, on 14 December 1993, represented an extraordinary effort by the EC to have an agreed allocation of the tariff quota well beyond any obligations that any Member might be deemed to have, under other circumstances, under Article XIII. None of the present Complaining parties could have claimed at the time to be entitled to any offer under Article XIII:2(d) for an agreed distribution of the tariff quota nor to any specific allocation under the same provision. Not Ecuador or

---

[123] See "Report of the First Session of the London Preparatory Committee of the United Nations Conference on Trade and Employment" (UN Document EPCT/33), October 1946, at 14.

[124] In the view of the Complaining parties, the "commercial considerations" principle was in any event made somewhat redundant with the introduction of the principle now set forth in the first sentence of Article XIII:2, which first appeared in the draft resulting from the New York Conference (January and February 1947). According to the Report of the New York Conference, subsequent redrafting of the other aspects of para. 2, including those pertaining to the two methods, were made "so as to make the provisions more clear and more consequential". "Report of the Drafting Committee of the Preparatory Committee of the UN Conference on Trade and Employment" (UN Document EPCT/34) Lake Success, NY, 5 March 1947, p.23.

[125] According to the EC, these criteria became obsolete after the Uruguay Round results were signed and no longer appear in the Agreement on Agriculture.

Honduras - which were not, as noted above, contracting parties; not Guatemala - which with 0.6 per cent share of trade in the year before the offer was made could have hardly been considered having an interest, let alone a substantial interest under Article XIII; not Mexico - which had never exported to the EC other than symbolic quantities; and not the United States which was neither producing more than a symbolic quantity nor *a fortiori* exporting to the EC. The EC agreed with the Complaining parties that under a rigorous interpretation of Article XIII the EC should have obtained agreement of all substantially interested parties. And this is exactly what it did when it passed an agreement with Colombia and Costa Rica. Unfortunately, none of the Complaining parties could at the time be reasonably included in that category.

4.185 In the end, the EC remarked, of the eight countries engaged in the negotiations and discussions with the EC[126], four accepted a country-specific tariff quota (Colombia, Costa Rica, Nicaragua and Venezuela) as well as the BFA. An allocation for non-traditional ACP bananas of 90,000 tonnes was also made.[127] What remained of the tariff quota was placed in the category "others". These results were then consolidated in the Uruguay Round Schedule and constituted, in the opinion of the EC, the outcome of a freely negotiated agreement. There was nothing to distinguish the EC's tariff quota on bananas from many other tariff quotas for agricultural products agreed in the Uruguay Round. Tariff quotas were allocated on a limited basis to a few countries and a category of "others" for the rest of the tariff quota. The other aspects of the BFA were also adjusted to the fact that only four countries now participated. Only these four countries could issue export licences that would need to be matched with EC import licences; only these were accorded transferability in case of under-utilization of their quota allocation as a result of *force majeure*.

4.186 With respect to the United States specifically, the EC noted that the United States, having no banana exports to the EC, could not claim any application of Article XIII:2(d), since they could not show having "a substantial interest" as indicated in that provision. Their export interests were therefore perfectly and duly protected under the "others" category in the EC tariff quota. The EC was of the opinion that the events described above clearly distinguished the present situation from the one taken into account by the panel in *Norway - Restrictions on Imports of Certain Textile Products*, adopted 18 June 1980, where no such offer had been made by Norway and no such refusal had been advanced by Hong Kong. Even less relevant was the quotation of the panel report *EEC - Quantitative Restrictions against Imports of Certain Products of Hong Kong*, adopted 12 July 1983, where the panel did not enter into any question concerning the alleged violation of Article XIII since it had already found that the relevant provisions of Article XI were not complied with.

4.187 The EC submitted specifically with respect to Guatemala, which had previous access to the EC market of around 1.5 per cent on average, that it failed to see how its inclusion – in the absence of any agreement – under the category "others" of the tariff quota which entitled the importation under the tariff quota of up to 49 per cent of the total tariff quota volumes, was by any means supposed to reduce Guatemala's opportunities to export its bananas to the EC. The EC further recalled that Mexico exported negligible quantities of bananas into the EC at the moment the Uruguay Round negotiations were concluded (and no significant change in the situation had occurred later on). No claim whatsoever by any of these Members was therefore admissible under Article XIII.

4.188 The Complaining parties noted that the EC, by its own admission, provided country shares to countries that it did not consider to have a "substantial interest" (Nicaragua and Venezuela, each of which exported on average, in the three years prior to 1993, just under 50,000 tonnes, and less than 50 tonnes, respectively). The EC had provided these countries guaranteed percentage allocations that were clearly out of proportion with their historical shipments. At the same time, the EC had also provided country-specific allocations to all the ACP

---

[126] Colombia, Costa Rica, Ecuador, Guatemala, Honduras, Nicaragua, Panama and Venezuela.

[127] According to the EC, this quantity of 90,000 tonnes could not just be added to the total of allocations for traditional bananas. This quantity fell under the tariff quota of 2.2 million tonnes and was treated exactly the same as other bananas under the tariff quota; normal tariff quota licences must be obtained for these quantities. Only their duty-free treatment was based on Article 168(2)(a)(ii) of the Lomé Convention.

suppliers, most of which had shipped quantities to the EC as small as, or even smaller than, Nicaragua's, under their preferential access arrangements. Most of the ACP countries had been provided allocations that greatly exceeded even their average recent shipments under the previous discriminatory national European regimes. They even exceeded their so-called "best ever" shipments, the criterion claimed to have been the basis for the EC's allocations.

4.189 According to the Complaining parties, the text of Article XIII:2 did not require a Member to refrain from according allocations to countries that did not have a "substantial interest in supplying" the product. However, the first sentence of Article XIII:2, which set out the overriding principle to be followed, circumscribed the manner and basis on which it could accord such allocations. A country might reach agreement with all substantially interested countries and also reserve part of its market for lesser suppliers. Under such an approach, any allocations to the lesser suppliers would need to aim at a distribution of trade approaching as closely as possible the shares that such countries might be expected to obtain in the absence of restrictions. The Complaining parties were of the view that the EC had failed to satisfy either of the two methods for countries the Complaining parties considered substantially interested parties, and had also failed to observe the first sentence of Article XIII:2 for those that it apparently did not consider to have a substantial interest.[128] It provided no allocation to Ecuador, a country with more trade than Colombia during what the EC considered the representative period, and thus had failed to reach an agreement pursuant to the first sentence. The fact that Ecuador was not party to the GATT at the time the BFA allocations were made did not obviate its present right as a Member to an agreed allocation or an allocation in accordance with the second sentence of Article XIII:2(d). With respect to other countries, none of the tariff quota allocations were based on an unrestricted representative period; moreover, they were provided to some countries and not others on a basis that could only be explained by political favouritism. As a practical matter, the access available to remaining Latin American exports (relegated to the "others" category in the EC's tariff quota for third countries) had fallen 27 per cent below the Complaining parties' access before Regulation 404/93 was implemented in the member States. Country-specific allocations provided to the BFA signatories were at the expense of the rest of Latin American countries.

4.190 With respect to the claim of the Complaining parties that access for the "others" category had fallen 27 per cent below the access level prior to Regulation 404/93, the EC indicated that calculations based on supply to the EC showed that between 1985 and 1990, the share of "others" in the supply of all Latin American bananas (short-hand for all non-ACP production, because it included very small quantities from Israel and the Philippines, for example) declined steadily every year from 61.7 per cent in 1985 to 50.7 per cent in 1990. This was a reduction of 11 percentage points, or 17.8 per cent of effective access. There was no reason to believe that this decline would not have continued in the absence of the speculation which occurred in 1991 and 1992 immediately prior to the entry into force of the EC regime, thus resulting in even lower access for the "others" category. The speculation resulted in a halt to the declining trend, and an upturn in supply, but not to previous levels. Equally if the situation was considered in terms of volume rather than percentages, the allocation under the EC tariff quota to "others", which currently stood at 1,201,818 tonnes was higher than any quantity supplied to the EC apart from during the highly speculative years 1991-93. In the EC's view it was not possible for the Complaining parties to argue that their access had been restricted as a result of the EC's policy.

4.191 Furthermore, the EC submitted that the EC negotiated its banana tariff quota in the context of the Uruguay Round at the time when neither Ecuador nor Honduras were a contracting party. The EC noted that nowhere did the Complaining parties contest the standard GATT notion of "substantial interest" as 10 per cent market share; any specific claim was in fact made only with regard to Ecuador, and no mention was made of Honduras (indeed, not even of Guatemala, which was a contracting party at the time). The EC further argued that under Article XII of the WTO Agreement "[a]ny State ... may accede to this Agreement, on terms to be agreed between it and the WTO". As the Protocol of Accession of Ecuador indicated, the WTO Agreement to which

[128] The EC claimed that Colombia and Costa Rica were the only GATT contracting parties in 1993 that were substantially interested suppliers.

Ecuador acceded included the Marrakesh Protocol to the GATT, i.e. the other Members' Uruguay Round schedules. No special terms concerning the EC Schedule, let alone its concession on bananas including country allocations, were present in Ecuador's Protocol of Accession. Ecuador had therefore, in the opinion of the EC, fully accepted the EC Schedule. Furthermore, the EC Schedule with regard to agricultural products contained market access concessions undertaken pursuant to the Agreement on Agriculture. These market access concessions, as set out in Article 4.1 of the Agreement, were composed of "bindings, reduction of tariffs" and "other market access commitments" – namely country allocations. In acceding to the WTO, Ecuador did not negotiate any special terms applicable to the EC market access concession on bananas. It accepted the EC Schedule as it was. In the view of the EC, Ecuador was attempting to go back on the engagement it took upon accession to the WTO. It claimed it was entitled to market access commitments that were the fruit of negotiations among the GATT contracting parties in the Uruguay Round, and which, paradoxically, Ecuador itself refused when they were offered by the EC. Ecuador did not negotiate any market access commitment on the occasion of its accession, and could not hope to obtain through dispute settlement what others were entitled to solely as a result of negotiations. In conclusion, the EC said, the Complaining parties' argument that Article XIII entitled Ecuador as a Member with a substantial interest to be allocated a country share upon its accession to the WTO was not relevant here, as the EC banana concession was a market access concession under the Agreement on Agriculture, which prevailed on the GATT. By accepting the EC Schedule, Ecuador had accepted the agricultural concessions as they were, and Article XIII (even in the case in which it should be considered applicable to acceding Members) could not be applied to them. On top of this overwhelming legal analysis, from a market access point of view, with the creation of the category of "others" in the tariff quota and the entry into force of the EC-wide banana market, some Complaining parties like Ecuador now had competition from fewer competitors than they did before, when they had to compete against all Latin American producers and also came up against the closed protected markets restricting access for their bananas.

4.192 As regards application of Article XIII to acceding Members concerning market access concessions negotiated prior to those Members' accession, the EC further submitted that: (i) either any allocation of a tariff quota under the GATT had obligatorily from the start to benefit all supplying countries, including non-Members of the WTO; or (ii) any late accession had to reopen the negotiation of all the schedules containing quotas or tariff quotas with the effect of annulling the legal certainty of all the schedules and of all the concessions negotiated with other Members. In the opinion of the EC, both suggestions contradicted the text of the GATT (Article XIII:2 talked about "all other contracting parties having a substantial interest") and the intention and the practise of the GATT and the WTO. Secondly, the EC argued, Ecuador itself had never relied on Article XIII to claim any "right". Ecuador acceded as from the 21 January 1996. In this particular context, Ecuador and the EC had signed an exchange of letters in which Ecuador had agreed "to seek remedy by bilateral negotiations" if it felt the EC regime "adversely affected Ecuadorian commercial interest". On 13 September 1995, while still not a Member, Ecuador requested negotiations. The Commission met with Ecuador on 21 November 1995, and replied that while happy to discuss at any time, it understood the commitment to apply when Ecuador became a Member. At that moment, it would hold negotiations. On 24 January 1996 (three days after joining), Ecuador wrote to the EC announcing its intention to seek formal consultations pursuant to WTO dispute settlement rules (because the EC had not agreed to hold bilateral negotiations). On 5 February 1996, it requested such consultations (with the other four complainants). A meeting took place between the Commission and Ecuador on 30 January, where no request for a share of a quota was made by Ecuador. The EC Commission met again with Ecuador on a number of occasions, including a visit to Quito by EC Commission officials. Ecuador never specified its requests, let alone requested an allocation of the quota. A further meeting took place in Miami on 9 April 1996. It was organized by USTR "to determine whether a mutually acceptable alternative to the current EU regime could be developed" (in the words of USTR's Chief, M. Kantor). In the course of the meeting, Ecuador announced that the decision to request a panel had already been taken. On 11 April, the five Complaining parties requested the panel. According to the EC, even beyond the formal application of WTO rules, the claims concerning the alleged violation of Article XIII while allocating the EC banana tariff quota were wrong and should be rejected. There had never been a genuine intention by Ecuador to find a negotiated solution to this issue.

4.193 According to Ecuador, a party acceding to the WTO was not required to reserve its rights to raise a claim under the GATT/WTO. Ecuador considered that the very purpose of a country's accession to the GATT was to enable it to claim the rights and obligations specified in the terms of the treaty, and that it would be a redundant and meaningless exercise for a country to issue a separate statement which provided that, upon its accession, it reserved the right to exercise all of its rights under the treaty. For example, a country clearly had a right to expect, upon its accession to the GATT, that an existing Member's tariff schedule accorded treatment under Article I of GATT, and it would be meaningless for the acceding country to be required to issue a separate statement reserving the right to challenge the tariffs under Article I. Ecuador submitted that no country could be expected to review every existing import regime for every single product in every country in the world before its accession to the GATT to determine whether any reservation of rights was necessary. Given the extraordinary burden such a requirement would impose, such a system would likely result in a gutting of the main purpose of the WTO system, i.e. to create a regime for enforcing rules and opening markets. Ecuador clarified, moreover, that the EC's statements concerning its exchange of letters with Ecuador were incorrect with respect to both process and substance. First, the exchange of letters took place on 19 May 1995, eight months before 21 January 1996, the date on which Ecuador acceded to the WTO. During the interim period, Ecuador requested the EC several times to begin bilateral negotiations, but the EC never responded to any of Ecuador's requests. Second, Ecuador noted that the text of the letters exchanged with the EC contained an agreement to attempt to find a solution through bilateral negotiations, but nowhere stated that Ecuador's membership in the WTO was a prerequisite to such negotiations. Indeed, with this understanding in mind, Ecuador presented several requests to the EC after May 1995 to negotiate an agreement that would address Ecuador's concerns regarding the illegalities of the EC banana regime, without result.

4.194 The Complaining parties considered that the EC had developed a new theory, without any support in the text of the GATT, that the newest Members of the GATT and WTO such as Honduras and Ecuador lost their GATT and WTO rights when they acceded without having obtained the elimination of all existing Members' illegal quota allocation schemes. They noted familiarity with the EC's previous efforts to delay Ecuador's accession to the WTO in order to obtain Ecuador's acceptance of the EC's banana regime. According to the Complaining parties, such efforts were inconsistent with all that was provided by WTO membership, and that the ordinary meaning of Article XIII was that it applied to all Members, old and new.

Representative period

4.195 The Complaining parties noted that Article XIII recognized that a country might not always be able to obtain an agreement with all substantially interested parties. In such cases it stated that shares could simply be assigned among suppliers, following the general principle of Article XIII that allocations had to approximate shares prevailing during a "representative" (unrestricted) period. The Complaining parties submitted that none of the country-specific allocations were based on shipments during a truly representative period, and even if one examined shipments during the restricted period of 1990-1992, it was clear that the EC had used no common criterion in allocating its market but political favouritism. The manner in which it had allocated its market clearly was inconsistent with Article XIII.

4.196 Mexico argued that the use of the period 1989-1991 by the EC was contrary to the meaning given to the "previous representative period" in the context of the GATT. The concept of previous representative period used in this particular Article was not precisely defined. However, under Article XXVIII of GATT and the Understanding on the Interpretation of Article XXVIII of GATT 1994 (*Article XXVIII Understanding*), it had been specified that it was the last three years for which data was available. Had the correct approach been followed, the period used would have been the triennium 1990-1992, instead of the triennium 1989-1991 used in the EC regime. The average of imports originating in non-ACP countries and non-traditional ACP countries during the triennium 1990-1992 exceeded the tariff quota imposed by the EC regime as a result of its own calculations. This access reduction was clearly contrary to the interests of the Members that were suppliers and, by analogy, to what was agreed in the *Article XXVIII Understanding.*[129]

4.197 As concerns the specific representative period used by the EC, the EC submitted in an answer to a question by the Panel, the second sentence under Article XIII:2(d) was not applicable to the specific situation of the allocation of the EC banana tariff quota since the pre-requisite of the existence of a party having a substantial interest not having agreed to an arranged allocation under the first sentence was not present. That pointed out, the EC nevertheless used criteria of allocation of the tariff quota when proposing an agreement under Article XIII:2(d) first sentence that were based on objective statistical data reproducing proportions of the total quantity of imports of bananas in the EC supplied by contracting parties (and even non-contracting parties) during a previous representative period. In this respect, Article XIII:2(d) set out two elements: (i) the period shall be previous: there was no obligation of taking into account any data at the very moment of the negotiation; and (ii) the period shall be representative. The word representative means "exemplary" or "emblematic" of a certain situation. To be logical in the connection with the word "previous" then, any allocating party must choose a criterium that could help to a distribution that is emblematic of a past reality. However, this past reality could not be, under the purpose of Article XIII, too far away from the moment of the actual allocation (otherwise it would not represent that reality) and at the same time could not be applied automatically, otherwise it could risk distorting the reality that it was deemed to represent. Moreover, and more importantly, the whole "representation" was deemed to describe the reality of the existing trade flows of a certain product between Members. The provision could not, on the contrary, be assumed as implying that the "previous representative period" should represent an abstract (and never existed) situation of theoretical "unrestricted" trade in that product. Following a practice known and applied by numerous Members in numerous circumstances, the EC decided therefore to distribute the tariff quota among those who were willing to reach an agreement on the basis of the latest statistical data of three years prior to the offer (1989 to 1991). The EC therefore applied "*à la lettre*" Article XIII:2(d). Although there were restrictions on the total volume of Latin American bananas which were permitted to enter those member States with protected markets prior to the creation of the common organization of the market for bananas, the restrictions did not discriminate between the different Latin American supplying countries. Proportions of bananas from those various supplying countries were not affected and were representative.

4.198 The EC also recalled that the only contracting parties having at the time a substantial interest in supplying the product concerned were Colombia and Costa Rica. None of the complainants could have be included in the category. Since the issue of the representative period was directly linked to the allocation of the tariff quota, the Complaining parties had then to show how they could possibly justify an interest to ask the Panel to address this issue without having a substantial interest pursuant to Article XIII:2(d). Secondly, and even more importantly, the EC continued, the level of the tariff quota was not – and could not be – at issue as it was bound in the Uruguay Round Schedule, precisely as a market access commitment (indeed the complainants did not openly claim that the level of the tariff quota violated any GATT or WTO rule, because they knew that such claim could not stand). Nevertheless, the EC could rebut the suggestions put forward by the Complaining parties that the EC should have used 1990-92 or 1991-93 as the representative period to establish the allocation of the tariff quota instead of the 1989-1991 period.

4.199 The EC submitted that when the volume of the tariff quota was fixed, statistics were not yet available for 1992, so 1989-91 represented the latest three years for which figures existed, and the tariff quota reflected the

[129] Mexico referred in particular to:

> "6. When an unlimited tariff concession is replaced by a tariff rate quota, the amount of compensation provided should exceed the amount of the trade actually affected by the modification of the concession. The basis for the calculation of compensation should be the amount by which future trade prospects exceed the level of the quota. ...
>
> (a) the average annual trade in the most recent representative three-year period increased by the average annual growth rate of imports in the same period, or by 10 per cent, whichever is the greater; or
>
> (b) trade in the most recent year increased by 10 per cent."

reality of the trading situation. The size of the original tariff quota was fixed in Regulation 404/93, adopted on 13 February 1993. The negotiations concerning the BFA, which resulted in the tariff quota being increased to a bound volume of 2.2 million tonnes, and also in the allocation of shares in the tariff quota to all contracting parties with a substantial interest, were conducted during the latter part of 1993, when final statistics for imports during 1992 were still not available.

4.200 The EC further submitted that even had 1992 statistics been available in time, it would not have been appropriate to use them, since 1992 was an abnormal year, and could in no way be considered a "representative period". 1992 was a peak year regarding imports to the EC, due to the strategic decisions of big players to flood the market in order to position themselves in preparation for the EC single market, which was scheduled to start in January 1993. This sudden increase in imports had a dramatic effect on prices which fell sharply. The Complaining parties themselves recognized "the kind of losses suffered by primary importers during the period of low prices in 1992-1993". The Commission's *Report on the Operation of the Banana Regime* made it very clear that 1992 was an abnormal year, both in the text, and also in the annexed statistics. Statistics showed that the importation of bananas from Latin America into the EC followed a continuously upward trend over many years, thanks to the EC member States import policies. Suggesting that the EC should have taken a different reference period would imply that the situation of the Complaining parties would have been worse off, while the EC used the most favourable period, representative of a previous normal trade flow between the Members.

4.201 Assuming that the allocation to the countries in the "other" category bore some relationship to import levels during the 1989-1991 reference period on which the EC purportedly relied in calculating the third-country tariff quota volumes, Ecuador was of the opinion that this period could not be considered "representative" of a period without restrictions on the importation of third-country bananas. The United Kingdom, Spain and France had effectively closed their markets to third-country imports during this time. Three other member States, Italy, Portugal and Greece, also limited the access of third-country bananas, though to a lesser extent. At the same time, the EC member States provided preferential treatment to imports of traditional ACP bananas. In any case, even though the market was partially closed to third-country bananas during this time, the EC allocation of the third-country tariff quota had actually reduced the share allotted to non-BFA third-country suppliers from 40 per cent of all EC-12 imports during the period 1989-1991 to less than 34 per cent in 1993.[130]

4.202 According to the Complaining parties, the first sentence of Article XIII:2 made clear that a "representative period" had to be one reflecting proportions of trade that might be expected to prevail in the absence of restrictions. Previous panel reports also provided guidance on how to establish a "representative" period. They had recognized that in determining a representative period in various GATT contexts, data had to be adjusted to take account of discriminatory quantitative restrictions. For example, in the 1980 panel report on *EEC - Restrictions on Imports of Apples from Chile,* the panel was faced with determining the representative period in connection with a restriction imposed under Article XI. The panel considered it appropriate, in keeping with GATT practice, to choose the three-year period immediately previous to the year in which the restriction was put into effect in 1979. However, it determined that the year 1976 should not be used "due to the existence of restrictions in 1976, and that the year immediately preceding 1976 should be used instead."[131] The EC's allocations to the ACP countries – on the basis of "best ever" shipments dating back over thirty years – were only one illustration of the manner in which the EC had ignored the concept of a "representative" base period. By definition, allocating the "best ever" amounts for selected countries was inconsistent with this principle.

4.203 The Complaining parties recalled that in 1963 a panel was established to render an advisory opinion in the dispute between the United States and the European Community regarding the re-negotiation of certain EC bound tariffs on poultry under Article XXIV:6, which required the determination of a representative reference period from which to assess the extent of compensation owed with respect to lost United States exports to Germany. The

[130] Adjusted Eurostat Import Data 1980-1994 (EC-12).

[131] "EEC - Restrictions on Imports of Apples from Chile", adopted 10 November 1980, BISD 27S/98, para. 4.8.

report provided some guidance about how to make appropriate adjustments to a reference period in order to make it "representative":

> The Panel was satisfied that it was in accordance with the normal practice of the GATT for a correction to be made to the figures for the reference period to take account of the discriminatory quantitative restrictions existing in the Federal Republic of Germany during that period. It was the Panel's view that, in the absence of quantitative restrictions, United States exports would have had a larger share of the existing German market. Moreover, the unrestricted entry of lower-priced United States poultry would have brought about an increase in German consumption and United States exports would also have had a share in this increase. The Panel then attempted to assess what the United States could reasonably have expected that the value of their exports would have been in the reference period had there been no discriminatory quantitative restrictions.[132]

The panel then went on to find that the United States would not have exclusively supplied any increase in consumption in Germany. In order to determine how exports from the United States would have fared against those of other suppliers, the panel used the shares of the various supplying countries in Switzerland, which was a "free and competitive" market, as the basis for calculating the trade that would have been obtained by the United States in the absence of restrictions. The approach of this panel demonstrated that it was possible to approximate a representative share by "subtracting out" the effect of illegal quantitative restrictions.

4.204 Furthermore, most recently, the first *Banana* panel had also examined the phrase "representative period" under Article XI in the light of long standing EC member State restrictions on bananas. The panel found that the EC was under the burden to demonstrate that shares allocated to imports reflected the proportionality of imports to domestic production that would have prevailed in the absence of restrictions during a "representative" period and that long standing restrictions that made this task difficult "could not excuse" the EC from demonstrating this condition.[133] The Complaining parties argued that in accordance with the above principles, the most recent time period that would be representative of unrestricted EC banana import levels would be the years just prior to Regulation 404/93, but only in those EC member States in which no GATT-inconsistent restrictions were in place. The EC should take the three most recent years prior to July 1993 for which data were available (1990 through 1992, or even mid-1991 to mid-1993) in the member States that had no GATT-inconsistent restrictions – Belgium, Denmark, Germany, Ireland, Luxembourg and the Netherlands – and use that data to determine what shares of these combined markets each supplying country had during that representative period. EC imports from Latin America in 1992 were not atypical, as confirmed by EC import data and prices on member States' markets. The Complaining parties observed that there was no evidence that EC imports of bananas in 1992 were unusually high; indeed, the data showed quite the contrary, i.e. growth slowed considerably in 1992 and was thereafter stopped by Regulation 404/93. On the basis of EC Commission data, the EC-12's growth rate of imports of Latin American bananas from 1991 to 1992 was under 1 per cent. This growth of 1 per cent was considerably lower than the rate of growth of EC-12 banana imports during the 1986-92 period, which was over 10 per cent per year. Likewise, price data demonstrated that supplies of Latin American bananas on the EC market in 1992 were not excessive. In its *Report on the Operation of the Banana Regime*, the Commission's data indicated that prices of "dollar zone bananas" (Latin American) on most member States' markets were about the same in 1989 and 1990 as they were in 1992. Considering that Austria, Finland and Sweden applied Regulation 404/93 beginning in 1995, a representative period to determine allocations to account for their EC membership would be average imports during 1992-94. The Complaining parties suggested that the EC could avoid the impact that such a drastic step would have on ACP suppliers by choosing not to allocate its tariff quota at all among supplying countries, and rely only on tariff differentials to provide preferential access to ACP suppliers.

---

[132] L/2088, reprinted in GATT, "Analytical Index: Guide to GATT Law and Practice" (Updated 6th edition, 1995) p.948.

[133] First *Banana* panel report, para. 338 citing "Japan - Restrictions on Certain Agricultural Products", adopted 2 February 1988, BISD 35S/163, para. 5.1.3.7.

4.205 With respect to the EC's claims that a representative period upon which allocations must be based need not be representative at all if a Member has always restricted its market, the Complaining parties considered that the text of Article XIII:2 and GATT practice confirmed the opposite – precisely to ensure that countries were not rewarded for maintaining GATT-inconsistent measures for a long period of time. In this context, the EC's position with respect to the representative period it selected to allocate shares to Latin America had become more extreme with the progress of this proceeding. At first, for example, the EC focused on imports during 1992 as being excessively high, pointing only to Chiquita's financial losses as evidence – since neither price nor import data indicated any oversupply during 1992. (In fact shipments from ACP and EC producers also increased during 1992.) The EC claimed without explanation that its imports from Latin America during the entire period of 1991 through 1993 were abnormal – again without supporting evidence based on import growth or price. The Complaining parties considered it was most convenient for the EC to seek to disregard these years because they showed a substantial growth by non-BFA suppliers in volume and relative share of EC imports. The Complaining parties went on to state that next they expected the EC to claim that in anticipation of the single market, the entire growth of Latin American imports beginning in the mid-1980s was due to big monopolies forcing EC consumers to eat bananas against their will. In fact, this growth only demonstrated the strong consumer demand for bananas, which should be taken into account in establishing a representative period.

4.206 The EC retorted that, contrary to the Complaining parties' statement, the *Report on the Operation of the Banana Regime* made it very clear that 1992 was an abnormal year, both in the text of the report and in the annexed statistics. For example, it stated that "1992 saw very low prices for bananas in Europe, largely as a result of banana companies' marketing strategies, many of whom made low profits or even losses in that year." The EC also noted that the first *Banana* panel report was been quoted. The EC stressed that the kind of affirmation found in that report was an extrapolation from a previous panel that had never examined Article XIII but only Article XI:2(c)(i). This was a very different provision indeed and nobody could be surprised if the contracting parties refused at that time to adopt the report. Having said that, the EC was astonished by the argument put forward by the Complaining parties: statistics showed quite evidently that the importation of bananas from Latin America into the EC followed a continuously upwards trend over many years. So, suggesting that the EC should have taken a different reference period would imply that the situation of the Complaining parties would have been worse off - the EC used the most favourable period representative of a previous normal trade flow between Members. The EC the added that none of the Complaining parties could have claimed, at the time the BFA was negotiated, to be entitled to any offer under Article XIII:2(d) for an agreed distribution of the EC tariff quota or to any specific allocation under the same provision. Neither Ecuador nor Honduras were contracting parties at that time. Guatemala could hardly be considered as having an interest, let alone a substantial interest, since it had only 0.6 per cent share of trade in the previous year. Mexico had never exported more than symbolic quantities to the EC and the United States produced only symbolic quantities and did not export any bananas at all.

Special factors

4.207 According to the Complaining parties, the second method for allocating country shares, i.e. that based on representative historical proportions, required the country promulgating the measure to take "due account" of any "special factors" which might have affected or might be affecting the trade in the product. The EC had not specifically invoked the special factors language to justify its allocations, but had it, such an invocation would, in the opinion of the Complaining parties, fail. As further discussed below, GATT text, GATT practice and GATT panel reports confirmed that the relevant factors that must be taken into account in establishing the allocations would require the EC to provide smaller allocations to countries whose production capacity was on the decline and larger allocations to countries whose production capacity was growing. The EC had not provided any evidence that it had considered the relative ability of countries to produce and export when establishing allocations. If it had, the EC clearly would have provided greater access to Latin American countries than to ACP countries, since Eurostat data in the EC's first submission made clear that Latin American countries were much more competitive than ACP countries. Indeed, even if the EC had used recent export performance trends, countries in the "others" category would have been provided much better access to the EC market than they in fact received. Countries in the "others" category had a much higher rate of export growth to the EC than both the ACP countries, for which the EC granted additional non-traditional allocations and the BFA countries. This was the case even though each of the ACP countries was shipping to its protected market, and the Latin American "others" countries had to compete for share.

4.208 According to the Complaining parties, the more favourable allocations for less competitive imports was consistent with the regime's overall policy of keeping the price of bananas in the EC high enough to avoid competition with other EC-grown fruit. In the EC's May 1992 options paper, the Commission observed that a regime based only on the bound tariff rate of 20 per cent would have a "prejudicial effect on other types of fruit on certain Community markets as a result of cheaper bananas and consequently higher demand."[134] The Complaining parties provided the following data concerning export growth in the years prior to Regulation 404/93:

Country	Growth of EC-12 imports 1990-1992 (percentage change)
Belize (ACP)	18.5
Cameroon (ACP)	42.6
Côte d'Ivoire (ACP)	53.7
Jamaica (ACP)	18.4
Colombia (BFA)	29.0
Costa Rica (BFA)	- 15.6
Nicaragua (BFA)	- 44.2
Venezuela (BFA)	- 10.0
Ecuador ("others")	92.3
Guatemala ("others")	299.2
Honduras ("others")	60.2
Mexico ("others")	24,263.0

4.209 The Complaining parties submitted that the Interpretative Note Ad Article XIII:4 clarified that the term "special factors" was to be read in light of the Interpretative Note Ad Article XI, which stated that the term included "changes in relative productive efficiency as between domestic and foreign producers, or as between different foreign producers, but not changes artificially brought about by means not permitted under the Agreement." The last phrase added specificity to the requirement in the first sentence of paragraph 2 of Article XIII that an allocation aimed to approximate the shares that Members would be expected to obtain in the absence of restrictions. In reviewing the analogous provision of the ITO Charter, a sub-committee at the Havana Conference had stated that:

> ... it was desirable to make clear that, in cases where separate import quotas were allotted to the various foreign suppliers, a country whose productive efficiency or ability to export had increased relatively to other foreign suppliers since the representative period on which import quotas were based should receive a relatively larger import quota.[135]

[134] "Setting up the Internal Market", para. 15.

[135] Havana Reports at 95-96.

4.210 The United States argued, moreover, that the EC was not free to consider political factors in providing a country-specific allocation and determining the precise allocation. A panel reviewing a United States reduction in Nicaragua's sugar allocation found it inconsistent with Article XIII:2 because "this reduction had not been motivated by any factor which might have affected or may be affecting trade in sugar."[136] The fact that signatories to the BFA agreed not to challenge the EC's banana regime in further GATT dispute settlement proceedings was not a factor under Article XIII that permitted the EC to favour such countries over others.

4.211 According to the Complaining parties, Article XIII:2(d) did not permit a Member to take a "special factor" into account for one supplier and disregard the same factor with respect to another. The EC had obviously made no effort to take productivity and export capacity of the "other" Latin American countries into account. Even if it had, the comparison would be unfair given that investment in Latin American countries was tempered by the restrictions in place prior to Regulation 404/93 and some (justified) uncertainty regarding the post-404/93 regime. For the record, however, banana investments prior to the new regime were hardly unique to the ACP. In Guatemala, for example, over $30 million were invested in the early 1990s for the rehabilitation of a port intended for banana exports. An equivalent amount was invested at that time for local banana infrastructure. Expansion plans were also under way to increase banana production in Guatemala by 3,000 hectares, all dedicated to production for the EC market. In Honduras, in 1991 and 1992 alone, well over $40 million were invested to improve infrastructure related to the banana sector. In Mexico, total investment of $6 million was made in Puerto Madero, in the state of Chiapas, to facilitate exportation of bananas from the Soconosco zone in that state. Other important investments were made in the Soconosco zone to improve production for export, as well as for other purposes. None of these or other investment activities of the Complaining parties (including those planned for the future) were taken into consideration by the EC in designing the banana regime.

4.212 The Complaining parties noted that they were not arguing that investment in any country's banana sector should be taken into account, in and of itself, as a special factor. It was the EC that had claimed that investments were relevant in its allocation of country shares. The point made by the Complaining parties was that such factors should not be permitted to be applied selectively. In the case of the ACP, the EC appeared not only to have taken into account "investments committed," but evidently also investments that might then have been envisioned for the future . In the case of Jamaica, for example, the EC apparently found a way to factor into its allocation that "many new plantings were necessary." In the case of Côte d'Ivoire, the EC took into account "that additional irrigation and drainage works were being planned." Judging simply by these unmeasurable considerations, the EC had seriously understated its admission that its allocations did not represent "an exact science." In the case of Venezuela, the EC went so far as to provide an allocation as a reward for not pursuing the illegalities in the regime. That allocation served to stimulate Venezuelan exports to the EC where none previously had occurred.

4.213 More to the point, though, the Complaining parties submitted, investments in themselves, investments "under way" or investments only in the minds of government officials did not constitute "special factors" that should be used to adjust historical shipments. The text of Article XIII stated that the only special factors to be taken into account were those "which may have affected or may be affecting the trade in the product," not those which might or would in the future affect trade in the product. Special factors included evidence of special productive efficiency and capacity to export that had made a particular country's exports more competitive than other exports on purely economic grounds; acts of *force majeure*, such as an earthquake,[137] that caused an uncharacteristic disruption during the base period; or, on the other hand, declines in a country's competitiveness or interest in supplying the product. Productive efficiency and capacity to export could, according to the Complaining parties, be measured by, among other factors, unit cost of production and output per hectare. Even if a country actually increased plantings in its banana sector in the years prior to Regulation 404/93, those investments would only contribute to increased production efficiency and export capacity if they were cost-effective relative to the production and export capacity of other producers. Looking strictly at productive

[136] "United States - Imports of Sugar from Nicaragua", adopted on 13 March 1984, BISD 31S/67 at 73.

[137] "EEC - Restrictions on Imports of Dessert Apples - Complaint of Chile", adopted 22 June 1989, BISD 36S/93, para. 12.24.

efficiency and export capacity, the EC's data on export growth and production costs would justify the EC's providing much greater access to Latin American countries than to ACP countries. The fact that several ACP and BFA countries could not even fill their allocations only underscored the EC's failure to observe the principles of Article XIII:2.

4.214 The EC submitted that the term "special factors which may have affected or may be affecting the trade in the product" was a very broad definition encompassing all situations that could not be considered the expression of a normal trade of a certain product between Members concerned. Those special factors were in particular the ones which, by abnormally affecting trade in that product at a certain moment, affected as well the possibility of representing objectively the past trade in that product in that previous period. The Note Ad Article XI (extended to Article XIII) did nothing more than precise that those special factors included equally changes in productive efficiency as between domestic and foreign producers, or as between different foreign producers. The Note did not exclude, on the contrary, factors such as abnormal speculative phenomena like the one that appeared in the banana trade to the EC in 1992 (and somehow continued in 1993). The volumes of bananas that were marketed in the EC in the years immediately prior to the creation of the banana regime, especially in those member States where only a tariff applied, were much higher than had ever previously been the case. This sudden large influx of tonnage was accompanied by dramatic price falls as supply significantly exceeded normal demand.

4.215 The EC continued that it was widely accepted and even acknowledged in companies' annual reports, that this market situation was caused by certain large companies deliberately oversupplying the market, in the hopes of increasing market share to strengthen their position for the implementation of the single market. Chiquita particularly suffered as a result of this strategy, incurring high debts to finance expansion, recording progressively reduced margins in 1991 and 1992 in spite of increased shippings, and culminating in a loss of $80 million in 1992. This situation could only be considered as a short-term strategy, since it was obvious that it was not sustainable for any company in the long term to continually incur losses of this nature in an attempt to capture an ever-increasing share of the market and to put pressure on competitors. This provided further justification for the EC's position that 1992 was an abnormal year and could not constitute an acceptable basis to represent "previous normal trade flows" in banana trade to the EC.

4.216 As far as a specific country that concluded the agreement under Article XIII:2(d) first sentence, Venezuela, the EC took into account the fact that substantial investment was under way in that country with the aim of exporting to the EC and, therefore, an appropriate portion of the allocation was destined to that country even though Venezuela did not export significant quantities to the EC during the period 1989-1991.

(b) Article XIII:1 of GATT

4.217 Ecuador argued with respect to Article XIII:1 that the EC had provided no rationale justifying why certain countries should be granted allocations far above their recent historical import levels while a basket of "other" countries had been given an allotment far below those countries' aggregate historical import levels. As a result of these measures, the EC banana regime did not "similarly prohibit or restrict" imports of third-country bananas, BFA signatory bananas, and ACP bananas, and therefore was not consistent with Article XIII:1.

4.218 Guatemala and Honduras submitted that the banana regime's differential volume restrictions by source fell squarely within the prohibition of paragraph 1 of Article XIII of GATT. Article XIII:5 specifically extended application of this principle to "any tariff quota instituted or maintained by any contracting party." According to Guatemala and Honduras, past panels had been rigorous in disallowing volume discrimination by source under Article XIII. In *EEC - Quantitative Restrictions against Imports of Certain Products from Hong Kong*, for example, the panel found that a differentiation by the EC in textile quota shares among suppliers according to their different geographical zones was contrary to the non-discrimination requirement of Article XIII.[138] Similarly, in

[138] BISD 30S/129, para. 33 (adopted 12 July 1983).

Norway - Restrictions on Imports of Certain Textile Products, the panel ruled that Norway had acted inconsistently with Article XIII when it implemented global import quotas on various textile items, but reserved certain market shares for other similarly situated countries.[139]

4.219 Applying these findings and the plain language of Article XIII:1 to the present facts, where there had been trade-expansive quantities set aside for designated ACP countries and a trade-restrictive overall tariff quota volume for other similarly situated import sources, the Panel should, according to Guatemala and Honduras, equally conclude that the "importation of the like product of all third countries [has not been] similarly ... restricted" in violation of Article XIII:1.

4.220 The EC submitted that, as stated above, Article XIII was relevant and applicable only in so far as one specific quota or tariff quota was concerned, and specifically its administration. No argument could, by contrast, be made under Article XIII, in particular XIII:1, alleging discrimination in the administration of two different regimes, which were independent one from the other and each legally justified on a different basis. Traditional ACP bananas had to be quantities traditionally supplied, as set out above, entered the EC at zero duty. This regime was covered by the Lomé waiver as set out below. The tariff quota regime was a direct result of the Uruguay Round and contained in Schedule LXXX - European Communities. The concessions were negotiated in the framework of the Agreement on Agriculture's specificity and, therefore, no violation of Article XIII of GATT 1994 could be claimed.

(c) Article I of GATT

4.221 Although Guatemala and Honduras considered Article XIII to be the most applicable principle of law to the present measure, they claimed that discriminatory tariff quota allocations were also unlawful under the Article I:1 prohibition against discriminatory "rules ... in connection with importation" that conferred an "advantage, favour, [and] privilege" to some foreign sources over others. Both the guarantee of market share for some, but not others, and the inflated assignment of shares to some over others represented distinct market advantages that had not been "immediately and unconditionally" conferred to all like foreign suppliers. *Per se* violations of Article I:1 of GATT had, in the opinion of Guatemala and Honduras, consequently occurred.

4.222 Guatemala and Honduras submitted that the access volume arrangements laid down under Regulation 404/93 *et seq.* had been imposed in two discrete stages, each of which was unlawfully discriminatory under the principles of the GATT. The first of the volume arrangements, which arose out of the regime's enabling regulations, provided terms of access that discriminated against Guatemala and Honduras in favour of traditional ACP suppliers. The second arrangement, effectuated a year and a half later with the signing of the BFA, created a distinct additional volume discrimination against Guatemala and Honduras, this time in favour of BFA signatory countries. Both layers of discrimination required independent analysis and condemnation under Articles I and XIII of GATT.

4.223 Guatemala and Honduras argued that the amount allocated under the tariff quota for imported bananas other than from traditional ACP sources had every year fallen far short of even the access that prevailed for such sources under the EC national regimes in effect prior to Regulation 404/93. Access under those regimes was at 2,431,118 tonnes in 1992,[140] which volume, if anything, was low relative to the preceding five-year robust annual growth pattern evidenced in the EC-12 for product from such sources. Under Regulation 404/93 *et seq.*, by using 1989-91 as reference period for tariff quota bananas, EC-12 access was capped for the latter half of 1993 at 1 million tonnes and for 1994 at 2.118 million tonnes. In 1995, when the EFTA-3 acceded, and again in 1996, the official volume for tariff quota bananas was roughly stagnant at 2.2 million tonnes, with a "transitional" (1995) and "autonomous" (1996) EFTA-3 volume authorized at 353,000 tonnes. That additionally authorized volume was 9

[139] BISD 27S/119, paras. 15-16 (adopted 18 June 1980).

[140] Eurostat Import Data.

per cent below the 1991-93 average EFTA-3 banana imports from tariff quota sources. The regime's highly restrictive volume methodology chosen for tariff quota sourced bananas was not applied to traditional ACP-sourced bananas. Products from traditional ACP origins were accorded, instead, access ceilings on a country-by-country basis that the EC characterized to have been set "in principle" as the individual ACP countries' "best ever" sendings up to and including 1990, which sendings were accomplished under the quota protection of the national regimes. However, the EC granted substantial, apparently discretionary additional allotments to ACP supplying countries even on top of this comparatively more favourable "best ever" methodology.

4.224 Guatemala and Honduras submitted that the source-specific quota and tariff quota volume requirements could also be seen to contravene the most-favoured-nation principle of Article I:1. Inequitable and discriminatory tariff quotas had been found in past GATT panel disputes to constitute "rules and formalities in connection with importation" that violated Article I:1. In *EEC - Imports of Beef from Canada*, for example, the panel found that an EEC regulation implementing a levy-free tariff quota on certain beef effectively denied access of like products from countries other than the United States in violation of Article I:1.[141] Here, where country-specific ACP volumes accorded a substantial, intended import advantage that had not been accorded by the EC on an "immediate and unconditional" basis to "the like product originating in ... the territories of all other contracting parties," an Article I:1 breach had also to be found.

4.225 Mexico argued that the difference between the granting of advantages (Article I) and the non-discriminatory application of measures (Article XIII) was of paramount importance for maintaining the structure and scope that the founders of the GATT gave to each of these concepts as distinct and independent Articles. A consequence of this was that there could, in the opinion of Mexico, be violation of Article I without automatic violation of Article XIII, and vice-versa. If the granting of an advantage were to be assimilated to the application of reverse discrimination, it would have made no sense to draw up provisions on non-discrimination because the latter would have been included in the former. Therefore, Article I should be examined independently of Article XIII.

4.226 The EC recalled the arguments set out above concerning the nature of the two distinct regimes which were legally justified on a different basis and could not be the subject of allegations of discrimination of the allocation within the tariff quota as compared to the traditional ACP allocation. As far as the alleged violation of Article I:1 was concerned, the ACP traditional allocation was covered, as set out below, by the Lomé waiver and no Member could claim an extension of that treatment outside the preferential framework that justified it. With respect to the bound tariff quota, the EC argued that the general most-favoured-nation treatment principle as expressed in Article I was part of Part I of GATT as was Article II concerning tariff concessions. Article II:7 clarified that "the schedules annexed to this Agreement are hereby made an integral part of Part I of this Agreement". As Article II:7 clearly indicated, the EC banana concession was an integral part of Part I of GATT and was therefore to be considered an integral part of Article I and Article II as appropriate. This entailed the consequence, in the opinion of the EC, that any application of the MFN principle set out in Article I could not prevail *per se* on the terms and conditions of the concession, in this case the EC banana concession, since this would mean giving priority to one part of Article I over other parts of the same Article, as supplemented by the concessions.

(d) The Lomé waiver

4.227 The general discussion of the Lomé waiver can be found in section IV.2(a)(i) above, dealing with issues concerning tariffs. In that section the EC submitted that it had shown that in order to fulfil its obligations with respect to the Lomé Convention in the case of bananas, it had implemented a series of measures as set out above. In the view of the EC, the Lomé waiver covered any measure taken by the EC in order to fulfil its legal obligations

[141] BISD 28S/92, paras. 4.1-4.3 (adopted 10 March 1981).

as indicated under the Lomé Convention with regards to any product originating in ACP countries, including bananas.

4.228 With respect to the arguments put forward by the Complaining parties concerning allocation issues, the EC recalled the general arguments set out earlier with respect to the nature of the two distinct regimes which were legally justified on a different basis and could not be the subject of allegations of discrimination of the allocation within the tariff quota as compared to the traditional ACP allocation. In addition, the EC argued that as far as the violation of Article I of GATT alleged by certain Complaining parties was concerned, the ACP traditional allocation was covered by the Lomé waiver and, therefore, no Member could claim the extension of that treatment outside the preferential framework that justified it.

4.229 In this light, however, the EC noted that the Complaining parties had raised the question concerning the actual coverage of the waiver as it referred to the quantities allocated to individual ACP countries under the ACP traditional allocation. As their reasoning went, no quantity above the "best ever" importation of bananas in the EC market by each individual ACP country should be admitted under the Lomé waiver. In the EC view, this argument was based on at least two errors and the resulting analysis of the legal and factual situation was therefore wrong and should be rejected: (i) it was not correct, as already demonstrated, that the EC obligations under the Lomé Convention were limited to the continuation of traditional access to the EC market and the advantages on this market: this misconception was rooted in the wrong belief that the Lomé waiver, as far as bananas were concerned, was limited to the application of Protocol 5 on bananas, thus failed to take into account the other obligations flowing from other provisions of the Convention; and (ii) it was not correct that, even if only the Protocol 5 to the Lomé Convention was considered, the preferential treatment should be calculated only the statistical individual "best ever" importation of bananas on the EC market. As noted above, in its meeting of 14-17 December 1992, the EC Council decided that:

> The Lomé commitments will be met by allowing tariff-free imports from each ACP State up to a traditional level reflecting its highest sendings "best ever" in any one year up to and including 1990. In cases where it can be shown that investment has already been committed to a programme of expanding production, a higher figure may be set for that ACP State.

The reasons for this decision were to be found not only in Protocol 5 itself - which concerned equally common ACP/EC measures to improve the conditions for the production and marketing of the bananas -but also in the obvious need not to waste EC public money and the trade opportunities that the EC financial intervention was trying to establish. In other words, the EC could not have restricted the advantages expected to accrue to some ACP countries as a result of the complete realization of projects aimed at improving and increasing banana production, which were well under way at the moment the decisions were taken and which were mostly financed together with the EC. The effects of these measures were therefore logically taken into account when allocating each individual part within the ACP traditional quota. Failure to do so would have resulted in providing no access to the increased production concerned and in violating the obligations of preserving the advantages already expected "at present" as a result of the application of the Lomé Convention. The alleged violation of Article I should, the EC argued, therefore be rejected.

4.230 In response to a question by the Panel, the EC submitted it had never claimed that the Lomé waiver was concerned with obligations under Article XIII. Whenever the Complaining parties had requested the extension of a particular regime or procedure profiting ACP bananas, however, the EC had evoked, where appropriate, the Lomé waiver to oppose any extension of the MFN clause, that is of Article I:1 of GATT and in accordance with the waiver.

4.231 In this light, the EC recalled that two factual and legal errors had to be avoided: no confusion could be allowed as for the totally separate nature of the two banana regimes of the Community: the ACP traditional allocation, on the one hand, and the EC regime for all other bananas, on the other hand. This reality was, in the EC view, a direct result of both the Uruguay Round negotiations and of the existence of the Lomé Convention(s) for a long time: any suggestion that it was a "carving up" of the market in order to "avoid a comparison of country treatment" under Article XIII was a legal and factual nonsense. On the contrary, the Complaining parties suggestion showed clearly their intention: to undermine the legal security of the Lomé waiver by the attempt to apprehend, under Article XIII (stretching its scope well beyond contracting parties' common will), what was waived by the waiver because it concerned Article I:1.

4.232 The Complaining parties noted that past GATT practice reflected a great reluctance to waive Article XIII obligations.[142] The Complaining parties noted that Article I of GATT was a separate Article from Articles X and XIII, and not even part of the same agreement as the Licensing Agreement. There was no legal basis whatsoever for assuming that a waiver with respect to Article I applied in any way, directly or indirectly, to other GATT articles that also prohibited distinctions based on country of origin.

4.233 The Complaining parties considered the issue of country-specific allocations to be conclusively addressed under Article XIII, making the Lomé waiver with respect to Article I violations irrelevant to these measures. Moreover, the EC had admitted in its answers to Panel questions that it did not consider the Lomé waiver covered violations of Article XIII. However, it was worthwhile to correct the record with respect to the EC's justification of its traditional ACP allocations. The EC had admitted that its ACP allocations exceeded "best ever" levels, but attempted to justify them on the basis that: (i) they were consistent with "other obligations flowing from other provisions of the Convention;" (ii) they fell within the "advantages on those markets ... at present" phrase of Protocol 5; (iii) the EC Council instructed that such allocations take into account "investment [that] has already been committed,"; and (iv) EC public money would be wasted had ACP allocations not been inflated. In the opinion of the Complaining parties, every one of those claims were either in error or irrelevant. The "other obligations" of the Lomé Convention relevant to traditional ACP allocations had not been specified by the EC and, as previously demonstrated, did not in any case exist in the area of banana trade. The "advantages on those markets ... at present" language of Protocol 5, under its plain meaning, could not be said to extend to any ACP investment activity that might have been under way or envisioned at the point of production. France and the United Kingdom certainly did not interpret the Protocol that way prior to Regulation 404/93. They accorded access to bananas of ACP origin solely on the basis of annual demand for bananas in their respective markets.[143] What the EC Council might have instructed in the way of supplementary ACP benefits was of no WTO consequence; after all, the EC Council had authorized the entire banana regime, which hardly made it WTO-consistent.

4.234 As to the concern that EC investments would have been wasted if the allocations had not been overstated, the same could just as easily be said of the national banana investments under way or planned in the Latin American supplying countries. Moreover, as already noted, the World Bank and other economists had pointed out that relative to "waste" that might derive from uncounted ACP investments, an EC funding waste of immensely greater magnitude had resulted from this EC regime, which had cost consumers $13.25 to transfer only $1.00 of benefit to ACP banana suppliers[144], and more to the point, other Members should not have to pay for the EC's budget mistakes.

[142] See Note by the Executive Secretary on "Questions Relating to Bilateral Agreements, Discrimination and Variable Taxes" (wherein it was stated "that in no case has a waiver on import restrictions authorized any deviation from the provisions of Article XIII"), L/1636, p.2. In fact, there has been one instance in which a waiver to Article XIII was permitted by the contracting parties (the Decision of 10 November 1952 on the "Waiver Granted in Connection with the European Coal and Steel Community", 1S/17, para. 3). The CONTRACTING PARTIES have otherwise refused to forgive discriminatory measures inconsistent with Article XIII. See e.g. Decision on "Problems Raised for Contracting Parties in Eliminating Import Restrictions Maintained During a Period of Balance-of-Payments Difficulties", BISD 3S/38, para. 2.

[143] First *Banana* panel, paras. 19-22 and 37-38.

[144] See "Beyond EU Bananarama", Annex (1) at 22; see also Brent Borrell, "EU Bananarama III", Policy Research Working Paper 1386, The World Bank (1994), Annex (2).

4.235 With respect to Article I of GATT, Guatemala and Honduras submitted that within the strict interpretive framework of waiver interpretation, the Lomé waiver could not be said to require discriminatory volume arrangements. By its express terms, all that the Lomé Convention required, or even contemplated, as to ACP trade in bananas was: (i) duty-free access for traditional ACP bananas under Article 168 of the Lomé Convention modified by Protocol 5 and Annex LXXIV; (ii) technical and financial assistance to traditional ACP suppliers to improve the production and marketing of bananas under Article 183 and Protocol 5, as modified by Annex LXXIV; and (iii) intervention from Stabex funds to stabilize export earnings for traditional ACP suppliers under Article 186.

4.236 Thus, in so far as the quantity preferences extended to ACP suppliers were well beyond the scope of tariff preferences and aid promised by the Lomé Convention – and the EC had itself confirmed that ACP volumes were not guaranteed by the Lomé Convention – these measures could hardly be said to fall within the sharply restricted reach of the Lomé waiver. What made this particularly so was that the differentiated volume treatment at issue had been structured for the stated purpose of curtailing Guatemala and Honduras' shipments, something the Lomé waiver expressly sought to avoid. Since the volume arrangements denied Guatemala and Honduras market access advantages that were otherwise being conferred to ACP bananas, and such advantages were not otherwise forgiven by the Lomé waiver, a breach of Article I:1 had occurred.

4.237 Guatemala and Honduras further considered that the Lomé waiver offered no justification for infractions concerning the allocation to BFA countries. As Costa Rica, Colombia, Nicaragua and Venezuela were not even the subject of the Lomé Convention, their receipt of discriminatory allocations could not be considered excused by the Lomé waiver. The Lomé waiver and the Lomé Convention were likewise irrelevant to tariff quota volume allocations for the non-traditional ACP suppliers – the Dominican Republic, Belize, Côte d'Ivoire, Cameroon and others. Protocol 5 and Annex LXXIV carefully circumscribed the extension of the Lomé Convention tariff preferences and direct aid to traditional ACP suppliers only. The application of quantity reserves for non-traditional suppliers, was, thus, manifestly beyond the scope of both instruments. Discriminatory tariff quota allocations were, in the opinion of Guatemala and Honduras, accordingly a breach of GATT's most-favoured-nation rule and had to be discontinued.

4.238 The EC reiterated that traditional ACP bananas had to be treated in accordance with Protocol 5 and the Joint Declaration in Annex LXXIV of the Lomé Convention. Non-traditional ACP bananas did not fall under the obligation to secure access to, and advantages on, the EC market at the level of the best year's performance by each ACP banana exporting country, but had to be given preferential treatment. This regime was covered by the Lomé waiver. For ACP bananas, the quantities traditionally supplied (according to the "best ever" criterion up to and including the year 1990) by various ACP States entered the EC, as before 1 July 1993, at zero duty.[145]

(ii) Reallocation of shortfalls

(a) <u>Article XIII of GATT</u>

4.239 The United States was of the view that the EC's provisions regarding shortfalls in BFA signatories' allocations were also inconsistent with the obligations in Article XIII. Paragraph 4 of the BFA provided that:

> [i]f a banana exporting country with a country quota informed the EC that it will be unable to deliver the quantity allocated to it, the short-fall shall be reallocated by the EC in accordance with the same percentage shares [provided by the BFA] (including "others").

However, paragraph 4 also provided that, nonetheless, "countries with country quotas may jointly request and the Commission shall agree to a different allocation amongst those countries". Article 2 of EC Regulation 478/95 implemented these provisions. In 1995, the first year of the BFA, both Nicaragua and Venezuela informed the EC

[145] Article 15(1) and the Annex of Regulation 404/93.

that they would not be able to fill their allocations. As a result of these countries' agreements with Colombia, all of Nicaragua's 3 per cent share and 70 per cent of Venezuela's 2 per cent share were transferred to Colombia for that year. In a similar arrangement for 1996, all of Nicaragua's 3 per cent share and 30 per cent of Venezuela's 2 per cent share were transferred to Colombia.[146] Thus, the EC provided additional access of 96,800 and 79,200 tonnes in 1995 and 1996, respectively, to Colombia alone instead of allocating these amounts on a non-discriminatory basis among all the historical suppliers, according to the EC's obligations in Article XIII. Permitting two BFA signatories to decide among themselves how to reallocate the shortfall was not, in the opinion of the United States, consistent with these obligations.

4.240 Ecuador considered that the preferential treatment of BFA-signatory countries referred to above was made even more egregious by operation of Article 2 of EC Regulation 478/95. On the basis of Article 2, the BFA signatory countries reallocated, according to Ecuador, among themselves their shares of the third-country tariff quota. For example, in 1995, all of Nicaragua's 3 per cent share and 70 per cent of Venezuela's 2 per cent share were transferred to Colombia.[147] Again, in 1996, all of Nicaragua's share and 30 per cent of Venezuela's share were transferred to Colombia.[148] The transferability of shares among the BFA signatory countries further removed these suppliers from the constraints placed on other third-country suppliers. The total third-country tariff quota and the share allocated to third countries in the "other" category were nominally (though not actually) based on recent historical import levels. However, the transferability of the country-specific tariff quotas among the BFA countries enabled these countries to tailor their shares to current commercial conditions. BFA transferability intensified, according to Ecuador, the discrimination inherent in the original BFA allocations by permitting certain BFA countries to obtain shares of the third-country tariff quota well in excess of their recent historical import levels.

4.241 Article 2 of Regulation 478/95 compounded, according to Guatemala and Honduras, these discriminatory allocations by entitling Costa Rica, Colombia, Nicaragua and Venezuela to transfer their tariff quota allocations among and between one another, in any manner approved by the Commission. That volume-shifting advantage had not been made available to other tariff quota suppliers. The BFA signatories had taken liberal advantage of the discriminatory quota-shifting allowance. All or much of the allotments accorded Nicaragua and Venezuela were transferred to Colombia in 1995 and again in 1996, largely because those countries did not have for these two years (or for any of the years before that) the production wherewithal to satisfy their artificially inflated allocations. The selectively applied transferability mechanism had thereby gained Colombia a market share in 1995 and 1996 on top of its already inflated original allocation of respectively 4.3 per cent and 3.6 per cent. Guatemala and Honduras submitted that the volume-shifting mechanism for BFA countries authorized by Regulation 478/95 did not observe either of the two quota apportionment rules of Article XIII:2(d). The transfer of quota shares among BFA countries was not predicated on the agreement of all substantial supplying interests, only the approval of the EC Commission and BFA signatory countries. Likewise, the source-exclusivity of that mechanism prevented, under any possible application, a quota distribution resembling the shares that various countries would have been expected to attain in an entirely unrestricted market (which the EC had never accorded its Latin American suppliers).

4.242 Mexico argued that the over-allocation of tariff quotas to all ACP countries, referred to above, was also applicable to BFA countries. Moreover, in this case, in contrast to what happens with non-ACP and ACP countries, BFA countries were allowed to make transfers among themselves of the tariff quota not used, which was clearly discriminatory against the other Members and contrary to the provision under which the distribution of trade should approach as closely as possible the shares which the various contracting parties might be expected to obtain in the absence of such restrictions.

---

[146] Commission Regulation (EC) No. 2568/95, 31 October 1995; Commission Regulation (EC) No. 356/96, 28 February 1996.

[147] Commission Regulation (EC) No. 703/95, 30 March 1995; Commission Regulation (EC) No. 1889/95, 28 July 1995.

[148] Commission Regulation (EC) No. 2568/95, 31 October 1995; Commission Regulation (EC) No. 356/96, 28 February 1996.

4.243 The EC rejected the allegations raised against the possibility, provided in the tariff quota, of transferring quotas or parts of a quota to each country party to the BFA to another BFA country, as compared to other supplying countries which, under the tariff quota, were not admitted to benefit from such transfers. According to the Complaining parties, this provision violated Articles XIII:2(d) and I:1 of GATT. The EC submitted that under Article XIII:2(d) "no conditions or formalities shall be imposed which would prevent any contracting party from utilizing fully the share of any such total quantity or value which has been allotted to it ... ." For the BFA countries, limitations of imports into the EC due to the allocation of quotas shared out by country would result in an unfair disadvantage if not assorted with the possibility of transferring quotas or part of quotas when unused. This was perfectly in conformity with Article XIII:2(d). The countries under "others" in the BFA disposed already, by the very nature of the non-shared out part of the tariff quota, of the widest possibility of transfer of the tariff quota or parts of the tariff quota. In this respect no violation of Article XIII:2(d) could be alleged. Due to the specific structure of the EC's tariff quota, the requested extension of access to the transfer of unused quota of the BFA countries by non-BFA countries would amount to an advantage for non-BFA countries which the EC did not intend to grant and which, in the view of the EC, would violate Article XIII.

4.244 According to the Complaining parties, the EC had failed to abide by Article XIII requirements by permitting a BFA signatory such as Colombia to obtain exclusive access to a shortfall in supply in Venezuela's allocation. The EC had claimed that the special quota transfer provisions of Regulation 478/95, Article 2, which permitted Costa Rica, Colombia, Nicaragua and Venezuela to shift market share among themselves, was in conformity with Article XIII:2(d) because the "others" suppliers had the "widest possibility of transfer of quota" and would be "advantaged" if special transfer provisions were not in place. However, Article XIII:2(d) provided specific rules for allocating quotas. Permitting a few countries (BFA signatories) to decide among themselves how to reallocate the quota was manifestly inconsistent with these principles. The suggestion that volume-shifting preferences were needed as a counter-balance to the inherent transferability afforded suppliers in the "others" category was not only irrelevant under Article XIII; it ignored the EC's exclusive provision of a distinct marketing advantage to selected supplying countries. The transfer measure only added to that discrimination, making it a separately identifiable violation of Article XIII:2(d) that had to be discontinued. The Complaining parties considered that the manner in which the EC continued to provide Colombia with portions of Venezuela's and Nicaragua's annual allocations contradicted its own original allocation of the third-country tariff rate quota. If Colombia was not entitled to a larger share of the EC's tariff-rate quota to begin with, it was not now entitled to be the exclusive recipient of an additional amount made available as a result of another country's shortfall in supply.

(b) Article I of GATT

4.245 Guatemala and Honduras submitted that the special quota transfer provisions contained in Regulation 478/95, compounded the discrimination created in the first instance by irregular tariff quota allocations. The BFA countries alone had been conferred the privilege of shifting market shares among and between BFA themselves if the Commission so approved. It's discriminatory application constituted a separately identifiable violation of Article I:1.

4.246 No violation of Article I:1 could, in the opinion of the EC, be claimed by the Complaining parties on this issue since, on the one hand, the transferability of the quota within the BFA country section amounted to equal the position of non-BFA countries with that of BFA countries, the former's position being likely to be otherwise better off under the present structure of the EC tariff quota. In other words, a non-advantage was not obligatorily extended on an MFN basis under the GATT. On the other hand, the actual structure of the EC tariff quota was part of the EC Schedule which was an integral part of Part I of GATT as indicated in Article II:7. No priority could be invoked for Article I under the GATT over the concessions consolidated in the GATT and accepted through their ratification by all the Members as argued in more detail elsewhere. The EC, referring to the complaints concerning the possibility of transferring quotas or parts of a quota allocated to each country party to the BFA to another BFA country only as compared to the other supplying countries, rejected the allegations that this provision violated Articles I:1 and XIII:2(d) of GATT.

c) *Import licensing issues*

4.247 This section presents the import licensing issues raised in the case. It first sets out the arguments of the Complaining parties concerning the import licensing regime as a whole, and continues with the EC responses to the claims, and subsequent arguments by the Complaining parties. This includes the preliminary issues raised by the EC: (i) the non-applicability of the Agreement on Import Licensing Procedures to tariff quotas; and (ii) the non-applicability of Articles III:4 and X of GATT to border measures. In addition, the EC reiterated its arguments set out earlier concerning horizontal issues: (i) the presence of two separate banana access regimes; and (ii) the applicability of the Lomé waiver to specific aspects of the Complaining parties' allegations. These issues are reverted to in relation to specific claims. Following the arguments presented concerning the import licensing regime as a whole, claims and arguments relating to individual aspects are recorded.

4.248 The Complaining parties argued that the EC's regulations imposed on imports from Latin America a licensing scheme that was highly complex. The system, both in its totality and in its individual elements, created highly unfavourable conditions of competition compared to the simple arrangements for traditional ACP bananas. Unnecessarily burdensome, discriminatory, trade-restrictive and trade-distortive, the licensing regime implicated both the basic provisions of the GATT and the newer Uruguay Round disciplines pertaining specifically to licensing procedures and trade-related investment measures. Ecuador also argued that the licensing regime was inconsistent with the Agreement on Agriculture, in particular.

(i) the licensing regime as a whole

(a) arguments of the Complaining Parties

4.249 On the basis of the following flow charts submitted by Ecuador, Guatemala, Honduras and the United States, the Complaining parties considered that the EC licensing regime for Latin American bananas was highly complex and burdensome for exporters and importers of bananas. That such layers of complexity were not required for administrative purposes was evident from the simple and transparent procedures applicable to traditional ACP bananas. Any investor or purchaser of bananas, seeing the two schemes, would quickly understand that the system for Latin American bananas amounted to a non-tariff barrier to trade.

Arrangement 1: EC Bananas

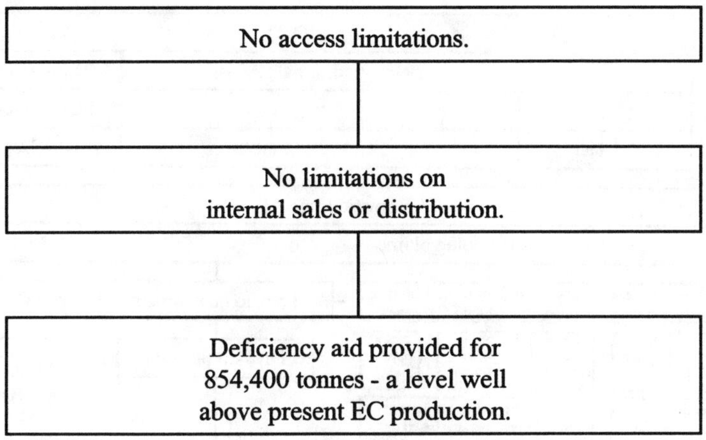

Arrangement 2: "Traditional ACP Bananas"

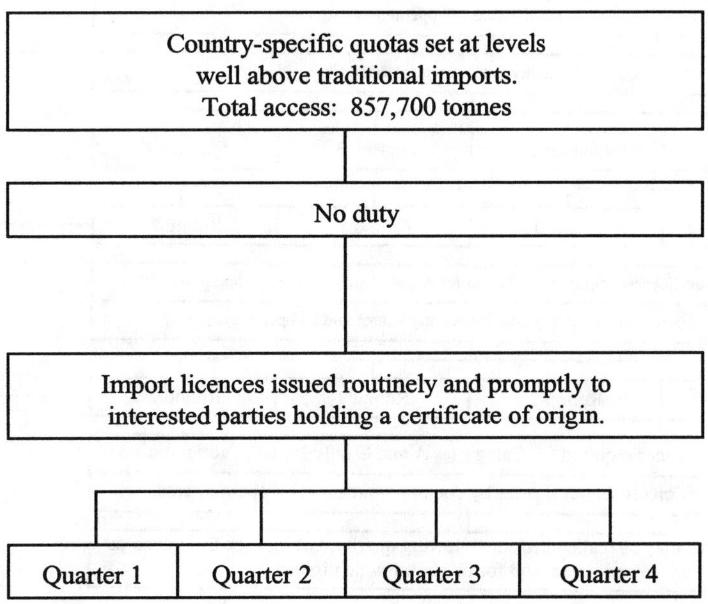

Arrangement 3: Third-Country and "Non-Traditional" ACP Bananas

Tariff quota total volume (2 million tonnes, increased to 2.2 million tonnes) set substantially below then-existing third-country EC-12 access. Tariff quota enlargement to cover former EFTA-3 volume is expected.

Further subdivision of that volume, some to specific countries, others to groups of countries. Reserve of 90,000 tonnes for both "non-traditional" and traditional ACP suppliers. Allocation transfers allowed among only certain countries.

Duty (1995)		
	"Non-traditional" ACP	Third country
1st Tier	0	ECU 75/tonne
2nd Tier	ECU 722/tonne	ECU 822/tonne

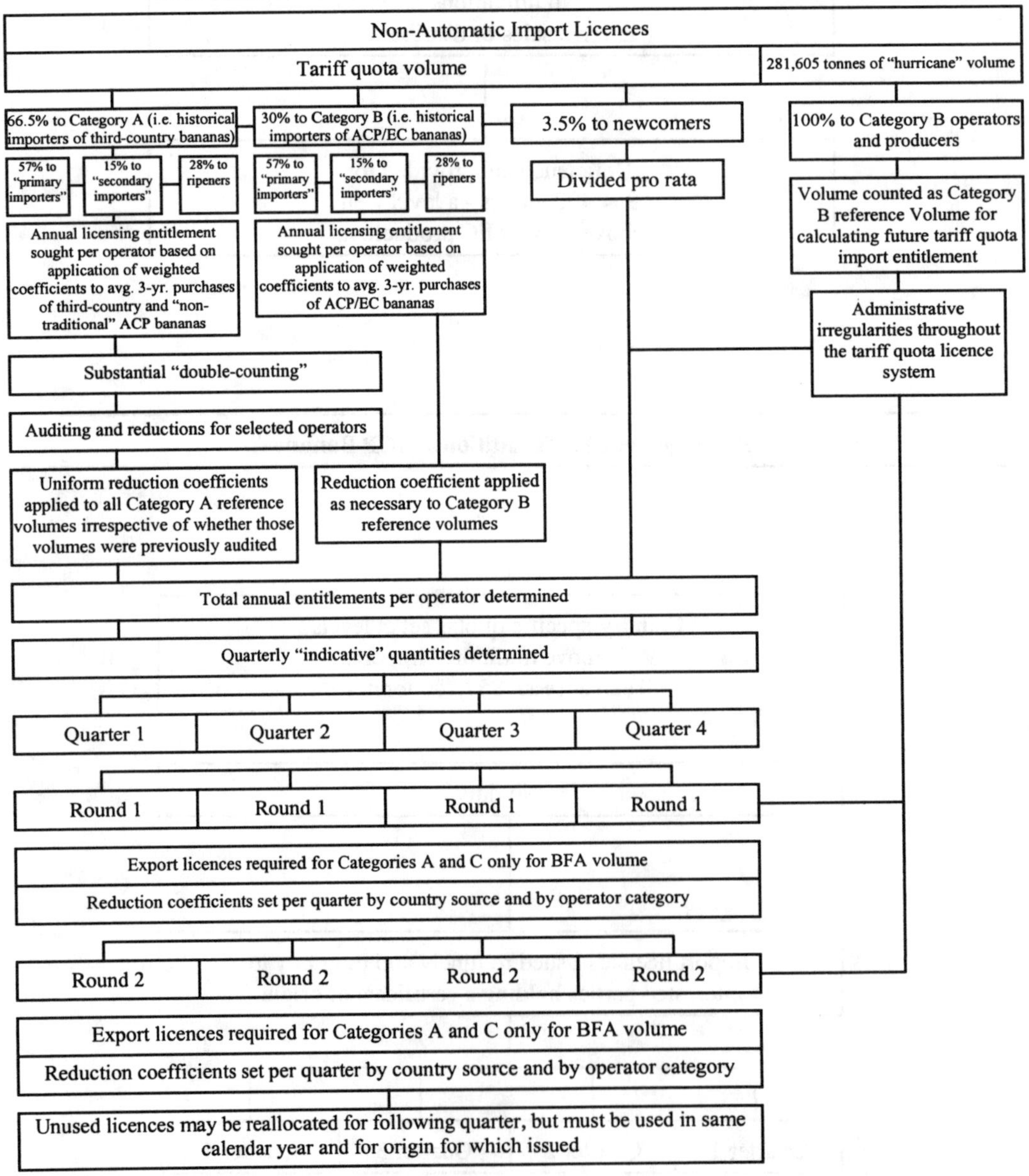

4.250 Ecuador argued that EC Regulation 1442/93 set out two separate application procedures - a procedure for obtaining licences to import traditional ACP bananas and a different procedure for obtaining licences to import third-country bananas. According to Article 14 of Regulation 1442/93, any operator wishing to import traditional ACP bananas would be able to do so after filing an application with the competent EC member State accompanied by a certificate of origin and bill of lading.[149] In contrast to this straightforward procedure, the application procedure for operators wishing to import third-country bananas was long and arduous, and involved the following major elements: (i) the allocation of the third-country tariff quota among BFA and non-BFA signatories; (ii) the allocation of the third-country tariff quota among operator categories; (iii) the allocation of operator category allocations among activity functions; (iv) the reduction of entitlement due to selective auditing and to application of inequitable reduction coefficients; (v) the two-round application procedure; (vi) the distribution and purchase of special export certificates; (vii) the reallocation of unused licences to a subsequent quarter of the year; and (viii) the issuance of hurricane licences to Category B operators. The differences in these two sets of application procedures clearly discriminated against third-country bananas and third-country operators and thus not only violated numerous provisions of the GATT as outlined elsewhere, but also of the Licensing Agreement.

4.251 Guatemala and Honduras submitted that the tariff quota licensing scheme was illegal, discriminatory and unfair when contrasted with the far simpler, essentially automatic traditional ACP licensing arrangement. Second, the scheme was discriminatory and unfair when contrasted with the free and open internal sale and distribution arrangement accorded EC bananas. Finally, because of both those forms of discrimination, and because of the overwhelmingly onerous requirements the tariff quota licensing scheme itself contained, the total tariff quota licensing arrangement restricted and distorted trade, and otherwise posed unnecessary administrative burdens in defiance of WTO law. According to Guatemala and Honduras, Regulation 404/93 *et seq*. subjected bananas from tariff quota sources to a complex, multi-layered, non-automatic licensing regime that dictated in micro-detail the entities and extensive procedures through which tariff quota bananas could be entered and distributed. Guatemalan and Honduran producers were not free to sell to purchasers of their choice, but had to sell to arbitrarily defined classes of "operators," over half of which had no experience in, or infrastructure for, the importation, distribution, and transport of Latin American bananas prior to the institution of Regulation 404/93. Moreover, tariff quota bananas could not be promptly distributed through such designated entities, but had to await multiple rounds of applications that confused the marketplace and precluded importation of the Complaining parties' bananas for the first three weeks of every quarter. The rules governing all such procedures and entities were voluminous and changed constantly. This unnatural, heavily constrained, and ever-changing distribution scheme for Latin American bananas had reconfigured historical distribution patterns, caused price distortions, curtailed delivery flexibility, and had created widespread uncertainty and confusion in the marketing of the Complaining parties' bananas.

4.252 By contrast, Guatemala and Honduras argued, traditional ACP-sourced bananas were subject to a distinctly different, greatly simplified, and essentially automatic licensing system. Traditional ACP bananas could be entered simply and promptly through any firm. The automatic licensing approach applied to traditional ACP bananas permitted commercial flexibility, simplicity, predictability, continuity and otherwise undistorted trade flow. The approach was so radically preferable to tariff quota licensing that EC importers, overwhelmed by the enormity and restrictiveness of tariff quota licensing rules, would over time place investment and marketing emphasis on traditional ACP sources if only to avoid the rigours and confusion of the tariff quota licensing system.

4.253 In contrast to the system for traditional ACP bananas, the United States argued, the EC banana regime subjected Latin American bananas to a multi-layered licensing scheme that operated to constrain importer flexibility at every turn. Latin American imports were subject to rules, e.g. distribution of licences on the basis of Category B operator criteria and activity functions (b) and (c), that attempted to shift imports away from those who had the skill, distribution networks and infrastructure to sell them, and toward those with little or no experience in importing bananas from Latin America, or in some cases, from anywhere else.

[149] Regulation 1442/93, Title II, Articles 14-17.

(b) arguments of the EC

4.254 The EC presented its arguments concerning the claims of the Complaining parties concerning import licensing issues firstly by submitting two preliminary issues: (i) the non-applicability of the Agreement on Import Licensing Procedures to tariff quotas; and (ii) the non-applicability of Articles III:4 and X of GATT 1994 to border measures. Details of these matters are set out below along with the arguments of the Complaining parties concerning them. In addition, as noted above, the EC reiterated its arguments set out earlier concerning horizontal issues: (i) the presence of two separate banana access regimes; and (ii) the applicability of the Lomé waiver to specific aspects of the Complaining parties' allegations. These issues are recorded in sections of the text dealing with specific claims. Finally, arguments concerning import licensing issues as they relate to the regime as a whole that have not been covered elsewhere are reported including those with respect to specific agreements and provisions.

(c) the non-applicability of the Agreement on Import Licensing Procedures to tariff quotas

4.255 In response to the allegations under the Agreement on Import Licensing Procedures (Licensing Agreement), the EC submitted that the text of Licensing Agreement itself specified that its scope was to regulate all the procedures, others than customs operations, prior to the importation. The provisions of that agreement appeared then as further specifications of some of the rules contained in Article XIII of GATT in which, *inter alia*, explicit reference was made in paragraph 3(a), "to import licences issued in connection with import restrictions". However, nothing in the Licensing Agreement specified (like Article XIII:5) that it applied also to cases where no import restriction was applied at the border and, therefore, it should not be deemed applicable to such cases as in the case of a tariff quota of the kind of the EC banana tariff quota.

4.256 The United States argued that the Licensing Agreement provided the most specific disciplines on import licensing among the various WTO agreements. In particular, as reflected in its preamble, it sought to place disciplines on non-automatic licensing, namely those licensing schemes where approval was not granted in all cases, such as the regime applicable to EC imports of bananas.

4.257 According to the Complaining parties, Article 1.1 of the Licensing Agreement, which defined its coverage, did not limit its provisions to absolute quotas. The reference to the licences being "a prior condition for importation" did not mean that the agreement did not apply to tariff quotas. A licence was required as a prior condition for importing fruit under the tariff item subject to the in-quota duty, which would always be the first to enter the market, while over-quota licence-free volumes would only be imported, if at all, when the tariff levels and other market conditions so allowed. Thus, the fact that licences were not required to import fruit at the over-quota rate was irrelevant.

4.258 In the view of the Complaining parties, the EC's claim that the Licensing Agreement applied solely with respect to "restrictions" overlooked the fact that Article 1.1 of the Licensing Agreement, setting out the scope of the agreement, made no mention of "restrictions". The expansive language of Article 1.1 clarified that it applied to all "administrative procedures used for the operation of import licensing regimes", whether or not an import restriction applied at the border. Other aspects of the Agreement tended, in the view of the Complaining parties, to support its application to tariff quotas. Article 3.3 conferred a very broad scope to the Agreement by referring specifically to licensing requirements "for purposes other than the implementation of quantitative restrictions". Although there were a few references to "restrictions", most references to quantitative limitations were to "quotas", which by definition included tariff quotas. Moreover, to the extent the word "restriction" was used in some instances, it should not be read in the sense of Article XI (which prohibited "restrictions", a term which in that context did not cover tariff quotas). Rather, the Agreement's use of the term "restriction", should be understood in the sense of its use in Article XIII of GATT, which made application to tariff quotas explicit.

4.259 Article XIII was closest in purpose to the Licensing Agreement in that it governed the administration of a measure, whereas Article XI simply prohibited restrictions and set forth exceptions to the prohibition. In this sense, given the judgment made by the contracting parties in 1947 that administrative disciplines applying to absolute quotas should be equally applicable to tariff quotas, there would be no reason to distinguish between them in an agreement that expanded upon those disciplines forty or fifty years later. The intent to cover tariff quotas could further be inferred from the reference in the Agreement's preamble to the "provisions of the GATT 1994 as they apply to import licensing procedures": the most explicit reference to import licensing was in Article XIII of GATT, which covered tariff quotas. Other parts of the GATT that applied more specifically to import licensing - among them Articles VIII and X - applied to tariff quotas as well. The purposes of the Licensing Agreement, as reflected in its preamble, did not reveal, in the opinion of the Complaining parties, any reason why tariff quotas would be removed from its coverage. Concerns such as implementation of licensing in a "transparent and predictable manner", "fair and equitable application", preventing the inappropriate use of licensing from impeding the "flow of international trade", and so on were all concerns that were just as valid with respect to tariff quotas.

4.260 In 1994, in the Import Licensing Committee under the Tokyo Round Code, the United States twice raised the discriminatory aspects of the EC's import licensing regime for bananas and the EC's failure to properly notify the Import Licensing Committee of the regime under the Import Licensing Agreement. Several countries expressed support for the United States' view. The EC did not contest the applicability of the Licensing Agreement to tariff quotas, stating only its confidence that the new regime was "in conformity with the new Agreement on Import Licensing Procedures."[150] Finally, the Complaining parties argued that the Agreement should be interpreted in light of the broader context of the Uruguay Round negotiations and the progress achieved in the agriculture negotiations in particular. A major achievement of the Uruguay Round agriculture negotiations was the large-scale conversion of non-tariff barriers to tariff quotas. Making tariff quotas an exception to the disciplines of the Licensing Agreement directly contradicted the trend toward transparency and predictability.[151] Unless the Licensing Agreement was rigorously applied consistent with its broad terms and disciplines, the major Uruguay Round advances in market access for agriculture intended by tariffication could be considerably undermined through arbitrary and burdensome licensing. This was surely not intended by the negotiators.

4.261 The EC argued that in addition to the points made earlier, Japan, in its third party submission had usefully introduced supplementary evidence justifying the EC interpretation. The EC, referring to the text of Article 1.1 of the Licensing Agreement, noted that the Agreement was of utmost clarity. The error the Complaining parties were making, according to the EC, was to relate the existence of the licence with the physical importation of bananas: those licences were only needed to benefit from a particular duty rate within the tariff quota but not to physically introduce bananas, from any origin, into the EC customs territory. Licences were therefore tradeable, and traded, and were not a prior condition to any importation; they were needed only for the application of a specific duty rate. This was why the fact that no limitation in quantities existed under the present GATT bound commitments was of paramount importance and should be sufficient to dismiss the Complaining parties insistence on the applicability of the Licensing Agreement to tariff quotas.

4.262 Further, the EC rejected the Complaining parties' analysis concerning the word "restriction". The EC submitted that if the word "restriction" which was found in Article XIII of GATT was to be interpreted differently than the same word used in Article XI, the specific provision of Article XIII:5 would not have been necessary at all, since the meaning of the word "restriction" found in Article XIII would already include, following the Complaining parties reasoning, not only volume restrictions but also the conditions applied in the administration of a tariff quota. According to the EC, however, this was not the case: without the explicit provision of Article XIII:5,

[150] See Minutes of the Meeting of the Committee on Import Licensing held on 5 May 1994, LIC/M/34, 10 June 1994 and Minutes of the Meeting of the Committee on Import Licensing held on 3 November 1994, LIC/M/35, 6 December 1994.

[151] The Complaining parties noted that it was also likely that negotiators of the Agreement on Agriculture would have stipulated such a major exception. Other exemptions were explicit such as in Article 13 of the Agreement on Agriculture, which exempted domestic subsidies from the Agreement on Subsidies and Countervailing Measures.

Article XIII would not have been applicable to tariff quotas simply because a tariff quota did not constitute a restriction to imports and the Article XIII language was equivalent in the letter and in the intention of the CONTRACTING PARTIES to the one used in Article XI. So when Article 3.3 of the Licensing Agreement referred to "restrictions" it meant what it said, i.e. the same concept as the one covered in Articles XI and XIII but without any provision equivalent to Article XIII:5. As mentioned before, the Licensing Agreement did not apply to tariff quotas but solely to quantitative restrictions. However, there was no loophole in the coverage of the GATT, since specific provisions in Article II:5 and Article XIII:2(d), last phrase, were applicable where appropriate.

4.263 In this light, in response to a question posed by the Panel, the EC submitted that where a tariff quota was bound in the appropriate schedule, Members expected then to be able to make full use of that tariff quota in accordance with the provisions of the appropriate schedule and, consequently, in compliance with Article II:1 of GATT. That principle could not be undermined by any provision concerning the administration of the quota, in particular any licensing procedure, that could modify the treatment the product was supposed to receive under the schedule. Article II:5, first part, further developed this principle through its reference to treatment to "a product". Moreover, and more specifically, Article XIII:2(d), last part, indicated that "no conditions or formalities shall be imposed which prevent any contracting party from utilizing fully the share of any such total quantity or value which has been allotted to it, subject to importation being made within any prescribed period to which the quota may relate". This provision, while reinstating the principle contained in Article II:1 and II:5, pointed more specifically to conditions and formalities which were normally related to a licensing scheme used, *inter alia*, to administer a tariff quota. It defined more clearly the general limits to which the principle of Article II:1 and II:5 was submitted with respect to formalities: Article XIII:2(d) in fact, accorded explicitly the possibility of taking any prescription related to the period to which the quota refers, in the opinion of the EC. By so doing, the practice of annual licences, for instance, was expressly acknowledged as been compatible with Article XIII:2(d) and, *a fortiori*, Article II:1 and II:5. This did not imply, however that, under Articles II and XIII, the treatment under the schedule included any commercial consideration, in particular with respect to licensing procedures. Ad Article XIII:2(d) stated: "no mention was made of 'commercial considerations' as a rule for the allocation of quotas because it was considered that its application by governmental authorities might not always be practicable". If this was not possible, and in any case not mandatory, for the allocation of shares of tariff quotas among supplying countries, it was certainly even less possible, and certainly not mandatory at all, when administering those tariff quotas. Commercial risk or any other commercial consideration could not and should not be taken into account when assessing the compliance with those Articles since it concerned the behaviour of operators on the market while the GATT, and in particular Articles II and XIII, was concerned only with the products while imported or exported.

4.264 The Complaining parties replied that the EC's argument that the GATT and Licensing Agreement did not apply to the EC preferential schemes for ACP and BFA countries because these schemes applied to importers and not to products was also without any support in the WTO. It was well established that advantages provided to particular producers on the basis of the country of origin of the product they handled (subsidies were a prime example) were considered to enhance the competitive opportunities for the product. Similarly any additional bargaining leverage provided by the regime to banana growers in some countries and not to others was discrimination against products on the basis of country of origin. Any benefits accruing to importers of ACP bananas that were not provided to importers of Latin American bananas also were discriminatory with respect to bananas. Moreover, as confirmed by numerous panels, the EC's arguments that these disadvantages had not had trade effects were legally irrelevant. With respect to the EC's artificial distribution of licences that were deliberately unconnected to import shares that would prevail in a free market, the Complaining parties considered them inconsistent with the general principle reflected in Article XIII against administrative measures based on factors other than economic efficiencies.

(d) the non-applicability of Articles III:4 and X of GATT to border measures

4.265 The EC emphasized that the Complaining parties addressed in their arguments the same issues with respect to import licensing both as violations of GATT provisions preventing discrimination in regard to measures taken at the border while importing bananas into the EC and as violations of the non-discrimination principle in the application of internal rules applicable after bananas had been cleared through customs and circulated within the EC market. The EC considered that the Complaining parties must choose which legal avenue they wished to follow but they could not have it both ways. In fact, a specific contested measure was objectively (and not merely relying on the particular ad hoc interest of a Complaining party) either a measure at the border or an internal measure. If the Complaining parties considered that some aspects of the EC regime fell within the first category while others fell within the other, the burden of proof lay on their shoulders to demonstrate what pertained to what. What was certainly unacceptable to the EC, and what should, in the EC's view, be rejected by the Panel, was the mixing of both issues, as if it were possible to escape this fundamental question. This was indispensable to a correct interpretation of the GATT. As far as the EC was concerned, it was its understanding that practically all measures concerning licensing rules and procedures in the administration of the EC banana tariff quota which concerned operators while importing bananas into the EC market were border measures and not internal rules applicable irrespectively to all bananas after they had been entered into the EC market.

4.266 As an illustration of the unacceptable confusion between border measures and internal measures, the EC referred to the claims of some Complaining parties that compared the licensing system needed for administering a legitimate tariff quota while importing bananas in the EC to a sale and distribution system of an internal product: the latter, evidently, did not cross any border and therefore did not need to be submitted to any licensing system. Many of the claims of the Complaining parties failed to indicate how rules under Articles III:4 and X of GATT could be applicable to border measures and, moreover, how they could be reasonably coupled with the allegations under Article 1.3 of the Licensing Agreement at the same time. As the 1958 Panel Report on *Italian discrimination against imported agricultural machinery* indicated, the purpose of Article III of GATT was "clearly to treat the imported products in the same way as the like domestic products once they have cleared trough customs. Otherwise indirect protection should be given". On the contrary, provisions like Articles XI and XIII and the Licensing Agreement (which provided precise rules concerning those Articles of GATT) applied clearly only to border measures at the moment of the importation or the exportation of a product and did not concern any alleged discrimination in the application of internal measures after the product had cleared through customs. Consequently, the EC submitted that, in GATT terms it was impossible to allege that a specific measure violated, at the same time, Articles III:4 and XIII of GATT and/or the Licensing Agreement. Finally, the EC was of the view that the legally correct interpretation of the EC banana licensing system, and in particular requirements under Article 19(b) of Regulation 404/93, as a border measure at the moment of the importation, did not imply that those measures violated any GATT rules and in particular not Articles 1.3, 3.2 and 3.5 of the Licensing Agreement.

4.267 The Complaining parties responded that the second *Banana* panel found that the Category B licences were inconsistent with the Article III national treatment requirement of GATT. The EC's licensing scheme also fell squarely within the first illustrative example of an Article III violation, set forth in the TRIM's Agreement. This example specified as an Article III violation any measure "compliance with which is necessary to obtain an advantage" (the advantage here being the receipt of an import licence), "and which require the purchase ... by an enterprise of products of domestic origin" (in this case EC bananas) "specified in terms of volume ... of products". The EC's treatment of this issue missed the point that an "advantage" provided could be in the form of a border measure, while the favour accorded to EC products could be one affecting purchasing and distribution decisions in the EC.

4.268 The Complaining parties further considered that Article III of GATT covered any regulation or requirement that affected internal conditions of competition in favour of EC bananas.[152] This was confirmed (not contradicted, as the EC contended) by the *Italian Discrimination Against Imported Agricultural Machinery* report:

> [t]he selection of the word "affecting" [in Article III:4] would imply, in the opinion of the Panel, that the drafters of the Article intended to cover in paragraph 4 not only the laws and regulations which directly governed the conditions of sale or purchase but also any laws or regulations which might adversely modify the conditions of competition between the domestic and imported products on the internal market.[153]

The condition upon which the EC granted Category B licences adversely modified the conditions of competition between the domestic and imported product on the internal market by providing a government benefit based on the purchases of the domestic product. Therefore, the second *Banana* panel report properly concluded that the provisions of Article III:4 applied to the EC banana import regime and the Category B licence was inconsistent with the EC's obligations under Article III:4.

4.269 Further, the Complaining parties noted that the laws and practices covered by Article X of GATT comprised all "trade regulations," which included, among many others, licensing regulations. Hence, there was an overlap between the Article X requirement that licensing rules and procedures be "uniform, impartial and reasonable", and the requirement in Article 1.3 of the Licensing Agreement that those same rules and procedures be "neutral", "fair", and "equitable". The EC's argument that Article X related solely to "internal rules" and hence was incompatible with a claim based on Article XIII of GATT was, according to the Complaining parties, not supported by the plain language of Article X or panel interpretations of its meaning. The scope of Article X was obvious from its first paragraph and its title: the Article X:3 obligation was applicable to all "trade regulations". The *Dessert Apples* report also clarified that Article XIII and Article X could apply to the same measure.[154]

4.270 In response to a question posed by the Panel, the EC noted that the Complaining parties had referred to a possible violation of Article III of GATT because "an advantage provided could be in the form of a border measure, while the favour accorded to EC products could be one affecting purchasing and distribution decisions in the EC". In the opinion of the EC, this affirmation was very important for two reasons: (i) the parties finally agreed with the EC that border measures were at issue and not internal measures: a further important reason to add to all those arguments the EC had produced demonstrating that the unadopted second *Banana* panel was wrong on this issue in its legal analysis; and (ii) the reasoning was also legally wrong. In this light, the EC provided an example: if country A wished to legally protect its domestic production on its market, it could use a border measure "*par excellence*", that is, it could impose punitive customs duties of, for instance, 1,000 per cent. This duty would certainly create an advantage which affected internal purchasing and distribution (domestic products would be immensely more competitive than imported ones on that market). However, nobody would ever contest this measure under Article III of GATT which, under constant practise and law, was concerned only with measures applicable after the product had cleared customs. Thus, to conclude the example, the EC submitted that if the introduction of the 1,000 per cent duty was made in compliance with the rules concerning that specific border measure (e.g. an Article XXVIII procedure), no other claim could be made against country A, even under Article III.

4.271 The Complaining parties rejected the EC's assertion that the incentive to purchase could not violate Article III:4 and its claim that Article III could not apply to anything connected to import licences because licences

---

152 Second *Banana* panel report, DS38/R, para. 148.

153 BISD 7S/60, para. 12 (adopted 23 October 1958). See also, United States - Section 337 of the Tariff Act of 1930, para. *5.10*; Report of the panel on "United States - Measures Affecting Alcoholic and Malt Beverages", adopted 19 June 1992, BISD 39S/206, para. *5.31*.

154 "Dessert Apples", para. 12.29.

were border measures. The Complaining parties considered that the EC's illustrative example, that a tariff of 1,000 per cent also would provide protection to domestic production but that such a tariff would not violate Article III:4, only confirmed their position, since tariffs were a GATT -consistent way to protect domestic production, while in contrast, non-tariff means of encouraging the internal purchases of domestic products were not. They were violations of Article III:4. In the view of the Complaining parties, the first illustrative example in the TRIM's Agreement established this with certainty. This example was intended to codify the findings of the panel in the EC *Parts and Components* dispute, in which the benefit for domestic products involved the suspension of certain anti-dumping procedures against companies agreeing to purchase domestic products. The point was that, regardless of the means the government used to provide an incentive to encourage the internal purchase of domestic goods, if it did not provide a similar incentive to purchase imports, the incentive violated Article III:4. It was not the form of the measure to which the incentive was connected, but the incentive it provided with respect to purchases within the EC that was at issue.

(e) Parties' subsequent arguments - the licensing regime as a whole

4.272 The EC reiterated that it was its understanding that practically all measures concerning licensing rules and procedures in the administration of the EC banana tariff quota which concerned operators while importing bananas into the EC market were border measures and not internal rules applicable to all bananas after they had been introduced into the EC market. Consequently the EC responded to the allegations within this legal framework. In addition, all the legal analysis with respect to the Licensing Agreement should be deemed to be under the general reservation that the Panel needed to solve the question of principle – the applicability of the Licensing Agreement to tariff quotas – prior to examining any other issue.

4.273 The EC argued that the first error the Complaining parties made was to consider that a tariff quota was an "import restriction" while the unadopted second *Banana* panel report had excluded this argument and no evidence of a different (inexistent) reality had been shown. Starting with the comparison between the EC tariff quota licensing system and the ACP traditional quota licensing system, it should first of all be noted that the Complaining parties did not explain how this comparison could be relevant. The EC recalled that the external aspects of the EC common organization of the markets for bananas consisted of two distinct regimes: the regime for so-called traditional ACP bananas which should be treated in accordance with the Lomé Convention and the Lomé waiver and be given preferential treatment; and a bound rate of duty for imports in excess of tariff quota quantities and a tariff quota allocation for all other bananas as instituted for many agricultural products by many Members.

4.274 With respect to import licensing issues, the EC submitted that any comparison between the tariff quota licensing system and the ACP traditional quota licensing system had no legal value and was not relevant. It was evident, in the view of the EC, that the fact that two separate and independent regimes, the ACP traditional and the EC tariff quota, had marginal differences in their respective licensing systems was neither in itself a violation of any GATT provision nor was it evidence of any violation of GATT provisions by any of the two systems. Secondly, as the tables below showed, the two systems did not create any substantial differences in their external effects on bananas imported from different sources; the only discrepancies that remained were on the side of the internal procedures to be followed by the competent authorities. The first table submitted by the EC was an annotated version of the chart submitted by the Complaining parties. The shaded parts in the EC's version of the chart which follows represent those that the EC considered to be erroneous and misleading.

Arrangement 3: Third-Country and "Non-Traditional" ACP Bananas

Tariff quota total volume (2 million tonnes, increased to 2.2 million tonnes) set substantially below then-existing third-country EC-12 access. Tariff quota enlargement to cover former EFTA-3 volume is expected.

Further subdivision of that volume, some to specific countries, others to groups of countries. Reserve of 90,000 tonnes for both "non-traditional" and traditional ACP suppliers. Allocation transfers allowed among only certain countries.

Duty (1995)		
	"Non-traditional" ACP	Third country
1st Tier	0	ECU 75/tonne
2nd Tier	ECU 722/tonne	ECU 822/tonne

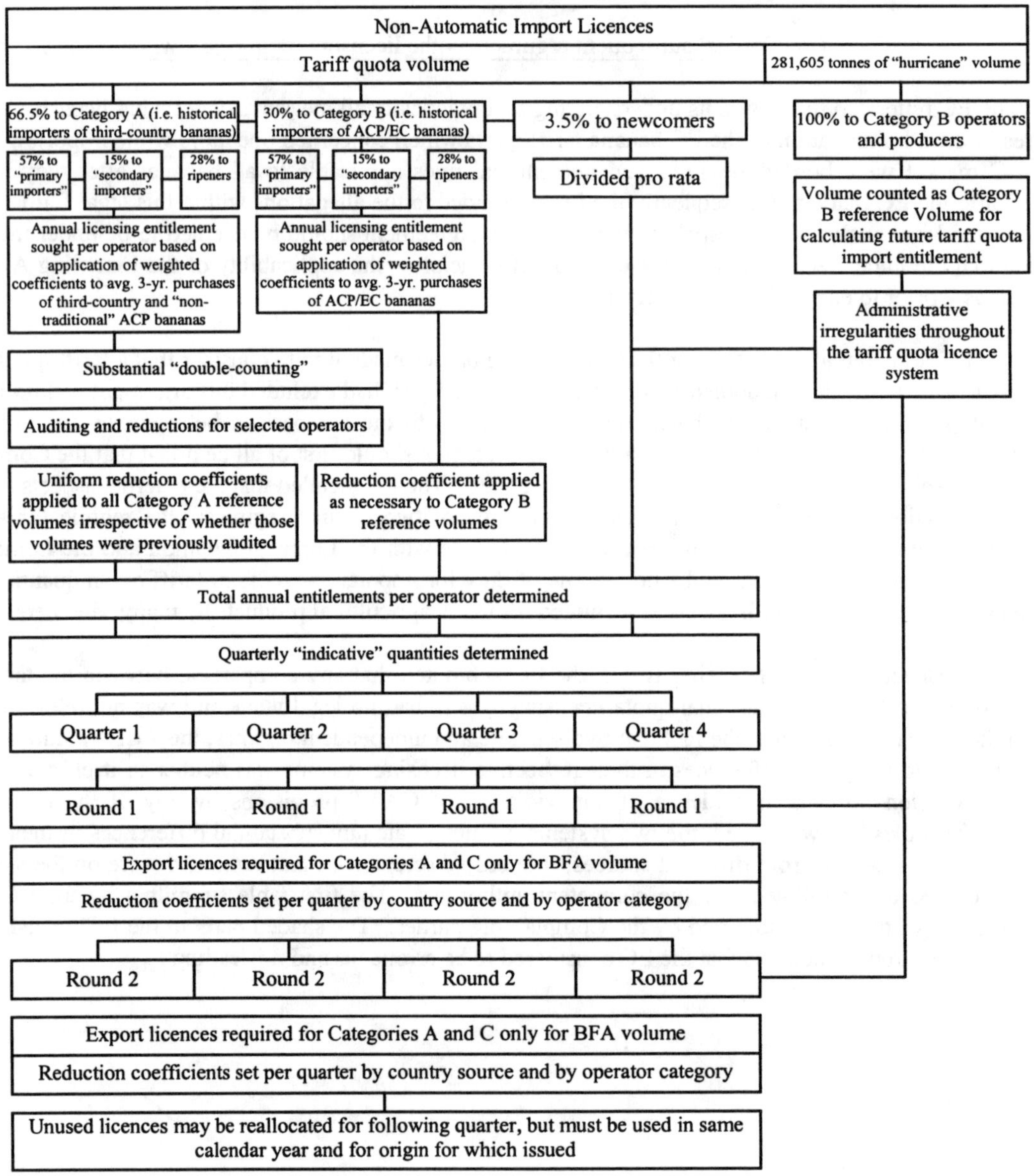

Imports under the tariff quota	Traditional ACP imports
1. Operator applies for a reference quantity by sending details of volumes bananas marketed in past three years to the relevant competent authority.	1. Operator obtains special certificates of origin from the issuing authority in the relevant ACP State.
(1.bis Optional: Operator obtains special export certificates (SEC's) if he wishes to import from Colombia, Costa Rica or Nicaragua with a Category A or C licence. (This stage applies to only 33 per cent of the volume of the tariff quota.)	
2. During the first 7 days of the month prior to the start of the quarter, operator applies for import licences for the quarter. SEC included if required.	2. During the first 7 days of the month prior to the start of the quarter, operator applies for import licences for the quarter. All applications must be accompanied by a special certificate of origin.
3. Import licences issued to operator; quantity requested reduced if required by the application of a reduction coefficient.	3. Import licences issued to operator; quantity requested reduced if required by the application of a reduction coefficient.
(3.bis Optional: If operator has not received all the quantity requested, he may apply for the balance during the second round.)	
4. Operator imports bananas.	4. Operator imports bananas.

4.275 The Complaining parties responded that although the procedures surely were also burdensome for the EC's "competent authorities", this did not make them any less burdensome for importers. Looking at the two procedures for administering imports, that for ACP bananas and that for Latin American bananas, the Complaining parties had no doubt as to which an investor or prospective marketer would choose to subject himself, given a choice.

4.276 The Complaining parties considered that the following comparison table clarified the differences in licensing treatment:

Latin America (LA)	African, Caribbean and Pacific (ACP)
1. Entitlement to the tariff quota is divided among A, B, C "operator" categories – 66.5%, 30%, 3.5%. This requires (1) historic importers of LA bananas either to lose traditional past access or buy back rights to import from companies with no past involvement in LA trade, or, for the longer term, rebuild their distribution structure in order to distribute bananas from EC or ACP areas, and (2) LA exporters to establish and/or restructure commercial relationships with firms not previously competitive in LA imports and persons, including EC farmers, without potential to become so.	1. No comparable provisions.
2. Licence eligibility is based on (a), (b), (c) "activity functions" ("primary importer", "secondary importer" and ripener). This shifts import entitlement away from traditional importers, and requires operators to expend significant resources to ensure adequate licence access, either by buying licences, thus entering into (forced) commercial arrangements with other licence grantees, or by expanding into additional activity functions to try to maintain historic reference volumes.	2. No comparable provision.
3. The operator applies for a reference quantity one year in advance by providing details of volumes and origins of bananas marketed in the past 3 years (beginning two years before current year) to the relevant competent authority.	3. No comparable requirement; historical shipments irrelevant to EC import licence distribution.
4. Due largely to ambiguous operator definitions developed through administrative fiats, over-filing of claims occurs. An across-the-board reduction coefficient is applied, regardless of auditing of some operators whose quantities have been adjusted or deemed correct, creating inequity and uncertainty regarding the operator's annual shipment entitlement, and constraining operator flexibility. Final operator entitlements, which are delayed until the third quarter of the actual year of import, have been well below provisional entitlement established prior to the year of import.	4. Because EC licence eligibility is not based on historical shipments, there are no competing claims regarding past activities. Occasionally, the EC has applied reduction coefficients for certain African countries where there is an over-subscription of bids to import.

5. Operator applies for import licences during the first 7 days in the month before the start of each quarter. Any Category A operator importing from Colombia, Costa Rica or Nicaragua must both obtain an export licence and be eligible for an import licence specifically applicable to that country ("matching") before an import licence for that country may be issued. Once obtained, the import licences must be physically distributed to ports of arrival for presentation to customs authorities for importation to be permitted. The "matching" requirement imposes significant costs, limits flexibility and creates market irregularities for all LA suppliers.	5. Operator applies for import licences during the first 7 days in the month before the start of each quarter. Applications require submission of ACP certificates of origin (which are obtained promptly - within a few weeks after application, and at no cost, from the issuing authority in the relevant ACP country). No "matching" is required. Licences are issued one week in advance of each quarter.
6. Once quarterly indicative quantities are set, a quarterly two-round licensing procedure is used. First-round applications are cut by reduction coefficients to force imports from specific sources. Second-round applications are not processed, and licences are not granted, until two weeks into the quarter. This procedure limits flexibility and creates uncertainty and irregularities in the market.	6. No comparable two-round system.
7. Because of ambiguities in eligibility criteria (see 4 above), following importation, the operator must gather and maintain for five years proof of production, transportation, insurance, EC sale, labelling and brand names to avoid losing future entitlement to that volume.	7. No comparable documentation requirements.

4.277 The Complaining parties argued that they had shown the licensing practices in their totality presented a burden on imports that was incomparable to any other licensing system on earth. The most telling evidence of its burden – and discriminatory nature – was that the EC had proposed moving non-traditional ACP bananas from this system to the simple system applicable to traditional ACP bananas. The responsive charts proffered by the EC only recorded the burden on Commission staff and conspicuously omitted the extraordinary constraints and adjustments imposed upon importers, reflecting attempts to hide unwelcome realities concerning these burdens.

4.278 The EC responded that although any comparison between the ACP traditional licensing system and the EC tariff quota licensing system was of no legal use, there was a need to concentrate on the table presented by the Complaining parties as set out above. The EC argued that it had shown the diagram originally submitted by the Complaining parties was erroneous and misleading. In submitting a second, much simpler diagram they had acknowledged the truth of this. However, they had still not got it right as the following corrected version showed, in the EC's opinion. The EC pointed out that it simply corrected the material errors in the Complaining parties' table to demonstrate how they had once again attempted to mislead the Panel. The EC had retained, as far as possible, the structure of their table, even though it included repetition and activities which were not the responsibility of operators. It does not represent, therefore, the real situation, which remained, as it has always been, as originally portrayed in the EC's table (see above, second table).

Tariff quota imports	Traditional ACP imports
1. Entitlement to import based on historic trade volumes and activity functions which spread licences throughout the marketing chain.	1. Entitlement to import based on obtaining a special certificate of origin. No *a priori* licence distribution therefore no direct comparison, but any operator at any point in the marketing chain may seek special certificates of origin
2. The operator applies for a reference quantity based on past trade.	2. The operator must obtain special certificates of origin
3. Licence entitlements calculated from reference quantities of previously imported bananas, which are verified to eliminate double counting. NB: verification of double counting is an activity by the competent authorities to tackle error and fraud in the declarations	3. Entitlement to import based on volume of special certificates of origin.
5. Quarterly indicative quantities set NB: activity of Commission that does not require operator's activity	5. Quarterly indicative quantities set
6. Operator applies for import licences during first 7 days of month prior to start of quarter, including special export certificate if required (for 35% of volume). Import licence must be presented to customs authorities to release fruit into free circulation.	6. Operator applies for import licences during first 7 days of month prior to start of quarter, including special certificate of origin (for 100% of volume). Import licence must be presented to customs authorities to release fruit into free circulation
7. Reduction coefficients applied to those origins where demand exceeds indicative quantity. Second round permits utilization of remaining quantities.	7. Reduction coefficients applied to those origins where demand exceeds indicative quantity.
8. Operator maintains normal commercial records, and submits them to apply for Category A reference quantity.	8. Operator maintains normal commercial records, and submits them to apply for Category B reference quantity.

(f) Claims under the GATT

- Article I:1 of GATT

4.279 The Complaining parties submitted that in addition to presenting other violations as set out below, the EC's licensing regime was subject to the more general discipline of Article I of GATT, which applied to all rules and formalities in connection with importation. The more favourable licensing rules applicable to traditional ACP country bananas constituted, in the opinion of the Complaining parties, a clear regulatory "advantage" that had not been accorded immediately and unconditionally to Latin American bananas in violation of Article I:1. The presence of an Article I:1 violation was supported by *Non-Rubber Footwear*, in which the panel found that Article I:1 strictly prohibited a contracting party from according a procedural or regulatory advantage to a product originating in one country, while denying that same advantage to the like product originating in the territories of other contracting parties.[155]

[155] "United States - Denial of Most-Favoured Nation Treatment as to Non-Rubber Footwear from Brazil", adopted 19 June 1992, BISD 39S/128, para. 6.11.

4.280 Mexico considered that Article I of GATT was applicable to the case under consideration by the Panel because the EC regime granted advantages, favours, privileges or immunities to products originating in certain WTO members (ACP countries and BFA countries) that were not granted to like products (bananas) originating in the territories of all other Members (non-ACP countries and non-BFA countries) through a regime that contained import formalities which was also related to certain issues referred to in paragraph 4 of Article III of GATT (Category B operators). In the view of Mexico, this had been confirmed by the second *Banana* panel.

4.281 The EC considered that a licensing system could not be considered by any means as an advantage, favour, privilege or immunity and therefore could not be covered by the provisions of Article I of GATT. If only for the sake of argument one might accept the idea that a licensing system could be considered an advantage within the scope of that Article, the EC maintained that the Lomé waiver was applicable to the particular licensing system used for the importation of bananas under the ACP traditional allocation, because the systems, in their respective regimes of application, responded to the need of preserving the advantages of the ACP countries on the EC market (Article 1 of Protocol 5 of the Lomé Convention) and to "improve the conditions for ... the marketing of bananas" (Article 2 of Protocol 5 of the Lomé Convention).

4.282 The EC recalled that the Lomé waiver covered any measure taken by the EC in order to fulfil its legal obligations as indicated under the Lomé Convention with regards to any product originating in ACP countries, including bananas. In the case of bananas, the legal obligations were fulfilled by the EC by: (a) creating a specific and separate system for the importation to the EC of the ACP traditional banana production; (b) by the allocation to ACP countries of a limited share of the bound tariff quota at a duty-free rate, that was lower that the MFN bound rate; (c) by a marginal reduction of the tariff rate applicable for the importation of bananas outside the tariff quota; and (d) by facilitating trade and commercial relations between the EC and the ACP countries through the creation of the so-called Category B operator licences to ensure that the quantities for which access opportunities were given could actually be sold and that the EC could thus fulfil its obligations to guarantee traditional ACP bananas their existing advantages, while not providing by this mean any incentive to purchase ACP bananas.

4.283 The EC's unexplained claim, in the view of the Complaining parties, that "a licensing system cannot be considered by any means as an advantage, favour, privilege or immunity" was contradicted, they asserted, by the EC's own *Report on the Operation of the Banana Regime*, in which the EC asserted that the proposal to subject non-traditional ACP bananas to the more favourable licensing rules applicable to traditional ACP bananas would provide "assistance" to certain non-traditional suppliers.[156]

4.284 Ecuador submitted that the preferential licensing scheme for traditional ACP bananas as a whole, and including with respect to advantages provided to Category B operators, could not be excused by the Lomé waiver which protected only certain historical tariff preferences given to traditional ACP suppliers.

4.285 Guatemala and Honduras considered that the Lomé waiver provided no cover for licensing discrimination by source. Its language had been carefully and narrowly drawn to waive Article I:1 of GATT only for that preferential treatment that was "required by the relevant provisions of the Lomé Convention" and that preferences be extended so as "not to raise undue barriers or to create undue difficulties for the trade of other contracting parties". In the view of Guatemala and Honduras, no provision of the Lomé Convention could be read to require the EC to confer a simple, prompt licensing arrangement on traditional ACP bananas while withholding such treatment for bananas from Latin American sources. Since the tariff quota licensing scheme denied Guatemala and Honduras a licensing advantage that was being conferred on bananas from other third countries, which advantage fell beyond the scope of the Lomé waiver, it had to be ruled down under the provisions of Article I:1 of GATT.

4.286 Referring to the EC claim that its preferential licensing rules as between traditional ACP and Latin American bananas were excused by the Lomé waiver pursuant to Articles 1 and 2 of Protocol 5 of the Lomé

[156] "Report on the Operation of the Banana Regime", p.19.

Convention, the Complaining parties, submitted that Article 2 of Protocol 5, contained no legal requirement to afford preferential licensing to traditional ACP suppliers, but set forth only non-binding objectives regarding traditional ACP banana marketing and production, making that Article irrelevant to the Lomé waiver. Although Protocol 5, Article 1, did contain a Lomé Convention requirement, that requirement did not, in the opinion of the Complaining parties, authorize the EC to go beyond permitting preferential access.[157] Neither Articles 1 nor 2 of the Banana Protocol could therefore be read to require discriminatory licensing rules that solely erected undue barriers to Latin American fruit.

4.287 In the Complaining parties' opinion, the EC's assertion in the alternative that the Lomé waiver excused such discriminatory licensing advantages misrepresented the Lomé requirements. The EC claimed that these advantages were required by Articles 1 and 2 of Protocol 5 of the Lomé Convention. However, Article 2 of Protocol 5 was irrelevant to the Lomé waiver, since it contained no legal obligation. Article 1 of that Protocol solely required the maintenance of a past "situation" as regards access and advantages. No past advantages existed for ACP products with respect to import licensing for Latin American bananas. If anything, with respect to import licensing generally, the Lomé requirements pertained to the facility of access for ACP fruit; they did not require discriminatory licensing rules that erected undue barriers to Latin American fruit to the entire EC market.

4.288 The EC submitted that a point of legal interest deserved to be highlighted: the Complaining parties had asserted that the licensing system devised by the EC to administer the ACP traditional allocation was, first of all, a preferential one and, secondly, it was not required by the Lomé Convention and therefore could not be covered by the Lomé waiver. The Complaining parties had concluded with the following: "neither Article 1 nor 2 of the Banana Protocol can therefore be read to require discriminatory licensing rules that solely erect undue barriers to Latin American fruit". According to the EC, the whole reasoning was flawed and should be rejected. The ACP traditional allocation was a specific regime that was governed by specific rules. As it had been repeatedly demonstrated, there was no fundamental difference between the ACP licensing system and the EC tariff quota system. However, the regime of access of the ACP traditional bananas was a preferential one and the licensing system was a means of administering it according to its specificity. To say that the Lomé Convention did not require "... licensing arrangements ... and does not guarantee specific levels of imports ..." was disingenuous. These measures were required in as much as they were essential in enabling the EC to provide the preferential treatment (access and advantages on traditional markets) specified in and required by Protocol 5. In this context it was covered by the Lomé waiver as part of the overall preference for ACP bananas. Moreover, the fact that a licensing system was not expressly required by the Lomé Convention might paradoxically go against what the Complaining parties considered their interest: they might be confronted with the request by the ACP States to abolish any kind of licensing. The reality was nevertheless simpler: the contracting parties to the Lomé Convention had recognized the need for a licensing system to ensure a correct and balanced implementation of the ACP traditional allocation. No barriers to Latin American fruit were erected as a consequence of the existence of a licensing system for ACP traditional bananas. Indeed, no barrier existed at all to the entry of any bananas of whichever origin: the only provisions concerned the licensing system administering the use of the EC tariff quota, which was not a restrictive regime.

4.289 Guatemala and Honduras considered that the Lomé waiver, was no answer to the EC's discriminatory export licence provisions. Selective export licensing requirements were for the exclusive benefit of Costa Rica, Colombia, and Nicaragua, countries that were entirely irrelevant to the Lomé Convention. With Article I:1 of GATT thereby violated, the export licences selectively mandated by Regulation 478/95 had to be ruled null and void, and deleted from the regime. Furthermore, according to Guatemala and Honduras, the Lomé waiver was irrelevant to the selective imposition of activity functions on tariff quota bananas. The recitals to Regulation 1442/93 themselves made clear that activity function requirements solely related to the distribution of tariff quota

[157] "Federal Republic of Germany v. Council of the European Union", para. 101.

bananas, not Lomé undertakings,[158] and so could not be seen as required to preserve traditional ACP banana access and advantages.

- Article III:4 of GATT

4.290 Guatemala and Honduras submitted that tariff quota bananas had to be sold through arbitrarily defined classes of operators, including those, such as ripeners, that fell squarely within the EC internal distribution chain, all in specifically prescribed amounts. Even then, tariff quota bananas might not be distributed promptly through such entities, but had to await several rounds of applications, which served at various points throughout the year to delay access for tariff quota bananas. The burden and complexity of these requirements, and the frequency with which they were changed, had served to distort the Complaining parties' prices, disrupt historical trade arrangements, interrupt trade flows, and surround the marketing of Latin American bananas with pervasive uncertainty, inflexibility and confusion. EC bananas, on the other hand, could be sold throughout the distribution chain entirely free of restriction. This enabled EC producers to sell to any purchaser on any schedule of their choosing, making the distribution and sale of EC bananas uncomplicated, flexible, transparent, predictable, uninterrupted, and otherwise commercially attractive. Given the choice between the EC sale and distribution arrangement and the tariff quota licensing arrangement, EC purchasers over time would inevitably opt to pursue the former because of its free-trade distribution advantages. By creating this gaping disparity in requirements affecting the sale and distribution of Latin American versus EC bananas, the EC had directly contravened, according to Guatemala and Honduras, the national treatment and fair trade regulation principles of Articles III:4 and X of GATT, and Article 1.3 of the Licensing Agreement.

4.291 According to Guatemala and Honduras, Article III:4 of GATT provided the essence of the national treatment principle in the GATT. This language had been interpreted consistently by previous panels as establishing the obligation to accord imported products "competitive opportunities" in the market place no less favourable than those accorded to domestic products.[159] Underscoring the importance of that obligation, panels had applied it broadly:

> not only [to] the laws and regulations which directly governed the conditions of sale or purchase but also [to] any laws or regulations which might adversely modify the conditions of competition between the domestic and imported products on the internal market.[160]

4.292 The obligation also broadly applied "whether imports from other contracting parties [are] substantial, small or non-existent."[161] Within that expansive context, the concept of less favourable "competitive opportunities" had been ruled to include regulations that created layers of domestic agents through which foreign,

---

[158] See recitals two and three.

[159] "United States - Taxes on Petroleum and Certain Imported Substances", BISD 34S/136, para. 5.1.9 (adopted 17 June 1987); "United States - Section 337 of the Tariff Act of 1930", BISD 36S/345, paras. *5.11-5.13* (adopted 7 November 1989); "United States - Measures Affecting Alcoholic and Malt Beverages", BISD 39S/206, para. *5.31* (adopted 19 June 1992); "EEC - Import Regime for Bananas", DS38/R, para. 146 (issued 11 February 1994).

[160] "Italian Discrimination Against Imported Agricultural Machinery", BISD 7S/60, para. 12 (adopted 23 October 1958).

[161] "Report of the Working Party on Brazilian Internal Taxes", BISD Vol. II/185, para. 16 (adopted 30 June 1949) as confirmed by "United States - Taxes on Petroleum and Certain Imported Substances", BISD 34S/136, para. 5.1.9 (adopted 17 June 1987); "EEC - Import Regime for Bananas", DS38/R, para. 146 (issued 11 February 1994).

but not domestic, products had to be sold.[162] The second *Banana* panel added that such opportunities might also arise from regulations that caused discriminatory price-distortions, irrespective of export effect.[163]

4.293 All such prior interpretation compelled, in the view of Guatemala and Honduras, a similar finding of Article III:4 inconsistency in the present action, where distortionary tariff quota licensing had unquestionably skewed conditions of competition in favour of EC bananas. EC producers could sell to any operator of their choosing, including directly to retailers, enabling them to bypass the middlemen altogether should they so desire. The Complaining parties' producers had been denied this option. They were forced to sell through micro-defined operators, such as ripeners, who fell within the internal EC marketing chain. The panels were clear in both the *Foreign Investment Review Act* and *United States Measures Affecting Alcohol* cases that distribution differentiation of this sort - requiring foreign interests to sell to designated middlemen, while exempting domestic interests from such requirement - was squarely contrary to Article III:4 of GATT. The price distortions being forced upon the Complaining parties' fruit by these differentiated arrangements were likewise recognized in the second *Banana* panel to be the type of competitive discrimination that fell within the Article III:4 proscription. Additionally, the tariff quota licensing requirements so overwhelmed EC operators that they were inevitably influenced to favour EC banana purchases. All such disadvantages accorded "less favourable" treatment in violation of Article III:4.

4.294 The EC argued that no sensible reason could be advanced for comparing the licensing system needed for administering a legitimate tariff quota to a sale and distribution system of an internal product: the latter did not cross any border and therefore did not need to be submitted to any licensing system. This was the reason why EC products were neither part of the tariff quota nor included in the EC banana schedule. This simple and undisputable reality had an important legal implication when applying the GATT: the internal sale and distribution system pertained to the internal rules applicable to that market and was relevant to the imported goods only if and when those goods had cleared customs. As the 1958 panel report on *Italian Discrimination against Imported Agricultural Machinery* indicated, the purpose of Article III of GATT was "clearly to treat the imported products in the same way as the like domestic products once they have cleared through customs. Otherwise indirect protection should be given". By contrast, provisions like Articles XI and XIII of GATT and the Licensing Agreement (which was destined to detail the rules concerning those Articles of GATT) applied clearly only to border measures at the moment of the importation or the exportation of a product and did not concern any alleged discrimination in the application of internal measures after the product had cleared customs. Consequently, in GATT terms it was impossible, according to the EC, to allege that a specific measure violated at the same time Article III:4 and Article XIII of GATT and/or the Licensing Agreement. The Complaining parties were therefore obliged to choose which legal avenue they were interested in pursuing, but the Panel should reject any mixing of the two legal issues.

- Article X of GATT

4.295 Guatemala and Honduras submitted that paragraphs 1 and 3 of Article X of GATT required all Members to administer:

> [l]aws [and] regulations ... pertaining to ... requirements, restrictions or prohibitions on imports ... or affecting their sale, distribution, transportation ... warehousing, [or] inspection ... in a uniform, impartial and reasonable manner....

[162] "United States - Measures Affecting Alcoholic and Malt Beverages", BISD 39S/206, para. *5.30* (adopted 19 June 1992); "Canada - Administration of the Foreign Investment Review Act", BISD 30S/140, para. 5.9 (adopted 7 February 1984).

[163] Second *Banana* panel DS38/R, para. 146 (issued 11 February 1994). Although the panel was asked to rule on whether the two distinctly different arrangements affecting the sale and distribution of tariff quotas and EC bananas constituted an Article III:4 violation, it declined to do so, focusing instead on the more narrow issue of whether operator categories violated Article III:4.

A 1968 Note by the Director-General interpreted this requirement as follows:

> [t]hese last words ["a uniform, impartial and reasonable manner"] would not permit ... the application of one set of regulations and procedures with respect to some contracting parties and a different set with respect to the others.[164]

Again, GATT rulings were clear that where such differential regulations by source could be shown, the burden shifted to the Member applying such regulations to prove that in spite of the differential treatment, the implicated GATT obligation was nevertheless satisfied.[165] Because the traditional ACP licensing scheme afforded more marketing stability, predictability, flexibility, uninterrupted product-flow, and price-neutrality than that accorded by the tariff quota licensing scheme, the EC could not prove, according to Guatemala and Honduras, that the "uniform, impartial and reasonable" standard of Article X had been met. Thus, Guatemala and Honduras submitted that the differentiation between Latin American and ACP bananas violated Article X:1 and X:3. Likewise, the differentiation between the tariff quota and EC banana distribution violated Article X. Where distinctly different distribution requirements could be shown, the burden of proof shifted to the Member responsible for that differentiation to demonstrate that the GATT obligation at issue had still been met.[166] Here, the EC would fail in that burden, as it could not in any respect show that the relative disadvantages in distribution, flexibility, predictability, trade flow, and price effect being forced upon the Complaining parties constituted "uniform, impartial and reasonable" treatment.

4.296 According to the United States, Article X:3 of GATT imposed a very basic obligation on Members that they administer regulations pertaining to requirements on imports in a "uniform, impartial and reasonable manner." The application of a burdensome set of import requirements to one group of countries and a simple system for others could not be considered "uniform" or "impartial" under any definition of such terms. The EC, while defending some member State's measures in a 1989 panel dispute, interpreted the uniformity and impartiality obligations in Article X:3 as meaning "in substance" that "the administration of trade measures .. should not be discriminatory among contracting parties."[167] A 1968 Note by the GATT Director-General had earlier recognized that "[t]hese [words] would not permit ... the application of one set of regulations and procedures with respect to some contracting parties and a different set with respect to others."[168] If Article X:3 had any meaning at all, it prohibited the EC's establishment of one set of rules for importing third-country bananas, and another more favourable set of import rules for importing traditional ACP bananas. As noted above, in the words of the EC, it was "discriminatory among contracting parties", and therefore violated this basic obligation.

4.297 Mexico argued that the fact that the EC imposed burdensome import requirements on a certain group of countries and another, simple, requirement for another group of countries could not be considered as "uniform" and "impartial" under any circumstance. The import requirements of the EC regime were discriminatory as among Members, because it applied rules for the importation of bananas from non-ACP which were different from the rules applied for the same purposes to imports of traditional ACP bananas. These requirements included the application for obtaining import licences. For non-ACP countries this procedure was both complicated and burdensome, whereas for traditional ACP imports the procedure was very simple. This constituted, in the opinion of Mexico, a violation of Article X:3(a) of GATT.

---

[164] L/3149 (29 November 1968). See also "EEC - Restrictions on Imports of Dessert Apples - Complaint by Chile", BISD 36S/93, para. 6.5 (adopted 22 June 1989) (wherein this passage was referenced).

[165] See "United States - Section 337 of the Tariff Act of 1930", BISD 36S/345, para. *5.11* (adopted 7 November 1989).

[166] Idem.

[167] Dessert Apples, p.117.

[168] L/3149, dated 29 November 1968.

4.298 The Complaining parties considered that Article X:3 of GATT required Members to administer trade rules in a "uniform, impartial and reasonable manner". With respect to the *prima facie* case required, the Complaining parties submitted that Article X:3 of GATT, like Article 1.3 of the Licensing Agreement, required at a minimum that the same rules and procedures apply to a product originating in one country and the like product originating in another, as had previously been expressed by the Director-General.[169] The EC's licensing arrangements, which differentiated on the basis of country of origin, violated that obligation. The Complaining parties did not argue that there was a lack of uniformity in the EC's treatment of bananas throughout the different member States that resulted in a violation of Article X. Rather, the Complaining parties considered that the lack of uniformity, impartiality and reasonableness between Members on the basis of the product's country of origin was a violation of Article X. The view of Article X requirements expressed by the Director-General in the quoted Note was that Article X:3 did not permit the application of one set of regulations and procedures with respect to products originating in some contracting parties and a different set with respect to products originating in others. The EC itself had argued in *Dessert Apples* that Article X:3(a) was intended to establish that "the administration of trade measures by the various administrations should not be discriminatory among contracting parties."[170] The Complaining parties were of the view that the application of Article X:3, as correctly explained in *Dessert Apples* by the EC, was obviously not satisfied by licensing measures such as these that explicitly and significantly discriminated among Members. Furthermore, the differences in the administration of the EC banana regime by country of origin did not constitute the kind of "minor administrative variations" that the panel found to be "minimal" (and therefore not inconsistent with Article X:3) in the *Dessert Apples* dispute.[171]

4.299 The EC replied that the position of the Complaining parties was based on numerous flawed legal arguments and should therefore be rejected. Among them were: (i) the quoted sentence of the 1968 Note of the Director-General of the GATT was not an authoritative interpretation of the GATT. The CONTRACTING PARTIES had never endorsed the statement save for an indecisive reference in an adopted panel report that could not, in the opinion of the EC, be considered as attributing a value of interpretation to the note. Moreover, there was no indication that such a generic reference, out of its context, corresponded here to anything useful for the solution of the present case; and (ii) Article X provided only for the procedural rules to be followed in the application of internal rules pertaining to custom's activities, including requirements, restrictions or prohibitions of imports. In the panel report *Republic of Korea - Restrictions on Imports of Beef* [172] the panel incidentally indicated that under Article X:

> laws, regulations, judicial decisions and administrative rulings of general application, made effective by any contracting party, pertaining to... rates of duty, taxes or other charges or to requirements, restrictions or prohibition of imports...shall be published promptly ...

while under Article XIII:3(b):

> in the case of import restrictions involving the fixing of quotas, the contracting party applying the restrictions shall give public notice of the total quantity or value of the products which will be permitted to be imported during a specific future period....

4.300 The EC considered that Article XIII and Article X of GATT did not and could not overlap, since the former was related to the administration of border measures involving a quota or a tariff quota while the latter concerned only the procedural rules to be followed in the application of internal rules pertaining to custom's activities, including requirements, restrictions or prohibitions of imports. The EC argued that practically all

[169] Note by the Director-General, L/3149 (29 November 1968).

[170] Dessert Apples, para. 6.5.

[171] Idem, para. 12.30.

[172] BISD 36S/268, adopted 7 November 1989.

measures concerning licensing rules and procedures in the administration of the EC banana tariff quota which concerned operators importing bananas into the EC market were border measures and not internal rules applicable irrespectively to all bananas after having been introduced in the EC market. It was not possible, therefore, to complain against alleged violations of Article X with respect to the same requirements, laws, regulations etc. for the same reason as a violation of Article XIII was contested. Moreover, Article X had not (and could not have) the effect of reintroducing an MFN obligation with respect to the separate regime applied to imports of traditional ACP bananas which was already waived by the CONTRACTING PARTIES, nor extend the scope of Article XIII beyond the limits the GATT had fixed for it. With respect to alleged discriminations between the tariff quota regime and the distribution of EC bananas, the EC recalled its arguments set out under claims concerning Article III:4 above.

4.301 The Complaining parties responded that the laws and practices covered by Article X comprised all "trade regulations", which included, among many others, licensing regulations. Hence, there was an overlap between the Article X requirement that licensing rules and procedures be "uniform, impartial and reasonable", and the requirement in Article 1.3 of the Licensing Agreement that those same rules and procedures be "neutral", "fair", and "equitable". The EC's argument that Article X related solely to "internal rules" and hence was incompatible with a claim based on Article XIII was, according to the Complaining parties, not supported by the plain language of Article X or panel interpretations of its meaning. The scope of Article X was obvious from its first paragraph and its title: the Article X:3 obligation was applicable to all "trade regulations". The *Dessert Apples* report also clarified that Article XIII and Article X could apply to the same measure.[173]

4.302 The Complaining parties added that the EC was mistaken in relying on *Republic of Korea - Restrictions on Imports of Beef* to support its claim that Articles X and XIII were incompatible. Although that panel did not consider it necessary to make formal findings under Articles X and XIII, its discussion of those provisions still supported the *Dessert Apples* conclusion that Articles X and XIII were compatible and cumulative obligations.

- Article XI of GATT

4.303 The Complaining parties, in their second submission, also noted that Article XI of GATT applied to import licensing:

> No prohibitions or restrictions other than duties, taxes or other charges, whether made effective through quotas, import or export licences or other measures, shall be instituted or maintained by any contracting party on the importation of any product of the territory of any other party ....[174]

Panels had confirmed that the term "restrictions" should be given the broadest possible reading to ensure coverage not only of quotas *stricto sensu*, but also of licensing and other restrictive measures that limit trade through means other than a simple duty at the border.[175]

4.304 The Complaining parties noted that preliminary 1995 EC-15 Eurostat data showed imports of only 2,471,700 tonnes from tariff quota origins, a volume approximately 9 per cent below the total volume amounting

[173] Dessert Apples, para. 12.29.

[174] GATT Article XI:1.

[175] See "EEC - Programme of Minimum Import Prices, Licences and Surety Deposits for Certain Processed Fruits and Vegetables", adopted 18 October 1978, BISD 25S/68, para. 4.9 (a minimum import price considered a restriction within the meaning of Article XI:1); "Japan - Trade in Semi-conductors", adopted 4 May 1988, BISD 35S/116, paras. 105 and 118 (a minimum import price and non-automatic licence system considered restrictions under Article XI:1); and "Canada - Import, Distribution and Sale of Alcoholic Drinks by Canadian Provincial Marketing Agencies", adopted 22 March 1988, BISD 35S/37, paras. *4.24-4.25* (Article XI:1 considered to include measures that restricted the number of marketing outlets for imported products).

to 2,708,765 tonnes authorized that year for tariff quota suppliers.[176] In a market that was otherwise characterized by robust growth before the institution of Regulation 404/93, the only possible conclusion from the data was that the tariff quota licensing arrangement had effected a restriction on the importation of bananas from tariff quota origins in violation of Article XI.

4.305 With respect to 1995 data, the EC indicated that no final data were available for 1995 from Eurostat, and that the only reliable figures concerning banana imports into the EC-15 for 1995 came from the tariff quota licence usage figures quoted by the Commission. These figures showed that a total of 2,653,441 tonnes of bananas were imported under the tariff quota in 1995, a volume 21 per cent above the EC's bound tariff quota of 2,200,000 tonnes, and representing 98 per cent utilization of the autonomously increased tariff quota. The EC also noted that even when validated final Eurostat figures for 1995 became available, it would still not be possible to determine the utilization of the tariff quota from this data source because there was no distinction between traditional and non-traditional ACP imports or between tariff quota and non-tariff quota imports. Moreover, in response to other claims the EC submitted in response to a question by the Panel that the tariff quota on bananas was not a restrictive measure: there were no restrictions imposed on imports and Members could import as many bananas as they wished into the EC market (see also paragraph *4.190*).

- Article XIII:1 of GATT

4.306 Guatemala and Honduras submitted that the Article XIII:1 obligation was unambiguous in prohibiting differentiated import restrictions by source. The title of Article XIII of GATT, *Non-discriminatory Administration of Quantitative Restrictions*, the stipulation in Article XIII:5 that tariff quotas were covered by this language, and the express reference in Article XIII:3(a) to import licensing "administration", individually and collectively made clear that the differences in licensing procedures for the tariff quota and ACP quotas herein at issue were fully covered by Article XIII:1. That such licensing procedures were covered under this provision was reinforced by the Licensing Agreement's recognition that "the flow of international trade could be impeded by the inappropriate use of import licensing procedures."[177] Thus, unless differential import licensing rules were included within the "restriction ... on the importation of product" language of Article XIII:1, an Article XIII loophole would exist through which trade-restrictive discrimination could be practised with impunity. Previous panels had confirmed that Article XIII:1 was breached by an import licensing administration that varied by supplying country. In *Dessert Apples*, the panel had ruled that applying one import licensing practice to Chilean apples and another to apple imports from all other sources constituted an Article XIII:1 illegality on the basis that like products of all third countries had not been similarly restricted.[178] Similarly, in *EEC - Quantitative Restrictions Against Imports of Certain Products from Hong Kong*, the panel made clear that import licensing measures that were differentiated by region implicated the prohibition of Article XIII.[179]

4.307 Guatemala and Honduras noted that the second *Banana* panel did not address the issue of whether the differences in import licensing rules as between traditional ACP and Latin American sources constituted an Article XIII:1 breach.[180] Nevertheless, the *dicta* of the second *Banana* panel fully supported a finding of illegality in the present action. The second *Banana* panel reasoned that discrimination in "the distribution of licences among supplying countries" would constitute an Article XIII restriction. Such discrimination among supplying countries was readily evident from the present facts. Regulation 404/93 licences were distributed for traditional ACP bananas routinely and promptly, with no restrictive limitations or impact. Regulation 404/93 licences were distributed for Latin American bananas non-automatically, with deeply restrictive limitations and impact. Latin

---

[176] This figure includes 2.2 million tonnes plus 353,000 tonnes EFTA-3 transitional volume, and 155,765 tonnes hurricane volume.

[177] Agreement on Import Licensing Procedures, recital eight.

[178] Dessert Apples, BISD 36S/93, paras. 12.20-12.21 (adopted 22 June 1989).

[179] BISD 30S/129, paras. 31-33 (adopted 12 July 1983).

[180] DS38/R, para. 66 (issued 11 February 1994).

American bananas could pass only through designated entities under cumbersome requirements that distorted price, complicated commercial transactions, and created instability and confusion in the marketplace. So restrictive was this licensing scheme that for the first three weeks of every quarter, the Commission delayed the issuance of licences for Latin American sourced bananas. A licensing scheme characterized by this level of restriction and disturbance, when contrasted with the simple licensing for traditional ACP fruit, inevitably depressed marketplace interest in bananas from Latin America. According to Guatemala and Honduras, Article XIII:1 expressly condemned substantive and procedural discrimination of this sort.

4.308 The EC replied that it was a mistake to consider that a tariff quota was an "import restriction" while the unadopted second *Banana* panel report excluded this argument and no evidence of a different reality had been shown. With respect to the comparison between the EC tariff quota licensing system and the ACP traditional quota licensing system the Complaining parties did not explain how this comparison could be relevant. It was evident that the fact that two separate and independent regimes, the ACP traditional and the EC tariff quota, had marginal differences in their respective licensing systems (as shown by the second table, above) was neither in itself a violation of any GATT provision, nor was there evidence of any violation of GATT provisions by any of the two systems. In the opinion of the EC, the two systems did not create any substantial differences in their external effects on the imported bananas from different origins; the only discrepancies remaining were on the side of the internal procedures to be followed by the competent authorities.

4.309 The EC reiterated that, as stated elsewhere, with regard also to the situation of companies, no one was losing traditional past access, being forced to buy back rights, or to rebuild their distribution structure. With regard to the activity function allocation, for instance, it was licence entitlement and not import entitlement which was being distributed. The consequence of this distinction was very important indeed: activity function allocation had not affected the volumes shipped by traditional importers, who continued to ship bananas for release into free circulation either by themselves, or by others, as they did previously.

4.310 In the view of the EC, the conclusion that Article XIII could not be applied simultaneously to the two different and separate parts of the EC banana regime, was confirmed by the interpretation of the scope of Articles I and XIII of GATT. While both Articles contained a general principle of non-discrimination with regards to the importation or the exportation of like products originating in all third countries, the evidence did not imply that the two provisions overlapped. Article XIII was concerned only with the administration of each of the parts of the regime, and, in particular, all the border measures related to the importation or exportation of the products subject to a specific quota. In the view of the EC, this implied that, in GATT terms, comparing, under the authority of Article XIII, the internal licensing requirements within the ACP traditional allocation to the requirements of the tariff quota bound in the EC Schedule was legally wrong.

4.311 Further, the EC was of the opinion that, if for the sake of argument, the impact on trade of the residual (and limited) differences between the two regimes were to be considered meaningful, no violation of Article XIII:1 could be claimed in this respect because this Article concerned the application of the principle of non-discrimination in the administration of a particular quota and was therefore not useful in determining any comparison between licensing systems applied under different licensing regimes and which responded to realities which were partially different. In this respect, the panel report on Chilean *Dessert Apples* was, in the view of the EC, not relevant to the present case. In that procedure, the panel was asked to consider, *inter alia,* whether the prohibition of imports of Chilean apples, issued by the EC seven days before the publication of import quotas, while like products of all third countries had not been similarly prohibited, was compatible with Article XIII:1 of GATT. The panel was then confronted with one single licensing system within which a different treatment was put in place distinguishing by the origin the same like product. The EC argued that it was quite clear that, contrary to the above-mentioned panel report, what the Panel had to find out in the present case was if the banana EC tariff quota licensing system responded to the rules concerning its administration set out in Article XIII. That should not be affected by the rules applicable in a separate regime, justified under separate and specific rules and conditions.

4.312 According to the Complaining parties, Article XIII:1 prohibited the application of a restriction to products of one Member that was not also applied to products of other countries. Although the EC insisted that the regime for administering the tariff quota was entirely separate, Regulation 404/93 only created one regime, not two. Regardless of how many regimes might be at issue, however, Article XIII still required that imports from all sources be similarly restricted. (In addition, as specifically discussed below a similar restriction was not in place as between BFA and non-BFA signatories, since BFA signatories could use export licences and non-BFA signatories could not.) The EC's reliance on the findings of the second *Banana* panel to deny the presence of licensing discrimination by country of origin misread, according to the Complaining parties, the findings of that report. That panel did not address the issue of whether the differences in import licensing rules as between traditional ACP and Latin American countries constituted an Article XIII violation. It only examined the licensing rules as they related to Latin American bananas (before the introduction of the BFA). To the extent the panel rejected an Article XIII claim, it did so on the basis that the distribution of licences was an "internal measure", a proposition with which the EC disagreed. The second *Banana* panel recognized that discrimination in "the distribution of licences among supplying countries" would constitute an Article XIII restriction.[181]

4.313 The Complaining parties further responded that the EC attempt to distinguish the *Dessert Apples* report on the basis that the report was only "confronted with one licensing system", as opposed to the two arrangements at issue here[182] was not appropriate. It was irrelevant under Article XIII how many structural arrangements may be present; the issue was only whether products of all origins were being similarly restricted. The panel in that case found that because "like products of all third countries had not been similarly prohibited" in the administration of import licences, the EC had acted inconsistently with its Article XIII obligations.[183]

4.314 The Complaining parties did not consider the concept of *lex specialis* to be relevant in this instance regarding the relation between the Licensing Agreement and Article XIII of GATT. Two separate agreements were involved, each of which were given equal force under the Marrakesh Protocol unless there was conflict between their provisions. Since there was no conflict between the provisions at issue, it was entirely permissible to assert a breach of Article XIII obligations in tandem with the Licensing Agreement violations discussed above. The Complaining parties argued that one of the primary purposes of the Licensing Agreement, "to ensure that import licensing procedures are not utilized in a manner contrary to the principles and obligations of GATT 1994,"[184] made clear that the Licensing Agreement was not intended to supplant, but rather to extend, clarify and complement existing GATT principles.

4.315 The EC rebutted that the Complaining parties seemed to confuse the allocation of a tariff quota with its administration. The former concerned the distribution of shares of the EC tariff quota to supplying countries, which is reflected in the EC Schedule, while the latter was concerned with the management of the importation of bananas under the terms and the conditions of that particular tariff quota.

(g) Claims under the Licensing Agreement

- Article 1.2 of the Licensing Agreement

4.316 Referring to the text of Article 1.2, Ecuador considered that the application procedures for obtaining licences to import third-country bananas were not in conformity with the GATT. Moreover, these procedures were also not implemented "with a view to preventing trade distortions". Consequently, the EC licensing procedures were not consistent with Article 1.2 of the Licensing Agreement. The EC licensing procedures were not consistent with the GATT since the principles in Articles I:1 and X were violated because the "rules and formalities", i.e. the

[181] Second *Banana* panel, paras. 141-142.

[182] First EC Submission at 59.

[183] Dessert Apples, para. 12.21.

[184] Recital seven.

licence application procedures, relevant to traditional ACP bananas were far less costly and burdensome than those applicable to third-country bananas.

4.317 The same aspects of the import licensing regime, Ecuador continued, which violated Articles I:1 and X of GATT also caused significant trade distortions. The complex import licence application regime applicable to third-country bananas imposed significant administrative costs on importers of third-country bananas, and thus created an important barrier to trade in such bananas. Furthermore, the excessive and unjustifiable delays in issuing the import licences for third-country bananas distorted trade by hindering access of third-country bananas to the EC market. The quarterly two-round application procedure generally spanned at least six weeks and was usually not concluded until at least three weeks into the quarter for which licences were to be issued. Imports of traditional ACP bananas were not burdened with such delays. The preferential treatment accorded to imports of traditional ACP bananas created a relatively cheap and easy means of access to the EC market, thereby creating an incentive to market such bananas rather than third-country bananas. The discriminatory licensing procedures applicable to imports of third-country bananas were, according to Ecuador, therefore, inconsistent with Article 1.2 of the Licensing Agreement.

4.318 Mexico also considered that since the EC regime violated Articles I:1, III:4, and X of GATT, it could not be in conformity with Article 1.2 of the Licensing Agreement, and all the more so when the regime not only did not prevent import distortions but reinforced them. Furthermore, the licensing procedures applied to traditional imports from ACP countries were less burdensome than those applied to non-ACP countries, including Latin American countries.

4.319 With respect to the claims of Ecuador and Mexico under Article 1.2 and in response to the EC's claims, the Complaining parties were of the view that this Article was not a generic reminder but a firm obligation, nor did it require proof of trade distortion. If the Panel examined the operation of the licensing procedures in light of the plain language and meaning of Article 1.2 it would find a clear violation.

4.320 With respect to the alleged violations of Article 1.2 of the Licensing Agreement, the EC stated that as no breach of the GATT provision cited could be proved the claims should be rejected.

- Article 1.3 of the Licensing Agreement

4.321 Referring to the Article 1.3 standard that "the rules for import licensing procedures ... be neutral in application and administered in a fair and equitable manner," the Complaining parties argued that the language in that Article was quite similar to the requirements in Article X:3 of GATT that regulations be "uniform, impartial and reasonable". Accordingly, past interpretations of Article X offered probative interpretive guidance for Article 1.3 of the Licensing Agreement. In the *Dessert Apples* case, the EC had agreed with the Director-General's Note concluding that the requirements of "uniformity" and "impartiality" were not satisfied by the application of one set of regulations and procedures with respect to products from one set of contracting parties and a different set with respect to the products of other contracting parties.[185] If such regulations and procedures were not uniform, impartial or reasonable, they should equally be said to lack "neutrality", "fairness", and "equity". Moreover, consistent with this view, once the licensing rules of any Member explicitly differentiated on the basis of country of origin alone, the burden shifted to that Member to prove that its differentiated rules and procedures reflected "neutrality", "fairness", and "equity." The differences in procedures for ACP and Latin American bananas presented, in the opinion of the Complaining parties, a *prima facie* case of an Article 1.3 violation. No justification could overcome the obvious substantial differences in the two procedures.

4.322 The United States argued that the EC banana regime explicitly imposed one set of import licensing rules on traditional ACP bananas, and another set of rules on third countries bananas. The EC Commission had

[185] Note of the Director-General, L/3149 (29 November 1968).

recognized that the treatment of ACP bananas was more favourable. Any definition of "neutral application" of licensing rules would have to preclude the application of different and less favourable rules to bananas from certain Members on account of their origin. Accordingly, in its totality the EC regime epitomized a violation of Article 1.3 of the Licensing Agreement.

4.323 Ecuador argued that the Licensing Agreement placed clear restrictions on how Members could administer import licensing regimes. Referring to Article 1 of the Licensing Agreement, Ecuador considered that the Licensing Agreement generally covered administrative procedures regarding the application for, and allocation of, licences to import bananas into the EC. Because the current Licensing Agreement was adopted as part of the Uruguay Round Agreements, no prior GATT panel had yet interpreted the requirements set out in Article 1.3. However, although the Licensing Agreement went well beyond the requirements of Article X of GATT, Ecuador was of the view that authoritative interpretations of Article X were helpful to shed light on the scope and intent of the principles set out in the Licensing Agreement. With regard to Article X, and referring to the Note of the Director-General of GATT,[186] Ecuador considered that Article 1.3 of the Licensing Agreement should be interpreted in a similar manner and should not permit Members to apply different sets of licence application procedures depending on the source of the product the applicant wished to import. This principle was particularly important when the different procedures imposed vastly different administrative burdens. As already mentioned, the application procedure for obtaining licences to import traditional ACP bananas was straightforward. In contrast, the application procedures for obtaining licences to import third-country bananas were extraordinarily complex and burdensome. Such disparate treatment was, in the opinion of Ecuador, not neutral, fair or equitable, and therefore was not consistent with Article 1.3 of the Licensing Agreement.

4.324 Guatemala and Honduras, referring to the text of Article 1.3, submitted that the EC bore the burden of proving that licensing rules that explicitly differentiated by source satisfied the "neutral", "fair and equitable" standard in application and administration.[187] The import instability, uncertainty, inflexibility, product interruption, and price distortion imposed by the tariff quota licensing scheme relative to the simple traditional ACP scheme made it impossible for the EC, in the opinion of Guatemala and Honduras, to satisfy that burden. A breach of Article 1.3 of the Licensing Agreement was accordingly present. Furthermore, as with the differentiated arrangement between tariff quota and traditional ACP - sourced bananas, the differentiated arrangement as between EC and tariff quota bananas also failed under Article 1.3 of the Licensing Agreement instruction that "[t]he rules for import licensing procedures ... be neutral in application and administered in a fair and equitable manner." The instability, uncertainty, inflexibility, product-flow interruption, and price distortion imposed by the tariff quota licensing scheme relative to the entirely unrestricted EC distribution arrangement made it impossible for the EC to demonstrate "neutrality", "fairness and equity" in these two arrangements. Guatemala and Honduras were of the view that the imposition of differential arrangements as between EC and Latin American bananas contravened, *inter alia*, Article 1.3 of the Licensing Agreement – the tariff quota licensing arrangement had to be considered illegal in its entirety to be replaced with an arrangement commercially and procedurally equivalent to the restriction-free arrangement being accorded to EC bananas.

4.325 Mexico argued that the EC regime explicitly prescribed the application of two different systems for granting licences within the tariff quota, depending on the origin of products, and the result was a very heavy and burdensome licensing system for imports originating in non-ACP countries, including Latin American countries, whereas this licensing system was not applied to countries, parties to the Lomé Convention, to which a simple system was applied. In the view of Mexico, it was clear that the absence of "neutrality", "fairness and equity" in the application of the licensing system resulted in a violation of Article 1.3 of the Licensing Agreement.

---

[186] L/3149. Also reference to this passage in Dessert Apples, BISD 36S/93 at 117, para. 6.5 (adopted 22 June 1989).

[187] See Note by the Director-General, L/3149 (29 November 1968); "United States - Section 337 of the Tariff Act of 1930", BISD 36S/345, para. *5.11* (adopted 7 November 1989).

4.326 The EC maintained, with respect to the claims under Article 1.3 of the Licensing Agreement, that the licensing system to administer the tariff quota was stable, certain, flexible, predictable and created no distortion on prices in the EC market which could be detrimental to bananas produced in the complaining countries. The structure of the tariff quota licensing system did not correspond under any possible circumstances to a distribution of licences to EC companies as opposed to foreign companies. "Neutrality", "fairness and equity" were in-built qualities of the EC tariff quota licensing system which was based on the application of objective criteria of eligibility to obtain tariff quota licences on the basis of past trade in bananas: trade volumes and not companies were the commanding principle of the system.

4.327 In reply to a question by the Panel, the EC noted that any direct comparison between the requirements of "uniformity, impartiality and reasonableness" in Article X:3(a) of GATT and those of "neutrality in application" and "fair and equitable administration" in Article 1.3 of the Licensing Agreement seemed inappropriate. The Licensing Agreement was concerned with import licensing procedures used for the operation of import regimes which required a specific documentation (other than that required for customs purposes) prior to the importation in the customs territory of the relevant product. On the other hand, Article X applied to "laws, regulations, judicial decisions and administrative rulings of general application, made effective by any contracting party, pertaining to the classification, or the valuation of products for customs purposes, or to rates of duty, taxes or other charges or to requirements, restrictions or prohibition of imports ..." or affecting "sale, distribution, transportation, insurance, warehousing inspection, exhibition, processing, mixing or other use ...." Even if Article X language, as compared to the Licensing Agreement was less precise, it appeared that it was more concerned with every operation related to customs (and in particular the activities of customs authorities) or the administrative activities after the product had cleared customs, and not so much with the procedures prior to customs clearance which concerned the possibility of importing the product as pre-requisite to any importation within the tariff quota (and customs operation).

4.328 Even though it compared Article XIII with Article X, the EC continued, the panel report *Republic of Korea - Restrictions on Imports of Beef*, adopted 7 November 1989, reasoned along these lines. The EC considered therefore that the Licensing Agreement, when applicable, and Article X did not overlap, since the former was related to the administration of import procedures while the latter concerned only the procedural rules to be followed in the application of provisions pertaining to customs activities or to internal rules applicable after a product had cleared customs. When applicable, Article 1.3 of the Licensing Agreement required neutrality in application: no discrimination of any kind should be admissible in the administration of a particular licensing scheme, notably with reference to the origin of the product. Moreover, "fair and equitable administration" was imposed: no unfair treatment of the operators concerned was admissible and possibility of complaint and remedy should be provided. Both were fully respected in the EC tariff quota licensing scheme and in its internal legal system in general.

4.329 Moreover, as far as the relation between the tariff quota and the internal EC bananas sale and distribution system was concerned, the EC recalled its view that no sensible reason could be advanced for comparing the licensing system needed for administering a legitimate tariff quota while importing bananas in the EC to a sale and distribution system of an internal product: the latter, evidently, did not cross any border and therefore was not to be submitted to any licensing system. At the same time, Article 1.3 of the Licensing Agreement was perfectly complied with.

4.330 The Complaining parties responded that the EC could not be considered to have satisfied its burden of showing that the licensing procedures were neutral in application and applied in a fair manner by merely asserting that the licensing system applicable to Latin American bananas "is stable, certain, flexible, predictable and creates no distortion on prices in the EC market which could be detrimental to bananas produced in the complaining countries."[188] This assertion did not even address the neutrality and equity requirements of Article 1.3. Nothing in the bananas themselves justified the inequity and discrimination in these procedures. Even the EC had admitted that "assistance" would flow to "non-traditional" ACP banana suppliers by moving them under the simpler traditional rules for ACP bananas.[189] The only justification provided by the EC with respect to the licences allocated to its own farmers (i.e. Category B operators performing the activity (a) function) was obviously protectionist and therefore lacking in neutrality and equity:

> Individual producers and producers' organizations which are not themselves necessarily "importers" of bananas have been allocated Category B licences. Since in general they have no interest in importing dollar bananas, these licences are sold, providing a supplement to their income in addition to the support provided by the provisions on aid to compensate for the loss of income.[190]

4.331 The EC was of the view that its licensing scheme did not violate Article 1:3 of the Licensing Agreement, where the emphasis of the Complaining parties was put on the alleged violation of the obligation of neutrality under that provision, while a correct and complete quote of the Article would disclose that: "The rules for import licensing procedures shall be neutral in application and administered in a fair and equitable way." The EC claimed that the CONTRACTING PARTIES had agreed on a text that explicitly required neutrality in the application and administration of the rules creating a particular licensing scheme. Nowhere in that Article had the CONTRACTING PARTIES committed themselves not to shape a particular import licensing procedure in the way the EC had done, where all operators of any country were freely competing within and among different categories set out in Article 19 of Regulation 404/93. Within that particular licensing scheme, neutrality was absolutely respected and no evidence had been shown to the contrary. Any operator could be eligible for any category of licence if the operator fulfilled the objective conditions therein. Furthermore, the EC was of the view that no evidence had been provided by the Complaining parties that the licensing scheme was administered in an unfair and inequitable manner. In the opinion of the EC, the Complaining parties should have demonstrated that the way the licensing scheme was administered was unfair and inequitable. The Complaining parties were on the contrary trying to demonstrate, through Article 1.3 of the Licensing Agreement, that the licensing scheme itself was unfair (which was in any case unfounded). In the opinion of the EC, this had nothing to do with the way the Licensing Agreement had been agreed upon and the common will of the CONTRACTING PARTIES that was expressed in that wording.

- <u>Articles 3.2 and 3.5(h) of the Licensing Agreement</u>

4.332 Ecuador claimed that the EC import licensing regime distorted trade and hindered the full utilization of the quota in violation of Article 3.2 of the Licensing Agreement. According to Ecuador, in the year immediately preceding the imposition of the tariff quota, imports of third-country bananas into the EC were 2,431,100 tonnes. However, the share allocated to third countries for 1993 and 1994 was set at only 1,000,000 tonnes for the second half of 1993[191] and 2,171,000 tonnes for 1994 (including the nominal 2.118 million tonnes allocated to third countries plus an additional 53,400 tonnes permitted to be imported under so-called "hurricane licences" issued to Category B operators). The allocation to third countries was thus set far below the third countries' historical

---

188 According to the Complaining parties, the EC's claim that the rules applicable to Latin American bananas contained "objective" criteria of eligibility, even if true, would provide no defence to the lack of neutrality. A measure could be based on measurable criteria for example, and still lack neutrality in application. Even if the licensing criteria were objective, the two licensing arrangements would still not be considered neutral, fair or equitable unless banana imports from all sources were subject to comparable rules, not just as to eligibility, but as to every aspect of the licensing system. The preferential licensing regime accorded to ACP imports definitively violated Article 1.3 of the Licensing Agreement.

189 "Report on the Operation of the Banana Regime", p.19.

190 "Report on the EC Banana Regime", European Commission, July 1994, pp.10-11.

191 See Regulation 1442/93, which opened the tariff quota for the second half of 1993.

import levels. Nevertheless, according to Eurostat statistics, imports of third-country bananas totalled only 967,161 tonnes during the second half of 1993.[192] During the full year of 1994, imports of third-country bananas totalled 2,043,100 tonnes, well below the third-country tariff quota volume. The fact that third-country imports failed to fill the tariff quota in those years, and that current import levels were significantly below historical import levels clearly demonstrated, in Ecuador's opinion, that the licensing regime had trade restrictive effects beyond those caused by the imposition of the tariff quota. The EC licensing regime thus directly violated Article 3.2 of the Licensing Agreement. According to Ecuador the fact that third-country imports failed to fill the third-country tariff quota also highlighted the inconsistency of the licensing regime with Article 3.5(h) of the Licensing Agreement which stated that Members "shall not discourage the full utilization of quotas".

4.333 Ecuador claimed further that the licensing procedures applicable to third-country banana imports were far more burdensome than absolutely necessary to administer the tariff quota. Twelve traditional ACP countries were given country specific allocations; yet the import licensing procedures applicable to traditional ACP bananas were far simpler than those for third-country bananas. For example, imports of traditional ACP bananas were not burdened with such requirements as matching import and export certificates. In fact, third-country bananas were the only product for which it was necessary to submit both export certificates and import licences in order to import into the EC. In the view of Ecuador, the EC could not claim that the complex licensing system for third-country banana imports was necessary to implement the tariff quota because the EC itself had devised regimes for administering quotas which were far less burdensome than that which it applied to administer the third-country tariff quota. For example, Council Regulation 520/94[193] set forth "General Administrative Principles" to govern quotas. Article 2 of this Regulation listed three specific methods under which quotas were to be administered: (i) a method based on traditional trade flows; (ii) a "first-come, first-served" method governing the order in which applications were submitted; and (iii) a method allocating quotas in proportion to the quantities requested when the applications were submitted. These alternative administrative procedures set out in Regulation 520/94 clearly demonstrated, according to Ecuador, that there were far less burdensome methods for administering a tariff quota than that which the EC used to administer the third-country tariff quota. The EC import licensing regime thus was not "absolutely necessary" to administer the tariff quota, and was consequently in direct violation of Article 3.2 of the Licensing Agreement.

4.334 Guatemala and Honduras submitted that Article 3.2 of the Licensing Agreement contained two instructions that were contravened by the tariff quota licensing scheme, that:

> [n]on-automatic licensing shall not have trade-restrictive or -distortive effects on imports additional to those caused by the imposition of the restriction ..." and "shall be no more administratively burdensome than absolutely necessary to administer the measure.

On a comparative or stand-alone basis, tariff quota licensing rules had trade-distortive effects on the Complainants' bananas well beyond those caused by the restrictive 2.2 million tonne first-tier quota. The Category B provisions that tied a licensing advantage to the purchase of bananas from certain sources on a rolling three-year basis meant sourcing distortions were both intended and inevitable. The assignment of tariff quota volume to arbitrarily defined middlemen too distorted the Complaining parties' prices and pre-Regulation 404/93 commercial relationships. The multi-round application procedures served to delay EC importation of the Complaining parties' bananas at various times of the year. The multitude of tariff quota licensing rules, and their frequency of change, created disincentives and confusion in the purchasing of tariff quota fruit. All such burdens and complexities of the tariff quota licensing scheme relative to the non-restrictive simplicity of the traditional ACP and EC arrangements skewed conditions of competition in favour of traditional ACP and EC bananas.

[192] According to Ecuador, imports of third-country bananas during the first half of 1993 were 1,186,862 tonnes.

[193] Council Regulation establishing an EC Procedure for Administering Quantitative Quotas.

4.335 Guatemala and Honduras argued further that in addition to being trade-restrictive and -distortive, the licensing scheme applicable to their bananas violated the Article 3.2 provision that non-automatic licensing "be no more administratively burdensome than absolutely necessary to administer the measure". That provision's use of the language "absolutely necessary" underscored, in the opinion of Guatemala and Honduras, the drafters' intention to tolerate only the most minimal administrative burdens. Indeed, the EC has instituted numerous tariff quotas at its border for a vast number of products, not a single one of which was administered by a licensing scheme that rivalled this level of administrative burden and confusion. Honduras and Guatemala suspected that few licensing schemes around the world matched this one for administrative burden. The burdens and adverse effects of this scheme had to be considered violative of the prohibitions against restriction, distortion, and unnecessary burden contained in Article 3.2 of the Licensing Agreement. In the opinion of Guatemala and Honduras, a conclusion ruling otherwise would render meaningless the new WTO licensing disciplines codified in Article 3.1 and give rise to a proliferation of comparable licensing schemes throughout the globe, undermining the reform, transparency, and predictability that Uruguay Round negotiators had intended to be accomplished by tariff quota conversions.

4.336 According to Mexico, EC banana imports originating in third countries, including Latin American countries, were subject to an import regime so complicated that the very existence of the regime, as well as the modalities of its administration, could not be considered as absolutely necessary. Mexico also considered that the complex system of licences applied by the EC discouraged the full utilization of tariff quotas allocated to non-ACP countries in violation of Article 3.5(h) of the Licensing Agreement.

4.337 The United States argued that the Licensing Agreement provided the most specific disciplines on import licensing among the various WTO agreements. In particular, as reflected in its preamble, it sought to place disciplines on non-automatic licensing, namely those licensing schemes where approval was not granted in all cases, such as the regime applicable to EC imports of bananas. Article 3.2 of the Licensing Agreement required, in the relevant part, that "[n]on-automatic licensing procedures ... shall be no more administratively burdensome than absolutely necessary to administer the measure". Article 3.5(h) further required that Members "shall not discourage the full utilization of quotas." The numerous layers of administrative complexity burdens applied to Latin American banana imports were not needed, in the opinion of the United States, to administer a quantitative limitation, let alone were they "absolutely necessary". In the first instance, the EC requirements for the Latin American tariff quota imports went beyond what was needed to administer imports of bananas subject to quantitative limitations, since a parallel import licensing system (for traditional ACP bananas) was a model of simplicity without any of the complex features applied to imports under the third-country tariff quota. ACP import licences were granted upon presentation of a certificate of origin, with a single reduction coefficient applied to all applicants if there was an over-subscription. The treatment afforded to traditional ACP bananas, the manner in which the current regime for third-country bananas developed, the manner in which member States administered quantitative limitations on bananas before Regulation 404/93, and international and EC general law and practice, all underscored why this regime did not need to be as burdensome as it was and why it violated Article 3.2. The complex scheme discouraged imports from Latin America, and was thus inconsistent with Article 3.5(h) as well.

4.338 The United States considered that the EC licensing regime for third-country bananas was also irregular under the EC's general legislation and practice. Council Regulation 520[194], establishing an EC procedure for administering "quantitative quotas," professed to set forth "General Administrative Principles" to govern quotas. Article 2 listed three specific methods under which quotas were to be administered, all of which, in contrast to the banana regime, appeared to resemble normal international practice: (i) a method based on traditional trade flows; (ii) a method based on the order in which applications were submitted (on a "first-come, first-served" basis); and (iii) a method allocating quotas in proportion to the quantities requested when the applications were submitted. Although Article 2 did not profess to set out an exhaustive list of methods that could be used, the specific examples highlighted that the means chosen by the EC to "administer" the tariff quota for third-country bananas was out of

[194] Regulation 520/94 establishing an EC Procedure for Administering Quantitative Quotas, 1994 O.J. (L 66) 1.

the ordinary. Although the EC maintained quantitative limitations on a variety of products, the banana import regime was unique in requiring both import and export certificate requirements on the same import. Indeed, the EC maintained several tariff quotas which were administered without either.[195] The banana regime was also the only regime distributing licences on the basis of "activity functions" and the resulting problems associated with competing claims and erosion of licensing entitlements. The combination of all these elements was hardly needed to administer the tariff quota.

4.339 The reason the EC did not abandon any one or more of these elements was not, in the opinion of the United States, because all were necessary to administer the tariff quota. Rather, the problem faced by the EC was that each element of its regime was conceived to effectuate EC policies unrelated to administrative concerns, among which were: keeping quota rents within the EC (use of import licences generally); providing business to EC-owned or controlled distribution companies (Category B criteria and activity functions); providing income in the form of quota rents to EC farmers (Category B criteria and distribution of hurricane licences); and attempting to prevent a WTO challenge to its entire regime (BFA export certificates). In the opinion of the United States, the Licensing Agreement did not permit Members to impose administrative requirements in an import licensing regime as a means of effectuating policies separate and apart from administrative concerns. In April 1996, the EC Commission issued a proposal for a Council Regulation to remove non-traditional ACP bananas from this licensing system and subject them to the simple system applicable to traditional ACP bananas.[196] The EC Commission had thus apparently recognized that the effect of the overall tariff quota licensing scheme was burdensome, discouraging purchases from third-country tariff quota sources, and that the scheme was not necessary for administrative purposes.

4.340 The United States argued that while import licensing systems were common in international practice, and while export certificates were employed occasionally in other instances, the Complaining parties in this dispute were unaware of any other instance anywhere in which they were required in combination. Indeed, the EC only added the export certificate requirement pursuant to the BFA (implemented in March 1995), almost two years after establishing the tariff quota. This additional layer could hardly be described as "necessary"; its object was to permit BFA signatories to enjoy quota rents so that they would cease challenging the EC's banana regime in the GATT or WTO. Before Regulation 404/93, several of the member States had permitted imports from Latin America on a limited basis. While import rights were often allocated exclusively to national companies, even these pre-1993 import regimes were frequently administered in a less cumbersome fashion than the current third-country tariff quota. For example, Italy used a first-come, first-served system. There was no administrative reason why a less onerous approach was not feasible EC-wide.

4.341 The EC replied that in order to demonstrate an alleged violation to Article 3.2 of the Licensing Agreement, the Complaining parties needed to prove, first, that the non-automatic licensing had "trade-restrictive or -distortive effects on imports additional to those caused by the imposition of the restriction." The Complaining parties should have demonstrated that bananas imported into the EC market were restricted by the administration of the tariff quota beyond the effects on trade of the very existence of the tariff quota, which was compatible with the GATT and part of the concessions accepted by all contracting parties was common practice in GATT agricultural negotiations. In the opinion of the EC, not a single evidence had been given of these supposed and totally unproved additional trade restrictive or distortive effects. Not a single evidence was shown, demonstrating any hindering in the access of the Complaining parties' bananas to the EC market whose parts of the tariff quota were immediately and completely used. The very existence of the tariff quota, however, was, in the opinion of the EC, a clear improvement in terms of market liberalization as compared to the situation prior to the conclusion of the Uruguay Round and created conditions for higher prices in the EC market as compared to world market prices and this was a benefit to the Complaining parties banana production.

---

[195] The United States mentioned mineolas and almonds as examples.

[196] Proposal for a Council Regulation amending Regulation 404/93 on the common organization of the market in bananas, 1996 O.J. (C 121) 9.

4.342 Secondly, the EC continued, the Complaining parties needed to demonstrate that the licensing system did not "correspond in scope and duration to the measure they are used to implement". No serious argument, in the opinion of the EC, had been brought contesting the EC's compliance with these obligations. The Complaining parties also needed to demonstrate that the licensing system administering the EC tariff quota was "more administratively burdensome then absolutely necessary to administer the measure". This third part of Article 3.2 of the Licensing Agreement could not, as already mentioned, be read in isolation but should be seen in the context of the whole paragraph (where reference was specifically made to "effects on imports") and to Article 1.1 of the Licensing Agreement (where the scope of the Agreement was limited to "regimes requiring the submission of an application or other documentation to the relevant body").

4.343 It was clear, the EC argued, that the Panel was not asked or given authority to decide in general and abstract terms what system, *in abstracto*, was absolutely necessary to administer a legitimate tariff quota (e.g. a banana tariff quota) but only if the burdens imposed on the operators of importing countries when making use of the tariff quota for the importation of their products were absolutely necessary to administer the measure. The administrative steps used in the case of the banana tariff quota were the following: (i) operators (firms) submitted evidence of their past trade in third countries, ACP and EC bananas. As a result of that data, annual rights to import were eventually given to each operator prior to the beginning of the calendar year; (ii) operators lodged a quarterly request to import, using part of their annual rights to import. As a result of that request, an import licence was delivered to each operator; and (iii) since the tariff quota was divided by country allocations, and in order to facilitate a full utilization of the different allocations and, hence, of the total tariff quota, whenever a specific country allocation was over-subscribed for a specific quarter, interested operators had the possibility of requesting to import from any other, non-fully subscribed origin in a second round of licence allocations (or withdraw their request without any charge). According to the EC, no other obligations or complexities existed. For operators with Category A or Category C licence rights willing to import from the BFA countries Colombia, Costa Rica and Nicaragua, a security had to be lodged, together with their quarterly request, in order to fulfil BFA obligations.

4.344 The EC believed that these administrative steps were not uncommon to any administration of existing tariff quotas in other sectors and they could not be considered as unnecessary for the correct functioning of the system since they responded to the specific needs of the tariff quota as bound in the EC Schedule. The EC concluded therefore that all requirements under Article 3.2 of the Licensing Agreement had been complied with and that the Complainant's allegations in this respect should be rejected. The EC further argued that claims concerning Article 3.5(h) of the Licensing Agreement should also be rejected. Indeed, this provision referred to administration of "quotas" and not to "tariff quotas" as was clearly indicated for instance in Article 3.5(a) where reference was made to "the administration of the restrictions". As had been underlined above (and equally stressed by the unadopted second *Banana* panel report), a tariff quota, as the EC banana tariff quota, was not a quantitative restriction and by its nature did not prevent importation or discourage use of import rights under the EC tariff quota or outside the EC tariff quota.

4.345 The Complaining parties reiterated that the whole tariff quota licensing scheme, *inter alia*, violated the various requirements of Article 3.2 of the Licensing Agreement. Contrary to the EC's suggestion, inconsistency with any one of the four requirements amounted to a violation. The tariff quota licensing rules had, first, "trade-distortive effects" and, second, "trade-restrictive effects" on Latin American bananas well beyond those caused by the tariff quota access limitations. Third, the rules did not "correspond in scope and duration to the measures they are used to implement". Fourth, they were more burdensome "than absolutely necessary" to administer the tariff quota.

4.346 The Complaining parties claimed that the use of the term "distortive effects" in Article 3.2 required under its ordinary meaning a demonstration that conditions of competition had been distorted or disrupted compared to what would otherwise have been the case absent those licences. The Complaining parties had shown that Regulation 404/93 and its implementing regulations subjected bananas from tariff quota sources to a complex licensing arrangement that dictated in detail the entities and extensive procedures through which tariff quota bananas could be entered and distributed. Latin American producers were not free to sell to purchasers of their choice, but had to sell to arbitrary classes of "operators" defined on the basis of the origin of their purchases and activities performed. Moreover, tariff quota bananas could not be distributed through such designated entities on a normal marketing cycle, but were forced every quarter through an uncommon two-round application procedure that required a matching of import licences to export licences and artificially segmented trade flows by country of origin and time. A substantial percentage of tariff quota quarterly licences was not distributed until two to three weeks into the quarter for which they applied. The rules governing all such procedures and entities were voluminous and changed constantly. This unnatural, heavily constrained distribution scheme for Latin American bananas had reconfigured historical distribution patterns, created an irregular marketing cycle, curtailed delivery flexibility and generated widespread uncertainty and confusion in the marketing of tariff quota bananas. By contrast, traditional ACP bananas could be entered simply and promptly through any firm. Unlike licences for Latin American bananas, the simple licensing approach that was applied to traditional ACP bananas permitted commercial flexibility and predictability.

4.347 The Complaining parties noted that Article 3.2 of the Licensing Agreement provided that "[n]on-automatic licensing shall not have trade-restrictive or distortive effects on imports additional to those caused by the imposition of the restrictions." The EC licensing regime amounted to a non-tariff barrier beyond the restriction caused by volume limitations. The regime's effects included the perpetual uncertainty regarding the volumes that would be available for import, and the sources from which those volumes could be obtained. Operators seeking to import under the tariff quota needed continuously to purchase licences, enter into marketing agreements with specific ripeners or invest in ripening facilities merely to avoid the licence erosion created by the administration of the regime, i.e. merely to maintain the same business as previously. In addition, throughout the year, they were uncertain as to their import volumes because of continuous auditing and the application of the reduction coefficient to address systematic over-filing. Moreover, all the way into the first few weeks of each quarter, the EC Commission would not have advised them of the results of the second round allocation, so that they could not ascertain in advance the volume and sources of their supplies. Since operators did not know their final entitlement until the third quarter of the actual year of entitlement, they were constrained from engaging in market planning and normal risk-taking. The Category B criteria also had distortive effects on trade by creating linkages between imports of Latin American bananas on the one hand, and ACP or EC banana purchases on the other. In combination, these elements (i.e. reduced operator flexibility, uncertainty and source-based linkages) acted as a non-tariff barrier that restricted and distorted the importation of third-country bananas beyond what might be expected from the mere operation of a tariff quota, in violation of Article 3.2 of the Licensing Agreement.

4.348 Addressing the fourth requirement of Article 3.2, the Complaining parties claimed that they had shown how the tariff quota licensing arrangement was "more administratively burdensome than absolutely necessary to administer the measure." The standard of proof for establishing a *prima facie* violation of this requirement clearly was satisfied by demonstrating that a much less burdensome set of licensing rules was applied to the same product from a different source, and where major components of the rules and procedure deviated sharply from customary licensing practice, or even the Member's own practices for other products. The administrative procedures at issue here were burdensome in an unprecedented way and highly discriminatory on the basis of product origin. No other procedures were designed to provide licence rights to those who had no capacity, or even showed any desire, to enter the business of importing from Latin America. As noted above: although the procedures surely were also burdensome for the EC's "competent authorities", this did not make them any less burdensome for imports. Looking at the two procedures for administering imports, that for ACP bananas and that for Latin American bananas, the Complaining parties had no doubt as to which an investor or prospective marketer would choose to subject himself to, given a choice. The burden thus shifted to the EC to demonstrate administrative necessity.

4.349 The EC reiterated that the Complaining parties needed to demonstrate that the licensing system administering the EC tariff quota was "more administratively burdensome then absolutely necessary to administer the measure". According to the EC, this provision was to be interpreted as referring to the burdensome character of the measure (the tariff quota) vis-à-vis the licensee importing the product concerned. This third part of Article 3.2

of the Licensing Agreement could not, in the opinion of the EC, be read in isolation but should be seen in the context of the whole paragraph (where reference was specifically made to "effects on imports") and to Article 1.1 of the Licensing Agreement (where the scope of the Agreement was limited to "regimes requiring the submission of an application or other documentation to the relevant body"). The Panel was not asked to decide in general and abstract terms what system was absolutely necessary to administer the banana tariff quota, but just if the burdens imposed on operators only (and not on internal custom administrations or other offices, independent from the operators activity) from importing countries when making use of the tariff quota for the importation of their products, were absolutely necessary to administer the measure.

4.350 In response to a question by the Panel, the EC submitted that the notion of "necessary" was already present in the GATT practise under Article XX(a) (b) and (d). In that context the recent Appellate Body Report *United States - Standards for Reformulated and Conventional Gasoline*, adopted on 29 April 1996, explicitly indicated that the chapeau of Article XX was "animated by the principle that while the exceptions of Article XX may be invoked as a matter of legal right, they should not be applied as to frustrate or defeat the legal obligations of the holder of the right under the substantive rules of the General Agreement".[197] It was in that context, therefore, that the notion of "necessary" had been developed as meaning a measure for which "no alternative measure which it could be reasonably expected to employ and which is not inconsistent with other GATT provisions is available to it".[198] The provision of Article 3.2 of the Licensing Agreement, on the contrary, was totally outside of that context since it was not an exception to any other WTO provision and did not imply that any GATT inconsistent rules was applied to the specific licensing system. The notion of necessity in this context was, therefore, governed by ordinary rules concerning the burden of proof under which the party that alleges a violation of a provision should provide for sufficient evidence demonstrating that violation. Nothing of the kind had been demonstrated by the Complaining parties: on the contrary, the EC had been able to show, by presenting facts and tables, that the burden on operators dependent from the administration of the tariff quota was reduced to its minimum and was needed to administer that measure.

4.351 Moreover, the EC submitted, contrary to any assertion by the Complaining parties, the banana traders' understanding of the system was totally satisfactory. The requirements on operators represented, in the view of the EC, an extremely small part of the administration of the total system. These requirements were straightforward and well known to all traders. For example, the requirement to apply for import licences during the first seven days of the month preceding the start of the relevant quarter existed since the start of the regime. Traders appeared to have no difficulty understanding the rules of the system, as shown by the almost complete utilization of the tariff quota, which would not be possible if operators were missing application deadlines or otherwise failing to claim their entire entitlement.

4.352 The Complaining parties responded that the separate use of the term "restrictive effects" in Article 3.2 required a present or potential trade flow impact on suppliers. As a recent economic report made clear, the tariff quota licensing scheme was creating precisely such an impact.[199] Preliminary 1995 EC-15 Eurostat data appeared to confirm the drop in demand for Latin American bananas arising from the licensing scheme. Those data showed imports of only 2,471,700 tonnes from tariff quota origins, a volume approximately 9 per cent below the total tariff quota (2.2 million tonnes), autonomous increase of 353,000 tonnes and "hurricane" volume (155,765 tonnes) amounting to 2,708,765 tonnes authorized that year for tariff quota suppliers.

4.353 Furthermore, the Complaining parties were unaware of any trader whose understanding of the system was "totally satisfactory". Moreover, they were unaware of any licensing scheme anywhere that subjected its participants to the collection of burdens present for third-country bananas. Even within the context of the banana

[197] WT/DS2/AB/R, p.22.

[198] L/6439, para. *5.26*.

[199] "Beyond Bananarama", p.25.

regime, the EC itself had obviously made the determination that the tariff quota licensing procedures were unduly burdensome, since they had exempted traditional ACP bananas from those rules and had proposed that non-traditional ACP bananas likewise be exempted from them. The fact that traditional ACP bananas were exempted from all such burdens was a clear violation of the "neutrality" standard of Article 1.3. Likewise, the burdens and adverse effects of the tariff quota licensing scheme were extreme and inconsistent with Article 3.2. If this system was not inconsistent with these new disciplines, it was hard to imagine systems that would come under their heading.

4.354 The EC retorted that the Panel should not overlook the fact that imports under the EC tariff quota in 1995 amounted to 123 per cent of the bound tariff quota volume and to 98 per cent of the autonomously increased tariff quota. The situation was similar in 1994. In the opinion of the EC trade had not been distorted and therefore the licensing system could not be accused of trade distortion.

(h) Claims under the Agreement on Agriculture

4.355 Ecuador argued that the EC import licensing regime was inconsistent with Article 4.2 of the Agreement on Agriculture. Ecuador claimed that the principal purpose of the Uruguay Round negotiations on agriculture was to eliminate the numerous systems throughout the world for agricultural protection which relied heavily on non-tariff barriers as a means of giving authorities discretion and latitude to control imports. Tariffication was seen as the first step in making agricultural protection transparent and subject to progressive reduction, both in the Uruguay Round and in subsequent global rounds of negotiations. Moreover, the preamble to the Agreement on Agriculture made it clear that an important purpose of the Agreement was to provide greater access for products of developing countries in the markets of developed countries, including "... the fullest liberalization of trade in tropical products ...".

4.356 Referring to Article 4.2 of the Agreement on Agriculture and its footnote, Ecuador considered that the threshold question was whether the import licensing regime set forth in Regulation 1442/93 constituted discretionary import licensing. If so, it was clear that under Article 4.2, Members were not permitted to maintain such measures. According to Ecuador, there were various features of the licensing regime which involved elements of discretion. But it was the totality of these features and the manner in which they interacted which resulted in granting Commission authorities exceedingly broad discretion to limit, control and even prevent imports. In the opinion of Ecuador, a good example was the interaction between the activity function allocation, the auditing procedure, and the uniform reduction coefficient. Since the very beginning of this system, total Category A operator reference volume claims of those applying for licences had exceeded actual banana imports by those same firms during the relevant reference period. As explained elsewhere, this over-filing (or double-counting) problem was due both to the confusion arising out of the definitions of "primary importer", "secondary importer" and "ripener" and to fraudulent over-claiming.

4.357 Regulation 1442/93 provided for two measures to address over-filing: the execution of audits and the application of a reduction coefficient. However, the Commission's auditing procedures were highly discretionary. The Commission apparently had broad latitude to select the operators to be audited, instruct the member States' authorities on the claims to be questioned and then rule on the legitimacy of those claims. There were no published guidelines or official explanations on how the Commission selected the operators that were to be audited. Although the Commission did not release information which would enable outside parties to verify this fact, it appeared that the auditing procedure was operated in such a way as to subject non-EC operators to greater scrutiny, thereby enabling EC-owned operators to continue benefiting from overfiling[200]. Those unfortunate enough to be audited were still subjected to the application of the reduction coefficient, even if the auditing revealed no overfiling, thereby making them pay for the overfiling of others, who were permitted to benefit from their own

[200] Ecuador noted that it was a reality that most of the direct importers were non-EC operators while the other operators involved in the marketing of bananas were European.

fraud. Although it was impossible for anyone except the Commission to verify these facts, the overall impact was clear: in practice the result of this process was the increase in the number of import licences in the hands of European operators.[201] Thus, the Commission was using a highly discretionary system to take away licences from many historical importers of Latin American bananas.

4.358 Ecuador further argued that another important discretionary weapon was the ability to delay licences. As explained elsewhere, it was normal practice not to grant the full licence quantity before the applicable quarter began. These unjustifiable delays hindered operators from marketing third-country bananas in a timely manner. As a result of this discretionary practice, in combination with the quarterly two-round procedure, a considerable volume of third-country bananas did not enter the market until at least three weeks into the quarter for which the licences were to be issued.[202] There was no official explanation for these frequent delays. One could assume, then, that this represented another discretionary practice to delay the entry into the EC of third-country bananas.

4.359 For these reasons, Ecuador considered that the discretionary import licensing regime violated Article 4.2 of the Agriculture Agreement. A finding to the contrary would permit governments to circumvent Article 4.2 merely by establishing a highly complex licensing system with a mix of discretionary and non-discretionary features, and then operating that system in a manner designed to make importation virtually impossible except under circumstances contemplated by the licensing authorities. The EC's use of a discretionary import licensing system had actually worsened, rather than improved, market access conditions compared to the situation pre-existing the new regime. Several major markets which were previously free from any licensing restrictions now faced a major non-tariff barrier. This deterioration in access was, according to Ecuador, obviously contrary to the purpose and objective of the Agreement on Agriculture.

4.360 The EC retorted that Ecuador's assertion should be rejected because the necessary elements to apply Article 4.2 of the Agreement on Agriculture were missing. The existing EC banana tariff was the result of the negotiation under the Uruguay Round after that the previous obsolete 20 per cent ad valorem rate had been de-consolidated. The tariff quota, that needed a licensing system to be administered, had not been required to be converted into ordinary custom duties but, on the contrary, was the result of a negotiated de-consolidation of an ad valorem customs duty. In addition, the EC import licensing was not a discretionary licensing system since it was based on strict and objective rules of general application which attributed individual rights to operators on the EC market and which were duly and thoroughly published. Certain aspects of the licensing system provided for administrative powers to be retained by the Commission as any other public authority in any other country administering any like procedure: these powers were, in any case, always awarded to the Commission by the EC applicable law. This did not and could not change at all the nature of a strictly legally bound licensing procedure.

4.361 In response to a question posed by the Panel, the EC recalled that, in its opinion, the Licensing Agreement did not apply to tariff quotas. The legal analysis concerning "non-automatic" and "discretionary" licensing was done, therefore, with the unique purpose of helping the Panel's interpretative tasks. In the EC view, the term "non-automatic licensing" referred to an administrative procedural step necessary to import a product in presence of a quantitative restriction or to profit from a tariff rate in presence of a tariff quota. As Article 3.5(e) of the Licensing Agreement pointed out, in this light, "any person, firm or institution which fulfils the legal and administrative requirements of the importing Member shall be equally eligible to apply and to be considered for a licence". The term "discretionary licensing", on the contrary, referred to a situation in which an administration of an importing Member retained the - full or partial - discretion on whether to distribute the licences and to whom. This administrative discretion was, in particular, concerned with the public interest as opposed to the rights of the individual operators: the authorities could therefore depart from pre-established criteria of distribution in order to

[201] Explanatory Memorandum of the Commission Proposal for a Council Regulation on the common organization of the market in bananas (COM (92) 359 final, 7 August 1992).

[202] According to Ecuador, because of the transit time through the Panama Canal, the time between loading and unloading was three weeks. Unloading took place at least four to five weeks after the time that the order was first placed by the importer.

take into account the existence of a specific public interest. Whatever the WTO provisions applicable to the EC tariff quota on bananas, the licensing system for administering it certainly fully corresponded to the definition of "non-automatic licensing" and not to that of "discretionary licensing".

4.362 As concerns the question of whether the terms "non-automatic licensing" and "discretionary licensing" were coterminous, the Complaining parties considered that they were not. The Licensing Agreement defined non-automatic licensing as a system which did not grant approval of licence applications in all cases. However, a non-automatic licensing system was not necessarily a discretionary system. In a non-automatic system, applicants could be subject to specific requirements with which they had to comply in order to receive an import licence. On the other hand, a discretionary licensing system was one in which an administrative body (in this case, the Commission) reserved to itself the right to deny a licence even if certain objective criteria were met. Ecuador had argued that the EC banana regime was a discretionary import licensing system because the EC had put in practice a system (through complicated distribution of licences, the two-round system, selective auditing and the application of reduction coefficients despite auditing having taken place) so as to allow it to decide to issue a licence or not based on non-objective, non-binding criteria.

(ii) operator category licence allocation

4.363 The Complaining parties argued that although the core of the import licensing system, i.e. the Category B operator criteria, was found to be discriminatory under Articles I and III of GATT by the second *Banana* panel, the EC had made no effort since that time to diminish that discrimination. As mentioned above, 30 per cent of the in-quota quantity for the tariff quota was allocated to companies, known as Category B operators, on the basis of three previous years' marketings of EC bananas and imports of ACP bananas. An obvious advantage, a highly valued import licence, was being provided as an incentive to purchase ACP and EC bananas. This represented the Article III:4 and Article I violations that the EC still had made no effort to address. Indeed, in the interim it also decided to provide additional advantages to those Category B operators, such as the exemption from export certificate requirements and the exclusive receipt of hurricane licences, which further favoured purchases of ACP and EC bananas.

4.364 The United States noted that on 11 February 1994, the second *Banana* panel found the Category B operator eligibility criteria to be inconsistent with Articles I:1 and III:4 of GATT, because they provided incentives to purchase other origin bananas.[203] The panel went on to say (in paragraph 145) that the GATT did not set forth specific provisions regarding the distribution of import licences, and that the EC could have chosen to allocate licences on the basis of importing companies' previous trade shares. It noted, however, that:

> The absence of any provisions in the General Agreement specifically regulating the allocation of tariff quota licences also meant that contracting parties, in allocating such licences, had to fully observe the generally applicable provisions of the General Agreement, in particular those of Article III:4, which prescribes treatment of imported products no less favourable than that accorded to domestic products, and Article I:1, which requires most-favoured-nation treatment with respect to internal regulations.

The panel concluded that the Category B eligibility criteria were inconsistent with both Article I:1 and Article III:4. In the opinion of the United States, the EC had done nothing to change the Category B criteria, or the incentives mentioned above, since the second *Banana* panel issued its report. Indeed, barely a month after the decision, the EC compounded the discrimination by insisting, in its negotiations with Colombia and Costa Rica, that Category B operators be exempted from its commitment to require the presentation of export certificates as a condition for

[203] Para. 144 of the second *Banana* panel report (DS38/R).

importing bananas from the BFA signatories that issued them. Implemented on 1 March 1995,[204] this exemption amounted to an additional violation of Articles I:1 and III:4 of GATT.

4.365 Ecuador recalled that Article I of GATT required that Members accord most-favoured-nation treatment to imports of products from other Members, while Article III of GATT required that Members accord national treatment to other Members' products. The second *Banana* panel report found that the Category B allocation violated both of these requirements. According to Ecuador, the EC had not amended the Category B licence allocation scheme since the 1994 panel report was issued. Therefore, the panel's reasoning that the Category B allocation violated the most-favoured-nation and national treatment provisions of the GATT remained persuasive.

4.366 The Complaining parties recalled that in its 1995 review of the operation of the banana regime, the EC Commission characterized the allocation of 30 per cent of the third-country tariff quota to operators on the basis of their past marketings of ACP and EC bananas (Category B) as "the result of a difficult political compromise in 1993". Commission documents used the term "cross-subsidization" to explain more specifically why it granted such rights to Category B firms, which had scarcely any history of distributing or transporting non-ACP and non-EC bananas:

> From the range of alternative methods that could be used ... the approach of cross-subsidisation, through issuing licences to import "dollar bananas" to those who traded in Community or ACP bananas, was chosen because it not only provides some financial compensation for the higher production costs of these bananas, but also acts as an incentive for the market to become more integrated, and to encourage operators to trade in both dollar and EC/ACP fruit.[205]

4.367 They further noted that the 66.5 per cent - 30 per cent - 3.5 per cent licensing distribution was now in effect for all EC-15 imports. Because Sweden, Austria and Finland imported bananas only from non-ACP third countries and non-traditional ACP countries, expanded application of the 66.5 per cent - 30 per cent - 3.5 per cent distribution to include EFTA-3 imports significantly increased Regulation 404/93's pre-accession cross-subsidization effect.

4.368 The EC submitted that the category allocation, in particular the Category B licence, was consistent with each of the provisions of the GATT and other agreements cited by the Complaining parties.

(a) claims under the GATT

- Article I of GATT

4.369 The United States claimed that the second *Banana* panel found the Category B operator eligibility criteria to be inconsistent, *inter alia*, with Article I:1 of GATT, to the extent that they provided an advantage to bananas from some countries (ACP beneficiaries), in the form of an incentive to purchase and market their fruit. Since the EC had not changed these criteria, the distribution of import licences based on historical purchases of ACP fruit remained, in the opinion of the United States, inconsistent with Article I. For the same reasons found by the second *Banana* panel with respect to the distribution of licences, exemption of Category B operators from the export certificate requirement with respect to imports from BFA countries was also inconsistent with Article I:1.[206]

4.370 Ecuador argued further that the MFN clause prohibited discrimination based on the origin of goods with respect, *inter alia*, to:

---

[204] Regulation 478/95.

[205] "Note for Information - Impact of Cross-Subsidization within the Banana Regime", European Commission. See also Report on the Operation of the Banana Regime, EC Commission, SEC(95)1565 p.11.

[206] Second *Banana* panel, paras. 146-147.

> all rules and formalities in connection with ... importation and exportation," to "internal charges of any kind in excess of those applied, directly or indirectly, to like domestic products,"[207] and to any "requirements affecting their internal sale, offering for sale, purchase, transportation, distribution or use.

The Category B allocation scheme required that operators market EC or traditional ACP bananas in order to obtain Category B licences. The Category B allocation scheme thus provided an incentive to purchase EC and/or traditional ACP bananas in order to obtain a larger share of the licences to import third-country bananas. The advantage given to ACP bananas through the Category B allocation mechanism thus directly violated Article I:1 of GATT.

4.371 Recalling Article 6 of the BFA and Article 3 of Regulation 478/95, Ecuador argued that Category B operators were excluded from the requirement to obtain special export certificates to import bananas from BFA signatory countries. This discrimination between operators violated, according to Ecuador, the GATT (and the Licensing Agreement). The fact that the BFA allocations were included as part of the EC's Uruguay Round Schedules could not excuse the GATT incompatibility of this discriminatory licensing requirement. The need for Category A and C operators to obtain special export certificates to import bananas from BFA signatory countries (except Venezuela) violated, in the view of Ecuador, Article I:1 of GATT. Any Category B operator could market bananas from Colombia, Costa Rica and Nicaragua without an export certificate. The export certificate "requirement" thus intensified the discrimination created by the original Category B allocation mechanism by providing an additional incentive to qualify for Category B licences by marketing EC bananas. This discrimination was a clear violation of Article I of GATT.[208]

4.372 Guatemala and Honduras submitted further that the second *Banana* panel analyzed the preferred allocation to Category B entities that purchased traditional ACP bananas and found it to be contrary to the Article I:1 requirement that any advantage accorded to one third country had to "be accorded immediately and unconditionally to the like product originating in ... the territories of all other contracting parties." As with Article III of GATT, the panel found that the incentive created under Category B to purchase ACP bananas accorded a clear ACP advantage that was disallowed by Article I:1. The panel reiterated that neither the trade flow impact of such incentive, nor the entitlement requirements of Category A, militated against this *per se* violation. The Lomé waiver likewise did not justify the violation. That decision excused the obligations of Article I:1 only to the most narrow extent "required" by the Lomé Convention. All that the Lomé Convention required, was that tariff preferences and certain forms of direct aid be afforded so that traditional ACP bananas were not placed in a less favourable position relative to the access and advantages previously accorded to them.[209] The ACP purchasing incentives linked to Latin American import entitlement constituted neither of these and, indeed, were nowhere to be found in the pre-Regulation 404/93 national regimes. Moreover, the primary underlying agenda for the Category B rules was to support privileged EC marketers, not Lomé undertakings. Thus, any interpretation that the Category B entitlement rules were required by the Lomé Convention, such that Article I:1 ceased to apply, would subvert the deliberately constrained language of the Lomé waiver and permit expansive discrimination in ways never intended by the contracting parties that approved the decision. Accordingly, Guatemala and Honduras were of the view that the Article I:1 ruling with respect to the Category B in the second *Banana* panel should stand.

4.373 Mexico considered that Article I of GATT was applicable to the incentive given in favour of ACP banana imports through the mechanism which reserved 30 per cent of total imports to Category B operators.

---

[207] See the direct reference in Article I of GATT incorporating Article III:2 and 4.

[208] Ecuador noted that the special export certificate requirement was not protected from scrutiny by the Lomé waiver since, at most, the waiver could cover certain historical tariff preferences given to traditional ACP bananas.

[209] Lomé Convention, Protocol 5, Article 1.

4.374 Guatemala and Honduras submitted that Regulation 404/93 stipulated that third country and non-traditional ACP bananas may only be entered and distributed within the quota by specifically defined "operator" categories. One substantial operator category, Category B, purchased only a *de minimis* volume of bananas from Latin America for entry and distribution in the EC prior to Regulation 404/93. The imposition of this category on Latin American bananas accordingly required that those suppliers terminate pre-Regulation 404/93 commercial relationships and forge entirely new ones. Guatemala and Honduras considered that this undesirable and inflexible commercial reconfiguration disrupted conditions of trade and market competitiveness for third country and non-traditional ACP bananas. Traditional ACP and EC suppliers, on the other hand, were accorded far different trade arrangements that had no such defined operator categories, enabling perfect continuity in trade flow and pre-existing commercial relationships for those sources. Guatemala and Honduras argued that other panels had considered that under Article I:1, a regulatory advantage may not be conferred to one foreign origin without conferring the same advantage to all others.[210] Yet, Regulation 404/93 *et seq.* conferred unlimited discretion to suppliers of ACP-sourced bananas to transact with entities of their choosing, while denying that same advantage to suppliers of bananas from tariff quota origins.

4.375 The EC noted that Regulation 404/93 provided in Article 19: "The tariff quota shall be opened from 1st July 1993 for: ... (b) 30% to the category of operators who marketed community and/or traditional ACP bananas;". All the Complaining parties had quoted the second *Banana* panel report (unadopted) in which the panel stated that "the absence of any provisions in the General Agreement specifically regulating the allocation of tariff quota licences also meant that contracting parties, in allocating such licences, had to fully observe the generally applicable provisions of the General Agreement, in particular those of Article III:4 which prescribes treatment of imported products no less favourable than that accorded to domestic products, and Article I:1, which requires most-favoured-nation treatment with respect to internal regulations". With respect to the claims concerning Article I:1, no evidence had, in the EC's opinion, been provided as to how the Category B reservation in the licensing administration of the EC tariff quota affected, if at all, the internal EC distribution market of bananas. On the contrary, it was all too logical that operators that had in the past traded in Community and ACP bananas would avail themselves of the opportunity to sell part of the tariff quota where the margins of profit were, in principle, higher than for EC or ACP traditional bananas. In any case, not a single piece of evidence had been provided demonstrating that the existence of the Category B licence had shifted trade from Latin American to ACP/EU bananas. The Category B licensing system did not create any incentive to purchase any particular product but only favoured the avoidance of the effects of oligopolistic trade by operators relying only on bananas of a particular origin, stimulating by so doing effective competition between operators trading in different sources of supply. This did not mean at all that imported bananas of any source were discriminated against or favourably in any sense since, whatever the nationality of the trader, provided that it qualified for the appropriate category under Regulation 404/93, any banana could be imported by that trader, whatever the origin (see also paragraphs *4.393* and *4.394*).

4.376 Nor was there any link between the allocation of licences, which were used "to cross the border", that was to put bananas into free circulation in the EC market, and the market share in processing or selling those bananas in the EC market. Moreover, the fact that licences were tradeable should not be disregarded and licences should not be confused with the physical handling of bananas either prior to their importation or when disposed of on the EC market. In these circumstances, it was difficult, if not impossible, to see what should be extended on an MFN basis to others in application of Article I:1, when not one single ACP traditional banana was traded on top of the existing separate ACP traditional regime and not a single Latin American banana less was imported under the EC tariff quota - which was constantly fully used by the application of Article 19(b) of EC Regulation 404/93. In fact, no advantage, favour, privilege or immunity was granted to any banana of whichever origin through the Category B licensing system.

---

[210] "United States - Denial of Most-Favoured-Nation Treatment as to Non-Rubber Footwear from Brazil", BISD 39S/128, para. 6.11 (adopted 19 June 1992).

4.377 However, if, for the sake of the argument, Article I:1 should be deemed applicable to the Category B licence category with regards to the ACP traditional bananas then Article 19 of EC Regulation 404/93 should be considered covered by the Lomé waiver in so far it reserved Category B licences for operators who could demonstrate they had imported ACP traditional bananas. Protocol 5, Article 1, of the Lomé Convention stated: "no ACP State shall be placed, as regards ... its advantages on those markets, in a less favourable situation than in the past or at present". The banana trade was of vital importance to many traditional ACP suppliers, not only in terms of revenue generation and employment, although this was frequently crucial, but also because of role of banana boats in importing essential supplies to isolated island nations. Consignments of bananas ensure regular shipping links, and also subsidize the cost of imports, because the boats are full both ways.

4.378 In an answer to a question posed by the Panel, the EC pointed to a CIRAD[211] study which demonstrated production costs were very close to, and in some cases even above the FOB prices received by ACP countries. This clearly showed that the tariff was not sufficient to compensate for the higher costs of banana production in ACP countries. The quality problems afflicting some ACP bananas also made them less attractive to the market, as an analysis of import and wholesale prices showed. Thus even if the tariff was set at a level which would equalise duty-paid import prices, Latin American bananas would still be more sought-after for the most part. Moreover, even with a much higher tariff than the current one, whilst some ACP production may be afforded sufficient protection to be traded, many suppliers would still be unable to compete in the view of the EC. Unfortunately, those least able to compete were also for the most part those countries which were most dependent on bananas, and so would experience the greatest effects on their entire economies from any disruption to the banana trade. In such cases, for example in the Caribbean, the degree of economic inter-dependence in the region would mean that any economic collapse would have an immediate knock-on effect on the economic stability of the region as a whole. This would threaten not only the banana industry of other islands dependent on shipping routes, but other industries, for example tourism, dependent on stable export earnings. It would also deter investment and jeopardise diversification efforts. The long-term economic survival and development of the region was inextricably linked to the continuation of the banana industry to provide a stable level of export earnings. It was therefore necessary, the EC argued, to take certain additional preferential measures in favour of importation of traditional ACP bananas so as to enable them actually to be sold on the market and give them a reasonable basis for competition with Latin America bananas.

4.379 In the opinion of the EC, the Category B licensing system, by providing a stabilized environment in the ACP banana trade, concurred in maintaining the "advantages", which were present before the entering into force of the EC banana regime, on the community markets and was therefore fully covered by the Lomé waiver. Moreover, reservation for traders who had systematically traded ACP bananas within the tariff quota licensing scheme served the purpose of avoiding the distortive effects of trading oligopolies based on the origin of the product and stimulated an increased presence of traders throughout all sources of supply. This mechanism favoured the economies of ACP countries by increasing the reliability of the trade chain of bananas bound for the EC market and fulfilled the obligation of the EC to avoid reductions in real terms of access of traditional ACP supplies (Article 1 of Protocol 5). No violation could thus be claimed concerning Article I:1 of GATT by the Category B licence system as no advantage, favour, privilege or immunity was granted to ACP bananas as compared with other sources bananas. In any case, Article I:1 was waived to the extent to permit the EC to fulfil its obligations vis-à-vis the ACP countries under Article 23 and Protocol 5, Article 1, of the Lomé Convention.

4.380 The Complaining parties argued that the EC's various claims with respect to the Category B allocation scheme were internally inconsistent. On the one hand, the EC asserted that Category B did not create any incentive to purchase product of ACP origins and that not one single ACP traditional banana was traded on top of the existing separate ACP traditional regime. On the other hand, it insisted that the "first and foremost aim of the [allocation] system [is] to help producers of ACP bananas." This was accomplished, it said, "by providing a stabilized environment in the ACP banana trade", "by increasing the reliability of the trade chain" for ACP

---

[211] Centre de Coopération Internationale en Recherche Agronomique pour le Développement, Montpellier.

bananas, and by otherwise ensuring that ACP quantities "would actually be sold on the market". The EC had argued that assistance of this sort was legally required by Protocol 5. Either way the EC tried to argue a legal need for Category B (trade neutrality or trade favouritism), in the opinion of the Complaining parties the Lomé waiver was inapplicable. The second *Banana* panel report confirmed that trade effects were irrelevant where a measure provided a competitive advantage; the preferred allocation of licences to operators who purchased bananas from ACP countries was inconsistent with Article I of GATT because it did not accord the same advantage to bananas from other sources.[212] This violation was not covered by the Lomé waiver, since the EC was not required by the Lomé Convention to go beyond simply permitting access opportunities and advantages for traditional ACP bananas. The EC Council of Ministers had confirmed that the Lomé Convention did not guarantee access for ACP quantities.[213] Hence, measures allegedly designed to guarantee that ACP quantities "would actually be absorbed in the market" had no basis in any Lomé Convention requirement and were therefore not covered by the waiver. Moreover, any obligation to maintain previous access and advantages applied with respect to sales of the ACP bananas themselves. It did not require providing an entirely unrelated advantage in connection with the import licensing procedures for Latin American bananas. In the opinion of the Complaining parties, the EC's 1992 options report provided additional evidence that Category B allocations were not a requirement of the Lomé Convention. Several options were considered in that report that would not have called for any such allocation. Although one of several options discussed was an approach that would have divided a Latin American quota, with 90 per cent to traditional Latin American marketers and 10 per cent to traditional ACP/EC marketers,[214] those proposed figures only confirmed how discretionary the final 30 per cent allocation in fact was.

4.381 The Complaining parties argued further that the distribution of Category B licences on the basis of ACP banana marketings was not required to fulfil any Lomé Convention obligation. The EC Court of Justice had already stated that under Protocol 5, the EC's only obligation was to "maintain the [prior] advantages, with respect to access of ACP bananas". The advantages being provided to ACP bananas under the current regime, from the excessive country-specific allocations, to the duty-free treatment for these amounts, to the special provisions for non-traditional ACP bananas, to the Category B licence criteria, and to the excessively burdensome import licensing system imposed on Latin American bananas, substantially exceeded the access and advantages provided by EC countries to ACP bananas under previous national regimes.

4.382 The EC asked the Panel to concentrate on the substance: the Lomé Convention was aimed at creating a preferential treatment in order to ensure that the ACP States, as regards access to their traditional banana markets and their advantages on those markets, "shall not be placed in a less favourable situation than in the past or at present". The EC had on numerous occasions during this procedure underlined the absolute need the ACP States had to dispose of a procedural mean (the Category B licence) which was aimed at maintaining the very existence of a regular trade chain for their bananas. Without this assurance, it would be impossible for the EC to ensure a no less favourable situation as regards access to its market and even less as regards the advantages on its market, for the simple reason that the ACP bananas would have their trade disrupted by the irregularity of the trade relations. The Category B licensing system provides a stabilized environment in the ACP banana trade.

4.383 The EC argued that it was one thing to support the ACP banana trade by appropriate means aimed at creating the conditions by which the bananas could reach the EC market in order to be allowed to preserve their access to that market and their advantages on that market. This was in clear conformity with Protocol 5, Article 1, and covered by the Lomé waiver. Moreover, this was the preservation of a real and effective opportunity to sell but by no means a guarantee of the selling of any specific volume of bananas nor of any minimum price on the EC market for the purchase of those bananas on that market. It was a completely different thing to claim that the Category B licensing intervened on the EC market, that is after the fruit had cleared customs. This was absolutely

[212] Second *Banana* panel, para. 147.

[213] "Report of the ACP-EEC Council of Ministers", Brussels, 25 July 1980, p.44, para. 2.1.2.4.

[214] "Setting Up the Internal Market", para. 61(a).

and thoroughly incorrect. Not a single ACP banana more was sold on the EC market because of the existence of the Category B licence. Not a single Latin American banana less was sold on the EC market because of the existence of the Category B licence.

- Article III of GATT

4.384 Ecuador argued that Article III:1 of GATT stated that internal laws, taxes and regulations "should not be applied to imported or domestic products so as to afford protection to domestic production." A requirement to purchase a domestic product in order to obtain the right to import a product at a lower rate of duty under the tariff quota clearly was a marketing incentive designed to "protect domestic production." The right to obtain Category B licences for importing third-country bananas was contingent upon the marketing of domestic or traditional ACP bananas. No similar incentive was provided for the marketing of Latin American fruit. The incentive to purchase EC fruit provided through the Category B allocation scheme thus violated the national treatment requirements of Article III of GATT.

4.385 The United States noted that the second *Banana* panel had drawn (in paragraph 146) the following conclusion with respect to the incentives provided to buy bananas from domestic sources:

> The Panel then proceeded to examine the EEC licensing scheme in the light of the incentive provided under the regulations to buy bananas from **domestic sources**. The Panel noted that Article III:4 had been interpreted consistently by previous panels as establishing the obligation to accord imported products competitive opportunities no less favourable than those accorded to domestic products. A previous panel has stated:
>
> > The words "treatment no less favourable" in paragraph 4 call for effective equality of opportunities for imported products in respect of the application of laws, regulations and requirements affecting the internal sale, offering for sale, purchase, transportation, distribution or use of products.[215]
>
> The Panel further noted that previous panels had found consistently that this obligation applies to any requirement imposed by a contracting party, including requirements 'which an enterprise voluntarily accepts to obtain an advantage from the government.'[216] In the view of the Panel, a requirement to purchase a domestic product in order to obtain the right to import a product at a lower rate of duty under a tariff quota is therefore a requirement affecting the purchase of a product within the meaning of Article III:4. The Panel further noted that, in judging whether effective equality of opportunities for imported products under Article III:4 was accorded, the trade impact of the measure was not relevant. The CONTRACTING PARTIES determined in 1949 that the obligations of Article III:4 'were equally applicable whether imports from other contracting parties were substantial, small or non-existent,'[217] and they have confirmed this view in subsequent cases.[218] Thus it was not relevant that, at present, the incentive under the EEC regulations to buy domestic or traditional ACP bananas may only result in raising their price, and not in reducing the exports of the third-country bananas, since these exports, because of the high over-quota tariff, were limited, de facto, to the amount allocated under the tariff quota. The

---

[215] Report of the panel on "United States - Section 337 of the Tariff Act of 1930", adopted 7 November 1989, BISD 36S/345 at 386 ("Section 337 of the Tariff Act of 1930").

[216] Report of the Panel on "EEC - Regulation on Imports of Parts and Components", adopted on 16 May 1990, BISD 37S/132 at 197.

[217] Report of the working party on "Brazilian Internal Taxes", adopted 30 June 1949 BISD Vol. II/181 at 185.

[218] Report of the panel on "United States - Taxes on petroleum and certain imported substances", adopted on 17 June 1987 BISD 34S/136, 158, para. 5.1.9; report of the panel on "United States - Measures affecting alcoholic and malt beverages", adopted on 19 June 1992, BISD 39S/206, para. *5.65*.

discrimination of imported bananas under the licensing scheme could therefore not be justified by measures on the importation that currently prevented, de facto, bananas from entering into the internal market. The Panel therefore found that the preferred allocation of part of the tariff quota to importers who purchase EEC bananas was inconsistent with Article III.4.

4.386 Mexico claimed that Article III:4 of GATT was applicable to the case under consideration by the Panel because the EC regime had a regulation with requirements affecting the internal sale, offering for sale, purchase, transportation, distribution or use of these products (imported bananas) in the internal market, granting them less-favourable treatment than that accorded to like products (EC bananas) in the domestic market. The less-favourable treatment for the importation of non-ACP bananas was due to the fact that according to the EC regime, 30 per cent of licences required to import non-ACP bananas within the tariff quota was reserved for the Category B operators, that is, those operators that historically had marketed EC or traditional ACP bananas, on a rolling three-year reference period basis. In conformity with the conclusions of the second *Banana* panel and in accordance with information from the EC itself, the mechanism relating to Category B operators resulted in an incentive in favour of EC bananas to the detriment of bananas imported from non-ACP countries. According to the second *Banana* panel, this incentive in favour of EC bananas was inconsistent with Article III:4 of GATT.

4.387 Mexico further claimed that there were other violations of Article III that were not examined by the second *Banana* panel because they did not exist then. These violations referred to the advantages accorded to EC banana producers through the EC regime to the detriment of imports. This included the exemption granted to Category B operators to import part of its banana imports from BFA countries without having to present the export certificates from those countries necessary for Category A and Category C operators. This created an incentive in favour of the purchase and marketing of EC bananas which was not enjoyed by imported bananas.

4.388 Guatemala and Honduras argued that the tariff quota category allocations violated Article III of GATT in three distinct ways. First, according to Guatemala and Honduras, Regulation 404/93 *et seq.* required Category B entities to purchase domestic and traditional ACP bananas in order to gain entitlement to import tariff quota bananas within the quota. That source-specific purchasing incentive had already been ruled inconsistent once in the second *Banana* panel and had to be ruled so again on the same, as well as new, grounds. The panel in the second *Banana* case carefully analyzed the preferred allocation to Category B entities that purchased EC bananas and found it to be inconsistent with Article III:4. Drawing from past case law, in which it was ruled that Article III:4 applied to requirements that "an enterprise voluntarily accepts to obtain an advantage from the government," the panel found that the Category B requirements to purchase EC bananas in order to obtain the right to import tariff quota bananas at the in-quota rate of duty constituted a requirement favouring the purchase of EC bananas in violation of Article III:4.[219] The panel arrived at this conclusion without regard to tariff quota trade impact. The panel stressed that because Article III:4 protected "equality of opportunities," even if the purchase incentive served only to raise EC banana prices, and not reduce tariff quota imports, Article III:4 was nevertheless violated. The panel added that Category A's entitlement based on historical tariff quota purchases in no way offset or legally justified the inconsistency of Category B with Article III:4. As no corrective actions had been taken by the EC to remove the Category B purchasing incentive, the second *Banana* panel ruling had, in the opinion of Guatemala and Honduras, to be sustained in the present action.

4.389 Guatemala and Honduras further submitted that Regulation 404/93 *et seq.* imposed on tariff quota banana producers the unique, unexpected burden of having to sell to specifically defined and arbitrarily allocated categories of operators. Fully 30 per cent of their already-restricted access was assigned to Category B firms and producers that historically had not been sufficiently competitive to import bananas from Latin American sources. That arbitrary Category B allocation, through which considerable tariff quota goods now had to flow, was distributed to firms and producers solely on the basis of their past purchases of traditional ACP and EC bananas

---

[219] Second *Banana* panel, DS38/R, para. 146 (issued 11 February 1994), citing "EEC - Regulation on Imports of Parts and Components", BISD 37S/132, para. *5.21* (adopted 16 May 1990).

under a rolling three-year reference period. The 30 per cent tariff quota licensing entitlement to Category B firms accordingly meant that Latin American suppliers had no choice but to use the various distribution, land transport, inspection, ripening and related services those firms supplied, even though such firms historically had no meaningful experience in the distribution and sale of Latin American bananas and were competitively unable to handle such fruit prior to receiving the 30 per cent licensing entitlement gift. EC suppliers, on the other hand, were given unlimited flexibility to sell and distribute bananas without disrupting historical distribution ties.

4.390 According to Guatemala and Honduras, Category B licences violated Article III in a third way, being distributed, among others, to EC producers to "cross-subsidize" the sale of EC bananas within the EC. The EC had itself explained how Category B import licences accomplished that benefit:

> Individual producers and producers' organizations which are not themselves necessarily 'importers' of bananas have been allocated Category B licences. Since in general they have no interest in importing dollar bananas, these licences are sold, providing a supplement to their income in addition to the support provided by the provisions on aid to compensate for the loss of income.[220]

Producers in Latin America did not share in this expressly admitted licensing benefit. Guatemala and Honduras were thereby being accorded differential, less favourable regulatory treatment than EC suppliers in disregard of Article III:4 of GATT and other WTO provisions.

4.391 As concerns Article III:4, Guatemala and Honduras submitted that that Article strictly prohibited Members from extending treatment to foreign suppliers "less favourable than that accorded to like products of national origin in respect of all laws, regulations, and requirements affecting their internal sale [or] offering for sale." That prohibition had been interpreted expansively to cover "any laws or regulations which might adversely modify the conditions of competition between the domestic and imported products on the internal market."[221] Here, as the EC openly conceded, Category B licences were intended to provide a competitive benefit to EC producers by providing a supplement to Regulation 404/93 deficiency payments. Other foreign sources were not receiving that same benefit. Thus, through the tool of Category B allocations, the EC had tipped conditions of competition in favour of domestic interests, thereby avoiding its Article III:4 national treatment obligation.

4.392 The EC submitted that paragraph 145 of the unadopted second *Banana* panel report was based in particular on the assumption that:

> the words treatment no less favourable in paragraph 4 call for effective equality of opportunities for imported products in respect of the application of laws, regulations and requirements affecting the internal sale, offering for sale, purchase, transportation, distribution or use of products.

---

220 See "Report on the EC Banana Regime", European Commission, July 1994, pp.10-11, prepared for the July 1994 Food and Agriculture Organization Conference in Jamaica.

221 "United States - Taxes on Petroleum and Certain Imported Substances", BISD 34S/136, para. 5.1.9 (adopted 17 June 1987); "United States - Section 337 of the Tariff Act of 1930", BISD 36S/345, paras. *5.11-5.13* (adopted 7 November 1989); "United States - Measures Affecting Alcoholic and Malt Beverages", BISD 39S/206, para. *5.31* (adopted 19 June 1992); "EEC - Import Regime for Bananas", DS38/R, para. 146 (issued 11 February 1994).

From this well known interpretation of Article III:4, which the EC agreed with and accepted, the panel went on with, in the view of the EC, an unjustified and incorrect consequence for the EC banana tariff quota that:

> a requirement to purchase a domestic product in order to obtain the right to import a product at a lower rate of duty under a tariff quota is therefore a requirement affecting the purchase of the product within the meaning of Article III:4.

The relevant parts of the quotations from the panel report ("a requirement to purchase a domestic product" and "a requirement affecting the purchase of the product within the meaning of Article III:4") -which was the essential link between the general and correct interpretation of Article III:4, and its actual concrete application to the EC banana tariff quota - was incorrect in the opinion of the EC. The licensing system as it functioned within the EC tariff quota did not concern the purchasing of any quantity of bananas on the EC market but provided the means to manage correctly, and according to the EC overall economic strategy, the importation of third-country bananas into that market in a required, satisfactory quantity. The bananas produced in the Complaining parties' countries entered the EC market and were sold at the EC market price, which was substantially higher than the average world price and profited largely any seller to that market.

4.393 In the view of the EC, in order to demonstrate a breach of Article III:4, even in the extended generous interpretation which ensured "equal competitive opportunities" in the banana market, the Complaining parties had to show that at least one single banana originating in one of their countries and importable within the legitimate tariff rate quota, as bound in the Uruguay Round Schedule LXXX, was actually not imported, or risked not being imported, or suffered a lower import price because of the existence of the Category B licence. However, nothing of the kind had ever been demonstrated or proven because such competitive disadvantage in the EC market did not exist.

4.394 The EC claimed that there was competition between over 2.2 million tonnes of low-cost, low-duty Latin American bananas and non-traditional ACP bananas on the one hand and a, de facto, limited quantity of EC bananas on the other hand, bananas which were high cost, but not subject to any duty. The mere existence of a duty was not relevant since tariffs were the basis of the GATT system and were legitimate trade means in trade relations between the Members. Outside the existence of the duty itself, the competitive relation was not affected by sharing out the amount of the quota between operators. There was no incentive not to sell the full quota of 2.2 million tonnes. On the contrary, the different production prices, totally in favour of imported, cheap Latin American bananas, ensured that the Latin American bananas were sold, probably sold first and certainly sold with a premium. Then, the EC continued, the suppliers of the EC market, wherever based, were free to market their bananas to whomever they wished, on whatever price or delivery terms, and there was no indication in the Complaining parties' allegations that banana exporters could not freely negotiate about price and delivery terms with those who had access to the tariff quota. Moreover, the EC said, no evidence had been provided of how the Category B reservation in the licensing administration of the EC tariff quota affected, if at all, the internal EC distribution of bananas. On the contrary, it was all too logical that operators that had in the past traded in EC and ACP bananas would avail themselves of the opportunity to sell part of the tariff quota, where margins of profit were in principle higher than for EC or ACP traditional bananas. In any case, not a single piece of evidence had, in the opinion of the EC, been provided, demonstrating that the existence of Category B licences had shifted trade from Latin American to ACP/EC bananas.

4.395 Nor was it possible for the Complaining parties to show, the EC argued, that any operator involved in trade in Latin American bananas was losing market share in the EC due to the existence of the Category B licences, since statistics tended to demonstrate quite the opposite, namely that these companies were actually increasing their market share of the primary import of ACP bananas and in marketing EC bananas. The above legal and factual analysis showed, according to the EC, that the unadopted second *Banana* panel report was not in conformity with reality: the licensing system for administering the EC banana tariff quota was not a law "affecting the internal sale, offering for sale, purchase, distribution or use" of EC and imported bananas. It was a law which was concerned with what happened at the moment of importation; it was not relevant to what happened after the bananas had passed customs. Moreover, it did not determine the sale or offering for sale of the 2.2 million tonnes tariff quota once these bananas were in the internal EC market and were therefore totally undistinguishable from bananas of any other source (EC or ACP traditional). Whatever the correctness of the interpretation given to Article III:4, *in abstracto*, by the unadopted second *Banana* panel report, that panel argued erroneously on the basis of that Article's applicability to, in particular, Article 19 of Regulation 404/93. The EC stressed that the licensing system for the administration of the EC banana tariff quota was applied at the border at the moment of importation and not after the bananas had cleared customs. As set out in the horizontal discussion concerning the applicability of Articles III:4 and X of GATT to border measures, the EC argued all the arguments based on Article III:4 should be rejected (together with the arguments based on Article X) - the allegations about which were, in any event, totally unfounded.

4.396 The Complaining parties responded that the second *Banana* panel found that the Category B licences were inconsistent with the Article III national treatment requirement, and nothing had occurred to change the validity of that Panel's conclusion. On the contrary: the EC's licensing scheme fell squarely within the first illustrative example of an Article III violation, set forth in the TRIM's Agreement as set out in the general discussion of the applicability of Articles III:4 and X of GATT to border measures. This example specified as an Article III violation any measure "compliance with which is necessary to obtain an advantage" (the advantage here being the receipt of an import licence), "and which require the purchase ... by an enterprise of products of domestic origin" (in this case EC bananas) "specified in terms of volume ... of products." The EC's treatment of this issue in its submission missed the point that an "advantage" provided could be in the form of a border measure, while the favour accorded to EC products could be one affecting purchasing and distribution decisions in the EC.

4.397 The Complaining parties further considered that Article III covered any regulation or requirement that affects internal conditions of competition in favour of EC bananas.[222] The condition upon which the EC granted the Category B licence adversely modified the conditions of competition between the domestic and imported product on the internal market by providing a government benefit based on the purchases of the domestic product. Therefore, the second *Banana* panel report properly concluded that the Category B licence was inconsistent with the EC's obligations under Article III:4. In this dispute, the granting of the Category B licences, the exemption from export certificates for Category B operators, and the special additional import licences given to Community producers when there was a natural disaster in a Community banana zone, all created an incentive for the purchase and marketing of EC bananas not enjoyed by imported bananas.

4.398 The Complaining parties considered that these were all plain violations of Article III of GATT and other WTO obligations. It was not necessary for them to show that the EC's violations had already resulted in lower imports from Latin America. As the EC well knew, the Article I and III obligations required the EC to preserve equal conditions of competition; trade effects were irrelevant to that question. Given that the EC reduced access for Latin American exports in 1993, in the hopes that EC and certain ACP bananas would eventually capture any growth in European consumption, fulfilment of the Latin America tariff quota might become even more difficult in the next few years.

- <u>Article X:3 of GATT</u>

4.399 Guatemala and Honduras submitted that the stipulation of Article X of GATT that all regulatory requirements be imposed in a "uniform, impartial and reasonable manner", was manifestly violated by the Category B licensing requirements that caused licensing rights to accrue solely on the basis of purchases from designated sources. This source-specific purchasing incentive was intentionally partial to EC and ACP interests. Article X disallowed this very type of partiality in the administration of trade regulations. Moreover, the "uniform, impartial and reasonable" standard arising out of paragraphs 1 and 3 of Article X was negated by a licensing

[222] Second *Banana* panel, para. 148.

allocation procedure that conferred an exclusive benefit on EC producers. Interpretive law had confirmed that a procedure that operated in one favourable way for certain interests and quite another, less favourable way, for others did not fulfil the uniformity requirement of Article X.[223] In short, every feature and effect of the Category B allocation - from its licensing tie to ACP/EC sources, to its comparatively burdensome import and distribution requirements, to its exemption from the need to obtain export certificates from BFA countries and finally, to its selective distribution of licences to EC producers - deprived the Complaining parties of their WTO right to non-discrimination, licensing fairness, and trade-neutrality. The EC was accordingly obliged under the WTO, in the view of Guatemala and Honduras, to discontinue this measure without delay.

4.400 Mexico also claimed that the relevant provisions of the EC regime made a clear differentiation between those provisions that would be applied to imports from non-ACP countries, including from Latin America, and those applicable to imports from traditional ACP countries. This differentiation resulted in the allocation of import licences to Category B operators for the importation of bananas from non-ACP countries on the condition of having marketed or imported bananas from traditional ACP countries. This differentiation of provisions relating to the supply source also violated Article X:3(a) of GATT because it could not be considered as "uniform" and "impartial".

4.401 The United States also considered these origin-based criteria to be inconsistent with Article X:3, which the EC had admitted prohibited discrimination as between contracting parties.

4.402 The EC recalled the general issue of the applicability of Articles III:4 and X of GATT to border measures and stressed that the licensing system for the administration of the EC banana tariff quota was applied at the border at the moment of importation and not after the bananas had cleared customs. Therefore, the EC argued, all the arguments based on Article X should be rejected along with those based on Article III:4.

4.403 As discussed earlier, the Complaining parties considered that Article X:3 of GATT required Members to administer trade rules in a "uniform, impartial and reasonable manner." The laws and practices covered by Article X comprised all "trade regulations," which included, among many others, licensing regulations.

- Article XIII of GATT

4.404 As set out with the arguments concerning Article I:1 of GATT, Guatemala and Honduras submitted that Regulation 404/93 stipulating the specifically defined "operator" categories, in particular Category B, required that tariff quota suppliers terminate pre-Regulation 404/93 commercial relationships and forge entirely new ones. This undesirable and inflexible commercial reconfiguration disrupted conditions of trade and market competitiveness for third country and non-traditional ACP bananas and was contrary to a number of GATT articles and WTO agreements. Article XIII:1 of GATT in particular banned all import restrictions that were differentiated on the basis of foreign origin by providing that:

> [n]o prohibition or restriction shall be applied by any contracting party on the importation of any product of the territory of any other contracting party ... unless the importation of the like product of all third countries ... is similarly ... restricted.

Previous panels had applied this principle to import licensing administration that varied by supplying country.[224] Although the second *Banana* panel reviewed category allocations and found that no discrimination among supplying countries occurred therefrom, the facts did not, according to Guatemala and Honduras, support an affirmation of that finding. The Complaining parties concurred with that panel's conclusion that the category

[223] Note by the Director-General, L/3149 (29 November 1968). See also Dessert Apples, BISD 36S/93, para. 6.5 (adopted 22 June 1989).

[224] Dessert Apples, BISD 36S/93, paras. 12.20-12.21 (adopted 22 June 1989); "EEC - Quantitative Restrictions Against Imports of Certain Products from Hong Kong", BISD 30S/129, paras. 31-33 (adopted 12 July 1983).

requirements, in strict isolation, did not themselves discriminate among supplying countries. Discrimination among supplying countries became readily apparent, however, when those allocation rules were contrasted with the import arrangement available for bananas of ACP origin. Tariff quota suppliers had to enter bananas through specially designated EC middlemen even though a substantial portion of those middlemen previously did not import and distribute tariff quota bananas. Traditional ACP suppliers had been permitted to maintain their historical commercial relationships across-the-board, sparing them the severe disruption effectuated by category allocations. Such import licensing discrimination among supplying countries could not be considered to be in conformity with Article XIII:1.

4.405 The EC recalled its view that it was a mistake to consider that a tariff quota was an "import restriction" while the unadopted second *Banana* panel report excluded this argument and no evidence of a different reality had been shown and also that it was evident that the fact that two separate and independent regimes, the ACP traditional and the EC tariff quota, had marginal differences in their respective licensing systems was neither in itself a violation of any GATT provision, nor was there evidence of any violation of GATT provisions by any of the two systems. Furthermore, in the opinion of the EC, the two systems did not create any substantial difference in their external effects on the imported bananas from different origins; the only discrepancies remaining were on the side of the internal procedures to be followed by the competent authorities.

4.406 As discussed above, the Complaining parties responded to this assertion by noting that Article XIII:1 prohibited the application of a restriction to products of one Member that was not also applied to products of other countries. Although the EC insisted that the regime for administering the tariff quota was entirely separate, Regulation 404/93 only created one regime, not two. Regardless of how many regimes might be at issue, however, Article XIII still required that imports from all sources be similarly restricted.

(b) claims under the Licensing Agreement

- Article 1.2 of the Licensing Agreement

4.407 Ecuador noted that Article 1.2 of the Licensing Agreement required that Members "ensure that administrative procedures used to implement import licensing regimes are in conformity with the relevant provisions of the GATT 1994 ... with a view to preventing trade distortions that may arise from an inappropriate operation of those procedures." The Category B allocation scheme, as explained above, did not comply with the GATT 1994 and created significant trade distortions. The EC's failure to eliminate this scheme was a direct violation of Article 1.2. As the previous discussion made clear, the allocation of licences to Category B operators was clearly not enacted "with a view to preventing trade distortions." In fact, the allocation of licences of Category B operators was in large part designed to create trade distortion by increasing the marketing of EC and traditional ACP bananas. Article 1.2 of the Licensing Agreement was designed precisely to prevent these types of trade distortive measures.

4.408 According to Ecuador, the exemption of the Category B operators from the requirement to match special export certificates with import licences as a condition for importing from BFA countries provided an extra incentive for operators to obtain Category B licences which in turn created trade distortions and reinforced the national treatment and MFN incompatibility inherent in the original allotment to Category B operators. Article 1.2 of the Licensing Agreement, which required that licensing procedures be in conformity with the GATT and implemented "with a view to preventing trade distortions," was devised precisely to prevent these types of trade distortive measures.

4.409 In the view of Mexico, by violating Article I:1 of GATT, the export certificate requirement needed for Category A and C operators to import bananas from BFA countries, also violated Article 1.2 of the Licensing Agreement.

4.410 The EC submitted that as no breach of the cited GATT provisions had been proved, the claims concerning Article 1.2 of the Licensing Agreement should be rejected.

- Article 1.3 of the Licensing Agreement

4.411 Ecuador recalled that Article 1.3 of the Licensing Agreement stated that the rules for import licensing procedures had to be neutral in application and be administered in a fair and equitable manner. Category B operators were not required to match their import licences with the special export certificates when they imported BFA bananas which eased the importation of third-country bananas for those operators. The exemption thus reinforced the incentive to market EC and traditional ACP bananas in order to obtain Category B licences. The exemption of Category B operators from the requirement to present special export certificates in order to import BFA bananas was, according to Ecuador, not neutral and was not administered in a fair and equitable manner, and was therefore in violation of, *inter alia*, Article 1.3 of the Licensing Agreement.

4.412 Guatemala and Honduras also claimed that licensing requirements that built in purchasing incentives for specified sources had equally to fail the standards of Article 1.3 of the Licensing Agreement that all licensing rules be "neutral in application and administered in a fair and equitable manner." As origin-specific purchasing incentives could not be considered "neutral," "fair," or "equitable" under any possible definition of those terms, the Category B provisions should, in the opinion of Guatemala and Honduras, be invalidated. Moreover, Guatemala and Honduras claimed, the source-discriminatory application of operator limitations likewise could not be said to satisfy the stipulation in Article 1.3 of the Licensing Agreement that licensing procedures be "neutral," "fair and equitable" in application and administration. Neutrality, fairness, and equity could hardly be considered present when the Complainants' bananas were subject to category allocations that constrained flexibility, disrupted trade flows, and distorted prices, while EC and traditional ACP banana importation and distribution were completely free of such constraints.

4.413 The United States argued that Article 1.3 of the Licensing Agreement provided in relevant part that "[t]he rules for import licensing procedures shall be neutral in application." Nothing could be further from "neutral" than a scheme which awarded nearly a third of the licences to import bananas from Latin America to entities based on their marketing of bananas from competing sources - EC members States or ACP countries. As such, the distribution of licences to Category B operators, and the exemption they were provided with respect to export certificate requirements, were blatantly inconsistent with Article 1.3.

4.414 The Complaining parties argued that the EC's licensing scheme had deliberately allocated third-country licences to firms with no history of importing from third countries, and therefore was inconsistent with the neutrality requirement of Article 1.3 of the Licensing Agreement.

4.415 The EC submitted that there was evidence that the Complaining parties were not very sure of the actual correctness of the legal analysis of the unadopted second *Banana* panel report. This was indicated by the fact that, while contesting the violation of Article III:4, and therefore considering that the EC banana licensing system was an internal measure, they had affirmed the violation by the same EC provisions of the Licensing Agreement and, in particular, Articles 1.3 and 3.2. These were certainly not related to internal measures since the Licensing Agreement provided for rules for "import licensing regimes requiring the submission of an application or other documentation ... to the relevant administrative body as prior condition for importation into the custom territory of the importing Member" (Article 1.1). Nevertheless, the EC was of the view that the legally correct interpretation of the EC banana licensing system as a border measure at the moment of the importation did not imply that those measures violated any GATT rules including Article 1.3 of the Licensing Agreement.

4.416 In respect of that Article, the EC argued that the Complaining parties had put the emphasis on the alleged violation of the obligation of neutrality under that provision, while a correct and complete quote of the Article would disclose that: "The rules for import licensing procedures shall be neutral in application and administered in a fair and equitable way." The CONTRACTING PARTIES had agreed on a text that explicitly required neutrality in the application and administration of the rules creating a particular licensing scheme. Nowhere in that Article the CONTRACTING PARTIES committed themselves not to shape a particular import licensing procedure in the way that the EC has adopted, where all operators of any country are freely competing within and among different categories as set out in Article 19 of EC Regulation 404/93. Within that particular licensing scheme, neutrality is absolutely respected and no evidence has been shown to the contrary. Any operator can be eligible for any category licence if it fulfils the objective conditions herein. No evidence had been further shown that the licensing scheme was administered in an unfair and unequitable manner. The word "manner" was normally defined, according to the EC, as "a way of doing something or a way in which a thing is done or happens" (American Heritage Dictionary of the English language). So the Complaining parties should have demonstrated that the way that licensing scheme (the "thing" in the definition) is administered ("happens" in the definition) is unfair and inequitable. The Complaining parties were, on the contrary, trying to demonstrate through Article 1.3 that the licensing scheme itself was unfair (which was in any case unfounded): but this had nothing to do with the way the Licensing Agreement was agreed upon or the common will of the CONTRACTING PARTIES that was expressed in the wording.

4.417 The Complaining parties retorted that the EC sought to satisfy its burden of explaining its discriminatory and burdensome regime by urging an unduly narrow reading of the Licensing Agreement to cover only licensing "procedures," which it defined to exclude operator eligibility criteria. The distinction between procedure and eligibility was, in the opinion of the Complaining parties, a false one. The EC's claim ignored the considerable administrative burdens associated with the tariff quota eligibility criteria. The EC had acknowledged the procedural character of licensing distributions by stating that Category B "provides the means to managing ... the importation of third-country bananas". Moreover because they were far more onerous on Latin American imports than on ACP imports they were not "neutral" under Article 1.3.

- Article 3.2 of the Licensing Agreement

4.418 The Complaining parties noted that Article 3.2 of the Licensing Agreement provided that "[n]on-automatic licensing shall not have trade-restrictive or distortive effects on imports additional to those caused by the imposition of the restrictions." The Category B criteria had distortive effects on trade by creating linkages between imports of Latin American bananas on the one hand, and ACP or EC banana purchases on the other.

4.419 Ecuador argued that for the same reasons that the Category B licence allocation scheme violated Article 1.2 of the Licensing Agreement, the scheme also violated Article 3.2. The trade distortive effects caused by the Category B allocation scheme were clearly in addition to those caused by the tariff quota itself. Whereas the tariff quota was designed to limit the access of foreign bananas, the Category B allocation scheme distorted trade by providing an incentive to market EC and traditional ACP bananas. The scheme therefore conflicted, according to Ecuador, with the requirements of Article 3.2.

4.420 Mexico argued that the very nature of the EC banana import licensing regime was designed to promote marketing of EC bananas and bananas from ACP countries at the expense of banana imports from other countries, including from Latin America. The requirement for Category B operators to market EC and ACP bananas in order to obtain licences to import non-ACP bananas, including Latin American bananas, was relevant here. This action distorted, according to Mexico, the EC import trade patterns by supply source because it granted a clear advantage to imports from ACP countries to the detriment of those originating in non-ACP countries, including the Latin American countries. The advantage for ACP countries had two different aspects: firstly, there was the requirement to import ACP bananas in order to be able to import non-ACP bananas, and secondly, there was the fact that ACP countries were not subject to the requirements imposed by the EC regime on non-ACP banana imports, relating to the allocation of licences to operators. The distribution of licences according to the type of operator, including Category B operators was not absolutely necessary according to Mexico.

4.421 Mexico was also of the view that the requirement of obtaining an export certificate to import bananas from BFA countries to the EC represented an element that contributed to the distortion of import trade for non-ACP countries, because besides discouraging Category A and C operators from importing bananas from BFA countries, it exempted Category B operators from this requirement. This violated Article 3.2 of the Licensing Agreement.

4.422 Guatemala and Honduras also considered that the proscription in Article 3.2 against "trade-distortive", non-automatic licensing was contravened by the Category B provisions. With non-automatic licensing provisions in place that tie a licensing advantage to the purchase of bananas from certain sources on a rolling three-year basis, sourcing distortions were both intended and inevitable. Moreover, those category allocations had rescinded pre-Regulation 404/93 commercial relationships and forced new ones with entities that were never sufficiently competitive to market Latin American bananas prior to Regulation 404/93; introduced price distortions by specifying arbitrarily defined categories of eligibility; curtailed import flexibility; and otherwise have thrown into disarray the marketing of Latin America bananas. Under any conceivable interpretation of the Article 3.2 standard, in the opinion of Guatemala and Honduras, these effects must be considered trade distortions additional to those arising from the tariff quota volume limitation at the border. When contrasted with the entirely unrestricted terms of purchase and distribution available to ACP and EC suppliers, these allocation requirements served to shift EC purchasing preferences towards ACP and EC sources, thereby restricting and distorting the trade of Guatemala and Honduras over time beyond that caused by the tariff quota volume limitation. The trade-restrictive and -distortive effects banned under Article 3.2 of the Licensing Agreement were, thus, squarely implicated by category allocations.

4.423 In contrast to the system for traditional ACP bananas, the United States argued, Latin American imports were subject to rules, e.g. distribution of licences on the basis of Category B operator criteria that attempted to shift imports away from those who had the skill, distribution networks and infrastructure to sell them, and toward those with little or no experience in importing bananas from Latin America, or in some cases, from anywhere else. These distributions were in themselves burdensome, and inconsistent with the general international principle of distributing licences to those who had performed and/or could efficiently perform, the actual importation.[225]

4.424 The EC recalled that in its view, the Complaining parties were not very sure of the legal analysis of the unadopted second *Banana* panel concerning Article III:4 - which considered that the EC banana licensing system was an internal measure - because they were claiming a violation by the same EC provisions of the Licensing Agreement and in, particular, Articles 1.3 and 3.2. These were certainly not related to internal measures. Nevertheless, the EC was of the view that the legally correct interpretation of the EC banana licensing system as a border measure at the moment of the importation did not imply that those measures violated any GATT rules, including Article 3.2 of the Licensing Agreement.

4.425 With respect to that Article, apart from unmotivated and unsubstantiated statements hinting that as a result of the Category B provisions, distortions were both intended and inevitable or that trade distortive effects were additional to those caused by the tariff quota itself, not a single concrete evidence was shown of these affirmations. The EC insisted that no violation of Article 3.2 had been committed and that no extra unnecessary burden for the operators at the border while importing was caused by the existence of the Category B licences. The same could be said for Article 3.5(h) of the Licensing Agreement: first this provision was not applicable and, in any case, no proof of violation whatsoever had been exposed.

4.426 In order to demonstrate an alleged violation to Article 3.2 of the Licensing Agreement, the Complaining parties needed to prove, first, that the non-automatic licensing had "trade-restrictive or -distortive effects on

[225] The United States noted that this principle was reflected in Article 3.5(h), (i) and (j) of the Licensing Agreement. The basis for the principle was an interest in preventing measures that interfere with economic efficiency, a policy reflected throughout the Licensing Agreement.

imports additional to those caused by the imposition of the restriction". The Complaining parties should have demonstrated that bananas imported into the EC market were restricted by the administration of the tariff quota beyond the effects on trade of the very existence of the tariff quota, which was a reality compatible with the General Agreement and part of the concessions accepted by all contracting parties, besides the fact that that was common practice in GATT agricultural negotiations. As noted above, in the opinion of the EC, not a single evidence had been given of these supposed and totally unproved additional trade restrictive or distortive effects. Not a single evidence was shown, demonstrating any hindering in the access of the Complaining parties bananas to the EC market whose parts of the tariff quota were immediately and completely used. The very existence of the tariff quota, however, was, in the opinion of the EC, a clear improvement in terms of market liberalization as compared to the situation prior to the conclusion of the Uruguay Round and created conditions for higher prices in the EC market as compared to world market prices and this was a benefit to the Complaining parties' banana production.

4.427 The EC further submitted that the effect of the EC institutional working procedures was that the management of the import licensing system was made by official acts (EC Commission Regulations) which were dutifully and timely published in the Official Journal of the EC. The entire structure of the licensing system was published in general EC Council and Commission regulations, which were also regularly and timely published. The framework regulations (404/93 and 1442/93) were the base for all subsequent management of EC Commission Regulations. The administrative activity of the EC tariff quota licensing system was governed by the law, i.e. by pre-determined criteria and rules which applied objectively to all bananas of whichever origin. The EC and its member States, the EC asserted, provided for full judicial review of all aspects of the licensing system, in particular its administration, allowing any operator's complaint to be examined in an independent and fair way and any individual right to be protected.

4.428 With respect to the separate "administrative burden" requirement of Article 3.2 of the Licensing Agreement, the Complaining parties argued that since the EC had acknowledged the procedural character of licensing distributions by stating that Category B "provides the means to managing ... the importation of third-country bananas," the associated procedures were hardly minimally burdensome or "absolutely necessary" to administer the tariff quota. The Complaining parties considered that the standard of proof for establishing a *prima facie* violation of this requirement clearly was satisfied by demonstrating that a much less burdensome set of licensing rules was applied to the same product from a different source, and where major components of the rules and procedure deviated sharply from customary licensing practice, or even the Member's own practices for other products. No other procedures were designed to provide licence rights to those who had no capacity, or even showed any desire, to enter the business of importing from Latin America.

4.429 The Complaining parties further argued that the discrimination and extraordinary burdens could not be justified by the EC's assertion that they were "not uncommon" or that "they respond to the specific needs of the tariff quota." The only specific need identified by the EC was a highly dubious explanation that the Category B licence criteria and the activity functions were driven by competition concerns -because the Latin American banana sector was alleged to be uniquely characterized by "oligopoly or even monopoly". This was not a legitimate justification for two reasons. First, competition concerns with respect to individual companies were more appropriately dealt with through competition laws and enforcement, which the EC had not been hesitant to use against multinationals in the past. The EC had provided no explanation for why its competition laws were not adequate to whatever task it claimed to have been trying to accomplish with the licensing regime. Second, as further elaborated below, the claim was obviously a *post hoc* rationalization that provided no basis or factual support for burdening imports of Latin American bananas.

4.430 The Complaining parties claimed that the Latin American banana distribution sector was in fact more competitive than distribution for other fruit in general, and for distribution of ACP bananas in France and the United Kingdom in particular. *Beyond EU Bananarama 1993* pointed out that banana trade was in reality less dominated by multinational corporations than were trade in wheat, maize, cotton, tobacco, coffee, cocoa beans, tea, timber, jute and jute products, copper, iron ore, bauxite, and other important products. If oligopoly concerns heavily influenced the banana tariff quota licensing scheme, it should further be asked whether the EC would likewise feel justified imposing the same or a similar regime on the wide array of other traded products that were more heavily controlled by trans-national companies than were bananas. In fact, however, even the EC Commission had recognized that healthy competition existed in the marketing of Latin American bananas. In surveying available options in anticipation of a common market, the Commission noted that:

> [t]here is a strong element of competition between these multinational companies and the independent suppliers [as to the sales of Latin American bananas], with the independents working hard to boost their share of the market at the expense of the multinationals.[226]

In fact, the world-wide trend was that up-and-coming distributors from Ecuador, Colombia and elsewhere had been steadily taking market share away from the traditional distributors, Chiquita, Dole Foods and Del Monte, during the 1980s and early 1990s. In the United States market, for example, Latin American-owned firms increased their market share from 12 per cent in 1981 to 47 per cent in 1993.

4.431 Moreover, legitimate competition concerns could hardly be the basis for the preferential licensing arrangements accorded to ACP bananas, in so far as the markets in which ACP fruit was primarily sold - France and the United Kingdom - were notoriously anti-competitive. Court decisions in both countries confirmed this pattern.[227] Also, a 1983 United Kingdom court proceeding, which upheld the United Kingdom's pre-404 banana regime as technically consistent with United Kingdom law, nevertheless criticized the United Kingdom's licence allocation system as promoting or reinforcing a near-monopoly.[228] The 90 per cent-plus entitlement to import Latin American bananas given to the "big three" in the United Kingdom market corresponded to their over-90 per cent share of ACP imports. Not only did these three firms dominate the importation of bananas into the United Kingdom, they were also highly vertically integrated, owning shipping fleets and, unlike the Latin American and United States firms, owning the firms that ripened their bananas.

4.432 This background suggested, according to the Complaining parties, that rather than having any basis in "legitimate" competition policy, the EC's arrangements were intended to perpetuate and extend for French and United Kingdom firms the uncompetitive conditions they enjoyed before Regulation 404/93. From the EC's perspective, the Latin American banana import market was perhaps too competitive for French and United Kingdom companies. Measures implemented to reduce that competitiveness did not amount to legitimate competition policy. The EC's current emphasis on competition policy was a new development. In the EC's *Report on the Operation of the Banana Regime*, the EC cited only three objectives of the regime, none of which related to competition policy:

> In completing the single market for bananas, the banana regime seeks to fulfil a range of objectives. Firstly, there are the commitments to Community producers as outlined in the Treaty .... Secondly, the Community's obligations to the ACP States as embodied by the Lomé Convention have to be honoured .... Finally, the regime has to ensure that the market (i.e. the consumer) is adequately supplied with bananas of good quality.[229]

Similarly in the second *Banana* panel proceeding, no reference was made to the competition policy objective.[230]

---

[226] "Setting up the Internal Market", para. 18.

[227] See "Decision of the French Competition Council Relating to Practices Found in the Banana Market" against the Banana Industry Interprofessional Committee ("CIB") and the Banana Industry Economic Interest Group ("GIEB"), 12 June 1990.

[228] "R. v. Secretary of State for Trade ex parte Chris International Foods Ltd.", Queen's Bench Division, Crown Office List, CO/1020/82.

[229] "Report on the Operation of the Banana Regime", pp.1-2 .

[230] Second *Banana* panel, paras. 10-16.

4.433 The Complaining parties further argued that if the EC did have a genuine interest in improving competition for bananas and other products, it could best achieve that by creating a large and open market in which competitive forces were allowed to prevail. Instead, it had distorted the market in favour of companies that had previously operated in a non-competitive market.

4.434 The EC submitted that the existence of the Category B licence, had nothing to do with the actual amounts of bananas that the EC had accepted to concede under its Schedule LXXX annexed to GATT 1994, nor with the bound duty applicable MFN to any imported bananas imported in excess of the tariff quota. In the presence or in the absence of Category B licences, the access of Latin American bananas to the EC market would be regulated in exactly the same way and opportunities of Latin American bananas would be exactly the same. In presence of a legitimate regulation by a Member of its importations of a product like bananas - such as in the case of the establishment of a tariff quota and the setting of relatively high out-of-quota tariff rates - the very existence of a licensing scheme created quota rents, irrespective of the system of distribution of the licences the Member in question had chosen. The same effect would be created, for instance, by a system of "first-come, first-served" which was extremely unpractical to manage. The existence of this quota rent had no link either with the GATT (which was never intended to regulate the flows of gains and losses of operators) or with the importation of bananas, for the simple reason that the importation of the product was not affected at all. The Complaining parties were still to indicate a provision of the GATT or other WTO agreement -apart from Article III of GATT that was not applicable in general to this matter and was not concerned with operators but only with products - which was violated by the Category B licensing system with respect to bananas (as opposed to operators and their gains and losses).

4.435 In addition, there was no physical link between a licence (or a Category B licence) and the importation of bananas from Latin America. Licences were transferable and tradable. The operators who traded EC bananas might choose to sell a Category B licence to another operator who might wish to use it to import Latin American bananas. In this example, the trader in EC bananas might gain part of a quota rent and the trader in Latin American bananas might benefit from less than the full quota rent. But not a single EC banana more would be sold on the EC market because of this commercial relation. Not a single Latin American banana less would be imported into the EC market because of these commercial relationships. The existence of Category B licences did not affect the volume of Latin American bananas sold on the EC market (the volume was governed by the size of the tariff quota), nor the country of origin of these bananas. Neither the amount of import duty due nor the price of bananas to EC consumers would change because of the existence of three types of licence for import under the tariff quota.

4.436 According to the EC, in application of existing EC general rules, any operator is entitled to a Category B licence. The Complaining parties referred themselves to unspecified statistics which indicated that EC-based operators have been issued 57 per cent of the Category B licences. Even if the argument were to be true, it would not demonstrate other than the correctness of the EC system. An EC-based company does not mean at all EC-owned: this of course means that many United States and foreign owned companies trade ACP and EC bananas from EC-based companies and the reference to EC-based companies does not show anything with respect to Category B licences. It should not be forgotten, in fact, that under Article 58 of the EC Treaty, a company established in one of the EC member States - irrespective of its ownership - is allowed to trade in any other EC member State. As a matter of fact, statistics show that United States companies and their subsidiaries inside and outside Europe receive a significant proportion of all Category B licences issued (see also paragraph *4.470*).

(c) claims under the Agreement on Trade-Related Investment Measures

- Articles 2.1 and 5 of the TRIM's Agreement

4.437 Ecuador argued that the Category B licensing system was inconsistent with Article 2 of the TRIM's Agreement. According to Ecuador, this Agreement set out specific restrictions on the Members' authority to implement investment measures related to the trade of goods. Referring to the national treatment provision in Article 2 of the TRIM's Agreement, Ecuador considered that the Category B allocation scheme directly violated

Article III of GATT. Referring to the Illustrative List of TRIM's in the Annex to the Agreement, Ecuador submitted, moreover, that Article 19(1) of Regulation 404/93 stated that 30 per cent of the licences for importing third-country tariff quota bananas were to be awarded to Category B operators. Regulation 404/93 thus made eligibility for a large portion of the licences to import third-country tariff quota bananas contingent upon the marketing of domestic bananas. This, in turn, required foreign operators to invest in EC production, ripening and marketing facilities in order to obtain access to Category B licences. This was precisely, in the opinion of Ecuador, the type of regulation specified in the Illustrative List as inconsistent with of Article 2 of the TRIM's Agreement. In addition, Article 5.1 of the TRIM'S Agreement required Members to notify to the Council on Trade in Goods, by the end of March 1995, TRIM's that they were applying that were not in conformity with the Agreement. Article 5.2 required that developed country members eliminate all such measures by the end of 1997. The EC had not notified the WTO of its measures providing advantages to Category B operators, but it was under no less of an obligation to eliminate them.

4.438 Guatemala and Honduras noted that the new national treatment discipline of the TRIM's Agreement applied to all "investment measures related to trade in goods ...". [231] Referring to the Illustrative List in the Annex to the Agreement, Guatemala and Honduras submitted that they had shown in their Article III:4 analysis of Category B that the very type of measure prohibited by Article 2, as further defined in the Annex to the TRIM's Agreement, arose in connection with the Category B rules. In order for Category B firms to obtain the right to import tariff quota bananas within the tariff quota, they were required to purchase bananas of domestic or ACP origin. Thus, for foreign investors to have any hope of becoming eligible for Category B licences, they had to first invest in EC and ACP bananas.

4.439 Guatemala and Honduras further submitted that Article 5 of the TRIM's Agreement set forth notification requirements for all non-consistent TRIM's and established a mandatory transition period for their elimination. The EC had, in their opinion, breached Article 5.1 by failing to notify the Council for Trade in Goods of its Article 2 violation arising out of Category B's trade-related investment measure. Pursuant to the language of Article 5.2, the EC, as a developed country Member, had, according to Guatemala and Honduras, until 1 January 1997, two years after the WTO Agreement entered into force, to eliminate this measure.

4.440 Mexico argued that the EC regime violated Articles 1 and 2 as well as the Illustrative List of the TRIM's Agreement. The Agreement was applicable to the case under consideration by the Panel because the EC regime affected those enterprises that imported bananas and, hence, the investment required to establish such enterprises or that would be required to establish them in the future. Moreover, such investment was related to trade in goods (bananas) and a GATT panel had already found that the EC banana regime violated Article III:4 of GATT. The EC regime was thus incompatible with the Agreement on TRIM's because it made the obtention of the advantages granted to Category B operators conditional on the purchase or use, by enterprises wishing to import bananas into the EC, of specified particular products of domestic origin or from domestic sources, in this case EC bananas. In the opinion of Mexico, violation of the TRIM's Agreement was even more evident when one considered that the only enterprises that were able to profit effectively from the advantages enjoyed by Category B operators were those enterprises that marketed significant volumes of EC bananas already before the entry into force of the EC regime, because these imports were based on past marketing by Category B operators and on reference periods that ensured their permanence. The 3.5 per cent share given to Category C operators (operators that began marketing in 1992) was so small and administratively cumbersome that it was economically unviable for new suppliers to use it.

4.441 The United States argued that for the reasons described in paragraph 146 of the second *Banana* panel report the Category B eligibility criteria were inconsistent with Article III:4 of GATT, to the extent that they provided rights to import bananas and exempted operators from the export certificate requirement. For the same reasons, these measures were also inconsistent with the TRIM's Agreement. Referring to Article 2.1 and to the illustrative list of TRIM's in the Annex to the Agreement, the United States argued that in the case at hand,

[231] TRIM's Article 1.

purchases of domestic bananas were required in order to obtain the advantages of: (i) future ability to import bananas within 30 per cent of the tariff quota; and (ii) future ability to import bananas from BFA countries without the additional burden of an export certificate requirement. As a practical matter, investment in either EC production or EC ripening facilities was required to obtain the benefit, year to year, of these advantages, since up to 57 per cent of licence entitlements based on the marketing of EC bananas was distributed to EC farmers or farmer cooperatives and 28 per cent to ripeners. The measures that linked marketing of domestic bananas to the advantages enjoyed by Category B licence-holders were thus, in the opinion of the United States, trade related investment measures inconsistent with the TRIM's Agreement.

4.442 Moreover, the United States continued, Article 5.1 of the TRIM's Agreement required Members to notify the Council on Trade in Goods by the end of March 1995 all TRIM's they were applying that were not in conformity with the Agreement. Article 5.2 required developed country Members to eliminate all such measures by the end of 1997. The EC had not notified its measures providing advantages to Category B operators to the WTO, but was under no less of an obligation to eliminate them.

4.443 The EC replied, quoting Article 2 of the TRIM's Agreement, that it was self-evident that the application of TRIM's was related to the application of Article III (national treatment) or XI (quantitative restrictions) of GATT. The Category B licence provided for in Article 19 of EC Regulation 404/93 did not fall within the scope of Article XI, since the Category B licence was part of a tariff quota that implied no quantitative restriction. Nor did it fall within the scope of Article III:4 because, as the EC had demonstrated, the EC banana licensing scheme was a border measure that concerned the operators at the moment of the importation of the bananas in the EC market, and not an internal measure affecting the EC rules of sale after imported bananas had cleared customs. The EC thus disputed the claims as the TRIM's Agreement was an extension, *inter alia*, of Article III of GATT, and that no Article III violation was present.

4.444 If, for the sake of the argument, the EC wanted to examine the applicability of Article 2 of the TRIM's Agreement to the subject matter, in order for the TRIM's Agreement to be applicable one needed, according to the EC: (i) an investment to be made within a particular country; and (ii) a purchase or use requirement by an enterprise of products of domestic origin in order to be allowed to make the investment.[232] Under the Category B licence requirement neither of these pre-requisites existed. While importing a certain amount of bananas using the EC tariff quota, no investment in the EC was made nor was it required; it was just a trade operation between a seller and a purchaser. Moreover, while selling imported Latin American bananas, the Complaining parties were not required to purchase any domestic good. Article 2 of the TRIM's Agreement was therefore, according to the EC, not applicable to the Category B licence provision of the EC banana tariff quota. As far as Article 5 of the TRIM's was concerned, the EC argued, the same remarks as for Article 2 of the TRIM's Agreement were appropriate although the EC considered the Article 5 claim inadmissible because it did not appear in the request made for the Panel. The EC was therefore of the opinion that this provision was not applicable either to the subject matter.

4.445 The Complaining parties submitted that they had shown that the Category B purchasing tie was squarely prohibited by Article 2 of the TRIM's Agreement and the Illustrative List annexed to the Agreement which, when read in combination, prohibited any law requiring "the purchase or use by an enterprise of products of domestic origin" in order "to obtain an advantage". The Complaining parties claimed to have already shown, however, that the 30 per cent Category B allocation directly contravened the national treatment obligations of Article III of GATT. According to the Complaining parties, the EC further misstated the relationship between Article III and the TRIM's Agreement. First, Article 2.2 of the TRIM's Agreement made it clear that a measure contained in the Annex to the TRIM's Agreement automatically violated Article III:4. It referred to the measures in the Annex to the TRIM's Agreement as an illustrative list of measures "that are inconsistent with the obligation of national treatment" in Article III:4. Second, Article 2.1 also made it clear that a Member did not cede any of its rights under

[232] In the same sense: the panel report on "Canada - Administration of the Foreign Investment Review Act", adopted on 7 February 1984.

Article III by raising a claim under the TRIM's. Thus, a Member was not restricted to arguing that a measure violated the TRIM's Agreement when there was an independent argument under Article III. Such measures were covered by both the TRIM's and the GATT, and not only by the TRIM's Agreement as *lex specialis*.

4.446 This attempted interpretive framework misstated, according to the Complaining parties, the coverage and reach of both Article III:4 of GATT and the TRIM's Agreement. The Complaining parties submitted that the first illustrative example of an Article III:4 violation in the TRIM's Agreement in fact corresponded to the kind of investment measure found inconsistent with Article III:4 by the panel in *EEC - Regulation on Imports of Parts and Components.*[233] In that case, the panel considered incentives provided by the EC to avoid companies' use of certain imported parts and materials. The panel found that "the comprehensive coverage" of Article III "suggests that not only requirement which an enterprise is legally bound to carry out, such as those examined by the *FIRA Panel* ... but also those which an enterprise voluntarily accepts in order to obtain an advantage from the government constitute 'requirements' within the meaning of that provision." In the TRIM's negotiations, the "advantage" language in the *Parts and Components* case was discussed extensively and formed the basis for the first illustrative example.

4.447 The Complaining parties submitted that in this case, the EC had provided, in the form of a valuable licence, an advantage or benefit connected to the purchase of domestic production that it had not provided with respect to the purchase of imported bananas, thus giving a competitive advantage to domestic products. Purchasing domestic product obviated the need to buy licences at a high price; therefore, one was required to purchase domestic products in order to obtain the government benefit of a free licence. The sale of licences at a high price indeed only confirmed the benefit accorded to domestic production; the purchase of domestic products ultimately enabled the domestic product to compete with a definite advantage not available to imports. As in the *Parts and Components* case, the Panel should conclude that the incentive provided to improve conditions of competition for domestic production unfairly skews conditions of competition for imports.

4.448 The Complaining parties submitted that if a measure described in the Illustrative List of the TRIM's Agreement was being applied, nothing more needed to be shown to establish an Article 2 violation. The TRIM's Agreement and its negotiating history drew no distinction between product-related trade measures and product-oriented trade-related investment measures. The negotiators recognized that if any Member, in whatever context, required the purchase by an enterprise of a domestic product in order to obtain an advantage, that requirement by definition had investment consequences for such an enterprise, putting the measure within the coverage of the TRIM's Agreement.[234] The investment implications of Category B were, according to the Complaining parties, manifestly apparent. The purchasing requirement had forced United States and Latin American firms importing and distributing in the EC, and those which had not historically chosen to purchase EC bananas, to invest by acquiring EC production, by acquiring Category B firms, or by entering into costly marketing arrangements simply to maintain their historical access to the EC market. The TRIM's Agreement applied to such investments whether undertaken by private enterprises or government enterprises. According to the Complaining parties, the *Foreign Investment Review Act* report recognized that government requirements or regulations making the grant of an advantage dependent on purchases by private enterprises or investors of domestic product in preference to imported goods were still also in breach of Article III:4 of GATT.[235] If Article III:4 applied to advantages made dependent on purchases by private enterprises or investors of a domestic product, so did the TRIM's Agreement.

---

[233] "EEC - Regulation on Imports of Parts and Components", adopted 16 May 1990, BISD 37S/132, para. *5.21*.

[234] See Submission by the European Communities to the Negotiating Group on Trade-Related Investment Measures, MTN.GNG/NG12/W/8, p.1 (23 June 1987) (wherein the EC recognized that certain measures e.g. local content, relating to access to goods result in foreign acquisitions in order to obtain such goods and therefore should be considered "investment measures").

[235] See "Canada - Administration of the Foreign Investment Review Act", adopted 7 February 1984, BISD 30S/140, para. 5.6; see also "EEC - Regulation on Imports of Parts and Components", adopted 16 May 1990, BISD 37S/132, para. *5.21*.

4.449 The Complaining parties further argued that even if an investment requirement were necessary to prove inconsistency with the TRIM's Agreement, the Category B licence criterion still fulfilled that pre-condition, since it necessitated an investment in EC or ACP bananas (either through marketing arrangements or direct production) in order to qualify for the direct receipt of those licences. Similarly, the activity function added an investment dimension to the licensing requirements. By the EC's own admission, the three-function approach required operators to purchase EC ripening rooms in order to obtain the "advantage" of retaining their historic reference volume, the only other option being the purchase of import licences in the marketplace:

> An operator who is efficient and competitive and so increases his business will obtain more licence in the future ... [It gives] a strong incentive for operators to change their trade patterns in order to maximize their licence allocation, e.g. by ripening bananas for the first time.[236]

As a practical matter, this has encouraged vertical integration for those who wished to remain importers of Latin American bananas. That private operators took the decision to invest in such ripening facilities did not negate the fact that a government measure, Regulation 1442/93, was effectuating an investment policy.

4.450 In reply to a question posed by the Panel, the EC considered that the arguments of the Complaining parties rested on a fundamental misinterpretation of the scope of the TRIM's Agreement. As the first preambular paragraph, quoting from the Punta del Este Declaration, puts it, the drafters of the TRIM's Agreement were concerned, according to the EC, about investment measures, when they had "trade-restrictive and distorting effects", and they wanted to draft further provisions in order "to avoid such adverse effects on trade". This orientation, which was confirmed in the last preambular paragraph, demonstrated that the TRIM's Agreement was not concerned with the investment effects of investments measures (i.e. the extent to which investment measures succeed in orienting investment in a particular way) and not even with the investment consequences of trade measures.

4.451 In the view of the EC, the TRIM's Agreement was exclusively concerned with the fact that certain measures concerning investment (i.e. measures which were linked to obtaining an investment permit or to obtaining investment premiums or investment tax rebates, etc.) could have a distortive effect on trade, because they were linked to e.g. local content requirements in the production or export performance requirements of the investment to be made. Such distortive effects on trade were contrary to Articles III or XI of GATT. However, the investment consequences of a measure were of no concern to GATT or the TRIM's Agreement (they were and are clearly outside the scope of both, and this was confirmed by the fact that investment was a subject beginning to be discussed *de lege ferenda* in the context of the OECD MAI negotiations and of the Singapore Ministerial Meeting); only the trade consequences of such a measure fall under the scope of GATT and the TRIM's Agreement.

4.452 Moreover, according to the EC, it is well-known that the TRIM's negotiations did not go a step beyond the measures which had already been condemned earlier under Articles III and XI of GATT. This was clearly confirmed by Article 2.1 of the TRIM's Agreement, where it was made clear that the Agreement merely prohibited "any TRIM that is inconsistent with the provisions of Article III or Article XI of GATT 1994". Even the illustrative list of TRIM's annexed to the Agreement self-avowedly did not go beyond these two Articles (see Article 2.2 of the TRIM's Agreement). Therefore, the drafters did not even care to specify the investment character of the measures mentioned in their illustrative list, unless they believed that the acronym TRIM's as defined in Article 1 said it all. Thus it was not specified that mandatory or enforceable investment measures were in the nature of investment permits or permits to import the necessary capital for investment. Nor is it clarified that the advantages of "measures compliance with which is necessary to obtain an advantage", were investment related advantages, such as investment premiums, tax holidays, etc. It is undisputable, however, that the measures

[236] "Working document, Determination of Reference Quantities from 1995 Onward", European Communities, 6 October 1993, VI.E.1, p.3.

themselves, as listed under (a) and (b) of paragraph 1 and under (a), (b), and (c) of paragraph 2 of the illustrative list are trade measures.

4.453 In the light of the above, the EC took the view that it was clear that the only difference between TRIM's and other similar measures prohibited under Articles III and XI of GATT was that the former were linked to the permission to invest or to other government advantages granted in connection with investment. The TRIM's Agreement merely confirmed what was already clear after the Canadian *FIRA* case, namely that measures which were ordinarily contrary to Articles III or XI were not taken out of the ambit of these Articles because they were investment-linked (in other words: investment as such may be outside the GATT and the WTO and be under exclusive national sovereignty, but in so far as investment measures have trade distortive and GATT incompatible consequences, they are not).

4.454 Therefore, the EC argued, trade measures which must be obeyed in order to obtain an investment permit or investment related advantages, were covered by both the TRIM's Agreement and by Articles III or XI of GATT (not by both Articles at the same time, because they were mutually exclusive). It followed from the above that the EC licensing system for bananas set conditions neither for investment as such (permit to invest or to import capital) nor for advantages related to investment (investment premiums, tax holidays, etc.) and could not possibly be contrary to the TRIM's Agreement.

4.455 Moreover, in the EC's opinion, the licensing system was a border measure, and as such not covered by Article III of GATT, and it related to a tariff quota and was not a quantitative restriction under Article XI. As the TRIM's Agreement did not go beyond these two Articles, this was another reason why the EC licensing system for bananas did not come under the TRIM's Agreement. In addition, and without prejudice to the above, there was no necessity for operators to comply, since import licences could be purchased on the market place. Furthermore, the investment measures subjected to the TRIM's Agreement were government measures (e.g. investment permits etc. made conditional on certain trade measures or trade performance goals to be observed by the prospective investor), whereas the Complaining parties' concern was with private investment and the effect that certain trade measures may have thereon. That issue was not covered by either the TRIM's Agreement or GATT in the view of the EC. It could only be covered by an investment agreement.

4.456 Finally, the EC pointed out that, as a matter of fact and without prejudice to what was said above, large firms registered as operators in both Category A and Category B (taking into account the fact that almost all the larger operators are registered in both categories) were vertically integrated to a significant extent prior to the creation of the regime, either through their subsidiary companies or through long-term links with commercial partners.

(iii) activity function licence allocation

4.457 The Complaining parties argued that the activity function rule, under which 43 per cent of the licences were distributed to parties other than primary importers, and the manner in which it was administered, additionally burdened and discriminated against imports from Latin America. By its nature, it increased transaction costs because it distributed licences to parties that did not previously import and who did not have the capacity to do so. The actual importers (those who were engaged in procuring the bananas from overseas) had to link up with particular ripeners or customs clearers ("licence pooling", as the EC admitted), or even invest in ripening facilities, in order not to lose a portion of their entitlement to import in the following year.

(a) <u>licence distribution issues</u>

4.458 The United States noted that according to the EC, the weighting coefficients assigned to each "activity" were based on the type of "risk" taken by the various operators in marketing bananas. The EC had, however, provided no explanation for the specific coefficients applied, any elucidation of "risk" or how any operators other than the primary importers assumed any risk at all. Moreover, the EC Commission had provided little explanation of the meaning of the three activities. Activity (a) appeared to designate the first entity established in the EC which purchased green bananas before they were entered into the customs territory of a member State, shipped them and sold them to others in the Community (for Category B, this function largely designated EC producers and producers' organizations). Activity (b) was in theory meant to designate the entity that cleared the bananas through a member State's customs authority (often following overland transport away from a European seaport) for subsequent sale to a ripener/distributor. However, there had been considerable confusion and disagreement between importers and ripeners as to which entities in the chain of distribution qualified for this function. An entity might for a short period have owned the bananas and released them for "free circulation" in the EC (i.e. cleared customs), but may not in fact have borne the risk of spoilage and loss - in which case both the original importer and this entity might have claimed entitlement to (b) licences for the same bananas. According to the United States, the activity function rule had also given import rights to ripeners that had never before imported bananas (activity (c)). The activity function rule had thus resulted in the further loss of import rights of firms that had imported Latin American bananas into the EC before the implementation of the regime.

4.459 At the establishment of the EC banana regime, an important element that was taken into account in relation to the creation and allocation of quota rent in the tariff quota system was the repercussions it might have on the different operators in the supply chain. In the EC view, to have handed the commercial and financial power associated with the tariff quota import licences to one particular category in the supply chain would have meant giving to such operators extraordinary powers of bargaining over their trading partners in the supply chain, which would have been detrimental to their negotiating ability and, hence, to their businesses. The whole internal EC banana market would have suffered from this unbalanced and potentially anti-competitive situation. Therefore, it was considered necessary, in determining the criteria which operators in the supply chain for bananas would have to meet in order to be considered as "operators" within the meaning of Regulation 1442/93 to: (i) take account of the complex and differing market structure in the member States; (ii) ensure that operators whose specialized business activity depended on access to the tariff quota, enjoyed such access without any disruption to normal trading relations; and (iii) take account of the different commercial burdens and risks taken by different traders in the marketing chain.

4.460 The EC thus explained that under EC Commission Regulation 1442/93, in particular Article 5, the quantities of bananas marketed in the EC by making use of the tariff quota through Category A and Category C licences - which were issued under the authority of Article 19 of Regulation 404/93 and its implementing legislation - should be multiplied by a coefficient, designed to reflect that level of commercial risk taken, depending on the economic activity as referred to in Article 3(1) of the Regulation. In order to be an "operator" in the technical sense, an operator must have performed at least one function in the marketing of bananas. "Marketing" meant placing on the market and did not include the wholesale and retail stages (Article 3.2 of Regulation 1442/93). The different functions could roughly be described as follows:

- activity (a): 57 per cent (primary importers: purchaser of green third-country and/or ACP bananas from the producer or, where applicable, the production, consignment and sale of such products in the EC);
- activity (b): 15 per cent (secondary importers: as owners, the supply and release for free circulation of green bananas and sale with a view to their subsequent marketing); and
- activity (c): 28 per cent (ripeners: as owners, the ripening of green bananas and their marketing within the EC).

4.461 In addition "operators" must have been established in the EC and have traded a minimum of 250 tonnes of bananas in one year of the reference period. The total quantity that any operator could actually import into the EC depended on the application of the above-mentioned coefficients. An operator's entitlement was based on the average volume of his trade in the reference period (for 1993, the years 1989-91, etc.) for each of the functions, multiplied by the weighting factor.

4.462 The EC set out the following, by way of example of how operators' reference quantities were be calculated: A primary importer who imported an average of 1,000 tonnes of bananas over the three year reference period would have a reference quantity of 1,000 x 0.57 = 570 tonnes. An operator ripening 1,000 tonnes on average over the reference period would have a reference quantity of 1,000 x 0.28 = 280 tonnes. For an operator performing the function of a secondary importer in the same circumstances, the reference quantity would be 150 tonnes. And an operator who performed all three functions for an average of 1,000 tonnes of bananas would receive a reference quantity based on his activities in all three categories and thus have 570 tonnes for his activity as a primary importer, plus 150 tonnes as a secondary importer and 280 tonnes for his ripening activities. Thus he would receive a total reference quantity of 1,000 tonnes. The weighting system also implied that primary, secondary importers and ripeners could pool their licences in order to obtain a quantity of bananas on which each of them could perform its functions. One import licence in the supply chain was sufficient to give all links in the chain work in respect of the quantity of bananas covered by that licence.

(b) claims under the GATT

- Article I of GATT

4.463 According to the Complaining parties, the activity function rule was not consistent with Article I of GATT, since the same complexities, constraints and uncertainties were not placed on ACP bananas. Even the EC Commission had acknowledged that this was not the normal way to distribute licences. The normal way was based on the criterion of effective importation. The EC's practices and procedures seemed designed to avoid applying this criterion as much as possible, with the effect that its procedures were more burdensome than necessary to administer the tariff quotas.

4.464 According to Ecuador, Article I of GATT prohibited Members from making a regulatory advantage available to imports from some countries while not making it available to others.[237] The activity function rule violated this principle because it imposed an administrative burden on products based on the origin of the bananas. The marketing and distribution of traditional ACP bananas was not constrained by the activity function rule. Rather, import licences were distributed among operators wishing to import traditional ACP bananas purely on the basis of efficiency and other market forces. These operators were not forced to alter their distribution patterns to conform to the requirements of an artificial marketing chain erected through EC regulations. In contrast, as the Commission itself had conceded, the activity function rule provided "a strong incentive for operators to change their trade patterns in order to maximize their licence allocation, e.g. by ripening bananas for the first time."[238] Because unintegrated operators were unable to import all of their bananas using their own import licences, the importation of third-country bananas was greatly hindered. The activity function rule adversely affected the importation of third-country bananas and thus was inconsistent with the requirements of Article I of GATT.

4.465 According to Guatemala and Honduras, all tariff quota volume entered and distributed by Category A and B firms had arbitrarily to be parcelled 57 per cent to "primary importers," 15 per cent to "secondary importers," and 28 per cent to "ripeners." Prior to Regulation 404/93, two of such activity providers, secondary importers, and ripeners, were merely subordinate agents in the EC distribution chain. Today, under the force of the activity function rule, 43 per cent of tariff quota bananas was assigned to such secondary importers and ripeners, a great many of which did not have the means to handle the commercial needs of tariff quota bananas. In the case of Portugal, a specially authorized derogation from the activity function rules meant that none of the volume entering that country had been allocated to firms that historically engaged in direct purchases from Latin American

[237] See "United States - Denial of Most Favoured Nation Treatment as to Non-Rubber Footwear from Brazil", BISD 39S/128, pp.150-152 (adopted on 19 June 1992).

[238] See "Working Document: Determination of Reference Quantities from 1995 Onward", European Commission, 6 October 1993, VI.E.1.

producers.[239] These activity rules and allowances should be analyzed in juxtaposition with the unencumbered arrangements afforded to EC and traditional ACP bananas, where no middleman was required. The unlimited flexibility given to traditional ACP suppliers to commercialize in ways they best saw fit greatly improved their market competitiveness relative to the complainants' fruit and should be disallowed under Article I:1, the most basic of all GATT non-discrimination rules.

4.466 The EC replied that, as far as Article I:1 was concerned, the source of violation should be found in the fact that the ACP traditional licensing system did not provide for a similar distinction among activity functions and therefore such an advantage, i.e. non-application of activity function should be extended on an MFN basis. In the EC's view, it was hard to understand how a technical device aimed at creating greater equality of treatment for the various types of operators in the EC could be perceived as a disadvantage affecting the bananas imported from any source as compared to the ACP traditional bananas whose better "status" should be extended on an MFN basis. The activity function allocation was another way of dealing with the problem of quota rent resulting from the tariff quota and the licences to allocate these quotas. The aim of the activity function was therefore not to concentrate the economic value related to import licences too much in a few hands, or in one part of the supply chain. Otherwise, the privileged recipients would have received a windfall dose of power and influence over their trading partners in the supply chain, for instance the dependence of independent ripeners on the big, integrated banana trading companies would have grown considerably, while it was already great. It would have meant a further blow to their negotiating ability vis-à-vis these companies, which dominated the banana trade already to a very great extent in large parts of the EC market. It was on this point that most clearly considerations of competition policy entered into the system.

4.467 Such considerations fell entirely outside the ambit of the WTO, however, as was clear from the preparatory discussions for the Singapore Ministerial Conference. It should be recalled that the notions of competitive opportunities that have played a role for quite a long time already in the GATT-system, did not have anything to do with the notions of domestic or EC competition policy, such as they entered into consideration here, when deciding about the desirability of allocating the windfall of economic bargaining power which would have gone automatically with the allocation of import licences. In practice, the activity function allocation reflected the value added to the chain of supply and had no impact at all on the importation of bananas from any source within the EC banana tariff quota. The system of licence pooling was by all means the best example of the neutrality of the activity function allocation in the importation process as a whole. According to the EC, the different reality in the two separate regimes - the ACP traditional and the EC tariff quota - justified the implementation of different policies partly due to different administrative and practical needs. The absence of an activity function allocation in the ACP traditional allocation could not be regarded as an "advantage, favour, privilege or immunity granted to [the] product" and hence Article I:1 of GATT was not applicable (nor violated) by it.

4.468 As discussed above, the Complaining parties argued that the discrimination and extraordinary burdens could not be justified by the EC's assertion that these licensing rules were "not uncommon" or that "they respond to the specific needs of the tariff quota." The only specific need identified by the EC was a highly dubious explanation that the Category B licence criteria and the activity functions were driven by competition concerns - because the Latin American banana sector was alleged to be uniquely characterized by "oligopoly or even monopoly." As set out earlier, competition concerns were not a legitimate justification for two reasons: (i) competition concerns with respect to individual companies were more appropriately dealt with through competition laws and enforcement, which the EC had not been hesitant to use against multinationals in the past - the EC had provided no explanation, in the view of the Complaining parties, for why its competition laws were not adequate to whatever task it claimed to have been trying to accomplish with the licensing regime; and (ii) the claim was obviously a *post hoc* rationalization that provided no basis or factual support for burdening imports of Latin American bananas. The Complaining parties further argued that if the EC did have a genuine interest in improving competition for bananas and other products, it could best achieve that by creating a large and open

[239] Regulation 1442/93, Article 3.1.

market in which competitive forces were allowed to prevail. Instead, it had not only distorted the market in favour of companies that had previously operated in a non-competitive market, it had encouraged market concentration. A system of activity functions did not increase competition or reduce marketing margins, as alleged by the EC. As long as the tariff quota's over-quota rate was prohibitive, the overall price level in the EC market was determined by EC demand (i.e. supply was fixed by the tariff quota, and only the quantity demanded could vary.) This price was above competitive market-clearing levels. If the internal allocation of the tariff quota reduced supply below the tariff quota level (i.e. the tariff quota was not fully utilized) the price was further increased and competition was reduced. By allocating rights to the tariff quota through the activity function system, the EC was creating such an inefficient system that the licence recipients were not able to market the entire tariff quota. The activity function was inefficient because it: (i) allocated rights to EC farmers - who, even the EC recognized, had no interest in importing bananas; (ii) gave rights to EC ripeners, which included hundreds of small entities dispersed throughout the EC and which had almost no prior record of purchasing bananas at source; and (iii) employed vague definitions that invited over-filing and double-counting, to which the EC responded by applying draconian reduction coefficients, further exacerbating importers' uncertainty regarding their actual licence entitlements.

4.469 According to the Complaining parties, the activity function rule was a political compromise between the EC member States, some of which wanted all licences to be issued to primary importers, others of which wanted all licences to be provided to ripeners, and still others of which proposed various formulae in between (for example, Belgium and the Netherlands had an interest in their distribution to primary importers because a large proportion of the EC's banana imports entered through Antwerp or Rotterdam). The final distribution among the activities most resembled the French proposal. The practical result of the application of the EC's activity function rule was to encourage vertical integration. Primary importers had addressed the problem by investing in ripening facilities, while both ripeners and primary importers had rushed to perform the customs clearance function in the individual member States so as to obtain future licence entitlement rights with respect to the (b) activity function.

4.470 The EC, in response to a question asked by the Panel, noted that it had stated that legitimate competition concerns played a role in fashioning the licensing system, but also made clear that these concerns were largely of a negative nature, namely averting that the quota rent which inevitably resulted from the creation of a tariff quota with import licences allocated to different exporting countries would exclusively, or to a very large extent, end up in the hands of those who already had a strong position on the import market, namely the big oligopolistic multinationals. The German market had already seen an abuse of dominant position by one firm vis-à-vis independent ripeners, in the view of the EC. This was a consequence of the structure of the import market for bananas - a small number of primary importers dealing with a large number of smaller ripeners. Economic theory demonstrated that in such a situation the powerful few tended to act as price-makers dictating terms to the large number of smaller dispersed firms. Giving or leaving all the licences for the tariff quota in the hands of these few big companies would have exacerbated the situation, giving more market power to the big companies and worsening the situation of the independent ripeners. It was a legitimate competition concern of the EC Council to prevent such incidental consequences of creating a licensing system. Article 42 of the EC Treaty gave the Council the power within the framework of Article 43 EC Treaty to include such competition concerns in its overall set-up of a common organization of the market for a specific agricultural product, in this case bananas.

4.471 A good example of the implicit competition aspects of Regulations based on Article 43 was the frequent stimulus given to the establishment of producers' organizations. This was apparent also in Regulation 404/93, in particular the fifth preambular paragraph. Other concerns of a competition nature featured in the 10th preambular paragraph ("maintaining traditional trade patterns as far as possible") and in the 14th preambular paragraph (not disrupting existing commercial links, while at the same time allowing some development of marketing structures). Similar concerns about not disrupting the relations between the various actors in the marketing chain were to be found in the second preambular paragraph of Regulation 1442/93 imply that competition issues and the distribution of quota rent were taken into account

- Article III of GATT

4.472 Guatemala and Honduras considered that the stipulation that tariff quota suppliers sell and distribute solely through those entities that satisfied the prescribed activity descriptions and allotments, such as ripeners - while authorizing EC suppliers to sell throughout the distribution chain to any entity of their preference, without going through, for example, designated ripeners - similarly constituted illegal discrimination under the edict of Article III:4 of GATT that the sale and distribution of imports be accorded "treatment no less favourable" than that accorded to domestic goods.

4.473 With reference to the argument that the activity function allocation "tilt(s) competitive opportunities in favour of domestic goods" because "foreign goods are required to be sold through middlemen, while domestic goods are not" and therefore the system allegedly violated Article III:4, the EC submitted that the absence of any evidence supporting such allegations coupled with the total misrepresentation of the system should deprive the allegation of any credit. It would certainly be interesting to know, in the EC's opinion, how the Complaining parties intended to sell (and to whom) green bananas without submitting them to a ripening process, and if they could expose to the other parties and the Panel any evidence showing that EC bananas were sold directly without any need of submitting them to a ripening process. It would also be interesting to know how the Complaining parties arrived at the conclusion that the "middlemen" were of a different nationality from the one of origin of the imported bananas and how it would be possible to submit EC bananas to import procedures while maintaining their character of EC domestic products. It sufficed, in the EC's opinion, that no serious allegation or evidence had been presented of a breach of Article III:4.

- Article X:3 of GATT

4.474 Ecuador recalled that Article X:3(a) of GATT required that a Member to "administer in a uniform impartial and reasonable manner all its laws, regulations, decisions and rulings ... ." and argued that this requirement had been interpreted to mean that Members could not permit, "in the treatment accorded to imported goods, discrimination based on country or origin, nor ... the application of one set of regulations and procedures with respect to some contracting parties and a different set with respect to others."[240] According to Ecuador, the activity function rule violated these principles because it applied only to imports of third-country and non-traditional ACP bananas and not to imports of traditional ACP bananas. The discrimination against third-country banana imports was thus a *prima facie* violation of Article X.

4.475 Guatemala and Honduras submitted that for comparable reasons as set out above, the source-differentiation in import distribution rules effectuated by activity functions disrespected Article X's instruction that Members administer regulations in a "uniform, impartial and reasonable manner." The Director-General's Note interpreted Article X to disallow one set of restrictive regulations applied to certain sources when a different set applied to others. The source-differentiation rules fell squarely within this prohibition and, accordingly, should be terminated.

4.476 Mexico considered that the activity function provisions also violated Article X:3(a) of GATT, because they applied exclusively to imports from non-ACP countries under the tariff quota, whereas imports originating from traditional ACP countries were not subject to a similar limitation.

4.477 The EC submitted that as far as Article X was concerned, the Complaining parties claimed a violation of paragraph 3(a), asserting that activity function allocation did not comply with the obligation of administering the internal regulations and laws in an "uniform, impartial and reasonable manner": this was all caused, in their opinion, by the so-called disparity of treatment between "sources". Nothing more was understandable from the claims which, in the EC's view, lacked in proof and clarity and did not go beyond the expression of an

---

[240] See Note by Director-General, 29 November 1968, L/3149; see also reference to this passage in Dessert Apples, para. 6.5.

uncircumstantiated statement. The EC maintained that the activity function allocation complied totally with Article X because within the EC banana tariff quota, the uniform, impartial and reasonable application of these rules was ensured by the competent authorities.

• Article XIII of GATT

4.478 Guatemala and Honduras further submitted that the legal standard of Article XIII:1 of GATT that import licensing restrictions could be applied only if "the importation of the like product of all third countries ... is similarly ... restricted" had been violated by the application of activity function licensing rules to only certain foreign origins. As noted above, Guatemalan, Honduran and other tariff quota suppliers had to enter their bananas through minutely-prescribed firms that were arbitrarily defined on the basis, inter alia, of "activities" performed. Many of these activity providers were not previously engaged, or competitive, in the actual importation and distribution of tariff quota bananas. Traditional ACP suppliers had been given full exemption from like import restrictions; they were free to enter their bananas through any enterprise of their preference, regardless of the activities that enterprise might have previously performed. Such import licensing discrimination against the Complaining parties could not be said to fulfil the Article XIII:1 principle expressed above.

4.479 The EC submitted that the Complaining parties were mistaking the application of the principle of non-discrimination between two separate and independent regimes under Article I:1 of GATT and the principle of non-discrimination in the administration of a given tariff quota under Articles XIII:1 and XIII:5. The allegations pertained fully to the first provision (that had already been examined) and not at all to the second. As no violation of Article XIII:1 was thus demonstrated, the EC rejected the claim. In any event, the EC argued that the activity function allocation of licences did not distort in any way and under any circumstance the importation of bananas of whichever origin: no evidence could be shown and had been shown by the Complaining parties that each share of the tariff quota that had been allocated to specific countries or to "others" was prevented from being fully utilized by the existence of the activity function allocation of the import licences: the activity function allocation had no impact on the importation of the bananas (the "product" referred to in Article XIII). No violation of Article XIII could be raised in this respect.

4.480 As discussed above, the Complaining parties responded that Article XIII:1 prohibited the application of a restriction to products of one Member that was not also applied to products of other countries. Although the EC insisted that the regime for administering the tariff quota was entirely separate, Regulation 404/93 only created one regime, not two. Regardless of how many regimes might be at issue, however, Article XIII of GATT still required that imports from all sources be similarly restricted.

4.481 The EC recalled in response to a question by the Panel concerning another claim that the tariff quota on bananas was not a restrictive measure: there were no restrictions imposed on imports and Members could import as many bananas as they wished into the EC market.

(c) claims under the Licensing Agreement

• Article 1.2 of the Licensing Agreement

4.482 Mexico argued that the provisions on activity functions, by violating Article X of GATT, also violated Article 1.2 of the Licensing Agreement.

4.483 Ecuador argued that activity functions were not only inequitable, they intensified the trade distortion already inherent in the system by depriving operators of a portion of their legitimate licence entitlement. The scheme was therefore in direct conflict with Article 1.2 (and Article 1.3) of the Licensing Agreement.

4.484 The EC recalled the issue of principle concerning the applicability of the Licensing Agreement to tariff quotas. In any event, the EC submitted it had shown no violations of GATT provisions existed; thus Article 1.2 of the Licensing Agreement was not violated. Further, as discussed above, the licensing system must serve the sole purpose of rendering the commitments under the schedules effective by allowing an organized access (in case of quotas) or an organized application of duties (in case of tariff quotas). Those commitments did not include either operators rights or importers commercial positions or interests on a certain market. The EC never committed under the GATT to the maintenance (or improvement) of commercial positions on its market of any specific company or operator, whichever its place of establishment or type of activity.

- Article 1.3 of the Licensing Agreement

4.485 Ecuador argued that the activity function allocation was inconsistent with the principles in Article 1.3 of the Licensing Agreement. The EC had stated that, in formulating the activity function rule, it was:

> guided by the principle whereby the licences must be granted to natural or legal persons who have undertaken the commercial risk of marketing bananas and by the necessity of avoiding disturbing normal trading relations between persons occupying different points in the marketing chain.[241]

However, the EC had not provided any definition of the term "commercial risk," nor had it explained how commercial risk was calculated for purposes of allocating licences among the three activity functions. In fact, it was unclear how much of the commercial risk was ever borne by secondary importers, whose task involved the largely administrative function of clearing the bananas through customs, and ripeners, who merely ripened the bananas for sale to retailers. Moreover, the actual investment of resources needed to perform the secondary importer or ripener functions was relatively minor compared to the investment required to perform the primary importer function. In any case, regardless of the commercial risk borne by the various operators, it was unclear why operators such as ripeners, which never before had imported third-country bananas, should have been allocated a substantial portion of the licences to import such bananas. In summary, far from "avoiding disturbing normal trading relations," the activity function allocation appeared to have fundamentally restructured the marketing chain.

4.486 Guatemala and Honduras submitted that, similar to category allocations, the source-specific application of activity function rules ran counter to the companion provision of Article 1.3 of the Licensing Agreement that licensing procedures be practised in a "neutral," "fair and equitable" manner. The requirements that the Complaining parties wedge their trade flow through specific activity providers that were otherwise unsuited in the pre-Regulation 404/93 market to enter and distribute such product, and that the Complaining parties did so in arbitrarily dictated quantities - while liberating EC and traditional ACP bananas from all such requirements - failed any possible standard of neutrality, fairness, and equity.

4.487 Mexico argued that the application of the activity function provisions of the EC's licensing scheme obliged Category A and B operators to buy import licences from ripeners (or otherwise to establish their own ripening installation) in order to maintain their percentage share in the tariff quota. These provisions were contrary to Article 1.3 of the Licensing Agreement, since they did not result in a just and fair administration of the procedures. Imports from ACP countries entered free from the activity function requirements which were applied only to imports originating in third countries, including Latin American countries.

4.488 The Complaining parties argued that the activity function rule, under which 43 per cent of licences were distributed to parties other than primary importers, and the manner in which it was administered, additionally burdened and discriminated against imports from Latin America. By its nature, it increased transaction costs because it distributed licences to parties that did not previously import and who did not have the capacity to do so. The actual importers (those who were engaged in procuring the bananas from overseas) had to link up with

[241] "Report on the EC Banana Regime", European Commission, July 1994, pp.10-11.

particular ripeners or customs clearers ("licence pooling", as the EC admitted), or even invest in ripening facilities, in order not to lose a portion of their entitlement to import in the following year as detailed elsewhere. This rule also created continued uncertainty as to the quantities that individuals would be permitted to import from Latin America. This practice was not equitable, as required by the Licensing Agreement, nor was it neutral.

4.489 The EC replied that the activity function allocation was applied in a neutral way, since no distinction of any sort, related to the origin of the bananas, was applied within the EC tariff quota. The activity function allocation was also administered in a fair and equitable manner because the coefficients of allocation were applied in an objective, statistical way with no reference, within the tariff quota, to the origin of the bananas.

4.490 The Complaining parties replied that the peculiar activity allocations of Regulation 1442 could not be explained or justified as neutral, equitable or objective. They represented an artificial allocation unconnected to import shares that would prevail in a free market. The obvious way to distribute import licences was on the basis of historical imports, with such imports easily ascertained by records. A Member that chose instead criteria that were not measurable or publicly verifiable, as had the EC here, should bear a heavier burden of showing that such procedures met the requirements of Article 1.3 of the Licensing Agreement.

- Article 3.2 of the Licensing Agreement

4.491 Ecuador, referring to the provisions of Article 3.2 of the Licensing Agreement, claimed that the activity function rule was not "absolutely necessary" to administer the third-country tariff quota. The activity function rule was, in the opinion of Ecuador, merely a means for further hindering the access of third-country bananas to the EC market. Moreover, Ecuador argued, the EC had at its disposal less trade distortive means for implementing a tariff quota. For example, in administering the allocations for traditional ACP bananas, the EC did not allocate import licences among categories of operators according to their activity function. In fact, the import licensing regime for third-country bananas was the only EC regime that distributed licences on the basis of "activity functions." The activity function allocation significantly distorted trade and could not be justified as necessary to implement the tariff quota. The scheme therefore directly conflicted with Article 3.2.

4.492 Guatemala and Honduras submitted that like the category allocation measures, activity function allocations - whether evaluated on a self-standing or relative basis - had "trade-restrictive [and] -distortive" consequences well beyond those arising out of the tariff quota volume limitation, rendering them illegal under Article 3.2 of the Licensing Agreement. Activity function allocations forced Guatemala and Honduras to use import and distribution agents that history had shown were not otherwise capable of commanding such services. The volumes to be directed through such agents were arbitrarily and inefficiently dictated, eliminating any possibility for economies of scale in the marketing of the Complainants' fruit. This led to adverse price consequences that dampened EC demand for the Complainants' bananas. No such ill effects had been forced upon EC and ACP suppliers, which could sell and distribute through any entity, with wide open economies of scale and no price distortion, significantly enhancing the marketing desirability of bananas from EC and ACP sources. Article 3.2 could not, in the opinion of Guatemala and Honduras, be read to permit licensing-specific trade restrictions and distortions of this kind.

4.493 The United States argued that under the activity function rule, historical importers had to incur costs additional to those flowing from the restriction simply to stay in business: to avoid losing up to 43 per cent of their business in the future, they had to purchase licences, enter into constraining marketing agreements with specific ripeners or even buy ripening facilities. The administration of the activity function rule resulted in continuous uncertainty as to the quantity an importer could hope to enter, since annual entitlements were only provisional and not finalized until well into the import year (usually the third quarter, following audits and reduction coefficients applied as a result of competing claims). In combination with other licensing measures, these unusual licensing requirements dramatically curtailed purchase, delivery and marketing flexibility for distributors of third-country bananas.

4.494 The United States argued that the EC had effectively conceded that the activity function rule had made its import procedures more administratively burdensome than necessary. Acknowledging that the rule had caused the banana trade to engage in "extremely complex" practices merely to stay in business, the EC Commission had in 1995 offered a proposal to change the scheme to one that was "simpler and more transparent" and allocated, "as is traditional in matters of trade, on the criterion of effective importation".

4.495 Further, the United States believed that these numerous layers of administrative complexity could hardly be "absolutely necessary" to administer a quantitative limitation. In the first instance, the EC requirements for the Latin American tariff quota imports went beyond what was needed to administer imports of bananas subject to quantitative limitations, since a parallel import licensing system (for traditional ACP bananas) was a model of simplicity without any of the complex features applied to imports under the third-country tariff quota. ACP import licences were granted upon presentation of a certificate of origin, with a single reduction coefficient applied to all applicants if there was an over-subscription. As a historical matter, Regulation 404/93 did not itself require the distribution of licences on the basis of activity functions. This feature was added by the EC Commission a few months later. The distribution of 43 per cent of import licences in Category A to entities, the vast majority of which had no practical experience in purchasing bananas abroad, could only be a hindrance, not a help, in administering the tariff quota. It could hardly be a feature that was "absolutely necessary" to administer imports.

4.496 The EC noted that Article 3.2 of the Licensing Agreement indicated, first, that a licensing regime should not "have trade -restrictive or -distortive effects on imports additional to those caused by the imposition of the restriction". No complaining party had proven that the activity function allocation distorted or restricted importation of bananas into the EC from any source beyond the effects of the legitimate EC banana tariff quota for the simple reason that, in the opinion of the EC, such effects did not exist and bananas, including Latin American bananas, entered the EC unhindered.

4.497 The EC further argued that Article 3.2 stated that non-automatic licensing procedures should not be more administratively burdensome than absolutely necessary to administer the measure. Coherently with what had been already indicated above when analysing this same Article about other aspects of the EC regime, the EC reiterated that the burdensome nature of the non-automatic licensing procedure had to be appreciated with respect to the operator at the moment of the importation of the bananas under the EC banana tariff quota. The asserted complexities of the activity function allocation were borne to a very large extent by the competent authorities of the member States of the EC which calculated the coefficients and applied the EC rules. What remained for the operators themselves was little indeed, and corresponded to the minimum absolutely necessary for the system to function correctly.

4.498 As discussed above, the EC was of the opinion that the legislation on competition was simply not relevant in the present case because the GATT was concerned with trade in goods (or even, in particular circumstances, competitive opportunities concerning those goods on a specific market, after the goods had cleared customs) but not with the operators' rights trading those goods. Furthermore, when the banana regime entered into force, only operators already active in the marketing supply chain were eligible to receive licences (apart from the 3.5 per cent of the tariff quota which was reserved for newcomers). Thus, importers and ripeners who had existing commercial and/or contractual arrangements, both received licences for a proportion of the bananas they had handled. A licence was only required once in order for the fruit to benefit from the bound duty under the tariff quota while clearing customs, and thus it was not necessary for both the importer and the ripener to hold a licence for a particular consignment. Since licences were distributed in proportion to existing trade, if the same commercial relationships continued, then those enterprises which already cooperated commercially would be able to handle the quantity of bananas represented by the sum total of their licences ("licence pooling"). This required no change in existing commercial relationships or practice. In the view of the EC, the regime did not oblige operators to maintain existing relationships *ad infinitum*. If operators choose to engage in new commercial relationships, it was incumbent upon them to ensure that one or other of the parties would be entitled to the necessary licence required to clear customs under the existing terms of the EC tariff quota. This was not a situation specific to banana trade, since it was an obligation which existed with regard to importing any product for which there was a tariff quota and an import licence regime.

4.499 The Complaining parties responded that the EC licensing regime amounted to a non-tariff barrier beyond the restriction caused by volume limitations. Operators seeking to import under the tariff quota needed continuously to purchase licences, enter into marketing agreements with specific ripeners or invest in ripening facilities merely to avoid the licence erosion created by the administration of the regime, i.e. merely to maintain the same business as previously. In combination with other licensing measures, these elements (i.e. reduced operator flexibility, uncertainty and source-based linkages) acted as a non-tariff barrier that restricted and distorted the importation of third-country bananas beyond what might be expected from the mere operation of a tariff quota, in violation of Article 3.2 of the Licensing Agreement.

4.500 The Complaining parties continued that the EC sought to satisfy its burden of explaining its discriminatory and burdensome regime by urging an unduly narrow reading of the Licensing Agreement to cover only licensing "procedures". With respect to activity functions, the EC had acknowledged that primary importers, secondary importers and ripeners often had to "pool their licences" to avoid loss of import entitlement. This "pooling" procedure was an excessive, perhaps even unprecedented, administrative burden to impose upon licensees, placing it well within the coverage of Article 3.2. Moreover, the record-keeping requirements needed to establish eligibility under the changing administration of the activity function rule were severe in themselves. The associated procedures were hardly minimally burdensome or "absolutely necessary" to administer the tariff quota.

4.501 As discussed above, the Complaining parties further argued that the discrimination and extraordinary burdens could not be justified by the EC's assertion that they were "not uncommon" or that "they respond to the specific needs of the tariff quota." The only specific need identified by the EC was a highly dubious explanation that the activity functions were driven by competition concerns - because the Latin American banana sector was alleged to be uniquely characterized by "oligopoly or even monopoly". This was not a legitimate justification in their view.

(d) issues concerning "over-filing" or "double-counting"

4.502 The Complaining parties observed that, because of competing claims for the same third-country banana imports, the total reference quantities accepted by the Commission for each of the marketing years since the introduction of the Community-wide regime had substantially exceeded, by a significant and growing amount, actual banana imports during the relevant reference period. The following table[242] showed the magnitude of the "over-filing" of reference quantities:

Licence allocation year	Reference period	Weighted per cent of over-filing
1993	1989-1991	13.9%
1994	1990-1992	14.7%
1995	1991-1993	18.3%
1996	1992-1994	28.6%

This over-filing was attributable, the Complaining parties argued, to confusion arising out of the "primary importer," "secondary importer" and "ripener" definitions, the lack of a publicly verifiable control point (such as

[242] Sources: European Community Banana Traders Association and Eurostat. Figures for 1996 were provisional.

customs clearance) and the lack of adequate controls by the EC Commission. The EC Commission had used two methods to address over-filing. First, the Commission instructed the particular member State to verify the legitimacy of claimed reference quantities by particular companies. It appeared that larger importers had received most of the audit attention. Second, after those audits were completed, normally mid-year (in time for the fourth quarter), it applied across-the-board reduction coefficients (reflected in the above table) to all individual operator reference quantities. The Commission applied these large reduction coefficients regardless of whether an operator's quantities had been certified as accurate in, or reduced as a result of, an audit. The system provided an incentive to operators to over-file by a percentage in excess of the projected annual reduction coefficient, thus enabling them to gain import rights to which they had no legitimate entitlement.

4.503 The Complaining parties considered that the EC's way of addressing over-filing - by applying a uniform reduction coefficient - was inequitable with respect to operators that had already been audited.[243] On top of these constraints, the EC Commission was unwilling to address the endemic over-filing for licences by many of the companies, a phenomenon due largely to its own confusing definitions. Instead the EC had continued to diminish eligibility for licences by applying an equal reduction coefficient that reflected these over-bids - even for operators whose quantities had already been reduced or deemed correct after audits. Over time, an operator importing from Latin America and making accurate declarations would lose licence rights. This rule also created continued uncertainty as to the quantities that individuals would be permitted to import from Latin America. This practice was not equitable, in the opinion of the Complaining parties, as required by the Licensing Agreement, nor was it neutral.

4.504 The United States submitted a graph to show that an operator making accurate declarations in the context of continued EC Commission reliance on inaccurate reference quantities would over time lose licence rights. These elements were inconsistent with the fundamental obligation in Article 1.3 of the Licensing Agreement that "rules for import licensing procedures ... be ... administered in a fair and equitable manner." For the same reason, the operation of the activity function was also inconsistent with the requirement under Article 1.3 that such rules be "neutral".

4.505 Ecuador argued that the EC's practice of auditing selected companies, and the penalization of operators through the application of a uniform reduction coefficient violated the principles set out in Articles 1.2 and 1.3 of the Licensing Agreement. The trade distortive effects of the activity function rules were intensified by the problem of "double counting" which arose through the practical application of the rule. Ecuador considered that the definitions of the various activity functions set out in the regulation were vague and had become even more confused by the promulgation of internal working documents from the Commission which provided additional guidelines for applying the activity function rule. The practical effect of the ambiguity in the definitions was that different operators claimed credit for marketing the same bananas. Because the operators' historical import levels were thus artificially inflated, the operators applied for more import licences than they were legitimately entitled to. Additional over-filing could also occur as a result of fraud.

4.506 Ecuador further said that the EC had attempted to reduce this problem by: (i) auditing the applications for licences in order to verify the claims made; and (ii) applying a reduction coefficient. Each of these measures, however, had been applied in a discriminatory manner to the detriment of operators involved in the importation and marketing of third-country bananas. According to Article 8 of Regulation 1442/93, "[t]he competent authorities shall conduct all necessary checks to verify the validity of applications and supporting documents submitted by operators ...". The authorities' auditing efforts were generally focused on the larger operators. These larger firms tended to be primary importers, many of which were non-EC owned firms such as Noboa. The

---

[243] The Complaining parties noted that this reduction coefficient differed from the rare reduction coefficients applied to some ACP imports in cases that country-specific allocations were exceeded since import eligibility was not based on records of historical shipments and involved no auditing. The effective rate of reduction for operators that have already been audited was much greater than the reduction for non-audited, inaccurate entitlement claims.

smaller firms, consisting mainly of ripeners and secondary importers, were usually EC-owned and were, according to Ecuador, generally not audited. The adverse discriminatory impact on non-EC entities was intensified by the fact that after the EC had conducted the audits to determine the average amount of over-filing, the EC fixed a uniform reduction coefficient for each category of operator. According to Regulation 1442/63, Article 6:

> Depending on the annual tariff quota and the total reference quantities of importers as referred to in Article 5, the Commission shall fix, where appropriate, a single reduction coefficient for each category of operators to be applied to operator's reference quantities to determine the quantity to be allocated to each.

Because the reduction coefficients were uniformly applied, the EC could audit a firm and find no evidence of over-filing, but still could impose a reduction coefficient on that firm's entitlement. The reduction coefficient system thus punished large firms which filed proper licence applications. However, it also rewarded smaller firms which tended to over-file on the expectation that they would not be audited.

4.507 Ecuador considered that this system was manifestly unfair on its face. Moreover, it created an enormous incentive for small firms to over-file in order to stay ahead of the uniform reduction coefficient and to obtain licences in excess of their legitimate entitlement. The effect of these uniform reductions was compounded over time since the reduced amounts were entered into the operators' three year rolling average for calculating licence entitlements. Consequently, application of the uniform reduction coefficients unfairly reduced the operator's entitlement in both the current year and in the future. According to Ecuador, this scheme was not only inequitable, but it intensified the trade distortion already inherent in the system by depriving operators of a portion of their legitimate licence entitlement. The scheme in its entirety was therefore in direct conflict with Articles 1.2 and 1.3 of the Licensing Agreement.

4.508 Guatemala and Honduras submitted that one prominent irregularity that even the EC acknowledged to be in need of attention was the widespread practice of over-filing by a percentage in excess of the projected annual reduction coefficient, thus enabling over-filers to gain undeserved import entitlement. That practice had led to substantial, annually increasing reduction coefficients that were applied uniformly, even to volumes that had been thoroughly audited. Because of the lingering, non-transparent nature of this practice, and the continuous, significant transfer of licensing entitlement effectuated by it, Guatemala and Honduras were left year-by-year, and even quarter-by-quarter, uncertain as to the volumes of bananas that had to be quickly reassigned to new EC firms. Guatemala and Honduras considered that this practice violated Articles 1.3 and 3.2 of the Licensing Agreement and Article X of GATT.

4.509 Mexico considered that the provisions concerning the application of auditing and reduction coefficients in the allocation of licences also violated Article 1.3 of the Licensing Agreement, and that their application to non-ACP countries within the tariff quota in particular also constituted a violation of Article 3.2 because it had distorting effects on imports.

4.510 The EC recalled its explanation of the activity function system. It noted that an operator's reference quantity thus calculated was multiplied by a reduction coefficient to determine the amount of the tariff quota to be allocated to that operator. In effect, the reference quantity was an indication of the operator's share of total EC trade in bananas of a particular category, e.g. traditional ACP and EC bananas, tariff quota bananas or non-traditional ACP bananas. An operator would receive an equivalent share, in percentage terms, of the tariff quota. Thus an operator who carried out 5 per cent on average of the trade in bananas in the EC in the reference period would receive 5 per cent of the available part of the tariff quota. The same mechanism was used for determining the quota allocation of both Category A and Category B licences. Category A licence allocation was based on past trade in third-country and non-traditional ACP bananas. Category B licence allocation was based on past trade in EC and traditional ACP fruit. Category C licences (for newcomers) did not have a reference quantity based on past trade; their allocation was dependent on the volume of applications for the portion for newcomers of the tariff quota. In addition, the EC explained that the existence of a reduction coefficient was an inherent part of the system, and not a result of double counting or over-filing. A reduction coefficient was a standard procedure that was universally used in import licensing systems the world over in cases where legitimate requests for licences exceeded the quantity available for distribution. If the aggregate total of reference quantities exceeded the volume available for import under the tariff quota, a reduction coefficient was applied without discrimination to the reference quantity of each operator to determine the operator's annual right to import.

4.511 The EC submitted that the licensing system under for the tariff quota imposed its heaviest burden on the administrations concerned, both of the member States and of the Commission, and this was true in particular for the task of verifying whether the figures transmitted by the member States were correct and could be explained on the basis of the underlying facts and declarations by operators in order to establish the reduction coefficient. In the EC view, it was important to realize that the Commission did not "audit" the operators concerned. The Commission was normally alerted to problems by discrepancies in the figures it received from the member States. The Commission had a number of means at its disposal to discuss these problems with the member States and to make them re-verify the factual data underlying the figures they had transmitted to the Commission. The first possibility was to discuss these problems in the Management Committee for bananas. During one particular period (July-December 1993) this Committee met 10 times, the EC continued, in order to discuss information which the Commission was requesting: the actual amount of reference quantities, the problem of double counting, the problem of certain operators registering in two different member States for the same function, the interpretation of Article 3(1)b of Regulation 1442/93 and the need for the member States to verify their figures submitted. At the occasion of such Committee meetings, bilateral or trilateral meetings with member States on some of these problems were organized. During the same period, Commission officials visited Germany, the Netherlands, Belgium and Italy. On the basis of all these activities the Commission was able to revise the aggregate reference quantities. Such revisions were made on the basis of information made available to the Commission by the member States and corrections were not made *a priori* and without fresh information to justify the correction made. Thus the Commission had not been collating and checking statistics relating to particular operators to achieve an aggregate national figure. The reverse process was followed: the Commission required that the national authorities re-examined their aggregate statistics and, if there were anomalies, worked back through the figures and proofs of particular undertakings. Only when that was done and errors and double-counting were identified were revisions in the numbers of the member States made.

4.512 This method of "working backward" with the help of national authorities ensured that "auditing" was not being used to "get at" or "to clear" a specific category of firms *a priori*. Cases in which anomalies in the figures showed that there might be double-counting or false claims may have led the national authorities back to certain firms.[244] The EC thus considered that the activity function allocation was administered in a fair and equitable manner because the coefficients of allocation were applied in an objective, statistical way with no reference, within the tariff quota, to the origin of the bananas.

4.513 The EC further explained that double-counting was a fraudulent practise by which an operator/importer attempted to increase its entitlement to import licences at the expense of the other operators/importers, by putting up reference quantities. When evidence of overfiling and double-counting were gathered by the competent authorities, they could decide to go ahead with an auditing procedure. As the name indicated, it was an enforcement action by which the competent authorities (of the member States of the EC) verified the correctness of the operator's behaviour, vis-à-vis, the customs and administrative authorities of that EC member State by examining their internal business documentation. No specific paperwork was requested by the EC from operators with respect to auditing procedures. The proof that such a procedure was needed, the EC submitted, was demonstrated by the case of the major Ecuadorian firm, where investigation of these documents showed that incorrect claims for reference quantities had been submitted. The claims had in fact been inflated by almost 20 per cent. Another case, which highlighted the necessity of establishing procedures permitting an in-depth analysis of

[244] This showed, the EC submitted, that the Ecuadorian allegations about selective auditing were groundless.

particular declarations, was that of one of the United States multi-nationals that consistently claimed to have supplied to one EC member State almost 50 per cent more bananas than that country's entire consumption. It should be stressed, the EC said, that a complete audit of any firm's operations had never been undertaken. Auditing was restricted to specific statistics concerning individually identified claims, contracts or transactions where double-counting or other incorrect declarations were suspected. A reduction coefficient was a totally different issue to double-counting. The application of a reduction coefficient was standard procedure that was universally used in import licensing systems the world over in cases where requests for licences exceeded the quantity available for distribution. The reduction coefficient was applied, without discrimination, to the reference quantity of each operator to determine the annual right to import. The reference quantity of a specific operator was adjusted only when over-filing had been identified.

4.514 The Complaining parties took issue with the EC's contention that the application of reduction coefficients was necessary solely because total historical imports were greater than the tariff quota. The EC had confused the issue of reduction coefficients. While it was true that a reduction coefficient was applied in customs practice where there were competing applications not based on historic entitlement, and that in this particular regime, the historic entitlements of all operators had been reduced equally in proportion to the initial reduction in access resulting from the application of the tariff quota, it was evident that with respect to a licence-holder making accurate declarations, the reduction coefficient was much greater than that which would apply simply because overall access to the EC market had been reduced. In fact, the reduction coefficients were necessary primarily to accommodate the extensive over-filing by the industry. As a simple example, the tariff quota in 1994 was 14 per cent lower than actual imports in 1992 (one of the reference years for the 1994 entitlement calculation). In addition to this difference between the tariff quota and imports during the reference year, the total of filed Category A reference volumes in 1992 was 24 per cent higher than the Category A allocation of the reduced tariff quota. The total loss to the Category A operators from these two factors alone was therefore 38 per cent. The Complaining parties further argued that it was the EC's confusing and imprecise definitions of "activities" that encouraged over-filing. Companies were either uncertain due to the ambiguities, or they recognized the EC would apply a reduction coefficient, so they "bid-ahead" and over-filed. Over-filing had been getting worse every year since 1993. The only disincentive provided by the EC system (except in cases of fraud) was with respect to honest operators who were audited and were still subject to an ever-increasing reduction coefficient. The EC created this problem -and even the Commission recognized it is a problem since it had proposed changing it - when it created this highly complicated system that allocated licences to various entities along the distribution chain, who were bound to compete against each other, instead of allocating licences in the logical and traditional way, which was to importers.

4.515 Ecuador considered that with respect to double-counting, every Ecuadorian company complied with the rules established by EC Regulation 1442/93, a fact that had been accepted by the competent authorities of the EC member States who had oversight of the actual shipments. The problem of incorrect claims cited by the EC arose when the EC Commission, instead of issuing licences to Ecuadorian companies, wrongly provided to European companies licences to import Ecuadorian bananas on the basis of an unpublished internal interpretive note (Ecuador added that the failure to publish this note also contravened Article X of GATT).

(iv) export certificates

4.516 The Complaining parties noted that the EC had taken the exceptional step of authorizing a select group of supplying countries to couple export licences with import licences in order to confer, in the EC's own words, "economic benefits" to those countries. In addition to presenting violations flowing from the fact that Category B operators were exempt from the export certificate requirement (see discussion above), the Complaining parties considered the requirement was a straight-forward violation of GATT and the Licensing Agreement.

4.517 The EC responded that Article 6 of the BFA concerning the possibility of BFA countries to deliver export certificates was introduced into the EC legislation through Article 3(2) of Commission Regulation 478/95. The EC implemented this further procedural step in the licensing system, that concerned only bananas originating in Colombia, Costa Rica and Nicaragua and which constituted an extra procedural burden for the exportation of the bananas from those countries, on specific demand by those countries. They had justified their request on the basis of internal needs concerning a better control of the export process of their domestic banana production. The EC had not had any reason to refuse such a request, a request that could be accorded to any other country which would manifest any specific need in this respect.

(a) claims under the GATT

- Article I:1 of GATT

4.518 The Complaining parties argued that the export licensing requirements of Regulation 478/95 violated the Article I:1 obligation that, "with respect to all rules and formalities in connection with importation ... any advantage ... granted by any contracting party" to products originating in one country had to be immediately and unconditionally accorded all others. The discriminatory advantages conferred by these export licensing rules were, in the opinion of the Complaining parties, obvious. As the EC best described it, the rules helped BFA countries, and no others, "share in the economic benefits of the tariff quota."[245] They did this by according export licence-holders in BFA countries bargaining leverage to extract a share of the quota rent for their fruit exported to the EC.

4.519 Guatemala and Honduras submitted that since 1995, selective tariff quota supplying countries -Costa Rica, Colombia and Nicaragua - had been permitted under Regulation 478/95 to issue export licences, which licences had to be obtained by Category A and C operators and coupled with import licences in order for bananas to enter the EC from those sources. Because preferential tariff quota volume shares had been laid down for those sources, Category A and C operators had no choice but to secure such export licences or risk rendering unusable significant portions of their import licensing entitlement. The requirement had, thus, given rise to the active purchase of export licences from these sources by Category A and C operators, the going price for which was now approximately $2.50 a box. As the EC itself had explained, the export licence authority thereby conferred on select sources covered by it a commercial advantage by helping such supplying countries "share in the economic benefits of the tariff quota."[246] Those economic benefits, like the benefits derived from preferential tariff quota allocations, were only granted by the EC on the condition that BFA recipients acquiesced to the provisions of Regulation 404/93 *et seq.* Such discriminatory application of export licensing authority was inconsistent with the most-favoured-nation provisions of Article I:1 of GATT. Costa Rica, Colombia and Nicaragua were being accorded a regulatory advantage that enabled them to share in the economic benefits of the tariff quota, while the Complaining parties were not.

4.520 It was no answer that Guatemala and Honduras, too, would have been accorded that advantage had they shown an interest in this discriminatory authority. The EC had made clear that the price-tag for such interest was full capitulation to the inconsistencies of the regime. The Complainants had repeatedly refused to buy into those inconsistencies, insisting, instead, on legitimate reforms that were consonant with WTO law. Such reforms could hardly be considered achieved by compounded managed-trade requirements of the sort represented by export licences, which practice inevitably served only to force regional investments into the business of trading licences, not bananas. The Lomé waiver, likewise, was no answer to this discrimination. Selective export licensing requirements were for the exclusive benefit of Costa Rica, Colombia and Nicaragua, countries that were entirely irrelevant to the Lomé Convention. With Article I:1 thereby violated, the export licences selectively mandated by Regulation 478/95 had to be ruled null and void, and deleted from the regime.

---

[245] See "Report on the EC Banana Regime, European Commission" (July 1994), p.12.

[246] Op. cit.

4.521 Mexico argued that the advantages granted to BFA countries, which related to the rent which resulted from the expedition of export certificates, were not granted to non-BFA countries and therefore were a violation of Article I:1 of GATT.

4.522 The United States noted that pursuant to the BFA and as implemented by Regulation 478/95, the EC recognized only those export certificates issued by BFA signatories as prerequisites for importing bananas into the EC. Because the BFA signatories' flexibility to issue such licences amounted to a "privilege" not enjoyed by other Members, it was inconsistent with Article I:1 of GATT.

4.523 According to the EC, the claim that the provisions of Article 3(2) of Commission Regulation 478/95 and the export certificate requirement for the BFA countries violated Article I:1 of the GATT, in so far as the existence of an export certificate enabled only the BFA countries to share in the economic benefits of the tariff quota while the other countries were excluded was unjustified. In order to justify the claim of a violation of Article I:1, it had to be proven, in the opinion of the EC, that the bananas from the BFA countries were receiving from the EC an advantage that was not accorded to the other Members of the WTO. The EC did not see this export certificate as an advantage. According to the EC, the extra procedural step created a situation by which bananas from the BFA countries were receiving licences after countries outside the BFA, i.e. mostly originating in the Complaining parties' countries. The result was that, for instance, Ecuador's, Honduras' and Mexico's parts of the EC tariff quota were very quickly overbooked. This showed clearly, in the opinion of the EC, that no Complaining party's production (or any other Member's production) was discriminated against by the export certificate provisions. Moreover, the banana production of the BFA countries was burdened by an extra procedural step that it was impossible to define as an advantage under Article I:1 of GATT.

4.524 The EC was aware that the administration by the BFA countries of the export certificates could create the possibility of quota rent but only among operators interested in trading in BFA bananas. According to the EC, it was a fact of life that any system of quotas created quota rents. Given that the agricultural sector was being liberalized largely by having recourse to a system of consolidated tariff quotas, there was no doubt that quota rents would play a certain role in the WTO system for some time to come. The GATT contained no rules on the sharing out of quota rents. Any government was entitled to pursue its own policy to distribute those quota rents provided that no discrimination between the products originating in the different Members' territories was created. It was inevitable that in allocating quota rent through a licensing system, in this case export licences, governments would also allocate a limited amount of financial power as between operators. However, on the one side, this phenomenon was not in breach of any WTO rule and, on the other side, did not affect in any sense either the volume of importation of the bananas into the EC market or the banana production and trade of the other countries. The EC was therefore of the opinion that no violation of Article I:1 of GATT was detectable in Article 3(2) of EC Commission Regulation 478/95. The related claims should therefore be rejected.

4.525 The EC rejected the allegation that bananas originating in Ecuador, Guatemala, Honduras and Mexico (the United States did not export bananas) might be affected in their trade with the EC by the imposition to Colombian and Costa Rican bananas of an export certificate necessary to obtain an import licence. Failing such evidence, no violation of any GATT rule could be advanced by the Complaining parties and this issue should be declared irrelevant. The EC was not responsible for the procedures set up by the BFA countries to administer their export certificates. This procedure had nothing to do with that and any eventual (and in the opinion of the EC, non-existent) violation of the GATT by those Members should be addressed by applying the relevant WTO provisions. The fact that not all import licences to import Colombian and Costa Rican bananas under the tariff quota were subject to this extra procedural step (Category B licences were excluded) could not, in the opinion of the EC, constitute a violation of any WTO rule, let alone Article I:1 of GATT. If that was the case, the non-existence of an export certificate for imports from the Complaining parties would also amount to a violation of that principle, meaning that the Complaining parties were benefiting from an advantage not extended on an MFN basis to the BFA countries. This would be an absurd consequence and should be rejected by the Panel.

4.526 The Complaining parties further submitted that the EC had also asserted that because the export licensing provisions caused bananas from BFA origins to be imported following the second round, they constituted a burden, not an advantage. However, the fact that export licences provided an advantageous opportunity would not be offset by any alleged burden. As found by previous panels, "an element of more favourable treatment would only be relevant if it would always accompany and offset an element of differential treatment causing less favourable treatment."[247] Moreover, the two-round system had created a greater burden for non-BFA countries because it permitted wide-spread licences "swapping" as described by Ecuador.

4.527 The Complaining parties considered that the EC had misunderstood the coverage of the GATT. In their opinion, any import rule, if it led to an advantage being conferred to products from one country and not others, was a *per se* infraction of Article I:1. The fact that money transfers might be involved did not diminish the effect of this measure on conditions of competition. The EC's claim that export licences, including the exemption for Category B operators, had had no trade impact was equally irrelevant. Actual trade effects were not relevant to determining conformity with Article I:1.[248]

4.528 The EC reiterated that it did not understand in which way bananas originating from Ecuador, Guatemala, Honduras and Mexico (the US do not export bananas) might be affected in their trade with the EC by the imposition, to Colombian and Costa Rican bananas, of an export certificate to be presented in order to obtain an import licence. Failing evidence, no violation of any GATT rule could be advanced by the Complaining parties and the issue should be declared irrelevant to the present dispute.

- Article X:3 of GATT

4.529 The Complaining parties submitted that since the rules concerning export certificates differed on the basis of the product's country of origin, they were inconsistent with the "uniform, impartial and reasonable" standard of Article X of GATT.

4.530 Guatemala and Honduras argued that the source-differentiation in the EC's export licence rules was outlawed, too, by Article X, which called on Members to administer regulations in a "uniform, impartial and reasonable manner." Two sets of rules applied in this area, one for BFA sources, another for all other tariff quota sources, a practice the 1968 Director-general's Note found to contravene in a direct way the administrative standard laid down in Article X.[249]

4.531 Mexico argued that the requirement of having to have an export certificate from BFA countries in order to import products from those countries constituted a violation of Article X:3(a) of GATT, since a standard was applied for imports of products originating from BFA countries which was different from the standard for imports originating in other countries.

4.532 As discussed above, the EC replied that the position of the Complaining parties was based on numerous flawed legal arguments and should therefore be rejected. Among them: Article X provided only for the procedural rules to be followed in the application of internal rules pertaining to custom's activities, including requirements, restrictions or prohibitions of imports. Furthermore, while rejecting completely any claim suggesting a possible breach of Article X, let alone on the basis of the authority of a note never endorsed by the CONTRACTING PARTIES and taken outside its context, the EC pointed out that Article X applied to laws and rules pertaining to custom activities of a country on exports from that country. In the case at hand, the export certificates were issued

---

[247] Second *Banana* panel, para. 148, citing "United States - Section 337 of the Tariff Act of 1930", adopted 7 November 1989, BISD 36S/345, para. *5.16*.

[248] *Id.*, para. 147.

[249] Note by the Director-General, L/3149 (29 Nov. 1968). See also Dessert Apples, BISD 36S/93, para. 6.5 (adopted 22 June 1989).

by BFA countries while imports from Complaining parties were not subject to the presentation of any export certificate. This affirmed that Article X of GATT was simply not applicable to the subject matter and therefore not violated.

4.533 The EC's argument that Article X related solely to "internal rules" and hence was incompatible with a claim based on Article XIII was, according to the Complaining parties, not supported by the plain language of Article X or panel interpretations of its meaning. As previously discussed, the scope of Article X was obvious from its first paragraph and its title: the Article X:3 obligation was applicable to all "trade regulations". The *Dessert Apples* report also clarified that Article XIII and Article X could apply to the same measure.[250]

4.534 The Complaining parties considered the EC's response - that export certificates were issued by BFA countries and were not required for non-BFA signatories - was a factual assertion that had no bearing on the legal obligation at issue. What was at issue were rules and procedures that conferred a discriminatory commercial advantage, augmented the incentives to purchase ACP and EC bananas, and otherwise disrupted regular marketing cycles. Thus, for the same reasons that Article 1.3 of the Licensing Agreement was breached, so too was Article X of GATT.

- <u>Article XIII:1 of GATT</u>

4.535 The Complaining parties submitted that Article XIII:1 of GATT required that imports from all sources be similarly restricted. A similar restriction was not in place as between BFA and non-BFA countries, because only BFA countries could use export certificates. The difference was material, since export certificates permitted a different allocation of quota rents than might occur without their use. Similarly, ACP countries were not subject to import licences based on any criteria other than possession of a certificate of origin. This requirement permitted producers in those countries to obtain a greater share of quota rents than they would if EC importers of their bananas received licences on the basis of historical shipments. These differences were analogous to the situation in the *Dessert Apples* case, in which the panel found that the EC had violated Article XIII:1 because it had applied an import licensing scheme to Chile, while entering into voluntary restraint agreements with other countries. In both instances, the difference in form amounted to a difference in substance. A voluntary restraint agreement permitted more quota rents to be obtained by the exporting countries, while import licences generally would provide quota rents to importers.[251] Thus, here, as in *Dessert Apples*, imports were being restricted in a different manner depending on origin, inconsistent with Article XIII:1.

4.536 As discussed earlier, the EC argued that the GATT contained no rules on the sharing out of quota rents. Any government was entitled to pursue its own policy to distribute those quota rents provided that no discrimination between the "products" originating in the different Members' territories was created. It was inevitable that in allocating quota rent through a licensing system, in this case export licences, governments would also allocate a limited amount of financial power as between operators. However, on the one side, this phenomenon was not in breach of any WTO rule and, on the other side, did not affect in any sense either the volume of importation of the bananas into the EC market or the banana production and trade of the other countries.

4.537 According to the Complaining parties, Article XIII of GATT still required that imports from all sources be similarly restricted. A similar restriction was not in place as between BFA and non-BFA signatories, since BFA signatories could use export licences and non-BFA signatories could not.

---

[250] Dessert Apples, para. 12.29.

[251] The Complaining parties were not arguing that the GATT provided an absolute right to quota rents. However, if a country permitted one trading partner to obtain more quota rents than another, by differentiated administration of restrictions, it was inconsistent with the non-discrimination requirement.

(b) claims under the Licensing Agreement

• Article 1.3 of the Licensing Agreement

4.538 The Complaining parties explained that it was important to clarify that they were not challenging in this dispute the export licence as issued by the BFA signatories; at issue was the export licence requirement as another condition of the EC's issuance of an import licence, as reflected in Article 3 of Regulation 478/95. The EC's limitation of this requirement to only four countries could not be considered "neutral in application" or otherwise fair or equitable, as required by Article 1.3 of the Licensing Agreement.

4.539 Guatemala and Honduras submitted that source-specific export licensing rules were equally proscribed by the provisions of Article 1.3 of the Licensing Agreement. If rules were established that provided a commercial advantage to certain sources and not to others, as was the case with export certificates, they definitionally had to be seen to fail the Licensing Agreement's neutrality, fairness, and equity instruction.

4.540 Mexico argued that the requirement that importers must have an export certificate to import BFA bananas to the EC was contrary to the "neutrality, fairness, and equity" standard of Article 1.3 of the Licensing Agreement.

4.541 According to the EC, the Complaining parties had claimed that the provisions of Article 3(2) of Commission Regulation 478/95 and the export certificate requirement for the BFA countries violated Article 1.3 of the Licensing Agreement because it allegedly constituted an unfair, unequal and non-neutral import licensing procedure should be rejected. The assertion was totally unfounded - the Complaining parties had no legal standing and no economic interest in requesting that an extra procedural step, that did not affect at all their production (which was on the contrary marginally advantaged by the existence of that extra burden on their competitors), should be declared in breach of Article 1.3 of the Licensing Agreement when that specific procedural step had been requested by the interested parties. Furthermore, the exemption for Category B operators when importing bananas from BFA countries put that category of licences in exactly the same condition as all the categories when importing from other Latin American countries. There was no trade distortion.

4.542 The EC's claim that the rules constituted an advantage, not a disadvantage, to the complaining parties reflected, in the Complaining parties' opinion, some legal confusion. If the EC's export licensing rules created trade advantages for products originating in certain countries and not others, they could not satisfy any possible test of neutrality. In fact, the export certificate requirement provided an extra bargaining chip to the exporter in dealings with the importer. The market price of export certificates ranged from $2.50 per box to $*3.00* per box. (The price of an import licence was about $*5.00* per box.) The exclusion of Category B operators from export licensing requirements, which added incentive to purchase bananas from ACP and EC origins, was also a breach of the neutrality standard. In addition, the manner in which the export licence requirement influenced the two-round system, by artificially segmenting imports of different origin by time, impaired normal supplying efficiencies for the Complaining parties' bananas. These procedures could not be considered "neutral in application".

• Article 3.2 of the Licensing Agreement

4.543 The Complaining parties claimed that they had shown that the EC's export licensing requirement was trade-disruptive and unduly burdensome under Article 3.2 of the Licensing Agreement. With respect to the trade distortion provision, the export licensing rules and procedures disrupted trade from its natural course by conferring a discriminatory commercial advantage to certain suppliers, by strengthening the incentive to purchase from ACP and EC countries and by disrupting customary marketing cycles.

4.544 Ecuador argued that the special export certificate requirement provided for in Regulation 3224/94 violated Article 3.2 of the Licensing Agreement. According to Ecuador, the special export certificates added a new layer to the already extraordinarily complicated licensing regime applicable to imports of Latin American bananas. The EC had failed to explain why the export certificates were necessary to administer only the BFA volumes allocated to Category A and C operators. In fact, the third-country tariff quota operated for two years without special export certificates, even though many countries had been given country-specific allocations. The special export certificate procedures therefore, were, in the opinion of Ecuador, inconsistent with Article 3.2 of the Licensing Agreement.

4.545 Guatemala and Honduras submitted that discriminatory export licence rules infringed both the non-distortion and non-burdensome disciplines contained in Article 3.2. As to the first of these, non-distortion, the export licence rules had led to "trade-distortive effects" additional to those caused by the tariff quota volume limitation by forcing source-selective cash transfers to producers in BFA countries in order to satisfy licensing match requirements. Those cash transfers flowing back to BFA producers amounted to a production aid, which was not made available to producers in other tariff quota source countries. Worse, the cash transfers were of such a substantial nature that they dried up productive regional investments in the banana sector, resulting in Latin American banana trade suffering.

4.546 Guatemala and Honduras argued that as to the second discipline, that non-automatic licensing "be no more administratively burdensome than absolutely necessary to administer the measure", export licences in tandem with import licences could not, according to Guatemala and Honduras, under any specific or general analysis be considered "absolutely necessary" to the administration of the tariff quota. For the first year and a half of the regime, export licences played no part in the tariff quota import licensing scheme, an obvious indication that they were not, even by EC's standards, considered "absolutely necessary". As further indication of non-necessity, the import licence/export licence combination had never been imposed on bananas from traditional ACP countries. In fact, Guatemala and Honduras were unaware of any other EC licensing regime for which the EC had deemed it "necessary" to couple export licences with import licences to administer a border measure. If this extraordinary combination of export and import licensing requirements was deemed by the Panel to be "absolutely necessary" to administer a tariff quota, Guatemala and Honduras considered that it would become virtually impossible to foresee the circumstances under which the "shall be no more administratively burdensome than absolutely necessary" limitation would be breached. In sum, the export licence feature of this regime had to be considered discriminatory, unnecessary, and distortive, compelling a Panel instruction that it be eliminated.

4.547 Mexico argued that in addition to other claims, the requirement of needing an export certificate to import BFA bananas into the EC was contrary to Article 3.2 of the Licensing Agreement, because this requirement was not absolutely necessary to administer the EC tariff quota.

4.548 The EC replied that in order to demonstrate an alleged violation to Article 3.2 of the Licensing Agreement, the Complaining parties needed to prove, first, that the non-automatic licensing had "trade-restrictive or -distortive effects on imports additional to those caused by the imposition of the restriction". The Complaining parties should have demonstrated that bananas imported into the EC market were restricted by the administration of the tariff quota beyond the effects on trade of the very existence of the tariff quota, which was a reality compatible with the GATT and part of the concessions accepted by all contracting parties, besides the fact that that was common practice in GATT agricultural negotiations. In the opinion of the EC, not a single evidence had been given of these supposed and totally unproved additional trade restrictive or distortive effects. Not a single evidence was shown, demonstrating any hindering in the access of the Complaining parties bananas to the EC market whose parts of the tariff quota were immediately and completely used.

4.549 The Complaining parties responded that undue administrative burden was apparent. The Complaining parties knew of no licensing system anywhere that required import licences for designated sources to be matched with export licences from designated sources. When the matching burden was coupled with the associated two-round application procedures, the collective process was certainly more administratively burdensome than absolutely necessary to administer the tariff quota. As discussed above, the Complaining parties noted that the export certificate requirement also provided an extra bargaining chip to the exporter in dealings with the importer with the market price of export certificates ranged from $2.50 per box to $*3.00* per box.

(v) publication of regulations and timing of licences

4.550 The Complaining parties noted that to date, Regulation 404/93 had been the subject of over a hundred implementing and amending regulations, the sum of which averaged out to one new regulation every ten days since July 1993. This extraordinary volume of regulations was made worse by the uncommon complexity of the rules being published. The reduction coefficient regulations typified that complexity. Numerous varieties of reduction coefficients were published, including: (i) an annual regulation fixing the provisional reduction coefficient for operator entitlements relating to third-country and non-traditional ACP bananas (set prior to the actual year of import); (ii) an annual regulation fixing the final reduction coefficient for such operator entitlements (usually not set until the middle of the actual year of import); and (iii) three types of reduction coefficient regulations published every quarter: a regulation fixing the quarterly indicative quantities, a regulation fixing the first-round reduction coefficients, and a regulation fixing the second-round reduction coefficients (with the first two published prior to the commencement of each quarter, and the latter published two weeks into each quarter.) Not only did this web of regulations violate the prohibitions of Article X:3 of GATT and of the Licensing Agreement against trade regulations that discriminated by country of origin; according to the Complaining parties, it also in several respects violated the Article X:1 requirement that regulations be published "promptly" to enable "traders to become acquainted with them". One aspect of these administrative procedures, the two-round system, was also inconsistent with Article XIII:2(d) of GATT.

4.551 As discussed above, the EC considered that Articles XIII and Article X of GATT did not and could not overlap, since the former was related to the administration of border measures involving a quota or a tariff quota while the latter concerned only the procedural rules to be followed in the application of internal rules pertaining to customs' activities, including requirements, restrictions or prohibitions of imports. It was not possible, therefore, to complain against alleged violations of Article X with respect to the same requirements, laws, regulations, etc., for the same reason as a violation of Article XIII was contested.

4.552 The EC's argument that Article X related solely to "internal rules" and hence was incompatible with a claim based on Article XIII was, according to the Complaining parties, not supported by the plain language of Article X or panel interpretations of its meaning. As previously discussed, the scope of Article X was obvious from its first paragraph and its title: the Article X:3 obligation was applicable to all "trade regulations". The *Dessert Apples* report also clarified that Article XIII and Article X of GATT could apply to the same measure.[252]

(a) claims under the GATT

- Article X of GATT

4.553 The Complaining parties submitted that, as a general matter, because of the extraordinary volume and complexity of the regulations being published, sufficient acquaintance with these regulations was simply not possible for most of the trade. Even those traders that committed substantial time and resources to familiarizing themselves with the relevant regulations did not have enough time to fully understand the workings of the rules under which they were being required to operate. This wide-spread level of uncertainty was made worse by the untimely publication of several key regulations, particularly those relating to reduction coefficients. One example was the regulation setting the final reduction coefficients for operator entitlements, which was not published until the middle of the actual year of import because of delays associated with unchecked "over-filing". This delay meant that operators were uncertain for the first half of every year what their permissible entitlement volume would be for that year, precluding any possibility of market planning.

4.554 Ecuador considered that the licensing procedures were not set out "in a manner as to enable governments and traders to become acquainted with them." Regulation 404/93 had been amended, clarified and derogated from in a mass of supplementary legislation since its enactment in 1993. Merely reading these myriad

[252] Dessert Apples, para. 12.29.

measures would be daunting enough. However, understanding these measures to the extent necessary to follow the application procedures and to determine the volume of bananas which a particular operator was entitled to import required a substantial commitment of time and resources.

4.555 Ecuador also argued that Article X:3(a) of GATT did not permit:

> in the treatment accorded to imported goods, discrimination based on country of origin, nor ... the application of one set of regulations and procedures with respect to some contracting parties and a different set with respect to others.[253]

Article X thus prohibited precisely the type of measures set out in Regulation 404/93 which imposed discriminatory and burdensome licence application procedures on operators wishing to import third-country bananas.

4.556 Guatemala and Honduras submitted that the stipulation of Article X of GATT that all regulatory requirements be imposed in a "uniform, impartial and reasonable manner," was manifestly violated by the administrative measures described above. No similar burdens or inequities were encountered by EC or traditional ACP suppliers. The administrative procedures at issue were not, in the opinion of Guatemala and Honduras, border-line violations. They were egregious in their unfairness, discrimination, and trade disruption.

4.557 Guatemala and Honduras considered that the predictable marketing of Guatemalan and Honduran bananas was also eroded by licensing regulations that were in an almost constant state of flux and uncertainty. Not only were rule changes routine, significant changes, such as implementation of tariff quota allocations and export licences, had been put into force with only a few days notice. Moreover, the quarterly two-round procedure was conducted over an uncommonly protracted six-week period and worked to deny tariff quota access for, at a minimum, the first three weeks of every quarter. That shut-out period had been extended even further in instances where the Commission had believed it necessary to encourage operators to engage more actively in the purchase of preferential hurricane licences. Such burdens and inequities, viewed on both an individual and a cumulated basis, created for Guatemalan and Honduran exporters a perpetual atmosphere of commercial unreadiness, confusion and deep cynicism with respect to the procedural scheme under which they were being forced to operate.

4.558 The Complaining parties noted that the quarterly reduction coefficient regulations also deprived traders of timely notice. Usually, at least three weeks of lead time was necessary to fill an order of bananas from Latin America. One week elapsed between the time when a producer received an order and the time when the boats were loaded for shipment. Actual shipment from Latin America to the European market usually took another two to three weeks. Traders were accordingly in no position to commit to customer orders unless all quarterly coefficient regulations were published three to four weeks in advance of the quarter. First-round licences, however, were not generally published until about ten days before the beginning of each quarter,[254] depriving traders of the notice necessary to satisfy their commercial needs. The Complaining parties considered that the second-round coefficients were even more untimely, since these were not published until at least two weeks into every quarter, amounting in practical effect to GATT-inconsistent backdating. The first quarter of 1996 was illustrative; the regulation publishing the second-round reduction coefficients for that quarter was not published until 13 January 1996, with a period of validity retroactive to 1 January. The panel in *Dessert Apples* explicitly found that the practice of backdating constituted a breach of the prompt publication and notification obligation of Article X:1 of GATT.[255]

---

[253] See Note of Director-General, 29 November 1968, L/3149; see also reference to this passage in Dessert Apples, BISD 36S/93, p.117, para. 6.5.

[254] According to the Complaining parties, the regulation issuing first round licences was published on 19 December 1995 for the first quarter of 1996, on 20 March 1996 for the second quarter and on 21 June 1996 for the third quarter.

[255] Dessert Apples, para. 12.29.

4.559 The EC recalled its strong doubts on whether Article X was applicable at all to management of a licensing system which was logically prior to and not immediately linked to customs related measures. However, irrespective of the outcome of that legal analysis, the EC considered that the management of the licensing system was transparent and administratively organized in such a way that no activity of the authorities in the allocation process was possible without a previously public and published EC decision. For example, for the quarterly management of the regime, a regulation was published giving details of the percentages of annual entitlements which could be applied for, and the percentages of each origin which were available ("indicative quantities"). The indicative quantities were always published and in force before the period when operators could apply for licences, and that period was fixed, i.e. operators knew they must apply between the 1st and 7th of the month preceding the start of the quarter.

4.560 The next step, the EC continued, was that a regulation was published stating what licences were to be issued. Operators thus received their first round licences (which always covered all bananas to be imported from the four relevant Complaining parties) at least a week before the start of the quarter, and two weeks before the expiry of the previous quarter's licences, so continuity of supply was ensured. This step did not imply any specific operators' activity. Operators also then knew what quantities were available for the second round because these were published in the Official Journal of the European Communities in the same regulation which gave reduction coefficients for the first round. The operators then had 10 working days to submit their second round applications to the competent authorities. The issuance of the second round licences by the competent authorities took place on the 17th day of the quarter, i.e. 10 days after the expiry of the previous quarter's licences, a period which represented approximately 11 per cent of a quarter.[256] Nobody could credibly, in the opinion of the EC, claim that only having first round licences available (and that was always the case) for such a short period could actually restrict commercial opportunities. Annual allocations could only go up unless double-counting (which was fraud committed by operators while requesting a licence) is identified which reduced an operator's reference quantity. All movements in the reduction coefficient throughout the year were to make it less constraining, not more so. What was indicated above showed, according to the EC, that the EC licensing system was managed in "uniform, impartial and reasonable manner" and that "all regulations and administrative rulings" concerning the management of the system were "published promptly in such a manner as to enable governments and traders to become acquainted with them".

4.561 Furthermore, the Complaining parties tried to apply Article X:3 of GATT at the same time to the ACP traditional allocation procedures and to the EC tariff quota. As the EC had already submitted to the Panel, the two regimes had to be treated separately. There was also no question of a violation of Article X:1 caused by a process of quota back-dating as in the case of *Dessert Apples*: as indicated, an EC Regulation, directly applicable in all EC member States, was published giving details of the percentages of annual entitlements which could be applied for, and the percentages of each origin which were available before the period when operators could apply for licences. The existence of a second round of distribution of the import licences served the purpose of giving a further

[256] The EC provided a list of the publications of regulations during 1996:

(a) Indicative quantities:
1st quarter (1st January): Reg. 2710/95 of *23.11*.95, entered into force on *24.11*.95;
2nd quarter (1st April): Reg. 357/96 of 28.2.96, entered in to force 29.2.96;
3rd quarter (1 July): 939/96 of 28.*5.96* entered into force 29.*5.96*;
4th quarter (1 October): 1563/96 of 30.7.96 entered into force 3.8.96.

(b) Regulations concerning issue of first round licences and availability for second round:
1st quarter: 2913/95 of 18.12.95, entered into force 19.12.95;
2nd quarter: 485/96 of 19.*3.96*, entered into force 20.*3.96*;
3rd quarter: 1111/96 of 20.6.96, entered in to force 21.6.96;
4th quarter: 1834/96 of 23.9.96 entered into force 24.9.96.

(c) Regulations concerning issue of second round licences:
1st quarter: 45/96 of 12.1.96, entered into force 13.1.96;
2nd quarter: 670/96 of 12.*4.96*, entered into force 13.*4.96*;
3rd quarter: 1371/96 of 16.7.96 entered into force 17.7.96.

opportunity to importers to fully utilize the quantities of bananas of those origins for which some volumes were still available: this operation was logically and practicably possible only when the rate of non-use was known, that was after the distribution of "first round" licences had occurred. The use of second round licences could not be described as a back dating, but was a practicable means of ensuring the total use of an already timely distributed tariff quota.

- Article XIII:2(d) of GATT

4.562 Guatemala and Honduras submitted that the two-round tariff quota licensing procedure constituted "conditions or formalities" proscribed by Article XIII:2(d) of GATT. That procedure was never concluded until three weeks into every quarter, causing the established term of validity for such licences to be cut short arbitrarily by at least twelve weeks out of every year. Although the fourth quarter in tariff quota licences remained valid for the first seven days of the following year, these few days fell far short of restoring a year-round tariff quota licensing validity period for fruit from tariff quota origins. The procedure had therefore to be said to prevent Guatemala and Honduras "from utilizing fully the share of any such quantity ... which has been allotted to it."

4.563 The EC replied that Article XIII:2(d), last phrase, provided that "[n]o conditions or formalities shall be imposed which would prevent any contracting party from utilising fully the share of any such total quantity or value which has been allotted to him". As the EC had explained previously, second round licences were a facilitating mechanism designed to assist exporting countries and operators to utilize all their indicative quantity or licence entitlement, respectively. There was never a period when valid licences for any origin were not available nor was there ever any backdating of the second round licences. The fact that they were distributed after the quarter had started responded exactly to the need to assess the non-requested entitlements for that quarter, which could not be known before the first round distribution had been completed. No violation could, therefore, be proved and, the EC submitted, the claim should be rejected.

4.564 Moreover, in order to assist the Panel in its deliberations, the EC had compiled the most accurate statistics possible concerning the utilization of the different allocations of the tariff quota in 1995. The utilization figures were related not to the EC's bound tariff quota of 2,200,000 tonnes, but to its autonomously increased volume of 2,553,000 tonnes, and obviously the utilization figures would be higher if the bound volume had been used. The EC also be noted that these figures represented an amalgamation of statistics from two distinct sources, member States customs' authorities for the first quarter, and competent authorities' declarations of licences used for the subsequent quarters, and thus a small margin of understatement was inevitable, although the figures provided a useful indication of the situation. The figures also excluded imports made using hurricane licences, which were also tariff quota imports, because these certificates did not include details of the origin of the bananas.

This statistical operation gave the following utilization rates:

	Percentage utilized
Framework Agreement signatories:	
Colombia	94
Costa Rica	fully utilized
Nicaragua	N/A
Venezuela	81
Others	98
Non-traditional ACP quantities:	
Dominican Republic	96
Belize	53
Cameroon	fully utilized
Côte d'Ivoire	99
Other ACP	60

For 1994, the EC continued, the EC's bound tariff quota was 2,100,000 tonnes, and a volume of 2,038,364 tonnes of bananas, equivalent to 97 per cent, was permitted entry under tariff quota conditions. It was clear therefore, in the EC's opinion, that there were no material obstacles or constraints imposed by the system which prevented exporting countries or operators from making full use of their rights or allocations to import.

4.565 The Complaining parties claimed that, all the way into the first few weeks of each quarter, the EC Commission had not advised them of the results of the second round allocation, so they could not ascertain in advance the volume and sources of their supplies. Since operators did not know their final entitlement until the third quarter of the actual year of entitlement, they were constrained from engaging in market planning and normal risk-taking. These delays (in issuing licences) substantially encroached on the term of validity for tariff quota licences and, hence, on the full usage of tariff quota allocations. The fact that many licences were issued before the quarter commenced was not a defence; a substantial portion were not. The Complaining parties further noted that the EC's assertion that the two-round procedure applied to all imports was erroneous, since traditional ACP sources were not subject to such procedures. It would not be a defence in any event: the Article XIII:2(d) requirement applied regardless. Moreover, it was of no consequence to say that import licences for the Complaining parties' bananas were issued in the first round; this may in most instances have been the case to date, but may not always be so.

4.566 In response, the EC submitted that the reality, as explained earlier, was: the annual entitlement to import from the tariff quota that entered into force 1 January 1995, per country or group of countries were known since 1995 (Regulation 478/95); the annual entitlement to import under the tariff quota per operator was known more than 1 month prior to the beginning of the year by a published Regulation; quarterly entitlements to import, per country and per operator, were known more than 1 month prior to the beginning of each quarter by published Regulations; the first round licence requests took place in the first week of the month prior to the beginning of the quarter; and if countries or groups of countries were oversubscribed in the first round, then in order to facilitate full utilization of the tariff quota, a second round took place to allow the remaining valid licence requests to choose another country or group of countries to import from. To conclude, complete and timely information was provided to operators on quantities available per country and on their entitlements to import, both on an annual and on a quarterly basis. Moreover, for 1995, the EC's bound tariff quota was 2,200,000 tonnes. As a result of the EC's autonomous increases in the tariff quota, a volume of bananas equivalent to 123 per cent of this was permitted entry under tariff quota conditions. The total quantity was 2,708,765 tonnes and represented a rate of utilization of the global tariff quota of 98 per cent.

(b) claims under the Licensing Agreement

- Article 1.3 of the Licensing Agreement

4.567 Guatemala and Honduras argued that the licensing administrative procedures were far from "neutral", "fair and equitable" in their operation. Neither the confusion and denial of access they created, nor the comparative burden they presented relative to the procedures for EC and traditional ACP bananas, could be viewed as fulfilling the Licensing Agreement Article 1.3 command.

4.568 Mexico also considered that the provisions concerning the two-round procedure that needed to be followed to get licences for importing bananas also violated Article 1.3 of the Licensing Agreement.

4.569 With respect to Article 1.3 of the Licensing Agreement, the EC maintained, as described above, that the licensing system to administer the EC tariff quota was stable, certain, flexible, predictable and created no distortion on prices in the EC market which could be detrimental to bananas produced by the Complaining parties. Neutrality, fairness and equality were in-built qualities of the licensing system which was based on the application of the objective criteria of eligibility to obtain tariff quota licences on the basis of past trade in bananas: trade volumes and not companies were the commanding principle of the system.

- Articles 3.2 and 3.5 of the Licensing Agreement

4.570 The Complaining parties noted that Article 3.2 of the Licensing Agreement provided that "[n]on-automatic licensing shall not have trade-restrictive or distortive effects on imports additional to those caused by the imposition of the restrictions." Throughout the year, operators were uncertain as to their import volumes because of continuous auditing and the application of the reduction coefficient to address systematic over-filing. Moreover, all the way into the first few weeks of each quarter, the EC Commission would not have advised them of the results of the second round allocation, so that they could not ascertain in advance the volume and sources of their supplies. Since operators did not know their final entitlement until the third quarter of the actual year of entitlement, they were constrained from engaging in market planning and normal risk-taking.

4.571 Mexico considered that the mechanism of two rounds for the granting of licences also constituted a violation of Article 3.2 of the Licensing Agreement because it had distorting effects on imports.

4.572 Guatemala and Honduras also argued that illegal trade restriction and distortion were best demonstrated by the two-round procedure, which halted tariff quota access and reserved the EC market for EC and ACP bananas for at least twelve weeks out of the year. With respect to the "administrative burden" provision of Article 3.2, Guatemala and Honduras considered that the two-round procedure constituted needless administrative burden, as proven by the very exclusion of EC and traditional ACP bananas from those same procedures.

4.573 The EC recalled its arguments that in order to demonstrate an alleged violation to Article 3.2 of the Licensing Agreement, the Complaining parties needed to prove, first, that the non-automatic licensing had "trade-restrictive or -distortive effects on imports additional to those caused by the imposition of the restriction". The Complaining parties should have demonstrated that bananas imported into the EC market were restricted by the administration of the tariff quota beyond the effects on trade of the very existence of the tariff quota, which was a reality compatible with the GATT and part of the concessions accepted by all contracting parties, besides the fact that that was common practice in GATT agricultural negotiations. In the opinion of the EC, not a single evidence had been given of these supposed and totally unproved additional trade restrictive or distortive effects. Not a single evidence was shown, demonstrating any hindering in the access of the Complaining parties bananas to the EC market whose parts of the tariff quota were immediately and completely used. The very existence of the tariff quota, however, was, in the opinion of the EC, a clear improvement in terms of market liberalization as compared to the situation prior to the conclusion of the Uruguay Round and created conditions for higher prices in the EC market as compared to world market prices and this was a benefit to the Complaining parties banana production. The EC also submitted that, the Complaining parties needed to demonstrate that the licensing system did not "correspond in scope and duration to the measure they are used to implement". No serious argument, in the opinion of the EC, had been brought contesting the EC's compliance with these obligations.

4.574 The Complaining parties claimed that the use of the term "distortive effects" in Article 3.2 required under its ordinary meaning a demonstration that conditions of competition have been distorted or disrupted compared to what would otherwise have been the case absent those licences. Tariff quota bananas could not be distributed through designated entities on a normal marketing cycle, but were forced every quarter through an uncommon two-round application procedure that required a matching of import licences to export licences and artificially segmented trade flows by country of origin and time. A substantial percentage of tariff quota quarterly licences was not distributed until two to three weeks into the quarter for which they applied. This unnatural, heavily constrained distribution scheme for Latin American bananas had reconfigured historical distribution patterns, created an irregular marketing cycle, curtailed delivery flexibility and generated widespread uncertainty and confusion in the marketing of tariff quota bananas. By contrast, traditional ACP bananas could be entered simply and promptly through any firm. Unlike licences for Latin American bananas, the simple licensing approach that was applied to traditional ACP bananas permitted commercial flexibility and predictability.

4.575 The Complaining parties argued that Article 3.2 of the Licensing Agreement further required that licensing rules and procedures correspond in "scope and duration" to the measures (i.e. the tariff quota allocations) they were used to implement. One reasonable benchmark for that standard was found in Article 3.5(h) of the Licensing Agreement (which applied to "quotas", including tariff quotas) and Article XIII:2(d) of GATT. Both of those provisions prohibited rules or procedures that would discourage or prevent any member from fully utilizing its share of the tariff quota. The Complaining parties had shown, in their opinion, that the two-round procedure - which was not concluded until, at least, two weeks into every quarter - contracted the period of validity of tariff quota import licences by at least eight weeks every year and otherwise amounted to backdating, making it a formality that did not correspond in "scope and duration" to the tariff quota.

(vi) licences provided to EC banana producers

4.576 The Complaining parties argued that the EC's licensing scheme had deliberately allocated third-country licences to firms with no history of importing from third countries, including many EC farmers with a direct conflict of interest toward the importation of more competitive Latin American bananas. Such an allocation was inconsistent with any notion of "neutrality" under Article 1.3 of the Licensing Agreement. It was one of the most protectionist ways licences could be distributed and was made even less neutral by the discriminatory exclusion of ACP imports from this rule.

4.577 According to the Complaining parties, the only justification provided by the EC with respect to the licences allocated to its own farmers was obviously protectionist and therefore lacking in neutrality and equity:

> Individual producers and producers' organizations which are not themselves necessarily "importers" of bananas have been allocated Category B licences. Since in general they have no interest in importing dollar bananas, these licences are sold, providing a supplement to their income in addition to the support provided by the provisions on aid to compensate for the loss of income.[257]

[257] "Report on the EC Banana Regime", European Commission, July 1994, pp.10-11.

4.578 Guatemala and Honduras submitted that the privileged licensing benefit to EC producers made possible by the Category B allocation of licences, including hurricane licences, also ignored the "neutral," "fair and equitable" stipulation of Article 1.3 of the Licensing Agreement. Neutrality, fairness, and equity were not served by licensing rules structured to provide a price compensation supplement exclusively to EC producers.

4.579 Mexico argued that the granting of Category B licences to EC producers and agriculture cooperatives, as well as the distribution of licences to EC territories, with the explicit objective of increasing the income of these entities through the sale of licences, compounded the violation of Article 3.5(h) of the Licensing Agreement, because the EC producers were the most interested in reducing imports, particularly of high quality products, such as the Latin American products.

4.580 The United States noted that over half of Category B import licences based on marketing of EC bananas were distributed to banana farmers or farm cooperatives (under the (a) activity function). The EC had recognized that the recipients of these licences had no interest (as well as no experience) in importing Latin American bananas and its principal objective in the distribution of these licences was to supplement their income, rather than to find a way to administer the tariff quota. This built-in, deliberate inefficiency was in itself evidence of lack of neutrality. However, the distribution of import rights to entities that had a long-term interest in reducing market access and skewing conditions of competition for imports was also inherently biased. Farm cooperatives were not only interested in exacting quota rents (in itself a built-in inefficiency) but also sought to reduce competition with their own fruit. This situation presented a clear conflict of interest that eroded normal incentives to purchase high quality imports, to market imports when they were in good condition, and to market them when prices were high. Accordingly, this distribution was inconsistent with Articles 1.3 and 3.5(h) of the Licensing Agreement and Article X:3 of GATT.

4.581 The EC maintained that the licensing system to administer the EC tariff quota was stable, certain, flexible, predictable and created no distortion on prices in the EC market which could be detrimental to bananas produced in the complaining countries. The structure of the EC tariff quota licensing system did not correspond under any possible circumstance to a distribution of licences to EC companies as opposed to foreign companies: arguments of this kind, advanced by the Complaining parties, were non-motivated and grossly misleading. The EC reiterated that neutrality, fairness and equality were in-built qualities of the EC tariff quota licensing system which was based on the application of the objective criteria of eligibility to obtain tariff quota licences on the basis of past trade in bananas; trade volumes, and not companies, were the commanding principle of the system. Furthermore, the EC was of the view that no evidence had been provided by the Complaining parties that the licensing scheme was administered in an unfair and inequitable manner. Moreover, there was no physical link between a licence (or a Category B licence) and the importation of bananas from Latin America. Licences were, not only in this field and not only in case of importation into the EC, transferable and tradable. The operators who traded EC bananas might choose to sell a Category B licence to another operator who might have wished to use it to import Latin American bananas. In this example, the trader in EC bananas might have gained part of a quota rent and the trader in Latin American bananas might have benefited from less than the full quota rent. But not a single EC banana more would have been sold on the EC market because of this commercial relation. Not a single Latin American banana less would have been imported into the EC market because of these commercial relationships. The existence of Category B licences did not affect the volume of Latin American bananas sold on the EC market (the volume was governed by the size of the tariff quota), nor the country of origin of those bananas. Neither the amount of import duty due, nor the prices of bananas to EC consumers would change because of the existence of three types of licence for imports under the tariff quota (Category A, Category B and newcomers) instead of one. In the context of another claim (see paragraphs 0 to 0), the EC also submitted that the initial holders of Category A licences were not absolutely separate from the initial holders of Category B licences. It was not companies which are categorized by the legislation, but trade volumes. Category A and Category B are therefore not mutually exclusive as demonstrated by the fact that all the larger operators were registered in both categories and hence receive both Category A and Category B import licences.

(vii) hurricane licences

4.582 The Complaining parties considered that another element of this convoluted licensing scheme was hurricane licences. Those compensatory licences were dispensed solely to EC and ACP suppliers and operators for the purpose of conferring a commercial advantage. The provision of these reflected obvious discrimination and inequitable licensing. As described above in the context of operator categories, the provision of these licences exclusively to Category B operators was inconsistent with various provisions of the WTO agreements.

4.583 Guatemala and Honduras noted that the producer benefit derived from hurricane licences is identical to that derived from the more general Category B distribution to those producers:

> Individual producers and producers' organizations which are not themselves necessarily "importers" of bananas have been allocated Category B licences. Since in general they have no interest in importing dollar bananas, these licences are sold, providing a supplement to their income in addition to the support provided by the provisions on aid to compensate for the lose of income.[258]

4.584 The EC noted that in order to compensate ACP producers which suffered from devastating natural phenomena like hurricanes, which hit on a regular basis a particular geographic area where a significant ACP banana production was located, the EC accorded to the ACP countries an import "over-quota" destined to replace exactly the loss in production caused by the hurricane. The measure aimed at maintaining a viable and functioning banana trade at the same level as the one corresponding to the normal production of that country, allowing therefore the banana trade to be reinstated as soon as the regular production conditions are back to normal. Those licences could also being sold, then replacing the lost income by another temporary source of income. In this respect, nothing was more normal then attributing these licences to the specific operators who could duly show a lost trade because of the hurricane that was among those who trade in ACP traditional bananas. These operators needed equally to show they "include or directly represent a specific banana producer affected by the tropical storm concerned" (EC Commission Regulation 2791/94, Article 2.1). This did not mean that any discrimination was occurring: the compensated loss in production was related only with the ACP traditional quota and any operator who traded in that quota. Therefore, those who had lost trade because of a hurricane were compensated within the limits of the lost part of the ACP traditional quota.

(a) claims under the GATT

- Article I:1 of GATT

4.585 Guatemala and Honduras argued that within the tariff quota licensing scheme, hurricane licences were yet another advantage conferred exclusively on Category B producers and operators. Such licences were intended to compensate for the volume of traditional ACP (and/or EC) bananas not marketed as a result of hurricanes or tropical storms.[259] Producer recipients of hurricane licences included those in select ACP supplying countries, most notably the Windward Islands (and in EC countries). The producer benefit derived from these licences was identical to that derived from the more general Category B distribution to those producers. Hence, ACP (and EC) producers that suffered the effects of inclement weather were given a boost in the form of licensing quota rent to help restore their competitiveness. Guatemalan and Honduran producers, who also commonly suffered crop damage as a result of weather conditions, were not given that advantage.

4.586 The EC submitted that the Lomé waiver was destined to permit the EC to provide preferential treatment for products originating in ACP States as required by the relevant provisions of the Lomé Convention. Protocol 5,

[258] "Report on the EC Banana Regime", European Commission, July 1994, pp.10-11.

[259] See e.g. Commission Regulation (EC) No. 2791/94, recital four.

Article 1, imposed on the EC not to place any ACP State as regards "... its advantages on those markets, in a less favourable situation than in the past or at present". Hurricane licences were licences to import additional quantities of bananas (from anywhere) for those who were part of the preferential system in favour of the Lomé countries and who had suffered demonstrable damage from hurricanes, which made it impossible for them to fill their normal, guaranteed quantities under the Lomé preference. Such compensatory licences were granted by the French and British authorities before the creation of the EC banana regime and hence had to be maintained pursuant to the guarantees given in the Banana Protocol to the Lomé Convention and the pertinent declaration contained in Annex LXXIV to that Convention. The EC should not therefore be required to extend the same treatment to any other contracting party.

4.587 Referring to the EC claim that because hurricane licences were granted by the French and British authorities before the creation of the Community banana regime, they represented advantages on those markets that had to be "maintained pursuant to the guarantees given in the Banana Protocol ... and ... Annex LXXIV", the Complaining parties submitted that the banana protocol and Annex LXXIV contained no such guarantee. Moreover, licences comparable to Regulation 404/93 hurricane licences had not been dispensed under the French and British regimes, as the EC claimed. National importers had occasionally been granted licensing authority to import additional volumes of Latin American bananas when there had been a shortfall of supplies. However, such licences had never been issued to ACP producers. They had been calculated on the basis of market demand, not overstated estimates of hurricane damage, and had not generated future licensing entitlement.[260]

4.588 The EC replied that contrary to the Complaining parties' claims both the United Kingdom and France had provided "hurricane licences" to their preferred suppliers in the event of natural disasters. In the United Kingdom, compensatory licences had been issued on the basis of estimates of the amount of the loss in each affected month. "Disaster licences" had then been issued to cover the lost volume to the affected operators, in proportion to the quantity of bananas that they would have supplied from traditional sources but for the disaster. These licences had been used to import fruit from Latin American sources. The most recent example of the use of these powers was the issue of disaster licences in 1989 following the destruction of the Jamaican banana crop caused by Hurricane Gilbert. Similar arrangements had been in force in France from the entry into force of the French national regime in 1962 until the creation of the EC single market for bananas on 1 July 1993. This authorized imports from other sources in the event of specific climatic disasters by those operators who had been affected by the disaster.

- Article III:4 of GATT

4.589 As discussed above, Guatemala and Honduras argued that within the tariff quota licensing scheme, hurricane licences were yet another advantage conferred exclusively on Category B producers and operators. Producer recipients of hurricane licences included those in EC sources (and in select ACP supplying countries, most notably the Windward Islands). The producer benefit derived from these licences was identical to that derived from the more general Category B distribution to those producers. Hence, EC (and ACP) producers that suffered the effects of inclement weather were given a boost in the form of licensing quota rent to help restore their competitiveness.

4.590 Mexico further claimed that there were violations of Article III that were not examined by the second *Banana* panel because they did not exist then. These violations referred to the advantages accorded to EC banana producers through the EC regime to the detriment of imports. This included increasing the tariff quota when there was a natural disaster in an EC banana production zone (hurricane licences). This created an incentive in favour of the purchase and marketing of EC bananas which was not enjoyed by imported bananas.

4.591 The EC stressed that the licensing system for the administration of the EC banana tariff quota was applied at the border at the moment of importation and not after the bananas had cleared customs. Therefore, the EC

[260] First *Banana* panel, paras. 19-22, 37-38.

argued, all the arguments based on Article III:4 of GATT should be rejected (together with the arguments based on Article X) - the allegations about which were totally unfounded. Moreover, the EC submitted that Article III:4 was not relevant to the subject matter since any aid given to EC domestic production was attributed to the producers and not according to preferential treatment of the product as compared to like imported products.

4.592 The Complaining parties rejected the EC's claim that licensing criteria could not be subject to Article III:4, noting that Article III covered any regulation or requirement that affects internal conditions of competition in favour of EC bananas.[261] This was confirmed, they argued, by the *Italian Discrimination Against Imported Agricultural Machinery* report.[262]

- Article X:3 of GATT

4.593 With respect to hurricane licences, too, Guatemala and Honduras claimed that the "uniform, impartial and reasonable" standard laid down in Article X of GATT could not be considered fulfilled by a licensing procedure that conferred a producer benefit on select sources only.

4.594 The EC stressed that the licensing system for the administration of the EC banana tariff quota was applied at the border at the moment of importation and not after the bananas had cleared customs. Therefore, the EC argued, all the arguments based on Article X of GATT should be rejected (together with the arguments based on Article III:4) - the allegations about which were totally unfounded. Moreover, the claims were unsubstantiated - there was no breach of Article X therefore the claim should be rejected.

4.595 As discussed above, the Complaining parties considered that Article X:3 of GATT required Members to administer trade rules in a "uniform, impartial and reasonable manner". The laws and practices covered by Article X comprised all "trade regulations," which included, among many others, licensing regulations.

(b) claims under the Licensing Agreement

- Article 1.3 of the Licensing Agreement

4.596 Guatemala and Honduras submitted that the privileged licensing benefit to EC producers made possible by the hurricane licences (and Category B allocations generally) ignored the "neutral", "fair and equitable" stipulation of Article 1.3 of the Licensing Agreement. Neutrality, fairness, and equity were not served by licensing rules structured to provide a price compensation supplement exclusively to EC producers.

4.597 In the view of Mexico, it was clear that the provisions regarding the allocation of "hurricane licences" violated the standard of neutrality, fairness and equity in the application of the licensing system established in of Article 1.3 of the Licensing Agreement.

4.598 As set out earlier, the EC was of the view that its licensing scheme generally did not violate Article 1.3 of the Licensing Agreement, where the emphasis of the Complaining parties was put on the alleged violation of the obligation of neutrality under that provision, while a correct and complete quote of the Article would disclose that: "The rules for import licensing procedures shall be neutral in application and administered in a fair and equitable way." Within the tariff quota licensing scheme, neutrality was absolutely respected and no evidence had been shown to the contrary. Any operator could be eligible for any category of licence if the operator fulfilled the objective conditions therein. Furthermore, the EC was of the view that no evidence had been provided by the Complaining parties that the licensing scheme was administered in an unfair and inequitable manner. In the opinion of the EC, the Complaining parties should have demonstrated that the way the licensing scheme was

---

[261] Second *Banana* panel, DS38/R, para. 148.

[262] Id. See also "United States - Section 337 of the Tariff Act of 1930", para. *5.10*; Report of the panel on "United States - Measures Affecting Alcoholic and Malt Beverages", adopted 19 June 1992, BISD 39S/206, para. *5.31*.

administered was unfair and inequitable. The Complaining parties were on the contrary trying to demonstrate, through Article 1.3 of the Licensing Agreement, that the licensing scheme itself was unfair (which was in any case unfounded). In the opinion of the EC, this had nothing to do with the way the Licensing Agreement had been agreed upon and the common will of the CONTRACTING PARTIES that was expressed in that wording.

4.599 The Complaining parties reiterated that the EC could not be considered to have satisfied its burden of showing that the licensing procedures were neutral in application and applied in a fair manner by merely asserting that the licensing system applicable to Latin American bananas "is stable, certain, flexible, predictable and creates no distortion on prices in the EC market which could be detrimental to bananas produced in the complaining countries."[263] This assertion did not even address the neutrality and equity requirements of Article 1.3. The only justification provided by the EC with respect to the licences allocated to its own farmers was obviously protectionist and therefore lacking in neutrality and equity.

C. General Agreement on Trade in Services (GATS)

1. Introduction

4.600 The Complaining parties claimed that the EC's banana regime went beyond WTO-inconsistent treatment of imported Latin American bananas. The regime's import licensing provisions directly targeted North and South American firms that distributed bananas. These licensing provisions provided definite competitive advantages to EC- and ACP-owned firms that wholesaled bananas vis-à-vis their competitors based in Latin America and the United States. Distribution companies of Latin America and the United States, such as Chiquita Brands (United States), Del Monte (Mexico), Dole Foods (United States) and Noboa (Ecuador) had played a leading role in developing the EC market for bananas dating from the early part of this century. They had invested hundreds of millions of dollars in infrastructure and services needed to bring bananas into and through the EC market efficiently, through entities they had established in the EC itself and in third countries. Even though the import licensing rules being challenged under the GATS were also contested under one or more Multilateral Agreements on Trade in Goods, WTO trade benefits accruing to Complaining parties' service suppliers under the GATS were distinct from the trade benefits relating to goods. The Complaining parties argued that these benefits were of great commercial importance to them and, as this was the first proceeding brought under the GATS, that the GATS issues should be addressed carefully by the Panel.

4.601 The Complaining parties claimed further that the Latin American and US firms that imported and sold bananas in the EC market were in the wholesaling business. Wholesale and retail trade services made up the larger category of distributive trade services. Distribution of goods was a huge service sector, on which millions of service jobs depended world-wide. In the GATS, the EC had undertaken specific commitments that covered both cross-border wholesaling activities and wholesaling activities based on a commercial presence within the EC. The combination of cross-border and commercial presence activities encompassed the entire process of wholesaling products from abroad into and through the EC. All of the main Latin American and US companies supplied wholesale trade services to the EC on a cross-border and commercial presence basis. Each such company provided wholesale services by acting as a middleman, purchasing bananas from other companies and reselling them to other wholesalers or retailers. This was in addition to the activities these companies performed in marketing their own bananas to and in the EC.

---

[263] According to the Complaining parties, the EC's claim that the rules applicable to Latin American bananas contain "objective" criteria of eligibility, even if true, would provide no defence for the lack of neutrality. A measure could be based on measurable criteria for example, and still lack neutrality in application. Even if the licensing criteria were objective, the two licensing arrangements would still not be considered neutral, fair or equitable unless banana imports from all sources were subject to comparable rules, not just as to eligibility, but as to every aspect of the licensing system. The preferential licensing regime accorded to ACP imports definitively violated Article 1.3 of the Licensing Agreement.

4.602 The United States argued that the EC banana regime employed discrete but compounding measures to reconfigure the Latin American banana service market in favour of EC and ACP suppliers, including through the use of: (i) operator category allocations, which granted the right to import 30 per cent of the Latin American banana tariff quota predominantly to EC and ACP firms; (ii) export certificates, which were made a requirement to import bananas from certain Latin American countries, unless the marketer belonged to the group of firms that were predominantly EC and ACP firms; (iii) hurricane licences (allowing additional imports in cases in which EC or ACP production was damaged due to storms), which were granted selectively to EC and ACP firms and which effectively increased these firms' entitlement to the Latin American banana tariff quota above the 30 per cent already set aside for them; and (iv) activity function allocations, which took the Latin American banana import rights that remained after the removal of 30 per cent under (i), and granted over 40 per cent of those remaining rights to predominantly EC firms that had ripened (but had not necessarily ever imported) bananas, or that had a role in importing bananas that was limited only to the administrative, frequently "paper-only" task of customs clearance. Notwithstanding the US and other non-EC/ACP suppliers' efforts to adjust to the EC's new discriminatory marketing regulations, accomplished at great cost, the EC's manipulation of the conditions of competition in favour of EC and ACP service suppliers continued to disadvantage US and other banana distribution firms.

4.603 The Complaining parties submitted that the four key components of the EC banana regime were inconsistent with the GATS. The first was the regime's operator category distinctions. Prior to Regulation 404/93, three large EC member States - France, Spain and the United Kingdom - had kept their markets almost entirely shut to bananas produced in Latin America.[264] Their markets were also largely shut to North and South American distribution companies. The companies that sourced and distributed bananas into the French, Spanish, and UK markets were almost exclusively owned by EC or ACP interests. When the EC decided to move to a common banana regime, it meant that these companies would for the first time be subject to competition from US and Latin American companies providing Latin American bananas. Over 95 per cent of Latin American bananas were sourced and distributed by companies that were owned or controlled by Latin American and US-based companies. These companies had made the necessary substantial commercial investments and had developed close relationships with Latin American suppliers. The companies distributed bananas into the other EC member States in relatively free-market conditions and their bananas were generally regarded as more cost-competitive than most EC and ACP bananas.

4.604 The Complaining parties noted that prior to the inception of Regulation 404/93, the French government required importers to obtain a licence from one of two government entities in order to import Latin American bananas into France. These entities granted licences to import Latin American bananas in extremely limited quantities to a small number of French companies whose primary business was importing EC and ACP bananas. The effect of the French licensing regime was to keep US and Latin American banana wholesalers largely out of the French banana market. The United Kingdom maintained a different, but no less restrictive, import regime. In the United Kingdom, the Banana Trade Advising Committee (BTAC), comprising representatives from three banana distributors (Geest, United Kingdom; Fyffes, Ireland; and Jamaica Producers, Jamaica) accounting for at least 90 per cent of the UK's ACP imports, as well as ACP producer organizations and the Ministry of Agriculture, assessed monthly supply and demand conditions and recommended the appropriate level of Latin American banana imports, whose recommendations the UK Government generally implemented. Not surprisingly, the UK Government issued banana import licences for Latin American bananas almost exclusively to its three largest banana distributors, in limited amounts, based on their previous share of EC and ACP banana trade. The UK licensing scheme kept other competitors out of the local banana wholesaling market. Spain prohibited all Latin American banana imports. The Spanish import regime effectively kept foreign-owned banana wholesaling firms out of its market.

[264] The Complaining parties submitted Eurostat data showing that bananas imported from Latin America into these three member States combined in each of the years 1990-92 were 4 per cent or less of total EC-12 imports from Latin America.

4.605 The Complaining parties asserted that, when the EC decided to create a common market for bananas in 1992, it was clear that those firms in the UK, French, and Spanish markets that had previously enjoyed government protection against competition from US and Latin American wholesalers would be required to compete with them. To protect those EC-owned (and ACP-owned) firms, the EC effectively recreated on an EC-wide basis - and thereby expanded many times over - the protection that the local French, UK and Spanish systems had formerly afforded by awarding those firms 30 per cent of all Latin American bananas imported into the EC. The EC did not have to look far for the precise mechanism to employ, as awarding rights to import Latin American bananas to firms who were in the business of importing EC or ACP bananas was a main feature of the French and UK regimes. However, the EC inflated this existing concept from less than 5 per cent of the EC's Latin American banana imports to 30 per cent.

4.606 The Complaining parties argued further that, to make sure that EC companies could compete with companies distributing Latin American bananas when the common regime went into effect, the EC gave its distribution companies a competitive advantage by handing them a share of the Latin American bananas and thus a share of the banana distribution business that they had never had. The EC imposed import licensing rules that guaranteed 30 per cent of the rights to import Latin American bananas to those companies that historically imported EC or ACP bananas. The EC was fully aware that its allocation scheme rearranged longstanding trade patterns for Latin American bananas and modified competitive conditions. Indeed, it had acknowledged in a formal judicial proceeding that the purpose of the 30 per cent set-aside was to "strengthen the competitive position" of marketers of EC/ACP bananas in comparison with their competitors who traditionally traded in Latin American bananas. Spain had been candid enough to state in a similar proceeding that a purpose of the regime was to reduce the alleged dominant role of non-European firms in banana distribution. This had been a polite way of saying that the regime was used to transfer business opportunities from Latin American and US firms to EC and ACP firms. The Complaining parties asserted that this type of reordering of the competitive environment in favour of domestic and ACP service suppliers was directly contrary to the principle of equality of competitive opportunities embodied in GATS Articles II and XVII. The manipulation of the import licensing rules through the 30 per cent set aside were applied on a company-by-company basis. The rules prescribed which companies got to bring Latin American bananas into the EC, and in what quantities. Short of an outright prohibition of wholesaling, it was difficult to imagine a measure having a more direct effect on the business of an international wholesaler than a measure that specified how much of the product the company would be entitled to import.

4.607 The Complaining parties claimed that a second key component through which the EC further transferred wholesale distribution business opportunities to its domestic service suppliers were the three activity functions. Under these, the EC awarded nearly half of the import rights of Latin American bananas to largely EC-controlled entities that had never been importers in any true sense. It awarded over 40 per cent of the import rights to what the EC called "secondary importers" which involved essentially only customs clearance, and to companies that ripened bananas, which was an activity that had no role in importation. Customs clearance and ripening were largely performed by EC-owned entities at the time Regulation 404/93 went into effect. The only entities that had "imported" Latin American bananas in any real sense were the US and Latin American banana distribution companies. The EC activity function system classified these firms as "primary importers". These primary importers obtained the Latin American bananas from their source in the tropics, arranged or even performed their transport to the EC, and sold them in the EC. In many instances, these companies also made sales arrangements with final retailers like supermarkets and carried out sales promotions and many other related activities. Nevertheless, ripeners were given 28 per cent of the import licences, and secondary importers 15 per cent, a total of 43 per cent. Thus, 43 per cent of the already-diminished rights to import Latin American bananas, and therefore, the means to provide wholesaling services with respect to Latin American bananas, were awarded not to the Latin American and US firms that had done the most to bring these bananas to the EC, but mostly to discrete classes of favoured EC-owned firms.

4.608 According to the Complaining parties, the EC thus manipulated these two features of the banana regime (the operator categories and activity functions) to strip opportunities for Latin American banana distribution business away from the firms that had traditionally supplied nearly all Latin American bananas into the EC market and award these opportunities to their competitors, which were EC or ACP-owned companies. By drastically altering competitive conditions in this manner, these aspects of the regime violated the principles of MFN and national treatment of Articles II and XVII of GATS. Two other aspects of the regime, selective export licence requirements (so-called "export certificates") and discriminatory grant of hurricane licences, further augmented the commercial advantages accorded to EC and ACP-owned operators. The Complaining parties asserted that each represented an independent violation of the GATS MFN and national treatment requirements.

4.609 The EC noted that the measures contested under the GATS remained the same as those contested under the GATT, i.e. the licensing system and, in particular, the allocation. In the opinion of the EC, these were measures directed at goods and except for some broad allegations on competitive conditions, the Complainants concerned did not substantiate that these measures related to trade in services. There was no clarity about the service suppliers which were allegedly discriminated against and whether they were indeed service suppliers of the Complainants involved. It was equally unclear if the service suppliers which were allegedly being advantaged by the contested measures were indeed service suppliers of the EC. No proof was offered. Unsubstantiated allegations about "taking away of market shares" abounded, without taking account of the fact that a licensing system was concerned with entitlement to import licences and not market shares. Assertions about "taking away quota rents" were rife, without taking account of the facts that such quota rents were created by the establishment of the (fully legitimate) tariff quota and that neither the GATT nor the GATS contained any obligation in respect of the allocation of quota rents.

4.610 The EC claimed that the facts of the licensing system demonstrated that there had been no transfer, as alleged by Ecuador and the United States, of a large portion of "the Latin American banana distribution market" from "Latin-American banana service suppliers" of the Complainants concerned to presumably EC "Latin American banana service suppliers", both because such was not the logical consequence of instituting a system of transferable licences and because there was, de facto, no appreciable change in market share for non-EC owned or controlled companies. Since there was a rise in market share for one such company and a decline for another, this alone was sufficient to demonstrate, according to the EC, that the system as such could not be the cause of the decline in market share of the latter. The difference had to be attributed to different strategic decisions and not to the measures related to goods described above.[265]

4.611 The EC argued further that the assertion by Ecuador and the United States that through the creation of the system of Category A, B, and C licences, market share was "taken away" from those who had traditionally traded in bananas from Central- and South America and "given" to those who had previously traded primarily in domestically and ACP-produced bananas, rested on the idea that the possession of import licences could be equated with actual physical importation or with market share. The most obvious characteristic of import licences was, however, that they were tradeable and therefore could, and did, end up in the hands of others than those to whom they had been issued. Moreover, it was sufficient to have one import licence in the chain of supply in order to be able to import the goods covered by that licence. Furthermore, apart from the possibility to trade licences, even the initial holders of Category A licences were not absolutely separate from the initial holders of Category B licences. The reference quantities which conferred eligibility to obtain tariff quota import licences were granted on the basis of past trade in bananas: Latin American bananas for Category A import licences and traditional ACP or EC bananas for Category B import licences. Thus it was not companies which were categorised by the legislation, but trade volumes. Categories A and B were therefore not mutually exclusive, as demonstrated by the fact that all the larger operators were registered in both categories, and hence received both Category A and B import licences.

---

[265] The EC submitted that, according to a report by *A.D. Little*, Dole's market share in the EC banana product market rose from 11 per cent (1991) to 15 per cent (1994), while Chiquita's declined from 25 per cent (1991) to 18.5 per cent (1994). Del Monte's market share rose from 7.5 per cent to 8 per cent in the same period (*A.D. Little*,"Etude de l'evaluation des effets de la mise en place de l'OCM bananes sur la filière dans l'Union européenne", 13 September 1995).

4.612 The European Commission (as well as the competent authorities of its member States), the EC continued, neither requested nor received information on the ownership of operators registered to receive banana import licences. Thus, they did not know the actual nationality of ownership of the operators, when issuing licences. As regards the firms referred to above, these received a substantial proportion of both Category A and B licences, and their subsidiaries included a number of companies trading exclusively in ACP or EC bananas. According to the above-mentioned *A.D. Little* study, a total of 380,000 tonnes or 28 per cent of EC/ACP production in 1994 was controlled by the big three integrated trading companies, Chiquita, Dole and Del Monte, the first two of which were US-owned or controlled.[266]

4.613 The EC argued further that the Mexican submission was inadequate and lacking in precision in respect of trade in services. It was restricted to a number of assertions about alleged infringements of Articles II and XVII of GATS, which were claimed to be basically identical to the infringements of Article III:4 of GATT. In the EC's view, Mexico could not invoke this identity of claims without demonstrating in which way the contested measures were "measures affecting trade in services" or "measures affecting the supply of services". There was a fundamental distinction between such measures and measures relating to goods. The GATS only governed the supply of services as such, after the goods in respect of which the services were supplied had entered the country. The EC claimed that Mexico had failed to explain whether there were any Mexican service suppliers active on the markets for the services which Mexico believed were the markets concerned. It was incumbent on Mexico to present a *prima facie* case and to demonstrate that the EC had nullified Mexico's benefits under the GATS. Mexico's submission on services fell far short of such a *prima facie* case.

2. *Issues of scope*

a) *The relationship between the GATS and the multilateral agreements on trade in goods*

4.614 According to the EC, there was no intention to create an overlap between the GATT and the GATS and certainly not with respect to the core provisions of both treaties: most-favoured-nation treatment and national treatment. The *raison d'être* of the GATS was that trade in services could not be covered by the GATT. Hence it was the intention of the negotiators in the Uruguay Round to create an instrument that would be distinct *ratione materiae* from, and complementary to, the GATT. The GATT was concerned with the treatment of imported products and not with the treatment of natural and legal persons. The GATS was concerned with the treatment of services and service providers. The GATS was about trade in services, i.e. there had to be a service transaction between a service seller and a buyer. There had to be a service which actually appeared on the market. In so far as the GATS covered the treatment of natural and legal persons, it did so only to the extent that they acted in their capacity as service providers trading in a marketable service. If they acted as persons who handled goods, the rules applicable to products, i.e. the GATT, its schedules and the other Multilateral Agreements on Trade in Goods, applied. Which services they could render with respect to these goods, in which quantity and under which conditions, was determined by the GATS.

4.615 The EC submitted that there were reasons to assume that with respect to transport and distribution the relationship between the GATT and the GATS was rather special and a clear distinction between goods and services, and thus between the GATT and the GATS, should be maintained. One should not too easily decide that matters related to the distribution and transportation of goods were covered by the GATS, as most goods, by the time they were put on the market, included or embodied transport or distribution services. Trade benefits related to goods arose under the rules of the GATT and the other Multilateral Agreements on Trade in Goods, including the concessions and commitments laid down in the GATT schedules. The extent of trade benefits or trade opportunities related to goods depended on the extent and importance of legitimate trade barriers, such as consolidated tariffs, including tariff quotas and their relevant licensing rules, any anti-dumping measures that might have been taken, and any countervailing duties or safeguard measures that might have been imposed.

---

[266] Op. cit.

4.616 The EC was of the view that benefits to services or service suppliers of other countries arose under the GATS and the commitments taken thereunder. They depended on the extent and importance of legitimate barriers to trade in services remaining under those commitments and properly inscribed under Article XVI of GATS, such as licences for service activities based on an economic needs test, or the limitation of foreign banks or insurance companies to a maximum turnover or a maximum percentage of total assets in the sector. For example, pursuant to limitations or conditions under Article XVI of GATS, computer services in a certain country might only be permitted to be provided by foreign companies in a joint venture with a national company of which there was only one, which indirectly led to very low imports of computers in that country, even though the tariff on computers was negligible. In such a case, the EC argued, one would not take the view that there was an infringement of the GATT. Similarly, it could not be claimed that there was an infringement of the GATS when US computer companies were able to provide hardly any installation or maintenance services through commercial presence in spite of a "no barriers" commitment in the GATS Schedule because computers from the United States had been struck by a prohibitive anti-dumping duty. Furthermore, there could be a legitimate domestic regulation under Article VI of GATS, such as authorizations, qualification requirements, licensing, etc. It appeared therefore that the cause of benefits or trade opportunities in the domain of goods and the domain of services was entirely different. Hence, the cause of the restriction or breach of these trade opportunities in the two different sectors had also to be different.

4.617 In the view of the EC, the GATS was concerned with trade in services as services, e.g. with the offer of road transport services on the EC market by road transport companies from non-EC States, not with the fact that in order to sell goods on the EC market someone had to transport them. Measures relating to the trade in bananas could certainly have repercussions on the transport of bananas, but such indirect and incidental repercussions of measures related to trade in goods were of no concern to the GATS. The GATS was concerned with measures which directly influenced the ability to perform a service, once a good involved in the service had been imported. If the GATS apprehended all kinds of indirect and incidental consequences of measures related to goods, there would be no security of scheduling whether under the GATS or under the GATT. Members were agreed that the services repercussions of their GATT measures needed not be included in their GATS Schedules.[267] The position of the Complaining parties amounted to saying that all Members should nevertheless have included these in order to be protected from "double jeopardy".

4.618 The EC argued that the same measures could not be condemned both under the GATT and the GATS since their coverage was intended to be mutually exclusive. The GATS did not cover the indirect quantitative consequences on the amount of services performed resulting from restrictions on the importations of goods but only such measures as related directly to services as such and to service suppliers in their capacity as service suppliers. If the measures relating to goods were covered by a GATT exception or by a GATT waiver, such exception or waiver could not be rendered ineffectual by bringing the measures relating to goods under the GATS and asserting that they were illegal in that framework. The reliability of exceptions and waivers would be reduced to naught. The Complainants could not now claim that the EC should also have obtained a GATS waiver for its goods measures relating to the Lomé Convention and its Banana Protocol, such as the preferential treatment and the licensing system in respect of bananas.

4.619 The Complaining parties responded that EC's assertion that a measure could not, as a matter of law, be covered by both the GATT and the GATS found no support in the text of either the GATT or the GATS. Had the negotiators intended to adopt a principle as fundamental as the one the EC put forward, they certainly would have provided for it in the text of the GATS or the WTO Agreement. It was true that the nature of the trade interests in the two agreements were different: GATT concerned trade in goods and the GATS trade in services. However, there was no reason why the same measure could not constitute discrimination with respect to both goods and services. It would not be uncommon for the same measure to violate more than one multilateral trade agreement for goods – so why not the GATT and the GATS? The WTO Agreement did not establish a *sub silentio* hierarchy

[267] See document MTN.GNS/W/164/Add.1, p.2.

of the GATT over newer agreements, such as the Agreement on Trade-Related Aspects of Intellectual Property Rights, the TRIM's Agreement, the Licensing Agreement and the Agreement on the Application of Sanitary and Phytosanitary Measures. In the absence of a specific indication to the contrary, or an irreconcilable conflict, neither of which the EC could point to here, those agreements had to be applied according to their terms. In the case of the GATS, Article XVII was plain: it applied if (i) the measure affected trade in services; (ii) the Member had entered a commitment in the relevant sector; and (iii) the measure provided less favourable treatment to foreign services or suppliers in comparison to like domestic ones. If this test was met, a violation of the GATS existed, whether or not the measure was "goods-related". Article II of GATS had a comparable test.

4.620 The Complaining parties argued further that accepting the EC's argument that measures related to goods were excluded from the GATS disciplines would produce anomalous results. First, it would effectively erase from the GATS schedules all service commitments made in the goods distribution sector for both wholesaling and retailing. The entire sector was devoted to the distribution of goods. Measures affecting those sectors were extremely likely to involve some connection to goods. The EC specifically, and voluntarily, committed not to discriminate in the area of wholesale trade services. It should not be permitted to renege on those commitments through a novel and unsupported theory that measures having a relationship to goods could not implicate the GATS. The EC's interpretation would allow discrimination against foreign service suppliers in all sectors, not only the distribution sector.

4.621 The Complaining parties submitted that the EC's discriminatory measures regulated the availability of goods to foreign service suppliers and had a real and direct effect on competitive conditions. Indeed, in the present case, the manipulation of marketplace competition was particularly direct, since the EC regime regulated the availability of the very merchandise (bananas) necessary for banana wholesalers to supply their service. The GATT had long recognized that measures governing services could be used to alter the terms of competition between domestic and imported goods. GATT Article III:4 prohibited less favourable treatment to imported goods "in respect of all laws, regulations and requirements affecting their internal sale, offering for sale, purchase, transportation, distribution, or use". The drafters of the GATT understood that they needed to cast their net broadly to ensure that the GATT did not permit countries to avoid their non-discrimination obligations based simply on the form of a measure. The same was also true of the GATS with respect to measures having a connection to goods, especially since the GATS covered entire services sectors and sub-sectors (e.g. distribution, freight transportation) devoted to the handling of goods.

4.622 The EC's claim that, if its banana measures were found to violate the GATS, all tariff quotas that restricted the volume of imports could be challenged under the GATS, vastly overstated the position of the Complaining parties. In their comments to the Panel, the Complaining parties clarified that their complaint was not based on the fact that the EC banana regime reduced the overall levels of Latin American imports but was instead based on service-related discrimination in the allocation of the remaining bananas available for importation under the EC regime, specifically, the EC's transferring of opportunities from Latin American and US service suppliers to ACP and EC firms. This type of discrimination was by no means inherent in tariff quotas generally. Indeed, tariff quotas, like the vast majority of other goods-related trade measures, would not generally raise GATS issues. Tariffs, quotas and tariff quotas on goods frequently did not distinguish between service suppliers at all, and when they did, they did not typically provide clear competitive advantages to service suppliers of particular countries at the expense of like suppliers of other countries. That was precisely what the EC's licensing regime did, however, awarding rights to Latin American bananas on a service-supplier-by-service-supplier basis, in a manner deliberately designed to favour its own and ACP companies.

4.623 The Complaining parties contested the EC's claim that the banana licensing rules had only indirect and incidental repercussions on service suppliers. The banana measures applied directly to service suppliers and regulated the quantity of imports they could directly obtain, and therefore, the cross-border wholesaling services they could provide. The EC's measures categorized firms according to how much wholesale services each had performed (that is, each "activity function" was defined in terms of buying and selling bananas into the EC market) and had the direct effect of skewing competitive conditions in favour of domestic and ACP service suppliers. In the wholesale distribution sector, an obvious way for governments to manipulate competitive conditions in favour of local firms was to manipulate supplies of goods in favour of local firms. If the EC's view of the GATS coverage that the GATS only governed measures directly regulating the manner in which a service was performed were adopted, it would allow governments simply to declare that foreign firms could no longer be supplied with goods, putting them completely out of business. Such an interpretation would effectively negate GATS commitments in the entire goods distribution sector. The Complaining parties submitted further that the import licensing measures were not GATT-compatible and were not covered by the Lomé Convention. Thus, the goal that the EC had put forward was hardly a legitimate one even under the GATT. Moreover, a GATT waiver would not permit the EC to discriminate against foreign service suppliers. The GATS had its own waiver provision which the EC had not invoked.

4.624 The EC responded that its position on the relationship between the GATT and the GATS had been mischaracterized by the complainants. It was not the EC's position that the GATT had to be exalted over the GATS. These were two agreements on the same level and precisely because there were no rules on collision between them, overlap should not be readily accepted. A careful distinction should be maintained between measures relating to goods and measures in respect of services trade. If this distinction was not maintained and it became clear that committing oneself in the distribution sector led to unforeseen consequences in the goods trade, a lack of further commitments in that sector might be the consequence.

4.625 The EC claimed that the Complainants' argument with respect to Article III:4 of GATT rebounded against themselves. There was no mirror image of GATT Article III:4 in the GATS. Article XVII of GATS did not contain a provision which gave equal weight to the repercussions of measures related to goods, let alone measures related to imported goods on service suppliers, as Article III:4 of GATT gave to the measures affecting internal sale, offering for sale, etc., of goods. All indications were that such an approach was not adopted.

4.626 The EC noted that the Complaining parties had recognized that measures which were lawful under the GATT, such as tariff quotas, should not be put in jeopardy under the GATS. They accepted that services related to imported goods were available pursuant to GATT rules. While they accepted this for tariff quotas, they attempted to make a distinction in respect of the licensing rules used to distribute the different portions of the tariff quotas. In the view of the EC, one could not make such a distinction without contradicting oneself. One could not argue that a particular measure relating to goods should not be covered by the GATS and another measure relating to goods, namely licensing rules, should be covered by the GATS. Complainants tried to circumvent this difficulty by arguing that import licences were given to companies which were service suppliers. This was, however, demonstrably incorrect. These licences were licences to import goods and were given to different categories of persons or companies on the basis of their past handling of bananas. It was a fact of life that import licences were granted to natural or juridical persons. This was true for all import licences and did not change goods-related measures into measures in respect of services. Moreover, the import licences for bananas were based on historical performance, not as service supplier, but as owner of bananas. In this respect they were not different from other import licences which were based on various economic criteria.

b) Standard of discrimination under the MFN and national treatment obligations

(i) measures affecting trade in services - Articles I:1 and XXVIII(c)

4.627 Ecuador recalled that according to Article I:1 of GATS, the Agreement covered any "measures by Members affecting trade in services". Article I:2 of GATS defined the scope of the Agreement to include measures affecting cross-border services into the EC and services performed through a commercial presence in the EC. Quoting Article I:2 of GATS, Ecuador considered that the GATS covered, among other things, those EC measures which affected such services as pre-shipment quality control services, wholesale distribution services, and rental and leasing services for shipping bananas to the EC. Moreover, referring to the text of Article I:3, Ecuador considered that this Article covered all regulatory measures affecting services, regardless of whether such measures were taken by national or sub-national bodies. Thus, according to Ecuador, the GATS extended to all measures taken by the EC or its member States which affected the provision of services. Ecuador noted that the EC had undertaken specific commitments to comply with the GATS in a large number of service sectors and sub-sectors, including the distribution, transportation, and business service sectors. Therefore, any measures taken by the EC or its member States which affected these services had to comply with the GATS.

4.628 The Complaining parties submitted that the scope provisions of the GATS were drafted in the broadest possible terms, using expressions such as "measures affecting trade in services" and "measures affecting the supply of services" that swept in any measure that affected the business of providing services through one of the four "modes" covered by GATS. The description of each of these key terms set out in Article XXVIII, while already very broad, was cast in illustrative, not exclusive, terms. Paragraphs (b) ("supply of a service") and (c) ("measures by Members affecting trade in services") used the term "include". Paragraph (a) ("measure") listed certain types of measures and then referred to measures in "any other form". This was in contrast to the other definitions in Article XXVIII which used the terms "means", "is", or "comprises", which denoted exclusiveness. These terms were drafted as non-exclusive illustrations purposefully, with the combined effect of making the scope of the GATS as sweeping as possible. Thus, the coverage of the GATS was very broad in the sense that it could potentially reach any measure that affected services or service providers, although it was precise in its articulation of the disciplines applicable to those measures.

4.629 The Complaining parties noted that Article XXVIII(b) provided that "'supply of a service' includes the production, distribution, marketing, sale and delivery of a service" and submitted that this illustrative list was far-reaching and included all aspects of the provision of a service. The definitions found in Article XXVIII(b) and (c) supplemented each other. One covered measures that affected the supply of a service, the other covered measures that affected the consumption of services, or commercial presence, since restrictions that affected any of these could have a direct impact on the business of service suppliers. Together, they reflected an effort by the negotiators to leave no type of measure outside the scope of scrutiny of the GATS, based simply on the form the measure might take. They did not seek to delimit, *a priori*, the universe of the types of measures subject to discipline. In the current case, the EC had allocated, on a discriminatory basis, the access to a product that was essential to the provision of a service. Indeed, the restrictions the EC had placed on the ability of US and Latin American banana wholesalers affected the full range of their services activities, including the "production, distribution, marketing, sale and delivery" of the service, as those terms were used in the illustrative list under "supply of a service". The GATS negotiators had chosen to include the term "affecting" in the phrase "measures affecting trade in services" to reflect the views set out in the *Italian Agricultural Machinery* case, which had interpreted the same term in GATT Article III:4 to include "not only the laws and regulations which directly governed the conditions of sale or purchase but also any laws or regulations which might adversely modify the conditions of competition between the domestic and imported products on the internal market".[268]

4.630 The EC argued that the illustrative definition of "measures affecting trade in services" in Article XXVIII(c) mentioned measures in respect of, *inter alia*, "the purchase, payment or use of a service" and "the presence ... of persons of a Member for the supply of a service" and not the supply of a good. The words "for the supply of a service" indicated that the measures had to be addressed to the natural or legal person in its capacity of service supplier or in its activity of supplying services. There could be a direct limitation on the quantity of services that it could provide, there could be a specific restriction (e.g. linked to nationality) on its licence as a service supplier or there could be a restriction of its corporate form as a service supplier. A restriction on the importation of the amount, and the allocation of this restricted amount, of products in respect of which certain services were to be provided could not be accommodated by this definition of "measures by Members affecting trade in services". These were measures related to products and hence fell under the GATT. Moreover, according to the EC, the broad meaning of the word "affecting" could not be transplanted out of its national treatment context

[268] Report of the panel on "Italian Discrimination Against Imported Agricultural Machinery", adopted on 23 October 1958, BISD 7S/60, para. 12.

in the GATT into a definition determining the scope of the whole of the GATS. The EC noted that in Article XXVIII(c) "affecting" was reduced to "in respect of", which was clearly a much narrower concept and indicated that the measures had to have the purpose and aim to regulate, or at the very least, directly influence services as services. That was not the case with the EC tariff quota and licensing rules for bananas. They merely had indirect consequences on services, in so far as the number of goods in respect of which services were rendered were regulated.

4.631 The Complaining parties responded that, by referring only to the types of market access restrictions listed in GATS Article XVI (e.g. limitations on the number of service suppliers, limitations on the total value of service transactions) as examples of measures that were covered by the GATS, the EC apparently implied that measures not falling within these particular categories were not covered by GATS disciplines. This argument was irrelevant because the Complaining parties' claims were not based on Article XVI, but on Articles II and XVII, which had entirely different standards. Article XVI made no mention of measures affecting trade in, or the supply of, services or to the notion of less favourable treatment. Rather, Article XVI was a list of certain specific types of measures that the drafters of GATS had considered so basic to obtaining access to other Members' service markets that (if scheduled) even non-discriminatory application of these measures would be prohibited. Thus, Article XVI provided no guidance to interpreting the coverage of Articles II or XVII, or of the overall scope of the GATS.

(ii) measures affecting trade in services - Article XVII:1

4.632 The United States submitted that a Member acted inconsistently with Article XVII if three elements existed: (i) the Member had undertaken a commitment in the relevant sector; (ii) the Member had adopted or applied a measure affecting the supply of services in that sector; and (iii) the measure accorded to services or service suppliers of any other Member treatment less favourable than that it accorded to the member's own like services or service suppliers. According to the United States, each of the above elements was present in this case.

4.633 The United States argued that the EC's banana marketing regime comprised a series of measures "affecting the supply of services" (Article XVII:1 of GATS). The term "affecting" was not defined in the GATS. However, the same term was used in Article III of GATT. Citing the first sentence of Article III:4 of GATT, the United States noted that past dispute settlement panels established to review the identically-worded Article III:4 of GATT 1947 had interpreted the term "affecting" as setting out a broad standard of measures that would be covered by national treatment obligations. The United States referred, in particular, to the *Italian Agricultural Machinery* case[269] which had found that: "The selection of the word 'affecting' would imply, in the opinion of the Panel, that the drafters of the Article intended to cover in paragraph 4 not only the laws and regulations which directly governed the conditions of sale or purchase but also any laws or regulations which might adversely modify the conditions of competition between the domestic and imported products on the internal market."

4.634 Thus, the use of the term "affecting" evinced, in the opinion of the United States, an intent on the part of the drafters of the GATS to sweep in a broad range of measures that could alter the competitive relationship between services suppliers. In the present case, each of the challenged aspects of the EC's banana import licensing rules was applied directly to firms that traded and marketed bananas. Thus, the measures directly governed the ability of firms to participate in the market for distribution services, as well as modifying the conditions of competition with respect to this services market. Each challenged aspect of the import licensing rules either redistributed market share from complainants' firms to EC or ACP firms; accorded a benefit predominantly to EC or ACP firms; or imposed a commercial burden predominantly on US and other non-EC/ACP firms.

[269] Op. cit., para. 12. See also report of the panel on "United States - Section 337 of Tariff Act of 1930", p.385 (citing the "Italian Agricultural Machinery" report, the panel found that measures used to enforce US patent law at the border were nevertheless covered by Article III:4, stating "If the procedural provisions of internal law were not covered by Article III:4, contracting parties could escape the national treatment standard by enforcing substantive law, itself meeting the national treatment standard, through procedures less favourable to imported products than to like products of national origin.").

4.635 In response, the EC referred to Article XXVIII on definitions, where "supply of a service" was defined as including the production, distribution, marketing, sale and delivery of a service. This definition confirmed the view of the EC that the GATS was concerned with regulating trade in services as such and not with services which formed part of an integrated supply chain, as in the case of trade in bananas. The measures to which national treatment had to be accorded were, therefore, measures which related to the supply of services as such, and not to indirect and incidental consequences on services in general. As to the meaning of "affecting", the EC did not agree with the interpretation presented by the United States. This interpretation was, in the opinion of the EC, not consistent with what the GATS drafters had written into the final text of the Article. Obviously they had known the *Italian Agricultural Machinery* case and wanted to take account of it. According to the EC, they had done so in paragraph 3 of Article XVII, which provided a further clarification of "no less favourable treatment". If the drafters had wanted to read the modification of competition into the word "affecting", they would certainly have clarified this in the text of the GATS, as they had done for the "no less favourable treatment" standard.

4.636 In the opinion of the EC, there was therefore, no particular reason in the text of the GATS to give a broad interpretation to the word "affecting" within the meaning of Article XVII of GATS. This phrase meant what it said, namely measures which had a direct influence on the sale, distribution, marketing or delivery of a service as such. National treatment in respect of the supply of services was not at stake, if there were indirect effects on services by measures which had as their object to regulate trade in goods. Disputes about such matters had to find their solution in the framework of the GATT. The EC considered that the contested measures in this case were measures regulating trade in goods and did not directly influence the supply of services. The EC argued that there had to be a direct link between the contested measures and the trade in services as such. Though the notion of supply of services or trade in services had to be broadly interpreted, the measures had to have some direct effect on the delivery of services. Measures affecting trade in goods were not (also) measures affecting trade in services, merely because they might have some indirect and incidental effect on services.

4.637 The Complaining parties submitted that Articles II and XVII of GATS were modelled after Article III of GATT which had long been interpreted to proscribe a wide variety of internal measures that accorded competitive advantages to domestic products. The concepts of "less favourable treatment" and "likeness" of Article II:1 and Article XVII:1 of GATS were the very same concepts as in Article III:4 of GATT. The substance of paragraphs 2 and 3 of Article XVII concerning formally identical or different treatment and modification of the conditions of competition was found in GATT panel reports interpreting Article III. In particular, in addition to the term "affecting", the phrase "modify the conditions of competition" came verbatim from the *Italian Agricultural Machinery* case. The *Section 337* panel[270] set out a standard comparable to the standard of the *Italian Agricultural Machinery* case. In its report, the *Section 337* panel found that "the words 'treatment no less favourable' in paragraph 4 of Article III of GATT called for effective equality of opportunities for imported products" and that that phrase "has to be interpreted as protecting expectations on the competitive relationship between imported and domestic products".[271]

4.638 The Complaining parties contended that much like Italy in the *Italian Agricultural Machinery* case, the EC was arguing for a restrictive interpretation of the scope of the GATS non-discrimination provisions to cover only measures that directly regulated the manner in which a service was provided. As in that case, adoption of the EC's interpretation would permit WTO Members to evade their GATS non-discrimination obligations, by drafting new measures that provided a competitive advantage to domestic service suppliers, but that did not directly regulate the provision of the service as such. Indeed, the EC's interpretation would permit governments to adopt the services analogue of the very type of measure at issue in the *Italian Agricultural Machinery* case, i.e. provision of credit facilities for the purchase of domestic services. The EC's interpretation would permit governments to adopt and maintain a host of other discriminatory actions, such as selectively taxing the real estate leased by

[270] Report of the panel on "United States - Section 337 of the Tariff Act of 1930", adopted 7 November 1989, BISD 36S/345 ("Section 337").

[271] Idem, paras. *5.11* and *5.13*.

foreign service suppliers who sought to establish themselves in a Member's territory, or shutting off their water supply or electricity. Measures such as these did not directly regulate the manner of providing the services but they could greatly restrict or even prevent a foreign firm from supplying a service. In this case, whether or not the EC's discriminatory allocation scheme dictated the precise manner of providing wholesale distribution services, it provided EC and ACP firms with tangible competitive advantages in the provision of services, at the expense of like Latin American and US firms. It thus fell within the scope of Articles II and XVII of GATS. The Complaining parties also contested the EC's claim that the term "measures affecting trade in services" must be interpreted to apply only to measures whose purpose and direct effect was to regulate services trade as such. The Complaining parties submitted that the EC's interpretation did not comport with the ordinary meaning of the phrase "measures affecting trade in services", in accordance with the "ordinary meaning" principle of interpretation of Article 31 of the Vienna Convention.

4.639 The EC rejected the Complainants' references to the *Italian Agricultural Machinery* case and its broad interpretation of the word "affecting" as meaning more than "governing". According to the EC, it was assuming too much that the drafters intended to transplant the broad meaning of the word "affecting" out of its national treatment context into a definition determining the scope of the whole GATS. The EC argued that the Complaining parties sought to scare the Panel with far-fetched examples, such as shutting off the electricity or water supply which would frustrate any economic activity, not merely of foreign service suppliers but of any foreign-owned establishment in a country. These examples had been addressed by Article XXVIII(c)(ii) of GATS and had no relevance for drawing the boundary line between the GATT and the GATS.

4.640 The Complaining parties responded that, while several of the Complaining parties' examples of the negative implications of the EC's restrictive interpretation of GATS, e.g. shutting off electricity or water, might be extreme, they would be permitted under the EC interpretation. Less extreme examples would equally be permitted under the EC's interpretation, and were also discriminatory. For example, a Member could impose a tax on real estate leases of foreign service suppliers, or a tax on cars that were repaired at foreign-owned car repair shops. These types of measures discriminated against foreign service suppliers even if they were "goods related" or did not regulate the provision of services as such. Under the EC's interpretation, a Member would be free to implement these types of measures.

(iii) standard of discrimination: Article II

4.641 The United States noted that Article II:1 of GATS set out Members' obligations with respect to MFN treatment for services.[272] According to the United States, a Member acted inconsistently with Article II if three elements existed: (i) the Member had adopted or applied a measure covered by the GATS; (ii) the Member could claim no MFN exemption as to that measure; and (iii) the measure accorded to services or service suppliers of any other Member treatment less favourable than that it accorded to the like services or service suppliers of any other country. Each of the above elements was, according to the United States, present in this case.

4.642 The United States argued that unlike the national treatment standard of Article XVII which applied only to the extent that a Member had made specific commitments in a particular sector or sub-sector, the MFN obligations applied "with respect to any measure covered by" the GATS, unless an exemption was specifically provided for in a Member's MFN exemption list. Article I:1 of GATS provided that: "[t]his Agreement applies to measures by Members affecting trade in services." Thus, "any measure covered by" the GATS was, according to

---

[272] The first two paragraphs of Article II provide as follows:

> "1. With respect to any measure covered by this Agreement, each Member shall accord immediately and unconditionally to services and service suppliers of any other Member treatment no less favourable than it accords to like services and service suppliers of any other country
>
> 2. A Member may maintain a measure inconsistent with paragraph 1 provided that such a measure is listed in, and meets the conditions of, the Annex on Article II Exemptions."

the United States, any measure by a Member affecting trade in services. The analysis above with respect to the meaning of the term "affecting" in the context of the GATS national treatment was, according to the United States, equally applicable in the context of the GATS MFN obligation.

4.643 The United States argued that the standard of Article II:1 of GATS was comparable to the formulation used in Article XVII of GATS with respect to national treatment. Article II:1 employed the same operative phrases "treatment no less favourable" and "like services and service suppliers" found in Article XVII:1. The text of Article XVII contained two additional paragraphs that amplified the basic national treatment standard, most notably through reference to a "conditions of competition" test. Comparable amplification was not provided in Article II. The amplification set out in Article XVII did not reflect, in the view of the United States, any deliberate differentiation between the two standards. Both standards were intended to prohibit discriminatory treatment of like services and service suppliers, in particular by prohibiting treatment that skewed the conditions of competition in favour of certain groups of competitors based on their nationality or ownership.

4.644 Ecuador recalled that Article II of GATS required that Members accord MFN treatment to services and service suppliers from other Members. Ecuador considered that the EC's MFN exemptions did not include the services provided by Ecuadorian and other third-country service suppliers for the marketing, distribution and sale of bananas in the EC. Therefore, all measures taken by the EC which affected these services had to comply with the MFN principle. The GATS was a new agreement adopted as part of the Uruguay Round and consequently the MFN provisions of Article II had never been interpreted or applied by a previous GATT/WTO panel. However, the "treatment no less favourable" standard set out in Article II:1 also appeared in Article III of GATT and the interpretation of this standard in this context should be considered when construing the standard set out in Article II:1.[273] In the Article III context, the "treatment no less favourable" standard had been interpreted to guarantee "effective equality of opportunities for imported products ...".[274] Moreover, "the previous practice of the Contracting Parties [to the GATT 1947] in applying Article III ... has been to base their decisions on the distinctions made by the laws, regulations or requirements themselves and on their potential impact, rather than on the actual consequences for specific imported goods."[275] The language of Article II of GATS parallelled that in Article XVII, which defined "less favourable" treatment as treatment which "modifies the conditions of competition in favour of services and service suppliers of the Member compared to like services and service suppliers of any other Member." Thus, in order to violate Article II of GATS, it needed not to be shown that the EC's import licensing regime created an actual distortion of trade but only that it modified the conditions of competition or created a risk of diminished opportunities for imported products.

4.645 The Complaining parties submitted that, like the GATT panels that had reviewed Article III:4, this Panel should interpret Article II of GATS in light of the language contained in Articles XVII:2 and 3 of GATS. Using such a standard, the conclusion would be that the EC's banana regime violated the EC's MFN obligations through its award of discriminatory competitive benefits to firms of ACP countries at the expense of those of Latin America and the United States.

4.646 The Complaining parties submitted further that Article II of GATS embodied the basic test -"no less favourable treatment" - of Article III:4 of GATT but did not contain the formulation used in Article I:1 of GATT concerning " ... any advantage, favour, privilege or immunity granted by any contracting party to any product originating in or destined for any other country ...". Although Article II of GATS did not contain the type of elaboration found in paragraphs 2 and 3 of Article XVII of GATS, concerning formally identical or different treatment and modification of conditions of competition, neither did the text of Article III:4 of GATT. GATT

[273] Article III:4 of GATT provides that "[t]he products of the territory of any contracting party imported into the territory of any other contracting party shall be accorded treatment no less favourable than that accorded to like products of national origin ...".

[274] Report of the panel on "United States - Section 337 of the Tariff Act of 1930", BISD 36S/345, at p.386, para. *5.11*.

[275] Idem, para. *5.13*.

panels had interpreted Article III:4 of GATT to include these latter concepts as a way to operationalize the very general "treatment no less favourable" standard of Article III:4. According to the Complaining parties, paragraphs 2 and 3 of Article XVII of GATS did not set up new substantive rules but rather served as guidance for the application of the national treatment rule articulated in the first paragraph. The first paragraph of Article XVII was in all relevant respects the same as the MFN rule set out in paragraph 1 of Article II of GATS.

4.647 The EC replied that Article II of GATS prescribed most-favoured nation treatment "with respect to any measure covered by this Agreement". Article I:1 stated that the GATS applied "to measures by Members affecting trade in services". The definition in Article XXVIII(c), in particular under subparagraph (i) thereof, indicated that the measures concerned had to affect trade in services as such and could not be measures with repercussions on services, such as measures on the purchase of goods. Moreover, the use of the words "in respect of" in the chapeau of Article XXVIII(c) demonstrated that, as in Article XVII, the word "affecting" had to be interpreted in a narrow sense and did not refer to measures which modified the conditions of competition. These elements of interpretation were directly based on the text and the context of Article II and were, thus, in conformity with the guidelines of Article 31 of the Vienna Convention.

4.648 The EC considered that, with respect to the "no less favourable treatment" standard, the interpretation should take account of the textual differences between Article II:1 and Article XVII:3 of GATS. Whereas the latter clause explicitly included the modification of competitive conditions as an element of "no less favourable treatment", Article II:1 did not. The drafters, through the inclusion of such elements as the "purchase, payment or use of a service" via the definition contained in Article XXVIII(c), had indeed included aspects of the national treatment clause as it figured in Article III:4 of GATT, into the most-favoured-nation clause of the GATS, but they had done so explicitly. If they had also wished to make the "modification of competitive conditions" requirement into an integral part of the "no less favourable treatment" test under the most-favoured-nation clause, they would have done so explicitly, as it was done for the national treatment clause in Article XVII:3 of GATS. Article XVII contained extensive explanations in paragraphs 2 and 3 thereof on what was meant by no less favourable treatment in the context of national treatment. Article II of GATS on the most-favoured-nation principle contained no such explanation. The conclusion could only be that this explanation did not apply to Article II. There was no reason to interpret the same words in the same way in different Articles. What was true for "like product" in the GATT could also be true for "no less favourable treatment" in the GATS. Therefore, the EC argued, under Article II of GATS there was less favourable treatment as between services and service suppliers of other Members of the WTO, if there was a difference in treatment (not including a modification of competitive conditions) with respect to any measure relating directly to the delivery of services as such.

4.649 For these reasons, the EC continued, it was at best possible to try to demonstrate that certain EC measures discriminated, de facto, against foreign services and/or services suppliers compared to EC services or service suppliers (national treatment), but where it concerned MFN-treatment it had to be shown that there was formally discriminatory treatment as between foreign services and between foreign service suppliers. The "no less favourable treatment" criterion extended, in the opinion of the EC, to the modification of competitive conditions in the national treatment provision but not in the most-favoured-nation clause. Since the entire analysis of the Complaining parties was in terms of competitive conditions, which the EC believed was not relevant, the complaint with respect to Article II should be dismissed.

4.650 The Complaining parties responded that GATS Article II was based on GATT Article III, and considered that there was no reason to suppose that the GATS negotiators had intended the reach of GATS Article II to be more narrow than that of GATT Article III. GATT Article III did not contain specific language on de facto discrimination. GATT panels had interpreted it to include this. They had done so because even facially neutral measures could in fact discriminate against foreign goods. Not to cover this would have allowed significant discrimination to continue as long as it was in the guise of a facially neutral measure. The same was true with respect to the GATS.

c) *Wholesale trade services*

4.651 Ecuador claimed that the EC had, in accordance with Article XVII:1 of GATS, inscribed in its Schedule sectors which included the services provided by Ecuadorian and other third-country suppliers in the transportation, marketing and distribution of bananas for sale in the EC. The national treatment commitments which the EC had scheduled included unqualified commitments in wholesale trade services with respect to cross-border supply and supply through a commercial presence.

4.652 The United States claimed that the entry of "None" under the column of "Limitations on National Treatment" in the GATS Schedule of the EC indicated that it had made an unqualified national treatment commitment for the provision of wholesale trade services by foreign service suppliers both on a cross-border basis and through a commercial presence within the EC. "Cross-border" commitments covered the supply of a service by non-resident service suppliers into another Member's territory.[276] Commitments with respect to commercial presence covered "the opportunities for service suppliers to establish, operate or expand a commercial presence in [another] Member's territory".[277] A "commercial presence" was "any type of business or professional establishment."[278] "Cross-border" wholesaling included, according to the United States, all activities associated with delivering bananas to the EC from abroad and reselling them there. Wholesale distribution on a "commercial presence" basis encompassed all activities associated with the marketing of bananas within the EC by commercial entities established there. Together, wholesaling on a cross-border and commercial presence basis included each of the steps of the banana distribution, but excluded banana production and retail sale. The EC's broad-ranging commitment in the area of wholesale trade services on both a cross-border and commercial presence basis meant, according to the United States, that the EC's national treatment commitments did apply to the aspects of the banana regime that affected any of the entire range of wholesale distribution services supplied by the Complaining parties' banana firms into and within the EC.

4.653 The United States noted that WTO Members had generally used the GATS Services Sector Classification List (SSCL) as the framework for the scheduling of national treatment (and market access) commitments.[279] The SSCL, in turn, referred to, and made use of, the United Nations Central Product Classification (CPC) codes, which described various services activities.[280]

4.654 The Complaining parties argued that in making its GATS national treatment commitments, the EC had used the CPC definition of wholesale trade services, i.e. CPC 622. Thus, the CPC was legally controlling as to the scope of the EC's commitments in wholesale trade services. Within CPC 622, there was a specific sub-category (CPC 62221) for "specialized wholesaling services of fresh, dried, frozen, or canned fruits or vegetables". This sub-category described banana wholesaling, although it should be noted, according to the Complaining parties, that the EC's commitment in wholesale trade services was general and thus covered wholesaling of all products. The headnote to the CPC section in which CPC 622 (and CPC 62221) was found provided a clear definition of wholesale trade services that included all activities associated with the re-sale of merchandise to entities other than the general public:

> ... selling merchandise to retailers, industrial, commercial, institutional or other professional business users, or to other wholesalers, or acting as agent or broker ... The principal services

---

[276] GATS, Guide to Reading the Schedules of Specific Commitments and the Lists of Article II (MFN) Exemptions ("GATS Guide"), p.1; GATS Article 1:2(a).

[277] Idem.

[278] GATS Article XXVIII(d).

[279] MTN.GNS/W/120 (10 July 1991).

[280] "Provisional Central Product Classification", Statistical Papers Series M No. 77, Department of International Economic and Social Affairs, Statistical Office of the United Nations (1991).

> rendered by wholesalers ... may be characterized as reselling merchandise, accompanied by a variety of related, subordinated services, such as: maintaining inventories of goods; physically assembling, sorting and grading goods in large lots; breaking bulk and redistribution in smaller lots; delivery services; refrigeration services; sales promotion services ....[281]

This broad definition included, in the opinion of the Complaining parties, all distribution and re-sale activities between the production and the retail stage. The definition was not limited to activities occurring just prior to the retail level. The definition explicitly included re-sale to other wholesalers, thus recognizing that there could be multiple wholesalers and multiple wholesale steps in the distribution chain for a particular product.

4.655 The Complaining parties submitted that the main Latin American and US banana distribution companies performed each of the activities listed in the above CPC definition, both when they distributed bananas from overseas into the EC, and within the EC itself, i.e.:

(a) *Reselling merchandise.* All of the main banana companies purchased a significant portion of the fruit they handled from local growers. This fruit was then resold in the market to other wholesalers, to ripeners or directly to retailers. In many instances, the profit realized in the reselling of the producers' fruit was shared with the producer. The profit-sharing arrangement between the grower and the re-seller was defined in the fruit purchase contract. In other instances, the main banana companies purchased green fruit in the market for reselling to ripeners or to ripen themselves for eventual resale (yellow) to retailers.

(b) *Maintaining inventories.* Banana companies maintained inventories in refrigerated containers after harvesting and before loading onto ships. During the time that the ship was on the water, the bananas were effectively in refrigerated inventory. By accelerating or delaying the ship's schedule, this inventory could be managed to respond to market conditions.

(c) *Physically assembling, sorting, grading in large lots, breaking bulk and redistribution in smaller lots.* After harvest, bananas were sorted to cull out bad fruit and separate saleable fruit by size and quality. The fruit was then weighed and packed in the appropriate boxes, based on label and size. The boxed fruit was then assembled into lots to fill individual containers or rail cars with the same type of fruit. These individual lots would typically contain about 1,000 boxes (18.2 tonnes). At the load port, the 1,000-box lots were then assembled into full ship loads. The loading of these individual lots in the ship's hold was done according to a precise stowage plan which recorded the exact location and class of each lot. Most ships trading to the EC had to load in more than one load port and typically carried from 200,000 to up to 350,000 boxes of bananas each week. The activity of assembling a full ship load of bananas therefore required careful coordination both within a given source country and between multiple source countries. When the ship was discharged, the process carried out at loading was essentially reversed, with customer-specified loads being assembled from the large inventory on the ship. The customer loads were assembled by sorting through the various blocks of like-class fruit in the ship's holds, breaking the bulk stowage using the stowage plan as a guide, and loading customers' lots for distribution to warehouses and ripening rooms. Any fruit that showed quality problems was sorted out for disposal. Fruit that was discharged directly into a refrigerated warehouse was also sorted into lots of like-class fruit to facilitate the assembling and redistribution of customer orders from the warehouse. Bananas were also sorted and graded in the ripening process where the additional parameter of "colour" was added. Assembling the retailer's load required sorting through the ripening rooms to obtain the quantity, classes/types, and degrees of ripeness that the customer had ordered.

---

[281] Op. cit., p.189.

(d) *Delivery services.* Delivery services were also performed at multiple stages of the distribution process, including: delivery from the packing station to the load port by rail or road, delivery from the load port to the market/discharge port by ship, delivery from the discharge port to other green wholesalers or ripeners by road or rail and delivery from the ripener to the retailer by road.

(e) *Refrigeration services.* Bananas had to be put under refrigeration within 36 hours of being cut and had to be held under continuous refrigeration until they were placed on the retail shelf. Refrigeration services were therefore a crucial part of the banana business and were carried out in refrigerated containers in the tropics, on the ship while sitting in the load ports, on the ship at sea, on the ship while sitting in the discharge ports, in refrigerated rail cars, containers and trucks in the markets, in refrigerated warehouses in the markets, and in refrigerated ripening rooms in the market.

(f) *Sales promotion services.* The main banana companies participated in sales promotions directed at other wholesalers and ripeners as well as at retail consumers. In their trade promotions, the banana companies used technical support, print advertising in trade publications, participation in trade conferences and exhibitions, sponsorship of trade events and continuous customer contacts to promote sales. The companies used television, print and radio advertising, and special events such as supporting social and sporting events to promote retail sales.

4.656 The EC replied that bananas could be marketed at different stages in the supply chain, for instance either before or after ripening. It was generally accepted, according to the EC, that in the banana trade the stage after the ripening process was the wholesale stage. The ripening stage was the stage during which for the last time considerable value was added to the product, when it was transformed from a largely starch-containing, indigestible green product into a largely sugar-containing, edible yellow product. Ripening could be seen as the last stage of the production process of bananas. It was only then that the product was ready for distribution to the final consumer through wholesalers and retailers. Wholesale services trade was described in CPC 622 and the only further indication of what wholesaling might mean was given in the heading of Section 6 of the CPC: "selling merchandise to retailers, to industrial, commercial, institutional or other professional business users, or to other wholesalers ... (wholesaling services)". This heading also mentioned that a wholesaler in the process of reselling merchandise might render a variety of services, such as assembling the goods, breaking bulk and redistribution in smaller lots, delivery, refrigeration, storage, sales promotion, etc. After having bought the bananas from the ripener, the wholesaler acted indeed in conformity with the description given above: he broke bulk, shipped the cartons of bananas in smaller quantities to bigger and smaller retailers and institutional consumers, such as hospitals, and maintained storage, refrigeration and a distribution network to that end.

4.657 The headnote to the CPC section on trade services was not very precise in its description of wholesale trade services but, in the view of the EC, it did place resale to retailers and industrial, commercial, institutional or other professional business users in the foreground. This clearly indicated that at this stage the good concerned (in this case, bananas) must be ready to be consumed: otherwise the retailer could not sell it or the hospital, for example, could not use it in the hospital meal. The EC was therefore of the view that wholesaling of fruit and vegetables, including bananas, consisted of the last trade layer before the retailer or institutional user. There might be horizontal sales at the same level of trade to other wholesalers but such sales were incidental to the true activity of a wholesaler who distributed goods in a consumption-ready state to retailers and institutional users.

4.658 In the view of the EC, the phrase in the description of wholesaling which stated that the resale of merchandise was "accompanied by a variety of related, subordinated services" could therefore no longer cause confusion and be stretched to the banana tree on the other side of the ocean. It was clear that keeping inventories, assembling, sorting, grading, (re)packaging, refrigerating, redistribution in smaller lots must concern goods which were ready for consumption and about to be delivered to the retailer. In the end, this was a service supplied to the retailer, or to institutional users.

4.659 The EC argued that it was important to adhere to a clear and well-circumscribed concept of wholesale services that was of general validity. Otherwise Members would not know what they were committed to under their Schedules: under one heading their commitment could be restricted to their own territory, and in others it could stretch half-way around the globe and include services that Members never dreamt could be "subordinate" to wholesaling.

4.660 The EC submitted further that cross-border wholesaling in the banana trade, although unusual in practice, could occur in Europe between the EC and neighbouring countries, such as the Czech Republic, Norway, Poland or Switzerland. This implied that the bananas which had been ripened in a ripening installation within the EC were subsequently distributed by a wholesaler to retailers or institutional consumers in these countries or vice versa. Bringing green fruit to the EC for ripening could not be described as cross-border wholesaling, which would stretch the notion of wholesaling well beyond the limits of its description as given in the heading to Section 6 of the CPC, as it should be applied to the banana trade. Assuming that wholesaling services through commercial presence were being supplied with respect to bananas within the EC, the Complaining parties had failed to demonstrate which companies, that were active in this area, were owned or controlled by interests of the Complainants involved and how these service suppliers were being discriminated by a measure relating to the way in which they provided their service within the EC. This would be difficult to demonstrate, according to the EC, since the wholesale and retail sectors were specifically excluded from the scope of the contested measures. Wholesalers and retailers were not "operators" within the meaning of Regulation 1442/93 (Article 3:2).

4.661 The EC argued that, if it was assumed that services which were incorporated into the banana sold on the EC market, could nevertheless be considered to be supplied at the same time as the banana was sold (*quod non*, according to the EC), the question arose which services were rendered prior to, or next to, the sale of the banana on the EC market. The EC asserted that, in the view of the Complainants, such incorporated services were (nearly) all wholesaling services. This choice, however, seemed primarily to have been determined by the fact that wholesaling services were largely free without restrictions under the first three modes, according to the EC Schedule. The following services would seem to be involved:

(a) *Picking bananas and transporting them to the packing station.* These were services incidental to agriculture (CPC 88110).[282]

(b) *Packaging at the packing station.* This was a packaging service in its own right (CPC 87600) or packing services incidental to transport (CPC 74). It was a service supplied to the banana plantation or to the transporter in the producing country, not to the retailer or the institutional user or even to another wholesaler in the EC.

(c) *Overland transport to loading wharf.* This was a service of its own right as freight transportation by railway (CPC 7112) or by truck (CPC 7123) which was rendered to the plantation or to the exporter, but not the retailer in the EC. Similarly, any storage or refrigeration that was necessary at this stage was done with a view to preparing goods for transport by sea. Such services were supplied to the plantation owner or to the transport company or exporters. It would be incorrect to regard these activities as services subordinate to wholesaling by arguing that they were referred to in the description of distribution services. These activities were not services rendered to the retailer in the framework of wholesaling.

[282] Op. cit., p.259.

(d) *Loading onto ship and administration connected thereto - other cargo handling services under supporting and auxiliary transport services (CPC 74190).* All specialized loading and unloading services, stowage techniques, etc., were provided in the port of exportation and the port of importation. These were services rendered to the shipper of the goods or to the ocean transport company. To regard these activities as services supplied to the retailer and institutional users as part of wholesaling on the basis that this amounts to assembling, sorting, breaking bulk, etc., was unwarranted. These were activities which were inherent in every ocean transport and were performed for different kinds of cargo. There was no reason to distinguish them and to regard them as part of wholesaling. Indeed, it was stated explicitly in the CPC that these activities were cargo handling, storage and warehousing services not subordinated to selling and classified in division 74 thereof.

(e) *Ocean transport - transportation of frozen and refrigerated goods (CPC 72121).* To qualify ocean transport as storage, refrigeration services or delivery service to the retailer or institutional user would imply that Members could dispense with a large part of negotiations on shipping services, once they had liberalized refrigerated storage. The CPC was a system of mutually exclusive categories and a specific commitment was valid for a specific category. Even if services may be linked, as in the case of advertising and market research, for example, one could not use liberalization in one sector in order to open up a sector which was (partially) closed. If this was true for service sectors which corresponded to CPC numbers, it must be true, *a fortiori,* for a term like "delivery" which was not defined and did not occupy a CPC heading. The EC argued that a services sector, such as ocean shipping, could not be opened up by making it into "delivery" under wholesale trade services. It was also unacceptable to determine what constituted wholesale trade services on the basis that a company regarded certain services as a package of wholesale services, including "delivery" by sea. The scope of certain services categories under the CPC, including wholesale services, could not vary with the fortuitous industrial structure in a particular sector, i.e. if there were large, integrated companies, wholesale comprised everything between the banana tree and the supermarket, and if this was not the case, wholesale covered only the last stage before retail. Such interpretation would lead to great uncertainty in scheduling because commitments would be entirely dependent on the fortuitous structure of the services company concerned.

(f) *Discharge from ship and related administrative services.* The points made under (d) above refer.

(g) *Land transport to the warehouser/ripener.* The points made under (c) above refer.

(h) *Ripening - Manufacture of food on a fee or contract basis (CPC 88411).*[283] Ripening was a kind of (re-)manufacturing process, comparable to turning raw lumber into dimension lumber, for which CPC 88411 was relevant.

(i) *Repacking for retail.* The points made under (b) above refer.

(j) *Advertising and Promotions* - Planning, creating and placement services of advertising (CPC 87120).

(k) *Transport to retail site.* The points made under (c) above refer.

(l) *Retail.* Retail sales of fruit and vegetables (CPC 63101).

[283] Op. cit., p.259.

4.662 The EC noted that it might be possible to regroup the services mentioned separately above under items (i), (j) and (k) and any incidental storage that might occur at those stages, into a service called "wholesale trade services of fruit and vegetables" (CPC 62221). This was possible to accept, on the basis of the introductory note to Section 6 of the CPC that these services might be related or subordinated to the activity of reselling bananas to the retailers as such services as delivery services, sales promotion, storage and sorting, grading and breaking bulk (i.e. repackaging) were explicitly mentioned.

4.663 In the view of the EC, if its interpretation of wholesaling under the CPC was correct and wholesaling was the (re-)sale of a good ready for consumption to retailers and institutional users (including some horizontal transactions with other wholesalers), the following conclusions could be drawn: (i) as regards Chiquita Brands, Del Monte, Dole Foods and Noboa, most, if not all of these companies probably did not engage in wholesaling as the EC defined it; (ii) the EC's granting of import licences did not extend to the wholesale stage as the EC defined it; and (iii) none of the other services referred to above were affected by the EC licensing rules.

4.664 The Complaining parties responded that the EC's argument that wholesaling was limited to activities that took place immediately prior to the retail stage was not supported by the CPC definition of wholesaling. The EC's claim was also based, according to the Complaining parties, on the faulty argument that ripening was actually part of the process of producing bananas. The point of the EC's argument was not clear since the EC's scheduled commitments applied to wholesaling of all merchandise, not only fresh fruit. Thus, if importers were not distributing bananas, they were distributing some other commodity that was also covered by the EC's commitments in wholesale trade services. Moreover, the Complaining parties contended, the argument that ripeners were "producers" contradicted the EC's own regulations and statements and would have bizarre implications: (i) Regulation 1442/93 included "production" of bananas in activity function (a) (primary importer) whereas ripening was in a separate activity function, activity function (c); (ii) the EC's 1994 Report on the EC Banana Regime described ripeners as "traders", not "producers" and, whereas ripening took place throughout the EC, that report noted that "EC production was concentrated in the peripheral areas of the EC..."[284]; (iii) if ripeners were producers, the United States would be the world's first or second largest producer of bananas because nearly all bananas consumed in the United States were ripened there. Yet this would be inconsistent with the EC's position that the US interest as a producer of bananas was so small as to justify excluding the United States altogether from the goods portion of this proceeding; and (iv) if ripeners were producers, they should be entitled to receive compensation for loss of income under Title III of Regulation 404/93; however, Title III limited compensation to entities located in the tropical and sub-tropical EC regions in which bananas were grown which was a further recognition that ripeners were not producers.

4.665 The Complaining parties claimed further that in arguing that wholesaling did not include trade in green bananas, the EC forgot that the entire "banana regime" as it affected imports, was applied to green, not yellow, bananas. The tariff quota was applied to green bananas; import licences were licences to import green bananas; the special export certificates issued by the BFA countries were certificates to export green bananas; and so forth. The EC also forgot that, in a working document leading up to the adoption of Regulation 1442/93 (which concerned activity functions), it described firms trading in bananas prior to ripening as "wholesalers of green bananas."[285] It was inconsistent, for the EC then to have argued that only yellow bananas were true "bananas," and only they could be "wholesaled".

4.666 In the context of its conclusions above, the EC recognized that its import licences covered green bananas and not yellow ones.

4.667 The Complaining parties continued that the EC had cited the CPC definition in making its national treatment commitments, and that this definition, which included all wholesaling, was legally controlled under the

[284] "Report on the EC Banana Regime", European Commission, July 1994, pp.2, 4.

[285] BANAN/TR/N/0015, 15 May 1993, p.2.

GATS. If this were not the case, significant distribution-related service activities would not be covered by the GATS disciplines, depending on the way some chose to use terms with respect to a particular industry at any particular time. Yet the GATS was, according to the Complaining parties, intended to cover all measures affecting trade in services.

4.668 The Complaining parties noted the EC's claim that its specific commitments for wholesale trade services did not include any banana distribution services provided from Latin America to Europe since such services necessarily involved ocean delivery and no GATS commitments in maritime transport services were currently applicable. This argument ignored the fact that the EC definition of wholesale trade services included delivery. In a cross-border context, delivery necessarily involved the movement of merchandise from abroad into the territory of a WTO Member, which could occur by air, land or sea. Of course, not all shippers were wholesalers. If a shipping company entered into a contract to deliver somebody else's cargo safely across the seas, that company was supplying maritime transport services, not wholesale trade services. If, on the other hand, a company bought the cargo, delivered it, resold it to a buyer on-shore in the territory of another Member, and engaged in the types of related activities listed in the CPC definition of wholesale trade services, these activities would clearly fall within the comprehensive coverage of cross-border wholesale trade services. The Complaining parties' GATS case against the EC was not founded on the theory that the EC had discriminated against United States or Latin American maritime transport operators, or United States or Latin American maritime transport services, in favour of EC shipping companies or EC ocean transport services. The EC would be correct to oppose such a case on the ground that it had no commitments in that sector. Rather, the Complaining parties' GATS case challenged what the EC banana regime had done to the business of international wholesaling of bananas into and within the EC. That business included an ocean delivery element. Many of the large banana distribution companies included overseas delivery as an integral element of their package of wholesaling services. Like any other aspect of wholesaling, the resale price of the merchandise reflected the value of this element of the wholesaling process. Delivery by sea should not be excluded simply because that activity could be offered as an independent commercial service. The CPC repeatedly defined services in a way that included subsidiary activities that some companies might perform as independent activities under other CPC categories. The commercial services described in the CPC did not overlap, although many of the physical activities carried out by firms in different categories were the same. Wholesalers bought and sold products. The transportation or delivery they engaged in or arranged for was incidental to, but inseparable from, their business as traders. Because such transportation was not offered as a discrete "service" to others, it could not itself be described as a "transportation service" any more than the use of a telephone could be deemed "telephone services." By contrast, "transportation services" entailed the discrete service of carrying others' goods from point to point. Applied to this case, the Complaining parties submitted that the EC's approach was inconsistent with the fact that wholesale trade services consisted of a package of activities, all directed toward bringing goods to the market. Indeed, the CPC described it in such terms, setting out a core activity (re-selling goods) and an inventory of related activities, explicitly including delivery, that all advanced the enterprise of wholesaling products.

4.669 The Complaining parties claimed that the EC itself not only accepted, but actually proposed, that wholesale trade services be defined to include some transport services, such as road and rail transport, that might be classified elsewhere in the CPC if performed as a separate service activity. The EC argued, according to the Complainants, that the Panel must draw the line at the water's edge, but provided no logical or principled reason why this should be so. The CPC contained no preference for rail and road delivery over ocean delivery in the context of wholesale trade services. The activities associated with the distribution of bananas from abroad into the EC, including ocean delivery, fitted the type of activities listed in the CPC definition of wholesale trade services. In addition, the EC was incorrect to argue that under the Complaining parties' interpretation of cross-border wholesale trade services, the scope of the service would vary from commodity-to-commodity, depending on whether distribution was done by vertically integrated firms or not. In a vertically integrated chain, one firm would do all the wholesaling for the product. In a non-integrated chain, multiple firms would perform the wholesaling. But the activities would be the same and they would all be wholesaling activities. With respect to the EC's claim that the Complaining parties had not demonstrated which companies were active in wholesale trade services the

Complaining parties referred to their discussion in the section below enumerating the evidence demonstrating the Latin American and United States firms engaged in this sector.

4.670 In response to the EC argument that Complaining parties' definition of wholesale trade services included services that "stretch half-way around the world", the Complaining parties observed that it was the nature of cross-border wholesale services that the service originated outside the particular Member at issue. Cross-border supply of wholesale trade services included services associated with buying bananas from abroad and bringing them into the EC. Thus, there was a connection to the EC market in any event.

4.671 The EC responded that it needed to be determined, if there existed a measure in respect of services, who the Member supplying the service was (in the case of direct trans-border services). Article I:2(a) of GATS was concerned with services supplied from the territory of another Member. This subparagraph contrasted with subparagraphs I:2(c) and (d) where the service supplier was relevant. This was confirmed by Article XXVIII(f)(i) of GATS. The comparison in cross-border trade was between like services from different Members, not between different service suppliers.

4.672 In the case of the supply of services through commercial presence, the question arose, according to the EC, who the service supplier in terms of the GATS was. In this regard, there were certain consequences resulting from the different structure of the GATS, as compared to that of the GATT. The GATS was about invisible trade. The EC argued that one could not rest content with assertions from one side, which stood as a *prima facie* case, if the other side did not contradict these. The complainants were not in a position to contradict because they could not get at the facts. One must have more clarity on whether the service providers of a country had actually provided the services that were claimed to be at issue (e.g. demonstration of statutory goal of the company; invoices or other proof showing that the company concerned engaged in the relevant services trade). In the view of the EC, it was unacceptable that the Panel give a kind of advisory opinion, such as: "If, as seems likely, service providers of X were performing service Y, the measures of Member Z are contrary to the GATS".

4.673 Another question was, according to the EC, where the service transaction was. It was an important prerequisite that the service be supplied "on the market and in competition with others". On this point, the documentation provided by Complainants was inadequate in the EC's opinion. Complainants asserted that the groups of companies concerned bought bananas from others. According to the EC, this did not demonstrate that these groups provided the services that followed (i.e. the whole string of services that Complainants listed) on the market. The companies concerned probably "labelled" the bananas and sold them as their own, providing services essentially within the companies. According to the EC, the situation was still unclear. Complainants wanted to play on two courts at the same time by arguing, on the one hand, that their companies provided a range of services from the banana tree to the supermarket and that it was all wholesale. The EC was of the view that it had demonstrated that this was not reasonably possible. First, this was not a proper interpretation of wholesale trade services on the basis of the heading to Section 6 of the CPC. Services provided within the country of exportation were not supplied to the retailer or institutional user in Europe. Second, shipping was a barrier, not only for lack of commitments but also because of the definition of shipping in Article XXVIII(f) of GATS. A shipping service was not a normal cross-border service: the flag of the vessel was decisive or the nationality of the person supplying the service through the operation of a vessel. Alternatively, the Complainants took the view that their companies were not integrated but that this did not matter since all relevant services were supplied in succession by service suppliers and "were caused to be supplied". The EC questioned who provided these discrete services, when and how. If it were true that the integrated companies caused the services to be supplied, they were no longer in the business of wholesaling which was concerned with physical distribution of goods and not with paper transactions. The EC argued that the Complainants wanted "to have their service and eat it": the real services were delivered by service suppliers (of unknown nationality, according to the EC) but, in addition, there was the undefined term "delivery" which allegedly entitled the Complainants' companies to the benefits of the commitments in the field of wholesale services.

4.674 Ecuador, Mexico and the United States claimed that, in addition to wholesale trade services, the EC had made relevant national treatment commitments with respect to freight transportation (CPC 71231) and rental of vessels with crew (CPC 72130). United States and other non-EC firms provided these types of services with respect to bananas sold in the EC on a commercial presence basis (for freight transportation) and a cross-border basis (for rental of vessels with crew). The discriminatory features of the EC banana regime had negatively altered the competitive conditions under which non-EC firms provided these related types of services as well.

4.675 The EC responded that it was mystified as to how the Complainants concerned could make any claims under the GATS in respect of freight transportation and rental of vessels with crew. These sectors were largely unbound, i.e. there were no commitments in these services sectors made by the EC and its member States. This meant that GATS Article XVII was not applicable. The fact that these sectors were mentioned in the Schedule did not mean that they were "inscribed" in the technical sense of a commitment having been made. Moreover, the Complainants involved had not a *prima facie* case that their service supplier had attempted to be active in the sector where there were no limitations on the third mode, namely rental of vessels with crew. The EC requested that under these circumstances the claims in respect of these two sectors must be rejected by the Panel.

3. *Operator category licence allocation*

a) *Article XVII*

4.676 The United States recalled that in its view, a Member acted inconsistently with Article XVII if three elements existed: (i) the Member had undertaken a commitment in the relevant sector; (ii) the Member had adopted or applied a measure affecting the supply of services in that sector; and (iii) the measure accorded to services or service suppliers of any other Member treatment less favourable than that it accorded to the Member's own like services or service suppliers. According to the United States, each of the above elements was present in this case.

4.677 The United States claimed that with regard to operator category allocations, firms that supplied distribution services for EC/ACP bananas were "like" those firms that supplied the same services for Latin American bananas. Their respective activities, equipment, types of personnel employed and marketing stages were either identical or virtually so and the extent to which they had competed directly with each other in the EC market had been limited only by the restrictive regulatory regimes established by certain member States (e.g. United Kingdom, France) and by traditional marketing relationships built up over time. Indeed, the EC itself had recognized this competitive relationship and had sought to rearrange it in favour of EC suppliers through its operator category allocations: "the [licensing] allocation formula is intended ... to strengthen the competitive position of operators who have previously marketed EC or ACP bananas, vis-à-vis their competitors who have previously marketed Latin American bananas ...".[286]

4.678 The United States argued further that paragraph 3 of Article XVII indicated that the "treatment no less favourable" element of the national treatment standard could be violated even where a Member had provided to foreign service suppliers "formally identical" treatment to that accorded to its own like service suppliers. That paragraph also indicated that a Member acted inconsistently with its obligations if a measure modified the conditions of competition in favour of services or service suppliers of the Member compared to like services or service suppliers of any other Member. Moreover, the EC's operator category allocations treated firms that had marketed Latin American bananas (Category A) less favourably than firms that had marketed EC or ACP bananas (Category B). Regulation 404/93 awarded a major portion (30 per cent) of the third-country tariff quota to service suppliers in Category B, even though Category B operators generally had little history of marketing Latin American bananas. There was no quantity set aside giving Category A operators new marketing rights for

[286] Written observations of the Council of the European Communities before the Court of Justice of the European Communities concerning the Application for Interim Relief pursuant to Articles 185 and 186 of the EEC Treaty, 14 June 1993, No. 435564, p.15.

EC/ACP bananas. According to the United States, the table below made clear that Category B service suppliers had been predominantly of EC nationality.

Company	Nationality/Ownership	Principal Operator Category
Chiquita Brands	United States	A
Dole Foods	United States	A
Noboa	Ecuador	A
Del Monte	Mexico[287]	A
Uniban	Colombia	A
Banacol	Colombia	A
Geest	United Kingdom	B
Fyffes	Ireland	B
Pomona	France	B
Compagnie Fruitière	France	B
CDB/Durand	France	B
Gipam	France	B
Coplaca	Spain	B
Bargoso SA	Spain	B
Others	EC	B
Jamaica Producers	Jamaica	B
Winban/Wibdeco	Windward Islands	B

[287] The United States submitted that there had been recent reports that Del Monte might be subject to a change of ownership.

4.679 Although the operator category distinctions appeared neutral as to nationality or ownership of service suppliers, the United States claimed that they were drawn in such a way as to accomplish precisely the same result as a measure based explicitly on nationality or ownership. The figures in the table below made clear, according to the United States, that operator category allocations effected a transfer of market share for the marketing of Latin American bananas from US, Ecuadorian and other non-EC/ACP firms to EC and ACP firms.

Latin American Banana Imports		
Principal Operator Category[288]	**1990-92 Share**	**1994 Import Entitlement under EC Regulation 404/93[289]**
Category A	**Over 95%**	**66.5%**
Category B	**Less than 5%**	**30%**

4.680 The United States noted that ECJ Advocate General Gulmann had found that "[i]t is ... a fact that the Regulation 404/93 uses means - the tariff quota and particularly the special rules for allocating it - which significantly interfere with existing patterns of trade; market shares for operators in certain member States [i.e. member States in which third-country marketing firms were primarily based] were reduced and considerable profit potential is transferred to operators in other member States. It was in my view to be foreseen that the regulation would lead to perceptible disturbances of trade in the markets which had hitherto been open, such as rising prices, falling turnover with the consequent risk of redundancies, under-utilization of installations both for the firms dealing directly with bananas and those transporting (shipping companies, ports and railways) and ripening bananas."[290]

4.681 According to the United States, the EC described its approach of issuing licences to import Latin American bananas to those who previously had traded only in EC or ACP bananas as "cross-subsidization." The EC Commission had been specific as to how it achieved cross-subsidization for its favoured domestic and foreign distribution firms by giving them a share of the market they had not earned: "The creation of a quantity-restricted market through a combination of tariffs and quotas results in internal price levels above the world price ... . [T]his results in a value being attached to licences to import (quota rent) ... . Reserving a proportion of tariff quota licences for those operators who have marketed ACP and/or EC bananas is a means of transferring some of this quota rent to them ...".[291] The EC had thus acknowledged not only that the allocation formula was intended to strengthen the competitive position of EC/ACP marketing firms vis-à-vis their

[288] The United States noted that this table focused on the activity function of "primary importer". EC firms' share of rights to import third-country bananas under the banana regime grew even greater if one factored in the large share of rights within Category A awarded to firms that engaged in the other two activity functions specified in Regulation 1442/93.

[289] The United States noted that the figures in this column were the tariff quota share percentages set down in Article 19 of Regulation 404/93. To reflect the exact respective import entitlement of the two sets of firms at issue, the figures would need to be adjusted to take account of the small amount of cross-over that existed between the two distribution segments. For example, the 1994 share of import entitlement for firms of principal operator Category B was 30 per cent, plus 1990-92 average volume of third-country bananas marketed by such firms x 0.665, minus 1990-92 average volume of EC/ACP bananas marketed by firms of the Latin American-banana distribution segment x 0.30. Because the cross-over was so small, and because the two adjustments tended to cancel each other out, the adjustments would, in the view of the United States, not significantly alter the figures listed in this column.

[290] Opinion of Advocate General Gulmann, 8 June 1994, "Federal Republic of Germany v. Council of the European Union", 26 ("Opinion of the Advocate General Gulmann").

[291] "Note for Information - Impact of Cross-Subsidization within the Banana Regime", European Commission, pp.1-2.

competitors but also that "the allocation formula may lead to a certain redistribution of respective market shares".[292]

4.682 The United States noted that the views of the EC and its member States were further elaborated by EC Advocate General Gulmann, as part of his opinion quoted above: "The [EC] Council does not deny that the 30 per cent share of the quota involves a transfer of resources to traders in Community/ACP bananas ... . The Spanish Government mentions in that connection that the transfer of a part of the quota to operators other than traditional dealers in third-country [i.e. Latin American] bananas helps also to reduce the dominant role which certain non-European companies have played in connection with marketing."[293] Thus, by the EC's own admissions and those of its member States, the 30 per cent set-aside for EC firms and selected, foreign-based firms provided less favourable treatment to non-EC firms that traditionally marketed Latin American bananas into the EC by: (i) transferring quota rent from Category A operators to Category B operators; (ii) strengthening the competitive position of Category B operators vis-à-vis Category A operators; (iii) redistributing market share from Category A operators to B operators; and (iv) helping to reduce the "dominant role" of non-European marketing firms. In sum, the allocation of licences to Category B operators affected the supply of a service (wholesale trade services) for which the EC had made an unrestricted national treatment commitment, and accorded less favourable treatment to non-EC service suppliers than the treatment accorded to like EC suppliers. This aspect of the EC banana regime violated the EC's obligations under Article XVII of GATS.

4.683 Mexico claimed that Article XVII was applicable in this case since the services in question (wholesale trade services, transport and rental of vessels with crew) were included in the EC's Schedule with certain conditions and exceptions, and the EC regime affected the supply of like services or suppliers of like services (distribution, transportation, and marketing of bananas from the country of origin to the European consumer), according them treatment that was formally different on the basis of the origin of the products.

4.684 Mexico argued that, at the level of service suppliers, the less favourable treatment accorded by the EC regime to services and service suppliers of other Members than the treatment it accorded to its own services and service suppliers was a result of the same factors cited to demonstrate the violation, at the level of goods, of Article III:4 of GATT. In other words, the less favourable treatment resulted from the fact that the EC had reserved 30 per cent of all import licences for Category B operators (service suppliers who had marketed EC or ACP bananas), with the result that Category B operators were service supplier enterprises owned by Europeans and, in two cases, by ACP countries. The incentive (or less-favourable treatment for non-European service suppliers) given to European service suppliers through the Category B operators was even more evident bearing in mind that Category A operators (non-European service suppliers) would have to reduce their share of European imports from 95 per cent in 1992 to the maximum of 66.5 per cent allowed to them under the EC regime. This redistribution of the market was not a random result of the EC regime but something that had even been recognized as a policy objective by the EC itself.

---

[292] Written observations of the Council of the European Communities before the Court of Justice of the European Communities concerning the Application for Interim Relief pursuant to Articles 185 and 186 of the EEC Treaty, 14 June 1993, No. 435564, p.15.
[293] Opinion of the Advocate General Gulmann, pp.22-23.

4.685 Ecuador argued that Category A operators generally included service providers from third countries while Category B operators were generally composed of ACP and EC service providers. The following table, submitted by Ecuador, listed the primary third-country and EC service suppliers and showed in which operator category these service suppliers fell:

Company	Nationality	Principal Operator Category
Chiquita Brands	United States	A
Dole Foods	United States	A
NOBOA	Ecuador	A
Del Monte	Mexico	A
Geest (purchased by Fyffes and Wibdeco)	United Kingdom	B
Fyffes	Ireland	B
Pomona	France	B
Companie Fruitière	France	B
CDB/Durand	France	B
Gipam	France	B

4.686 The services provided by the third-country operators on the one hand and the ACP/EC operators on the other hand were, according to Ecuador, virtually identical. However, the EC regime did not treat these two groups of operators in the same way. Rather, the EC regime effectively hindered third-country operators while facilitating the access of ACP/EC bananas to the EC market. The EC had, in fact, admitted that: "the [licensing] allocation formula is intended ... to strengthen the competitive position of operators who have previously marketed Community or ACP bananas, vis-à-vis their competitors who have previously marketed Latin American bananas ...".[294] Ecuador considered that Regulation 404/93 distorted competition in the services sector by shifting 30 per cent of the third-country banana market to service suppliers which previously had no involvement in the importation, marketing, and distribution of third-country bananas. The table above illustrated, according to Ecuador, the extent of the market disruption which Regulation 404/93 had wrought.

4.687 On the basis of the citations above, Ecuador claimed that the clear and acknowledged effect of the operator category allocation was to transfer large portions of the market from third-country suppliers to EC and ACP suppliers. This discriminatory treatment of third-country operators directly violated the national treatment requirements of Article XVII of GATS.

4.688 The Complaining parties submitted that the EC's import allocations provided discriminatory advantages to EC and ACP banana distributors even though they appeared neutral on their face. Transferring business opportunities from importers of Latin American bananas to importers of EC/ACP bananas and to customs clearers and ripeners was the equivalent of an explicit transfer to EC and ACP firms. At the time of Regulation 404/93, the vast majority of EC/ACP banana importers and customs clearers and ripeners were EC-

[294] Written observations of the Council of the European Communities before the Court of Justice of the European Communities concerning the Application for Interim Relief pursuant to Articles 185 and 186 of the EEC Treaty, 14 June 1993, No. 435564, p.15.

or ACP-owned firms. Articles II and XVII of GATS had adopted established GATT doctrine that a measure need not discriminate on its face against imported products in order to discriminate. The *Section 337* panel report observed that: "On the one hand, contracting parties may apply to imported products different formal requirements if doing so would accord to imported products more favourable treatment. On the other hand, it also has to be recognized that there may be cases where application of formally identical legal provisions would in practice accord less favourable treatment to imported products and a contracting party might thus have to apply different legal provisions to imported products to ensure that the treatment accorded them was in fact no less favourable."[295]

4.689 It was no coincidence that the term "formally identical" which appeared in the *Section 337* panel report reappeared in Article XVII:2. Indeed, drawing on GATT precedent, paragraph 2 of Article XVII made explicit that facially neutral measures could provide less favourable treatment to foreign service providers just as surely as explicit discrimination based on the country of origin of the providers. In sum, by adopting the GATT approach to discrimination, the GATS negotiators recognized that, over the years, the GATT had developed a coherent and workable test of what it meant to discriminate. This Panel should employ that test in applying Article XVII of GATS to the EC's import licensing rules in this case.

4.690 The Complaining parties claimed that the companies that controlled the UK market had lobbied hard for the market-share-transferring aspects of the regime, fully aware of the windfall these aspects represented for their business. Market investors and other observers universally had recognized the economic advantages that the EC banana regime represented for EC firms, such as Geest and Fyffes. Those advantages were so substantial and so obvious that it was possible to chart the firms' share prices simply by observing the status of the adoption and implementation of the banana regime. According to the Complaining parties, in December 1992, when the deal to establish the regime was struck, share prices of Geest and Fyffes rose substantially.[296]

4.691 The EC submitted that Article XVII of GATS enjoined the EC in the sectors inscribed in its Schedule (according to Complainants, in this case the wholesale trading sector) not to grant any less favourable treatment to services or service suppliers of the Complaining parties than it granted to its own services or service suppliers. Such less favourable treatment could consist of treatment which modified the conditions of competition in favour of services or service suppliers of the EC compared to service and service suppliers of the Complaining parties. The only direct cross-frontier service that might be involved was ocean-shipping of bananas and there were no MFN commitments in this sector. Similarly, with respect to the third mode of services supply, through commercial presence, if the service sector concerned was wholesale trading, this sector was not covered by the EC measures, which in any case were measures relating to goods. If nevertheless it were considered possible for the EC licensing system for bananas to touch third mode services activities related to bananas, the Complaining parties would have to make a *prima facie* case that companies owned or controlled by them were active on the relevant EC services market and that such companies did not or could not *de iure* or *de facto* fall under the category of operators who marketed EC bananas or under any of the categories of ripeners or secondary importers. Such a *prima facie* case had, in the opinion of the EC, not been made. The remarks on transferability of licences that were made above were also applicable in this case.

4.692 As concerns "nationality" of companies for GATS purposes, the EC argued, incorporation in the EC did not necessarily imply EC ownership or control within the meaning of the relevant GATS provisions. The

---

[295] "Section 337" panel report, para. *5.11*.

[296] Financial Times, *Bananas*, 1 September 1992; The Times, "European Import Deal Zips Up Great Banana Split", 19 December 1992; Irish Times, 11 February 1993; Lloyds List, "EC Banana Deal Sends Geest Shares Soaring", 16 February 1993. Similar reports are found at: Supermarketing, UK: "Banana Benefit for Geest - EC Quotas", 2 April 1993; Supermarketing, UK: "Super Marketing Share Watch: Sainsbury's and Argyll Bounce Back", 11 December 1992; Lloyds List, Eire: "Fisher Rumoured to have Interest in Fyffes Stake", 20 April 1993; The Guardian, "EC Court Puts the Skids under Germany in Latest Banana War", 30 June 1993; Reuters Financial Service, "Banana Ruling Seen Positive for Fyffes", 29 June 1993.

EC was suffering from the same handicaps of confidentiality as the Complainants and hence did not make general affirmations about company ownership. It would not be acceptable to the EC if this led to the Panel accepting without any further proof the assertions of the Complainants. Moreover, the EC has submitted evidence (supported by the *A.D. Little* study) that, in 1994, 28 per cent of EC/ACP imports were controlled by Chiquita, Dole and Del Monte. The EC reiterated that Regulations 404/93 and 1442/93 specifically excluded from their scope bananas at the wholesale and retail stage. In the opinion of the EC, the Complaining parties concerned had not made a serious attempt to set out which companies of the Complainants involved were engaging in wholesale trade services of fruit in the EC. The tables in paragraphs 0 and 0 above were not demonstrably linked to wholesale trade services. Its indications of nationality and ownership were not corroborated by any evidence. Its utilization of the "principal operator category" was misleading because it ignored the fact that many of the firms concerned, and certainly the three large, integrated banana traders, received considerable allocations of both A and B licences. The EC claimed that the Complaining parties made allegations which, at least for the UK market, were incorrect or contradictory. In 1991, 137,739 tonnes or 28 per cent of total banana imports into the United Kingdom were of Latin American origin which represented 6 per cent of total Latin American banana imports into the EC. The EC considered that, in light of these figures, either the companies that brought bananas to the UK market were not almost all owned or controlled by EC interests or it was incorrect to claim that 95 per cent of Latin American bananas were sourced and distributed by companies owned or controlled by United States or Latin American persons.

4.693 The EC argued that the available evidence indicated that, with respect to the assertions relating to the alleged redistribution of market share and quota rents as well as the competition policy reasons underlying the allocation of quota rents, companies which were United States-owned or controlled had not lost market share. Moreover, they had the considerable advantage of being able to sell their bananas for prices which were higher in the EC market than on the world market and in this way had the possibility of making a handsome profit on their bananas from Central and South America which normally had lower production costs than ACP or EC bananas.

4.694 The EC submitted that there were growing indications that Del Monte, originally claimed to be a service provider of Mexico, was not, or no longer, a service supplier of that country. There were strong indications that Del Monte had been sold to a Palestinian/Jordanian business group. In the view of the EC, this could imply that Del Monte was no longer a service supplier of Mexico within the meaning of Article XXVIII of GATS, in particular paragraphs (m)(ii) and (n) thereof. The EC argued that this should result in the incapacity of Mexico to advance a claim under the third mode of service supply.

4.695 Mexico responded that, in its opinion - and this opinion was supported by several previous panels - there was no need for a Member to demonstrate adverse commercial effects in order to claim the fulfillment of obligations under the WTO by other Members. To follow such criteria would imply that Members with more trade would have more rights than the rest of the Members. And what was even worse, that those Members that did not have trade, would never have rights, only obligations. If one conceded without accepting that there was a need to demonstrate commercial effects in order to claim Mexico's rights under the WTO, it would have been necessary to analyze whether Del Monte was a Mexican company when the EC regime was established, and not whether Del Monte was still a Mexican company. Otherwise, the possibility that the EC regime could have been so harmful for non-European companies that some of these companies had preferred to go out of business would have been left aside, or an argument could have been made that a Member had no right to claim because in the future it might not have a company trading its product in a given market. However, given the interest of the EC in this matter, Mexico noted that Del Monte was and continued to be 100 per cent Mexican-owned.

4.696 The Complaining parties disagreed with the EC's assertion that they had not provided *prima facie* evidence of a GATS violation. The Complaining parties referred, *inter alia*, to (i) Exhibit E of their Joint rebuttal submission, which listed the companies of Complainants established in the EC that supplied wholesale trade services for bananas, and (ii) the information set out above, which indicated with specificity the types of wholesale trade services that Complainants' service suppliers engaged in, and (iii) documents they had submitted which demonstrated that Complaining parties' banana wholesalers distributed bananas they did not produce themselves. With regard to an indication of which activities were performed by which companies in the EC, the EC had not explained why this type of detail was necessary to establish a *prima facie* case under the GATS. The Complaining parties noted that this type of information was very likely to implicate confidential business information. GATS Article III *bis* provided that a Member was not required to submit such information. Moreover, the EC did not seriously question the fact that, before Regulation 404/93 went into effect, Latin American and United States firms distributed nearly all Latin American bananas into the EC, and EC and ACP firms distributed the vast majority of EC and ACP bananas into the EC. The Complaining parties observed that the EC alleged that three major Latin American or United States wholesaling firms "controlled" 28 per cent of EC/ACP banana production in 1994 citing the *A.D. Little* report. The EC purported to base this allegation on a report commissioned by an European banana producer association, but had not provided the study or the underlying data contained in it to the Panel. More importantly, the 28 per cent figure pertained to the period after the regime went into effect and was thus irrelevant to whether the regime had modified competitive conditions. The Complaining parties noted further that the *A.D. Little* report itself indicated that the share of EC and ACP banana production controlled by the three main North American banana distribution companies prior to the EC banana regime was only 6 per cent. If one assumed, *arguendo*, that the 6 per cent figure was accurate, it supported Complaining parties' contention that Latin American bananas and EC/ACP bananas were distributed by separate groups of firms prior to Regulation 404/93.

4.697 The Complaining parties further questioned whether the EC's arguments regarding sufficiency of evidence could be taken seriously when the EC had not submitted any of its own information to contest Complaining parties' data, even though as administrator of the banana regime it was the keeper of all data on license allocations given to companies established in the EC, and despite Complaining parties' requests during consultations for such information. The Complaining parties also questioned how the EC could plausibly say that all of its actions were motivated by the desire to curtail the "Latin American banana oligopoly", and then claim that it did not know whether these firms are engaged in the EC banana market at all. Although maintaining that they had provided adequate information, the Complaining parties offered to provide additional information if the Panel felt it required further clarification to assist its deliberations.

4.698 The EC argued that its import licensing system was not a measure related to the supply of services. It was a measure aimed at regulating the entry of goods into the EC market and the allocation of the right of importation of these goods among different operators. Even the criteria of allocation were based on the quantities of bananas marketed and not on services supplied. In order to obtain licences under the Category B licence system, one had to have marketed bananas on one's own account (Article 19 of Regulation 404/93) or as "owner" (Article 3.1 of Regulation 1442/93). It did not suffice to have rendered services in respect to bananas. For this reason alone, the EC argued, the attempt to apply the GATS to the system of Category B licences failed.

4.699 The Complaining parties recalled their argument above that the regime categorized firms by the amount of wholesale trade services each supplied, in that each of the activity functions were defined in terms of buying and selling bananas into the EC market.

4.700 The EC continued that the Complaining parties tried to incorporate the licensing system into the GATS with the assertion that it modified competitive opportunities. The EC considered, however, that such assertion alone did not determine whether a measure was covered by the GATS instead of the GATT. First it had to be demonstrated that the measure in question was one that concerned not goods but services. In the view of the EC, one could not argue that import licensing rules which clearly concerned the importation of products became measures affecting trade in services because licences were distributed to companies. It was obvious that import licensing rules were covered by the GATT and, since the Tokyo Round, by the Import Licensing Agreement which were both agreements on trade in goods. There was no reason to assume that after the

Uruguay Round rules on import licensing had suddenly become measures affecting trade in services. The EC considered that the kind of licences covered by the GATS was of a fundamentally different nature than import licensing rules. Article VI:4 of GATS referred to "licensing requirements" which should not constitute "unnecessary barriers to trade in services" and which were "not in themselves a restriction on the supply of a service". In the same way, Article XVI of GATS indicated that the kind of restrictions which could be maintained, *inter alia*, through licences were all in the nature of restrictions on the provision of services as services. The import licences at issue were not of this nature.

4.701 The EC considered that if the import licences concerned were to be considered licences within the ambit of the GATS, they should fall under Article VI:4 and 5. The licensing requirements mentioned in that Article were of a fundamentally different nature, however, because they related to "the competence and the ability to supply the service"; they aimed to ensure "the quality of the service" (Article VI:4 of GATS). Import licensing requirements were not of this nature; they were measures relating to goods. In the EC's view, Article VI of GATS, and the way in which it approached licences, demonstrated that the GATS was not intended to cover import licences at all. If the Panel were nevertheless to take another view, that is to say that import licences were measures affecting trade in services, then the EC considered that the import licensing rules for bananas were covered by Article VI of GATS. In that case the EC would be in the non-violation situation of Article VI:5. In that case, the Complaining parties should, first, show that licensing requirements had been used so as to nullify or impair specific commitments of the EC in one of the ways indicated in paragraph 4 of Article VI and, second, that this could not have reasonably been expected of the EC when it made its commitments in the distribution services sector. The EC noted that when the EC commitments in this sector entered into force, the EC banana regulations and its licensing system had been in force for years and that hence no reasonable expectations on the part of the Complaining parties could exist.

4.702 The Complaining parties contested the EC's claim that the phrase "measures affecting trade in services" must be interpreted narrowly to exclude import licences, and to include only those licences that pertain to Article XVI and those described in Article VI of GATS. According to the Complaining parties, the test for whether a measure was covered by the non-discrimination provisions of GATS Article XVII, and Article II, was whether the measure affected trade in services. In contrast, to the extent that GATS Article VI applied to governmental licences, it was meant primarily to address certain non-discriminatory, but potentially trade-restrictive, procedures pertaining to the issuance of permits and licences to engage in professional services. These obligations were in addition to, and separate from, the non-discrimination rules applicable to all measures affecting trade in services in scheduled sectors. Thus, Article VI could not be read to restrict the meaning of the phrase "measures affecting trade in services." With respect to Article XVI, the Complaining parties referred to their arguments above concerning that article in the context of the meaning of "measures affecting trade in services" of GATS Articles I:1 and XXVIII(c).

4.703 The EC reiterated that the objective of the operator category system was to ensure that the advantages that ACP countries had enjoyed on the market of the EC were safeguarded. The banana producing countries, pursuant to Protocol 5 of the Lomé Convention, were in need of some mechanism that would permit their bananas to have a fair chance to be sold on the EC market in view of their higher production cost. This was only possible by giving importers of ACP bananas a right to import a part of the tariff quota for bananas. The import licences were transferable and did not necessarily allocate market share. The only way for the EC to fulfil its legal duties to the ACP countries was by working through importers and in this way have the desired guarantees for ACP producers. What was given to these importers were rights to import bananas and these were clearly measures relating to goods and not to trade in services. In so far as these rights affected wholesale services, such effects were a consequence of the availability of goods and had to be accepted, in so far as that limited availability was a consequence of measures in conformity with the goods agreements of the WTO. Such situations were covered, in the opinion of the EC, by footnote 9 to Article XVI(2)(c) of GATS, which, according to this footnote, did not cover measures of Members which limited inputs for the supply of services. The (re)distribution of competitive opportunities in the sector of wholesale services was therefore not at issue.

4.704 The EC recalled that two questions were relevant for the question of possible discrimination under Article XVII, namely what the relevant market and what the relevant period were. According to the EC, the relevant market was certainly not the market for wholesaling Latin-American bananas: it was either wholesaling fruit and vegetables or wholesaling bananas. The relevant period started on 1 January 1995 with the entry into force of the GATS. The situations to be compared were those before and after that date.

4.705 The Complaining parties responded that two key factual issues were relevant to the question of whether the EC's import licensing rules violated the GATS national treatment and MFN requirements: (i) what conditions of competition had prevailed in the cross-border and domestic EC market for banana wholesaling services prior to the EC banana regime; and (ii) whether the EC rules had modified those conditions in favour of domestic and ACP banana wholesalers. The EC attempted to deflect attention away from these fundamental inquiries by pointing to various ways in which the Latin American and United States firms could endeavour to recoup some of the business they lost due to the regime. The EC asserted, according to the Complaining parties, that North and South American banana importers could buy the right to import back from the EC firms to which their former share of the market had been awarded, or invest in plantations in EC or ACP areas and thereby start to generate their own Category B rights after several years. In fact, if the Latin American and United States firms had to buy their businesses back it was only because they were the victims of a continuing discriminatory market reallocation in favour of EC and ACP firms. In stark contrast, EC and ACP firms were permitted to continue their traditional contractual relations with EC and ACP producers, and were given substantial additional business in the Latin American banana sector. The Complaining parties did not agree that traditional suppliers of Latin American bananas did not lose business as a result of the banana regime. The EC itself had predicted such an effect in EC Court of Justice proceedings. However, like the GATT, the GATS was ultimately not concerned with actual market effects, since this could be the result of many factors other than a given measure. Instead, drawing from GATT practice, the GATS focused on whether the regulatory framework established by a measure changed the competitive environment in a manner that served to protect domestic service providers. The GATS thereby avoided an analytically dubious inquiry into investment flows or market performance. Applying the test that the GATS negotiators intended to be applied under Articles II and XVII, both of which were based on GATT Article III, it was clear that the EC's banana framework had radically altered pre-existing conditions of competition in the banana wholesale services market in favour of EC and ACP firms. The manner in which the regime altered the situation that existed just prior to it showed that the regime was discriminatory. There was no "grandfathering" provision in the GATS that would permit Members to maintain discriminatory regimes upon entry into force of the GATS in January 1995. The fact that the regime continued to this day brought it within the disciplines of the GATS.

4.706 The EC argued that any system of quotas created quota rents. Given that the agricultural sector was being liberalized largely by having recourse to a system of consolidated tariff quotas, there was no doubt that quota rents would play a certain role in the WTO system for some time to come. The GATT contained no rules on the sharing out of quota rents. Obviously, the GATS had even less reason to include such rules, as tariff quotas on goods did not fall under its ambit. Therefore it was pushing the GATS too far to argue that it was intended to regulate government behaviour with respect to the allocation of quota rents. Any government which instituted tariff quotas created a windfall of quota rents. Nobody had a right to a quota rent that was newly created. There might be rules of domestic law which governed this problem but there were no applicable rules in the law of the WTO. It was inevitable that in allocating quota rent through a licensing system, governments would also allocate a limited amount of financial power as between operators, but this was the unavoidable result of having a tariff quota. In the present case, by far the largest share of the quota rent (66.5 per cent) was handed to established traders in bananas from Central and Latin America, including the two large, integrated United States owned banana trading companies. If a smaller amount of this quota rent was given to traders in bananas from ACP and EC countries, it was partly for reasons related to the EC's obligations under the Lomé Convention's Banana Protocol, to ensure that the quantities for which access was given would also be marketed; partly for reasons related to the integration of the internal market, to ensure that marketing of ACP bananas and Latin American bananas would not continue in two closed circuits; and partly for reasons of competition policy, to ensure that not all of the windfall quota rent would end up with the companies which already had a very strong oligopolistic position on the EC market. All these reasons would, in the opinion of the EC, seem to be entirely consonant with WTO rules or, as in the case of competition, fall entirely outside the scope of the WTO.

4.707 The EC submitted further that the issue of quota rent transfer was one related to the general protection of investment or treatment of companies and not to the sector of wholesale services or wholesale service suppliers. Therefore, quota rents which were linked to the transferable import rights distributed through the licensing system were not covered by the GATS. The EC claimed that the Complaining parties were seeking a general protection of competitive opportunities to investors and not one which was limited to competitive opportunities to provide services. Competitive opportunities in the field of wholesale trade services arose because of commitments (subject to Article VI regulation) and the rules of the GATS and neither the commitments nor the rules contained anything with respect quota rents. In the view of the EC, it was entirely legitimate to consider a fair (re)distribution of quota rent to counteract the concentration of such "windfall" in a few (already powerful) hands. Otherwise, the "windfall" would be given to the party which happened to be in the strongest position on the market at the moment. According to the EC, it was not possible to apply MFN or national treatment principles to quota rent and it was not necessarily fair to use the criterion of the existing trade patterns.

4.708 The Complaining parties replied that the EC's licence allocation redistributed opportunities to engage in wholesale trade. The 30 per cent set aside as well as the allocations to ripeners and customs clearers gave EC and ACP firms the means to enter the business of cross-border wholesaling of Latin American bananas. The EC effected this transfer of competitive opportunities at the direct expense of the Latin American and United States firms whose business it had previously been. The Complaining Parties submitted that there was no difference between a measure designed (in the EC's words) to "strengthen the competitive position" of domestic service suppliers, and one designed to "modify the conditions of competition in favor of" domestic service suppliers, as provided in GATS Article XVII. Because the tariff quota restricted the availability of bananas in the EC market it created quota rents and those rents were awarded, also on a discriminatory basis, along with banana import rights. The fact that some quota rents were (or were not) transferred along with import rights did not change the fact that the transfer of business opportunities from Latin American and United States banana wholesalers to EC and ACP wholesalers modified the terms of competition in favour of the latter in violation of Articles II and XVII of GATS. The Complaining parties disagreed with the EC's assertion that the Complaining parties were attempting to protect their Latin American "investment" interests and not services interests within the scope of the GATS. The Latin American and United States banana wholesalers provided wholesale trade services on a cross-border basis from Latin American Members to the EC, and within the EC, in a manner directly covered by GATS Article I:2(a) and (c), which concerned services provided on a cross-border and commercial presence basis.

4.709 The Complaining parties contested the EC's claim that its banana regime was implemented in pursuit of legitimate, country-neutral goals, and was not an effort to discriminate on the basis of service suppliers. The EC claim that it was motivated by the need to ensure an integrated market was irrelevant as a GATS matter (and unsupported by the facts). GATS Article V governed market integration. Article V did not relieve the EC from its national treatment obligations, or its MFN obligations vis-à-vis ACP service suppliers. The EC's competition policy claim supported Complaining parties' contention that the regime was in fact intended to alter competitive conditions.

b) Article II

4.710 Ecuador submitted that prior to the imposition of the EC banana regime, the overwhelming percentage of all third-country bananas imported into the EC were imported, distributed and marketed by third-country service suppliers, though the ripening of these bananas was largely performed by EC operators. However, the EC banana regime fundamentally altered this pattern of trade. The operator category allocations set out in Regulation 404/93 violated, according to Ecuador, the MFN principle by allocating a substantial portion of the market in third-country bananas to operators from ACP countries which had never before been involved in the transportation, marketing, and sale of such bananas. The operator categories set out in Regulation 404/93 generally corresponded to the two classes of service providers described above. Category A operators included mainly service providers from third countries, while Category B operators were largely composed of ACP and EC service providers. Although Category A operators imported virtually all of the third-country bananas marketed in the EC prior to the imposition of the banana regime, Regulation 404/93 deprived these operators of 30 per cent of their market. This 30 per cent share was reallocated to Category B service providers which had never before imported such bananas. Not only did this arbitrary reallocation unjustifiably provide a windfall for traditional ACP service providers, but Regulation 404/93 provided nothing in return to compensate the third-country service providers for their loss. Regulation 404/93 thus left the sheltered market for ACP operators intact while cutting the market for third-country service suppliers almost in half. In the opinion of Ecuador, a more direct violation of the MFN principles set out in Article II of GATS would be difficult to imagine.

4.711 Mexico argued that, at the level of service suppliers, the violation of Article II of GATS resulted from the same reasons as those mentioned to demonstrate other violations, at the level of goods, of several Articles of GATT. In this case, the violation of Article II of GATS was the result of the advantages granted to ACP enterprises that historically marketed traditional ACP bananas and therefore were registered as Category B operators with all the consequent benefits that this implied, i.e. exemption from the requirement of export certificates when importing bananas from BFA countries and the import licences granted to them in addition to the tariff quota in the event of natural disasters (hurricane licences).

4.712 The United States argued that the 30 per cent set aside for Category B operators had altered the conditions of competition in favour of ACP marketing firms in comparison with other non-EC banana distribution firms. Certain ACP banana marketing firms (e.g. Jamaica Producers and Winban/Wibdeco) had been clear and deliberate beneficiaries of the operator category regime. Because these firms had, along with EC firms, traditionally marketed ACP-produced bananas for sale in the EC, they were handed part of the 30 per cent allocation reserved for Category B operators. United States, Ecuadorian and other non-EC/ACP firms that had historically marketed the vast majority of Latin American bananas but had marketed few ACP (or EC) bananas sold in the EC were stripped of a portion of their market share, and that portion was awarded, in part, to marketers of selected other countries. According to the United States, the EC had conceded, and other neutral authorities had recognized, that the operator category allocations were instituted to provide, and had the predictable consequence of providing, commercial advantage to those non-EC marketing firms that historically handled EC/ACP bananas as compared to those who historically handled Latin American bananas. The allocation of licences to Category B operators thus provided less favourable treatment to United States and other third-country banana distribution firms than was provided to like ACP firms and was therefore contrary to the EC's MFN obligations under GATS Article II.

4.713 The United States noted that the EC had made no entries on its list of MFN exemptions that covered any of the measures at issue with respect to the Complaining parties' GATS claims. Although the EC had obtained a limited waiver from Article I of GATT for implementation of certain preferences required under the Lomé Convention with respect to goods, this waiver did not apply to any of the EC's obligations under the GATS.

4.714 The EC responded that Article II of GATS obliged the EC to grant no less favourable treatment of services of third countries (first mode) and of service suppliers of third countries (third mode). In the present case, as far as the first mode was concerned, direct trans-frontier services with respect to bananas could not be treated differently as services whether they were services of the Complaining parties or services of any of the

ACP States. Since the only direct trans-frontier service involved was ocean shipping where there were so far no MFN obligations or commitments, this was a purely theoretical question. Where it concerned the third mode, Article II of GATS obliged the EC not to treat service suppliers of the Complaining parties any different than service suppliers from any of the ACP States. The EC recalled that the EC licence distribution system was a measure affecting trade in goods and not a measure affecting trade in services. Even under the assumption that the licence distribution system was a measure affecting trade in services, the Complaining parties had to make a *prima facie* case that there were companies owned or controlled by them operating in the third mode on the EC market and that such companies did not or could not *de iure* fall under the category of operators who marketed traditional ACP bananas or under any of the categories of ripeners or secondary importers. This the Complaining parties had not done. But even if this were to be the case, the EC was of the view that the Complaining parties had not been able to counter the argument that the licences in question were tradeable and therefore could be bought if necessary. As the EC had argued above, such buying and selling of tradeable import licences was a question of shifting around the quota rent, which was not a matter covered by the GATS.

4.715 The EC considered that the argument resorted to by the United States in relation to an alleged lack of MFN treatment under the GATS was an argument that the EC had altered the conditions of competition as between marketing firms (probably wholesale trade services firms) of ACP bananas and "other non-EC banana distribution firms". According to the EC, the real complaint of the United States was about the origin of the bananas, not about the origin of the services; in other words, the dispute was about goods and not about services. As was demonstrated in the section on "Standard of Discrimination: Article II" above, the alteration of competitive conditions was not, in the view of the EC, part of the "no less favourable treatment standard" under Article II:1 of GATS. Hence, there was no basis for the United States complaint on this point, quite apart from the other reasons already mentioned above, for rejecting the idea that the quota allocation system had a direct link with the supply of services as such. Moreover, the contested measures did not cover the wholesale trade services sector (see also paragraph *4.610* above).

4. *Activity function licence allocation - Articles II and XVII*

4.716 The Complaining parties recalled their claim, as set out above, that a key component through which the EC transferred wholesale distribution business opportunities to its domestic service suppliers were the three "activity functions".

4.717 The Complaining parties claimed that the specific shares chosen by the EC for the three activity functions gave the false impression of precision or rationality. In fact, the EC had never explained how it arrived at these particular numbers. Moreover, whereas the EC's directives mentioned such considerations as level of commercial risk and scale of business activity, it had never explained how these considerations justified awarding nearly half the import rights on the basis of customs clearance and ripening. The EC thus manipulated the two features of the banana regime described - the operator categories and activity functions - to strip opportunities for Latin American banana distribution business away from the firms that had traditionally supplied nearly all Latin American bananas into the EC market and awarded these opportunities to their competitors, which were EC or ACP-owned companies. By drastically altering competitive conditions in this manner, these aspects of the regime violated the principles of MFN treatment and national treatment of Articles II and XVII of GATS.

4.718 The Complaining parties submitted that in order to assess whether the EC had impermissibly modified competitive conditions, Article XVII of GATS required an examination of, first, the competitive environment that existed at the time Regulations 404/93 and 1442/93 (which established activity function allocations) went into effect, and second, whether the EC had altered that environment in favour of its own firms. At the time Regulations 404/93 and 1442/93 took effect the situation was as follows:

(i) Latin American and United States firms were virtually alone in providing cross-border wholesaling services for Latin American bananas sold into the EC market. These firms purchased the bananas from Latin American suppliers, took physical delivery, assumed commercial risk, arranged for, or performed, ocean transportation and found wholesale buyers for Latin American bananas sold into the EC. The EC designated these firms as primary importers under activity function (a) and awarded them only 57 per cent of those Latin American banana import rights not already transferred to EC or ACP banana firms.

(ii) The vast majority of banana ripeners were EC-owned firms, frequently small, and located close to retail points of sale. According to information submitted by the Complaining parties, at the time the EC regime took effect, over 80 per cent of the EC's banana imports were ripened by EC-owned firms. Ripening played no role in actual importation. The EC designated ripening firms as performing activity function (c) and awarded them 28 per cent of the import rights for Latin American bananas.

(iii) Customs clearance for Latin American bananas was performed by different types of entities, such as: (a) agents (generally EC nationals or firms) on behalf of United States and Latin American importers, in some cases technically taking title to the bananas for purposes of customs clearance procedures; (b) larger ripeners, or entities related to ripeners; and (c) the importers themselves. Customs clearance was largely a paperwork exercise that was independent of the actual physical and commercial process of importation. Nevertheless, firms that had performed customs clearance for Latin American bananas received 15 per cent of remaining EC licences for those bananas.

4.719 The United States claimed that firms whose activities were classified within the three activity functions were "like service suppliers". Each activity was part of the overall wholesale distribution chain for Latin American bananas sold in the EC. The right granted to firms under the three activity functions was the same, i.e. the right to import Latin American bananas. The EC's grant of such rights placed firms engaging in the named activities in direct competition with the others for the provision of wholesale distribution services. For example, the 28 per cent import share gave ripeners the means to engage in the import side of the wholesale distribution business in competition with the firms from which their market share was extracted.

4.720 According to the United States, the EC had explained that in establishing the activity function allocations the Commission had been guided by "the principle whereby the licences had to be granted to natural or legal persons who had undertaken the commercial risk of marketing bananas and by the necessity of avoiding disturbing normal trading relations between persons occupying different points in the marketing chain".[297] The EC had also explained that the weighting percentages (57/15/28 per cent) for the three activity functions were designed "to take account of the scale of business concerned and of the commercial risks incurred".[298] The United States was of the view that none of these rationales provided a sustainable basis for the EC's allocation of banana importation in a manner favouring its domestic service providers. The EC had never stated why it selected the criterion of commercial risk nor, so far as the United States knew, had the EC ever made clear how it defined commercial risk in this context or what methodology it used to assess such risk.

[297] Regulation 404/93, recital 15.

[298] Regulation 1442/93, recital 3.

The EC had likewise never disclosed its basis for deciding that all importers, customs clearers, and ripeners assumed a marketing risk and precisely how it allocated the percentage of risk between those three groups.[299] Similarly, the EC had not explained how the scale of business concerned was an appropriate criterion for allocating import licences and how this criterion justified allocating over 40 per cent of the import rights to activity functions (b) and (c). Activity function (c) required only a modest commercial investment and activity function (b) required none. The overwhelming majority of commercial investments required arose in connection with the so-called primary importer activities. The United States further observed that, while the EC had also claimed that its allocation of import rights for Latin American bananas was meant to avoid disturbing normal trading relations, in fact the EC's overall and specific allocation schemes were calculated to radically rearrange the trading relationships that pertained prior to the imposition of the tariff quota.

4.721 The Complaining parties argued that there were few if any independent firms whose primary business was clearing Latin American bananas through customs. Thus, this activity did not meet the EC's own test for allocating according to activity function, i.e. that the rules "ensure that the various types of operators whose specialized business activity is directly dependent on access to the quota enjoy such access without any consequent disruption to normal trade between the various actors in the marketing chain."[300] It was not clear whose "specialized business activity" the EC was referring to in the case of customs clearance. Rather, in the view of Complaining parties, the secondary importer category was an entirely artificial construction created by the EC to shift more licence entitlement away from the primary importers. Although ripeners could be identified as discrete commercial entities, their market risk and scale of activity were minor compared to primary importers. In theory, banana ripeners that obtained title to their fruit assumed the risk of price drops that might occur in the five-to-seven day period in which they held bananas. However, this risk was more theoretical than real, since it was common practice for ripeners to recoup from the primary importers any losses resulting from sudden price drops that occur over those several days. Indeed, because of their minimal commercial risk, ripeners generally did not experience the kind of losses suffered by primary importers during the period of low prices in 1992-93. By contrast, the long-term contracts and other arrangements that United States and Latin American banana wholesalers concluded with Latin American growers made them vulnerable to fluctuations in market conditions. Moreover, the scale of commercial activity involved in the marketing of bananas from tropical growing areas to Europe was vastly greater than that of banana ripening. The EC described how ripeners ripened bananas and "often carry out additional controls of quality and re-packing before selling either to wholesalers or to distributors, such as supermarkets." By contrast, for a given shipment of bananas the primary importers generally performed each of the activities listed in the CPC definition of wholesale trade services not just once, but multiple times and in multiple locations, as they distributed the bananas from the tropics to and through the EC. The fact that the EC had not explained the actual percentage allocations between the three activity functions (or the discrimination inherent in stripping import rights only from US and Latin American firms) confirmed that the allocations were politically motivated, made in direct response to a polling of the Member States, each of which generally put forward allocations designed to favor local interests.

4.722 The EC responded that the activity function allocation was another way of dealing with the problem of quota rent created by the tariff quota and the licences. The aim of the activity function was not to concentrate the economic value related to import licences in a few hands or in one part of the supply chain. Otherwise, the privileged recipients would receive a "windfall dose of power" and influence over their trading partners in the supply chain. For instance, the dependence of independent ripeners on the large, integrated banana trading companies, which was already great, would have grown considerably. It would have meant a further blow to their negotiating ability vis-à-vis these companies, which dominated the banana trade to a very great extent in

[299] The United States remarked that in the banana distribution business, like the distribution business for other fruit, it was commonly known that commercial risk "flowed backward". Firms further down the distribution chain (such as ripeners, customs clearers) incurred vastly fewer commercial risks than those firms that undertook to procure and ship bananas from overseas locations to the EC.

[300] Regulation 1442/93, recital 2.

large parts of the European market. It was on this point that considerations of competition policy most clearly entered into the EC banana regime. Such considerations fell, in the opinion of the EC, entirely outside the ambit of the WTO as was clear from the preparatory discussions for the Singapore Ministerial Conference. The notion of competitive opportunities that had played a role for quite a long time already in the GATT system had nothing to do with the notions of domestic or EC competition policy, such as they entered into consideration here, when deciding about the desirability of allocating the windfall of economic bargaining power which automatically went along with the allocation of import licences.

4.723 The EC recalled that, in its view, the allocation of import quotas was a goods-related measure and thus not covered by the GATS. In relation to the licence allocation to the ripening sector, it was the view of the EC that the measures at issue did not touch the supply of wholesale trade services since the wholesale trade services sector, which was the sector concerned, was the sector following the ripening stage in the supply chain. In so far as the case under Article II was based on the assertion that the EC measures on activity function allocation had modified the conditions of competition, the EC recalled that Article II did not include this notion. For these reasons, the activity function allocations were not covered by the GATS or, otherwise, were in any case in conformity with Articles II and XVII of GATS.

4.724 The EC submitted further that the activity function system which required only one import licence as between the different operators made it entirely possible to continue with the existing relationships between so-called primary and secondary importers and ripeners. If the existing business relationships were maintained, the requisite bananas could be imported by a licence somewhere in the chain (whether by a ripener or a primary importer). The only difference would be that the windfall quota rent would not all go to the importers and that the independent ripeners would have some bargaining power vis-à-vis importers intending to rely on the ripener's import licence. In the opinion of the EC, no shift in competitive opportunities between importers and ripeners occurred. Otherwise, the position of primary importers would have become even stronger than it already was, because of the windfall of quota rent. The same was true *mutatis mutandis* for the secondary importers. The EC considered it entirely legitimate to address these likely competitive consequences of its own regulation in the regulation itself. There was no need to await individual abuses of the increased bargaining power of primary importers in order to act.

4.725 The Complaining parties replied that the EC's justification was simply a *post hoc* explanation for protectionism. The Complaining parties argued: (i) the EC could have addressed such concerns through its competition laws, which were the normal route for addressing competition issues and which had previously been used by the EC without hesitation in the banana trade; (ii) the EC did not mention competition concerns or oligopolies in any of the relevant directives, the 1995 report on the operation of the banana regime, or during the second banana GATT panel proceedings; (iii) the Latin American banana distribution sector was in fact more competitive than the distribution sector for other fruit for which the EC had not constructed comparable discriminatory regimes; (iv) the EC did not impose the same import restrictions on distributors of ACP bananas even though the markets in which the ACP bananas were primarily sold, France and the United Kingdom in particular, were notoriously non-competitive; (v) the activity function allocations did not promote competition in any event; and (vi) the EC transferred import opportunities away from all US and Latin American wholesalers, regardless of their competitive position in the EC banana wholesale market.

4.726 The EC was of the view that it had shown that its concerns regarding competition were explicitly mentioned in the preambular paragraphs of the relevant acts. The EC legislator considered that it would leave ripeners and specialist customs clearers in a difficult position if cooperation with them was not necessary in order to import the tariff quota bananas into the EC. They were given some bargaining power to remedy this situation and since the ripening sector had always been penetrated by foreign suppliers of ripening services or of ripeners for the account of integrated firms (around 20 per cent, according to the EC), it was very difficult to see what de facto discrimination might have occurred. Competition concerns were not raised in the second banana panel because the activity function system was not at issue in that case.

4.727 The Complaining parties submitted that the EC's claim that the activity function allocations were necessary to protect downstream entities was based on economically unsound reasoning. There was no economic difference, in so far as ripeners were concerned, between the primary importers in fact importing the bananas and primary importers being allocated the legal right to do so. By contrast, allocating a significant share of licences to ripeners did alter existing economic conditions by affording the ripeners the means to enter the cross-border banana wholesaling business. If access to banana imports was critical for downstream firms under the tariff quota, why did the EC choose not to provide allocations to customs clearers and ripeners with respect to their imports of ACP bananas? The fact that the EC did not allocate licences to import ACP bananas suggested that those firms were not disadvantaged by the tariff quota in the first place.

5. Hurricane licences - Articles II and XVII

4.728 Ecuador recalled that, since the inception of the banana regime, the EC Commission had made available a total of 281,605 tonnes of supplemental "hurricane" licensing entitlements exclusively to Category B operators and producers. Volumes imported using hurricane licences were used in calculating a firm's future entitlement to licences as a Category B operator. No comparable licence replacement benefit had been conferred on Category A operators. Hurricane licences which were generally either sold or used to import Latin American bananas essentially increased the entitlement of Category B operators above the 30 per cent given to them under Regulation 404/93. The additional volume represented by hurricane licences gave Category B operators a distinct commercial advantage in comparison to Category A operators. Ecuador considered that the measure had skewed the conditions of competition in favour of EC and ACP services and service suppliers in comparison to like services and service suppliers of the United States, Mexico and Ecuador. As such, the measure was inconsistent with the EC's national treatment obligations under Article XVII of GATS and the EC's MFN obligations under Article II of GATS.

4.729 The United States noted that the EC Commission had granted hurricane licences to Category B distributors and producers entitling them to import bananas from any source. These bananas entered over the established third-country tariff quota. Operators used these licences primarily to import additional Latin American bananas, in light of the otherwise restrictive tariff quota applicable to these bananas. Bananas imported using hurricane licences were counted in calculating a firm's future entitlement to Category B licences under the EC's rolling three-year reference period. No comparable benefit had been conferred on Category A operators. The United States was of the opinion that, by according less favourable treatment to non-EC service suppliers as compared to like EC service suppliers, hurricane licences were inconsistent with the EC's national treatment obligations under Article XVII of GATS. By according less favourable treatment to non-EC/ACP banana distribution firms vis-à-vis like ACP distribution firms, these licences were likewise inconsistent with the EC's MFN obligations under Article II of GATS.

4.730 The Complaining parties submitted that the EC's grant of hurricane licences only to firms that historically traded in EC and ACP bananas (Category B operators) represented a further discriminatory allocation to EC and ACP companies of the right to import Latin American bananas. While firms that traditionally traded in ACP bananas were eligible for hurricane licences, United States and Latin American banana wholesalers were not. The EC's hurricane licence allocation scheme thus represented, according to the Complaining parties, a further discriminatory alteration of the terms of competition in the wholesale bananas services market. The EC had acknowledged that any B operator, not only banana farmers, could receive hurricane licences: "... nothing is more natural than attributing these licences to the specific operators who can duly show a lost trade because of the hurricane that is among those who trade in ACP traditional bananas. These operators must equally show they 'include or directly represent[301] a specific banana producer affected by the tropical storm concerned'."

[301] Regulation 2791/94, Article 2.1.

4.731 The EC replied that hurricane licences were licences to import additional quantities of bananas (from anywhere) for those who were part of the preferential system in favour of the Lomé countries and who had suffered demonstrable damage from hurricanes which made it impossible for them to fill their normal, guaranteed quantities under the Lomé preference. Such compensatory licences had been granted by the French and British authorities before the creation of the EC banana regime and hence had to be maintained pursuant to the guarantees given in the Banana Protocol to the Lomé Convention and the pertinent declaration contained in Annex LXXIV of the Lomé Convention. Since they served to import goods, namely bananas, hurricane licences did not relate to the supply of services or the trade in services. It was equally unclear how hurricane licences related to trade in wholesale services. Hence, they were not covered by the GATS and in any case could not be contrary to Articles II and XVII thereof.

4.732 As described above, the Complaining parties argued that the EC's Lomé waiver was limited to goods and was inapplicable to GATS obligations.

6. *Export certificates - Articles II and XVII*

4.733 Ecuador argued that the special export certificate procedures violated Articles II and XVII of GATS. The principles of Article II and XVII were directly violated by the requirement set out in the BFA and Regulation 478/95 that Category A and C operators, but not Category B operators, apply for a special export certificates to import bananas from the BFA signatory countries. Obtaining special export certificates imposed a significant administrative burden on Category A and C operators and forced these operators to incur large additional transaction costs which Category B operators were not required to bear. These costs arose in part from the fact that Category A and C operators from non-BFA signatory countries frequently had to purchase the special export certificates from those producers and service suppliers in the signatory countries which were awarded special export certificates from their national governments. This process essentially forced the Category A and C operators, but not the Category B operators, to subsidize the BFA entities which sold the export certificates. The EC had recognized that the special export certificates "help [BFA] supplying countries to share in the economic benefits of the tariff quota."[302] Additional administrative costs were incurred by the Category A and C operators to ensure that the operators could match the import and export certificates in order to import BFA bananas into the EC.

4.734 Ecuador noted that firms that were principally Category B service suppliers were composed virtually entirely of EC and ACP firms, while Category A service suppliers consisted of third-country firms. Thus, the additional costs imposed on Category A and C service suppliers were, de facto, imposed in a discriminatory manner on the basis of the nationality of the service or service suppliers. The special export certificate requirement consequently imposed costs on third-country service suppliers but did not impose similar costs on EC and ACP firms. The special export certificate system thus directly violated, according to Ecuador, the MFN and national treatment requirements of the GATS.

4.735 Mexico argued that the EC regime violated Article II of GATS because it provided the benefit of the quota rent from export certificates only to the suppliers of services of BFA countries and not to all service suppliers of the other Members, because enterprises marketing non-ACP bananas faced an administrative licensing system which was extremely complex and costly and which was not applied to enterprises marketing ACP bananas.

4.736 The United States noted that EC Regulation 478/95 implemented provisions of the BFA by requiring that Category A and C licence-holders to present export certificates as a condition for importing bananas from three of the four BFA countries (Colombia, Costa Rica and Nicaragua).[303] Category B licence-holders (i.e.

---

[302] "Report on the EC Banana Regime", European Commission, July 1994, p.12.

[303] Regulation 478/95, Article 3.2.

predominantly EC and ACP firms) were exempted from this requirement. The requirement to obtain and present an export certificate for bananas sourced in certain countries added expense and administrative burden for firms that imported Latin American bananas to the EC. Category A applicants had to obtain certificates from the authorities of the exporting country and had to match these certificates with an import licence entitlement obtained from the EC before they could import bananas from these countries. Both steps entailed substantial administrative and financial costs. For example, Category A operators frequently had to purchase export certificates from producers or marketing firms in the producing countries. Category B operators, in applying for licences to import Latin American bananas from the same source countries, were free of such burdens.

4.737 According to the United States, the EC had recognized the commercial effect of the export certificate requirement. The EC Commission had explained that Regulation 478/95's delegation of authority to issue export certificates to the relevant exporting countries was made in order to "help [BFA] supplying countries to share in the economic benefits of the tariff quota."[304] The economic benefits to which the EC Commission referred were a share of the quota rent associated with the marketing of Latin American bananas. Entities in the BFA countries realized these quota rents by, for example, selling the export certificates to Category A operators. By excluding Category B licence-holders from the export certificate requirement, the EC ensured that BFA countries' share of quota rent would come only from Category A (and C) operators. Thus, the EC had not only given Category B firms 30 per cent of the Latin American tariff quota, but had also made it much easier and more financially profitable for Category B firms to market this share as compared to Category A firms. The EC's selective application of an export certificate requirement accorded, in the opinion of the United States, less favourable treatment to non-EC banana distribution firms as compared to like EC firms, and was therefore inconsistent with the EC's national treatment obligations under Article XVII of GATS. This feature of the EC banana regime also accorded less favourable treatment to United States and other non-EC/ACP banana distribution firms vis-à-vis like ACP firms and was therefore inconsistent with the EC's MFN obligations under Article II of GATS as well.

4.738 The Complaining parties submitted that the EC's requirement that certain types of operators had to obtain export certificates, in addition to import licences, in order to import bananas from three of the BFA countries, amounted to further less favourable treatment for Latin American and United States banana wholesale service suppliers beyond that created by the 30 per cent set aside. The EC required export certificates from firms that traditionally traded in Latin American bananas (Category A) but not from firms that traditionally traded in EC or ACP bananas (Category B). A Category A licence-holder's need to obtain export certificates from authorities in the BFA countries and to match the certificates with EC-issued import certificates entailed substantial administrative and financial costs. A Category B licence-holder could import the same bananas from the same BFA countries without having to incur these costs. Thus, the EC's export certificate requirement accorded a competitive advantage to EC/ACP firms (Category B) in relation to Latin American and United States firms (Category A). The EC did not explain why it required export certificates only from Category A operators, that is, predominantly United States and Latin American firms, but not Category B operators. In the view of the Complaining parties, the export certificate requirement, like the 30 per cent set-aside for EC and ACP wholesalers, directly altered the terms of market competition in favour of those same companies by imposing import costs solely on Latin American and United States firms. The export certificate requirement thus equally violated Articles II and XVII of GATS.

4.739 The EC replied that the Complaining parties' approach to the so-called discrimination relating to export certificate requirements rested on a number of assumptions which were unwarranted or were insufficiently established. First, the Complainants assumed that the measures concerning export certificates were measures relating to the supply of services or to trade in services. In the opinion of the EC, there could be no doubt that regulations concerning the export certificates related to trade in goods. An export certificate was

[304] "Report on the EC Banana Regime", European Commission, July 1994, p.12.

a document showing that a certain good had been exported from a certain country. It was not certifying that a particular service had been exported from that country. Hence, rules in respect of export certificates did not come under the GATS. Second, the EC reiterated that neither the GATT nor the GATS contained any rules with respect to the allocation of quota rents. The export certificate requirement was the best example that the Complaining parties, or at least their service suppliers, were interested primarily in quota rents. They protested against a burden which had been imposed on other countries than their own, which, at least with respect to the speed with which one could dispose of one's bananas, was an advantage to some of the Complaining parties. It appeared to the EC that it was the quota rent that was the problem, not the possibility to provide services. Third, the Complainants seemed to assume that Category A licence-holders were all non-EC and non-ACP owned and that Category B licence-holders were all either EC or ACP owned or controlled. In the view of the EC, Category A and B licences were spread over both categories of ownership. The requirements with respect to export certificates were, in the opinion of the EC, not contrary to Articles II and XVII of GATS.

V. ARGUMENTS PRESENTED BY THIRD PARTIES

A. ACP Third Parties

1. Introduction

5.1 Belize, Cameroon, Côte d'Ivoire, Dominica, the Dominican Republic, Ghana, Grenada, Jamaica, Saint Lucia, Saint Vincent and the Grenadines, Senegal, and Suriname (the "ACP third parties") submitted that not all of the 70 ACP States which were signatories to the Lomé IV Convention (the "Lomé Convention") were involved in the production of bananas and their export to the EC. However, the issues at stake in this dispute went beyond bananas. They concerned the interests of all ACP States, whether banana producing or not, which were Members of the WTO and benefited from the Lomé Convention and the Lomé waiver. Moreover, for those Caribbean and African ACP States which were involved in the production and marketing of bananas, it was an essential aspect of their livelihoods. The banana industry provided high levels of employment and fundamental transport and communication infrastructure in these countries. In addition, for all banana producing ACP States, but especially those which were islands, the weekly shipping service which the banana industry provided was a lifeline without which many of their other industries would collapse.

5.2 The national regimes which operated before the introduction of the EC banana regime afforded significantly greater protection to the ACP banana growers than the current regime. Latin American bananas were admitted to supplement ACP supplies in volumes that would not deprive ACP bananas of a remunerative return from the market. Under its banana regime, the EC had, for the first time, imposed quantitative limits on duty-free imports from the ACP States which were not necessitated by the Lomé Convention. The highest volume of exports from traditional ACP countries amounted to 919,606 tonnes (FAO) or, providing for corrections in the cases of Cameroon and Côte d'Ivoire, 940,000 tonnes. This compared to traditional duty-free imports fixed at a maximum of 857,700 tonnes in Regulation 404/93. These figures did not suggest a "design to shift" banana supplies from Latin American bananas to ACP and EC sources.

5.3 The ACP third parties argued that the establishment of a common market organization for bananas in the EC was complicated by several factors. First, the costs of production in the EC and the ACP States were greatly in excess of the costs of production of Latin American bananas. In Ecuador, costs of production were approximately US$2.95 per box compared to approximately US$12.38 per box in Martinique. ACP costs of production reached up to US$10-11 per box. Secondly, ACP and EC producers faced other inherent disadvantages which necessitated a system, such as the Category B licence arrangement, in order to ensure continued production, distribution and marketing in the EC. These disadvantages included the following:

(i) Severely limited export capacity: One of the key financial considerations in banana importation was shipping cost. No ACP State produced a quantity of bananas which allowed for optimal shipping efficiency. The limited production capacity of the ACP States meant that any ship was involved in up to four port loadings per voyage. Apart from the resulting extra cost and time delay, this also led to uneconomic use of hold space.

(ii) Limited production resulting in additional overhead costs: The limited production capacity in the ACP States increased significantly the overhead costs of companies producing or purchasing bananas from these sources.

(iii) Increased risk of climatic disasters and disastrous consequences of production shortfalls: All ACP banana producing regions were vulnerable to climatic hazards such as chill, floods, blow-downs, disease and most particularly, hurricanes. The banana producing islands of the Caribbean were most vulnerable to severe disruptions due to climatic conditions. Similarly, production in Côte d'Ivoire was frequently adversely affected by heavy rains and tornadoes.

(iv) Inability to benefit fully from productivity gains: The limited volumes of production (whether due to the size of the allocation or physical constraints) imposed dis-economies of scale. The limitation on access from ACP sources restricted the ability to improve productivity per hectare and thereby reduce unit costs of production.

(v) Inability to market ACP bananas throughout the EC: With the exception perhaps of Spain, the consumers in the 15 member States of the EC were familiar with the size, shape and trademarks associated with Latin American bananas. On the other hand, wholesalers in some markets were unfamiliar with ACP bananas and had, to date, shown a complete reluctance to handle such fruit.

5.4 Thirdly, the ACP third parties claimed that the banana market was highly concentrated and oligopolistic. Prior to the introduction of Regulation 404/93, two relatively distinct markets for bananas existed in the EC: EC and ACP bananas were sold primarily in the markets of Italy, Portugal, Greece, the United Kingdom, Spain and France; Latin American bananas accounted for approximately 2 million tonnes and predominated in the Northern European countries of Germany, the Netherlands, Belgium, Luxembourg and Ireland.

5.5 The ACP third parties claimed that the Latin American markets were dominated, from production to ripening, by three multinational companies which had a unique level of vertical integration from source to retail level. European legislators' concern about the potential for market abuses or existing market distortions as a result of the strength of such integrated companies in the production and marketing of Latin American bananas was heightened by the fact that the largest of these companies had a lengthy history of abuses of its market power. In contrast to the vertical integration of large multinationals in the EC market for Latin American bananas, the EC market for EC and ACP bananas was, despite the significant presence of both Dole and Del Monte, fragmented and notable for its lack of vertical integration. Moreover, the EC and ACP bananas were dependent on the individual markets into which they had traditionally supplied their bananas.

5.6 These differences in market structure meant, in the view of the ACP States, that importers were likely to abandon ACP suppliers unless the new regime provided sufficient incentives for trade to continue. Because of the vulnerability of the EC market to anti-competitive practices, an open system would have enabled any powerful vertically integrated multinational company to eliminate those of its competitors with less flexibility and resources. The ability of large multinationals to distort the market was demonstrated prior to the introduction of the new regime. 1992 saw the peak of speculative or below cost trading in bananas by major multinationals. Volumes reached unsustainably high levels with correspondingly low prices at all stages in the marketing chain. In 1992, Chiquita lost at least US$52.5 million on its banana sales in Europe and its total declared losses were US$284 million. In the same year, Colombia announced that its producers had suffered losses totalling US$70 million. The EC was faced with a situation in which there were concerted efforts "to weed out" weaker players in the lead up to the new market regime. The depressed market in 1991/92 and the first half of 1993 could not therefore be taken into account for the purposes of establishing the EC third-country tariff quota.

5.7 For the EC to fulfil its commitments to ACP producers (and indeed to consumers who would ultimately bear the cost), it had to ensure that the oligopolistic structure of the market would not undermine the operation of the new regime. The concept of Category B licences was ultimately found to be the only way to achieve this.

5.8 The ACP third parties argued that as demonstrated above, trading in ACP bananas was more difficult, more risky and much less profitable than trading in Latin American bananas. It was the Category B licence system which provided an incentive for operators to continue importing from ACP countries. In the view of the ACP third parties, it was only by this means that the EC could fulfil its Lomé Convention commitment that traditional ACP suppliers should be no worse off than under the preceding national arrangements.

5.9 Licences to import ACP bananas into the EC were awarded on the basis of a special certificate of origin obtained from the competent authority in the respective ACP country. These special certificates of origin had the potential to operate in the same way as the export certificates issued by the Latin American countries pursuant to the BFA. It was incorrect to state that the exemption of Category B licence-holders from the export certificate requirement for imports from Costa Rica and Colombia favoured EC and ACP traders, since by far the majority of the companies purchasing Colombian and Costa Rican bananas and using Category B licences were the so-called non-EC and non-ACP companies, namely Dole, Del Monte, and Chiquita. The great majority of Category B licences were purchased by these companies and they therefore benefited from the exemption from the export certificate requirement. Moreover, similar certificates were required for importing ACP bananas.

5.10 With regard to hurricane licences, the ACP third parties refuted the claim by the Complaining parties that these licences were given exclusively to Category B operators. Nowhere in the relevant regulations was there any reference to Category B operators. Hurricane licences were awarded to banana producer organizations regardless of whether they were Category B operators. Failure to protect the producers with hurricane licences would have resulted in financial disaster and the loss of their relationship with the traditional wholesalers/shippers and the possible loss of the vital shipping arrangements.

5.11 Furthermore, hurricane licences were necessary to fulfil obligations under Protocol 5 of the Lomé Convention since they maintained benefits accorded to ACP producers prior to the EC banana regime. Both the United Kingdom and France had arrangements pre-existing Regulation 404/93 which "safeguarded the interests of operators who are victims of such exceptional events" (fifth recital to Regulation 2791/94). These arrangements were therefore one of the advantages that ACP producers enjoyed on their traditional markets and were, as such, covered by the Lomé waiver. Contrary to suggestions by the Complaining parties that the hurricane licences favoured Category B licence-holders, a comparison between the pre-1993 arrangements and the new banana regime revealed a clear shift from granting licences to importers to "operators who represent banana producers".

2. *Preliminary matters*

5.12 The ACP third parties recalled that at the beginning of the panel process, they requested that they should be granted enhanced third party status in the proceedings of the Panel with:

(i) The right to ask questions and respond to questions raised by the parties at the first and second substantive meetings;

(ii) the right to make written rebuttals; and

(iii) the right to attend the second substantive meeting of the parties; to present submissions at that meeting; and to be heard, ask questions and respond to questions raised by the parties at that meeting.

5.13 The ACP third parties argued that, as signatories to the Lomé Convention, the ACP States would be directly and severely affected by any decision in this dispute which was favourable to the Complaining parties. The enormity of the threat posed by the United States and Latin American complaint to the livelihoods of these countries and to their survival in the world economy could not be overstated. In fighting to ensure the continued application of the commitment undertaken by the EC in the Lomé Convention, the ACP States were, without exaggeration, fighting for their economic survival. Considerations of this kind had on several occasions been taken into account by the International Court of Justice in similar circumstances. Panels historically had recognized the special status of countries in situations analogous to the one faced by the ACP States.[305]

5.14 The ACP third parties submitted that Belize, Dominica, the Dominican Republic, Ghana, Grenada, Saint Lucia, Saint Vincent and the Grenadines, Senegal, and Suriname were not afforded the opportunity to attend the organizational meeting on 13 June 1996 and make their own presentations concerning their rights of representation. The proper procedure for the Panel to have followed would have been to hold an organizational meeting to consider the question of which parties had sufficient "substantial interest" to be accorded third party status. Parties should have been accorded the proper opportunity to be heard on such matters. Having decided who "the parties" to a panel request were, the Panel should have held organizational meetings with all "the parties" or "consulted" with them, to decide upon the proper working procedures, taking into account all the circumstances, including the complexity and seriousness of the complaint, and the potential impact for the parties.

5.15 The denial of these rights was a breach of Article 10.1 of the DSU which required that "the interests of the parties to a dispute and those of other Members under a covered agreement at issue in the dispute shall be fully taken into account during the Panel process". The Panel's misinterpretation of the system established by Article 12.1 of the DSU had led to the ACP third parties' interests not being "fully taken into account during the panel process".

5.16 The ACP third parties argued, furthermore, that it was incorrect for the Panel to assume that the consent of the parties was required for it to grant the enhanced status sought by the ACP States. Article 12.1 of the DSU merely empowered the Panel to "consult" the parties in making its decision on the matter; "to consult" did not mean to secure their consent. The Panel, in this regard, transferred powers to the parties which the DSU had expressly reserved for the Panel itself. In the view of the ACP third parties, the Panel's decision on the level of their participation was prejudicial to their interests. The Panel should therefore review its decision of 25 June 1996 and find it null and void. The right to be heard in a manner consistent with one's

[305] See "European Community - Tariff Treatment on Imports of Citrus Products from Certain Countries in the Mediterranean Region" (L/5776, 7 February 1985); "United Kingdom - Dollar Area Quotas", adopted on 30 July 1973 (BISD 20S/230).

interests was a fundamental principle of natural justice and this right of the ACP States as third parties, set forth in Articles 10 and 12.1, had been breached.

5.17 The ACP third parties submitted that they were given inadequate time to prepare and present their arguments and submissions. This was in breach of Articles 12.2 and 12.4 of the DSU which required that panel procedures provide sufficient flexibility so as to ensure high quality reports and that the panel shall provide sufficient time for the parties to prepare their submissions. Moreover, it was in breach of Article 12.10 which specifically provided that, when examining a complaint against a developing country, a panel must accord sufficient time for the developing country Member to prepare and present its argumentation.

5.18 The ACP third parties requested the Panel to dismiss the complaint and to terminate the proceedings since, in their view, the Complaining parties' request for establishment of a panel failed to meet the requirements of Article 6.2 of the DSU.

5.19 The ACP third parties argued that the request for the establishment of the panel provided neither "a brief summary of the legal basis of the complaint sufficient to present the problem clearly", as required by Article 6.2 of the DSU, nor "the greatest degree of precision", as required in the report of the panel *United States - Imposition of Anti-Dumping Duties on Imports of Fresh and Chilled Atlantic Salmon*. Instead of identifying the "specific measures at issue", the Complaining parties merely cited the "regime for the importation, sale and distribution of bananas". They also failed to explain how specific measures allegedly were inconsistent with specific WTO obligations.

5.20 The ACP third parties requested further that, if the panel were not to dismiss the entire proceedings, Mexico and the United States should be dismissed as complainants because they had no trade interest.

5.21 The ACP third parties argued that Mexico's principal alleged justification for appearing as a complainant in this dispute, namely Mexican ownership of Del Monte, had disappeared on 11 June 1996 when Del Monte was sold to the IAT Group, a Jordanian holding company that also controlled United Trading Company of Santiago, Chile. Moreover, Mexico did not export bananas to the EC and was not actively seeking to do so. Mexico had therefore no trade interest in goods and services in this proceeding. Mexico's only available claim was that it might export bananas to the EC in the future. Such hypothetical trade interest fell short of the standards established in Article XXIII:1 of GATT and the DSU. The use of the term "benefit" in Article XXIII:1 of GATT and Article 3.3 of the DSU required that there be actual trade or an active attempt to trade. Further support for requiring all complainants to have a tangible and present trade interest in a dispute was found in the domestic legal regimes of most, if not all, Members, referred to usually as the requirement of "*locus standi*".

5.22 Similarly, in the ACP third parties' view, the United States' interest in the dispute was not a trade interest in goods or services; any possible interest was an investment interest. Chiquita Brands exported no bananas from the United States to the EC. Neither Chiquita nor Dole supplied any service in, or from, the United States relating to trade in bananas. The only connection that the United States had to this dispute was that Chiquita and Dole, which produced bananas in, and shipped them from, various Central and Latin American countries, happened to be owned by United States interests. The GATT did not address investment interests.[306]

5.23 The ACP third parties argued that the United States sought to salvage its status as a Complaining party by alleging an interest under the GATS regarding the marketing of bananas. However, repeated references to firms that were in the business of marketing bananas could not obscure the reality that the United States interest

[306] "Report of the panel on Canada - Administration of the Foreign Investment Review Act", adopted 7 February 1984 (BISD 30S/140, para. 5.1).

did not fall within the scope of Article I of GATS. Article I provided that, as in the case for trade in goods under the GATT, GATS covered trade in services between one Member and another. The supply of a service could occur in one of four different ways, but in each instance the trade in the service was between the territory of the complainant and the territory of the respondent. The scope of Article I of GATS did not extend to a service provided between a third country and the respondent based on the fact that the service provider happened to be owned by a national of the complainant. This was an investment interest which was not within the scope of the GATS.

5.24 The ACP third parties also requested that the Panel dismiss Ecuador's claim with regard to an alleged breach by the EC of the Agreement on Agriculture. In their view, Ecuador had failed to comply with the requirements of Article 6.2 of the DSU to provide a sufficient explanation of the legal basis in its request for the establishment of a panel. When Ecuador identified its allegation in its first submission, it claimed that the EC licensing regime was inconsistent with footnote 1 to Article 4.2 of the Agreement on Agriculture. Article 4.2 was part of the overall commitment in that Agreement to "tariffy" existing quantitative restrictions. Footnote 1 provided an illustration of the types of measures associated with existing quantitative restrictions. The EC banana regime was "tariffied". It was based on tariff quotas which were expressly permitted under the Agreement on Agriculture. Article XIII of GATT as well as the Licensing Agreement recognized that import licensing regimes were necessary to implement tariff quota schemes. To read footnote 1 to Article 4.2 of the Agreement on Agriculture as vitiating this approved method of tariffication was absurd.

5.25 In the view of the ACP third parties, the Agreement on Agriculture gave specificity to the rights and obligations of Members in respect of agriculture. In the event of a conflict between the Agreement on Agriculture and GATT, the provisions of the former prevailed. This was central to an understanding of the market access bindings, quotas, and other commitments under the Agreement on Agriculture. However, these market access commitments were consolidated concessions within GATT and in this case, there was no conflict. Even if the Panel were to find that Ecuador had properly identified the legal basis of its allegation, the claim that the EC licensing regime was inconsistent with footnote 1 to Article 4.2 of the Agreement on Agriculture should therefore be dismissed by the Panel for lack of substance.

3. The Lomé Convention and the Lomé waiver

5.26 The ACP third parties submitted that the Fourth Lomé Convention, signed by the European Community, its member States and the ACP States in 1989 and ratified in 1990, had a duration of approximately 10 years, expiring on 29 February 2000. There were 70 ACP signatories to the Convention which represented almost half of the WTO Members.

5.27 The various Lomé Conventions were designed to stimulate the development of the ACP States through, *inter alia*, the promotion of trade of the ACP countries. They provided a margin of preferences but were not intended to create undue difficulties for the trade of any other Member. The ACP group of countries contained some of the smallest and least developed countries in the world. Article 167 of the Convention provided as follows:

> In the field of trade co-operation, the object of this Convention is to promote trade between the ACP States and the Community .... In pursuit of this objective, particular regard shall be had to securing effective additional advantages for ACP States' trade with the Community, and to improving the conditions of access for their products to the market in order to accelerate the growth of their trade and, in particular, of the flow of exports to the Community ....

5.28 The ACP third parties claimed that the obligations of the EC to banana producers in ACP States under the Lomé Convention were not limited to Article 1 of Protocol 5. They were much more extensive and included the following:

> (i) Article 167 obliging the EC to improve market access and otherwise contribute to the growth of ACP trade, including trade in bananas from any ACP source;
>
> (ii) Articles 168 and 169, conferring free movement of goods into the EC;
>
> (iii) the special undertaking on bananas contained in Article 183 and Protocol 5 on bananas;
>
> (iv) Article 186, providing that the Stabex provisions applied to fresh bananas;
>
> (v) provisions establishing obligations with respect to trade cooperation, in particular in relation to the island ACP States.

5.29 Article 168 prohibited the imposition of customs duties, or charges having equivalent effect, on goods being imported from ACP States into the EC. Article 169 prohibited quantitative restrictions. Article 168(2)(a)(ii) specified that the EC was obliged, in relation to products originating in the ACP States, to "take the necessary measures to ensure more favourable treatment than that granted to third countries benefiting from the most-favoured-nation clause for the same products". These provisions applied without distinction to traditional and non-traditional ACP products. The suggestion that the Lomé Convention did not require any preferential treatment for non-traditional ACP bananas was therefore incorrect in the view of the ACP third parties.

5.30 The imposition of customs duties or quantitative restrictions was, however, made subject to Article 168(2), which provided that if the EC subjected the products to a common organization of the market, as it did for bananas by way of Regulation 404/93, it reserved the right to adapt the import treatment for products originating in the ACP States. However, Article 168(2)(a)(ii) applied to any adaptation of the import arrangements and obliged the EC to "ensure more favourable treatment than that granted to third countries benefiting from the most-favoured-nation clause for the same products". This covered the preferential tariff treatment and the quantitative allocations accorded to both traditional and non-traditional ACP bananas.

5.31 Article 183 provided that "in order to permit the improvement of the conditions under which bananas originating in the ACP States are produced and marketed, the contracting parties agree to the objectives set out in Protocol 5". Article 183 did not draw a distinction between traditional and non-traditional bananas, although a distinction relating to "traditional suppliers" and "traditional markets" was introduced in certain aspects of Protocol 5, to which the Article referred. The preamble to Protocol 5 provided that the EC agreed to the following objectives:

> ... continuing the advantages enjoyed by traditional suppliers in accordance with the undertakings of Article 1 of this Protocol.

Article 1 stated that:

> In respect of its banana exports to the Community markets, no ACP State shall be placed, as regards access to its traditional markets and its advantages on those markets, in a less favourable situation than in the past or at present.

5.32 The EC was thus under the obligation to preserve the traditional markets and advantages enjoyed "in the past or at present". The same terms had been used in the banana protocols of the Lomé Conventions since

Lomé I in 1975. Given that no limitation on the time period to be taken into account was specified in the banana protocols, the term "in the past or at present" could only be construed as meaning that the traditional markets and advantages enjoyed at any time before 1991 must be matched. The ACP third parties understood that, rather than taking into account all years prior to 1991, the EC used the reference period 1976 to 1991 in establishing the traditional quantities set out in Regulation 404/93. The reason for this restriction on the reference period was not apparent from the wording of the Lomé Convention and was inconsistent with the EC's obligations under Protocol 5. The restriction had the effect of disadvantaging certain ACP countries, such as Jamaica, whose exports to EC member States prior to 1976 were higher than the quantity allocated to them in Regulation 404/93.

5.33 ACP bananas were not only allowed unlimited duty free access to the EC, but in certain of them, namely the "traditional" markets, they were in effect "guaranteed" a market. In the view of the ACP third parties, the protection afforded to ACP producers in terms of "access to, and advantages in" traditional markets prior to Regulation 404/93 included the following:

(i) Imports of cheaper Latin American bananas were prohibited if their imports would reduce the market price below a level considered adequately remunerative for ACP producers.

(ii) ACP producers were free to increase production and to compete in the more liberalized markets of Northern Europe, with the only advantage being the preferential tariff.

(iii) There were no restrictions on the quantities they could produce and market. In particular, this meant that any growth in consumer demand was for their benefit.

(iv) ACP producers had the assurance of significant financial aid in the event of natural disasters.

5.34 The ACP third parties considered that the EC was under a legal obligation to preserve the advantages which ACP banana suppliers enjoyed in the past as regards "markets" and "access". A loss of such access and advantages, even if made up by subsidies, would constitute of breach of the requirements of Protocol 5 since prior to Regulation 404/93 ACP banana producers derived their income from the market. Moreover, a policy of aid instead of trade would be wholly inconsistent with the spirit of the Lomé Convention, given that one of the stated objectives was to promote economic development and increase exports from its ACP signatories to the EC. The provisions of Regulation 404/93 concerning Category B licences were therefore vital to the continued existence of the ACP banana industries. The reasons for the necessity of the Category B licences included the production, shipping and marketing disadvantages which could not simply be remedied by a tariff advantage or subsidy. Moreover, the Category B licence system was necessary due to the concerns relating to the potential for market manipulation and distortion. If these latter concerns were not addressed, the banana industries of the ACP States would not survive.

5.35 The ACP countries submitted further that the EC had obligations in relation to trade co-operation, in particular in relation to island ACP States. Title I of Part Three of the Lomé Convention contained numerous obligations regarding trade cooperation and general trade arrangements. For example, paragraph 1 of Article 167 stated the EC's obligation to "promote trade between the ACP States and the Community". Paragraph 2 stated, more specifically, that the EC shall pay:

> particular regard to securing effective additional advantages for ACP States' trade with the Community and to improving the conditions of access for their products to the market in order to accelerate the growth of their trade and, in particular, of the flow of their exports to the Community and to ensure a better balance in the trade of the contracting parties.

These provisions established a general obligation on the part of the EC to improve market access and otherwise contribute to the growth of ACP trade, including trade in bananas from any ACP source.

5.36 Finally, the Lomé Convention established specific obligations with respect to island ACP States. According to Article 335:

> Specific provisions and measures shall be established to support island ACP States in their efforts to overcome the natural and geographical difficulties and other obstacles hampering their development, so as to enable them to step up their respective rates of development.

The ACP States most heavily dependent on banana exports were small island developing States which were extremely vulnerable to natural hazards and constrained by geographic characteristics.

5.37 With regard to the Lomé waiver, the ACP third parties submitted that the second *Banana* panel had pointed to a waiver under Article XXV:5 of GATT to remedy any possible conflict between the obligations of the EC under the Lomé Convention and those under the GATT:

> The Panel wishes to point out, however, that the contracting parties have at their disposal other procedures under the General Agreement, including Articles XXIV:10 and XXV:5, that are designed to allow contracting parties to take into account, in view of the Panel, economic and social considerations. The adoption of this report would not prevent the contracting parties from taking action under any of these Articles.

5.38 On 9 December 1994, Complaining parties and other GATT contracting parties, at the request of the EC, granted the Lomé waiver to allow the EC to meet its commitments to the ACP States embodied in the Lomé Convention (GATT document L/7604, refers). It was abundantly clear to all WTO Members, in particular the United States which supported the waiver, that one of its purposes was specifically to remedy the possible inconsistencies between the GATT and Regulation 404/93. The Complaining parties and, in particular, the United States had ample opportunity to raise, at the time the waiver was being debated, questions as to whether it fully covered Regulation 404/93. They did not do so. It was a standard principle of legislative interpretation that an instrument should be interpreted in light of the circumstances giving rise to its adoption. The ACP third parties considered that the Panel must be cautious in interpreting the waiver in a manner which could undermine its obvious purpose of protecting Regulation 404/93 as it stood prior to the adoption of the waiver.

5.39 In the recitals to the waiver decision, the contracting parties recognized that the Lomé Convention was aimed at improving the standard of living and economic development of the ACP States and that the granting of preferential treatment for ACP products under the Lomé Convention was consistent with the provisions of the GATT.

5.40 The scope of the EC's obligations under the Lomé Convention was extensive. The scope of the Lomé waiver was coterminous and thus was very broad, too. Paragraph 1 provided:

> Subject to the terms and conditions set out hereunder, the provisions of paragraph 1 of Article 1 of the General Agreement shall be waived, until 29 February 2000, to the extent necessary to permit the European Communities to provide preferential treatment for products originating in ACP States as required by the relevant provisions of the Fourth Lomé Convention, without being required to extend the same preferential treatment to like products of any other contracting party.

5.41 The ACP third parties considered that Complaining parties attempted to curtail the scope of the waiver by asserting that it applied only to "preferential treatment ... required by" the Lomé Convention. The Complaining parties would limit the waiver only to those preferences "absolutely" required by the Lomé Convention. This reading of the Lomé waiver was incorrect and misleading. The text of the waiver read in relevant part "preferential treatment ... as required by" the Lomé Convention. The word "required" and the phrase "as required by" were not used as terms of restriction, but as terms of definition. They informed the definition of "preferential treatment" by tying it to the provisions of the Lomé Convention. The Lomé waiver empowered the EC to establish preferences in order to meet its obligations to ACP countries under the terms of the Lomé Convention. Absent the waiver, the EC might be caught between its obligations under the WTO and the Lomé Convention. The phrase "as required by" communicated to the reader that the waiver was granted expressly to resolve this dilemma, providing the EC the authority to meet its Lomé Convention obligations, without at the same time violating GATT Article I:1. The same was true of the phrase "to the extent necessary" in the waiver.

5.42 The phrases "to the extent necessary" and "as required", even if interpreted as limitations rather than definitions did not limit the EC to one methodology or regime of preferences. The waiver saved from inconsistency with Article I:1 any means necessary to implement the preferential treatment required by the Lomé Convention. However, the phrases "to the extent necessary" and "as required" did not limit the mechanism(s) used to effect the preferences to only one (i.e. to the "required" or "necessary" one). Rather, the waiver permitted the EC to develop and select any regime to create the preferences, as required or necessary to implement the EC's commitments under the Lomé Convention. Therefore, the possibility of other regimes or ways to achieve the preferential treatment did not render Regulation 404/93 "unnecessary". The EC had created, in Regulation 404/93, a regime with provisions that "provide preferential treatment to products originating in ACP States as required by" the Lomé Convention. Even if the Lomé Convention waiver permitted the EC only to provide the "minimal" preferential treatment as required by the Lomé Convention, the preferences contained in Regulation 404/93 would fall within this "minimal" requirement. Therefore, Regulation 404/93, in its entirety, and each of its provisions were covered by the terms of the Lomé waiver.

5.43 The phrase "without being required to extend the same preferential treatment to like products of any other contracting party" was, in the view of the ACP third parties, significant. Even accepting the Complaining parties' argument that the waiver extended only to "required" and "necessary" measures, the fact that the mechanism chosen to effect the preferential treatment under the Lomé Convention resulted in discriminatory treatment for other contracting parties was irrelevant to the question of whether the mechanism was "required" to implement that treatment. This was so because the waiver itself operated to save the discriminatory treatment from inconsistency with Article I:1 by building in discrimination and making it inherent in the implementing mechanism for the preferential treatment. Therefore, a case could not be made against the mechanism or measure on the grounds that it was restrictive or could be less restrictive in the extent to which it discriminated against other contracting parties, or could be less discriminatory against other contracting parties. The Lomé waiver anticipated that discrimination would occur and expressly saved it from inconsistency with Article I:1 of GATT.

5.44 The ACP third parties argued that it would be inappropriate for the Panel in its consideration of the Lomé Convention to act as the final arbiter on the interpretation of its provisions. Serious juridical and legal confusion would arise if the Panel were to carry out that role, quite apart from the practical difficulties it would have in undertaking the requisite detailed legal analysis. The role of the Panel should be akin to that of a court judicially reviewing the acts of an administration, i.e. that it should not substitute itself for the administration, but should rather evaluate the reasonableness of the challenged acts.

4. *Article I of GATT*

5.45 The ACP third parties noted that Regulation 404/93 established different tariff rates for ACP and third-country bananas. Different tariff rates were also established for in-quota and over-quota imports of bananas from each source. The tariff rates established preferences, first, for traditional ACP bananas, second, for non-traditional ACP bananas, and, third, for third-country bananas.

5.46 The tariff rates were "customs duties and charges of any kind imposed on or in connection with the importation" of bananas and also represented a "method of levying such duties and charges". Therefore, they fell under the ambit of Article I:1 of GATT. As the preferential tariff rates were necessary to achieve the Lomé Convention's "no less favourable situation" commitment, they were therefore within the scope of the Lomé waiver. To the extent that the current in-quota tariff of ECU 75 per tonne was less than the previous 20 per cent, the EC had afforded advantages to the Complaining parties with respect to maintaining historical advantages.

5.47 The ACP third parties submitted that the quota allocations to ACP States were not subject to Article XIII of GATT but fell under GATT Article I:1 and were therefore within the scope of the Lomé waiver.

5.48 Country-specific allocations were inherent in the preferential treatment required by Protocol 5 of the Lomé Convention. Article 1 of Protocol 5 obliged the EC to ensure that "no ACP State" was placed in a less favourable situation. The EC's commitment to provide "no less favourable treatment" was thus, by definition, to each ACP State individually and, to meet these individual obligations, the EC had to set country-specific allocations. The EC, taking account of the trade interest of the non-ACP banana exporting countries, had established a tariff quota for these countries based on their historical performance over a representative period. Thus, the EC had restricted itself in establishing the allocation in a manner which took account of the concerns of non-ACP banana exporters.

5.49 The Complaining parties' allegation that the country-specific allocations for certain traditional ACP suppliers exceeded what was required under the Lomé Convention was incorrect. The commitment contained in the Lomé Convention to guarantee the benefits "past or present" required consideration of the highest export from those countries and was not limited to exports after 1976. In addition, the EC had to give, as a minimum, full consideration to investments made "at present".

5.50 The hitherto unrestricted rights to increase production for the traditional markets had been removed and exports had been capped in some cases, such as Jamaica, at levels well below the historical best. In 1966, Jamaica exported bananas to the United Kingdom in excess of 200,000 tonnes, which compared to an allocation of 105,000 tonnes in Regulation 404/93. In 1961, Cameroon's banana exports totalled approximately 140,000 tonnes. In the years preceding the introduction of the EC banana regime, substantial investments, exceeding US$20 million, took place in the banana industry. These investments were capable of resulting in banana exports considerably in excess of 155,000 tonnes allocated to Cameroon. It was therefore incorrect to suggest that the allocation exceeded the minimum obligations of the EC to Cameroon. The traditional quantity of Côte d'Ivoire contained in Regulation 404/93 was based on the highest quantities of exports to the EC before 1991 as well as specific investments made in banana production in the period preceding Regulation 404/93. The highest previous exports of Côte d'Ivoire took place in 1978 (143,000 tonnes). Accordingly, the quota of 155,000 tonnes allocated to Côte d'Ivoire was wholly consistent with the EC's obligations under the Lomé Convention. In the case of Belize, the traditional quantity contained in Regulation 404/93 was 40,000 tonnes which was less than production in 1994 (59,000 tonnes). The allocation was established on the basis of the "best ever" exports and investments of US$100 million. These investments led to improvements in both quantities and quality of bananas.

5.51 With the adoption of the EC Regulation implementing the BFA, and its incorporation into its Schedule of GATT concessions, non-traditional ACP imports to the EC were capped at 90,000 tonnes. At that time, the exports of non-traditional quantities from Cameroon, Côte d'Ivoire and the Dominican Republic were considerably in excess of 90,000 tonnes. The limitation of non-traditional exports ensured that any further increases in the third-country tariff quota benefited exclusively the Latin American suppliers to the detriment of ACP suppliers, which was not required by the Lomé Convention or GATT rules and was a further concession granted to Latin American suppliers.

5.52 The ACP third parties submitted that the EC licensing regime as a whole, and each of its constituent parts, fell within the scope of GATT Article I:1 as the regime established "rules and formalities in connection with importation". The fact that the licensing regime was a "formality in connection with importation" within the scope of Article I:1 was made clear by reference to Article VIII of GATT which was entitled "Fees and Formalities Connected with Importation and Exportation". Paragraph 4(c) of Article VIII explicitly listed licensing as a formality imposed in connection with importation.

5.53 The ACP third parties considered that, since the licensing regime fell within the scope of Article I:1 of GATT and was necessary for the EC to meet its Lomé Convention obligations, it was covered by the Lomé waiver. The licensing regime as a whole, and the Category B licences in particular, were the minimum necessary to preserve the historically favourable treatment of the ACP States' banana exports. Without the 30 per cent set aside for Category B operators, there would be insufficient incentives for operators to ship, import, ripen and market ACP bananas.

5.54 The hurricane licence provisions were also crucial to ensure the ACP States' continued access to the EC banana market and for the EC to meet its obligations and commitments which existed prior to the EC banana regime. Without the protection of legislation covering future hurricanes, the operating companies could not maintain their trading links with the ACP States that were vulnerable to hurricanes. To do so in such circumstances would be imprudent and irresponsible to the companies' shareholders. For both reasons, the hurricane licence provisions were required for the EC to meet its "no less favourable situation" obligation and, thus, fell within the scope of the Lomé waiver.

5.55 The ACP third parties noted that Article I:1 of GATT subsumed the national treatment obligation of Article III:4 of GATT by providing that:

> ... with respect to all matters referred to in paragraphs 2 and 4 of Article III, any advantage, favour, privilege or immunity granted by any contracting party to any product originating in or destined for any other country shall be accorded immediately and unconditionally to the like product originating in or destined for the territories of all other contracting parties.

Assuming, *arguendo*, that the licensing regime did not establish "rules and formalities in connection with importation" of bananas under GATT Article I:1, it was a law, regulation or requirement affecting the internal sale, offering for sale, purchase, transportation, distribution, or use of a good (i.e. an internal requirement within the scope of Article III:4 of GATT). Viewed as an internal requirement, all aspects of the licensing regime which were deemed to provide preferences to ACP imports were "advantages" that were not accorded to all Members. Thus, they were within the scope of Article I:1 and hence were within the scope of the Lomé waiver. In other words, the licensing regime was within the scope of Article I of GATT even if, as the second *Banana* panel ruled, the measures were internal measures rather than rules in connection with their importation.

5. *Article XIII of GATT*

5.56 The ACP third parties submitted that country-specific allocations for traditional ACP banana exports did not fall within the scope of Article XIII of GATT. These allocations were an integral part of the preferential treatment that the EC was required to provide by the Lomé Convention, which was saved by the Lomé waiver from inconsistency with Article I:1 of GATT. Article I of Protocol 5 to the Lomé Convention obligated the EC to ensure that:

> In respect of its banana exports to the Community markets, no ACP State shall be placed, as regards access to its traditional markets and its advantages on those markets, in a less favourable situation than in the past or at present.

The EC had chosen a reasonable mechanism to implement this obligation. It coupled preferential tariff treatment for traditional ACP exports with country-specific allocations at levels reflecting historical ACP export volumes. Where the allocated quantity exceeded the previous exports, this reflected investments made. This was confirmed by the higher quantities exported to the EC within a short time of the establishment of the allocations.

5.57 Not only were the country-specific allocations an integral part of the preferential treatment, they also served to limit the extent of the preferential treatment. By virtue of the Lomé waiver, the EC could have established a preferential regime for ACP bananas with virtually no limit. The EC did not do so. Instead, the EC limited the advantages accorded to traditional ACP bananas by capping preferences at certain quantities for each ACP State. By limiting the degree of GATT Article I:1 discrimination, the EC sought to fulfil the terms of the Lomé waiver. In the view of the ACP third parties, the measures introduced by the EC were the very minimum which it could have taken in order to meet its legal obligations.

5.58 Likewise, according to the ACP third parties, quantitative allocations for non-traditional ACP banana exports did not fall within the scope of Article XIII of GATT. They were an integral part of the preferential treatment required to fulfil the EC's obligations under the Lomé Convention, which was saved from possible inconsistency with Article I:1 of GATT by the Lomé waiver. The obligations of the EC under the Lomé Convention extended beyond merely preserving historical access. Article 168 combined with Article 169 obliged the EC to maintain preferences for ACP banana exports. This applied to all ACP bananas, whether traditional or non-traditional. It also applied to preferences in respect of quantitative restrictions. Article 167 of the Lomé Convention established a general obligation on the part of the EC to "secure effective additional advantages for ACP States' trade with the Community", by improving market access for ACP products and otherwise contributing to the growth of ACP trade. Article 335 required specific additional provisions and measures to enhance the economic development of the island ACP States.

5.59 Without the combination of preferential tariffs and a specific allocation for non-traditional ACP banana exports, these bananas would never reach the EC market because they were much more costly to produce and distribute than Latin American bananas. The only way the EC could fulfil its obligations under the Lomé Convention to secure effective additional advantages for the banana trade in ACP countries was to couple preferential tariff treatment with a specific quantitative allocation for non-traditional ACP exports. As with regard to traditional ACP exports, the Lomé waiver saved the preferential treatment provided to non-traditional ACP exports and required to fulfil the EC's obligations under the Lomé Convention, from inconsistency with Article I:1 of GATT.

5.60 According to Article 3.5(j) of the Licensing Agreement:

> ... Consideration shall also be given to ensuring a reasonable distribution of licences to new importers, taking into account the desirability of issuing licences for products in economic quantities. In this regard, special consideration should be given to those importers importing products originating in developing country Members and, in particular, in the least-developed country Members ....

The EC's allocation for non-traditional ACP banana exports fulfilled the responsibilities established by this exhortation to provide special consideration to developing and least-developed countries which otherwise would be excluded from markets, such as the EC banana market.

5.61 The ACP third parties considered that the EC allocation of licences based on operator categories and activity functions was not inconsistent with Article XIII of GATT. Although the allocation of tariff quota licences was made on the basis of past marketing of bananas by the operator concerned, each licence could be used to purchase bananas from any source. Therefore, Regulation 404/93 did not discriminate among supplying countries.

6. *Article X of GATT and the Licensing Agreement*

5.62 The ACP third parties submitted that the Complaining parties' claims under Article X of GATT and the Licensing Agreement were improperly characterized as arguments directed at Regulation 404/93. They were of the view that the Complaining parties chose this approach since they recognized that any possible challenge would be under Article I:1 of GATT. Any inconsistency with Article I:1 of GATT would be covered by the Lomé waiver and they therefore sought to escape this restriction by recasting their allegations independently of Article I:1.

5.63 The ACP third parties argued that some differentiation with regard to the procedural requirements faced by importers of Latin American versus ACP bananas was to be expected given the "dictates" of the Lomé Convention. The Lomé Convention required the EC to distinguish between ACP and non-ACP imports in order to ensure ACP States' continued access to the EC market. It also required the EC to carefully monitor imports of Latin American bananas in order to ensure such continued access. Without monitoring, the producers and importers of the more competitive Latin American bananas would "upset" the EC market for ACP bananas.

5.64 The ACP third parties claimed that the Complaining parties had asserted under Article X:3(a) of GATT that the procedural requirements for importing bananas from their countries exceeded those faced by importers of ACP bananas. The correct measure to assess this claim was the extent of the additional burden faced by importers of bananas from the Complaining parties, which was not significant. This approach was followed by the panel of *European Economic Community Restrictions on Imports of Dessert Apples - Complaint by Chile* (BISD 36S/93). The panel found that the variations in the EC regulation raised by the complainant "... were minimal and did not in themselves establish a breach of Article X:3".

7. *The GATS*

5.65 ACP third parties submitted arguments that Mexico and the United States must be dismissed as Complaining parties because they had no trade interest (either as to goods or services) in this proceeding.

5.66 The ACP third parties claimed further that the United States' complaint had failed to produce any evidence that the provision of services, *qua* services by United States companies, was restricted, prejudiced, or discriminated against, by virtue of the measures adopted by the EC. The United States had confused the provision or offering of services with trade in goods. The United States could not point to any restrictions or discrimination in respect of the provision of shipping services, wholesaling services, distribution services, or ripening services. EC preferences for goods of a certain origin did not directly or indirectly affect the provision of services relating to those goods. If the Panel were to uphold the United States' complaint on these grounds, every waiver and every tariff quota, which had an impact on the movement of goods, would also constitute a restriction on the provision of services in relation to those goods.

5.67 The ACP third parties refuted the claim that the EC was, de facto, discriminating against US companies by virtue of preferences given to ACP bananas and thereby ACP service companies. The ACP third parties submitted that so-called US companies were substantially involved in the supply of ACP bananas to the EC and their distribution within the EC. US companies and Del Monte had a dominating position in supplying ACP African bananas to the EC market. Both Dole and Del Monte had, at present, substantial interests in banana production in Cameroon. In Côte d'Ivoire, approximately 30,000 to 35,000 tonnes of bananas were marketed by companies associated with Dole, Del Monte and Chiquita. In Jamaica, Dole controlled, at present, 35 per cent of the Jamaican producers' banana market company which held approximately 18 per cent of the UK market. In 1993, Chiquita exported some 25,000 tonnes of bananas from the Dominican Republic to the EC. On the whole, at present, almost 355,000 tonnes of EC and ACP bananas were supplied to the EC market by Chiquita, Dole and Del Monte. Besides Chiquita's ownership of Fyffes (at present, the largest supplier of ACP bananas to the EC) prior to the introduction of the EC banana regime, US companies had considerable control over the major import and distribution companies in France: Chiquita had a 50 per cent shareholding in Compagnie de Banane (which it had since increased to a 100 per cent shareholding) and Dole had a 33 per cent shareholding in Compagnie Fruitière. These two French companies accounted for the major proportion of ACP bananas imported into France from Africa.

5.68 The ACP third parties claimed that the very basis of the allegation that so-called "Latin American banana segment firms" handled less than 10 per cent of the distribution and related marketing of ACP/EC bananas into the EC prior to the institution of the EC banana regime was therefore factually incorrect and misleading.

5.69 However, even assuming that the trade was trade in services (which it was not): (i) the Complaining parties had failed to discuss, much less establish, the required elements; and (ii) a review of the facts demonstrated that Regulation 404/93 did not violate GATS Article II. To establish non-conformity with Article II of GATS, the Complaining parties had to, first, identify an affected service or service supplier. Second, the Complaining parties had to identify the treatment provided by the EC to that discrete service or service provider when it was supplied from, or in the territory of, an ACP country, through commercial presence of an ACP service supplier in the EC, or through the temporary presence of an ACP service supplier in the EC. Third, the Complaining parties had to prove that the EC accorded less favourable treatment to a like service or a supplier of a like service when that discrete service was supplied from, or in the territory of, a non-ACP country, through the commercial presence of a non-ACP service supplier, or through the temporary presence of a non-ACP service supplier in the EC. The Complaining parties had avoided a careful analysis of the requirements of the GATS. They had only used the argument that the word "affecting" in Article I:1 of GATS should be broadly interpreted as, they claimed, two previous panels had done with regard to Article III:4 of GATT.[307] The Complaining parties' attempt to base their entire argument on one word failed because a number of elements were needed to establish non-conformity with Article II of GATS and the Complaining parties had failed to prove any of them.

5.70 The ACP third parties argued that they subscribed to what they considered to be the common concept of wholesaling, which was the last stage before retail sale, i.e. the stage at which bulk shipments were stored in inventory and then broken-up into smaller lots for resale to retailers.

5.71 The ACP third parties argued that the United States had acknowledged that the EC regulations were neutral on their face and did not discriminate, *de iure,* on the basis of nationality of the service provider. The United States had claimed de facto discrimination, but offered no facts in support of this allegation. None of the Complaining parties identified the nature of the wholesaling services involved or the entity that provided them. They had suggested that third-country bananas imported by Category B operators could and would only

[307] "Italian Discrimination against Imported Agricultural Machinery", BISD 7S/60, and "United States - Section 337 of the Tariff Act of 1930", BISD 36S/345.

be wholesaled by ACP providers of wholesale services. The experience of the regime had shown that this was incorrect. Most Latin American bananas, irrespective of whether imported with Category B licences, were "wholesaled" in the north European countries by the same wholesalers which marketed imported bananas with Category A licences. The mere fact that, historically, a certain group of wholesalers might have handled the last pre-retail stage of ACP banana distribution in the EC was irrelevant. The issue was whether the manner in which the EC distributed licences to import third-country bananas served to preclude non-ACP wholesalers from entering or expanding the provision of wholesale services. There were, however, no restrictions on wholesalers which traditionally imported Latin American bananas from offering these services in relation to ACP/EC bananas.

5.72 With regard to Category A licence allocations, the ACP third parties submitted that the United States had failed to point out that, while 66.5 per cent of these licences were granted to so-called Latin American banana companies, the balance of 30 per cent was given to any company which imported EC or ACP bananas. There was no restriction whatsoever on so-called Latin American companies importing EC and ACP bananas. Dole and Del Monte significantly benefited from this arrangement. On the other hand, access to 66.5 per cent of the licences was restricted to those with an historic involvement in marketing third-country bananas.

5.73 With regard to export certificates, there appeared to be an attempt by the United States to suggest that nationality or categorisation of a company would confer on it benefits of exemptions from the export certificate requirement. This was incorrect. Any company, whether of EC, United States or ACP nationality, which had a Category A licence was subject in the relevant Latin American countries to the possible requirement of export certificates. Equally, any company, regardless of nationality or categorisation, which wished to utilize Category B licences in the relevant Latin American countries was exempt from the export certificate requirement. Chiquita, Dole, and Del Monte possessed substantial quantities of Category B licences and, in each of case, these companies were exempted from the export certificate requirement when importing into the EC using Category B licences.

5.74 With regard to hurricane licences, these licences were effectively replacement licences for the shortfall from ACP or EC origin when production was destroyed by hurricanes. Licences were issued essentially to the producer organizations and not to operators and certainly not to operators on the basis of their nationality.

5.75 In the view of the ACP third parties, Ecuador's argument with regard to the rental of seagoing vessels with crew was fundamentally flawed. Neither the EC nor any other Member had any MFN, national treatment or market access obligations as to any maritime transport service since the legal conditions set out in the GATS "Annex on negotiations on Maritime Transport Services" had not yet been fulfilled. Accordingly, the Panel should dismiss this claim.

8. *Conclusion*

5.76 In summary, the ACP third parties requested the Panel to find that:

- The Lomé waiver provided the legal basis for the preferential treatment granted to ACP banana exports to the EC and comprehensively met its purpose, namely to ensure "legal certainty". Thus, the Panel should find that the EC banana regime did not violate Article I of GATT because the regime fell within the scope of the Lomé waiver.

- The quota allocations to the ACP States and the licensing measures did not violate the relevant provisions of GATT nor those of other instruments of Annex 1A of the WTO Agreement.

- The EC banana regime was fully consistent with the GATS and in any case did not discriminate between the ACP and non-ACP service suppliers.

B. Canada

5.77 Canada submitted that it had a substantial interest in several legal issues relating to the interpretation of the GATT and the GATS which had been raised by the parties to the dispute. The first was the relationship between the General Agreement on Tariffs and Trade 1994 and other Multilateral Agreements on Trade in Goods, and the General Agreement on Trade in Services. The second was the effect to be given to a waiver under Article XXV of GATT and the Understanding in Respect of Waivers of Obligations under the General Agreement on Tariffs and Trade 1994.

1. *The relationship between trade in goods and trade in services*

5.78 Canada stated that its interest in the case stemmed from the fact that it was the first opportunity for a WTO dispute settlement panel to deal with the interrelationship between treatment of imported products under GATT and the treatment of service suppliers under GATS. The Panel's consideration of the relationship between rights and obligations arising out of WTO agreements relating to trade in goods and rights and obligations arising out of the GATS with respect to measures affecting trade in services was thus of significance for Canada as a party to the WTO agreements. Previous GATT 1947 panels had clearly indicated that GATT applied not only to the importation of goods but also to internal terms and conditions attached to the distribution and sale of products which might have adversely modified the conditions of competition between imported goods and domestic goods within the internal, domestic market. One of the primary reasons for reaching this conclusion was the explicit language of GATT Article III:4, the first sentence of which stated that:

> ... products of the territory of any contracting party imported into the territory of any other contracting party shall be accorded treatment no less favourable than that accorded to like products of national origin in respect of all laws, regulations and requirements affecting their internal sale, offering for sale, purchase, transportation, distribution or use.

5.79 There was a well-developed line of cases which considered the application of GATT disciplines and the consistency with GATT disciplines of internal laws or practices in terms of whether such measures accorded national treatment to imported products.[308] Canada considered that it was noteworthy that a number of these cases specifically considered the issue in the context of distribution measures. In their submissions in this case, Ecuador, the United States and Mexico had specifically raised distribution issues as being a contravention of GATS in addition to being a contravention of GATT.

5.80 In Canada's view, any consideration of the GATS implications of such measures had to be assessed in the light of what effect, if any, the result would have for the interpretation of GATT, the relationship between the two agreements and the interpretation of the WTO agreements as a whole.

[308] See for example: "Italian Discrimination against Imported Agricultural Machinery", adopted 23 October 1958, BISD 7S/60; "Canada - Administration of Foreign Investment Review Act", adopted 7 February 1984, BISD 30S/140; "Canada - Import, Distribution and Sale of Certain Alcoholic Drinks by Canadian Provincial Marketing Agencies", adopted 22 March 1988, BISD 35S/37; "United States - Section 337 of the Tariff Act of 1930", adopted 7 November 1989, BISD 36S/345; "Thailand - Restrictions on Importation of and Internal Taxes on Cigarettes", adopted 7 November 1990, BISD 37S/200; "Canada - Import, Distribution and Sale of Certain Alcoholic Drinks by Provincial Marketing Agencies", adopted 18 February 1992, BISD 39S/27; "United States - Measures Affecting Alcoholic Drinks and Malt Beverages", adopted 19 June 1992, BISD 39S/206.

2. *The Lomé waiver*

5.81 Canada also expressed its interest in the dispute as it, in Canada's view, raised a unique opportunity to consider whether measures inconsistent with a waiver granted under GATT were "justiciable" in a WTO dispute settlement and whether measures arising from such a waiver that caused nullification or impairment were "justiciable". Canada noted that the determination of these questions may well have implications beyond the facts of the particular dispute.

5.82 The Lomé waiver explicitly noted that it was not to "... preclude the right of affected contracting parties to have recourse to Articles XXII and XXIII of the General Agreement". Past GATT panels had considered whether a measure was or was not consistent with a waiver granted by the CONTRACTING PARTIES.[309] In addition, Canada noted that paragraph 3 of the "Understanding in Respect of Waivers of Obligations under the GATT 1994" provided that a Member considering that a benefit accruing to it under the GATT was being nullified or impaired as a result of (a) the failure of the Member to whom the waiver was granted to observe the terms and conditions of the waiver; or (b) the application of a measure consistent with the waiver, may invoke the dispute settlement provisions of Article XXIII of GATT. Thus, the issue of whether or not a measure was consistent with a waiver was a matter that could be properly submitted to a panel under both GATT practice and now under WTO rules.

5.83 In Canada's view, there may be some question as to whether or not the "Understanding in Respect of Waivers of Obligations under the GATT 1994" was intended to codify the existing practice or to modify it with respect to the ability to assert claims with respect to violations of the GATT. In the *United States Sugar Panel* the panel concluded that while a waiver did not necessarily indicate a decision by the contracting parties that a measure consistent with the waiver was inconsistent with the General Agreement, both the substantive obligation and the relief provided under Article XXV:5 in the form of a waiver were part of the GATT and thus a measure consistent with the waiver could not constitute a failure by a Member to carry out its obligations under the GATT within the meaning of Article XXIII:1(a).[310] In that case, the claim that the measure in question was a violation of the Agreement was rejected.

5.84 In the case referred to in the previous paragraph, the panel had then considered whether a measure consistent with a waiver could constitute nullification and impairment of benefits accruing to a Member within the meaning of Article XXIII:1(b) of GATT (i.e. "non-violation" nullification and impairment). The panel concluded that the fact that the measures found to be inconsistent with the GATT were consistent with the waiver did not preclude a claim being brought pursuant to Article XXIII:1(b), but that in such a case the complainant bore the burden of demonstrating such nullification or impairment resulting from the application of the measure.[311]

5.85 The text of the "Understanding in Respect of Waivers of Obligations under the GATT 1994" did not distinguish between violation and non-violation claims pursuant to Article XXIII. Canada questioned, therefore, whether it should be interpreted as only including non-violation claims or whether the drafters had intended to modify existing practice. The drafters would have been familiar with the existing case law and thus it would not be unreasonable to conclude that the lack of language explicitly distinguishing between violation and non-violation cases indicated an intention to modify the law. Before so concluding, however, Canada submitted that the Panel should consider whether such a significant result could be justified through interpretative inference. Canada further asked for reflection on whether in cases where the drafters were aware

[309] For example: "United States - Restrictions on the Import of Sugar and Sugar-Containing Products Applied Under the 1955 Waiver and Under the Headnote to the Schedule of Tariff Concessions", adopted on 7 November 1990, BISD 37S/228.

[310] Idem, paragraph *5.18*, p.260.

[311] Idem, para. *5.20*, p.261.

of the law and practice and intended to modify that law and practice, it was reasonable to expect that such intention be clearly indicated by explicit language in order to avoid an interpretation that the text was not intended to be declaratory of the previous law. Further, where the previous law was embodied in the text of an agreement, relatively minor wording differences may carry significant interpretative weight, but should this also be the case where the law was embodied in such things as decisions of the parties and panel findings? In Canada's view, in the latter case there should, perhaps, be a presumption that if the matter could not be resolved based upon the explicit language of the text, the text should be regarded as codifying the existing law and practice.

3. *Conclusion*

5.86 Canada urged the Panel to give serious consideration to the various systemic issues raised by the case and, in particular, the issues relating to the interpretation of the interrelationship of the various WTO agreements, and the appropriate interpretation to be given to the scope of the "Understanding in Respect of Waivers of Obligations under the GATT 1994".

C. Colombia, Costa Rica, Nicaragua and Venezuela

1. *Introduction*

5.87 Colombia, Costa Rica, Nicaragua and Venezuela recalled that during the Uruguay Round, the EC established a tariff quota for a quantity of bananas and allocated it among supplying countries. The allocation followed long negotiations between the EC and the principal banana supplying countries. During the negotiations, the EC had offered a tariff quota allocation to all countries interested in the EC banana market in accordance with the principles set out in Article XIII of GATT. The negotiations resulted in a market access commitment in the schedule of concessions of the EC, including an allocation of a tariff quota to all Members. This concession was based on the Banana Framework Agreement ("BFA") negotiated between the EC and countries that figured among the most important suppliers of bananas to the EC, namely Colombia, Costa Rica, Nicaragua and Venezuela. In the complaint on the EC's regime for the importation, sale and distribution of bananas, Ecuador, Guatemala, Honduras, Mexico and the United States challenged, *inter alia*, the legality of those parts of the EC's banana regime that implemented the BFA. In the view of Colombia, Costa Rica, Nicaragua and Venezuela, their main complaint was not that the EC banana regime was inconsistent with the market access commitment the EC had accepted in respect of bananas, but that the regime was inconsistent with other, more general obligations that all Members had accepted in respect of all products. The complaint therefore raised the fundamental question of whether a specific market access commitment for agricultural products of the type included in the schedules of many Members was *lex specialis* in relation to the more general obligations assumed under the WTO agreements, or whether such a commitment could be challenged in the light of such general rules.

5.88 Colombia, Costa Rica, Nicaragua and Venezuela noted their interest in the dispute as both signatories of the BFA and exporters of agricultural products interested in the stability and balance of the legal framework governing trade in agriculture. The principal legal argument of Colombia, Costa Rica, Nicaragua and Venezuela was that it was legally incorrect to examine those parts of the EC banana import regime that reflected the EC market access commitment on bananas in the light of the GATT because, under the provisions of the Agreement on Agriculture, market access commitments had to be carried out as specified in the schedule of the Member and these provisions overrode those of the GATT. Subsidiarily, they also argued that the tariff quota allocation and its administration was consistent with the GATT because the provisions of the BFA on the allocation of the banana tariff quota in the EC Schedule constituted an agreement between the EC and all banana supplying countries Members of the WTO within the meaning of Article XIII:2(d) and because the provisions of the BFA on the allocation of export licences did not affect trade levels or shares but concerned the distribution of financial benefits that did not accrue under the GATT.

2. *Principal legal arguments*

5.89 Colombia, Costa Rica, Nicaragua and Venezuela recalled that the Uruguay Round produced a fundamental systemic change in the field of agriculture - from a situation of many non-tariff measures to a tariff-only regime. Two principles had governed the negotiations: first, all non-tariff measures had to be transformed into tariffs and, second, the market access opportunities that were already available prior to the conclusion of the Round had to be maintained and certain minimum market access opportunities had to be provided. Many Members made commitments on market access opportunities in the form of tariff quotas allocated to specific countries, and many had included in their schedules commitments on the administration of the tariff quotas. In the view of Colombia, Costa Rica, Nicaragua and Venezuela, the Agreement on Agriculture acknowledged that a market access concession may relate not only to a tariff concession but also to commitments governing the implementation and administration of tariff quotas. This followed from Article 1(g) of the Agreement on Agriculture, which defined the term "market access concessions" as including "... all market access commitments undertaken pursuant to this Agreement" and Article 4.1, which stated that "[m]arket access concessions contained in Schedules relate to bindings and reductions of tariffs, and to other market access commitments as specified therein".

5.90 Colombia, Costa Rica, Nicaragua and Venezuela argued that the negotiators of the Agreement on Agriculture had agreed that any tariff quota, including the applicable tariff rate and any other conditions related to the tariff quota, should be specified in Section I-B of Part I of the schedule of each of the Members concerned. The EC had included in Section I-B of Part I of its Schedule LXXX the following market access commitment: "Initial and final quota quantity and in-quota tariff rate: 2,200,000 tonnes - ECU 75 per tonne subject to the terms and conditions as indicated in the Annex". This Annex set out the BFA. The EC's market access commitments thus comprised the provisions on tariff quota allocation and administration set out in the BFA and were part of the EC's market access commitments under the Agreement on Agriculture.

5.91 Colombia, Costa Rica, Nicaragua and Venezuela argued that in accordance with the general interpretative note to Annex 1A of the WTO Agreement[312] and Article 21 of the Agreement on Agriculture, the Agreement on Agriculture overrode the GATT. In their view, these provisions made it clear, that the provisions of the GATT applied only to the extent that the Agreement on Agriculture did not provide otherwise. Thus, the drafters of the Agreement on Agriculture had clearly expressed their intention that a commitment on subsidies or market access contained in a Member's schedule was *lex specialis* in relation to the more general obligations under WTO agreements other than the Agreement on Agriculture.

5.92 Colombia, Costa Rica, Nicaragua and Venezuela noted that from a strictly legal perspective, the market access commitments as well as the export subsidy commitments established in each Member's schedule, were an integral part of the GATT as modified by the Agreement on Agriculture. Articles 1, 3, 4, 6, 7, 8 and 9 thereof permitted the qualification of general obligations through scheduled commitments. In their view, these provisions modified Article II:1(b) of GATT. They argued that it would thus be legally incorrect and contrary to the purpose and objective of the Agreement on Agriculture to examine those parts of the EC banana import regime that reflected the EC market access commitment on bananas in the light of GATT.

5.93 They argued, furthermore, that unlike the GATT and the GATS that established the obligation to accord treatment no less favourable than that provided in the schedule, Article 4.1 of the Agreement on Agriculture specifically required Members to carry out their market access commitments "as specified in their schedules", not as provided for under the GATT. Consequently, Colombia, Costa Rica, Nicaragua and Venezuela argued that the question the Panel needed to examine was whether the EC banana regime was consistent with its market access commitment on bananas, not whether it was consistent with the GATT.

---

[312] "In the event of a conflict between the provisions of the [GATT 1994] and the provisions of another agreement in Annex 1A to the [WTO Agreement], the provisions of the other agreement shall prevail to the extent of the conflict."

5.94 Colombia, Costa Rica, Nicaragua and Venezuela submitted that unlike the GATT, the Agreement on Agriculture permitted the qualification of general obligations through scheduled commitments. The tariff concessions made under the GATT 1947 resulted in most instances from protocols accepted only by the contracting parties that made the concessions. Since a treaty could not create either obligations or rights for non-signatory States without their consent,[313] these GATT 1947 tariff protocols could only be used to assume obligations in addition to those set out under the GATT 1947 - not to diminish the rights of third contracting parties under that Agreement. Moreover, Article II:1(b) merely permitted a Member to make a tariff concession in its schedule "subject to the terms, conditions or qualifications set forth in that schedule", which made clear that it was only the tariff concession and not the obligations under the GATT 1994 that could be qualified through schedule provisions. For these reasons, Colombia, Costa Rica, Nicaragua and Venezuela argued that the 1989 panel report on *United States - Restrictions on Imports of Sugar*[314] correctly rejected the contention of the United States that a note in its Schedule in which it had reserved the right to impose quota limitations on imports of sugar justified import restrictions on sugar inconsistent with Article XI of GATT 1947. The Complaining parties' reference to this panel was not pertinent.

5.95 In contrast, they argued, the market access commitments under the Agreement on Agriculture were part of the WTO agreements which all Members, including the Complaining parties, had accepted - there were no non-signatory, third Members in respect of such market access commitments. Furthermore, the Agreement on Agriculture was based on a legal concept fundamentally different from that of the GATT, i.e. the Agreement on Agriculture regulated the relationship between it and the schedule commitments in a different manner. According to Colombia, Costa Rica, Nicaragua and Venezuela, this was reflected by the fact that the GATT was essentially a framework agreement for the incorporation of the results of tariff negotiations into schedules while the Agreement on Agriculture and the scheduled commitments negotiated under it constituted together the result of a negotiation on the first stage of agricultural reform.

5.96 Colombia, Costa Rica, Nicaragua and Venezuela submitted that the participants in the Uruguay Round were therefore permitted to use the process of scheduling commitments on particular products to both add to and qualify obligations that they would have had under the Agreement on Agriculture in the absence of scheduled commitments for these specific products. Thus, according to Article 8 of the Agreement on Agriculture, the general prohibition of export subsidies did not apply to a Member that accorded a subsidy in accordance "with commitments as specified in that Member's Schedule" -a qualification of general obligations regarding export subsidies. The same applied, in their view, to the market access commitments assumed in addition to a tariff concession. These commitments, too, were, according to Article 4.1 of the Agreement on Agriculture, "as specified" in each Member's schedule irrespective of whether they corresponded to obligations set out in WTO agreements other than the Agreement on Agriculture. The words "as specified" implied that the "other market access commitments" - meant and understood to relate to country-specific tariff quota allocations - had to be carried out exactly as set out in the schedules.

5.97 Colombia, Costa Rica, Nicaragua and Venezuela considered that while one may regret that the drafters of the Agreement on Agriculture decided to permit Members to include in their schedules specific provisions that overrode or qualified provisions in WTO agreements establishing general obligations, the role of the Panel was not to assess the manner by which the drafters of the Agreement on Agriculture expressed their intention. What was important for the Panel was that the drafters of the Agreement on Agriculture had clearly expressed their intention that a commitment on subsidies or market access contained in a Member's schedule was *lex specialis* in relation to more general obligations under WTO agreements other than the Agreement on Agriculture.

---

[313] See Article 34 of the Vienna Convention on the Law of Treaties.

[314] BISD 36S/342-343.

5.98 Colombia, Costa Rica, Nicaragua and Venezuela submitted that the market access commitments made under the Agreement on Agriculture constituted in large part settlements of disputes on: the interpretation and application of the provisions of GATT 1947 that had arisen prior to the Uruguay Round; disagreements in the course of the Uruguay Round about the adherence to the guidelines for negotiations; and potential future disputes about the precise implementation of the market access commitments. The provisions relating to the BFA in the EC's market access commitments had precisely these functions: they were not designed to circumvent GATT provisions. If the Panel were to decide to review the BFA provisions in the light of the provisions of the GATT, it would, in their view, effectively decide that all market access commitments could be subject to such a review and would therefore reopen the "Pandora's Box" of endless disputes that the negotiators of the Agreement on Agriculture had succeeded closing after long and arduous negotiations. Each of the commitments that governed the allocation and administration of the tariff quotas resulted from a negotiation in which not only the Member that assumed the commitment, but also those Members that benefited from them, had made compromises. In many cases, the beneficiary Members had agreed to a proposed tariff quota level on the condition that issues regarding the allocation and administration of the quota were clearly settled. The provisions of Article 4.1 of the Agreement on Agriculture made clear that in such cases both the tariff concession (that is the tariff quota level and in-quota tariff level) and the related market access commitments (that is the allocation of the quota among countries) had the same legal status.

5.99 Furthermore, under the WTO agreements, the legal status of a market access commitment did not depend on its conformity with the criteria and procedures used to negotiate it. The proposal to include in the Agreement on Agriculture a provision with that effect was specifically rejected. The legal status of market access commitments inserted in a schedule was governed by the same rules that governed the legally binding nature of all other provisions of the WTO Agreement: i.e. they were accepted and ratified as a single undertaking[315] and with no reservations, except as otherwise provided in the Multilateral Trade Agreements[316]. The law did not distinguish between treaty provisions that were inserted at an early stage of the negotiations and those which were inserted in the final stage. It followed from the above that any shortcomings that may have arisen during the negotiating process could have been corrected only during the negotiating process. Neither WTO law nor general international law permitted a State to accept the WTO Agreement and subsequently invoke a failure to follow the procedures for its negotiation as grounds for its invalidity.

5.100 In reference to Guatemala's claims, Colombia, Costa Rica, Nicaragua and Venezuela submitted that whatever rights Guatemala had during the Uruguay Round negotiations such as the right to raise the issue of alleged shortcomings in the verification process in the Trade Negotiations Committee or the right to decide not to join the WTO, were lost as a result of its acceptance of the WTO Agreement because that acceptance could not be made subject to a reservation concerning the EC's Schedule.[317] Given the fact that Guatemala could not at the same time be a Member and make a valid reservation with respect to the EC market access commitment, its letter to the Director-General could have only one of the following legal consequences: either Guatemala's acceptance of the WTO Agreement was null and void and Guatemala was not a Member of the WTO or Guatemala's reservation was null and void because of Article XVI:5 of the WTO Agreement.

5.101 Colombia, Costa Rica, Nicaragua and Venezuela argued that if the Panel were to decide to review the market access commitments in the light of the provisions of the GATT, it would review the legal status of only that part of the negotiated compromise which was beneficial to the exporting Members, not the part that was beneficial to the importing Member. The Panel would then potentially create a legal situation under which Members would be deprived of the security of the market access benefits they had negotiated under the Agreement on Agriculture without having any possibility to change the level of tariff concessions they had accepted to obtain that security. This would, in the view of Colombia, Costa Rica, Nicaragua and Venezuela,

---

[315] WTO Agreement, Article II.

[316] Idem, Article XVI:5.

[317] Idem.

produce an enormous imbalance in the rights and obligations under the Agreement on Agriculture. Not only would it be inconsistent with the wording of the provisions of Agreement on Agriculture but also contrary to their purpose and objective.

3. Subsidiary legal arguments

5.102 Colombia, Costa Rica, Nicaragua and Venezuela argued that, although the principles on non-discrimination set out in Article XIII of GATT were difficult to apply in the case of an allocation of tariff quota shares among supplying countries, the allocation of the banana tariff quota in the EC Schedule was consistent with Article XIII since it reflected an allocation agreed by all Members, including all banana supplying country Members, and met the requirements for a unilateral allocation. Although ideally the allocation of a tariff quota among supplying countries should result in a distribution of trade equivalent to the distribution that would prevail in the absence of the quota, that distribution was never known and the introductory sentence of Article XIII:2 therefore merely obliged Members to aim "as closely as possible" at that distribution. According to Article XIII:2(d), Members may base the allocation on the shares during "a previous representative period ... due account being taken of any special factors which may ... be affecting the trade in the product ...". Since it was difficult to determine which previous period was "representative" and which "special factors" called for a modification of the allotted share, this method was difficult, if not impossible to apply. The example was given of a Member which transformed an import prohibition into a tariff quota allocated among supplying countries. In that case an allocation based on a previous representative period was not possible.

5.103 According to Colombia, Costa Rica, Nicaragua and Venezuela, these inherent difficulties in allocating quotas among supplying countries led the drafters of the GATT to decide that the preferred method of allocating import quota shares would be an agreement with the supplying countries. Article XIII:2(d) therefore provided that:

> In cases in which a quota is allocated among supplying countries the contracting parties applying the restrictions may seek agreement with respect to the allocation of shares in the quota with all other [Members] having a substantial interest in supplying the product concerned.

An allotment in accordance with a previous representative period should be used according to Article XIII:2(d), second sentence, only when an allocation by agreement was "not reasonably practicable".

5.104 Colombia, Costa Rica, Nicaragua and Venezuela argued that in the case at hand, the provisions on the allocation and administration of quotas of the BFA had not only been agreed among the signatories of the BFA but had been formally accepted by all Members. They therefore constituted an agreement on the allocation of tariff quota shares within the meaning of Article XIII:2(d). Colombia, Costa Rica, Nicaragua and Venezuela noted that the allocation of the tariff quota shares, while formally accepted by all Members, did not satisfy all of them. Each banana supplying country buttressed with statistics had claimed to be entitled to a greater share of the tariff quota. Thus, neither the signatories of the BFA nor any of the other countries had come out of the negotiations fully satisfied but the advantage of making the tariff quota allocation part of an agreement accepted by all Members was that legal security and predictability of conditions of trade could be created for all of them. The law did not distinguish between treaty provisions that were accepted willingly and those that were accepted reluctantly.

5.105 Colombia, Costa Rica, Nicaragua and Venezuela considered that, even if the allocation of shares set out in the EC Schedule were not regarded as an agreed allocation within the meaning of Article XIII of GATT 1994, it would nevertheless fall within the range of discretion which this provision accorded to importing

Members that allotted quota tariff shares on the basis of a unilateral decision. Article XIII:2(d) stated that, if an allocation by agreement was not reasonably practicable, the Member shall allot to the Members:

> having a substantial interest in supplying the product shares based on the proportions, supplied by such [WTO Members] during a previous representative period, of the total quantity or value of imports of the product, due account being taken of any special factors which may have affected or may be affecting the trade in the product.

Article XIII:4 stated that:

> the selection of the representative period for any product and the appraisal of any special factors affecting the trade in the product shall be made initially by the [Member] applying the restriction; *Provided* that such [Member] shall, upon the request of any other [Member] having a substantial interest in supplying that product ..., consult promptly ... regarding the need for an adjustment of the proportions determined or of the base period selected, or for a reappraisal of the special factors involved ....

Under these two provisions, it was thus up to the EC to initially select a previous representative period, appraise any special factors affecting trade in bananas, allot shares to the substantially interested Members accordingly and to then stand ready to consult on its decisions with those Members. According to Colombia, Costa Rica, Nicaragua and Venezuela, the EC selected, consistent with recognized GATT 1947 practice,[318] an appropriate previous representative period, i.e. the three previous years with normal trade flows. In their view, the EC had chosen from among several legitimate and reasonable options the period of 1989-1991 because it was the most recent period with reliable data on exports and imports, and because during that period the speculative distortions in trade patterns due to the expectation of a unified EC banana market had not yet taken place. Moreover, that period corresponded to the period the EC had chosen for the establishment of the total tariff quota. It was true that the period of 1989-1991 was not a period free of restrictions and therefore did not give a precise indication of the shares that could reasonably be expected in the absence of restrictions,[319] but a comparison of the distribution of imports into the whole of the EC during 1989-1991 with the distribution of imports into the six EC member States that did not maintain restrictions during that period (see the following table) showed the differences were only very small. This was a further indication that the reference period chosen was a reasonable one.

[318] See the panel reports in BISD 27S/116 and 36S/130-131.

[319] Colombia, Costa Rica, Nicaragua and Venezuela noted that six of the twelve member States had restrictive regimes in place during that period, potentially affecting the distribution of imports among supplying countries.

Origin[1]	EC-12 (%)	EC-6 (%)
Colombia	20.3	19.7
Costa Rica	25.4	25.3
Ecuador	19.6	17.8
Guatemala	1.5	1.0
Honduras	6.9	6.0
Nicaragua	2.2	2.4
Panama	23.3	25.0
Others[1]	0.8	2.9

[1]Non-preferential imports only.
Source: Calculations based on COMEXT.

5.106 Furthermore, Colombia, Costa Rica, Nicaragua and Venezuela claimed that the EC had offered tariff quota allocations to all countries having a substantial supplying interest. GATT did not define the term "substantial interest"; it merely stated in the context of the withdrawal or modification of a concession that these terms were meant to cover only those Members which had "a significant share in the market".[320] This had been interpreted in practice under GATT 1947 as referring to contracting parties that could "absorb at least 10 per cent of the market".[321] The only GATT contracting parties that qualified at the time of the allotment of the tariff quota shares as contracting parties with a trade share of more than 10 per cent were Colombia and Costa Rica. Thus, in the view of Colombia, Costa Rica, Nicaragua and Venezuela, the EC would have fulfilled its obligations under Article XIII if it had determined its tariff quota allotments only in consultation with these two countries. Nevertheless, the EC had offered tariff quota allocations not only to Colombia and Costa Rica but to all countries that had expressed an interest in supplying the EC banana market, including all complainants in the GATT 1947 panel proceedings on the EC banana regimes, and several non-contracting parties to GATT 1947. The table below showed that the country quotas offered to the other interested suppliers corresponded, with the exception of Venezuela, approximately to the share they had in the EC market during the reference period chosen.

[320] See para. 7 of the Note Ad Article XXVIII.

[321] See the GATT Secretariat description of this practice in document MTN.GNG/NG7/W/9.

Country-quotas offered to other interested suppliers				
Country	**GATT 1947 status**	**1989-91 NPI EC-12 (%)[1]**	**Quota offered December 1993 (%)[2]**	**BFA (%)**
Ecuador	Not contracting party	19.6	20.2	
Panama	Not contracting party	23.3	19.7	
Honduras	Not contracting party	6.9	6.8	
Guatemala	Complaining party	1.5	1.5	
Nicaragua	Complaining party	2.2	1.9	3.0
Venezuela	Complaining party	0	"others"	2.0

NPI: Non-Preferential Imports.
Source: [1]Calculations based on COMEXT.
[2]EC offer on agriculture, 14 December 1993.

5.107 In the case of Venezuela, the EC had, consistently with the principles set out in Article XIII, taken into account special factors that affected that country's trade in bananas, according to Colombia, Costa Rica, Nicaragua and Venezuela. Although Venezuela had not previously exported bananas to the EC in significant amounts, large Venezuelan banana growers had made significant investments since early 1993 to cultivate additional acreage specifically for export to the EC and the United States. On the basis of feasibility studies and expectations of the trend and market access conditions in the EC, they had invested US$28.6 million over a period of three years to expand production for export. This fundamental commercial interest explained why Venezuela had participated as a complainant in the proceedings of the two GATT 1947 panels on the EC banana regime and in the context of the Uruguay Round in the bilateral market access negotiations that led to the BFA.

5.108 Furthermore, Colombia, Costa Rica, Nicaragua and Venezuela submitted, that the EC had allocated, in conformity with the practice of many Members under Article XIII of GATT, a quota share not only to major named supplying countries but also a residual quota to all other supplying countries. The residual quota amounted to 50.6 per cent less the 90,000 tonnes allocated to non-traditional bananas from the ACP countries. This percentage reflected the share of the other supplying countries during the reference period.

5.109 Colombia, Costa Rica, Nicaragua and Venezuela noted that country-specific quota allocations established, in general, not only the minimum but also the maximum quantity which may be exported. Any shortfall by one of the countries to which such an allocation had been made could not normally be made up by another such country. This put such countries at a disadvantage in relation to the "other" countries benefiting from a common residual quota because each of these countries could export the quantities not exported by another. In the case in point, however, they noted that the EC had decided to put the named countries and the "other" countries on the same footing in this respect by making the quota allocations transferable among the named countries. This transferability of the country-specific tariff quota shares raised the level of imports into the EC by ensuring that, over time, each country-specific quota was fully utilized in line with the spirit of Article XIII:2 of GATT. The transferability had led merely to small, transitory changes that did not affect the overall distribution of imports into the EC and that did not go beyond what was required to ensure a full utilization of the country-specific quotas. The EC had thus distributed the resulting trade shares "as closely as possible" in proportion to the shares that might be expected in the absence of the quota limitations, taking into account the legal requirement to permit a full utilization of each quota allotment.

5.110 In evaluating the EC's allotment of shares, Colombia, Costa Rica, Nicaragua and Venezuela submitted that the Panel should take into account the enormous difficulties the EC had faced in applying the principles of Article XIII of GATT 1947 to its transformation of the diverse import regimes of its member States into an EC-wide regime. Six of its member States had applied restrictions for a long period of time and the expectation of the transformation had given rise to speculative transactions. Moreover, changes in production patterns in Latin America, in particular in Venezuela, had taken place. Both the determination of a representative period and the appraisal of the special factors that affected trade in bananas were therefore extremely difficult to make. Against this background, any objective observer could not but conclude that the offer of tariff quota shares by the EC constituted an appropriate exercise of the discretion it was entitled to exercise in accordance with Article XIII:2 and 4 of GATT had it not successfully sought an agreement to settle the difficult issue with all Members in the context of the Uruguay Round in accordance with Article XIII:2(d).

5.111 According to Colombia, Costa Rica, Nicaragua and Venezuela, the Complaining parties' argument that the administration of the tariff quotas, in particular the export certificate system applicable to signatories of the BFA, was inconsistent with Article XIII of GATT was based on a misconception of the benefits accruing under this provision and the GATT generally. Article XIII, like the other non-discrimination provisions of the GATT, obliged Members to extend advantages accorded to any product to similar products originating from, or destined for, the territories of all Members; Article XIII did not oblige Members to extend to the producers of all Members the benefits extended to one of them. The terms of Article XIII referred only to the distribution of shares of trade, not shares in quota rents, and the same applied to the Licensing Agreement. Also Articles I, III, and XI of GATT applied solely to the treatment of products not to the treatment of producers or investors. It was correct to say that Article I of GATT applied to all rules and any advantage, but the Complaining parties had overlooked that Article I applied only to rules in connection with importation and only to advantages accorded to products. In their view, the Complaining parties had not explained how the export certificate system could be regarded as according an advantage to a product in connection with importation. They agreed that Article III applied only to measures that distinguished between like products of domestic and foreign origin, not measures distinguishing between producers, as the two tuna/dolphin panels had confirmed. In their view, the same applied to the Licensing Agreement whose principal purpose was "to ensure that import licensing procedures are not utilized in a manner contrary to the principles and obligations of the GATT". For these reasons, Members were free to allocate the in-quota licences to any enterprise from any Member as long as that allocation did not entail discrimination between products of different origins or destinations. Colombia, Costa Rica, Nicaragua and Venezuela claimed that the export certificate system served solely to distribute the financial benefits arising from the quota system which were matters not covered by the GATT and the Licensing Agreement. It did not affect in any way the level of imports of bananas into the EC nor the distribution of trade among exporting countries. The system thus dealt with the distribution of benefits that simply did not accrue under the GATT.

5.112 Furthermore, the Agreement on Safeguards made it perfectly clear that the allocation of trade shares had to be distinguished under the GATT from the allocation of the financial benefits associated with the administration of quota regimes. Article 2.2 of that Agreement stipulated that "[s]afeguard measures shall be applied to a product being imported irrespective of its source." However, footnote 3 to Article 11 of that Agreement provided that:

> An import quota applied as a safeguard measure in conformity with the relevant provisions of the GATT 1994 and this Agreement may, by mutual agreement, be administered by the exporting Member.

The drafters of this Agreement thus had considered that the treatment of products under an import quota system had to be distinguished from other aspects of the administration of quota system and that a quota allocation could be consistent with Article XIII of GATT even if the administration of the quota system varied between Members.

5.113 Moreover, Colombia, Costa Rica, Nicaragua and Venezuela, claimed that the Panel should consider the broad implications that an acceptance of the interpretations advanced by the Complaining parties would entail. Most Members that allocated tariff quotas among supplying countries did so by allocating a share to named countries constituting the main suppliers and a residual share to "other countries". The producers of the named countries could easily obtain the financial benefits associated with a quota regime by forming an export cartel or by asking their government to channel exports through a single agency in accordance with Articles XVII and XX(d) of GATT; the "other countries" needed to cooperate with one another to secure that financial benefit, which was inherently more difficult. In spite of this different impact on producers of different countries, this method of allocating trade shares among countries had never been challenged in the whole history of the GATT. If, as the Complainants had suggested, Article I or Article XIII of GATT were to be interpreted to oblige countries not only to afford equal trade opportunities but also equal opportunities to obtain the financial benefits arising from the administration of quotas, a quota allocation mechanism used by practically all Members that use quotas, including the United States, would be illegal.

5.114 According to Colombia, Costa Rica, Nicaragua and Venezuela, the claim that the administration of the tariff quota was inconsistent with the Licensing Agreement was equally based on a total misconception of the objective of the Agreement. The Agreement prescribed in Article 3.5(e) that "any person, firm or institution which fulfils the legal and administrative requirement of the importing Member shall be equally eligible to apply and to be considered for a licence". Neither this nor any other provision of the Licensing Agreement constrained the right of importing Members to determine who could obtain an import licence. As its name indicated, the Agreement merely obliged Members to administer whatever legal and administrative requirements they adopted in a transparent, predictable and least burdensome manner. Colombia, Costa Rica, Nicaragua and Venezuela claimed, however, that all the evidence the Complaining parties had submitted to the Panel to support their claim that the EC had violated the Licensing Agreement related to the legal and administrative requirements imposed by EC legislators and not to the application of the requirements by EC administrators. Moreover, some of the Complaining parties' allegations related to the requirements imposed not by the EC, but by banana exporting countries and therefore did not concern the matter before the Panel.

5.115 Colombia, Costa Rica, Nicaragua and Venezuela further submitted that the United States had brought the complaint against the EC banana regime not to defend its trade interests in bananas, which were minimal, but to defend the investment interests of United States enterprises in other countries, and it was now trying to make the Panel accept interpretations that would turn the provisions of GATT on the treatment of products into provisions on the treatment of investors. The Panel should, in the view of Colombia, Costa Rica, Nicaragua and Venezuela, take the interpretations that had been proposed by the Complaining parties for what they were, an attempt to turn a trade agreement into an investment agreement, and reject them accordingly.

4. *Conclusions*

5.116 Colombia, Costa Rica, Nicaragua and Venezuela requested the Panel to reject the Complaining parties' argument that those parts of the EC banana import regime that implemented the provisions of the BFA set out in the EC's market access commitment were inconsistent with the EC's obligations under the WTO agreements. They stated that, just as the Complainants, they would have preferred the access to the EC banana market to be free and unencumbered by a complex tariff quota allocation scheme. However, in contrast to the Complaining parties, Colombia, Costa Rica, Nicaragua and Venezuela recognized that this goal could only be attained by negotiation. The GATT clearly permitted the EC to impose high tariffs, establish tariff quotas and allocate of such quotas to specific countries which may secure the financial benefits generated by the quotas through export monopolies, and the CONTRACTING PARTIES to the GATT 1947 granted the EC the right to accord preferential treatment to ACP bananas. A fundamental change in that regime could therefore not be achieved through the WTO dispute settlement procedures. Colombia, Costa Rica, Nicaragua and Venezuela therefore sought an agreement with the EC committing it to a stable and predictable administration of the regime it was legally entitled to introduce.

5.117 The GATT rules governing the quota allotments were extremely difficult to apply and left the importing Member substantial discretion in the choice of the previous representative period and in the appraisal of special factors. Moreover, if a WTO panel considered a Member's quota allotment to be inconsistent with Article XIII of GATT, it could not prescribe a specific new quota allotment because it would thereby take away the Member's right to exercise the discretion accorded by this provision. A negative finding of a panel on a specific quota allotment could therefore be followed by a new dispute on the allotment put in place to replace the original illegal allotment, and so on. Members facing tariff quotas therefore had a legitimate interest in settling by agreement all the complex issues to which the administration of the tariff quotas gave rise. The legitimacy of that interest was recognized in Article XIII:2 of GATT, which declared quota allotments by agreement to be the preferred method of allocation, and Article 4.1 of the Agreement on Agriculture which put tariff concessions and market access commitments related to the implementation of the tariff concessions on an equal legal footing. The Panel, too, should recognize the legitimacy of settling thorny quota allocation and administration issues as part of a negotiation on tariffs and tariff quotas.

5.118 Furthermore, Colombia, Costa Rica, Nicaragua and Venezuela claimed that the issue before the Panel was the legal status of all such settlements included in market access commitments exchanged under the Agreement on Agriculture, not merely those reflected in the BFA. At issue was the basic question of whether the Agreement on Agriculture was interpreted as an essentially self-standing agreement settling the extremely difficult and complex question arising in the allocation and administration of tariff quotas and providing legal certainty in agricultural trade, or as an agreement whose content could be endlessly challenged in the light of the provisions of other WTO agreements. If the Panel's reasoning were to permit such endless challenges, it could rule in favour of the Complaining parties only if it were to deny Members the right to settle quota allocation issues by agreement and if it were to rule that the benefits accruing under the GATT went beyond the treatment of products and those accruing under the Licensing Agreement went beyond procedural issues. It would be extremely serious for the Panel to fail to recognize the broad implications of the rulings it had been asked by the Complaining parties to make.

5.119 The WTO's dispute settlement system "serves to preserve the rights and obligations of Members"[322]. The main function of the interpretative process panels were engaged in must therefore be to ascertain and confirm the understandings that had been reached during the Uruguay Round, not to unravel these understandings. According to Colombia, Costa Rica, Nicaragua and Venezuela, an interpretation leading to a one-sided elimination of specifically negotiated and clearly expressed commitments on the grounds that they ran counter to more general commitments would be contrary to this principle and therefore would cast serious doubts on the credibility of the WTO's dispute settlement process and the political acceptability of the decisions that emerged from it.

D. India

5.120 India noted that the EC market for imported bananas was the largest in the world, with imports in 1995 totalling approximately 30 per cent of all bananas traded globally. Although not a significant exporter of bananas, India was the world's largest producer of the product, with production totalling about 9.5 million tonnes in 1995 out of total world production of 54.5 million tonnes. India had, therefore, an understandable interest in the EC import regime for this product.

[322] Article 3 of the DSU.

1. The Lomé Convention and the Lomé waiver

5.121 The preferential treatment given to the ACP developing countries by the EC in its import regime for bananas was based on the provisions of the Fourth Lomé Convention, signed on 15 December 1989, and notified to the GATT on 16 December 1992. The parties to the Lomé Convention initially claimed that the Lomé Convention was genuinely compatible with Article XXIV and Part IV of GATT 1947. India noted that during the GATT Council discussions on the Lomé Convention, it was generally agreed that the Lomé Convention was, by any standard, the most comprehensive ever signed between a group of industrial countries of the North and a group of developing countries of the South, and that there was general recognition among GATT contracting parties that its objectives were commendable. The Lomé Convention was not concerned solely with providing ACP States preferential access to the EC market. Article 4 of the Lomé Convention stated that support would be provided in ACP-EEC cooperation for the ACP States' efforts to "achieve comprehensive self-reliant and self-sustained development, based on their cultural and social values, their human capacities, their national resources and their economic potential in order to promote the ACP States' social, cultural and economic progress and the well-being of their populations, through satisfaction of their basic needs ...". With specific reference to bananas, India noted that Protocol 5 of the Lomé Convention stipulated: "In respect of its banana exports to the Community markets, no ACP State shall be placed as regards access to its traditional markets and its advantages on those markets, in a less favourable situation than in the past or at present" (Article 1). Under this provision, the ACP States appeared to have a legal right to obtain preferential treatment for their exports of bananas to the EC market.

5.122 India recalled that the parties to the Lomé Convention made a joint request to the GATT Council for a waiver from the obligations of the EC under Article I:1 on the basis of Article XXV:5 of GATT 1947, with respect to the "granting of preferential treatment for products originating in the ACP countries as foreseen under the relevant provisions of the Fourth Lomé Convention, for the duration of the Convention". The GATT Council granted a waiver for the period up to 29 February 2000, "to the extent necessary to permit the European Communities to provide preferential treatment for products originating in ACP States as required by the relevant provisions of the Fourth Lomé Convention, without being required to extend the same preferential treatment to like products of any other contracting party". India further recalled the reasoning given by the representative of the ACP contracting parties in seeking this waiver, i.e. for the "legal certainty" of the trade of vulnerable developing countries.

2. Conclusion

5.123 Against the background given above, India requested the Panel to look at the dispute in the light of the waiver jointly obtained by the EC and the ACP States so that the legal certainty derived out of the waiver decision in respect of the significant market access preferences extended to the ACP countries was not diluted or impaired.

E. Japan

5.124 Japan submitted that one of the main issues addressed in this dispute concerned the consistency of the EC's tariff quota system for the importation, sale and distribution of bananas with the Agreement on Import Licensing Procedures (the "Licensing Agreement").

1. Non-applicability of the Agreement on Import Licensing Procedures to tariff quota systems

5.125 Japan noted that paragraph 1 of Article 1 of the Licensing Agreement defined "import licensing" as "administrative procedures used for the operation of import licensing regimes requiring the submission of an application or other documentation (other than that required for customs purposes) to the relevant administrative body as a prior condition for importation into the customs territory of the importing Member".

5.126 According to Japan, however, a tariff quota was a system in which the in-quota tariff rate was applied for the imports within the quota and an over-quota tariff rate was applied for the imports beyond the quota. Under these systems, imports could be made beyond the quota quantity by paying the over-quota tariff. In this respect, a tariff quota system was clearly distinct from an import quota (quantitative restriction) system in which an import licence was a prior condition for importation. Thus, in the view of Japan, obtaining an allocation of a tariff quota was not a prior condition for importation within the meaning of paragraph 1 of Article 1 of the Licensing Agreement. Accordingly, Japan was of the view that tariff quota systems were not covered by the Licensing Agreement.

5.127 Furthermore, Japan submitted that the notification practice under the Tokyo Round Agreement on Import Licensing Procedures (the "Tokyo Round Agreement") supported this interpretation. Japan believed that in responding to the questionnaire on import licensing procedures under the Tokyo Round Agreement, at the beginning of its implementation, no contracting party notified its tariff quota systems as import licensing procedures. Therefore, Japan considered that contracting parties at that time did not hold any recognition or interpretation that the tariff quota system was covered by the Tokyo Round Agreement. The current Licensing Agreement was largely based on the text of the Tokyo Round Agreement. The definition of "import licensing" in paragraph 1 of Article 1 of the current Agreement was almost identical. The only difference between the two, in Japan's view, was very technical, i.e. "the importing country" at the end of the sentence of paragraph 1 of Article 1 of the Tokyo Round Agreement, had been replaced with "the importing Member". Japan submitted it did not see any reason to change the interpretation with the entry into force of the WTO Licensing Agreement, given such an identity of texts.

2. *Conclusion*

5.128 For these reasons, Japan believed that the Licensing Agreement was not applicable to tariff quota systems. Japan therefore requested that the Panel find that the tariff quota system at dispute was not covered by the Licensing Agreement and thereby did not cause any consistency problem with respect to the Licensing Agreement.

F. The Philippines

5.129 As a major banana exporting country, the Philippines stated that it attached great importance to the developments in the global trade of the product, particularly with respect to the influence of EC policies on trade in bananas in other markets. The Philippines claimed that the EC measures had a negative influence on prices in other markets supplied by the Philippines. While the Philippines sympathized with the extension of developmental assistance and recognized the value of non-reciprocal advantages accorded by developed countries to developing countries, the Philippines emphasized that Members must fully conform with the rules and disciplines of the multilateral trading system.

1. *Preliminary arguments*

5.130 According to the Philippines, the EC had pointed out in its submissions, that by virtue of Article II:7 of GATT, its concession on bananas was an integral part of Articles I and II of the Agreement. As such, Article I of GATT could not be made to prevail on the terms and conditions of the concession as this would mean giving priority to a part of Article I over other parts of the same Article, as supplemented by the concession. The EC had concluded that no claim could therefore be made on its concession with regard to a violation of Article I. According to the Philippines, the EC further stated that the other provisions of the GATT were also to be applied taking into account at the same time two elements: the content of the concessions, and the MFN principle as supplemented by the concession. The EC had also excluded, according to the Philippines, the applicability of Article XIII of GATT to its concession on bananas as it claimed that all parties had agreed in the Uruguay Round negotiations to the concession.

5.131 The Philippines considered that, with regard to Article I, the inconsistency of the concession *per se* with the MFN principle was not the relevant issue in this case. Rather, the issue, as far as the MFN principle related to the EC concession, rested essentially on the manner of administration of such a concession. The Philippines believed that the consequences of Article II:7 did not render the other provisions of the GATT inapplicable to the terms and conditions of the concession. The *Report of the Review Working Party on Other Barriers to Trade* (BISD 3S/225), which was adopted by the CONTRACTING PARTIES in 1955, concluded that:

> ... there was nothing to prevent the Contracting Parties, when they negotiate for the binding or reduction of tariffs, from negotiating on matters, such as subsidies, which might affect the practical effects of tariff concessions, and from incorporating in the appropriate schedule annexed to the Agreement the results of such negotiations; provided that the results of such negotiations should not conflict with other Articles of the General Agreement.

5.132 Furthermore, the *Sugar Headnote*[323] panel took note of the above statement by the Review Working Party and concluded that, whether as a policy recommendation or as a confirmation of a legal requirement, the proviso in the Review Working Party's decision supported the conclusion that contracting parties did not envisage that qualifications in schedules justified measures inconsistent with the other Articles of the Agreement. In the Philippines' opinion, both the conclusions by the Review Working Party and the *Sugar Headnote* panel confirmed that other provisions of the GATT were applicable to the terms, conditions and qualifications attached to the concessions as specified in the schedules.

5.133 The Philippines also submitted that the EC had contended that all parties had agreed to the EC concession on bananas in the Uruguay Round. In the view of the Philippines, this was not a factual reflection of the situation. It was well known that some contracting parties had registered their concerns. In fact, Guatemala and Honduras had submitted written reservations to the Director-General of the GATT. When acceding to the WTO Agreement, these countries had maintained their disagreement with the EC concession on bananas and had reserved their rights to bring the matter to the appropriate WTO body.

5.134 According to the Philippines, the EC had argued that the scope of the Lomé Convention, which was covered by the Lomé waiver, was not limited to extending preferential treatment only to traditional ACP banana exports, but covered exports from all ACP countries. Moreover, the EC had claimed that the Lomé Convention allowed for the adoption of all possible measures that would enable the EC to provide preferential treatment to ACP countries. The Philippines submitted that, by its own terms, the Lomé waiver was limited in application only to EC measures inconsistent with Article I:1 of GATT and which were required by the Lomé Convention. The Lomé waiver thus did not cover measures inconsistent with other provisions of the GATT.

[323] BISD 37S/228.

2. *Specific legal arguments*

5.135 In the view of the Philippines, the EC tariff quota distribution did not conform with GATT Article XIII which required that the distribution of quotas should approach as close as possible the shares which Members might be expected to obtain in the absence of the restriction. The Philippines found the EC allocation lacked in historical or commercial basis and that the EC had failed to present any other objective rational for its allocation. The Philippines considered inappropriate the use of the latest three years prior to implementation (1989-1991) as the representative period, considering that these were precisely years when the inconsistent measures were in place in the EC. The 1980 report of the *Apple Panel*[324] stated:

> Due to the existence of restrictions in 1976, the Panel held that that year could not be considered as representative, and that the year immediately preceding 1976 should be used instead.

5.136 Moreover, the Philippines believed that having allocated import quotas to some Members but failing to do so for others which had equal if not more substantial supplying interest on trade in the product constituted a violation of GATT Article XIII by the EC. In the case of major supplying countries, in particular Ecuador, Honduras and Guatemala, the Philippines believed that the EC had failed to honour its obligations relevant to the specific requirement prescribed in subparagraph (d) of Article XIII:2. Having merely sought agreement with these countries was not sufficient for the EC to claim it had fulfilled entirely the requirements of Article XIII. In the view of the Philippines, the EC was clearly not able to comply with the alternative method prescribed in Article XIII:2(d) with respect to substantially interested parties, and thereby had failed to fulfil its obligations with respect to that provision.

5.137 Further, in the view of the Philippines, maintaining a fairly advantageous import licensing rule for ACP countries while imposing a less favourable procedure for other countries clearly ran counter to Article 1.3 of the Licensing Agreement which prescribed that import licensing rules shall be applied in a neutral, fair, and equitable manner. The Philippines believed that the EC had no reason not to apply the less complicated licensing system on the tariff quotas of third-country banana exporters. Alternative procedures, which were the usually accepted procedures, included: (i) a first-come, first-served basis; (ii) the method based on traditional trade flows; and (iii) the allocation of quotas in proportion to the quantities requested. The Philippines summarized that the EC system was more complicated and unnecessarily burdensome for non-ACP countries.

5.138 The Philippines also maintained that the second *Banana* panel findings concerning the EC's banana import regime remained valid in the present dispute. That panel had concluded that the EC's category allocation of import licences violated Articles I and III of GATT. By maintaining the scheme for Category B licences (i.e. making the marketing of EC and ACP bananas the criteria for eligibility to obtain a licence for third-country bananas), the EC continued to violate, in the view of the Philippines: (i) Article I of GATT by awarding incentives to operators for the marketing of bananas from ACP countries and not from other exporting countries; and (ii) the national treatment requirement of Article III of GATT by protecting domestic production through the award of incentives for the marketing of EC bananas. Indeed, the 1978 Panel Report on *EEC - Measures on Animal Feed Proteins*[325], in reference to the EEC scheme requiring domestic producers or importers of vegetable proteins to purchase a certain quantity of surplus skimmed milk powder held by intervention agencies, had concluded that the measures provided for by the EC with a view to ensuring the sale of a given quantity of skimmed milk powder protected the product in a manner contrary to Article III:1 and III:5 of GATT. In the view of the Philippines, the EC allocation of licences linked to operator categories greatly restricted competition for third-country bananas in the EC market while conferring on, and maintaining

---

[324] "EEC - Restrictions on Imports of Apples from Chile" ("Apple Panel"), BISD 27S/98.

[325] BISD 25S/49.

advantages for, preferred suppliers. The scheme, which had trade distortive and trade restrictive effects, was also prohibited under Articles 1.2 and 3.2 of the Licensing Agreement.

3. Conclusion

5.139 In light of the above, the Philippines requested the Panel to find the EC regime in violation of Articles I, III and XIII of GATT, and Articles 1 and 3 of the Licensing Agreement.

VI. INTERIM REVIEW

6.1 On 2 April 1997, the European Communities, Ecuador, Guatemala, Honduras, Mexico and United States requested the Panel to review in accordance with Article 15.2 of the DSU precise aspects of the interim reports that had been issued to the parties on 18 March 1997. The European Communities also requested the Panel to hold a further meeting with the parties on the issues identified in its written comments. The Panel met with the parties on 14 April 1997 in order to hear their arguments concerning the interim reports. We carefully reviewed the arguments presented by the EC and by the Complaining parties, jointly or individually, and the responses offered by the other side.

6.2 With respect to procedural matters, the Complaining parties commented on the Panel's interpretation of the requisite degree of specificity of a panel request in light of the requirements of Article 6.2 of the DSU. They also raised concerns as to the Panel's refusal to consider claims made or endorsed by one or more of them after the filing of the first written submissions. As regards those claims which the Panel had found unnecessary to address, the Complaining parties further argued that several of them, e.g., allegations regarding overfiling under the activity function rules and the distribution of licences to producers, were not issues of secondary importance and should be addressed by the Panel in addition to those aspects of the licensing procedures which had been found to be inconsistent with WTO rules. Furthermore, they suggested several drafting changes. We carefully considered these arguments and where we agreed, we modified the Findings in response in paragraphs *7.40*, *7.42* and *7.49*.

6.3 The EC and the Complaining parties asked for a number of specific modifications or additions to those paragraphs in the Findings which summarize their legal arguments. Since these proposed changes concerned the representation of the parties' own legal arguments, we generally accepted them. In particular, in reaction to suggestions by the EC, we modified or expanded paragraphs *7.65*, *7.78*, *7.104*, *7.169*, *7.200*, *7.205*, *7.224*, *7.287*, *7.301* and *7.313*. In our view, these adjustments in general did not entail repercussions for the legal analysis in the Findings. However, in the context of the applicability of the Lomé waiver to licensing procedures and of the interpretation of Article II of GATS, we added more detail to the legal reasoning in paragraphs *7.198* and *7.301-7.302*.

6.4 In respect of the discussion of Article XIII in the Findings, the Complaining parties asked the Panel to expand its findings on "Members with a substantial interest" and "New members". The EC commented on the Panel's treatment of issues such as "previous representative period", "special factors" or the EC enlargement. To the extent we accepted these suggestions, we adjusted the Findings, e.g., in paragraphs *7.91-7.94*.

6.5 The Complaining parties also commented on the application of the Lomé waiver to Article XIII, on the one hand, and to the tariff treatment of non-traditional imports of ACP bananas, on the other. To the extent that we agreed with those comments, we made adjustments to paragraphs *7.104-7.110* and paragraphs *7.135* and *7.139*. The EC also raised arguments concerning the interpretation of the coverage of the waiver. In response to the EC's comments, we revised paragraphs *7.197-7.199*.

6.6 Both sides requested the Panel to expand the factual discussion of the differences between the licensing procedures applied to traditional ACP imports as opposed to those applied to third-country and non-traditional ACP imports. We broadly followed these suggestions by adding more factual information from, or cross-referring to, specific parts of the descriptive section of the panel report on which our findings are based. We inserted additions in paragraphs *7.190-7.192*. Other modifications along the same lines are reflected in paragraphs *7.211*, *7.221* and *7.230*.

6.7 With respect to the part of the Findings dealing with GATS issues, the Complaining parties proposed several specific drafting changes. We accepted these suggestions where we considered them appropriate and modified language in the discussion of "measures affecting trade in services", (paragraphs *7.281*, *7.282* and *7.285*), of "wholesale trade services" (paragraphs *7.287* and *7.291*) and of certain other issues (see, e.g., paragraphs *7.316*, *7.324*, *7.347*, *7.377* and *7.391*). Further to that, the Complaining parties also commented on the application of the concept of "conditions of competition" to services. We revised the report accordingly in paragraphs *7.335-7.236* where we found merit in the suggestions. Finally, they clarified their claims as being based on allegations of less favourable treatment accorded to their service suppliers, not their services. In light of this, we modified the Findings accordingly, particularly in paragraphs *7.294*, *7.297*, *7.298*, *7.306*, *7.314*, *7.317*, *7.324*, *7.329*, *7.341* and *7.353*.

6.8 The EC commented extensively on the part of the Findings dealing with GATS issues. Paragraphs *7.301-7.302* and *7.308* reflect our responses to the EC's concerns about the interpretation of Article II of GATS and the effective date of GATS obligations.

6.9 With respect to the sections addressing specific claims under Articles II and XVII of GATS against certain aspects of its licensing procedures, the EC suggested that the factual information it had submitted was not sufficiently reflected and discussed in the Findings of the interim report. In particular, the EC referred to information concerning nationality, ownership or control of trading companies and ripeners. Moreover, the EC asked the Panel to take more account of the information it had provided concerning the evolution in recent years of market shares of suppliers of EC/ACP origin as opposed to suppliers of Complaining parties' origin in the EC/ACP and the third-country market segments. In response to these comments, we significantly revised paragraphs *7.329-7.339* and also changed paragraphs *7.362-7.363*. The revised paragraphs address in more detail the information submitted by the EC and indicate specifically how we evaluated it. We also expanded our discussion of exactly why the Panel draws conclusions from the information submitted by the parties which are different from the conclusions advocated by the EC.

6.10 In respect of the interim reports' descriptive section, the EC and the Complaining parties suggested further changes which we took into account in re-examining that part of the reports. As to the EC's request for a section describing the EC's view of the facts, we were of the view that the EC's interpretation of the facts is already reflected in a comprehensive manner in the section of the panel report which contains the legal arguments. However, where we saw the need to follow specific suggestions for changes by either side, we revised the descriptive section of the interim reports.

6.11 Ecuador also raised concerns about our description of its share of the EC banana market. We examined these concerns and concluded that no changes in the description were necessary.

VII. FINDINGS

7.1 This case is an exceedingly complex one. There are six parties (one representing 15 member States) and 20 third parties, meaning that almost one-third of Members are involved in the case. In addition to claims under the General Agreement on Tariffs and Trade 1994, claims are made for the first time in dispute settlement under four other WTO agreements: The Agreement on Agriculture, the Agreement on Import Licensing Procedures, the Agreement on Trade-Related Investment Measures and the General Agreement on Trade in Services. The submissions by the Complainants[326] and the EC totalled several thousand pages. Moreover, the unprecedented number and complexity of the claims and arguments has meant that the organization and presentation of our work has not been easy.

7.2 The findings are divided into three main parts. First we address various organizational issues that arose in the course of the Panel's work. Second, we consider preliminary issues raised by the EC concerning the validity of the establishment of this Panel and the lack of a legal interest in some issues on the part of the United States. Finally, we address the substantive issues presented by this case.

A. Organizational Issues

7.3 In the course of these proceedings, we considered two issues related to the organization of our work. These concerned the extent of the participatory rights to be afforded third parties and the presence in Panel meetings of private lawyers representing third parties.

1. Participation of third parties

7.4 At the meeting of the Dispute Settlement Body on 8 May 1996, Belize, Cameroon, Colombia, Costa Rica, Côte d'Ivoire, Dominica, Dominican Republic, Ghana, Grenada, Jamaica, Nicaragua, Saint Vincent and the Grenadines, Saint Lucia, Senegal, Suriname and Venezuela requested to be allowed to participate more fully in the work of the Panel, i.e., these Members requested to be present at all meetings between the Panel and the parties to the dispute; to be able to present their point of view at each of these meetings; to receive copies of all submissions and other written material; and to be allowed to present written submissions both to the first and to the second meetings of the Panel. While the DSB took note of these statements, there was no consensus on such participation.[327] Several of these countries later confirmed their requests in letters addressed to the Chairman of the DSB.

7.5 Subsequently, we considered the above requests. The rights of third parties are dealt with in Article 10 and Appendix 3 of the Dispute Settlement Understanding. Article 10 provides that third parties "shall have an opportunity to be heard by the panel and to make written submissions to the panel". It also provides that third parties are entitled to receive the submissions of the parties made to the first substantive panel meeting. Paragraph 6 of Appendix 3 specifies that third parties shall be invited "to present their views during a session of the first substantive meeting of the panel set aside for that purpose. All such third parties may be present during the entirety of this session". Under prior GATT practice, more expansive rights were granted to third parties in

[326] Our use of the term Complainants in these Findings is explained in para. 7.0 infra. In respect of organizational and preliminary issues, it is used to refer to all five Complaining parties.

[327] WT/DSB/M/16, item 1, pp. 1-5.

several disputes, including the two prior disputes involving bananas and in the *Semiconductors* case.[328] In those cases, however, the extension of such rights had been the subject of agreement between the parties at that time. No such agreement existed between the parties in the present dispute.

7.6 Having considered representations by the Complainants, the EC and third parties, we decided prior to our first substantive meeting with the parties that, in addition to the rights specifically provided for in the DSU, third parties in this dispute would be invited to observe the whole of the proceedings at that meeting and not just the one session thereof set aside for hearing third-party arguments.

7.7 At the first substantive meeting of the Panel, the EC requested that third parties be allowed to participate in future panel meetings as set out above. The Complainants expressed the view that third party rights were sufficiently safeguarded by the normal procedures as set out in Article 10 of the DSU. We consulted the parties on this issue, but they maintained their opposing viewpoints.

7.8 We thereafter ruled as follows:

a) The Panel has decided, after consultations with the parties in conformity with DSU Article 12.1, that members of governments of third parties will be permitted to observe the second substantive meeting of the Panel with the parties. The Panel envisages that the observers will have the opportunity also to make a brief statement at a suitable moment during the second meeting. The Panel does not expect them to submit additional written material beyond responses to the questions already posed during the first meeting.

b) The Panel based its decision, *inter alia*, on the following considerations:

(i) the economic effect of the disputed EC banana regime on certain third parties appeared to be very large;

(ii) the economic benefits to certain third parties from the EC banana regime were claimed to derive from an international treaty between them and the EC;

(iii) past practice in panel proceedings involving the banana regimes of the EC and its member States; and

(iv) the parties to the dispute could not agree on the issue".

As a consequence of our ruling, the third parties in these proceedings enjoyed broader participatory rights than are granted to third parties under the DSU.

7.9 Following the second substantive meeting of the Panel with the parties, several of the third parties asked for further participatory rights, including participation in the interim review process. We consulted the parties and found that, as before, they had diverging views on the appropriateness of granting this request. We decided that no further participatory rights should be extended to third parties, except, in accord with normal

[328] Panel Report on "EEC - Import Regime for Bananas", issued on 11 February 1994 (not adopted), DS38/R, p.4, para. 8; Panel Report on "EEC - Member States' Import Regimes for Bananas", issued on 3 June 1993 (not adopted), DS32/R, p.2, para. 9; Panel Report on "Japan - Trade in Semiconductors", adopted on 4 May 1988, BISD 35S/116, 116-117, para. 5. See also Panel Report on "EEC - Tariff Treatment on Imports of Citrus Products from Certain Countries in the Mediterranean Region", issued on 7 February 1985 (not adopted), L/5776, p.2, para. 1.5; Interim Panel Report on "United Kingdom - Dollar Area Quotas", adopted on 30 July 1973, BISD 20S/230, 231, para. 3.

practice, to permit them to review the draft of the summary of their arguments in the Descriptive Part. In this regard, we noted that Article 15 of the DSU, which deals with the interim review process, refers only to parties as participants in that process. In our view, to give third parties all of the rights of parties would inappropriately blur the distinction drawn in the DSU between parties and third parties.

2. Presence of private lawyers

7.10 At the beginning of the Panel's first substantive meeting on 10 September 1996, one of the Complainants objected to the alleged presence of private lawyers in the Panel meeting. In accordance with Article 12.1 of the DSU and the Working Procedures of Appendix 3, we held consultations with the Complainants and the EC on this issue and the Complainants expressed opposition to allowing private lawyers to be present.

7.11 We thereafter asked parties and third parties to observe the guidelines contained in our working procedures and that only members of governments (including the European Commission and an international civil servant of the ACP Secretariat) attend the Panel meeting. We based our request on the following considerations:

(a) It has been past practice in GATT and WTO dispute settlement proceedings not to admit private lawyers to panel meetings if any party objected to their presence and in this case the Complainants did so object.

(b) In the working procedures of the Panel, which were adopted at the Panel's organizational meeting, we had expressed our expectation that only members of governments would be present at Panel meetings.

(c) The presence of private lawyers in delegations of some third parties would be unfair to those parties and other third parties who had utilized the services of private lawyers in preparing their submissions, but who were not accompanied by those lawyers because they assumed that all participants at the meeting would comply with our expectations as expressed in the working procedures adopted by the Panel at its organizational meeting.

(d) Given that private lawyers may not be subject to disciplinary rules such as those that applied to members of governments, their presence in Panel meetings could give rise to concerns about breaches of confidentiality.

(e) There was a question in our minds whether the admission of private lawyers to Panel meetings, if it became a common practice, would be in the interest of smaller Members as it could entail disproportionately large financial burdens for them.

(f) Moreover, we had concerns about whether the presence of private lawyers would change the intergovernmental character of WTO dispute settlement proceedings.

7.12 We noted that our request would not in any respect adversely affect the right of parties or third parties to meet and consult with their private lawyers in the course of panel proceedings, nor to receive legal or other advice in the preparation of written submissions from non-governmental experts.

B. Preliminary Issues

7.13 First, the EC claims that the consultations held in this matter between the Complainants and the EC did not fulfil their minimum function of affording a possibility for arriving at a mutually satisfactory solution and a clear setting out of the different claims of which a dispute consists. Second, it claims that the request for the establishment of this Panel was unacceptably vague and failed to comply with the requirements of Article 6.2 of the DSU. Third, it claims that the United States has no legal right or interest in a resolution of certain of its claims and therefore should not be permitted to raise them. Fourth, the EC claims that it is entitled to separate panel reports under Article 9 of the DSU.

7.14 As the Appellate Body has made clear in its first two decisions, under Article 3.2 of the DSU the starting point for the interpretation of treaty provisions is the Vienna Convention on the Law of Treaties (the "Vienna Convention").[329] Article 31 of the Vienna Convention provides in relevant part as follows:

> 1. A treaty shall be interpreted in good faith in accordance with the ordinary meaning to be given to the terms of the treaty in their context and in light of its object and purpose.
>
> ...
>
> 3. There shall be taken into account, together with the context: ... (b) any subsequent practice in the application of the treaty which establishes the agreement of the parties regarding its interpretation; ....

Article 32 of the Vienna Convention permits recourse to

> supplementary means of interpretation ... in order to confirm the meaning resulting from the application of article 31, or to determine the meaning when the interpretation according to article 31 (a) leaves the meaning ambiguous or obscure; or (b) leads to a result which is manifestly absurd or unreasonable.

7.15 In addition, Article XVI of the Marrakesh Agreement Establishing the World Trade Organization provides as follows:

> Except as otherwise provided under this Agreement or the Multilateral Trade Agreements, the WTO shall be guided by the decisions, procedures and customary practices followed by the CONTRACTING PARTIES to GATT 1947 and the bodies established in the framework of GATT 1947.

7.16 In light of this framework for interpretation, we turn to the arguments of the EC.

1. Adequacy of the consultations

7.17 Consultations under Article 4 of the DSU are normally required as the first step in the WTO dispute settlement process.[330] Article 4.2 of the DSU requires a Member "to accord sympathetic consideration to and afford adequate opportunity for consultation regarding any representations made by another Member ...". Article 4.5 of the DSU specifies that "[i]n the course of the consultations ... before resorting to further action under this Understanding, Members should attempt to obtain satisfactory adjustment of the matter". However, if consultations fail to settle a dispute within 60 days of the request for consultations, Article 4.7 of the DSU authorizes the complaining party to request the DSB to establish a panel.[331]

---

[329] Appellate Body Report on "Japan - Taxes on Alcoholic Beverages", adopted on 1 November 1996, WT/DS8/AB/R, WT/DS10/AB/R, WT/DS11/AB/R, AB-1996-2, pp.10-12; Appellate Body Report on "United States - Standards for Reformulated and Conventional Gasoline", adopted on 20 May 1996, WT/DS2/AB/R, AB-1996-1, pp.16-17.

[330] Under Article 8.10 of the Agreement on Textiles and Clothing, a matter may be taken to the DSB without prior consultations under the DSU.

[331] If there is a failure to consult, Article 4.3 of the DSU provides that a panel may be requested after 30 days.

7.18 The EC argues that the consultations that were held in this matter between the Complainants and the EC did not fulfil their minimum function of affording a possibility for arriving at a mutually satisfactory solution and a clear setting out of the different claims of which a dispute consists. The Complainants argue that Article 4.5 of the DSU only requires that an "attempt" be made to resolve the matter. Since consultations were held on 14-15 March 1996, the Complainants argue that they complied with the DSU and were authorized to request the DSB to establish a panel when those consultations failed to produce a mutually agreed solution to the dispute. We note that the EC did not raise this issue in the DSB.[332]

7.19 Consultations play a critical role in the WTO dispute settlement process as they did under GATT. Experience under the DSU to date has shown that consultations frequently enable disputes between Members to be resolved without resort to the dispute settlement panel process.[333] Since the DSU provides in Article 3.7 that "[a] solution mutually acceptable to the parties to a dispute and consistent with the covered agreements is clearly to be preferred", disputing parties should consult in good faith and attempt to reach such a solution. Consultations are, however, a matter reserved for the parties. The DSB is not involved; no panel is involved; and the consultations are held in the absence of the Secretariat. In these circumstances, we are not in a position to evaluate the consultation process in order to determine if it functioned in a particular way. While a mutually agreed solution is to be preferred, in some cases it is not possible for parties to agree upon one. In those cases, it is our view that the function of a panel is only to ascertain that consultations, if required, were in fact held or, at least, requested.[334]

7.20 As to the EC argument that consultations must lead to an adequate explanation of the Complainants' case, we cannot agree. Consultations are the first step in the dispute settlement process. While one function of the consultations may be to clarify what the case is about, there is nothing in the DSU that provides that a complainant cannot request a panel unless its case is adequately explained in the consultations. The fulfilment of such a requirement would be difficult, if not impossible, for a complainant to demonstrate if a respondent chose to claim a lack of understanding of the case, a result which would undermine the automatic nature of panel establishment under the DSU. The only prerequisite for requesting a panel is that the consultations have "fail[ed] to settle a dispute within 60 days of receipt of the request for consultations ...".[335] Ultimately, the function of providing notice to a respondent of a complainant's claims and arguments is served by the request for establishment of a panel and by the complainant's submissions to that panel.

7.21 **We reject the EC's claim that the Complainants' case should be dismissed because the consultations held concerning this dispute did not perform their minimum function of affording a possibility for arriving at a mutually satisfactory solution and a clear setting out of the different claims of which a dispute consists.**

2. *Specificity of the request for panel establishment*

   a) *Article 6.2 and the request for establishment of the Panel*

7.22 Article 6.2 of the DSU provides in relevant part as follows:

> The request for the establishment of a panel shall be made in writing. It shall indicate whether consultations were held, identify the specific measures at issue and provide a brief legal basis of the complaint sufficient to present the problem clearly.

---

[332] Minutes of DSB Meeting of 24 April 1996, WT/DSB/M/15, item 1, pp.1-2; Minutes of DSB Meeting of 8 May 1996, WT/DSB/M/16, item 1, pp.1-5.

[333] WT/DBS/8, p.17 (1996 Annual Report of the DSB).

[334] DSU, art. 4.3.

[335] DSU, art. 4.7.

....

The EC claims that the request for the establishment of the Panel in this case fails to "identify the specific measures at issue" and does not "provide a brief legal basis of the complaint sufficient to present the problem clearly.

7.23 The relevant parts of the Complainants' request for the establishment of this Panel read as follows:

> The European Communities maintains a regime for the importation, sale and distribution of bananas established by Regulation 404/93 (O.J. L 47 of 25 February 1993, p. 1), and subsequent EC legislation, regulations and administrative measures, including those reflecting the provisions of the Framework Agreement on bananas, which implement, supplement and amend that regime. The regime and related measures appear to be inconsistent with the obligations of the EC under, *inter alia*, the General Agreement on Tariffs and Trade 1994 ("GATT 1994"), the Agreement on Import Licensing Procedures, the Agreement on Agriculture, the General Agreement on Trade in Services ("GATS") and the Agreement on Trade-Related Investment Measures ("TRIM's Agreement").
>
> [Description of consultations omitted]
>
> The Governments of Ecuador, Guatemala, Honduras, Mexico and the United States, acting jointly and severally, each in the exercise of the rights accruing to it as a member of the WTO, therefore, respectfully request the establishment of a panel to examine this matter in light of the GATT 1994, the Agreement on Import Licensing Procedures, the Agreement on Agriculture, the GATS, and the TRIM's Agreement, and find that the EC's measures are inconsistent with the following Agreements and provisions among others:
>
> (1) Articles I, II, III, X, XI and XIII of the GATT 1994,
> (2) Articles 1 and 3 of the Agreement on Import Licensing Procedures,
> (3) The Agreement on Agriculture,
> (4) Articles II, XVI and XVII of the GATS, and
> (5) Article 2 of the TRIM's Agreement.
>
> These measures also produce distortions which nullify or impair benefits accruing to Ecuador, Guatemala, Honduras, Mexico and the United States, directly or indirectly, under the cited Agreements; and these measures impede the objectives of the GATT 1994 and the other cited Agreements.[336]

b) *The arguments of the parties*

7.24 The EC claims that the Complainants' request for the establishment of this Panel fails to comply with the requirements of Article 6.2 of the DSU. The EC notes that the request refers specifically to only one EC regulation and describes that regulation and related, but unspecified, measures as a "regime". The EC further notes that while the request refers to some specific agreements and provisions, it suggests that there might be other unspecified provisions and agreements that are relevant, and that it fails to explain which part of the EC regime is inconsistent with the requirements of which provision of which agreement. The EC argues that for these reasons the panel request is inadequate to serve as the basis for the terms of reference of the Panel and inadequate to give appropriate notice to the EC and potential third parties of which claims may be put forward by the Complainants. In support of its arguments, the EC cites two panel reports issued under the Tokyo Round

[336] WT/DS27/6.

Agreement on the Interpretation of Article VI (the "Tokyo Round Anti-Dumping Code"), one of which was adopted by the Committee on Anti-Dumping Practices and one of which was not.[337]

7.25 In response, the Complainants argue that their request refers to the basic EC regulation that establishes the EC rules on banana imports and that this reference is sufficient to identify the measures at issue. They argue, in addition, that Article 6.2 does not require a panel request to tie each part of a contested measure to a specific provision of a WTO agreement that it is inconsistent with, but rather that submissions to panels serve that purpose. The Complainants further argue that the Tokyo Round Anti-Dumping Code cases are irrelevant. Moreover, they note that the EC did not raise this issue at either DSB meeting at which the panel request was presented and cannot now claim that it was prejudiced by not knowing the claims of the Complainants. Finally, the Complainants argue that this Panel may not rule on this claim because it is outside the Panel's terms of reference.

c) Analysis of the Article 6.2 claim

7.26 We examine first the argument by the Complainants that we have no authority to consider the EC claim. As noted above, panels under GATT 1947 and the Tokyo Round agreements considered similar claims.[338] We see no reason to deviate from that practice. Because of the application of "reverse" consensus decision-making applicable in the case of panel establishment in the DSB, the DSB is not likely to be an effective body for resolving disputes over whether a request for the establishment of a panel meets the requirements of Article 6.2 of the DSU. Therefore, as a practical matter only the panel established on the basis of the request (and thereafter the Appellate Body) can perform that function. Moreover, the issue we are asked to resolve can be viewed in essence as a decision on the scope of our terms of reference, which is clearly a proper subject for consideration by a panel.[339] We turn therefore to an analysis of the EC claim in light of the interpretative rule of the Vienna Convention and of Article XVI of the WTO Agreement. In this connection, we examine (i) the ordinary meaning of the terms of Article 6.2, (ii) the context of the terms of Article 6.2, (iii) the object and purpose of Article 6.2 and (iv) past practice under Article 6.2 and its predecessor.

(i) ordinary meaning of treaty terms

7.27 Article 6.2 of the DSU requires that the "specific measures at issue" be "identif[ied]" and that there be "a brief summary of the legal basis of the complaint sufficient to present the problem clearly". The EC challenges the panel request on both grounds. As to the first requirement, the panel request does identify the basic EC regulation at issue by place and date of publication. In our view, this complies with the requirements of Article 6.2. While the request does not identify the subsequent EC legislation, regulations and administrative measures that further refine and implement the basic regulation, we believe that the "banana regime" that the Complainants are contesting is adequately identified.

---

[337] Panel Report on "United States - Anti-Dumping Duties on Imports of Fresh and Chilled Atlantic Salmon from Norway", adopted on 26 April 1994, ADP/87, p. 99, paras. 333-335; Panel Report on "EC - Anti-Dumping Duties on Audiotapes in Cassettes Originating in Japan", issued on 28 April 1995, ADP/136, p. 53, para. 295.

[338] Panel Report on "United States - Denial of Most-Favoured Nation Treatment as to Non-Rubber Footwear from Brazil", adopted on 19 June 1992, BISD 39S/128, pp. 147-148, paras. 6.1-6.2. Panels under Tokyo Round agreements include: Panel Report on "European Communities - Imposition of Anti-Dumping Duties on Imports of Cotton Yarn from Brazil", adopted on 4 July 1995, ADP/137, pp. 105-109, paras. 438-466; Panel Report on "United States - Countervailing Duties on Imports of Fresh and Chilled Atlantic Salmon from Norway", adopted on 27 April 1994, SCM/153, pp. 68-69, paras. 208-214; Panel Report on "United States - Anti-Dumping Duties on Imports of Fresh and Chilled Atlantic Salmon from Norway", adopted on 26 April 1994, ADP/87, p. 99, paras. 333-335; Panel Report on "United States - Anti-Dumping Duties on Imports of Gray Portland Cement and Cement Clinker from Mexico", issued on 7 September 1992, ADP/82, pp. 49-50, para. *5.12*.

[339] The Appellate Body has considered terms of reference issues. Appellate Body Report on "Brazil - Measures Affecting Desiccated Coconut", issued on 21 February 1997, WT/DS22/AB/R, AB-1996-4, p.22.

7.28 As to the second requirement of Article 6.2, a complete elaboration of the complainant's legal argument is not required. Article 6.2 specifies only that the request must include a "summary" of the legal basis of the complaint and that the summary need only be "brief". However, Article 6.2 does require that summary to "present the *problem* clearly". In undertaking an analysis of whether the panel request in this case complies with the terms of Article 6.2 of the DSU, we find it useful to divide the request into three categories of specificity. First, in most cases, the request alleges that the EC banana regime is inconsistent with the requirements of a specific provision of a specific agreement. Second, in the case of the Agreement on Agriculture, the request simply alleges that the regime is inconsistent with that agreement. Third, the panel request indicates that the list of provisions specified in the request is not exclusive. We examine the compliance of the request with Article 6.2 in each of these three situations.

7.29 Where the panel request alleges that the banana regime is inconsistent with the requirements of a specific article of a specific agreement, we believe that the request is sufficiently specific to comply with the minimum standards established by the terms of Article 6.2 of the DSU. For example, the request claims that the regime is inconsistent with the requirements of six GATT provisions: Articles I, II, III, X, XI and XIII, as well as inconsistent with the requirements of specific provisions of the Agreement on Import Licensing Procedures, the Agreement on Trade-Related Investment Measures and the General Agreement on Trade in Services. Generally, each of these provisions is concerned with a distinct obligation. For example, Article I of GATT bans discrimination on the basis of origin in respect of certain specified matters. A fair reading of the panel request's reference to Article I would be that there is an allegation that the EC banana regime is inconsistent with the requirements of Article I because it contains elements that discriminate in favour of some countries to the detriment of Members. Such an allegation can be described as a "brief summary of the legal basis of the complaint", which arguably presents the "problem" clearly, i.e. there is discrimination on the basis of product origin which is inconsistent with the requirements of Article I. However, a panel request that does no more than identify a measure and specify the provision with which it is alleged to be inconsistent is, in our view, at the outer limits of what is acceptable under Article 6.2. Nonetheless, particularly in light of our analysis below of the object and purpose and of the context of Article 6.2 and of past GATT and WTO practice, we believe that this conclusion is the appropriate interpretation of the terms of Article 6.2. In this regard, we note that there is no explicit requirement in Article 6.2 to explain how the measure at issue is inconsistent with the requirements of a specific WTO provision and the EC concedes in its response to our questions that a simple listing of the provision and agreement alleged to have been violated may suffice for the purposes of Article 6.2.[340]

7.30 The panel request alleges an inconsistency with the requirements of the Agreement on Agriculture, without specifying any provision thereof. It also states that "the EC's measures are inconsistent with the following Agreements and provisions *among others*", suggesting that there may be inconsistencies with unspecified agreements and inconsistencies with unspecified provisions of the specified agreements. In these two situations, it is not possible at the panel request stage, even in the broadest generic terms, to describe what legal "problem" is asserted. While a reference to a specific provision of a specific agreement may not be essential if the problem or legal claim is otherwise clearly described, in the absence of some description of the problem, a mere reference to an entire agreement or simply to "other" unspecified agreements or provisions is inadequate under the terms of Article 6.2. Accordingly, we find that references to a WTO agreement without

[340] In its response, the EC seems to accept that the following panel requests under the DSU meet the requirements of Article 6.2 even though they only list the WTO provisions that the challenged measures are alleged to be inconsistent with, without explaining why: Canada - Certain Measures Concerning Periodicals, Request for the Establishment of a Panel, 24 May 1996, WT/DS31/2; EC - Measures Concerning Meat and Meat Products (Hormones), Request for the Establishment of a Panel, WT/DS26/6; EC - Trade Description of Scallops, Request for the Establishment of a Panel by Chile, WT/DS14/5; EC - Trade Description of Scallops, Request for the Establishment of a Panel by Peru, WT/DS12/7; EC - Trade Description of Scallops, Request for the Establishment of a Panel by Canada, WT/DS7/7. We would note that at least one of the EC's three panel requests under the DSU has mentioned only the agreement and provisions alleged to have been violated, i.e., United States - Tariff Increases on Products from the EC, Request for the Establishment of a Panel by the EC, WT/DS39/2.

mentioning any provisions or to unidentified "other" provisions are too vague to meet the standards of Article 6.2 of the DSU.

7.31 Thus, we preliminarily find that, given the ordinary meaning of the terms of Article 6.2 of the DSU, the panel request made by Complainants was generally sufficient to meet its requirements. We note, however, that since the invocation of the Agreement on Agriculture in the panel request did not indicate a specific provision thereof, we will not consider the claim raised by Ecuador in its first written submission under that Agreement. We will also not consider the claims raised by Ecuador, Guatemala and Honduras, and the United States in their first written submissions under Article 5 of the TRIM's Agreement since the panel request referred only to Article 2 of the TRIM's Agreement.[341] We now consider whether this preliminary finding is supported by the context and the object and purpose of Article 6.2. We also consider past practice under Article 6.2 and its predecessor.

(ii) context

7.32 The terms of Article 6.2 of the DSU must be interpreted in light of their context in the WTO dispute settlement system. First and foremost, that system is designed to settle disputes.[342] Article 3.2 of the DSU specifies that "[t]he dispute settlement system of the WTO is a central element in providing security and predictability to the multilateral trading system. ...". Article 3.3 continues in the same vein (emphasis added):

> The *prompt* settlement of situations in which a Member considers that any benefits accruing to it directly or indirectly under the covered agreements are being impaired by measures taken by another Member is essential to the effective functioning of the WTO and the maintenance of a proper balance between the rights and obligations of Members.

In our view, the DSU must be interpreted so as to promote the prompt settlement of disputes, without adopting a reading of DSU provisions that would prolong disputes unnecessarily or make the DSU overly difficult for Members, including developing country Members, to use. A clear test of specificity, such as we apply in this case, is required.

7.33 The problems presented by other interpretations of Article 6.2 are readily apparent in this case. While no one would contest that there is a real dispute between the Complainants and the EC over the EC's import regime for bananas, if we were to rule that the panel request did not meet the requirements of Article 6.2 of the DSU and that the Complainants' panel request was accordingly invalid, the resolution of this dispute would be delayed by at least 6 or 7 months. Yet, what purpose would that serve? Once the Complainants filed their first submission, there could be no doubt exactly what their claims were. To the extent that a respondent could legitimately claim surprise in what was contained in a complainant's submission, the efficient solution would be to grant the respondent several more weeks to file its initial submission, not to start the entire consultation/panel request process over. This is particularly true given that a reading of Article 6.2 of the DSU such as the EC proposes could result in some parts of the case being accepted, while others were relegated to a different proceeding, something completely contrary to the DSU's philosophy of resolving all related issues

---

[341] Given that the request for consultations did list Article 5 of the TRIM's Agreement, the omission of that article in the panel request could be understood as a decision by the Complainants not to pursue this claim in the light of a more thorough legal assessment and/or the consultations.

[342] Appellate Body Report on "United States - Measure Affecting Imports of Woven Wool Shirts and Blouses from India", issued on 25 April 1997, WT/DS33/AB/R, AB-1997-1, p. 19.

together, as expressed in Article 9 of the DSU.[343] Moreover, such a reading could make it more difficult for Members, and particularly developing-country Members, to use the dispute settlement system, except by incurring the expense of private legal experts at the earliest stage of the proceedings.

7.34 Thus, a consideration of the context of the terms of Article 6.2 supports the preliminary finding reached above.

(iii) object and purpose

7.35 We see three purposes for Article 6.2 of the DSU. First, the request for the establishment of a panel under Article 6.2 will usually serve to set the terms of reference of the panel under Article 7 of the DSU. Second, the request informs the responding Member of the scope of the case against it. Third, the request informs potential third parties of the scope of the case, so that they can better decide whether they wish to assert third-party rights.

7.36 In this case, we believe that the request for establishment of a panel adequately serves these three purposes. First, we have already found that Article 6.2 of the DSU requires a complainant to specify the provision of the WTO agreements that it is relying upon by agreement and article. Thus, a panel will always be able to understand which claims it is required to examine under its terms of reference. Given this interpretation of Article 6.2, we understand our terms of reference without difficulty in this case.

7.37 Second, it appears that the panel request adequately informed the EC of the case against it. We reach this conclusion in light of the facts that the EC did not complain about the request's specificity until it filed its first submission, it did not ask for time beyond the normal periods indicated in the DSU to file its submission and it did not claim in its written submissions that its defence was prejudiced in any particular way by a lack of specificity in the panel request. The EC stated at the Panel's hearings, however, that it had been prejudiced in that the lack of minimal clarity handicapped the EC in the preparation of its defence. However, as pointed out by the Complainants, the EC's oral presentation at the first meeting of the Panel, its responses to our questions and its rebuttal submission essentially followed the line of argument made in its initial submissions, suggesting that it had sufficient time to develop its line of defence. In these circumstances, we believe that the object and purpose of Article 6.2 of the DSU was served by the Complainants' panel request, suggesting that such request was adequately specific under Article 6.2.

7.38 Third, it appears that the panel request adequately informed third parties of the case against the EC, as 20 third parties participated in this panel process.[344]

7.39 Thus, a consideration of the object and purpose of Article 6.2 supports the preliminary finding reached above.

---

[343] Article 9 of the DSU provides that "1. Where more than one Member requests the establishment of a panel related to the same matter, a single panel may be established to examine these complaints taking into account the rights of all Members concerned. A single panel should be established to examine such complaints whenever feasible. ... 3. If more than one panel is established to examine the complaints related to the same matter, to the greatest extent possible the same persons shall serve as panelists on each of the separate panels and the timetable for the panel process in such disputes shall be harmonized".

[344] Belize, Cameroon, Canada, Colombia, Costa Rica, Côte d'Ivoire, Dominica, Dominican Republic, Ghana, Grenada, India, Jamaica, Japan, Nicaragua, Philippines, Saint Vincent and the Grenadines, Saint Lucia, Senegal, Suriname and Venezuela. Thailand indicated a third-party interest in the proceedings, but later withdrew.

(iv) past practice

7.40 Article XVI:1 of the WTO Agreement provides, as noted above, that the "WTO shall be guided by the decisions, procedures and customary practices" of GATT. In the case of adopted panel reports, the Appellate Body has indicated that

> Adopted panel reports are an important part of the GATT *acquis*. They are often taken into account by subsequent panels. They create legitimate expectations among WTO Members, and, therefore should be taken into account where they are relevant to any dispute. However, they are not binding, except with respect to resolving the particular dispute between the parties to that dispute.[345]

There are two GATT/WTO cases that consider issues related to the one we face here. In 1992 a panel declined to consider claims based on GATT Articles X and XXIII(b)-(c) because they were not within its terms of reference, which it noted were defined by the request for the establishment of the panel.[346] More recently, a WTO panel reached a similar result in respect of a claim that consultations had not been properly held under Article XXIII, rejecting the claim because a fair reading of the documents that were used to establish its terms of reference showed that the issue had not been raised in those documents.[347] Although treated as a "terms of reference" issue in both cases, the results were in effect determined on the basis of the panel request. The terms of reference were found not to encompass the claim because the provision or issue had not been referred to in the panel request (and related documents in one case), which in both cases had served to establish the panels' terms of reference. Our reading of the terms of Article 6.2 of the DSU is not inconsistent with these past GATT/WTO panel decisions, nor with a recent Appellate Body decision affirming the above-mentioned WTO panel decision.[348] In this connection, we note that the power of a panel to interpret its terms of reference is not negated by the requirement in Article 7.2 of the DSU that a panel address the "relevant" provisions of covered agreements cited by the parties.

7.41 With respect to practice of GATT contracting parties and Members in requesting panels, numerous examples may be found in the period from 1989[349] to date of panel requests containing only an allegation that a measure is inconsistent with the requirements of a specific provision of a specific agreement, without a more detailed description of the problem.[350] Indeed, as noted above, the EC concedes as much in its response to our

---

[345] Appellate Body Report on "Japan - Taxes on Alcoholic Beverages", adopted on 1 November 1996, WT/DS8/AB/R, WT/DS10/AB/R, WT/DS11/AB/R, AB-1996-2, p. 14.

[346] Panel Report on "United States - Denial of Most-favoured-nation Treatment as to Non-rubber Footwear from Brazil", adopted on 19 June 1992, BISD 39S/128, 147-148, paras. 6.1-6.2.

[347] Panel Report on "Brazil - Measures Affecting Desiccated Coconut", issued on 17 October 1996, WT/DS22/R, pp. 77-78, paras. 286-290.

[348] Appellate Body Report on "Brazil - Measures Affecting Desiccated Coconut", issued on 21 February 1997, WT/DS22/AB/R, AB-1996-4, p.22.

[349] In 1989, the GATT CONTRACTING PARTIES adopted Improvements to the GATT Dispute Settlement Rules and Procedures (BISD 36S/61), including the following language, which is quite similar to that contained in Article 6.2 of the DSU:

> "F.(a) The request for a panel or a working party shall be made in writing. It shall indicate whether consultations were held, and provide a brief summary of the factual and legal basis of the complaint sufficient to present the problem clearly".

There were no specific rules on the form of requests for the establishment of panels prior to 1989.

questions where it examines panel requests in eight WTO cases and finds that in most cases there is no specific explanation given as to how the contested measure is inconsistent with the requirements of the specified provisions of the specified agreements. To date, no GATT or WTO panel has found such requests to be inadequate, except in respect of the antidumping and countervailing duty claims discussed in the following paragraph. Thus, our reading of the terms of Article 6.2 of the DSU is consistent with the practice followed by GATT contracting parties and WTO Members in requesting panels under Article 6.2 and the similar language of its predecessor provision, which was adopted by the GATT CONTRACTING PARTIES in 1989.

7.42 It can be argued, however, that our reading of the terms of Article 6.2 may not be consistent with several panel decisions (adopted and unadopted) under the Tokyo Round Agreement on Implementation of Article VI (the "Tokyo Round Anti-Dumping Code").[351] We find these cases to be of limited relevance in the interpretation of the terms of Article 6.2 of the DSU. In the first place, the Tokyo Round Anti-Dumping Code had different rules for the initiation of panel procedures than were applicable in the case of GATT 1947 panels. More fundamentally, Article 15 of the Tokyo Round Anti-Dumping Code required a so-called conciliation procedure, involving the disputing parties and the Committee charged with supervising the operations of the Code, between the end of the consultation period and the filing of a request to establish a panel. The practice under this conciliation procedure involved the preparation of a detailed statement of issues by the complaining party, which was circulated to the members of the Committee so that they might attempt to solve the dispute through conciliation. Article 15.5 of the Tokyo Round Anti-Dumping Code referred to the conciliation process as involving a "detailed examination by the Committee". In order to make the conciliation process meaningful, it may have been appropriate to insist that all claims brought before a panel have been considered in the conciliation process. Such a conciliation requirement does not exist under the DSU and did not exist under GATT 1947 rules. There has never been a practice of preparing such a statement of claims. Moreover, the nature of antidumping cases is different from this case.

7.43 In any event, we recognize that past practice under the Tokyo Round Anti-Dumping Code may have been inconsistent with the result we reach. We recall that Article 3.3 of the DSU states that the prompt settlement of disputes is essential to the effective functioning of the WTO and we believe that our interpretation of Article 6.2 of the DSU best achieves that objective.

---

[350] See examples cited in note Error! Bookmark not defined. supra. See also EC - Measures Affecting Livestock and Meat (Hormones), Request for the Establishment of a Panel, WT/DS48/5; Brazil - Measures Affecting Desiccated Coconut, Request for the Establishment of a Panel, WT/DS22/2; European Communities - Duties on Imports of Grains, Request for the Establishment of a Panel, WT/DS13/2; Japan - Taxes on Alcoholic Beverages, Request for the Establishment of a Panel by the United States, WT/DS11/2; European Communities - Duties on Imports of Cereals, Request for the Establishment of a Panel, WT/DS9/2; United States - Standards for Reformulated and Conventional Gasoline, Request for the Establishment of a Panel, WT/DS4/2; United States - Measures Affecting the Importation and Internal Sale and Use of Tobacco, Recourse to Article XXIII:2 by Argentina, DS44/8; EEC - Restrictions on Imports of Apples, Communication from Chile, DS39/2 & DS41/2.

[351] Panel Report on "United States - Anti-Dumping Duties on Imports of Fresh and Chilled Atlantic Salmon from Norway", adopted 26 April 1994, ADP/87, paras. 333-335; Panel Report on "European Communities - Imposition of Anti-Dumping Duties on Imports of Cotton Yarn from Brazil", ADP/137, adopted on 4 July 1995, paras. 438-466; Panel Report on "United States - Anti-Dumping Duties on Imports of Gray Portland Cement and Cement Clinker from Mexico", issued on 7 September 1992 (not adopted), ADP/82, para. *5.12*; Panel Report on "EC - Anti-Dumping Duties on Audiotapes in Cassettes Originating in Japan", issued on 28 April 1995 (not adopted), ADP/136, para. 295. In addition, there was one case involving this issue under the Tokyo Round Agreement on Interpretation and Application of Articles VI, XVI and XXIII. Panel Report on "United States - Countervailing Duties on Imports of Fresh and Chilled Atlantic Salmon from Norway", adopted 27 April 1994, SCM/153, paras. 208-214 (following the approach of the Salmon antidumping case cited above). A claim of non-compliance with Article 6.2 was made in the Panel Report on "Measures Affecting Desiccated Coconut", dated 17 October 1996, WT/DS22/R, para.290, but the panel did not reach the Article 6.2 issue, except as noted above, by finding that the failure to allege that a measure was inconsistent with the requirements of a specific provision of GATT meant that a claim based on that provision was not within the panel's terms of reference, a result which we follow.

(v) cure

7.44 Finally, we note that at the second substantive Panel meeting, we expressed the preliminary view that even if there was some uncertainty whether the panel request had met the requirements of Article 6.2, the first written submissions of the Complainants "cured" that uncertainty because their submissions were sufficiently detailed to present all the factual and legal issues clearly. We considered that at the time that the EC filed its first written submission to the Panel, it had complete knowledge of the Complainants' case through their submissions. In light of our analysis of the panel request and Article 6.2 as outlined above, we confirm our preliminary view.[352]

7.45 **We therefore find that the panel request made by the Complainants was sufficient to meet the requirements of Article 6.2 of the DSU to the extent that it alleged inconsistencies with the requirements of specific provisions of specific WTO agreements.**

7.46 **In light of the foregoing finding, since the invocation of the Agreement on Agriculture in the panel request did not indicate a specific provision thereof, we will not consider the claim raised by Ecuador in its first written submission under that Agreement. We will also not consider the claims raised by Ecuador, Guatemala and Honduras, and the United States in their first written submissions under Article 5 of the TRIM's Agreement since the panel request referred only to Article 2 of the TRIM's Agreement.[353]**

3. *Requirement of legal interest*

7.47 The EC argues that the US claims concerning trade in goods should be rejected because US banana production is minimal, its banana exports are nil and that for climatic reasons this situation is not likely to change. As a result, the EC suggests that the United States has not suffered any nullification or impairment of WTO benefits in respect of trade in bananas as required by Article 3.3 and 3.7 of the DSU.[354] Moreover, the EC argues that the United States would have no effective WTO remedy under Article 22 of the DSU. With no effective remedy and absent any notion of a declaratory judgment or advisory opinion in the WTO dispute settlement system, the EC claims that the United States cannot raise "goods" issues because it has "no legal right or interest" therein. The EC argues that there must be a requirement in the WTO dispute settlement system that a complaining party have such a "legal interest" because the absence of such a requirement would undermine the DSU by leading to litigation "by all against all". The EC also suggests that the interests of Members in any given case can be adequately protected through assertion of a third party interest in the case.

7.48 In response, the Complainants argue that there is no basis in the DSU for the EC's claim and that their claims are covered by the Panel's terms of reference. They argue that Article 3.8 of the DSU presupposes a finding of infringement prior to a consideration of the nullification-or-impairment issue, suggesting that even if no compensation were due, an infringement finding could be made. Moreover, they argue that it is inappropriate to try to define potential trade. They also mention that in a past case the EC advanced a broad notion of nullification or impairment, which if generally accepted would permit the Complainants to claim nullification or impairment in this case.

---

[352] We exclude from this confirmation any suggestion that the panel request was sufficient to allow claims based on the Agreement on Agriculture and Article 5 of the TRIM's Agreement since as to those provisions, the panel request did not comply at all with the requirements of Article 6.2 and, accordingly, there was no uncertainty that could be cured.

[353] The panel request listed Article XI of GATT, but no claims under Article XI were pursued by the Complainants.

[354] Article 3.3 of the DSU provides that the prompt settlement of disputes is essential "in situations where a Member considers that benefits accruing to it directly or indirectly under the covered agreements are being impaired". Article 3.7 of the DSU requires Members to exercise judgment as to whether invocation of the DSU would be "fruitful".

7.49 In examining this issue, we note that neither Article 3.3 nor 3.7 of the DSU nor any other provision of the DSU contain any explicit requirement that a Member must have a "legal interest" as a prerequisite for requesting a panel. The reference in Article XXIII of GATT to nullification or impairment (or the impeding of the attainment of any GATT objective) does not establish a procedural requirement. Moreover, Article 3.8 of the DSU provides that nullification or impairment is normally presumed if there is an infringement of the obligations of a WTO agreement.[355]

7.50 We fail to see that there is, or should be, a legal interest test under the DSU. This view is corroborated by past GATT practice, which suggests that if a complainant claims that a measure is inconsistent with the requirements of GATT rules, there is not a requirement to show actual trade effects. GATT rules have been consistently interpreted to protect "competitive opportunities" as opposed to actual trade flows. For example, in the 1949 Working Party Report on Brazilian Internal Taxes, a number of the members of the working party took the view that

> the absence of imports from contracting parties ... would not necessarily be an indication that they had no interest in the exports of the product affected by the tax, since their potentialities as exporters, given national treatment, should be taken into account.[356]

This view was confirmed in the 1958 *Italian Agricultural Machinery* case, where the panel noted that Article III of GATT applied to "any laws or regulations which might adversely modify the conditions of competition between the domestic and imported products".[357] The *Section 337* case notes that Article III is concerned with "effective equality of opportunities for imported products".[358] These cases confirm that WTO rules are not concerned with actual trade, but rather with competitive opportunities. Generally, it would be difficult to conclude that a Member had no possibility of competing in respect of a product or service. The United States does produce bananas in Puerto Rico and Hawaii. Moreover, even if the United States did not have even a potential export interest, its internal market for bananas could be affected by the EC regime and that regime's effect on world supplies and prices. Indeed, with the increased interdependence of the global economy, which means that actions taken in one country are likely to have significant effects on trade and foreign direct investment flows in others, Members have a greater stake in enforcing WTO rules than in the past since any deviation from the negotiated balance of rights and obligations is more likely than ever to affect them, directly or indirectly. Since the United States is likely to be affected by the EC regime, it would have an interest in a determination of whether the EC regime is inconsistent with the requirements of WTO rules. Thus, in our view a Member's potential interest in trade in goods or services and its interest in a determination of rights and obligations under the WTO Agreement are each sufficient to establish a right to pursue a WTO dispute

---

355 See Panel Report on "United States - Taxes on Petroleum and Certain Imported Substances", adopted on 17 June 1987, BISD 34S/136, 158, para. 5.1.9.

356 GATT/CP.3/42, adopted 30 June 1949, II/181, 185, para. 16.

357 Panel Report on "Italian Discrimination Against Imported Agricultural Machinery", adopted 23 October 1958, 7S/60, 64, para.12.

358 Panel Report on "United States - Section 337 of the Tariff Act of 1930", adopted on 7 November 1989, BISD 36S/345, 386-387, para. *5.11*.

settlement proceeding. Moreover, we note that this result is consistent with decisions of international tribunals.[359]

7.51 As to the EC's suggestions that the absence of a legal interest test (defined to exclude the US "goods" claims in this case) would undermine the DSU because it would lead to litigation "by all against all" and that the interests of Members in any given case can be adequately protected through assertion of a third party rights in the case, we note that all Members have an interest in ensuring that other Members comply with their obligations. That interest is not completely served by the possible assertion of third party rights since there may be no occasion to assert such rights unless another Member initiates a DSU proceeding and since third party rights are more limited than the rights of parties. The likelihood of litigation by all against all seems unlikely, as Members are admonished by Article 3.7 of the DSU to exercise restraint in bringing cases and the cost of bringing cases is such, especially in a case like this one, that this admonition is likely to be followed. In our view, it is also unlikely that significant numbers of cases will be initiated by Members that have no immediate trade interest in their results.

7.52 **Thus, we find that under the DSU the United States has a right to advance the claims that it has raised in this case.**

4. *Number of panel reports*

7.53 The EC requested the Panel, pursuant to Article 9 of the DSU, to prepare four panel reports in this case-one each for the claims of Ecuador, Guatemala and Honduras (who filed a joint first submission), Mexico and the United States. The Complainants suggested that, even if the EC had a right to insist on separate reports under Article 9, it should not do so because of the increased administrative burden that would be placed upon the Panel. Moreover, they requested that the Panel should make the same findings and conclusions with respect to the same claims.

7.54 Article 9 of the DSU provides in relevant part as follows:

> 1. Where more than one Member requests the establishment of a panel related to the same matter, a single panel may be established to examine these complaints taking into account the rights of all Members concerned. ...
>
> 2. The single panel shall organize its examination and present its findings to the DSB in such a manner that the rights the parties to the dispute would have enjoyed had separate panels examined the complaints are in no way impaired. If one of the parties to the dispute so requests, the panel shall submit separate reports on the dispute concerned. ....

---

[359] The International Court of Justice has not defined the concept of legal interest in specific terms. However, a number of its cases would support finding a legal interest in this case. For example, in the *Wimbledon* case, the Permanent Court of International Justice found that a state could raise a claim with respect to the Kiel Canal even though its fleet did not want to use it, suggesting that a potential interest was sufficient for a legal interest. PCIJ (1923), Ser. A, no. 1, 20. In *Northern Cameroon's* (*Preliminary Objections*), the ICJ stated:

> "The function of the Court is to state the law, but it may pronounce judgment only in connection with concrete cases where there exists at the time of adjudication an actual controversy involving a conflict of legal interest between the parties. The Court's judgment must have some practical consequence in the sense that it can affect existing legal rights or obligations of the parties, thus removing uncertainty from their legal relations" (ICJ Reports (1963), 33-34).

Here, our decision will have such an effect to the extent that the EC is obligated to revise the challenged measures. See also Part II of the Draft Articles on State Responsibility, art. 40.2(e)-(f), provisionally adopted by the Drafting Committee of the International Law Commission. A/CN.4/L.524, 21 June 1996.

7.55 We interpret the terms of Article 9 to require us to grant the EC request. However, in light of the fact that the Complainants presented joint oral submissions to the Panel, joint responses to questions and a joint rebuttal submission, as well as the fact that they have collectively endorsed the arguments made in each other's first submissions, we must also take account of the close interrelationship of the Complainants' arguments.

7.56 In our view, one of the objectives of Article 9 is to ensure that a respondent is not later faced with a demand for compensation or threatened by retaliation under Article 22 of the DSU in respect of uncured inconsistencies with WTO rules that were not complained of by one of the complaining parties participating in a panel proceeding. Our reports must bear this objective in mind.

7.57 For purposes of determining whether a Complainant in this matter has made a claim, we have examined its first written submission, as we consider that document determines the claims made by a complaining party. To allow the assertion of additional claims after that point would be unfair to the respondent, as it would have little or no time to prepare a response to such claims. In this regard, we note that paragraph 12(c) of the Appendix 3 to the DSU on "Working Procedures" foresees the simultaneous submission of the written rebuttals by complaining and respondent parties, a procedure that was followed in this case. To allow claims to be presented in the rebuttal submissions would mean that the respondent would have an opportunity to rebut the claims only in its oral presentation during the second meeting. In our view, the failure to make a claim in the first written submission cannot be remedied by later submissions or by incorporating the claims and arguments of other complainants.

7.58 **Accordingly, we have decided that the description of the Panel's proceedings, the factual aspects and the parties' arguments should be identical in the four reports. In the "Findings" section, however, the reports differ to the extent that the Complainants' initial written submissions to the Panel differ in respect of alleging inconsistencies with the requirements of specific provisions of specific agreements. Thus, to take an example, the report for Guatemala and Honduras does not discuss GATS issues because their initial written submission did not allege inconsistencies with the requirements of GATS provisions.**

7.59 In light of the foregoing, in the "Findings" we use the term "the Complainants" to refer to all of the Complaining parties who have made a particular claim. In discussing the claim, when we refer to the Complainants' arguments, we mean all arguments made in support of the claim by the various Complaining parties, who have incorporated each other's arguments into their own. Thus, the term "the Complainants" in this report means Ecuador and one or more of the other Complaining parties.

7.60 As explained above, when one of the Complaining parties has not claimed that a specific provision of a specific agreement has been violated in its initial written submission to the Panel, we do not discuss our findings with respect to that claim in the report for that party. However, for the convenience of readers of the four reports, we have used the same paragraph numbers and footnote numbers for the substantive discussions of the same issues in the four reports. Where an issue has not been raised by Ecuador, we indicate in this report which reports and which paragraph numbers in those reports discuss that issue.

C. Substantive Issues

7.61 We now turn to an examination of the substantive issues raised by the Complainants in respect of the EC's regime for the importation, sale and distribution of bananas. We first address claims related to the EC's quantitative allocations for bananas, including the shares assigned to the ACP countries and to signatories of the Framework Agreement on Bananas ("BFA"). Second, we consider tariff issues, including preferences afforded to imports of certain ACP bananas. We then consider the claims made in respect of the EC licensing procedures for bananas. Finally, we examine the claims raised in respect of the General Agreement on Trade in Services.

7.62 Before doing so, we consider whether bananas from the EC, ACP countries, BFA countries and other third countries are "like" products for purposes of the claims made in respect of Articles I, III, X and XIII of GATT. The factors commonly used in GATT practice to determine likeness, such as, for example, customs classification, end-use, and the properties, nature and quality of the product, all support a finding that bananas from these various sources should be treated as like products.[360] Moreover, all parties and third parties to the dispute have proceeded in their legal reasoning on the assumption that all bananas are "like" products in spite of any differences in quality, size or taste that may exist.

7.63 **We find that bananas are "like" products, for purposes of Article I, III, X, and XIII of GATT, irrespective of whether they originate in the EC, in ACP countries, in BFA countries or in other third countries.**

1. The EC market for bananas: Article XIII of GATT

7.64 As of 1995, bananas could be marketed in the EC as follows:

a. First, up to 857,700 tonnes of bananas were permitted to enter duty-free from traditional ACP suppliers.

b. Second, pursuant to its GATT Article II Schedule, the EC permitted the entry of a total of up to 2.2 million tonnes of bananas at a tariff of 75 ECU per tonne. This quota was allocated as follows: (i) 49.4 per cent to the countries who are parties to the BFA; (ii) 90,000 tonnes to ACP countries in respect of amounts that they did not traditionally supply to EC member States (admitted duty-free); and (iii) the rest (46.5 per cent) to other banana exporters. In 1995 and 1996, the EC increased the 2.2 million tonne tariff quota by 353,000 tonnes to take account of the enlargement of the EC to include Austria, Finland and Sweden, although no change has been made in the EC's Schedule. Additional quantities were permitted at the in-quota tariff via hurricane licences.

c. Third, imports of bananas in excess of the above-mentioned amounts were subject in 1995 to a tariff of 822 ECU per tonne (722 ECU for ACP bananas). The 822 ECU per tonne tariff will fall in equal instalments to 680 ECU per tonne on full implementation of the EC's Uruguay Round commitments.

d. Finally, bananas from EC territories could be sold on the EC market without restriction. In 1995, 658,200 tonnes of such bananas were marketed in the EC.

7.65 The Complainants claim that the EC has failed to allocate country-specific tariff quota shares to those Complainants that export bananas to the EC and that the EC's allocation of tariff quota shares to the ACP and BFA countries is inconsistent with the requirements of the tariff quota allocation rules of Article XIII of GATT. The EC responds that it has complied with the terms of Article XIII. In particular, the EC argues that the preferences it provides to traditional ACP bananas are permitted under the Lomé waiver and its treatment of BFA and other bananas is provided pursuant to the EC's Schedule into which the BFA is incorporated.

---

[360] For a general discussion of relevant factors for determining the likeness of products, see Panel Report on "Japan - Taxes on Alcoholic Beverages", adopted on 1 November 1996, WT/DS8/R, WT/DS10/R & WT/DS11/R, pp. 111-114, paras. 6.20-6.23, as modified by, Appellate Body Report on "Japan - Taxes on Alcoholic Beverages", adopted on 1 November 1996, WT/DS8/AB/R, WT/DS10/AB/R & WT/DS11/AB/R, pp. 19-21.

7.66 We first consider how Article XIII of GATT should be interpreted and whether the EC's banana tariff quota shares conform to its requirements. We then consider whether any inconsistencies with Article XIII are waived by the Lomé waiver or permitted as a result of the negotiation of the BFA and its inclusion in the EC's Schedule.

a) Article XIII

7.67 Article XIII of GATT generally regulates the administration of quotas and tariff quotas. In relevant parts, it provides as follows:

Article XIII
Non-discriminatory Administration of Quantitative Restrictions

1. No prohibition or restriction shall be applied by any Member on the importation of any product of the territory of any other Member or on the exportation of any product destined for the territory of any other Member, unless the importation of the like product of all third countries or the exportation of the like product to all third countries is similarly prohibited or restricted.

2. In applying import restrictions to any product, Members shall aim at a distribution of trade in such product approaching as closely as possible the shares which the various Members might be expected to obtain in the absence of such restrictions and to this end shall observe the following provisions:

...

(*d*) In cases in which a quota is allocated among supplying countries the Member applying the restrictions may seek agreement with respect to the allocation of shares in the quota with all other Members having a substantial interest in supplying the product concerned. In cases in which this method is not reasonably practicable, the Member concerned shall allot to Members having a substantial interest in supplying the product shares based upon the proportions, supplied by such Members during a previous representative period, of the total quantity or value of imports of the product, due account being taken of any special factors which may have affected or may be affecting the trade in the product. No conditions or formalities shall be imposed which would prevent any Member from utilizing fully the share of any such total quantity or value which has been allotted to it, subject to importation being made within any prescribed period to which the quota may relate.*[361]

...

[361] Note Ad Article XIII, Paragraph 2(d), reads: "No mention was made of 'commercial considerations' as a rule for the allocation of quotas because it was considered that its application by governmental authorities might not always be practicable. Moreover, in cases where it is practicable, a Member could apply these considerations in the process of seeking agreement, consistently with the general rule laid down in the opening sentence of paragraph 2".

4. With regard to restrictions applied in accordance with paragraph 2 (*d*) of this Article or under paragraph 2 (*c*) of Article XI, the selection of a representative period for any product and the appraisal of any special factors*[362] affecting the trade in the product shall be made initially by the Member applying the restriction; *Provided* that such Member shall, upon the request of any other Member having a substantial interest in supplying that product or upon the request of the [CONTRACTING PARTIES], consult promptly with the other Member or the [CONTRACTING PARTIES] regarding the need for an adjustment of the proportion determined or of the base period selected, or for the reappraisal of the special factors involved, or for the elimination of conditions, formalities or any other provisions established unilaterally relating to the allocation of an adequate quota or its unrestricted utilization.

5. The provisions of this Article shall apply to any tariff quota instituted or maintained by any Member, and, in so far as applicable, the principles of this Article shall also extend to export restrictions.

7.68 The wording of Article XIII is clear. If quantitative restrictions are used (as an exception to the general ban on their use in Article XI), they are to be used in the least trade-distorting manner possible. In the terms of the general rule[363] of the chapeau of Article XIII:2:

> In applying import restrictions to any product, Members shall aim at a distribution of trade in such product approaching as closely as possible the shares which the various Members might be expected to obtain in the absence of such restrictions ....

In this case, we are concerned with tariff quotas, which are permitted under GATT rules, and not quantitative restrictions *per se*. However, Article XIII:5 makes it clear, and the parties agree, that Article XIII applies to the administration of tariff quotas. In light of the terms of Article XIII, it can be said that the object and purpose of Article XIII:2 is to minimize the impact of a quota or tariff quota regime on trade flows by attempting to approximate under such measures the trade shares that would have occurred in the absence of the regime. In interpreting the terms of Article XIII, it is important to keep their context in mind. Article XIII is basically a provision relating to the administration of restrictions authorized as exceptions to one of the most basic GATT provisions-the general ban on quotas and other non-tariff restrictions contained in Article XI.

7.69 While previous panels have dealt with specific aspects of Article XIII, this is the first case in which a broad challenge to a quota or tariff quota system has been made. Therefore, we must in the first instance consider in general terms how the various subdivisions of Article XIII work together. Article XIII:1 establishes the basic principle that no import restriction shall be applied to one Member's products unless the importation of like products from other Members is similarly restricted. Thus, a Member may not limit the quantity of imports from some Members but not from others. But as indicated by the terms of Article XIII (and even its title, "Non-discriminatory Administration of Quantitative Restrictions"), the non-discrimination obligation extends further. The imported products at issue must be "similarly" restricted. A Member may not restrict imports from some Members using one means and restrict them from another Member using another means.

---

[362] Note Ad Article XIII, Paragraph 4, provides: "See note relating to 'special factors' in connection with the last subparagraph of paragraph 2 of Article XI". That note reads as follows: "The term 'special factors' includes changes in relative productive efficiency between domestic and foreign producers, or as between different foreign producers, but not changes artificially brought about by means not permitted under the Agreement".

[363] At the 1955 Review Session, a working party considering amendments to Article XIII stated: "The Working Party ... agreed to recognize that the general rule contained in the introduction to paragraph 2 governed the various sub-paragraphs of that paragraph including those of sub-paragraph (d)". Working Party Report on "Quantitative Restrictions", adopted on 2, 4 and 5 March 1955, BISD 3S/170, 176, para. 24.

The only directly relevant panel report dealt with this issue briefly, but confirms this interpretation of Article XIII:1. The report found an inconsistency with the requirements of Article XIII:1 where a GATT contracting party negotiated export restrictions on imports of products from some countries but imposed unilateral import restrictions on the like products from another country. The report also noted differences in administration (import restrictions versus export restraint) and in transparency between the two measures.[364]

7.70 Article XIII's general requirement of non-discrimination is modified in one respect by Article XIII:2(d), which provides for the possibility to allocate tariff quota shares to supplying countries. Any such country specific allocation must, however, "aim at a distribution of trade ... approaching as closely as possible the shares which Members might be expected to obtain in the absence of such restrictions" (chapeau of Article XIII:2(d)).

7.71 Article XIII:2(d) further specifies the treatment that, in case of country-specific allocation of tariff quota shares, must be given to Members with "a substantial interest in supplying the product concerned". For those Members, the Member proposing to impose restrictions may seek agreement with them as provided in Article XIII:2(d), first sentence. If that is not reasonably practicable, then it must allot shares in the quota (or tariff quota) to them on the basis of the criteria specified in Article XIII:2(d), second sentence.

7.72 The terms of Article XIII:2(d) make clear that the combined use of agreements and unilateral allocations to Members with substantial interests is not permitted. The text of Article XIII:2(d) provides that where the first "method", i.e., agreement, is not reasonably practicable, then an allocation must be made. Thus, in the absence of agreements with all Members having a substantial interest in supplying the product, the Member applying the restriction must allocate shares in accordance with the rules of Article XIII:2(d), second sentence. In the absence of this rule, the Member allocating shares could reach agreements with some Members having a substantial interest in supplying the product that discriminated against other Members having a substantial interest supplying the product, even if those other Members objected to the shares they were to be allocated.

7.73 The question then is whether country-specific shares can also be allocated to Members that do not have a substantial interest in supplying the product and, if so, what the method of allocation would have to be. As to the first point, we note that the first sentence of Article XIII:2(d) refers to allocation of a quota "among supplying countries". This could be read to imply that an allocation may also be made to Members that do not have a substantial interest in supplying the product. If this interpretation is accepted, any such allocation must, however, meet the requirements of Article XIII:1 and the general rule in the chapeau to Article XIII:2(d). Therefore, if a Member wishes to allocate shares of a tariff quota to some suppliers without a substantial interest, then such shares must be allocated to all such suppliers. Otherwise, imports from Members would not be similarly restricted as required by Article XIII:1.[365] As to the second point, in such a case it would be required to use the same method as was used to allocate the country-specific shares to the Members having a substantial interest in supplying the product, because otherwise the requirements of Article XIII:1 would also not be met.

7.74 The allocation of country-specific tariff quota shares to all supplying countries on the basis of the first method (agreement) may in practice be difficult since there will likely be demand for more than 100 per cent of the tariff quota and, furthermore, there would be no possibility to make provision for new suppliers. This would leave the second method as the only practical alternative-a result that, however, runs counter to the

[364] Panel Report on "EEC - Restrictions on Imports of Apples from Chile", adopted on 10 November 1980, BISD 27S/98, 114, 116, paras *4.11*, *4.21*. See also Panel Report on "EEC - Quantitative Restrictions Against Imports of Certain Products from Hong Kong", adopted 12 July 1983, BISD 30S/129, 139-140, para. 33.

[365] See Panel Report on "EEC Restrictions on Imports of Apples from Chile", adopted on 10 November 1980, BISD 27S/98, 114, 116, paras. *4.11*, *4.21*.

provision of Article XIII:2(d) to first seek agreement with all Members having a substantial interest in supplying the product concerned.

7.75 The consequence of the foregoing analysis is that Members may be effectively required to use a general "others" category for all suppliers other than Members with a substantial interest in supplying the product. The fact that in this situation tariff quota shares are allocated to some Members, notably those having a substantial interest in supplying the product, but not to others that do not have a substantial interest in supplying the product, would not necessarily be in conflict with Article XIII:1. While the requirement of Article XIII:2(d) is not expressed as an exception to the requirements of Article XIII:1, it may be regarded, to the extent that its practical application is inconsistent with it, as *lex specialis* in respect of Members with a substantial interest in supplying the product concerned.

7.76 In so far as this in practice results in the use of an "others" category for all Members not having a substantial interest in supplying the product, it comports well with the object and purpose of Article XIII, as expressed in the general rule to the chapeau to Article XIII:2. When a significant share of a tariff quota is assigned to "others", the import market will evolve with the minimum amount of distortion. Members not having a substantial supplying interest will be able, if sufficiently competitive, to gain market share in the "others" category and possibly achieve "substantial supplying interest" status which, in turn, would provide them the opportunity to receive a country-specific allocation by invoking the provisions of Article XIII:4. New entrants will be able to compete in the market, and likewise have an opportunity to gain "substantial supplying interest" status. For the share of the market allocated to Members with a substantial interest in supplying the product, the situation may also evolve in light of adjustments following consultations under Article XIII:4. In comparison to a situation where country-specific shares are allocated to all supplying countries, including Members with minor market shares, this result is less likely to lead to a long-term freezing of market shares. This is, in our view, consistent with the terms, object and purpose, and context of Article XIII.

7.77 In this case, we are confronted with the following situation: with respect to its common market organization for bananas, the EC reached an agreement on shares in its bound tariff quota for bananas with the BFA countries, allocated shares of that tariff quota in respect of non-traditional ACP bananas and created an "others" category in that tariff quota for other Members (and non-Members). In addition, it also allocated tariff quota quantities to traditional ACP suppliers of bananas. To evaluate this situation in light of the foregoing discussion of Article XIII, it is necessary to consider (i) whether the EC market organization for imported bananas should be analyzed as one or two regimes for purposes of Article XIII, (ii) which Members could be considered to have had a substantial interest in supplying bananas to the EC at the time the EC regulation was put in place and how they were treated by the EC, (iii) how Members without such a substantial interest were treated and (iv) the position of new Members.

(i) separate regimes

7.78 The EC has one common market organisation for bananas established by Regulation 404/93. It has argued, however, that it has two separate regimes for imported bananas - one for bananas traditionally supplied by certain ACP countries, and one for bananas from non-traditional ACP, BFA and other third-country sources. In its view, the Panel should separately examine the consistency of each of these regimes with the requirements of Article XIII. The EC claims that the regime for traditional supplies of ACP bananas has a different legal basis than the bound tariff quota for bananas because it is a preferential regime in that different tariff rates apply to ACP bananas as compared to other bananas. The Complainants argue that nothing in the language of Article XIII supports such a distinction, that recognizing it would undermine the purpose of that Article and that Article implies that there cannot be separate regimes because if there were, imports under the separate regimes would not be similarly restricted as required by Article XIII:1.

7.79 We note that Article XIII:1 provides that no restriction shall be applied by any Member on the importation of any product of another Member "unless the importation of the like product of all third countries ... is similarly ... restricted". Article XIII:2 requires Members when allocating tariff quota shares to "aim at a distribution of trade ... approaching as closely as possible the shares which the various Members might be expected to obtain in the absence of such restrictions". By their terms, these two provisions of Article XIII do not provide a basis for analysing quota allocation regimes separately because they have different legal bases or because different tariff rates are applicable. Article XIII applies to allocations of shares in an import market for a particular product which is restricted by a quota or tariff quota. In our view, its non-discrimination requirements apply to that market for that product, irrespective of whether or how a Member subdivides it for administrative or other reasons. Indeed, to accept that a Member could establish quota regimes by different legal instruments and argue that they are not as a consequence subject to Article XIII would be, as argued by the Complainants, to eviscerate the non-discrimination provisions of Article XIII.

7.80 Similarly, in our view, the existence of different tariff rates does not imply that the EC import measures applied to bananas must or should be treated as two separate regimes. The object and purpose of Article XIII:2 is to attempt to approximate under a tariff quota regime the trade shares that would have occurred in the absence of the tariff quota. To the extent that a preferential tariff benefits imports from certain countries, their trade shares should already reflect that preference. Thus, the fact that different tariff rates may apply to imports from different Members does not justify separate analysis of the allocation of tariff quota shares on the basis of the tariff applicable to the Member in question, without reference to the allocations to Members subject to a different tariff rate. While it is true that non-beneficiaries of the tariff preference by definition cannot benefit from that preference, they may be affected by the way in which tariff quota shares benefitting from the tariff preference are allocated. For example, an allocation of shares could be made in a way that would allow beneficiaries of the tariff preference to compete more effectively than would the tariff preference alone. Not to apply Article XIII in such a situation would mean that preferential treatment in addition to the tariff preference was being afforded to those Members.

7.81 Past GATT and WTO practice suggests that Members have typically distinguished between tariff preferences and non-tariff preferences. For example, in the so-called Enabling Clause, preferential tariff treatment on a unilateral basis is authorized for developing countries in general terms in accordance with the Generalized System of Preferences, while non-tariff preferences are permitted only to the extent governed by instruments multilaterally negotiated under GATT/WTO auspices.[366] As noted below, most current waivers allowing preferential treatment have been limited to preferential tariff treatment. The "separate regimes" argument of the EC blurs these distinctions and would result in a tariff preference providing preferential treatment in addition to a tariff advantage.

7.82 **We find that the EC has only one regime for banana imports for purposes of analysing whether its allocation of tariff quota shares is consistent with the requirements of Article XIII.**

(ii) Members with a substantial interest

7.83 The following statistics supplied by the EC indicate the shares of suppliers to the EC banana market during the 1989-1991 period. We use 1989-1991 statistics because the EC claims that at the time it negotiated the BFA, 1992 statistics were not available. Although the Complainants contest this assertion, they have not convinced us that such statistics were in fact available.

---

[366] Decision of the CONTRACTING PARTIES of 28 November 1979 on "Differential and More Favourable Treatment, Reciprocity and Fuller Participation of Developing Countries", BISD 26S/203.

GATT Contracting Party 1993	1989-1991 Average Volume (tonnes)	1989-1991 Average of Shares %
Costa Rica	508,957	19.7
Colombia	409,153	15.7
St. Lucia	114,445	4.5
Côte d'Ivoire	98,908	3.8
Cameroon	82,938	3.1
St.Vincent & the Grenadines	70,464	2.7
Jamaica	57,505	2.2
Dominica	52,628	2.0
Nicaragua	44,840	1.7
Suriname	28,465	1.1
Guatemala	28,128	1.2
Belize	23,412	0.9
Grenada	8,215	0.3
Dominican Republic	4,789	0.2
Venezuela	90	0.0
Madagascar	23	0.0
other ACP countries	1,215	0.1
Total	1,534,062	59.2

Non - GATT Contracting Party 1993	1989-1991 Average Volume (tonnes)	1989-1991 Average of Shares %
Panama	465,701	18
Ecuador	401,419	15.2
Honduras	136,858	5.4
Somalia	41,751	1.7
Cape Verde	2,820	0.1
Total	1,048,549	40.4

The EC argues that only Colombia and Costa Rica had a "substantial interest in supplying the product" in the sense of Article XIII:2(d), in that they were the only GATT contracting parties at the time with market shares of more than 10 per cent and that, analogously to practice under Article XXVIII of GATT, a market share of 10 per cent could be considered as the threshold for a country to establish a substantial interest.[367] The other major suppliers to the EC market-Ecuador and Panama-were not GATT contracting parties at the time. The remaining suppliers had relatively minor shares. The Complainants argue that the EC cannot claim compliance with Article XIII:2(d), first sentence, because there were GATT contracting parties with which the EC did not reach agreement and that they in some cases had more significant market shares of EC banana imports than some of the countries with which the EC did reach agreement in the BFA.

7.84 We do not find it necessary to set a precise import share for determination of whether a Member has a substantial interest in supplying a product. A determination of substantial interest might well vary somewhat based on the structure of the market.[368]

7.85 **Given the particular circumstances of this case, we find that it was not unreasonable for the EC to conclude that at the time the BFA was negotiated Colombia and Costa Rica were the only contracting parties that had a substantial interest in supplying the EC banana market in terms of Article XIII:2(d). We also find that it is not reasonable to conclude that at the time the BFA was negotiated Nicaragua and Venezuela had a substantial interest in supplying the EC banana market in the terms of Article XIII:2(d).**

7.86 Before turning to the consequences of the above finding, we must consider whether it would be possible for other Members to challenge an agreement reached under Article XIII:2(d), first sentence. The EC argues that since it negotiated an agreement with Colombia and Costa Rica in compliance with Article

[367] Paragraph 7 to the Note Ad Article XXVIII:1 states that "[t]he expression 'substantial interest' is not capable of a precise definition ... It is, however, intended to be construed to cover only those Members which have ... a significant share in the market ...". It was indicated in 1985, however, that a 10 per cent rule has been applied generally. Analytical Index: Guide to GATT Law and Practice, 6th rev. ed. 1995, p. 941, citing TAR/M/16, p. 10.

[368] We note that in the case of Article XXVIII, the Uruguay Round Understanding on the Interpretation of Article XXVIII of the General Agreement on Tariffs and Trade 1994 provides that the Member which has the highest ratio of exports affected by the concession to its total exports shall be deemed to have principal supplying interest in the product at issue for purposes of negotiations under Article XXVIII. There is so far no similar understanding applicable to Article XIII.

XIII:2(d), first sentence, the provisions of that agreement may not be challenged as not complying with other provisions of Article XIII. However, even though the EC did negotiate an agreement as foreseen in Article XIII:2(d), first sentence, it is necessary to keep in mind that the goal of any such agreement is provided in the general rule in the chapeau to Article XIII:2. We would not rule out the possibility that an agreement that does not generally achieve this goal may be open to challenge by Members who are not parties to the agreement, even if there is no requirement to include such Members in the negotiations because they do not have a substantial interest in supplying the product concerned. For example, in our view, it would be possible for other Members to challenge an agreement between the EC, Colombia and Costa Rica if it divided the bound tariff quota between only Colombia and Costa Rica. Support for allowing for the possibility of such a challenge is found in past GATT practice.[369]

7.87 In this case, however, we find it unnecessary to specify in detail under what circumstances an agreement reached pursuant to Article XIII:2(d) may be challenged. If our findings on the use of separate regimes (para. 7.0), on the shares assigned to Members without a substantial interest (*infra*) and the rights of new Members under Article XIII (*infra*), as well as those relating to the EC's licensing procedures, are adopted by the DSB, it will be necessary for the EC to reconsider its treatment of banana imports, including the allocation of tariff quota shares.

7.88 **Accordingly, we make no finding on whether the allocation of shares to Colombia and Costa Rica is consistent with the requirements of the general rule in the chapeau to Article XIII:2(d).**

(iii) Members without a substantial interest

7.89 As noted above, Article XIII:1 would permit the EC to allocate a tariff quota share to all supplying Members without a substantial interest in the form of an "others" category, without specific shares. In this case, the EC allocated tariff quota shares by agreement and assignment to some Members (e.g., ACP countries (in respect of traditional and non-traditional exports), Nicaragua and Venezuela) without allocating such shares to other Members (e.g., Guatemala). Moreover, under the BFA, the BFA countries were given special rights in respect of reallocation of tariff quota shares[370] that were not given to other Members (e.g., Guatemala). For the reasons noted above (paragraphs 7.0 and 7.0), such differential treatment of like products from Members is inconsistent with the requirements of Article XIII:1.

---

[369] For example, in a case involving Norwegian quotas on textiles products, the panel found that Norway had reached agreement on the limitation of textiles imports from six countries, but not Hong Kong. The panel found that the quantitative restrictions limiting Hong Kong exports were subject to Article XIII:2 and ruled that

> "Norway's reservation of market shares for these six countries therefore represented a partial allocation of quotas under an existing regime of import restrictions of the product in question and that Norway must therefore be considered to have acted under Article XIII:2(d). ... The Panel was of the view that to the extent that Norway had acted with effect to allocate import quotas for these products to six countries but had failed to allocate a share to Hong Kong, its ... action was inconsistent with Article XIII".

This report's conclusion was based in part on the fact that Hong Kong had a substantial interest in supplying most of the products at issue. Nonetheless, the report supports the argument that Article XIII:2(d) agreements may be challenged by Members not having a substantial interest, as the panel report drew no distinction between products where Hong Kong had a substantial interest and those where it did not. Panel Report on "Norway - Restrictions on Imports of Certain Textiles Products", adopted on 18 June 1980, BISD 27S/119, 125-126, paras. 15-16.

[370] Under the BFA, there is a general provision that provides that if a country with a country-specific share of the tariff quota indicates to the EC that it will be unable to deliver the allocated quantity, the amount of the short-fall is to be allocated in accordance with the BFA allocations (including to the "others" category). The BFA also provides that countries with country-specific shares of the tariff quota may jointly request the EC to allocate the short-fall differently, in which case the EC is required to do so. As a result, according to the Complainants, in 1995 and 1996, all of the tariff quota share allocated to Nicaragua, and 70 and 30 per cent, respectively, of the share allocated to Venezuela, have been reallocated to Colombia.

7.90 **Accordingly, we find that (i) the EC's allocation of tariff quota shares by agreement and by assignment to some Members not having a substantial interest in supplying bananas to the EC (including Nicaragua and Venezuela and certain ACP countries in respect of traditional and non-traditional exports) but not to other Members (such as Guatemala) and (ii) the tariff quota reallocation rules of the BFA, are inconsistent with the requirements of Article XIII:1.**

(iv) new members

7.91 We now consider the position of a Member who acceded to the WTO or GATT after the implementation of the EC common market organization for bananas (a "new" Member). As noted above, the general rule in the chapeau to Article XIII:2 indicates that the aim of Article XIII:2 is to give to Members the share of trade that they might be expected to obtain in the absence of a tariff quota. There is no requirement that a Member allocating shares of a tariff quota negotiate with non-Members, but when such countries accede to the WTO, they acquire rights, just as any other Member has under Article XIII whether or not they have a substantial interest in supplying the product in question.

7.92 Thus, although the EC reached an agreement with all Members who had a substantial interest in supplying the product at one point in time, under the consultation provisions of Article XIII:4, the EC would have to consider the interests of a new Member who had a substantial interest in supplying the product if that new Member requested it to do so.[371] The provisions on consultations and adjustments in Article XIII:4 mean in any event that the BFA could not be invoked to justify a permanent allocation of tariff quota shares. Moreover, while new Members cannot challenge the EC's agreements with Colombia and Costa Rica in the BFA on the grounds that the EC failed to negotiate and reach agreement with them, they otherwise have the same rights as those Complainants who were GATT contracting parties at the time the BFA was negotiated to challenge its consistency with Article XIII. Generally speaking, all Members benefit from all WTO rights.

7.93 **In this connection, we find that the failure of Ecuador's Protocol of Accession to address banana-related issues does not mean that Ecuador must accept the validity of the BFA as contained in the EC's Schedule or that it is precluded from invoking Article XIII:2 or XIII:4.**

(v) other arguments

7.94 In light of our findings in respect of Article XIII:1, we find it unnecessary to address the claims and arguments in respect of the interpretation of Article XIII:2(d), second sentence (e.g., the use of a "previous representative period" and "special factors") or in respect of the EC's enlargement to include Austria, Finland and Sweden.[372] We would note, however, that in order to bring its banana import regulations into line with Article XIII, the EC would have to take account of Article XIII:1 and XIII:2(d). In order to allocate country-specific tariff quota shares consistently with the requirements of Article XIII, the EC would have to base such shares on an appropriate previous representative period[373] and any special factors would have to be applied on a non-discriminatory basis (see *infra*).

---

[371] While the provisions of Article XIII:4 on consultations and adjustments seem to be primarily aimed at adjustments to quota shares allocated pursuant to Article XIII:2(d), second sentence, they also apply in the case where agreements were reached pursuant to Article XIII:2(d), first sentence, with Members having a substantial interest in supplying the product concerned. In addition, in so far as a new Member has a substantial interest in supplying that product, its share of the "others" category can be viewed, for purposes of Article XIII:4, as a provision established unilaterally relating to the allocation of an adequate quota.

[372] The Appellate Body has stated that "[a] panel need only address those claims which must be addressed in order to resolve the matter in issue in the dispute". Appellate Body Report on "United States - Measure Affecting Imports of Woven Wool Shirts and Blouses from India", issued on 25 April 1997, WT/DS33/AB/R, AB-1997-1, p. 19.

[373] In this regard, we note with approval the statement by the 1980 *Chilean Apples* panel:

b) The allocation of tariff quota shares to ACP countries: The Lomé waiver

7.95 In light of the finding that the EC's allocation of country-specific tariff quota shares for bananas to the ACP countries for both traditional and non-traditional bananas is not consistent with the requirements of Article XIII, we now consider whether that inconsistency is covered by the Lomé waiver. In this connection, we recall the findings of the second *Banana* panel report.[374] It found that (i) the specific duties levied by the EC on imports of bananas were inconsistent with Article II, (ii) the preferential tariff rates for banana imports from ACP countries were inconsistent with the requirements of Article I and (iii) certain procedures regarding the allocation of licences were inconsistent with the requirements of Articles I and III. It also found that the then effective EC rules did not discriminate between sources of supply in the sense of Article XIII because the licences issued to import bananas could be used to import bananas from any source. After the issuance of the panel report, which was not adopted by the GATT CONTRACTING PARTIES, the EC and the ACP countries that were GATT contracting parties requested a waiver (although they were and still are of the opinion that such a waiver is not needed) of the EC's Article I:1 obligations in order to permit the EC to provide preferential treatment to the ACP countries as required by the Lomé Convention.[375]

7.96 Subsequently, the Lomé waiver was adopted by the GATT CONTRACTING PARTIES in December 1994 and was extended by the WTO General Council in October 1996.[376] Under the operative paragraph of the Lomé waiver,

> the provisions of paragraph 1 of Article I of the General Agreement shall be waived, until 29 February 2000, to the extent necessary to permit the European Communities to provide preferential treatment for products originating in ACP States as required by the relevant provisions of the Fourth Lomé Convention, without being required to extend the same preferential treatment to like products of any other contracting party.

In order to determine whether the EC may allocate tariff quota shares to the ACP countries inconsistently with the requirements of Article XIII, we must determine whether those allocations are covered by the Lomé waiver. This determination involves resolving two interpretative issues. First, what preferential treatment in respect of bananas is "required" by the Lomé Convention? Second, does the Lomé waiver, which refers only to Article I:1 of GATT, encompass a waiver of Article XIII obligations as well?

"[I]n keeping with normal GATT practice, the Panel considered it appropriate to use as a 'representative period' a three-year period previous to 1979, the year in which the EC measures were in effect. Due to the existence of restrictions in 1976, the Panel held that that year could not be considered as representative, and that the year immediately preceding 1976 should be used instead. The Panel thus chose the years 1975, 1977, 1978 as a 'representative period'".

Panel Report on "EEC Restrictions on Imports of Dessert Apples - Complaint by Chile", adopted on 10 November 1980, BISD 27S/98, 113, para. 4.8. In the report of the "Panel on Poultry", issued on 21 November 1963, GATT Doc. L/2088, para. 10, the panel stated: "[T]he shares in the reference period of the various exporting countries in the Swiss market, which was free and competitive, afforded a fair guide as to the proportion of the increased German poultry consumption likely to be taken up by United States exports". See also Panel Report on "Japan - Restrictions on Imports of Certain Agricultural Products", adopted on 22 March 1988, BISD 35S/163, 226-227, para. 5.1.3.7.

374 Panel Report on "EEC - Import Regime for Bananas", issued 11 February 1994 (not adopted), DS38/R, p. 52, paras. 169-170.

375 The EC's Uruguay Round Schedule substituted a specific tariff in place of its prior *ad valorem* tariff binding for bananas. The consistency of that substitution with GATT rules is examined in para. 7.137 *et seq.* of the Guatemala-Honduras report. In respect of the panel's finding that the EC regime was inconsistent with the requirements of Article III, the EC did not change the regime and we examine that issue in para. 7.0.

376 EC - The Fourth ACP-EEC Convention of Lomé, Waiver Decision of 9 December 1994, L/7604, 19 December 1994; Extension of the Waiver, Decision of 14 October 1996, WT/L/186. Although the Lomé waiver was initially approved by the GATT CONTRACTING PARTIES until 29 February 2000, it was necessary for the WTO General Council to consider whether to extend it because under the Uruguay Round Understanding in Respect of Waivers of Obligations under the General Agreement on Tariffs and Trade 1994, all waivers in effect on the entry into force of the WTO Agreement expired two years thereafter (i.e., on 1 January 1997) unless extended.

(i) preferential treatment required by the Lomé Convention

7.97 As a preliminary matter, the EC and the ACP countries argue that the Panel is not authorized to interpret the Lomé Convention. We accept that we are not directed in our terms of reference to interpret the Lomé Convention. We recall that we have found that the EC's allocation of tariff quota shares to ACP countries is inconsistent with the requirements of Article XIII. However, in order to determine whether or not the EC's Article XIII obligations are waived, we must determine whether or not the Lomé waiver applies. That requires an interpretation of the Lomé waiver, which is a decision of the GATT CONTRACTING PARTIES, later extended by a WTO General Council decision. Since the waiver applies to action "necessary ... to provide preferential treatment ... *as required by the relevant provisions of the Fourth Lomé Convention*" (emphasis added), we must also determine what preferential treatment is required by the Lomé Convention.

7.98 The EC argues that the Panel must accept the EC and the ACP countries' interpretation of the Lomé Convention as valid since they are the parties to the Lomé Convention. We note that since the GATT CONTRACTING PARTIES incorporated a reference to the Lomé Convention into the Lomé waiver, the meaning of the Lomé Convention became a GATT/WTO issue, at least to that extent. Thus, we have no alternative but to examine the provisions of the Lomé Convention ourselves in so far as it is necessary to interpret the Lomé waiver. Moreover, we note that in their submissions to us, it appears that the EC and the ACP countries are not in accord on some aspects of what is required by the Lomé Convention.

7.99 We note that the Lomé Convention permits the EC to limit duty-free ACP country exports to the EC of products subject to common market organizations in the EC, i.e., many agricultural products. In respect of those products, Article 168(2)(a)(ii) of the Lomé Convention requires the EC to:

> take necessary measures to ensure more favourable treatment than that granted to third countries benefitting from the most-favoured-nation clause for the same products.

Moreover, in the case of bananas, Protocol 5 to the Lomé Convention places some restraints on the EC's right to limit imports of ACP bananas. It specifies in Article 1:

> In respect of banana exports to the Community markets, no ACP State shall be placed, as regards access to its traditional markets and its advantages on those markets, in a less favourable situation than in the past or at present.

Since the Lomé Convention was signed in 1989 and was expected to enter into force in 1990, we believe that the words "at present" should be interpreted to refer to 1990. A Joint Declaration to Protocol 5 provides that "Article 1 of Protocol 5 does not prevent the Community from establishing common rules for bananas as long as no ACP State, traditional supplier to the Community, is placed as regards access to, and advantages in, the Community in a less favourable situation than in the past or at present". The fact that the EC has done so obviously makes the meaning of Protocol 5 more difficult to ascertain since what was a system of individual EC member State markets has been transformed into one EC-wide market.

7.100 In allocating country-specific shares of the banana tariff quota to traditional ACP banana supplying countries, the EC set the shares at the level of each ACP country's "best-ever" exports to the EC, adjusted for certain other factors. The issue is whether it was required to do so by the Lomé Convention. The Complainants correctly point out that Protocol 5 does not guarantee that a certain level of banana exports will be achieved, and in response to questions of the Panel, the EC did not disagree. We recall that generally speaking, ACP countries formerly competed for the most part on either the French or UK markets and that on these markets they were protected by and large from import competition from other banana exporters. Given this degree of market access and advantage, the issue is how the EC could fulfil its obligations under Protocol 5 on an EC-wide market.

7.101 It appears that prior to Regulation 404/93 there were no set maximum levels for ACP exports to EC member State markets. While the ACP countries did not have specific quotas, they generally did enjoy protected access to one EC member State market (e.g., France, in the case of Cameroon and Côte d'Ivoire; Italy, in the case of Somalia; the UK, in the case of several Caribbean ACP countries).[377] Access to these markets was essentially controlled by ad hoc decisions.[378] We think that it can be reasonably contended that an EC-wide equivalent of the market access and advantages enjoyed by ACP countries in the past would be a country-specific tariff quota share, which may be assimilated to the past advantage of a protected EC member State market, set at their pre-1991 best-ever export levels. We note that since the pre-1991 best-ever export levels of the ACP countries occurred in different years for different countries (and in some cases, many years ago), there was no way for the EC to provide tariff quota shares covering such amounts consistently with the requirements of Article XIII:2, which requires shares to be based on a previous representative period, which has generally been interpreted to mean the most recent three years.[379] If the EC had (i) provided only a non-country-specific share for ACP countries or (ii) set shares for ACP countries at a level lower than their pre-1991 best-ever levels, an ACP country with the ability to export at its pre-1991 best-ever level might have been effectively prevented from doing so either by lack of the protected market provided by a specific-country share allocation or by the volume limit of its share allocation. Thus, in order not to place an ACP country in a less favourable situation as regards access to and advantages on its traditional markets, which is the EC's obligation under the Lomé Convention, it was not unreasonable for the EC to conclude that the Lomé Convention requires the allocation of country-specific tariff quota shares to the ACP countries in an amount of their pre-1991 best-ever exports of bananas to the EC. We accept that interpretation for purposes of our analysis of this issue.

7.102 There is, however, nothing in Protocol 5 that suggests that the EC is required to apply other factors to increase the shares of ACP countries above their best-ever export levels prior to 1991. While the Lomé Convention contains various provisions concerning trade promotion and assistance to ACP countries, there are no specific provisions established in the Lomé Convention that can be said to require country-specific tariff quota shares in excess of past exports. Thus, in our view, the EC is not required by the Lomé Convention to assign tariff quota shares to ACP countries in excess of their pre-1991 best-ever exports to the EC.

7.103 **Accordingly, we find that it was not unreasonable for the EC to conclude that the Lomé Convention requires the EC to allocate country-specific tariff quota shares to traditional ACP banana supplying countries in an amount of their pre-1991 best-ever exports to the EC. However, we do find that the allocation of tariff quota shares to ACP countries in excess of their pre-1991 best-ever exports to the EC is not required by the Lomé Convention.**

(ii) application of the Lomé waiver to the EC's Article XIII obligations

7.104 The Lomé waiver, as quoted above, permits the EC to provide preferential treatment to ACP countries as required by the Lomé Convention. However, by its terms, the Lomé waiver only waives compliance with the provisions of Article I:1. Thus, the issue arises whether the EC's obligations under Article XIII are also waived in connection with preferential treatment required by the Lomé Convention. The Complainants argue that they are not and that such an interpretation would be unprecedented. Indeed, the EC has not argued that the Lomé waiver should be interpreted to waive its obligations under Article XIII. In its response to a question from the Panel, the EC stated that it did not claim and "has no need to suggest" that the Lomé waiver covers a violation of Article XIII. Rather the EC argued that (i) it has not acted inconsistently with the requirements of Article XIII and (ii) the Lomé waiver permits the preferential treatment required by the Lomé Convention.

---

[377] Panel Report on "EEC - Member States' Import Regime for Bananas", issued on 3 June 1993 (not adopted), DS32/R, p. 3, para. 12.

[378] Id., pp. 4-5, 7, paras. 19-22, 37-38.

[379] See Panel Report on "EEC - Restrictions on Imports of Apples from Chile", adopted on 10 November 1980, BISD 27S/98, 113, para. 4.8.

Since we have rejected the EC's argument that it has complied with Article XIII and have found that the EC's allocation of country-specific shares to ACP countries is inconsistent with Article XIII, we believe that it is appropriate to consider also whether this inconsistency is covered by the Lomé waiver. In this regard, we note that the EC has also argued that where aspects of a measure have been found to be covered by the waiver for purposes of Article I, they should not be found to violate another GATT provision imposing MFN-like obligations similar to those that have been waived (see paragraph *7.224*).

7.105 In interpreting the scope of the Lomé waiver, we are mindful that the only GATT panel to interpret a waiver recalled that waivers are to be granted only in exceptional circumstances[380] and concluded that "their terms and conditions consequently have to be interpreted narrowly".[381] The waiver at issue in that case had no expiration date and permitted imposition of restrictions on a number of important agricultural products. A GATT working party on the waiver noted:

> Since the Decision [approving the waiver] refers to the provisions of Articles II and XI of the Agreement, it does not affect the obligations of the United States under any other provisions of the Agreement. In particular, as its obligations under Article XIII are not affected, the United States would acquire no right by virtue of this waiver to deviate from the rule of non-discrimination provided for in that Article.[382]

In light of this practice, we now consider the scope of the Lomé waiver, and, in particular, whether it waives the obligations of the EC under Article XIII in respect of the allocation of tariff quota shares based on the best-ever exports of bananas by the ACP countries to the EC.

7.106 We recall that Article 168(2)(a)(ii) of the Lomé Convention requires some preferential treatment for products from ACP sources. As we have found above, Protocol 5 to the Lomé Convention expands this general obligation in respect of traditional ACP banana exports in that it is not unreasonable for the EC to interpret it to require the EC to provide access opportunities to the EC market for the ACP countries in a volume no greater than their pre-1991 best-ever exports to the EC. As explained above, this can be accomplished only by country-specific tariff quota shares and by tariff quota shares that are larger than would be allowed under Article XIII (assuming that the best-ever exports did not occur within a representative period). If the Lomé waiver is interpreted to waive only compliance with the obligations of Article I:1, the waiver would effectively limit preferential treatment to tariff preferences. In our view, in light of the 75 ECU per tonne rate applicable to the EC's bound tariff quota, tariff preferences alone would not allow the EC to provide market access opportunities and advantages required of it by the Lomé Convention. In other words, in order to give real effect to the Lomé waiver, it needs to cover Article XIII to the extent necessary to allow the EC to allocate country-specific tariff quota shares to the ACP countries in the amount of their pre-1991 best-ever banana exports to the EC. Otherwise, the EC could not practically fulfil its basic obligation under the Lomé Convention in respect of bananas, as we have found that it was not unreasonable for the EC to conclude that the Lomé Convention may be interpreted to require country-specific tariff quota shares at levels not compatible with Article XIII. Since it was the objective of the Lomé waiver to permit the EC to fulfil that basic obligation, logically we have no choice therefore but to interpret the waiver so that it accomplishes that objective. In fact, such an interpretation would be consistent with the terms of this particular waiver as it applies to preferential

[380] GATT, art. XXV:5; WTO, art. IX:3-4.

[381] Panel Report on "US - Restrictions on the Importation of Sugar and Sugar-Containing Products Applied Under the 1955 Waiver and Under the Headnote to the Schedule of Tariff Concessions", adopted on 7 November 1990, BISD 37S/228, 256-257, para. 5.9.

[382] Working Party Report on "Import Restrictions Imposed by the United States Under Section 22 of the United States Agricultural Adjustment Act", adopted on 5 March 1955, BISD 3S/141, 144, para. 10.

treatment generally and not, as is mostly the case with other currently effective waivers, only to preferential *tariff* treatment.[383]

7.107 Such an interpretation is also supported by the close relationship between Articles I and XIII:1, both of which prohibit discriminatory treatment. Article I requires MFN treatment in respect of "rules and formalities in connection with importation", a phrase that has been interpreted broadly in past GATT practice,[384] such that it can appropriately be held to cover rules related to tariff quota allocations. Such rules are clearly rules applied in connection with importation. Indeed, they are critical to the determination of the amount of duty to be imposed. To describe the relationship somewhat differently, Article I establishes a general principle requiring non-discriminatory treatment in respect of, *inter alia*, rules and formalities in connection with importation. Article XIII:1 is an application of that principle in a specific situation, i.e., the administration of quantitative restrictions and tariff quotas. In that sense, the scope of Article XIII:1 is identical with that of Article I.

7.108 The foregoing considerations suggest that the Lomé waiver should be interpreted so as to waive compliance with the obligations of Article XIII, to the extent indicated above. We must consider, however, whether such a conclusion is consistent with past GATT practice that waivers are to be interpreted narrowly. Our interpretation of the Lomé waiver is narrow in the sense that the Lomé waiver itself has been qualified by the fact that it is applicable only to preferential treatment "required" by the Lomé Convention and does not extend to all preferential treatment that the EC might wish to give to the ACP countries. Thus, there is no danger of an overly broad interpretation of its scope. In our view, we only acknowledge what is implied in the decision to grant the waiver in the first place.

7.109 In reaching this conclusion, however, we note our view that the scope of the Lomé waiver lacks precision. Future waiver negotiations will have to deal more precisely with the issues raised in this case in order to reduce differences in interpretation.

7.110 **In light of these factors, to the extent that we have found that the EC has acted inconsistently with the requirements of Article XIII:1 (*infra*), we find that the Lomé waiver waives that inconsistency with Article XIII:1 to the extent necessary to permit the EC to allocate shares of its banana tariff quota to specific traditional ACP banana supplying countries in an amount not exceeding their pre-1991 best-ever exports to the EC.**

c) The allocation of tariff quota shares to BFA countries

7.111 In our general discussion above of Article XIII, we found that the EC's allocation of shares in its tariff quota to the BFA countries not having a substantial interest in supplying bananas and in respect of non-traditional ACP bananas is inconsistent with the requirements of Article XIII. In this section, we consider whether any such inconsistency may be permitted because of (i) the inclusion of the banana tariff quota allocation to BFA countries and in respect of non-traditional ACP bananas in the EC's Schedule attached to the Marrakesh Protocol or (ii) the priority provision of the Agreement on Agriculture.

---

[383] There are three other waivers now in force for preferential treatment to groups of developing countries. These waivers cover Canadian preferences to Caribbean countries and US preferences to Caribbean countries and to Andean countries. In each of these three cases, the waiver is limited by its terms to preferential *tariff* treatment. CARIBCAN, WT/L/185; Caribbean Basin Economic Recovery Act, WT/L/104; Andean Trade Preference Act, WT/L/184. The waiver in respect of United States - Former Trust Territory of the Pacific Islands, WT/L/183, applies also to non-tariff preferential treatment.

[384] Panel Report on "United States - Denial of Most-favoured-nation Treatment as to Non-rubber Footwear from Brazil", adopted on 19 June 1992, BISD 39S/128, 150, para. 6.8 (Article I:1 applies to rules for revocation of countervailing duties).

(i) inclusion of the BFA tariff quota shares in the EC Schedule

7.112 The EC argues that even if the tariff quota share allocations to the BFA countries and in respect of non-traditional ACP bananas do not satisfy the requirements of Article XIII, they are consistent with GATT rules because of their inclusion in the EC's Schedule as a result of the Uruguay Round negotiations. The Complainants argue that a prior adopted GATT panel report (the so-called *Sugar Headnote* case)[385] supports the conclusion that tariff bindings in schedules cannot justify inconsistencies with the requirements of generally applicable GATT rules. The EC responds that the Uruguay Round Schedules are of a different nature than past GATT tariff protocols, thereby undermining the legal reasoning underpinning the *Sugar Headnote* case, and that, in any event, the inclusion of the BFA tariff quota shares in its Schedule overrides Article XIII because of the priority provision of the Agreement on Agriculture.

7.113 The panel in the *Sugar Headnote* case found that qualifications on tariff bindings do not override other GATT provisions after an analysis of the wording of Article II, its object, purpose and context, and the drafting history of the provision. Although it made no mention of the Vienna Convention, it seems to have followed closely Articles 31 and 32 thereof.[386] Its analysis was as follows:

> 5.1 ... The United States argues that the proviso "subject to the terms, conditions or qualifications set forth in that Schedule" in Article II:1(b) permits contracting parties to include qualifications relating to quantitative restrictions in their Schedule. The United States had made use of this possibility by reserving in its Schedule of Concessions the right to impose quota limitations on imports of sugar in certain circumstances. Since the restrictions on the importation of sugar conformed to the qualifications set out in the Schedule of the United States, and the Schedules of Concessions were, according to Article II:7, an integral part of the General Agreement, the restrictions were consistent with the United States obligations under that Agreement. Australia argues that qualifications to concessions made in accordance with Article II:1(b) cannot justify measures contrary to other provisions of the General Agreement, in particular not quantitative restrictions inconsistent with Article XI:1.
> ...
>
> 5.2 The Panel first examined the issue in the light of the wording of Article II. It noted that in Article II:1(b), the words "subject to the ... qualifications set forth in that Schedule" are used in conjunction with the words "shall ... be exempt from ordinary customs duties in excess of those set forth in [the Schedule]". This suggests that Article II:1(b) permits contracting parties to qualify the obligation to exempt products from customs duties in excess of the levels specified in the Schedule, not however to qualify their obligations under other Articles of the General Agreement. The Panel further noted that the title of Article II is "Schedules of Concessions" and that the ordinary meaning of the word "to concede" is "to grant or yield". This also suggests in the view of the Panel that Article II permits contracting parties to incorporate into their Schedules acts yielding rights under the General Agreement but not acts diminishing obligations under that Agreement.
>
> 5.3 The Panel then examined the issue in the light of the purpose of the General Agreement. It noted that one of the basic functions of the General Agreement is, according to its Preamble, to provide a legal framework enabling contracting parties to enter into "reciprocal and mutually advantageous arrangements directed to the substantial reduction of tariffs and other barriers to trade". Where the General Agreement mentions specific types of negotiations, it refers to negotiations aimed at the reduction of barriers to trade

[385] Panel Report on "US - Restrictions on Imports of Sugar", adopted on 22 June 1989, BISD 36S/331, 341-343, paras. 5.2-5.7.

[386] These provisions of the Vienna Convention are quoted in para. 7.0 supra.

(Articles IV(d), XVII:3 and XXVIII bis). This supports in the view of the Panel the assumption that Article II gives contracting parties the possibility to incorporate into the legal framework of the General Agreement commitments additional to those already contained in the General Agreement and to qualify such additional commitments, not however to reduce their commitments under other provisions of that Agreement.

5.4 The Panel then examined the issue in the context of the provisions of the General Agreement related to Article II. It noted that negotiations on obstacles to trade created by the operation of state-trading enterprises may be conducted under Article XVII:3 and that a note to that provision provides that such negotiations

> may be directed towards the reduction of duties and other charges on imports and exports or towards the conclusion of any other mutually satisfactory arrangement consistent with the provisions of this Agreement (See paragraph 4 of Article II and the note to that paragraph) (emphasis added).

The negotiations foreseen in Article XVII:3 are thus not to result in arrangements inconsistent with the General Agreement, in particular not quantitative restrictions made effective through state-trading that are not justified by an exception to Article XI:1. The Panel saw no reason why a different principle should apply to quantitative restrictions made effective by other means.

5.5 The Panel then examined the issue in the light of the practice of the CONTRACTING PARTIES. The Panel noted that the CONTRACTING PARTIES adopted in 1955 the report of the Review Working Party on Other Barriers to Trade, which had concluded that:

> there was nothing to prevent contracting parties, when they negotiate for the binding or reduction of tariffs, from negotiating on matters, such as subsidies, which might affect the practical effects of tariff concessions, and from incorporating in the appropriate schedule annexed to the Agreement the results of such negotiations; provided that the results of such negotiations should not conflict with other provisions of the Agreement." (emphasis added) (BISD 3S/225).

Whether the proviso in this decision is regarded as a policy recommendation, as the United States argues, or as the confirmation of a legal requirement, as Australia claims, it does support, in the view of the Panel, the conclusion that the CONTRACTING PARTIES did not envisage that qualifications in Schedules established in accordance with Article II:1(b) could justify measures inconsistent with the other Articles of the General Agreement.

5.6 The Panel finally examined the issue in the light of the drafting history. It noted that the reference to "terms and qualifications" was included in a draft of the present Article II:1(b) during the Second Session of the Preparatory Committee of the United Nations Conference on Trade and Employment. The original draft had referred only to "conditions". This amendment was proposed and adopted "in order to provide more generally for the sort of qualifications actually provided in the form of notes in the specimen Schedule. A number of these notes are, in effect, additional concessions rather than conditions governing the tariff bindings to which they relate" (E/PC/T/153 and E/PC/T/W/295). Schedule provisions qualifying obligations under the General Agreement were not included in the specimen Schedule nor was the possibility of such Schedule provisions mentioned by the drafters. The

Panel therefore found that the drafting history did not support the interpretation advanced by the United States.

5.7 For the reasons stated in the preceding paragraphs, the Panel found that Article II:1(b) does not permit contracting parties to qualify their obligations under other provisions of the General Agreement and that the provisions in the United States GATT Schedule of Concessions can consequently not justify the maintenance of quantitative restrictions on the importation of certain sugars inconsistent with the application of Article XI:1.

7.114 We agree with the analysis of the *Sugar Headnote* panel report and note that Article II was not changed in any relevant way as a result of the Uruguay Round. Thus, based on the *Sugar Headnote* case, we conclude that the EC's inclusion of allocations inconsistent with the requirements of Article XIII in its Schedule does not prevent them from being challenged by other Members. We note in this regard that the Uruguay Round tariff schedules were prepared with full knowledge of the *Sugar Headnote* panel report, which was adopted by the GATT CONTRACTING PARTIES in the middle of the Round (June 1989). This is particularly significant in light of the Appellate Body's statement that "[a]dopted panel reports are an important part of the GATT *acquis*. They are often taken into account by subsequent panels. They create legitimate expectations among Members, and, therefore should be taken into account where they are relevant to any dispute".[387]

7.115 The EC further argues that the principle of *pacta sunt servanda* supports its position that the BFA should override GATT rules. However, in our view, that principle applies as well to Article II, as interpreted by the *Sugar Headnote* case. We cannot accept that a conflict between Article II and the BFA should necessarily be resolved in the BFA's favour. It was to ensure consistency with the basic GATT rules that the *Sugar Headnote* panel reached the conclusions it did. As that panel stated (paragraph 5.2): "Article II permits contracting parties to incorporate into their Schedules acts yielding rights under the General Agreement but not acts diminishing obligations under that Agreement". That rule is a basic agreement of the Members that must be enforced.

7.116 The EC also notes that Article II:7 of GATT incorporates schedules into Part I of GATT, which contains Articles I and II, and argues that one provision of Part I such as Article II may not be given priority over another (i.e., the schedules). However, we are of the opinion that if there is a conflict between a schedule and GATT rules, it is necessary to resolve it, and that is what the *Sugar Headnote* panel did.[388]

7.117 Finally, the EC argues that the result in the *Sugar Headnote* case was necessary under GATT practice because tariff protocols, which added tariff commitments to schedules, were not accepted by all GATT contracting parties. It further argues that such a result is not necessary in the context of the WTO because all Members accepted all the results of the Uruguay Round. The *Sugar Headnote* panel's analysis was, in our view, a straightforward exercise in treaty interpretation under Vienna Convention principles. It made no mention that the result it reached was "necessary" under GATT practice. Moreover, the US measure at issue in the *Sugar Headnote* case first appeared in the Annecy and Torquay Protocols, both of which were signed by all GATT contracting parties at the time.[389] Thus, these Protocols were in this respect similar to the schedules attached to the WTO Agreement.

---

[387] Appellate Body Report on "Japan - Taxes on Alcoholic Beverages", adopted on 1 November 1996, WT/DS8/AB/R, WT/DS10/AB/R, WT/DS11/AB/R, AB-1996-2, p.15.

[388] The incorporation of schedules into Part I was done only because "it was intended that Part II [of GATT] would be immediately superseded by the [Havana] Charter provisions when the Charter entered into force". Analytical Index: Guide to GATT Law and Practice, 6th rev. ed. 1995, p.99.

[389] Contracting Parties to the General Agreement on Tariffs and Trade, Status of Legal Instruments, pp. xxi, 3--2.1-2.4, 3--3.1-3.4.

7.118 **Thus, we find that the inclusion of the BFA tariff quota shares in the EC's Schedule does not permit the EC to act inconsistently with the requirements of Article XIII of GATT.**

[7.119 Used in the Guatemala-Honduras report.]
7.119 Since we have found that the inclusion of the BFA in the EC's Schedule does not permit the EC to act inconsistently with the requirements of Article XIII of GATT, we do not need to address Guatemala's argument that it reserved its rights in respect of the inclusion of the BFA tariff quotas in the EC's Schedule at the time it accepted the WTO Agreement. In respect of this argument, we would note, however, that Article XVI:5 of the WTO Agreement does not permit reservations.

(ii) Agreement on Agriculture

7.120 The EC argues that the provisions of the Agreement on Agriculture prevail over GATT rules such as Article XIII and that the inclusion by the EC of the BFA tariff quota shares in its tariff schedules means that they prevail over Article XIII, even if the *Sugar Headnote* case remains a valid interpretation of GATT rules.

7.121 In examining this argument, we note that the Agreement on Agriculture was intended to make agricultural products subject to strengthened and more operationally effective GATT rules. In the Preamble to the Agreement, Members recall:

> their long-term objective as agreed at the Mid-Term Review of the Uruguay Round "is to establish a fair and market-oriented agricultural trading system and that a reform process should be initiated through the negotiation of commitments on support and protection and through the establishment of strengthened and more operationally effective GATT rules and disciplines."

7.122 In some cases, the results of the agricultural negotiations were not consistent with the rules found in other WTO agreements. For example, Article 4.2 of the Agreement on Agriculture prohibits the use of certain measures that might otherwise be authorized by Article XI:2 of GATT; Article 5 of the Agreement on Agriculture permits the use of certain measures that might otherwise be questioned under Articles II and XIX of GATT and the Agreement on Safeguards. In order to establish priority for rules of the Agreement on Agriculture, Article 21.1 of that Agreement specifies:

> The provisions of GATT 1994 and of other Multilateral Trade Agreements in Annex 1A to the WTO Agreement shall apply subject to the provisions of this Agreement [i.e., the Agreement on Agriculture].

It is clear from Article 21.1 that the provisions of the Agreement on Agriculture prevail over GATT and the other Annex 1A agreements. But there must be a provision of the Agreement on Agriculture that is relevant in order for this priority provision to apply. It is not the case that Article 21.1 of the Agreement on Agriculture means that no GATT/WTO rules apply to trade in agricultural products unless they are explicitly incorporated into the Agreement on Agriculture. We note that one of the purposes of the Agreement on Agriculture is to bring agriculture under regular GATT/WTO disciplines. It is against this background that we consider the EC's argument.

7.123 There is no provision of the Agreement on Agriculture that incorporates tariff bindings related to agricultural products into the Agreement on Agriculture. While the Annexes to the Agreement are incorporated into the Agreement by Article 21.2 thereof, tariff bindings are not. Indeed, under paragraph 1 of the Marrakesh Protocol, the Uruguay Round schedules attached to that protocol, which include the agricultural tariff bindings, are explicitly made schedules to GATT.

7.124 An examination of the Agreement on Agriculture reveals that most of its provisions and annexes are concerned with domestic support and export subsidies and do not relate to market access concessions generally except for Articles 4 (market access) and 5 (special safeguard provisions) and Annex 5 (special treatment with respect to paragraph 2 of Article 4). Since we are not concerned here with special treatment or special safeguard measures, only Article 4 itself might be relevant. It reads as follows:

> 1. Market access concessions contained in Schedules relate to bindings and reductions of tariffs, and to other market access commitments specified therein.
>
> 2. Members shall not maintain, resort to, or revert to any measures of the kind which have been required to be converted into ordinary customs duties [footnote omitted], except as otherwise provided for in Article 5 and Annex 5.

In our view, Article 4.1 is not a substantive provision, but is a statement of where market access commitments can be found. The definition of "market access concessions" (Article 1(g) of the Agreement on Agriculture) makes it clear that the Schedules annexed to Article II of GATT also contain the import quota commitments undertaken pursuant to Annex 5 of the Agreement on Agriculture (as well as an identification of the tariff lines which are eligible for the special safeguard provisions of Article 5 of the Agreement on Agriculture). If the Agreement on Agriculture would have allowed for country-specific allocations of tariff quotas there would have been a specific provision to this effect in deviation from Article XIII:2(d) as with the special treatment provisions of Annex 5. In contrast, Article 4.2 is a substantive provision in that it prohibits the use of certain non-tariff barriers, subject to certain qualifications. As a substantive provision, it prevails over such GATT provisions as Article XI:2(c).

7.125 Moreover, neither Article 4.1 nor 4.2 of the Agreement on Agriculture provides that agricultural tariff bindings have a special standing vis à vis other tariff bindings or that a market access commitment included therein is absolved from complying with other GATT rules. Indeed, we note that there are a number of provisions in the Agreement on Agriculture which simply refer to other agreements or decisions that are not incorporated into the Agreement on Agriculture. The reference in Article 14 to the Agreement on Sanitary and Phytosanitary Measures is one example; the reference to the Decision on Measures Covering the Possible Negative Effects of the Reform Programme on Least-Developed and Net Food-Importing Developing Countries in Article 16 is another example. These "cross-reference" provisions may be explained by the attempt of the framers of the Agreement on Agriculture to provide a complete overview of the Uruguay Round results in agriculture, since these matters are referred to generally in the preamble to the Agreement.

7.126 Finally, we note that, pursuant to Article 21 of the Agreement on Agriculture, GATT rules apply "subject to" the provisions of the Agreement on Agriculture, a wording that clearly suggests priority for the latter. But giving priority to Article 4.1 of the Agreement on Agriculture, which simply "relates" market access concessions to Members' goods schedules as attached to GATT by the Marrakesh Protocol, does not necessitate, or even suggest, a limitation on the application of Article XIII. The provisions are complementary, and do not clash. Thus, Article 21 of the Agreement on Agriculture is not relevant in this case.

7.127 **Accordingly, we find that neither the negotiation of the BFA and its inclusion in the EC's Schedule nor the Agreement on Agriculture permit the EC to act inconsistently with the requirements of Article XIII of GATT.**

d) Tariff quota share allocations and Article I:1

[7.128-7.130 Used in the Guatemala-Honduras report.]

7.128 Guatemala and Honduras claim that the EC's tariff quota share allocations to the ACP and BFA countries and the reallocation rules of the BFA are inconsistent with the requirements of Article I:1 because they constitute "rules and formalities" in connection with importation and are applied on a non-MFN basis. The EC responds that these issues should be dealt with under Article XIII.

7.129 These matters may fall within the definition of "rules and formalities" as that term is used in Article I:1. In our view, however, it is more appropriate to consider these issues under Article XIII because that is the more specific provision. This is in accord with past GATT practice, where panels have resolved similar issues under Article XIII, without resort to Article I.[390]

7.130 Accordingly, we make no finding on the compatibility of the EC's tariff quota share allocations and BFA reallocation rules with Article I:1.

2. *Tariff issues*

7.131 The Complainants have not challenged the tariff preferences accorded by the EC to traditional ACP bananas, i.e., bananas in traditional amounts from ACP countries that traditionally supplied the EC market. They have, however, claimed that the tariff preferences granted by the EC to non-traditional ACP bananas, i.e., bananas from ACP countries that have not traditionally supplied the EC market and bananas from historical suppliers in excess of their traditional supplies, are inconsistent with the requirements of Article I:1 of GATT. The tariff preference in the case of non-traditional ACP bananas imported under the relevant EC tariff quota share (90,000 tonnes) is 75 ECU per tonne (0 versus 75 ECU), while for over-quota bananas it is 100 ECU per tonne (in 1995: 822 ECU versus 722 ECU). The EC responds that to the extent that these tariff preferences are inconsistent with Article I:1, the inconsistency is permitted by the Lomé waiver.

7.132 Article I:1 provides in relevant part as follows:

> With respect to customs duties and charges of any kind imposed on or in connection with importation ..., any advantage, favour, privilege or immunity granted by any Member to any product originating in ... any other country shall be accorded immediately and unconditionally to the like product originating in ... the territories of all other Members.

7.133 It is clear that the above-described tariff preferences for ACP bananas are inconsistent with Article I:1 since ACP and other bananas are like products and the lower tariffs on ACP-origin bananas are not provided unconditionally to bananas from other Members. The issue is whether the Lomé waiver covers the inconsistency. As noted above, the Lomé waiver provides:

> the provisions of paragraph 1 of Article I of the General Agreement shall be waived, until 29 February 2000, to the extent necessary to permit the European Communities to provide preferential treatment for products originating in ACP States as required by the relevant provisions of the Fourth Lomé Convention, without being required to extend the same preferential treatment to like products of any other contracting party.[391]

7.134 In this regard, we note that Article 168(2)(a)(ii) of the Lomé Convention provides that the EC:

> shall take the necessary measures to ensure more favourable treatment than that granted to third countries benefitting from the most-favoured-nation clause for the same products.

[390] Panel Report on "EEC Restrictions on Imports of Apples from Chile", adopted on 10 November 1980, BISD 27S/98, 112, para. 4.1, Panel Report on "EEC - Restrictions on Imports of Dessert Apples - Complaint by Chile", adopted on 22 June 1989, BISD 36S/93, 133, para. 12.28.

[391] EC - The Fourth ACP-EEC Convention of Lomé, Waiver Decision of 9 December 1994, L/7604, 19 December 1994; Extension of the Waiver, Decision of 14 October 1996, WT/L/186.

While Members in granting the Lomé waiver could have limited the extent to which the EC could provide preferential tariff treatment under Article I:1, they did not do so. Thus, even though waivers must be interpreted strictly,[392] it seems to us that the preferential tariff for non-traditional ACP bananas is clearly a tariff preference of the sort that the Lomé waiver was designed to cover. In our view, in light of the requirement of Article 168(2)(a)(ii) of the Lomé Convention, the Lomé waiver permits the EC to grant tariff preferences to ACP countries on non-traditional bananas.

7.135 The Complainants argue, however, that the EC Court of Justice has ruled that Protocol 5 of the Lomé Convention supersedes Article 168(2)(a)(ii) with the result that the EC is not required to give non-traditional ACP bananas more favourable treatment pursuant to that provision. We do not agree with this characterization of the Court of Justice decision.[393] In the part of the decision cited by the Complainants, the Court of Justice rejected the argument that the EC Council could not rely on Article 168(2)(a) in adopting the EC banana regime. Indeed, the Court states "the import of bananas from ACP States falls under Article 168(2)(a)(ii) of the Lomé Convention". The issue in the case was whether the Lomé Convention required that all ACP bananas had to be admitted duty-free, and the Court ruled that Protocol 5 did not require that. It did not rule that Article 168(2)(a)(ii), which generally requires some preferential treatment of ACP products, did not apply to bananas not covered by Protocol 5.

7.136 **Accordingly, we find that to the extent that the EC's preferential tariff treatment of non traditional ACP bananas is inconsistent with its obligations under Article I:1, those obligations have been waived by the Lomé waiver.**

[7.137-7.141 Used in the Guatemala-Honduras report.]

7.137 Guatemala challenges the EC tariffs as being inconsistent with the EC's pre-Uruguay Round tariff binding on bananas of 20 per cent ad valorem, which it asserts was not properly modified through negotiations under Article XXVIII of GATT 1947. Guatemala recalls that despite the EC's former tariff binding of 20 per cent ad valorem on bananas, in 1993, the EC established a tariff quota for bananas and implemented a duty on in-quota bananas of 100 ECU per tonne and on over-quota bananas of 850 ECU per tonne. It later notified the GATT Secretariat of its intention to renegotiate its pre-Uruguay Round tariff binding on bananas under Article XXVIII. The EC responds that its 20 per cent tariff binding was replaced by the inclusion of the new tariff binding in its Uruguay Round Schedule.

7.138 The second *Banana* panel report found that the new EC duties were inconsistent with the requirements of Article II.[394] We agree with that finding. The issue for this Panel is whether that inconsistency was cured by the inclusion in the EC's Uruguay Round Schedule of a new binding in respect of bananas, which establishes an in-quota duty of 75 ECU per tonne and an over-quota duty of 850 ECU per tonne, falling to 680 ECU per tonne at the end of the implementation period for the Uruguay Round commitments.

7.139 The purpose of tariff schedules is to make it clear what tariff commitments Members have made and Article II requires Members to adhere to those commitments. In the Uruguay Round of Multilateral Trade Negotiations, all original Members participated and a complex new set of agreements and commitments was entered into, replacing GATT 1947 and various related side agreements. In this connection, many changes in tariff bindings were made, including certain tariff increases, and it was for all prospective members of the

[392] Panel Report on "US - Restrictions on the Importation of Sugar and Sugar-Containing Products Applied Under the 1955 Waiver and Under the Headnote to the Schedule of Tariff Concessions", adopted on 7 November 1990, BISD 37S/228, 256-257, para. 5.9.

[393] Germany v. Council, Case C-280/93, para. 101 (Judgment of 5 October 1994).

[394] Panel Report on "EEC - Import Regime for Bananas", issued on 11 February 1994 (not adopted), DS38/R, pp.38-40, paras. 132-136.

WTO to decide whether they would accept the new agreements, including the new bindings proposed by other participants. Under Article XVI:5 of the WTO Agreement, reservations are not permitted, except to the extent provided for in a WTO agreement; there is no such provision in GATT 1994. In this regard, we recognize the importance of not undermining the stability and predictability of tariff bindings. In light of the foregoing, in our view, the tariff rates specified in the EC's Uruguay Round Schedule are the valid EC tariff bindings in respect of bananas.

7.140 Furthermore, we note that there is a basic difference between this finding in respect of *tariff rates* and our finding in respect of the BFA tariff quota *allocations*. Under Article II of GATT, the purpose of the tariff schedules is to set clearly the tariff rate maxima that must be respected. As interpreted in the *Sugar Headnote* case, as discussed above, Article II of GATT does not allow Members to qualify their *non-tariff* obligations in their tariff schedules in a way that is inconsistent with WTO obligations.

7.141 We find that the tariff rates specified in the EC's Uruguay Round Schedule are the valid EC tariff bindings in respect of bananas.

3. The EC banana import licensing procedures

7.142 We turn now to an examination of the EC's banana import licensing procedures.[395] We give an overview of the claims of the Complainants and explain how we will organize our discussion of the numerous issues raised by those claims.

7.143 Altogether, the Complainants, jointly or severally, have raised more than 40 different claims against the EC licensing regime in general, or against specific elements thereof, under provisions of GATT, the Licensing Agreement and the TRIM's Agreement.[396]

7.144 We begin by considering three general issues: (i) whether the Licensing Agreement covers licences relating to tariff quotas; (ii) the relationship between claims under GATT 1994 and the Annex 1A Agreements in light of the General Interpretative Note to Annex 1A; and (iii) whether the EC licensing procedures should be analysed as one or two regimes.

a) General issues

(i) scope of the Licensing Agreement

7.145 The first general interpretative issue is whether the Licensing Agreement applies to tariff quotas. The Complainants argue that the administration of tariff quotas is subject to the disciplines embodied in the Licensing Agreement and have raised claims under Articles 1.2, 1.3, 3.2 and 3.5 of that Agreement. The EC takes the opposite view. It argues that the Licensing Agreement applies to "import restrictions". Since in its view tariff quotas do not constitute import restrictions, tariff quotas are not subject to the provisions of the

[395] The EC common organization of the banana market, including the licensing regime and its administrative application, encompass more than 100 different regulations. The most important ones are: Council Regulation (EC) No. 404/93 of 13 February 1993 on the common organization of the market in bananas (O.J. L 47/1 of 25 February 1993); Commission Regulation (EEC) No. 1442/93 of 10 June 1993 laying down detailed rules for the application of the arrangements for importing bananas into the Community (O.J. L 142/6 of 12 June 1993); Council Regulation (EC) No. 3290/94 of 22 December 1994 on the adjustments and transitional arrangements required in the agricultural sector in order to implement the agreements concluded during the Uruguay Round of multilateral trade negotiations (O.J. L 349/105 of 31 December 1994); and Commission Regulation (EC) No. 478/95 on additional rules for the application of Council Regulation (EEC) No. 404/93 as regards the tariff quota arrangements for imports of bananas into the Community and amending Regulation (EEC) No. 1442/93 (O.J. L 49/13 of 4 March 1995).

[396] We recall that we decided not to consider claims under Article 5 of the TRIM's Agreement and under Article 4.2 of the Agreement on Agriculture because they were not or not adequately raised in the request for the establishment of the Panel. See para. 7.0 supra.

Licensing Agreement. It also argues that import licences are tradeable and are not a "prior condition for importation" within the meaning of Article 1.1 of the Licensing Agreement since import licences are required only for the purpose of benefitting from the in-quota duty rate.

7.146 We therefore turn to an examination of the terms of the Licensing Agreement, interpreted in light of their context and of the object and purpose of the Agreement. Article 1.1 of the Licensing Agreement provides (footnote omitted):

> For the purpose of this Agreement, import licensing is defined as administrative procedures used for the operation of import licensing regimes requiring the submission of an application or other documentation (other than that required for customs purposes) to the relevant administrative body as a prior condition for importation into the customs territory of the importing Member.

7.147 The terms of Article 1.1 do not explicitly include, or exclude, the administration of tariff quotas from the coverage of the Licensing Agreement. Its terms define "import licensing" as "administrative procedures used for the operation of import licensing regimes". However, footnote 1 to Article 1.1 further defines "administrative procedures" to include "those procedures referred to as 'licensing' as well as other similar administrative procedures". Accordingly, irrespective of whether the term "licensing" is used, in our opinion, administrative procedures are covered by the Licensing Agreement provided that they have a purpose similar to licensing. In other words, Article 1 of the Licensing Agreement, as further elaborated by footnote 1 thereto, clearly follows a functional approach. It embodies a comprehensive coverage of the Licensing Agreement, except as specifically limited.

7.148 Two limitations on the scope of the Licensing Agreement may be derived from the terms of Article 1.1. First, the notion of "import licensing" is limited to procedures "requiring the submission of an application or other documentation (other than that required for customs purposes) to the relevant administrative body". The licensing procedures used by the EC for the administration of the in-quota imports of bananas meet the terms of this limitation because they require the submission of an application, as well as other documentation.

7.149 Second, Article 1.1 limits "import licensing" to regimes requiring the "submission of an application or other documentation" as a "prior condition for importation into the customs territory of the importing Member". In our view, the requirement to present an import licence upon importation constitutes a "prior condition for importation", irrespective of whether that requirement applies to the administration of a quantitative restriction or a tariff quota. The mere possibility to import a particular product at a higher tariff rate outside a tariff quota without being subjected to the same or any licensing requirement does not alter the fact that the importation of a particular product within a tariff quota at a lower duty rate is made dependent upon the presentation of an import licence as a prior condition for importation at that lower rate.[397]

7.150 Thus, while Article 1.1 does not specifically include licences for tariff quotas within its scope, it does not exclude them. Indeed, the general definition of the scope of application in Article 1.1 of the Licensing Agreement is formulated in a comprehensive manner: import licensing procedures are mentioned without any reference to the underlying measure for whose administration they are employed. Moreover, procedures which

[397] According to Article 18 of Regulation 1442/93, imports outside of the EC bound tariff quota are subject to automatic licensing.

are not in explicit terms labelled as "licensing" but pursue a similar purpose are included in the scope of the Licensing Agreement by virtue of footnote 1 to Article 1.1.[398]

7.151 Article 3.1 of the Licensing Agreement also defines the coverage of the Agreement by providing that non-automatic licensing is covered by the Agreement as follows:

> The following provisions, in addition to those in paragraphs 1 through 11 of Article 1, shall apply to non-automatic import licensing procedures. Non-automatic import licensing procedures are defined as import licensing not falling within the definition contained in paragraph 1 of Article 2.

Article 2:1 of the Licensing Agreement, in turn, reads:

> Automatic import licensing is defined as import licensing where approval of the application is granted in all cases, and which is in accordance with the requirements of paragraph 2(a).

Given that the approval of an application for an import licence is not, in the sense of Article 2.1 of the Licensing Agreement, granted by the relevant administrative bodies in all cases, the EC licensing procedures fall within the category of non-automatic import licensing.

7.152 Further indication of the scope of Article 3 of the Licensing Agreement can be derived from the wording of the first sentence of Article 3.2:

> Non-automatic licensing shall not have trade-restrictive or -distortive effects on imports additional to those caused by the imposition of the *restriction* (emphasis added).

This raises the question whether the term "restriction" should be interpreted narrowly so as to encompass only quantitative restrictions, or whether it should be read to include also other measures such as tariff quotas.

7.153 In this context, Article 3.3 of the Licensing Agreement offers implicit guidance:

> In the case of licensing requirements for purposes other than the implementation of quantitative restrictions, Members shall publish sufficient information for other Members and traders to know the basis for granting and/or allocating licences.

The phrase "other than the implementation of quantitative restrictions" makes clear that the coverage of Article 3 of the Licensing Agreement is not limited to procedures used in the implementation of quantitative restrictions. On the contrary, the wording of Article 3.3 implies that the disciplines concerning non-automatic licensing also cover procedures used for the administration of other measures.

7.154 Moreover, the use of the term "restriction" in Article 3.2 is not a reason to give a narrow reading to the scope of the Licensing Agreement. Past GATT panel reports support giving the term "restriction" an expansive interpretation.[399] The introductory words of Article XI of GATT provide as follows:

---

[398] While it is true that the EC import licences for bananas are transferable and tradeable, it is also clear that a trader, regardless of whatever his classification might be with respect to operator categories and/or activity functions, at some point in time has to file an application for an import licence. That trader can use the licence he has obtained or sell it on the marketplace. Thus the trader who applies for a particular import licence is not necessarily the one who actually effectuates the importation of bananas. However, there is no requirement under Article 1.1 of the Licensing Agreement that the natural or legal person who files the application for a licence must also carry out the transaction of actually importing bananas. Moreover, in respect of transferability and tradability of licences, there is no difference between the administration of quantitative restrictions and of tariff quotas.

> No prohibitions or restrictions other than duties, taxes or other charges, whether made effective through quotas, import or export licences or other measures ....

Thus, tariffs and tariff quotas are restrictions as that term is used in Article XI, although "duties, taxes or other charges" are excepted from Article XI's requirements. A similar reading is appropriate in the case of the Licensing Agreement. Article 3.2 of the Licensing Agreement refers to "restrictions" and Article 3.3 of the Licensing Agreement applies to "licensing requirements for purposes other than the implementation of quantitative restrictions". Accordingly, we find that licensing procedures used for the implementation of measures other than quantitative restrictions, including tariff quotas, are subject to the disciplines of the Licensing Agreement.[400] We also note that our argument that tariff quotas are "restrictions" does not imply that they are not, in principle, legitimate trade measures under the agreements covered by the WTO in the same sense that tariffs are.

7.155 This finding is in accord with a consideration of the object and purpose and the context of the Licensing Agreement. The preamble to the Licensing Agreement makes it clear that the Licensing Agreement is to further the objectives of GATT. It is equally explicitly noted that the provisions of GATT apply to import licensing and then stated that Members desire that import licensing procedures not be used contrary to the principles and objectives of GATT. Since one of the principal GATT provisions dealing with import licensing is Article XIII, which by the explicit terms of Article XIII:5 applies to tariff quotas, it follows from the preamble to the Licensing Agreement that the Licensing Agreement should also apply to tariff quotas. There would not seem to be any reason to treat licensing procedures for quantitative restrictions differently from those for tariff quotas. The concerns raised in the preamble about the possible negative consequences of the inappropriate use of import licensing regimes would apply equally to both.

7.156 **Accordingly, we find that the Licensing Agreement applies to licensing procedures for tariff quotas.**

(ii) GATT 1994 and the Annex 1A Agreements

7.157 The Complainants have raised claims in respect of the EC's import licensing regime under GATT 1994, the Licensing Agreement and the TRIM's Agreement. Having found that the Licensing Agreement applies to tariff quotas, a further threshold question is whether both GATT 1994, as well as the Licensing Agreement and the TRIM's Agreement, apply to the EC's import licensing procedures. This requires us to consider the interrelationship of GATT 1994, on the one hand, and the Licensing Agreement and the TRIM's Agreement, on the other.

7.158 The General Interpretative Note to Annex 1A of the Agreement Establishing the WTO ("General Interpretative Note") reads:

> In the event of conflict between a provision of the General Agreement on Tariffs and Trade 1994 and a provision of another agreement in Annex 1A to the Agreement Establishing the WTO ... , the provision of the other agreement shall prevail to the extent of the conflict.

Both the Licensing Agreement and the TRIM's Agreement are "agreement[s] in Annex 1A to the Agreement Establishing the WTO".

---

[399] Panel Report on "Japan - Trade in Semiconductors", adopted on 4 May 1988, BISD 35S/116, 153, paras. 104-105; Panel Report on "EEC - Programme of Minimum Import Prices, Licences and Surety Deposits for Certain Processed Fruits and Vegetables", adopted on 18 October 1978, BISD 25S/68, 98-100, para. 4.9.

[400] We note that past GATT/WTO practice in respect of this issue is not helpful in clarifying the meaning of the Licensing Agreement.

7.159 As a preliminary issue, it is necessary to define the notion of "conflict" laid down in the General Interpretative Note. In light of the wording, the context, the object and the purpose of this Note, we consider that it is designed to deal with (i) clashes between obligations contained in GATT 1994 and obligations contained in agreements listed in Annex 1A, where those obligations are mutually exclusive in the sense that a Member cannot comply with both obligations at the same time, and (ii) the situation where a rule in one agreement prohibits what a rule in another agreement explicitly permits.[401]

7.160 However, we are of the view that the concept of "conflict" as embodied in the General Interpretative Note does not relate to situations where rules contained in one of the Agreements listed in Annex 1A provide for different or complementary obligations in addition to those contained in GATT 1994. In such a case, the obligations arising from the former and GATT 1994 can both be complied with at the same time without the need to renounce explicit rights or authorizations. In this latter case, there is no reason to assume that a Member is not capable of, or not required to, meet the obligations of both GATT 1994 and the relevant Annex 1A Agreement.

7.161 Proceeding on this basis, we have to ascertain whether the provisions of the Licensing Agreement and the TRIM's Agreement, to the extent they are within the coverage of the terms of reference of this Panel, contain any conflicting obligations which are contrary to those stipulated by Articles I, III, X, or XIII of GATT 1994, in the sense that Members could not comply with the obligations resulting from both Agreements at the same time or that WTO Members are authorized to act in a manner that would be inconsistent with the requirements of GATT rules. Wherever the answer to this question is affirmative, the obligation or authorization contained in the Licensing or TRIM's Agreement would, in accordance with the General Interpretative Note, prevail over the provisions of the relevant article of GATT 1994. Where the answer is negative, both provisions would apply equally.

7.162 Based on our detailed examination of the provisions of the Licensing Agreement, Article 2 of the TRIM's Agreement as well as GATT 1994, we find that no conflicting, i.e. mutually exclusive, obligations arise from the provisions of the three Agreements that the parties to the dispute have put before us. Indeed, we note that the first substantive provision of the Licensing Agreement, Article 1.2, requires Members to conform to GATT rules applicable to import licensing.

7.163 **In the light of the foregoing discussion, we find that the provisions of GATT 1994, the Licensing Agreement and Article 2 of the TRIM'S Agreement all apply to the EC's import licensing procedures for bananas.**

(iii) separate regimes

7.164 The EC argues that for purposes of Article I:1 of GATT and other non-discrimination provisions the traditional ACP licensing procedures should not be compared with the third-country and non-traditional ACP licensing procedures because they are separate regimes. We note that licensing procedures applicable to all

[401] For instance, Article XI:1 of GATT 1994 prohibits the imposition of quantitative restrictions, while Article XI:2 of GATT 1994 contains a rather limited catalogue of exceptions. Article 2 of the Agreement on Textiles and Clothing ("ATC") authorizes the imposition of quantitative restrictions in the textiles and clothing sector, subject to conditions specified in Article 2:1-21 of the ATC. In other words, Article XI:1 of GATT 1994 prohibits what Article 2 of the ATC permits in equally explicit terms. It is true that Members could theoretically comply with Article XI:1 of GATT, as well as with Article 2 of the ATC, simply by refraining from invoking the right to impose quantitative restrictions in the textiles sector because Article 2 of the ATC authorizes rather than mandates the imposition of quantitative restrictions. However, such an interpretation would render whole Articles or sections of Agreements covered by the WTO meaningless and run counter to the object and purpose of many agreements listed in Annex 1A which were negotiated with the intent to create rights and obligations which in parts differ substantially from those of the GATT 1994. Therefore, in the case described above, we consider that the General Interpretative Note stipulates that an obligation or authorization embodied in the ATC or any other of the agreements listed in Annex 1A prevails over the conflicting obligation provided for by GATT 1994.

banana imports are embodied in the same Regulation 1442/93. Furthermore, administrative decisions applying the EC banana import procedures are not always contained in separate regulations depending on whether they relate to traditional ACP licensing or third-country and non-traditional ACP licensing procedures. This would also suggest that all EC licensing procedures for banana imports constitute a single regime.

7.165 Moreover, we have refuted the same argument above in the context of Article XIII's application to allocation of tariff quota shares. The object and purpose of Article I, Article X, Article XIII and similar non-discrimination provisions are to preclude the creation of different systems for imports from different Members, as explained in a 1968 Note by the GATT Director-General on Article X:3(a).[402] We discuss this Note in more detail above, but in our view, it is clear that the object and purpose of the non-discrimination provisions would be defeated if Members were permitted to create separate regimes for imports of like products based on origin.

7.166 This is not to say that Members may not create import licensing regimes that vary in technical aspects. For example, the information required to establish origin for purposes of demonstrating an entitlement to a preferential tariff rate may differ from the information collected generally to establish origin. However, the measures for implementing a preferential tariff permitted under WTO rules should not in themselves create non-tariff preferences in addition to the tariff preference.

7.167 **Accordingly, we find that the EC licensing procedures for traditional ACP bananas and third-country and non-traditional ACP bananas should be examined as one licensing regime.**

(iv) examination of the licensing claims

7.168 In light of the foregoing, we organize our examination of the EC's import licensing procedures for bananas as follows.[403] In respect of each of the four principal components of the procedures to which the Complainants have objected - operator categories, activity functions, export certificates and hurricane licences, we first consider whether the EC's procedures are inconsistent with the general non-discrimination rules of Articles I and III of GATT. We then examine their consistency, where necessary, with Articles X:3 and XIII of GATT and the more specific provisions of the Licensing Agreement. We treat the claims under Article 2 of the TRIM's Agreement together with our consideration of the claims under Article III of GATT. We discuss the claims relating to operator categories in section (b), those relating to activity functions in section (c), those relating to export certificates in section (d) and those relating to hurricane licences in section (e). The remaining claims in respect of the EC licensing procedures are addressed in section (f).

b) Operator categories

7.169 For purposes of the distribution of licences the EC established three types of "operators": operators who have during a preceding three-year period marketed third-country bananas and non-traditional ACP bananas are classified in Category A. Those who have marketed bananas from EC and traditional ACP sources during a preceding three-year period fall within Category B. Operators who have marketed third-country and non-traditional ACP bananas as well as traditional ACP and EC bananas qualify for both categories. New market entrants who start marketing third-country or non-traditional ACP bananas may qualify as Category C operators. Article 19 of EC Regulation 404/93 earmarks 66.5 per cent of the licences allowing imports of third-country and non-traditional ACP bananas at the lower tariff rates within the tariff quota for Category A operators. Another 30 per cent is allocated to Category B operators, while 3.5 per cent is reserved for the new market entrants of Category C. Subject to limitations, import licences for third-country and non-traditional ACP bananas are transferable and tradeable within and between operator categories.

---

[402] Note by the Director-General of 29 November 1968, L/3149.

[403] In considering how to organize our findings, we note that Article 1.2 of the Licensing Agreement requires Members to conform to GATT rules applicable to import licensing procedures.

7.170 The Complaining parties raise claims against the operator category rules under Articles I, III, X and XIII of GATT and Article 2 of the TRIM's Agreement, as well as claims under the Licensing Agreement. In the case of Ecuador, we consider the claims it has raised under Article III of GATT, Article 2 of the TRIM's Agreement and Article I of GATT.

(i) Article III:4 of GATT

7.171 The Complainants claim that the rules introducing operator categories, the eligibility criteria for Category B operators and the allocation to Category B operators of 30 per cent of the licences required for the importation of third-country and non-traditional ACP bananas at the lower duty rate within the bound tariff quota are inconsistent with Article III:4 of GATT because this licence allocation amounts to a requirement or incentive to purchase EC bananas in order to be eligible to import the bananas of Complainants' origin.

7.172 The EC responds that the licensing regime applied to third-country imports within the tariff quota does not force any trader to purchase any quantity of EC bananas, but provides a tool for managing correctly the importation of third-country bananas according to the demand on the EC market. Likewise, the operator category rules and the allocation of 30 per cent of the licences required for imports from third-country sources form part of the EC's overall economic strategy and do not affect the volume of imports from third-country sources. Moreover, the EC reiterates that the licensing regime is applied at the border at the moment of importation, and not after the bananas have cleared customs and that, accordingly, all allegations concerning operator category rules under Article III are unfounded.

7.173 The relevant part of Article III:4 of GATT provides:

> The products of the territory of any Member imported into the territory of any other Member shall be accorded treatment no less favourable than that accorded to like products of national origin in respect of all laws, regulations and requirements affecting their internal sale, offering for sale, purchase, transportation, distribution or use.

7.174 In addressing these claims concerning licensing procedures, we first examine the issue whether import licensing procedures are subject to the requirements of Article III. In this regard, we note that a GATT panel considered "... that the intention of the drafters of the Agreement was clearly to treat the imported products in the same way as the like domestic products once they had been cleared through customs. Otherwise indirect protection could be given."[404] In view of this interpretation of Article III:4, the fact that imported products may be subject to the collection of tariffs or the imposition of a licensing requirement taken as such, whereas the marketing of domestic products is obviously not, cannot per se violate Article III:4 of GATT.

7.175 The next question that arises is whether the EC procedures and requirements for the allocation of import licences for foreign products to eligible operators are measures that are included in the notion of "all laws, regulations and requirements affecting their internal sale, offering for sale, purchase ..." in the meaning of Article III:4. In our view, the word "affecting" suggests a coverage of Article III:4, beyond legislation directly regulating or governing the sale of domestic and like imported products. We further have to take into account the context of Article III, i.e., the Interpretative Note Ad Article III which makes clear that the mere fact that an internal charge is collected or a regulation is enforced in the case of an imported product at the time or point of

[404] Panel Report on "Italian Discrimination against Imported Agricultural Machinery", adopted on 23 October 1958, BISD 7S/60, 63-64, para. 11.

importation does not prevent it from being subject to the provisions of Article III.[405] A GATT panel interpreted the Note as follows:

> The fact that Section 337 is used as a means for the enforcement of United States patent law at the border does not provide an escape from the applicability of Article III:4; the interpretative note to Article III states that any law, regulation or requirement affecting the internal sale of products that is enforced in the case of the imported product at the time or point of importation is nevertheless subject to the provisions of Article III. Nor could the applicability of Article III:4 be denied on the ground that most of the procedures in the case before the Panel are applied to *persons* rather than *products*, since the factor determining whether persons might be susceptible to Section 337 proceedings or federal district court procedures is the source of the challenged products, that is whether they are of United States origin or imported.[406] (emphasis added)

This interpretation is in line with the interpretation of the term "affecting" in other past GATT panel reports.[407]

7.176 We further note that our interpretation is confirmed by the fact that the coverage of Articles I and III with respect to governmental measures is not necessarily mutually exclusive, as demonstrated by Article I:1's incorporation into the GATT most favoured nation clause of "all matters referred to in paragraphs 2 and 4 of Article III". To put it differently, under GATT internal matters may be within the purview of the MFN obligations and border measures may be within the purview of the national treatment clause.

7.177 In the light of the foregoing, we have to distinguish the mere requirement to present a licence upon importation of a product as such from the procedures applied by the EC in the context of the licence allocation which are internal laws, regulations and requirements affecting the internal sale of imported products. In the alternative, if the mere fact that the EC regulations on the introduction of the common market organization for bananas include or are related to a border measure such as a licensing requirement would mean that the Article III cannot apply, it would not be difficult to evade the GATT national treatment obligation. Such a result would run counter to the object and purpose of Article III, i.e., the obligation of Members to accord foreign products no less favourable treatment than like domestic products in the application of any measure affecting the internal sale of products, regardless of whether it applies internally or at the border.

7.178 In turning to the specific measures at issue, we note that operators address claims for reference quantities of bananas marketed during a preceding three-year period and applications for the allocation of quarterly licences to competent member State authorities. The administration of the licence allocation procedures is carried out in cooperation between these authorities and the European Commission within the EC territory. Consequently, although licences are a condition for the importation of bananas into the EC at in-quota tariff rates, we find that the administration of licence distribution procedures and the eligibility criteria for the allocation of licences to operators form part of the EC's internal legislation and are "laws, regulations and requirements affecting the internal sale, ... purchase, ... distribution" of imported bananas in the meaning of Article III:4. Therefore, the argument that licensing procedures are beyond the purview of the GATT national treatment clause cannot, in our view, be sustained in light of the wording, context, object or purpose of Article III or with the findings of past GATT panel reports.

---

[405] "... any law, regulation or requirement of the kind referred to in paragraph 1 which applies to an imported product and to the like domestic product and is ... enforced in the case of the imported product at the time or point of importation, is nevertheless to be regarded as ... law, regulation or requirement of the kind referred to in paragraph 1, and is accordingly subject to the provisions of Article III."

[406] Panel Report on "US - Section 337 of the Tariff Act of 1930", adopted on 7 November 1989, BISD 36S/345, 385, para. *5.10*.

[407] Panel Report on "Italian Discrimination against Imported Agricultural Machinery", adopted on 23 October 1958, BISD 7S/60, 63-64, para. 11; Panel Report on "EEC - on Imports of Parts and Components", adopted on 16 May 1990, BISD 37S/132, 197, paras. *5.20-5.21*.

7.179 Turning now to the basic Article III claim of Complainants in respect of operator categories, we first recall the findings of the panel on *EEC - Import Regime for Bananas*[408] ("second *Banana* panel"), which held with regard to operator categories:

> 144. The Panel first examined the operation of the EEC import licensing system and noted the following. The quantity of bananas that an operator may import, pursuant to licences granted under the tariff quota, depends on the origin of the bananas that the operator has marketed during the preceding three-year period.[409] In particular, 30 per cent of the tariff quota is apportioned among operators who, during the preceding period, have purchased bananas from domestic or traditional ACP sources. As a result, operators wishing to increase their future share of bananas benefiting from the tariff quota would be required to increase their current purchases of EEC or traditional ACP bananas.
>
> 145. The Panel noted that the General Agreement does not contain provisions specifically regulating the allocation of tariff quota licences among importers and that contracting parties are, therefore, in principle free to choose the beneficiaries of the tariff quota. They could, for instance, allocate the licences to enterprises on the basis of their previous trade shares. However, the absence of any provisions in the General Agreement specifically regulating the allocation of tariff quota licences also meant that contracting parties, in allocating such licences, had to fully observe the generally applicable provisions of the General Agreement, in particular those of Article III:4, which prescribes treatment of imported products no less favourable than that accorded to domestic products, and Article I:1, which requires most-favoured-nation treatment with respect to internal regulations.
>
> 146. The Panel then proceeded to examine the EEC licensing scheme in the light of the incentive provided under the regulations to buy bananas from domestic sources. The Panel noted that Article III:4 had been interpreted consistently by previous panels as establishing the obligation to accord imported products competitive opportunities no less favourable than those accorded to domestic products. A previous panel has stated:
>
>> The words "treatment no less favourable" in paragraph 4 call for effective equality of opportunities for imported products in respect of the application of laws, regulations and requirements affecting the internal sale, offering for sale, purchase, transportation, distribution or use of products.[410]
>
> The Panel further noted that previous panels had found consistently that this obligation applies to any requirement imposed by a contracting party, including requirements 'which an enterprise voluntarily accepts to obtain an advantage from the government'.[411] In the view of the Panel, a requirement to purchase a domestic product in order to obtain the right to import a product at a lower rate of duty under a tariff quota is therefore a requirement affecting the purchase of a product within the meaning of Article III:4. The Panel further noted that, in judging whether effective equality of opportunities for imported products under Article III:4 was accorded, the trade impact of the measure was not relevant. The CONTRACTING

[408] Panel Report on "EEC - Import Regime for Bananas", issued on 11 February 1994 (not adopted), DS38/R.

[409] Council Regulation (EEC) No 404/93, Article 19 (original footnote).

[410] Report of the panel on United States - Section 337 of the Tariff Act of 1930, BISD 36S/345, 386, para. *5.11*, adopted on 17 June 1987 (original footnote).

[411] Report of the panel on EEC - Regulation on Imports of Parts and Components, BISD 37S/132, 197, para. *5.21*, adopted on 16 May 1990 (original footnote).

PARTIES determined in 1949 that the obligations of Article III:4 'were equally applicable whether imports from other contracting parties were substantial, small or non-existent',[412] and they have confirmed this view in subsequent cases.[413] Thus it was not relevant that, at present, the incentive under the EEC regulations to buy domestic or traditional ACP bananas may only result in raising their price, and not in reducing the exports of the third-country bananas, since these exports, because of the high over-quota tariff, were limited *de facto* to the amount allocated under the tariff quota. The discrimination of imported bananas under the licensing scheme could therefore not be justified by measures on the importation that currently prevented, *de facto,* bananas from entering into the internal market. The Panel therefore found that the preferred allocation of part of the tariff quota to importers who purchase EEC bananas was inconsistent with Article III:4.

147. The Panel then examined the EEC licensing scheme in the light of the incentive provided under the regulations to buy bananas of ACP origin in preference to other foreign origins. The Panel noted that Article I:1 obliges contracting parties, with respect to all matters referred to in Article III:4, to accord any advantage, granted to any product originating in any country, to the like product originating in the territories of all other contracting parties. As under Article III, the Panel considered that actual trade flows were not relevant to determine conformity with Article I:1. The Panel therefore found that the preferred allocation of licences to operators who purchase bananas from ACP countries was inconsistent with the EEC's obligations under Article I:1.

148. The Panel noted that the EEC's licensing system, by reserving 66.5 per cent of the tariff quota to operators who had marketed third-country or non-traditional ACP bananas during a preceding period, included also incentives to continue importation of third-country bananas, even though these incentives may not have trade-distorting effects at present in view of the undisputed greater competitiveness of these third-country bananas. The Panel was of the view that, regardless of the trade effects, the apportioning of 66.5 per cent of the tariff quota to operators who had marketed third-country or non-traditional ACP bananas could not offset or legally justify the inconsistencies of the licensing system with Articles III:4 and I:1. The Panel agreed in this respect with a previous panel that had found that 'an element of more favourable treatment would only be relevant if it would always accompany and offset an element of differential treatment causing less favourable treatment'.[414]

7.180 While the second *Banana* panel report was not adopted by the GATT CONTRACTING PARTIES, the Appellate Body has stated in another context:

[W]e agree with the panel's conclusion ... that unadopted panel reports "have no legal status in the GATT or WTO system since they have not been endorsed through decisions by the CONTRACTING PARTIES to GATT or WTO Members."[415] Likewise, we agree that "a

[412] Report of the working party on Brazilian Internal Taxes, BISD II/181, 185, para. 16, adopted on 30 June 1949 (original footnote).

[413] Report of the panel on "United States - Taxes on petroleum and certain imported substances", BISD 34S/136, 158, para. 5.1.9, adopted on 17 June 1987; Report of the panel on "United States - Measures affecting alcoholic and malt beverages", DS23/R, para. *5.65*, adopted on 19 June 1992 (original footnote).

[414] Report of the panel on "United States Section 337 of the Tariff Act of 1930", BISD 36S/345, 388, para. *5.16*, adopted on 7 November 1989 (original footnote).

[415] Panel Report on "Japan - Taxes on Alcoholic Beverages", adopted on 1 November 1996, WT/DS8/R, WT/DS10/R, WT/DS11/R, pp.106-107, para. 6.10 (original footnote).

panel could nevertheless find useful guidance in the reasoning of an unadopted panel report that it considered to be relevant."[416] [417]

Neither the EC nor the Complainants have claimed that the rules concerning operator categories have significantly changed[418] since the second *Banana* panel report was issued on 11 February 1994 in a way that would affect the soundness of that panel's findings and conclusions with respect to Article III:4. Nor does the adoption of the Lomé waiver by the GATT CONTRACTING PARTIES and its extension by the WTO General Council, in our view, affect our examination of the allocation of licences to different operator categories in the light of Article III:4. Accordingly, we adopt the findings of the second *Banana* panel on Article III:4 of GATT in respect of operator categories as our own findings.

7.181 However, before finding whether the allocation to Category B operators of 30 per cent of the licences allowing the importation of third-country and non-traditional ACP bananas at in-quota tariff rates is inconsistent with Article III:4, we need to consider that Article III:1 is a "general principle that informs the rest of Article III", as the Appellate Body has recently stated.[419] Since Article III:1 constitutes part of the context of Article III:4, it must be taken into account in our interpretation of the latter. Article III:1 articulates a general principle that internal measures should not be applied so as to afford protection to domestic production.[420] As noted by the Appellate Body, the protective application of a measure can most often be discerned from the design, the architecture, and the revealing structure of the measure.[421] We consider that the design, architecture and structure of the EC measure that provides for allocation to Category B operators of 30 per cent of the licences allowing the importation of third-country and non-traditional ACP bananas at in-quota tariff rates all indicate that the measure is also applied so as to afford protection to EC producers.

7.182 **Thus, we find the allocation to Category B operators of 30 per cent of the licences allowing the importation of third-country and non-traditional ACP bananas at in-quota tariff rates is inconsistent with the requirements of Article III:4 of GATT.**

(ii) Article 2 of the TRIM's Agreement

7.183 Proceeding on the assumption that the operator category rules are inconsistent with the requirements of Article III:4, the Complainants allege that the conditions for operator B eligibility and the 30 per cent tariff quota allocation for Category B operators are inconsistent with Article 2.1 of the TRIM's Agreement. The fact that the allocation of 30 per cent of the licences required for the importation of third-country bananas is contingent upon the marketing of EC (and traditional ACP) bananas amounts, in the view of the Complainants, to a purchasing requirement which falls within the first category of the Illustrative List in the Annex to the TRIM's Agreement of those trade-related investment measures which are inconsistent with Article III:4 of GATT.

---

[416] Ibid.

[417] Appellate Body Report on "Japan - Taxes on Alcoholic Beverages", adopted on 8 November 1996, WT/DS8/AB/R, WT/DS10/AB/R, WT/DS11/AB/R, AB-1996-2, pp.14-15.

[418] While provisions such as Article 19 of Regulation 404/93 of 13 February 1993 and Articles 3 and 4 of Regulation 1442/93 of 12 June 1993 have been implemented and modified through subsequent EC legislation, these rules are still in essence in force in the EC legal order without having been affected by subsequent legislation.

[419] Appellate Body Report on "Japan - Taxes on Alcoholic Beverages", *op. cit.*, p.18. The Report states: "The purpose of Article III:1 is to establish this general principle as a guide to understanding and interpreting the specific obligations contained in Article III:2 and in the other paragraphs of Article III, while respecting, and not diminishing in any way, the meaning of words actually used in the texts of those other paragraphs".

[420] *Ibid.*, p.18.

[421] *Ibid.*, p.29.

7.184 In the EC's view, no breach of Article 2 of the TRIM's Agreement can be found because no breach of Article III:4 has occurred. In the alternative, the EC argues that rules establishing operator categories do not fall within the ambit of the TRIM's Agreement because there is no requirement to make an investment within a particular country; nor is there a requirement for purchase or use by an enterprise of products of domestic origin or from any domestic source in order to be allowed to make the investment.

7.185 In considering these arguments, we first examine the relationship of the TRIM's Agreement to the provisions of GATT. We note that with the exception of its transition provisions[422] the TRIM's Agreement essentially interprets and clarifies the provisions of Article III (and also Article XI) where trade-related investment measures are concerned. Thus the TRIM's Agreement does not add to or subtract from those GATT obligations, although it clarifies that Article III:4 may cover investment-related matters.

7.186 We emphasize that in view of the importance of the TRIM's Agreement in the framework of the agreements covered by the WTO, we have examined the claims and legal arguments advanced by the parties under the TRIM's Agreement carefully. However, for the reasons stated in the previous paragraph, we do not consider it necessary to make a specific ruling under the TRIM's Agreement with respect to the eligibility criteria for the different categories of operators and the allocation of certain percentages of import licences based on operator categories. On the one hand, a finding that the measure in question would not be considered a trade-related investment measure for the purposes of the TRIM's Agreement would not affect our findings in respect of Article III:4 since the scope of that provision is not limited to TRIM's and, on the other hand, steps taken to bring EC licensing procedures into conformity with Article III:4 would also eliminate the alleged non-conformity with obligations under the TRIM's Agreement.

7.187 **Therefore, we do not consider it necessary to make a specific ruling under the TRIM's Agreement with respect to the allocation to Category B operators of 30 per cent of the licences allowing the importation of third-country and non-traditional ACP bananas at in-quota tariff rates.**

(iii) Article I of GATT

7.188 The Complainants claim that (i) the conditions for operator B eligibility based on marketing of ACP bananas, (ii) the exemption of traditional ACP imports from operator category rules and (iii) the allocation of 30 per cent of the licences allowing imports of third-country bananas at in-quota tariff rates to Category B operators, are inconsistent with the requirements of Article I:1 of GATT. They argue: (a) that the comparatively less complex licensing procedures that apply to imports of bananas from traditional ACP sources are an "advantage" that the EC fails to accord to imports of third-country bananas, and (b) that these aspects of the EC licensing system provide an incentive or requirement to purchase bananas from traditional ACP sources over those originating in third countries. The EC responds that the existence of Category B licences *per se* does not create an incentive to purchase any particular product, but is designed to mitigate the effects of oligopolistic market structures and to stimulate competition between operators. Since licences allocated to particular operators are tradeable, the EC concludes that such licences do not constitute an impediment to imports from any specific source. In the alternative, the EC maintains that the Lomé waiver covers any inconsistency with the requirements of Article I:1 because Category B licences are required under the Lomé Convention in order to maintain existing advantages for traditional ACP bananas on the EC market.

7.189 Article I:1 provides as follows:

> With respect to customs duties and charges of any kind imposed on or in connection with importation or exportation or imposed in the international transfer of payments for

[422] We have already dismissed the Complainants' claim under the transition provisions of Article 5 of the TRIM's Agreement because Article 5 was not listed in the request for the establishment of the Panel as required by Article 6.2 of the DSU, see para. 7.0.

> imports or exports and with respect to the method of levying such duties and charges, and with respect to all rules and formalities in connection with importation and exportation, and with respect to all matters referred to in paragraphs 2 and 4 of Article III, any advantage, favour, privilege or immunity granted by any Member to any product originating in or destined for any other country shall be accorded immediately and unconditionally to the like product originating in or destined for the territories of all other Members.

In our view, import licensing procedures, including the operator category rules, are "rules and formalities in connection with importation" in the meaning of Article I:1. A panel found, for example, that comparatively more favourable rules for revoking countervailing duties were an "advantage" for purposes of Article I:1 and that "making a regulatory advantage available to imports from some countries while not making it available to others" is inconsistent with Article I:1.[423]

7.190 In our view, the operator category and activity function rules contained in the licensing procedures for third-country and non-traditional ACP bananas require substantially more data to be submitted to show entitlement to a licence for third-country and non-traditional ACP bananas than is required by the procedures applicable to traditional ACP bananas. This is clearly demonstrated by comparing the data that needs to be maintained and submitted under the two systems.

7.191 In respect of traditional ACP bananas, we note that, according to the EC,[424] operators need only to obtain special certificates of origin from the issuing authority in the relevant ACP State for traditional ACP imports. In this regard, Article 14(4) of Regulation 1442/93 on "Detailed Rules Applicable to Imports of Traditional ACP Bananas" (as amended by Regulation 875/96) provides:

> 4. Import licence applications shall only be admissible where:
>   (a) they are accompanied by the original of a certificate drawn up by the competent authorities of the ACP country concerned testifying to the origin of the bananas ...
>   (b) they contain:
>   - the words 'traditional ACP bananas – Regulation (EEC) No 404/93' ...
>   - an indication of the country of origin ..."

7.192 In contrast, in respect of third-country and non-traditional ACP imports, operators need to apply for a reference quantity by sending details of banana volumes marketed during a preceding three-year period to the relevant competent authority. Article 19(2) of Regulation 404/93 on "Detailed Rules for the Application of the Tariff Quota Arrangements" provides in respect of imports of third-country and non-traditional ACP bananas that:

> On the basis of separate calculations for each of the categories of operators ... each operator shall obtain import licences on the basis of the average quantities of bananas that he has sold in the three most recent years for which figures are available. For the category of [A] operators ..., the quantities to be taken into consideration shall be the sales of third-country and/or non-traditional ACP bananas. In the case of category [B] operators ..., sales of traditional ACP and/or Community bananas shall be taken into consideration. ....

Article 4 of Regulation 1442/93 provides:

---

[423] Panel Report on "US - Denial of MFN Treatment as to Non-Rubber Footwear from Brazil", adopted on 19 June 1992, BISD 39S/128, 150-151, paras. 6.8-6.11.

[424] See the first item on the chart submitted by the EC which is reproduced at para. *4.274*.

> 1. The competent authorities of the Member States shall draw up separate lists of operators in Category A and B and the quantities which each operators has marketed in each of the three years prior to that preceding the year for which the tariff quota is opened, broken down according to economic activity as described in Article 3(1).
> Operators shall register themselves and shall establish quantities they have marketed by submitting individual written applications on their own initiative in a single Member State of their choice.
> ...
>
> 2. The operators concerned shall notify the competent authorities at the latest by ... each year thereafter of the overall quantities of bananas marketed in each of the years referred to in paragraph 1, breaking them down clearly:
> (a) according to origin, pursuant to the definition laid down in Article 15 of Regulation (EEC) No 404/93,[425] as follows:
> - of imports from non-ACP third countries and non- traditional imports from ACP States,
> - traditional imports from ACP States within the quantities set out in the Annex to Regulation (EEC) No. 404/93, specifying the quantities by State,
> - Community bananas, specifying the region of production;
>
> (b) according to the economic activity as described in Article 3(1).
>
> 3. The operators concerned shall make the supporting documents specified in Article 7 available to the authorities.

Article 7 of Regulation 1442/93 provides:

> At the request of the competent authorities of the Member States, the following documents may be submitted to establish the quantities marketed by each operator in Category A and B registered with them:
> - the copy delivered to the importer of the Single Administrative Document (SAD) or, where applicable, his copy of the document for simplified declarations,
> - a copy of the T2 declaration issued pursuant to ... for transactions effected during the reference period,
> - original sales invoices or certified copies thereof,
> - any relevant supporting documents such as national import documents issued and used before the entry into force of these arrangements,
> - import licences issued pursuant to this Regulation and documents testifying to the marketing of bananas produced in the Community.

The information required to support claims in respect of activity functions (e.g., ripening) is not specified in this provision, but such information also must be maintained and submitted. We further note that the filing of data concerning the past volumes of traditional ACP and/or EC bananas marketed for purposes of the calculation of reference quantities for Category B operators relates to the eligibility of such operators for the allocation of licences allowing the importation of third-country and non-traditional ACP bananas at in-quota tariff rates. However, this filing of data on past banana volumes marketed is not a prerequisite for the

[425] Article 15 of Regulation 404/93 provides for definitions of, *inter alia*, "traditional imports from ACP States"', "non-traditional imports from ACP States", "imports from non ACP-third countries", "Community bananas".

importation of traditional ACP bananas, for the issuance of traditional ACP import licences, or for the marketing of EC bananas.

7.193 From the foregoing, in our view, it is clear that the procedural and administrative requirements for imports of third-country and non-traditional ACP bananas arising from the application of the operator category rules differ from, and go significantly beyond, those required in respect of traditional ACP bananas. Thus, we believe that the licensing procedures applied by the EC to traditional ACP banana imports, when compared to the licensing procedures imposed on third-country and non-traditional ACP imports with its operator category rules, can be considered as an "advantage" which the EC does not accord to third-country and non-traditional ACP imports. The EC thereby acts inconsistently with the requirements of Article I:1.

7.194 In addition, Article I:1 obliges a Member to accord any advantage granted to any product originating in any country to the like product originating in the territories of all other Members, in respect of matters referred to in Article III:4. The matters referred to in Article III:4 are "laws, regulations and requirements affecting [the] internal sale, offering for sale, purchase, transportation, distribution and use [of a product]". In our view, the allocation to Category B operators of 30 per cent of the licences allowing for the importation within the tariff quota of third-country bananas means *ceteris paribus* that operators who in the future wish to maintain or increase their share of licences for the importation of third-country and non-traditional ACP bananas at in-quota tariff rates would be required to maintain or increase their current purchases and sales of traditional ACP (or EC) bananas in order to claim that they market traditional ACP (or EC) bananas for purposes of the operator category rules. Such a requirement to purchase and sell a product from one country (i.e., a source of traditional ACP imports) in order to obtain the right to import a product from any other country (i.e., a third country or a source of non-traditional ACP imports) at a lower rate of duty under a tariff quota is a requirement affecting the purchase of a product within the meaning of Articles III:4 and I:1. The allocation of licences allowing imports of third-country and non-traditional ACP bananas at in-quota tariff rates to operators who purchase and sell traditional ACP bananas is inconsistent with the EC's obligations under Article I:1 because it constitutes an advantage of the type covered by Article I that is accorded to traditional ACP bananas but which is not accorded to like products from all Members (i.e., non-traditional ACP and third-country bananas). We note that this result was also reached in the second *Banana* panel report as quoted above.[426]

7.195 **Thus, we find that the application in general of operator category rules in respect of the importation of third-country and non-traditional ACP bananas at in-quota tariff rates, in the absence of the application of such rules to traditional ACP imports, and in particular the allocation to Category B operators of 30 per cent of the licences allowing the importation of third-country and non-traditional ACP bananas at in-quota tariff rates, are inconsistent with the requirements of Article I:1 of GATT.**

(iv) application of the Lomé waiver to the EC's Article I obligations

7.196 In light of the foregoing finding that the operator category rules contained in the EC's licensing procedures for bananas are inconsistent with the requirements of Article I:1, we must consider whether the EC's obligations in this respect have been waived by the Lomé waiver. We have already found that the Lomé waiver covers (i) tariff preferences that the EC currently affords to traditional and non-traditional ACP bananas, which would otherwise be inconsistent with its obligations under Article I:1 (*infra*) and (ii) to a limited extent, the banana tariff quota share allocations made by the EC to certain ACP countries, which would otherwise be inconsistent with its obligations under Article XIII (*infra*). As we noted in our discussion of this issue in the context of Article XIII, we must first determine whether the EC licensing procedures that we have found to be

[426] Panel Report on "EEC - Import Regime for Bananas", issued on 11 February 1994 (not adopted), DS38/R, p.42ff, paras. 143-148, especially para. 147.

inconsistent with the requirements of Article I:1 are required by the Lomé Convention. If it is not, then the Lomé waiver is not applicable.

7.197 We recall that the operative paragraph of the Lomé waiver provides as follows:

> the provisions of paragraph 1 of Article I of the General Agreement shall be waived, until 29 February 2000, to the extent necessary to permit the European Communities to provide preferential treatment for products originating in ACP States as required by the relevant provisions of the Fourth Lomé Convention, without being required to extend the same preferential treatment to like products of any other contracting party.

For purposes of examining the issue of what is required by the Lomé Convention, we must examine the provisions of Article 168 and Protocol 5 of the Lomé Convention. In addition, we also consider whether the Lomé waiver should be interpreted to cover other provisions of the Lomé Convention that might be read to require such licensing procedures for ACP countries.

7.198 Article 168 of the Lomé Convention requires in general that ACP products be admitted duty-free to the EC. However, in the case of products, such as bananas, that are subject to specific rules as a result of the common agricultural policy, under Article 168(2)(a) they are to be (i) accorded duty-free treatment if there are no non-tariff measures applicable to their import or (ii) if (i) is not applicable (as is the case for bananas), given "more favourable treatment than that granted to third countries benefitting from the most-favoured-nation clause for the same products". The importation of traditional ACP bananas and non-traditional ACP bananas within the EC tariff quota is duty-free. Thus, for those imports, the basic requirement of Article 168, as expressed in its first paragraph, has been met, and we see no requirement in Article 168 that the EC must provide favourable treatment beyond such duty-free treatment. The Lomé waiver should not be interpreted to permit breaches of WTO rules that are not clearly required to satisfy the provisions of the Lomé Convention. This reading is confirmed by the terms of the waiver itself, which states in its fourth preambular paragraph: "Considering that the preferential treatment ... required by the Convention is designed ... not to raise undue barriers or to create undue difficulties for the trade of other contracting parties". In our view, the EC licensing procedures at issue do create undue difficulties for the trade of other Members. Accordingly, since Article 168 of the Lomé Convention does not specifically require these licensing procedures, it cannot be invoked as a justification for applying the Lomé waiver to such procedures.

7.199 Protocol 5 of the Lomé Convention provides:

> In respect of banana exports to the Community markets, no ACP State shall be placed, as regards access to its traditional markets and its advantages on those markets, in a less favourable situation than in the past or at present.

Protocol 5 suggests that each ACP country must be protected as regards its traditional markets and advantages thereon, nothing in the Lomé Convention specifically requires a licensing system for third-country and non-traditional ACP banana imports, such as is provided by the application of the operator category-activity function system to third-country and non-traditional ACP imports. It is, however, necessary to consider whether these licensing procedures were one of the advantages, as that term is used in Protocol 5, formerly enjoyed by the ACP countries under member States' banana import regimes.

7.200 The first *Banana* panel report provided detailed information on the licensing systems that were applied in the EC member States prior to the implementation of its common market organization for bananas. Prior to the implementation of Regulation 404/93, ACP bananas were primarily imported by France and the United Kingdom.[427] The panel report described the French regime as follows:

> 19. A banana import regime was first established in France by a Decree of 9 December 1931. This provided for the imposition of temporary quotas on imports of bananas from third countries. It was complemented by a law of 7 January 1932, on safeguard of production of bananas in colonies, protectorates or territories under French mandate. By Decree No. 60-460 of 16 May 1960, a special import regime was established for countries of the "zone franc" (i.e. former colonies). By an *arbitration* of the President of the Republic of 1962, the general supply of the French market was divided as follows: two thirds for national production (Guadeloupe, Martinique) and one third for imports from African suppliers (Cameroon, Côte d'Ivoire and Madagascar). Bananas from the Latin American countries were imported only to make up for any shortfall from the regions or countries mentioned above. When imported, the Latin American bananas were subject to the bound 20 per cent tariff and to licences.
>
> 20. In order to manage the banana market, an Interprofessional Committee for Bananas (Comité Interprofessionnel Bananier "CIB") was established on 5 December 1932. It was recognized as an agricultural interprofessional organization on 1 April 1989. The CIB brought together producers and importers, ripeners and distributors, including representatives of the African producers, as well as associated members (i.e., transporters). Since 1970, the GIEB (Groupement d'Intérêt Economique Bananier - Banana Economic Interest Group) has administered the existing quotas and import licences.
>
> 21. The CIB was responsible for assessing the demand for bananas on the French market on a yearly basis. A restricted Committee *(Conseil d'Administration)* of the CIB met every month to examine the quantities to buy the following month and to make a forecast for two months. In case of shortage of supply from one of the domestic or African sources, the CIB requested the GIEB to import from other third countries. In addition, the Ministry of Economics and Finance published notices to importers concerning the opening of quotas administered through licences. These licences were valid for a period of six months and were primarily designed to cover indirect imports made through other member States, as direct imports were made by the GIEB.
>
> 22. Import licences were granted to the GIEB by the government. The GIEB was exclusively responsible for purchasing and importing bananas directly from third countries. Imported quantities were then sold by the GIEB at the domestic market price. The "mark-up" was transferred to the Treasury. In addition to the national market organization, France was authorized, under the provisions of Article 115 of the Treaty of Rome, not to grant EEC treatment to bananas originating in certain third countries and put into free circulation in another EEC member State.[428]

It described the regime of the United Kingdom as follows:

> 37. The banana import regime dated back to the early 1930's when the United Kingdom introduced preferential duties on imports of British Empire bananas. Traditionally, and before it joined the EEC, the United Kingdom imported most of its bananas from the Windward Islands and Jamaica, formerly part of the British Empire. These countries were

[427] Panel Report on "EEC - Member States' Import Regimes for Bananas", issued on 3 June 1993 (not adopted), DS32/R, p.3, para. 12.

[428] Ibid., pp.4-5, paras. 19-22.

now regarded as ACP countries under the Lomé Convention. Imports of bananas from ACP countries entered in unrestricted quantities and duty free. Between 1940 and 1958, there was a total ban on imports of bananas from Latin American countries. Thereafter, imports from third countries, usually Latin American bananas, had been subject to a quota, since 1985 an annual quota, and a licensing system, as well as the common external tariff of 20 per cent. Licences were granted under Section 2 of "The Import of Goods (Control) Order" of 1954. There was a guaranteed minimum quantity for third country banana imports which, in 1992, amounted to 38,868 tons. Additional imports from third countries occurred when there was a short-fall of supplies. Upon its accession to the EEC, the United Kingdom was authorized, by the Commission of the EC, under Article 115 of the Treaty of Rome, to apply restrictions to imports, through other member States, of bananas from third countries, put into free circulation in the EEC.

38. At the beginning of every calendar year, the government authorities fixed the level of bananas that could be imported from all suppliers, according to the domestic needs determined by the Ministry of Agriculture, Fisheries and Food. On the basis of these parameters, monthly supply and demand conditions were established by the Banana Trade Advisory Committee (BTAC), set up in 1973 as a consultative committee for trade in bananas. Under the existing rules, the Department of Trade and Industry (DTI) was responsible for administering the import licensing system which controlled the quantity of banana imports from third country suppliers. The DTI issued public notices to importers. Since 1985, this took the form of an annual Notice to Importers, inviting applications for licences for the importation of bananas of non-preferential origin. Importers who fulfilled certain well-established criteria were eligible to obtain these licences. Once licences were allocated, for the annual basic import quota, management of further imports from third countries was done on a monthly basis. The BTAC met to consider updated forecasts of supply and demand. The DTI was then advised on the issue of further licences to cover shortfalls in supply and increases in demand.[429]

Based on the foregoing description of the UK and French procedures, it appears that when licences for banana imports were used, they were issued on a discretionary basis from time to time to established importers. Thus, prior to or as of 1990 (the reference period in the Lomé Convention for past or present advantages), neither the French nor the UK procedures appears to contain anything at all similar to the operator category-activity function system. Thus, in our view, licensing procedures of the kind presently applied were not an "advantage" that ACP countries formerly enjoyed in the EC or in individual member State markets.

7.201 In this connection, the EC argues that its licensing system is necessary to provide that the quantities for which access opportunities were given could actually be sold thereby guaranteeing traditional ACP bananas their existing advantages. We note that it appears that the ACP countries have enjoyed greater collective success on the EC market under Regulation 404/93 than in the years prior to 1993.[430] In any event, we believe that there are other methods consistent with WTO rules by which the EC could assist the ACP countries to compete on the EC market. As noted above, in our view, the Lomé waiver should not be interpreted to permit breaches of WTO rules that are not clearly required to satisfy the provisions of the Lomé Convention. This reading is, in our view, confirmed by the terms of the waiver itself, which states in its fourth preambular paragraph: "Considering that the preferential treatment ... required by the Convention is designed ... not to raise undue barriers or to create undue difficulties for the trade of other contracting parties". In our view, these

[429] Ibid., p.7, paras. 37-38.

[430] According to statistics submitted by the EC, the ACP countries' average share of the EC-12 market for imported bananas averaged 611,000 tonnes in the years 1989-1992, or 22.8 per cent. For 1993-1994, it averaged 737,000 tonnes, or 25.4 per cent. The Complainants suggest that the ACP share is understated in the EC statistics.

licensing procedures do create undue difficulties for the trade of other Members. Since licensing procedures are not an advantage formerly enjoyed by ACP countries and they are not required to provide access to traditional markets, such procedures are not covered by the Lomé waiver.

7.202 There are other provisions of the Lomé Convention, such as Articles 15(a) and 167, that call for the promotion of trade between the EC and ACP countries. However, they are too general to impose specific requirements on the EC. Thus, we do not agree that those provisions can be read to require a particular licensing system such as the operator category-activity function system.

7.203 Finally, we note that a finding that the Lomé waiver does not apply to the EC's licensing procedures for banana imports is in accordance with past panel practice that waivers should be interpreted narrowly.[431]

7.204 **Thus, we find that the Lomé waiver does not waive the EC's obligations under Article I:1 of GATT in respect of licensing procedures applied to third-country and non-traditional ACP imports, including those related to operator category rules.**

(v) Article X:3(a) of GATT

[7.205-7.212 Used in the Guatemala-Honduras, Mexico and United States reports.]

7.205 The Complainants claim that the EC licensing procedures are inconsistent with the requirements of Articles X:3 of GATT because they are not administered in a uniform, impartial and reasonable manner. The EC responds that Article X:3 only applies to internal measures and therefore is not applicable in this case. Alternatively, it argues that a system permitted under Article I by the Lomé waiver cannot be found to breach another GATT provision imposing MFN-like obligations similar to those waived. We note that we found in the preceding section that the EC licensing procedures were not permitted under Article I by the Lomé waiver.

7.206 Article X:3(a) provides:

> Each Member shall administer in a uniform, impartial and reasonable manner all its laws, regulations, decisions and rulings of the kind described in paragraph 1 of this Article.

Article X:1 defines the coverage of Article X:3(a) as follows:

> Laws, regulations, judicial decisions and administrative rulings of general application, made effective by any Member, pertaining to the classification or the valuation of products for customs purposes, or to rates of duty, taxes or other charges, or to requirements, restrictions or prohibitions on imports or exports or on the transfer of payments therefor, or affecting their sale, distribution, transportation, insurance, warehousing, inspection, exhibition, processing, mixing or other use ....

Given that this provision enumerates national legislation regarding border measures as well as internal measures, and customs tariffs as well as quantitative measures, the coverage of Article X could hardly be more comprehensive. Accordingly, internal laws regulating border measures constitute "... requirements ... on imports ..." in the meaning of Article X:1 and cannot be excluded from its scope.

---

[431] Panel Report on "US - Restrictions on the Importation of Sugar and Sugar-Containing Products Applied Under the 1955 Waiver and Under the Headnote to the Schedule of Tariff Concessions", adopted on 7 November 1990, BISD 37S/228, 256-257, para. 5.9.

7.207 **Consequently, we find that the EC import licensing procedures are subject to the requirements of Article X of GATT.**

7.208 More specifically, the Complainants claim that the rules establishing operator categories on the basis of the source of bananas marketed during a preceding three-year period are inconsistent with the requirements of Article X:3(a) because the EC applies them to imports of third-country and non-traditional ACP bananas but not to traditional ACP imports. According to the Complainants, these rules are inconsistent with the standards of "uniform, impartial and reasonable administration" of domestic laws, regulations, decisions and rulings and thus are inconsistent with the requirements of Article X:3(a). The EC maintains that the rules applying operator categories are administered in a uniform, impartial and reasonable manner among the third countries which are subject to that separate licensing regime and that the Complainants have failed to provide evidence to the contrary.

7.209 The Complainants support their argument by referring to a 1968 Note by the GATT Director-General, which stated that Article X:3(a)

> would not permit, in the treatment accorded to imported goods, discrimination based on country of origin, nor would they permit the application of one set of regulations and procedures with respect to some contracting parties and a different set with respect to the others.[432]

The EC responds that the 1968 Note cannot be considered as an authoritative interpretation of GATT rules because it was never endorsed by a formal decision of the CONTRACTING PARTIES.

7.210 We note that a prior panel in discussing the interpretation of Article X:3(a) found that its terms would be met if regulations were applied "in a substantially uniform manner, although there were some minor administrative variations, e.g. concerning the form in which licence applications could be made and the requirement of pro-forma invoices".[433] In that case, the panel found that such differences were minimal and did not in themselves establish a breach of Article X:3(a).

7.211 In our view, the Director-General's Note correctly describes the reach of Article X:3(a) and is consistent with the quoted panel decision. While minor "administrative variations" in the application of regulations may not be inconsistent with the requirements of Article X:3(a), as suggested by the above-mentioned panel report, two different sets of rules would be inconsistent with the requirements of Article X:3(a). In this case, we are confronted with a system for the importation of bananas into the EC with two different origin-based sets of import licensing procedures. These sets of licensing procedures differ significantly from one another, depending on whether imports of bananas are from traditional ACP sources or from third countries and non-traditional ACP sources, particularly with respect to the application of the rules on operator categories. The operator category (and activity function) rules contained in the licensing procedures for third-country and non-traditional ACP bananas (but not in the procedures applicable to traditional ACP

---

[432] Note by the GATT Director-General of 29 November 1968, L/3149.

[433] Panel Report on "EEC - Restrictions on Imports of Dessert Apples", Complaint by Chile, adopted on 22 June 1989, BISD 36S/93, 133, para.12.30. In the descriptive part of the *Chilean Apples* case, "concerning Article X:3, Chile argued that there were differences among the ten member States of the EEC as to the requirements they imposed on applications for licences for imports of dessert apples. It cited examples, such as a French requirement for licence applications to be accompanied by a pro forma invoice, which effectively meant that licences could not be applied for until after ships had been loaded. Other examples cited by Chile included acceptance of telexed licence applications by some member states and not others; differing procedures for bank guarantees; and the refusal by one member state to accept a licence issued by another". Idem at p.116, para. 6.3.

bananas) mean that substantially more data must be maintained and submitted to show entitlement to a licence for third-country and non-traditional ACP bananas (see paragraphs 7.0 *et seq.*). These differences are not consistent with Article X:3(a)'s requirement of "uniform" administration.

7.212 **As a result, we find that the application of operator category rules in respect of the importation of third-country and non-traditional ACP bananas at in-quota tariff rates, in the absence of the application of such rules to traditional ACP imports, is inconsistent with the requirements of Article X:3(a) of GATT.**

(vi) other claims

7.213 In light of the foregoing findings on operator category rules and the allocation of certain percentages of import licences on the basis thereof, we do not consider it necessary to address the other claims raised by the Complaining parties against these EC measures. We further note that a finding that operator category rules are or are not inconsistent with the requirements of other provisions of GATT or the Licensing Agreement would not affect the findings we have made in respect of operator category rules.

c) Activity functions

7.214 Activity function rules apply to Category A operators as well as to Category B operators. Article 3 of Regulation 1442/93 defines three categories of economic activities, i.e. (1) "primary" importers, (2) "secondary" importers and (3) ripeners. Fixed percentages of the licences required for the importation of bananas from third countries or non-traditional ACP sources at lower duty rates within the tariff quota are allocated on the basis of these "activity functions": Article 5 of Regulation 1442/93 provides for a weighting coefficient of 57 per cent for "primary" importers, 15 per cent for "secondary" importers, and 28 per cent for ripeners of bananas. The EC notes that "the Commission is guided by the principle whereby the licences must be granted to natural or legal persons who have undertaken the commercial risk of marketing bananas and by the necessity of avoiding disturbing normal trading relations between persons occupying different points in the marketing chain".[434]

7.215 The Complaining parties raise claims against the activity function rules under Articles I, III, X and XIII of GATT as well as claims under the Licensing Agreement. In the case of Ecuador, we consider the claims it has raised under Articles I and X of GATT.

(i) Article III:4 of GATT

[7.216-7.219 Used in the Guatemala-Honduras report.]

7.216 The Complainants claim that, while the reservation to ripeners of 28 per cent of the Category A and B import licences required for the importation of third-country bananas does not necessarily force operators to alter their trade and distribution pattern, the activity function rules provide nevertheless a strong incentive for operators to change the pattern of their economic activities with a view to maximizing their licence allocation. In the Complainants' view, the activity function rules require marketing through "middlemen"[435] and are inconsistent with Article III:4 of GATT.

7.217 The EC explains that the licence distribution on the basis of "activity functions" is indispensable in order to avoid that certain operators in the supply chain would obtain extraordinary bargaining powers over

---

[434] Recital 15 of Council Regulation 404/93.

[435] Panel Report on "Canada - Administration of the Foreign Investment Review Act", adopted on 7 February 1984, BISD 30S/140, 160, para. *5.10.*

their trading partners due to the commercial and financial power associated with the allocation of import licences for the tariff quota. The EC further submits that the Complainants failed to provide evidence as to how rules establishing activity functions could tilt competitive opportunities in favour of domestic products.

7.218 We note that the classification of companies according to the economic activities they perform applies to both Category A and B operators. Thus, for the application of the activity function rules, it does not matter whether economic actors have previously traded in third-country and non-traditional ACP bananas, on the one hand, or traditional ACP and EC bananas, on the other. Consequently, the rules establishing activity functions as such do not discriminate against bananas from third-country and non-traditional ACP sources. Unlike the case of the Category B operators, the right to import bananas at in-quota tariff rates is not tied to the purchase of domestic products. Thus, in respect of activity function rules, third-country and non-traditional ACP bananas are not treated less favourably than EC bananas in the terms of Article III:4.

7.219 **Consequently, we find that the use of activity functions in connection with the allocation of licences allowing the importation of third-country and non-traditional ACP bananas at in-quota tariff rates is not inconsistent with the requirements of Article III:4 of GATT.**

(ii) Article I:1 of GATT

[7.20-7.23 Used in the Ecuador, Guatemala/Honduras, and United States report.]

7.220 The Complainants claim that activity function rules are inconsistent with the requirements of Article I:1 because import licences for bananas from third countries are issued to Category A and B operators according to the economic activities performed by them, while the licensing system applied to imports of traditional ACP bananas does not utilize activity functions as a criteria for issuing licences. The EC argues that it is necessary to issue licences on the basis of activity functions so that certain operators in the supply chain do not obtain extraordinary bargaining power due to the commercial and financial power associated with import licences and that the use of activity functions as a criteria for issuing licences has no direct impact on the imports of bananas from any source. In the EC's view, the absence of a licence allocation based on activity functions under the traditional ACP licensing procedures cannot be regarded as an "advantage" in the meaning of Article I and thus there is no inconsistency with the requirements of Article I. In the alternative, the EC takes the position that activity function rules are covered by the Lomé waiver.

7.221 In our view, import licensing procedures, including the activity function rules, are "rules and formalities in connection with importation" in the meaning of Article I:1. For example, a panel found that comparatively less favourable rules for revoking countervailing duties were an "advantage" for purposes of Article I:1 and that "making a regulatory advantage available to imports from some countries while not making it available to others" is inconsistent with Article I:1.[436] As noted earlier, in our view, the procedural and administrative requirements for imports of third-country and non-traditional ACP bananas arising from the application of the activity function rules differ from, and go significantly beyond, those required in respect of traditional ACP bananas. More specifically, the activity function rules contained in the licensing procedures for third-country and non-traditional ACP bananas (but not in the procedures applicable to traditional ACP bananas) mean that substantially more data must be maintained and submitted to show entitlement to a licence for third-country and non-traditional ACP bananas. In particular, in respect of past banana imports, Article 4(2) of Regulation 1442/93 requires a breakdown by origin, by category *and* activity function. Thus, we believe that the licensing procedures applied by the EC to traditional ACP banana imports, when compared to the licensing procedures imposed on third-country and non-traditional ACP imports with its activity function rules, can be considered as an "advantage" which the EC does not accord to third-country and non-traditional ACP imports..

[436] Panel Report on "US - Denial of MFN Treatment as to Non-Rubber Footwear from Brazil", adopted on 19 June 1992, BISD 39S/128, 150-151, paras. 6.8-6.14.

7.222 We consider that imports of third-country and non-traditional ACP bananas are treated less favourably than traditional ACP imports since the latter are not subject to activity function rules. Finally, for the reasons given above, we reiterate our finding that the Lomé waiver does not waive the EC's obligations under Article I:1 in respect of licensing procedures (*infra*).

7.223 Accordingly, we find that the application of activity function rules in respect of the importation of third-country and non-traditional ACP bananas at in-quota tariff rates, in the absence of the application of such rules to traditional ACP imports, is inconsistent with the requirements of Article I:1 of GATT.

(iii) Article X:3(a) of GATT

[7.224-7.231 used in the Ecuador, Guatemala/Honduras and Mexico report.]

7.224 The Complainants claim that the differences in the licensing procedures applied by the EC to traditional ACP imports and those applied to third-country and non-traditional ACP imports and in particular the rules establishing activity functions are inconsistent with the requirements of Article X:3 of GATT because they are not administered in a uniform, impartial and reasonable manner. The EC responds that Article X only applies to internal measures and therefore is not applicable in this case. Alternatively, it argues that a system permitted under Article I by the Lomé waiver cannot be found to breach another GATT provision imposing MFN-like obligations similar to those waived. The EC maintains that the activity function rules are administered in a uniform, impartial and reasonable manner among the third countries which are subject to that separate licensing regime and that the Complainants have failed to provide evidence to the contrary.

7.225 Article X:3(a) provides:

> Each Member shall administer in a uniform, impartial and reasonable manner all its laws, regulations, decisions and rulings of the kind described in paragraph 1 of this Article.

Article X:1 defines the coverage of Article X:3(a) as follows:

> Laws, regulations, judicial decisions and administrative rulings of general application, made effective by any Member, pertaining to the classification or the valuation of products for customs purposes, or to rates of duty, taxes or other charges, or to requirements, restrictions or prohibitions on imports or exports or on the transfer of payments therefor, or affecting their sale, distribution, transportation, insurance, warehousing, inspection, exhibition, processing, mixing or other use ....

Given that this provision enumerates national legislation regarding border measures as well as internal measures, and customs tariffs as well as quantitative measures, the coverage of Article X could hardly be more comprehensive. Accordingly, internal laws regulating border measures constitute "... requirements ... on imports ..." in the meaning of Article X:1 and cannot be excluded from its scope.

7.226 Consequently, we find that the EC import licensing procedures are subject to the requirements of Article X of GATT.

7.227 More specifically, the Complainants claim that the rules establishing activity functions are inconsistent with the requirements of Article X:3(a) because the EC applies them to imports of third-country and non-traditional ACP bananas but not to traditional ACP imports. According to the Complainants, these rules are inconsistent with the standards of "uniform, impartial and reasonable administration" of domestic laws, regulations, decisions and rulings and thus are inconsistent with the requirements of Article X:3(a). The EC maintains that the rules applying activity functions are administered in a uniform, impartial and reasonable manner among the third countries which are subject to that separate licensing regime and that the Complainants have failed to provide evidence to the contrary.

7.228 The Complainants support their argument by referring to a 1968 Note by the GATT Director-General, which stated that Article X:3(a)

> would not permit, in the treatment accorded to imported goods, discrimination based on country of origin, nor would they permit the application of one set of regulations and procedures with respect to some contracting parties and a different set with respect to the others.[437]

The EC responds that the 1968 Note cannot be considered as an authoritative interpretation of GATT rules because it was never endorsed by a formal decision of the CONTRACTING PARTIES.

7.229 We note that a prior panel in discussing the interpretation of Article X:3(a) found that its terms would be met if regulations were applied "in a substantially uniform manner, although there were some minor administrative variations, e.g. concerning the form in which licence applications could be made and the requirement of pro-forma invoices".[438] In that case, the panel found that such differences were minimal and did not in themselves establish a breach of Article X:3(a).

7.230 In our view, the Director-General's Note correctly describes the reach of Article X:3(a) and is consistent with the quoted panel decision. While minor "administrative variations" in the application of regulations may not be inconsistent with the requirements of Article X:3(a), as suggested by the above-mentioned panel report, two different sets of rules would be inconsistent with the requirements of Article X:3(a). In this case, we are confronted with a common regime for the importation of bananas into the EC with two different origin-based sets of import licensing procedures. These sets of licensing procedures differ from one another, depending on whether imports of bananas are from traditional ACP sources or from third countries and non-traditional ACP sources, including with respect to the application of activity function rules. As noted earlier, (e.g., [discussion of: *ed.*] Article 4:2(b) of Regulation 1442/93), in our view, the procedural and administrative requirements for imports of third-country and non-traditional ACP bananas arising from the activity function rules differ from, and go significantly beyond, those required in respect of traditional ACP bananas. More specifically, the activity function rules contained in the licensing procedures for third-country and non-traditional ACP bananas (but not in the procedures applicable to traditional ACP bananas) mean that substantially more data must be maintained and submitted to show entitlement to a licence for third-country and non-traditional ACP bananas. These differences are not merely minor administrative variations in the application of regulations but are two different sets of rules which are inconsistent with the requirement of "uniform" administration as required by Article X:3(a).

7.231 **As a result, we find that the application of activity function rules in respect of the importation of third-country and non-traditional ACP bananas at in-quota tariff rates, in the absence of the application of such rules to traditional ACP imports, is inconsistent with the requirements of Article X:3(a) of GATT.**

---

[437] Note by the GATT Director-General of 29 November 1968, L/3149.

[438] Panel Report on "EEC - Restrictions on Imports of Dessert Apples", Complaint by Chile, adopted on 22 June 1989, BISD 36S/93, 133, para. 12.30. In the descriptive part of the *Chilean Apples* case, "concerning Article X:3, Chile argued that there were differences among the ten member states of the EEC as to the requirements they imposed on applications for licences for imports of dessert apples. It cited examples, such as a French requirement for licence applications to be accompanied by a pro forma invoice, which effectively meant that licences could not be applied for until after ships had been loaded. Other examples cited by Chile included acceptance of telexed licence applications by some member states and not others; differing procedures for bank guarantees; and the refusal by one member state to accept a licence issued by another". Idem at page 116, para. 6.3.

(iv) other claims

7.232 In light of the foregoing findings on activity function rules under Articles I and X, we do not consider it necessary to address the other claims raised by the Complaining parties against these EC measures. We further note that a finding that activity function rules are or are not inconsistent with the requirements of other provisions of GATT or the Licensing Agreement would not affect the findings we have made in respect of activity function rules.

d) BFA export certificates

7.233 As part of the EC import licensing procedures, Category A and C operators are required, for imports from Colombia, Costa Rica or Nicaragua, to present export certificates issued by these countries. Category B operators are exempted from this requirement.

The relevant part of Article 6 of the BFA provides that:

> ... supplying countries with country quotas may deliver special export certificates for up to 70% of their quota, which, in turn, constitute a prerequisite for the issuance, by the Community, of certificates for the importation of bananas from said countries by "Category A" and "Category C" operators. ....

The relevant part of Article 3.2 of EC Regulation 478/95 reads as follows:

> For goods originating in Colombia, Costa Rica or Nicaragua, the application for an import licence of category A or C ... shall also not be admissible unless it is accompanied by an export licence currently valid for a quantity at least equal to that of the goods, issued by the competent authorities listed in Annex II.[439]

In light of these provisions, we consider the claims raised the Complaining parties, who have alleged that the export certificate requirement is inconsistent with the requirements of Articles I, III and X of GATT and Articles 1.2, 1.3 and 3.2 of the Licensing Agreement. In the case of Ecuador, we consider the claim it raised under Article I.

7.234 Initially, the EC argues that a consideration of export certificates is outside the Panel's terms of reference because such certificates are not issued by the EC and therefore not part of the EC banana import regime. We agree that to the extent that the administration of export certificates is carried out by the authorities of Colombia, Costa Rica or Nicaragua, as appropriate,[440] it is not within the terms of reference of this Panel. However, we cannot agree with the EC's argument that export certificates are completely outside the EC's sphere of competence and their legal examination thus entirely excluded from the mandate of this Panel. On the contrary, Article 3 of Regulation 478/95 states clearly that an application for an EC import licence is not admissible unless it is accompanied by an export certificate. Thus the requirement to match EC import licences with BFA export certificates and the exemption of Category B operators therefrom are part of the EC legal system and, accordingly, are within our terms of reference, to the extent they fall within the EC's responsibility.

---

[439] Regulation No. 478/95 of 1 March 1995 on additional rules for the application of Council Regulation (EEC) No. 404/93 as regards the tariff quota arrangements for imports of bananas into the Community and amending Regulations (EEC) No. 1442/93, O.J. L 49/13 of 4 March 1995.

[440] According to Annex II of Regulation 478/95, the bodies authorized to issue special export certificates are: for Colombia: Instituto Colombiano de Comercio Exterior; for Costa Rica: Corporación Bananera S.A.; and for Nicaragua: Ministerio de Economia y Desarrollo, Dirección de Comercio Exterior.

(i) Article I:1 of GATT

7.235 The Complainants claim that the fact that the EC recognizes only export certificates issued by BFA signatories as prerequisites for importation, amounts to the conferral of a "privilege" (i.e., a commercial benefit) not enjoyed by other Members. This is alleged to be inconsistent with the requirements of Article I:1.

7.236 The EC responds that the Complainants have failed to prove that the export certificate requirement constitutes an "advantage" in the meaning of Article I:1 accorded to BFA signatories which is not conferred on other third countries. The EC concedes that the administration of the export certificates by BFA signatories can generate quota rents, but only among operators who are interested in marketing BFA bananas. However, the EC takes the position that the WTO agreements do not contain rules on the sharing and allocation of quota rents, e.g., by means of a licensing scheme. Therefore, in its view, any government is entitled to pursue its own policies in the distribution of quota rents provided that there is no discrimination between products originating in different Members.

7.237 The issue presented is whether the export certificate requirement constitutes an advantage in respect of rules and formalities in connection with importation accorded to BFA bananas that is not accorded to third-country bananas as required by Article I:1.

7.238 On its face, it would appear that there is discrimination against BFA bananas because they are subject to a requirement that is not imposed on other third-country bananas. However, closer analysis suggests that the export certificate requirement may in fact constitute a favour, advantage, privilege or immunity in the meaning of Article I. It is a commonplace, which no party to the dispute contests, that tariff quotas are likely to generate quota rents. The allocation of licences used in the administration of such tariff quotas can be viewed as a mechanism for the distribution of such rents. In fact, the parties do not contest that the export certificate requirement serves the purpose, or at least has the effect, of transferring part of the quota rent which would normally accrue to initial EC import licence holders to the suppliers who are initial holders of export certificates for bananas originating in the three BFA countries. The EC argues that the WTO agreements do not contain any rules governing the distribution of quota rents which are generated by trade measures, e.g., tariff quotas, whose imposition is legitimate under those agreements. We nevertheless have to ascertain whether the particular mechanisms implemented for the purposes of rent transfer directly or indirectly entail inconsistencies with the obligations Members have to respect under the WTO agreements.

7.239 The requirement to match EC import licences with BFA export certificates means that those BFA banana suppliers who are initial holders of export certificates enjoy a commercial advantage compared to banana suppliers from other third countries.[441] We note that it is not possible to ascertain how many of the initial BFA export certificate holders are BFA banana producers or to what extent the tariff quota rent share that accrues to initial holders of BFA export certificates is passed on to the producers of BFA bananas in a way to create more favourable competitive opportunities for *bananas* of BFA origin. However, we also note that the possibility does exist to pass on tariff quota rent to BFA banana producers in such a way, whereas there is no such possibility in respect of non-BFA third-country banana producers. Thus, the EC's requirement affects the competitive relationship between *bananas* of non-BFA third-country origin and bananas of BFA origin. It is certainly true that Article I of GATT is concerned with the treatment of foreign *products* originating from different foreign sources rather than with the treatment of the suppliers of these products. In this respect, we note that the transfer of tariff quota rents which would normally accrue to initial holders of EC import licences to initial holders of BFA export certificates does occur when *bananas* originating in Colombia, Costa Rica and

---

[441] "Whereas the framework agreement provides that the signatory countries are authorized to issue export licences for seventy per cent of their allocations, which licences are to be presented in order to obtain import licences of Category A and C for import into the Community, *in conditions which may improve the regularity and stability of commercial transactions* and guarantee the absence of any discriminatory treatment among operators" (emphasis added). Recital 8 of Regulation No. 478/95.

Nicaragua are, at some point, traded to the EC. Therefore, in our view, the requirement to match EC import licences with BFA export certificates and thus the commercial value of export certificates are linked to the *product* at issue as required under Article I. In practice, from the perspective of EC *importers* who are Category A or C operators, bananas of non-BFA third-country origin appear to be more profitable than bananas of BFA origin. This is confirmed by the fact that EC import licences for non-BFA third-country bananas and Category B licences for BFA bananas are typically oversubscribed in the first round of licence allocations, while Category A and C licences for BFA bananas are usually exhausted only in the second round of the quarterly licence allocation procedure. The EC argues that the fact that licences allowing the importation of non-BFA bananas at in-quota tariff rates are usually exhausted in the first round amounts to an advantage for bananas of Complainants' origin. While we do not endorse the EC's view, even if this were to constitute an advantage, we note "that Article I:1 does not permit balancing more favourable treatment under some procedure against a less favourable treatment under others".[442]

7.240 Indeed, one could argue that if the export certificate requirement is beneficial to BFA countries, non-BFA third countries could autonomously introduce a similar requirement in order to reap quota rent benefits. In this case, however, since the allocation of the "others" category of the BFA is not country-specific under the current EC regime, operators could switch to alternative sources within this category which are not subject to an export certificate requirement. Therefore, we consider that the requirement to match BFA export certificates with EC import licences in connection with the country-specific allocation of tariff quota shares under the BFA is an advantage or privilege in the terms of Article I:1 in respect of rules and formalities in connection with importation. Since the EC accords this advantage to products originating in Colombia, Costa Rica and Nicaragua "while denying the same advantage to a like product originating in the territories of other [Members],"[443] i.e., the Complainants' countries, the requirement to match EC import licences with BFA export certificates as provided for in Article 3 of Regulation 478/95 is inconsistent with Article I:1.

7.241 **For these reasons, we find that the requirement to match EC import licences with BFA export certificates is inconsistent with the requirements of Article I:1 of GATT.**

(ii) other claims

7.242 In light of our finding that the requirement to match EC import licences with BFA export certificates is inconsistent with the requirements of Article I:1, one of the fundamental provisions of GATT, we consider it unnecessary to make specific rulings on the other claims raised by the Complaining parties with respect to the same EC measures, including the claim that the exemption of Category B operators from the matching requirement violates Article I also. A finding that these measures are or are not inconsistent with the requirements of Articles III and X of GATT and the Licensing Agreement would not affect our findings in respect of Article I. Moreover, steps taken by the EC to bring the measures into conformity with Article I should also eliminate the alleged non-conformity with these other obligations.

---

[442] "The Panel ... considered that Article I:1 does not permit balancing more favourable treatment under some procedure against a less favourable treatment under others. If such a balancing were accepted, it would entitle a contracting party to derogate from the most-favoured nation obligation in one case, in respect of one contracting party, on the ground that it accords more favourable treatment in some other case in respect of another contracting party. In the view of the Panel, such an interpretation of the most-favoured-nation obligation of Article I:1 would defeat the very purpose underlying the unconditionality of that obligation". Panel Report on "United States - Denial of Most-favoured-nation Treatment as to Non-rubber Footwear from Brazil", adopted on 19 June 1992, BISD 39S/128, 151, para. 6.10. Likewise, in the context of Article III a panel found that "an element of more favourable treatment would only be relevant if it would always accompany and offset an element of differential treatment causing less favourable treatment." Panel Report on "United States - Section 377 of the Tariff Act of 1930", adopted on 7 November 1989, BISD 36S/345, 388, para. *5.16*.

[443] Panel Report on "United States - Denial of Most-favoured-nation Treatment as to Non-rubber Footwear from Brazil", adopted on 19 June 1992, BISD 39S/128, 151, para. 6.11.

e) Hurricane licences

7.243 Hurricane licences[444] authorize operators who include or represent EC and ACP producers, or producer organizations "to import in compensation third-country bananas and non-traditional ACP bananas for the benefit of the operators who directly suffered damage as a result of the impossibility of the supplying the Community market with bananas originating in affected producer regions" because of the impact of tropical storms.[445] In the aftermath of the hurricanes Debbie, Iris, Luis and Marilyn, 281,605 tonnes[446] of third-country or non-traditional ACP imports were authorized between November 1994 and May 1996. The Complaining parties have raised claims under Article I, III and X of GATT and Articles 1.2, 1.3 and 3.5(h) of the Licensing Agreement. In the case of Ecuador, it did not raise any of these claims.

(i) Article III:4 of GATT

[7.244-7.250 Used in the Guatemala-Honduras and Mexico reports.]

7.244 The Complainants allege that the issuance of hurricane licences by the EC is inconsistent with the requirements of Article III:4 of GATT because EC producers are treated more favourably than third-country suppliers. The EC argues that the distribution of hurricane licences does not discriminate against bananas from third countries because hurricane licences are used for the importation of third-country or non-traditional ACP bananas.

7.245 We recall that it is the purpose of the national treatment clause to protect foreign *products* from being treated less favourably than like domestic products. Therefore, we have to examine whether the EC, by issuing hurricane licences, treats third-country bananas less favourably than domestic bananas.[447] We note that hurricane licences can be used to import third-country bananas or non-traditional ACP bananas. Therefore, by issuing hurricane licences, the EC in effect authorizes imports of third-country (and non-traditional ACP) bananas at the lower duty rates in addition to the imports under the EC bound tariff quota.

---

[444] See, e.g., Commission Regulation (EC) No. 2791/94 of 16 November 1994 on the exceptional allocation of a quantity additional to the tariff quota for imports of bananas in 1994 as a result of tropical storm Debbie. Commission Regulation (EC) No. 510/95 of 7 March 1995 on the exceptional allocation of a quantity additional to the tariff quota for imports of bananas during the first quarter of 1995 as a result of tropical storm Debbie. Commission Regulation (EC) No. 1163/95 of 23 May 1995 on the exceptional allocation of a quantity additional to the tariff quota for imports of bananas during the second quarter of 1995 as a result of tropical storm Debbie. Commission Regulation (EC) No. 2358/95 of 6 October 1995 on the exceptional allocation of a quantity additional to the tariff quota for imports of bananas during the fourth quarter of 1995 as a result of tropical storms Iris, Luis and Marilyn. Commission Regulation (EC) No. 127/96 of 25 January 1996 on the exceptional allocation of a quantity additional to the tariff quota for imports of bananas during the first quarter of 1996 as a result of tropical storms Iris, Luis and Marilyn. Commission Regulation (EC) No. 822/96 of 3 May 1996 on the exceptional allocation of a quantity additional to the tariff quota for imports of bananas during the second quarter of 1996 as a result of tropical storms Iris, Luis and Marilyn.

[445] "Whereas ... these measures should be to the benefit of the operators who have directly suffered actual damage, without the possibility of compensation, and as a function of the extent of the damage." Recital 9 of Commission Regulation (EC) No. 510/95 of 7 March 1995 on the exceptional allocation of a quantity additional to the tariff quota for imports of bananas during the first quarter of 1995 as a result of tropical storm Debbie.

[446] Total quantities of authorized third-country and non-traditional ACP imports:

Regulation No. 2791/94 of 18 November 1994:	53,400 tonnes
Regulation No. 510/95 of 7 March 1995:	45,500 tonnes
Regulation No. 1163/95 of 23 May 1995:	19,465 tonnes
Regulation No. 2358/95 of 6 October 1995:	90,800 tonnes
Regulation No. 127/96 of 25 January 1996:	51,350 tonnes
Regulation No. 822/96 of 3 May 1996:	21,090 tonnes
Total:	281,605 tonnes

[447] The exception of Article III:8(b) of GATT could be relevant where production aids to domestic production would accrue only to the producers, but not to processors of a domestic product. However, no such defense was raised in this case.

7.246 In turning to the substance of this claim, we note that only operators including or directly representing EC (or traditional ACP) banana producers or producer organizations who have suffered damage caused by a tropical storm are eligible for the allocation of hurricane licences. We consider that it is not possible to ascertain to what extent such operators pass on the tariff quota rents linked to the hurricane licences to EC (or ACP) banana producers in a way to create more favourable competitive opportunities for *bananas* of EC (or traditional ACP) origin. However, we also note that it is the object and purpose of the EC hurricane licence regulations to pass on tariff quota rents to EC (or ACP) producers, whereas no such possibility exists in respect of third-country banana producers. Thus, competitive opportunities for *bananas* of Complainants' origin are less favourable than those that the EC provides to bananas of EC (or traditional ACP) origin, additional production of which may be encouraged in hurricane-prone regions because of the reduced risk of financial losses for such EC (or traditional ACP) banana producers in the event of a tropical storm.

7.247 Furthermore, since hurricane licences are issued only to operators who include or directly represent EC (or ACP) producers or producer organizations affected by a tropical storm,[448] Category A operators who have historically marketed third-country and non-traditional ACP bananas will not be allocated hurricane licences at all, irrespective of whether they include or represent third-country producers affected by a hurricane. Therefore, the fact that hurricane licences are issued only to operators who include or directly represent EC (or ACP) producers affected by a hurricane, although such licences might be used for the immediate importation of third-country (or non-traditional ACP) bananas, may provide an incentive for operators to market more EC (or traditional ACP) bananas grown in hurricane-prone areas than they otherwise would, in preference to third-country bananas, since the issuance of hurricane licences to eligible operators ensures that they can maintain, or do not lose, reference quantities for the purpose of establishing their entitlements to Category B licences in the future. Consequently, even if tariff quota rents linked to the hurricane licences are not fully passed on to producers by initial holders of hurricane licences who may only represent affected EC (or ACP) banana producers without being producers themselves, the greater incentive to market such EC (or traditional ACP) bananas arising from the fact that losses of such bananas caused by tropical storms can be expected to be compensated for through the allocation of hurricane licences, nevertheless, adversely affects conditions of competition for *bananas* of Complainants' origin in respect of which the risk of loss due to hurricanes cannot be expected to be reduced by the EC's hurricane licence allocations.

7.248 In light of the foregoing, we now consider whether the above-described practice of issuing hurricane licences is inconsistent with the requirements of Article III:4. To establish an inconsistency with Article III:4, it would be sufficient for the Complainants to show that third-country bananas are treated less favourably than EC bananas in respect of a law, regulation or requirement affecting their internal sale, etc. We recall that we have agreed with the findings of the second *Banana* panel, which stated: "A requirement to purchase a domestic product in order to obtain the right to import a product at a lower rate of duty under a tariff quota is therefore a requirement affecting the purchase of a product within the meaning of Article III:4". We note that this is the case in respect of the conditions attached to eligibility for hurricane licences. Since the practice of issuing hurricane licences may create an incentive for operators to purchase bananas of EC (and ACP) origin for marketing in the EC

[448] "1.The quantities referred to in Article 1(2) shall be allocated to the operators who:

- include or directly represent banana producers affected by tropical storm Debbie.
- and who, during the last quarter of 1994, are unable to supply, on their own account, the Community market with bananas originating in the regions or countries referred to 1(2) on account of the damage caused by tropical storm Debbie.

2. The competent authorities in the Member States concerned shall determine the beneficiary operators who meet the requirements of paragraph 1 and shall make an allocation to each of them pursuant to this Regulation on the basis of:

- the quantities allocated to the producer regions or countries referred to in Article 1(2) and of
- the damage sustained as a result of tropical storm Debbie.

3. The competent authorities shall assess the damage sustained on the basis of all supporting documents and information collected from the operators concerned." Article 2 of Commission Regulation No. 2791/94 of 16 November 1994 on the "exceptional allocation of a quantity additional to the tariff quota for imports of bananas in 1994 as a result of tropical storm Debbie.

rather than bananas of third-country origin, this practice is an advantage accorded to bananas of EC origin that is not accorded to bananas of third-country origin. Thus, in terms of Article III:4, third-country bananas are treated less favourably than EC (and ACP) bananas in respect of a law, regulation or requirement affecting their internal sale.

7.249 However, before deciding whether the practice of issuing hurricane licences is inconsistent with Article III:4, we need to consider that Article III:1 is a general principle that informs the rest of Article III, as the Appellate Body has recently stated.[449] Since Article III:1 constitutes part of the context of Article III:4, it must be taken into account in our interpretation of the latter. Article III:1 articulates a general principle that internal measures should not be applied so as to afford protection to domestic production.[450] According to the Appellate Body, the protective application of a measure can most often be discerned from the design, the architecture, and the revealing structure of the measure.[451] We consider that the design, architecture and structure of the EC practice of issuing hurricane licences all indicate that the measure is applied so to afford protection to EC (and ACP) producers.

7.250 **Thus, we find that the issuance of hurricane licences exclusively to EC producers and producer organizations or operators including or directly representing them is inconsistent with the requirements of Article III:4 of GATT.**

(ii) Article I:1 of GATT

[7.251-7.259 Used in the Guatemala-Honduras report.]

7.251 The Complainants claim that hurricane licences provide an "advantage" to ACP producers which is not unconditionally and immediately accorded to third-country producers as required by Article I:1 of GATT. The EC argues that the distribution of hurricane licences does not discriminate against bananas from third countries because hurricane licences are used for the importation of third-country or non-traditional ACP bananas. In the alternative, the EC submits that any inconsistency with Article I would be covered by the Lomé waiver.

7.252 We note that it is the purpose of the MFN clause to protect foreign *products* from being treated less favourably than like products of any other foreign origin. Therefore, we have to examine whether the EC, by issuing hurricane licences, accords bananas of Complainants' origin less favourable treatment than traditional ACP bananas. We share the view that hurricane licences are in general used to import third-country bananas or non-traditional ACP bananas. Therefore, by issuing hurricane licences, the EC in effect authorizes imports of third-country (and non-traditional ACP) bananas at the lower duty rates in addition to the imports under the EC bound tariff quota.

7.253 In turning to the substance of this claim, we note that only operators including or directly representing ACP (or EC) banana producers or producer organizations who have suffered damage caused by a tropical storm are eligible for the allocation of hurricane licences. We consider that it is not possible ascertain to what extent such operators pass on the tariff quota rents linked to the hurricane licences to ACP (or EC) banana producers in a way to create more favourable competitive opportunities for *bananas* of traditional ACP (or EC) origin. However, we also note that it is the object and purpose of the EC hurricane licence regulations to pass on tariff quota rents to

---

[449] Appellate Body Report on "Japan - Taxes on Alcoholic Beverages", *op. cit.*, p.18. The Report states: "The purpose of Article III:1 is to establish this general principle as a guide to understanding and interpreting the specific obligations contained in Article III:2 and in the other paragraphs of Article III, while respecting, and not diminishing in any way, the meaning of words actually used in the texts of those other paragraphs".

[450] Ibid., p.18.

[451] Ibid., p.29.

ACP (and EC) producers, whereas no such possibility exists in respect of third-country banana producers. Thus, the EC modifies the competitive relationship between *bananas* of Complainants' origin and bananas of traditional ACP (or EC) origin, additional production of which is encouraged in hurricane-prone regions because of the reduced risk of financial losses for such traditional ACP (and EC) banana producers in the event of a tropical storm.

7.254 Furthermore, since hurricane licences are issued only to operators who include or directly represent ACP (or EC) producers or producer organizations affected by a tropical storm, Category A operators who have historically marketed third-country and non-traditional ACP bananas are unlikely to be allocated hurricane licences at all, irrespective of whether they include or represent third-country producers affected by a hurricane. Therefore, the fact that hurricane licences are issued only to operators who include or directly represent ACP (or EC) producers, although such licences might be used for the immediate importation of third-country (or non-traditional ACP) bananas, may provide an incentive for operators to market more traditional ACP (or EC) bananas grown in hurricane-prone areas than they otherwise would, in preference to third-country bananas, since the issuance of hurricane licences to eligible operators ensures that they can maintain, or do not lose, reference quantities for the purpose of establishing their entitlements to Category B licences in the future. Consequently, even if tariff quota rents linked to the hurricane licences are not fully passed on to producers by initial holders of hurricane licences who may only represent affected ACP (or EC) banana producers without being producers themselves, in a way to constitute an advantage for bananas of traditional ACP (or EC) origin grown in hurricane-prone regions, the greater incentive to market such traditional ACP (or EC) bananas arising from the fact that losses of such bananas caused by tropical storms can be expected to be compensated for through the allocation of hurricane licences, nevertheless, is an advantage that the EC does not accord to bananas of Complainants' origin in respect of which the risk of loss due to hurricanes cannot be expected to be reduced by the EC's hurricane licence allocations.

7.255 In light of the foregoing, we now consider whether the above-described practice of issuing hurricane licences is inconsistent with the requirements of Article I.1. To establish an inconsistency with Article I:1, it would be sufficient for the Complainants to show that bananas of ACP origin are accorded an advantage in respect of matters referred to in Article III:4 that is not accorded to bananas of third-country origin. We have already found that this is a matter referred to in Article III:4 (*infra*). Since the practice of issuing hurricane licences may create an incentive for EC operators to purchase bananas of ACP (and EC) origin for marketing in the EC rather than bananas of third-country origin, this practice is an advantage in terms of Article I:1 accorded to bananas of ACP origin that is not accorded to bananas of third-country origin.

7.256 **Therefore, we find that the issuance of hurricane licences exclusively to traditional ACP producers and producer organizations or operators including or directly representing them is inconsistent with the requirements of Article I:1 of GATT.**

(iii) application of the Lomé waiver

7.257 The EC maintains that the practice of issuing hurricane licences to ACP countries derives from historic British and French schemes whose preservation is required by Protocol 5 of the Lomé Convention and covered by the Lomé waiver. The EC submits that under the UK scheme, "disaster licences" were issued to the affected operators to cover the volume lost, in proportion to the quantity of bananas that they would have supplied from traditional sources but for the disaster.[452] Similar arrangements were in force in France beginning in 1962 which, according to the EC, in the event of specific climate disasters authorized imports from other sources by those operators who had been affected by the disasters.

[452] According to the EC, the most recent example was the issue of disaster licences in 1989 following the destruction of the Jamaican banana crop caused by Hurricane Gilbert.

7.258 We recall that the Lomé waiver provides that:

> ... the provisions of paragraph 1 of Article I of the General Agreement shall be waived, until 29 February 2000, to the extent necessary to permit the European Communities to provide preferential treatment for products originating in ACP States as required by the relevant provisions of the Fourth Lomé Convention ....

In this connection, we further recall that Protocol 5 of the Lomé Convention requires that in respect of banana exports to the EC market, "no ACP States shall be placed, as regards access to its *traditional* markets and *its advantages* on those markets, in a less favourable situation than in the past or at present" and the Joint Declaration to Protocol 5[453] provides that "... no ACP State, *traditional* supplier to the Community, is placed as regards access to, and advantages in, the Community, in a less favourable situation than in the past or at present". Since the possibility of obtaining hurricane licences existed under the historic French and UK licensing schemes, hurricane licences can be viewed as advantages in the meaning of the Lomé Convention enjoyed by ACP States in the past in respect of their access to their traditional markets. As such, in terms of the Lomé waiver, the issuance of hurricane licences may be viewed as preferential treatment required by the Lomé Convention and thus is within the coverage of the Lomé waiver.

7.259 **Accordingly, we find that it was not unreasonable for the EC to conclude that the Lomé waiver waives its obligations under Article I:1 of GATT in respect of the issuance of hurricane licences to traditional ACP producers and producer organizations.**

(iv) Article 1.3 of the Licensing Agreement

[7.260-7.264 Used in the Guatemala-Honduras, Mexico and United States reports.]

7.260 The Complainants claim that the issuance of hurricane licences by the EC exclusively to EC and ACP producers and producer organizations as well as operators who include or directly represent them is inconsistent with the requirements of Article 1.3 which requires the neutral application and the fair and equitable administration of import licensing procedures. The EC argues that no discrimination occurs in connection with the issuance of hurricane licences because the eligibility for hurricane licences is based on objective criteria.

7.261 Article 1.3 of the Licensing Agreement provides:

> The rules for import licensing procedures shall be neutral in application and administered in a fair and equitable manner.

To apply Article 1.3, we must interpret the terms "neutrality" in application, as well as "fairness" and "equity" in administration. In this regard, we recall our interpretation of Article X:3(a) of GATT (*infra*). Using the reasoning developed there, we interpret the phrase "neutrality in application" to preclude the imposition of one system of import licensing procedures in respect of a product originating in certain Members and a different system of import licensing procedures on the same product originating in other Members.[454] In particular, we consider that the issuance of hurricane licences exclusively to ACP and EC producers and organizations or operators including or directly representing them in respect of bananas lost to hurricanes, but not to third-country producers and producer organizations or operators including or directly representing them, is inconsistent with the requirement of neutral

---

[453] Annex LXXIV - Joint declaration relating to Protocol 5 of the Fourth Lomé Convention.

[454] We recall that we considered that minor "administrative variations" in the application of regulations may not be inconsistent with Article X:3(a) of GATT (para. 7.0). In our view, the same consideration applies in the context of Article 1.3 of the Licensing Agreement.

application as contained in Article 1.3. In the light of the foregoing, we find it unnecessary to consider whether the EC hurricane licensing system meets Article 1.3's requirement of "fairness" and "equity".

7.262 The question then becomes whether the Lomé waiver applies so as to waive the EC's obligations under Article 1.3 in this regard. We note that the Lomé waiver was initially approved by the CONTRACTING PARTIES of GATT 1947, who had no power over the Tokyo Round Agreement on Import Licensing Procedures, which, at the time, was administered by a committee of signatories and contained no waiver provision. In the light of these considerations, the Lomé waiver from Article I of GATT cannot be read to waive the EC's obligations under Article 1.3 of the Licensing Agreement. We also note that the extension of the waiver by the General Council of the WTO has not altered that fact.

7.263 **As a result, we find that the issuance of hurricane licences exclusively to ACP and EC producers and producer organizations or operators including or directly representing them is inconsistent with the requirements of Article 1.3 of the Licensing Agreement.**

(v) other claims

7.264 In light of our findings that the issuance of hurricane licences exclusively to EC and ACP producers and producer organizations or operators including or directly representing them is inconsistent with the requirements of Article III:4 of GATT and Article 1.3 of the Licensing Agreement, we consider it unnecessary to make specific rulings on the other claims raised by the Complaining parties with respect to the same EC measures. We further note that a finding that these measures are or are not inconsistent with the requirements of Article X:3(a) of GATT or Article 3:5(h) of the Licensing Agreement would not affect the findings we have made in respect of hurricane licences. Moreover, steps taken by the EC to bring the measures into conformity with the requirements of these articles should also eliminate the alleged non-conformity with Article X:3(a) of GATT and Article 3:5(h) of the Licensing Agreement.

f) Other claims

(i) general

7.265 In light of the findings we have made on operator categories, activity functions, export certificates and hurricane licences under Articles I, III and X of GATT, we do not consider it necessary to address the other claims raised by the Complaining parties against the EC licensing procedures. These claims are largely dependent on the existence of the operator category and activity function rules. For example, the alleged overfiling and unnecessary burdens and the alleged restrictive and distortive effects claimed to be inconsistent with the requirements of Article 3.2 of the Licensing Agreement and the alleged discouragement of tariff quota use claimed to be inconsistent with the requirements of Article 3.5(h) of the Licensing Agreement arise from the application of those rules. We further note that a finding that these EC measures are or are not inconsistent with the requirements of other provisions of GATT or the Licensing Agreement would not affect the findings we have made in respect of the EC licensing procedures.

7.266 We examine only the claim based on Article 1.2 of the Licensing Agreement, which we are required to do by Article 12.11 of the DSU since the claim relates to developing country Members.

(ii) Article 1.2 of the Licensing Agreement

7.267 The Complainants allege that the EC import licensing regime in general and the distribution of licences on the basis of operator categories as well as the application of activity function rules to operators importing third-country and non-traditional ACP bananas in particular, are inconsistent with the requirements of Article 1.2 of the Licensing Agreement. Moreover, in their view, economic development purposes and financial and trade needs of developing country Members are not sufficiently taken into account by the EC licensing procedures. In response, the EC recalls its position that the Licensing Agreement does not apply to tariff quota regimes, and furthermore submits Article 1.2 is merely a generic reminder that import licensing procedures should be in conformity with GATT rules. In the EC's view, Article 1.2 does not in itself create obligations additional to those arising from GATT.

7.268 Article 1.2 reads:

> Members shall ensure that the administrative procedures used to implement import licensing regimes are in conformity with the relevant provisions of GATT 1994 including its annexes and protocols, as interpreted by this Agreement, with a view to preventing trade distortions that may arise from an inappropriate operation of those procedures, taking into account the economic development purposes and financial and trade needs of developing country Members.[455]

This provision derives from the 1979 Tokyo Round Agreement on Import Licensing Procedures which was negotiated as a self-standing agreement without a formal legal link to GATT 1947. Accordingly, membership was open not only to GATT contracting parties and the European Communities, but also to any other government.[456] Therefore, provisions of GATT 1947 applied between the signatories of the 1979 Licensing Agreement, by virtue of that agreement, only to the extent that they had been explicitly referred to and incorporated into the 1979 Licensing Agreement. In this context, Articles 1.10 and 4.2 of the 1979 Licensing Agreement mention, *inter alia*, Articles XXI, XXII and XXIII of GATT 1947. Accordingly, the general rule that administrative procedures used to implement import licensing regimes had to conform with the relevant GATT provisions in fact added only to the obligations which any non-GATT contracting parties among the signatories of the 1979 Licensing Agreement would have been subject to.[457]

7.269 The wording of Article 1.2 remained unchanged in the Uruguay Round. Given that the Agreement Establishing the WTO and all the agreements listed in Annexes 1 through 3 thereto constitute a single undertaking, however, Article 1.2 of the WTO Licensing Agreement has become largely duplicative of the obligations already provided for in GATT, except for the reference to developing country Members. Given this context, Article 1.2 of the WTO Licensing Agreement has lost most of its legal significance.

7.270 However, the Appellate Body has endorsed the principle of effective treaty interpretation by stating that "an interpreter is not free to adopt a reading that would result in reducing whole clauses or paragraphs of a treaty to redundancy or inutility".[458] In light of this, we have to give effect and meaning to Article 1.2 of the Licensing Agreement.

7.271 **For this reason, to the extent that we find that specific aspects of the EC licensing procedures are not in conformity with Articles I, III or X of GATT, we necessarily also find an inconsistency with the requirements of Article 1.2 of the Licensing Agreement.**

---

[455] The footnote to Article 1.2 of the Licensing Agreement provides: "Nothing in this Agreement shall be taken as implying that the basis, scope and duration of a measure being implemented by a licensing procedure is subject to question under this Agreement."

[456] 1979 Licensing Agreement, Article 5.

[457] In fact, there were no such signatories.

[458] Appellate Body Report on "US - Standards for Reformulated and Conventional Gasoline", adopted 20 May 1996, AB-1996-1, WT/DS2/AB/R, p.23.

7.272 With respect to Article 1.2's requirement that account should be taken of "economic development purposes and financial and trade needs of developing country Members", the Licensing Agreement does not give guidance as to how that obligation should be applied in specific cases. We believe that this provision could be interpreted as a recognition of the difficulties that might arise for developing country Members, in imposing licensing procedures, to comply fully with the provisions of GATT and the Licensing Agreement. In the alternative, Article 1.2 could also be read to authorize, but not to require, developed country Members to apply preferential licensing procedures to imports from developing country Members. In any event, even if we accept the latter interpretation, we have not been presented with evidence suggesting that, in its licensing procedures, there were factors that the EC should have but did not take into account under Article 1.2.

7.273 **Therefore, we do not make a finding on whether the EC failed to take into account the needs of developing countries in a manner inconsistent with the requirements of Article 1.2 of the Licensing Agreement.**

4. *The EC banana import licensing procedures and the GATS*

a) *Introduction*

7.274 The Complainants[459] claim that the EC regime for the importation, sale and distribution of bananas is inconsistent with the EC's obligations under Articles II (Most-Favoured-Nation Treatment) and XVII (National Treatment) of GATS in that it discriminates against distributors of Latin American and non-traditional ACP bananas in favour of distributors of EC and traditional ACP bananas. The Complainants consider such distributors to be suppliers of "wholesale trade services", a service sector in which the EC has undertaken a full commitment on national treatment in its Schedule. They also consider both groups of distributors to be "like" service suppliers within the meaning of Articles II and XVII. The Complainants have made claims with respect to four specific measures of the EC regime that we have analyzed in the preceding section on import licensing procedures: operator category allocations, activity function rules, BFA export certificates and hurricane licences.

7.275 The EC rejects the claims with respect to the GATS arguing, *inter alia*, that the measures in respect of which the Complainants have made claims were measures directed at trade in goods and not trade in services. Therefore, they could not be considered "measures affecting trade in services" within the meaning of the GATS. Moreover, the EC argues that "wholesale trade services" covers only the distribution of ripened (yellow) bananas, while the measures at issue relate to the import of unripened (green) bananas. In addition, the EC contests that the Complainants' services and service suppliers have been given less favourable treatment in the meaning of the GATS. In its view, the Complainants are contesting the allocation of tariff quota rents, a matter not dealt with by the GATS.

7.276 In our consideration of the claims raised under the GATS, we first examine seven general issues: (i) whether the four measures cited by the Complainants constitute "measures affecting trade in services" within the meaning of the GATS; (ii) the definition of "wholesale trade services"; (iii) the supply of services through different modes; (iv) the scope of Article II obligations; (v) the scope of Article XVII obligations; (vi) the effective date of GATS obligations; and (vii) the admissibility of Mexico's claims. Second, we examine the consistency of four specific measures - operator category allocations, activity function rules, BFA export certificates and "hurricane licences - with the EC's obligations under Article II and its commitments under Article XVII.

[459] In this section on services, the term "Complainants" refers to Ecuador and the United States, and to Mexico except in respect of claims under Article XVII of GATS concerning activity function rules, export certificates and hurricane licences.

(b) General issues

(i) measures affecting trade in services

7.277 The EC claims that the four measures complained against by the Complainants are not "measures affecting trade in services" since they regulate the importation of goods and not the provision of services. The EC argues that the objective of the GATS is to regulate trade in services as such and that it covers the supply of services as products in their own right. Furthermore, it argues the GATS is not concerned with the indirect effects of measures relating to trade in goods on the supply of services.

7.278 The EC also argues that a measure could not be covered by both GATT and the GATS since the coverage of the two agreements was intended, in the EC's view, to be mutually exclusive. In this connection, the EC notes that if a measure relating to trade in goods was covered by a GATT exception or a waiver, such exception or waiver could be rendered ineffectual by a finding against the measure relating to goods under the GATS and asserting its illegality in that context. The EC also considers that the illustrative definition of "measures affecting trade in services" in Article XXVIII(c) of GATS mentions measures as they relate to the supply of services and not the supply of goods. In the EC's view, in Article XXVIII(c), the term "affecting", which is used in Article I to define the scope of the GATS, should be interpreted narrowly so as to mean "in respect of", which is a much narrower concept indicating that the measure in question has to have the purpose and aim of regulating, or at least directly influencing, services as services.

7.279 In examining these issues we note the following: Article I (Scope and Definition), which defines the scope of the GATS, states in paragraph 1:

> This Agreement applies to measures by Members affecting trade in services.

Article XXVIII(c) of GATS further defines the term by stating:

> measures by Members affecting trade in services' *include* measures in respect of:
> (i) the purchase, payment or use of a service;
> (ii) the access to and use of, in connection with the supply of a service, services which are required by those Members to be offered to the public generally;
> (iii) the presence, including commercial presence, of persons of a Member for the supply of a service in the territory of another Member;" (emphasis added).

7.280 In accordance with Article 31 of the Vienna Convention on the Law of Treaties,[460] we note that the ordinary meaning of the term "affecting", in Article I:1 of GATS, does not convey any notion of limiting the scope of the GATS to certain types of measures or to a certain regulatory domain. On the contrary, Article I:1 refers to measures in terms of their effect, which means they could be of any type or relate to any domain of regulation. Like GATT, the GATS is an umbrella agreement which applies to all sectors of trade in services and all types of regulations. We also note that the definition of "measures by Members affecting trade in services" in Article XXVIII(c) has been drafted in an illustrative manner by the use of the term "include". Sub-paragraphs (i)-(iii) do not contain a definition of "measures by Members affecting trade in services" as such, but rather are an illustrative list of matters in respect of which such measures could be taken. In other words, the term "in respect of" does not describe any measures affecting trade in services, but rather describes what such measures might regulate. For example, sub-paragraph (i) refers to "the purchase, payment or use of a service", which are matters that could be regulated by different types of measures affecting trade in services, such as licensing requirements, numerical limitations, foreign exchange regulations or others. We, therefore, do not agree with the view of the EC that Article XXVIII(c) narrows the meaning of the term "affecting" to "in respect of".

---

[460] See para. 7.0 supra.

7.281 In accordance with Article 32 of the Vienna Convention,[461] we note that the preparatory work of the GATS confirms the foregoing interpretation. In the Uruguay Round, the drafters of the GATS were aware that the term *affecting* had been interpreted in prior GATT panel reports to cover not only laws and regulations which directly govern the conditions of sale or purchase but also any laws or regulations which might adversely modify conditions of competition between like domestic and imported products on the internal market.[462] Another indication of the wish of the drafters to widen the scope of the GATS in terms of the regulatory measures it covers is the use of the concept of "supply" of services rather than "delivery". The text of Article XXVIII(b)[463] as well as the preparatory work[464] indicate that the choice of the term "supply of a service" involved the coverage of a wider range of activities than the case would have been had the drafters chosen to use the term "delivery". That has made a wider range of regulations subject to the application of the GATS. In sum, we believe that, consistently with their general approach, the drafters consciously adopted the terms "affecting" and "supply of a service" to ensure that the disciplines of the GATS would cover any measure bearing upon conditions of competition in supply of a service, regardless of whether the measure directly governs or indirectly affects the supply of the service.

7.282 With respect to the claim by the EC that GATT and the GATS cannot overlap, we note that such a view is not reflected in any of the provisions of the two agreements. On the contrary, the provisions of the GATS referred to above explicitly take the approach of being inclusive of any measure that affects trade in services whether directly or indirectly. These provisions do not make any distinction between measures which directly govern or regulate services and measures that otherwise affect trade in services.

7.283 Furthermore, it is our view that if we were to find the scope of the GATS and that of GATT to be mutually exclusive, in other words, if we were to find that a measure considered to fall within the scope of one agreement could not at the same time fall within the scope of the other, the value of Members' obligations and commitments would be undermined and the object and purpose of both agreements would be frustrated. Obligations could be circumvented by the adoption of measures under one agreement with indirect effects on trade covered by the other without the possibility of any legal recourse. For example, a measure in the transport sector regulating the transportation of merchandise in the territory of a Member could subject imported products to less favourable transportation conditions compared to those applicable to like domestic products. Such a measure would adversely affect the competitive position of imported products in a manner which would not be consistent with that Member's obligation to provide national treatment to such products. If the scope of GATT and the GATS were interpreted to be mutually exclusive, that Member could escape its national treatment obligation and the Members whose products have been discriminated against would have no possibility of legal recourse on account that the measure regulates "services" and not goods. It is also our view that if the drafters of the GATS had intended to impose such a serious limitation on its scope, particularly in the light of how the term "affecting" had been interpreted in past GATT panel reports and their deliberate choice of the concept of "supply" as explained above, they would have provided for the limitation explicitly in the text of the GATS itself or in the provisions of

---

[461] See para. 7.0 supra.

[462] MTN.GNS/W/139 (Definitions in the Draft General Agreement on Trade in Services - Note by the Secretariat), p.4, para. xii, states: "The term 'affecting' has been interpreted in Article III of the GATT to mean an effect on the competitive relationship between like products, not on the subsequent trade volumes in those products (BISD 36S/345 at paragraph *5.11*; BISD 34S/136 at paragraph *5.19*)". For example, in the *Italian Agriculture Machinery* case, the panel report stated: "[T]he drafters of [Article III] intended to cover in paragraph 4 not only the laws and regulations which directly govern the conditions of sale or purchase but also any laws or regulations which might adversely modify the conditions of competition between the domestic and imported products on the internal market". Panel Report on "Italian Discrimination Against Imported Agricultural Machinery", adopted on 23 October 1958, BISD 7S/60, 64, para. 12. This interpretation has also been confirmed in subsequent GATT panel reports.

[463] Article XXVIII(b) provides: " 'supply of a service' includes the production, distribution, marketing, sale and delivery of a service".

[464] MTN.GNS/W/139 (Definitions in the Draft General Agreement on Trade in Services), p.3, para. xi, states: "The notion of 'supply' is intended to encompass the whole range of activities necessary to produce and deliver a service. The definition is illustrative, not comprehensive. The use of the term 'supply', in place of 'delivery' in prior versions of the text, suggests a wider range of activities than the word delivery".

the Agreement Establishing the World Trade Organization. In the absence of such a provision, it is our view that the claim by the EC that the scope of the GATS and GATT cannot overlap has no legal basis.[465]

7.284 With respect to the EC's view that bringing a measure relating to goods under the GATS might undermine the effectiveness of an exception or a waiver under GATT, we note that there are no applicable exceptions or waivers at issue under the GATS claims in this case.[466] In the case of waivers, the problem raised by the EC could be avoided by appropriate drafting of waivers. In the case of exceptions, we note that Articles XII, XX and XXI of GATT and Articles XII, XIV and XIVbis of GATS are similar, thus reducing the likelihood of a conflict between GATT and GATS provisions. In any event, we need not decide in this case how to resolve a conflict that may never arise.

7.285 In the light of the above, we find that, in principle, no measures are excluded *a priori* from the scope of the GATS as defined by its provisions. The scope of the GATS encompasses any measure of a Member to the extent it affects the supply of a service regardless of whether such measure directly governs the supply of a service or whether it regulates other matters but nevertheless affects trade in services.

***7.286* We therefore find that there is no legal basis for an *a priori* exclusion of measures within the EC banana import licensing regime from the scope of the GATS.**

(ii) wholesale trade services

7.287 The EC takes the view that, in the banana trade, wholesale trading starts only after the ripening process is completed and that any activity prior to ripening should not be defined as wholesaling of bananas, but rather as part of their production or "remanufacturing" process. The EC further argues that the normal meaning of wholesale is distributing goods with a view to sale to the consumer and, therefore, in a form which is ready for the consumer. In the EC's view, the wholesale trade stage for bananas was excluded from the scope of the contested measures since the importation of bananas normally takes place before they are ripened. The EC further argues that wholesalers, who according to this definition would only be trading in yellow bananas, are not operators within the meaning of the EC regime since import licences cover only green bananas and not yellow ones.

7.288 In addressing this issue we need to examine the definition of "wholesale trade services" for the purposes of this case. In this respect we note the following: The sectoral coverage of the GATS is, in principle, universal. Article I establishes this in paragraph 3(b) where it states:

> 'Services' include any service *in any sector* except services supplied in the exercise of governmental authority (emphasis added).

Exceptions to this principle are explicitly provided for in the text of the GATS, such as in the case of "services supplied in the exercise of governmental authority" (Article I:3(b)) and "services directly related to the exercise of traffic rights" (Annex on Air Transport Services, para. 2(b)). No such exceptions exist for "wholesale trade services". Therefore, "wholesale trade services" are in principle fully covered by the GATS.

7.289 In the Uruguay Round negotiations participants agreed to follow a set of guidelines for the scheduling of specific commitments under the GATS.[467] With respect to the classification of services sectors for the purpose of scheduling commitments, the guidelines encouraged participants to use the Services Sectoral Classification List

---

[465] For support of this view, see Panel Report on "Canada - Certain Measures Concerning Periodicals", issued on 14 March 1997 (not adopted, subject to appeal), WT/DS31/R, pp.69-71, paras. *5.13-5.19*.

[466] We have found that the Lomé waiver does not cover the EC licensing measures which are at issue under the GATS (para. 7.0).

[467] MTN.GNS/W/164 & Add. 1 (Scheduling of Initial Commitments in Trade in Services: Explanatory Note).

developed during the Uruguay Round,[468] which is largely based on the United Nations Central Product Classification system (CPC). Although the use of the Services Sectoral Classification List is not mandatory, most Members, including the EC, have adopted it as the basis for scheduling their commitments. Furthermore, in scheduling commitments on "wholesale trade services", the EC inscribed the CPC item number (622) in its services schedule. Therefore, any breakdown of the sector should be based on the CPC. Consequently, any legal definition of the scope of the EC's commitment in wholesale services should be based on the CPC description of the sector and the activities it covers.

7.290 The CPC classification describes "wholesale trade services" as a sub-set of the broader sector of "distributive trade services" which is described in a headnote to section 6 as:

> Distributive trade services consisting in selling merchandise to retailers, to industrial, commercial, institutional or other professional business users, or to other wholesalers, or acting as agent or broker (wholesaling services) or selling merchandise for personal or household consumption including services incidental to the sale of the goods (retailing services). The principal services rendered by wholesalers and retailers may be characterized as *reselling merchandise*, accompanied by a variety of related, subordinated services, such as: maintaining inventories of goods; physically assembling, sorting and grading goods in large lots; breaking bulk and redistribution in smaller lots; delivery services; refrigeration services; sales promotion services rendered by wholesalers ... (emphasis added; underlining original).

Under this section, the CPC contains a sub-sector entitled "wholesale trade services of food, beverages and tobacco" (6222). A further breakdown of this sub-sector includes a separate item relating to "wholesale trade service of fruit and vegetables" (CPC 62221) which is described as:

> Specialized wholesale services of fresh, dried, frozen or canned fruits and vegetables (Goods classified in CPC 012, 013, 213, 215).

Item (013) of the CPC classification of goods relates to "fruit and nuts" and under its sub-classification (01310) it refers to:

> dates, figs, *bananas*, coconuts, brazil nuts, cashew nuts, pineapples, avocados, mangoes, guavas, mangosteens, fresh or dried" (emphasis added).

7.291 The CPC description of "wholesale trade services" is based on the identification of a core activity, that is "reselling merchandise", which could be accompanied by a variety of other related subordinate activities the objective of which would be to facilitate the delivery of the described services (i.e., reselling merchandise). In many instances, in order to resell merchandise it may be necessary to maintain inventories of goods, to sort and grade goods, to break bulk, refrigerate, and deliver goods to the purchaser. Thus, the subordinate activities listed in the headnote to CPC section 6 (such as maintaining inventories, breaking bulk, etc.), when they accompany the reselling of merchandise and are not performed as a separate service in their own right, are within the scope of

---

[468] MTN.GNS/W/164 (Scheduling of Initial Commitments in Trade in Services: Explanatory Note), para. 16, states: "The legal nature of a schedule as well as the need to evaluate commitments, require the greatest possible degree of clarity in the description of each sector or sub-sector scheduled. In general the classification of sectors and sub-sectors should be based on the Secretariat's revised Services Sectoral Classification List[3]. Each sector contained in the Secretariat list is identified by the corresponding Central Product Classification (CPC) number. Where it is necessary to refine further a sectoral classification, this should be done on the basis of the CPC or other internationally recognised classification (e.g., Financial Services Annex). The most recent breakdown of the CPC, including explanatory notes for each sub-sector, is contained in the UN Provisional Central Product Classification[4].

[3]Document MTN.GNS/W/120, dated 10 July 1991.

[4]Statistical Papers Series M No. 77, Provisional Central Product Classification, Department of International Economic and Social Affairs, Statistical Office of the United Nations, New York, 1991".

wholesale trade service commitments. However, a distinction is made between performing any of these subordinate activities as a component of supplying a "wholesale trade service" and performing any of them as a service in its own right. In the case of the latter, that activity is classified in a separate CPC category with a different number and would be treated under the GATS as such.

7.292 Finally, we note that the CPC descriptions do not make any distinction between green and ripened bananas. As mentioned above, item 62221 of the CPC relating to "wholesale trade services of fruit and vegetables" cross refers to goods classified in CPC 013 which in turn refers in its sub-classification CPC 01310 to "bananas" without making any distinction between green and ripened bananas.

***7.293* We find that the distribution of bananas, regardless of whether they are green or ripened, falls within the scope of category CPC 622 "wholesale trade services" as inscribed in the EC's GATS Schedule of Commitments so long as it involves the sale of bananas to retailers, to industrial, commercial, institutional or other professional business users, or other wholesalers.**

(iii) modes of supply

7.294 Article I:2 of GATS defines its coverage as including four modes of supply of services: cross-border supply, consumption abroad, commercial presence and presence of natural persons.[469] The Complainants submit that the measures of the EC banana regime that they have challenged have an impact on the wholesale trade services they can supply through commercial presence. Such impact is claimed to be inconsistent with the unqualified national treatment commitment in the EC's Schedule covering the supply of "wholesale trade services" in relation to that mode. It is also claimed to be inconsistent with the EC's obligations under Article II of GATS. In the view of the Complainants, the supply of wholesale trade services through commercial presence includes all activities associated with delivering bananas to the EC from abroad and reselling them there. That would cover all the activities associated with reselling bananas as described in the headnote to Section 6 of the CPC (e.g., maintaining inventories, physically assembling, sorting, grading in large lots, breaking bulk, redistribution in smaller lots, refrigeration and delivery services).

---

[469] Article I:2 of GATS provides:

"For the purposes of this Agreement, trade in services is defined as the supply of a service:

(a) from the territory of one Member into the territory of any other Member;

(b) in the territory of one Member to the service consumer of any other Member,

(c) by a service supplier of one Member, through commercial presence in the territory of any other Member

(d) by a service supplier of one Member, through presence of natural persons of a Member in the territory of any other Member".

7.295 With respect to supply through commercial presence, we note that Article I:2(c) of GATS[470] defines supply through commercial presence as the supply of a service by a service supplier of one Member, through commercial presence, in the territory of another Member. Article XXVIII(f)(ii)[471] defines a "service of another Member" in the case of a supply of a service through commercial presence as a service which is supplied by a service supplier of that other Member. In addition to these provisions, explanation of the modes of supply has been provided in the explanatory note on the scheduling of commitments referred to above.[472] These definitions as well as the explanation of the supply of a service through commercial presence in the explanatory note rely on the territorial presence of the service supplier as a basis for drawing distinctions between modes. In other words, in the case of supply through commercial presence, the service supplier would have to be physically present in the territory where the service is being supplied. In such cases, the origin of the service is to be determined on the basis of the origin of the supplier. And the origin of the service supplier is to be determined on the basis of the definitions laid down in Article XXVIII(g), (j), (m) and (n) which provide:

> (g) 'service supplier' means any person that supplies a service;[11]
>
> (j) 'person' means either a natural person or a juridical person;
>
> (m) 'juridical person of another Member' means a juridical person which is either:
> (i) constituted or otherwise organized under the law of that other Member, and is engaged in substantive business operations in the territory of that Member or any other Member; or
> (ii) in the case of the supply of a service through commercial presence, owned or controlled by:
> 1. natural persons of that Member; or
> 2. juridical persons of that other Member identified under subparagraph (i).
>
> (n) a juridical person is:
> (i) 'owned' by persons of a Member if more than 50 per cent of the equity interest in it is beneficially owned by persons of that Member;
> (ii) 'controlled' by persons of a Member if such persons have the power to name a majority of its directors or otherwise legally to direct its actions;
> (iii) 'affiliated' with another person when it controls, or is controlled by, that other person; or when it and the other person are both controlled by the same person.
>
> --------------------------
>
> [11]Where the service is not supplied directly by a juridical person but through other forms of commercial presence such as a branch or a representative office, the service supplier (i.e. the juridical person) shall, nonetheless, through such presence be accorded the treatment provided for service suppliers under the Agreement. Such treatment shall be extended to the presence through which the service is supplied and need not be extended to any other parts of the supplier located outside the territory where the service is supplied.

---

[470] See note 476 supra.

[471] Article XXVIII(f) provides: "'service of another Member' means a service which is supplied,

(i) from or in the territory of that other Member, or in the case of maritime transport, by a vessel registered under the laws of that other Member, or by a person of that other Member which supplies the service through the operation of a vessel and/or use in whole or in part; or

(ii) in the case of the supply of a service through commercial presence or through the presence of natural persons, by a service supplier of that other Member".

[472] MTN.GNS/W/164 (Scheduling of Initial Commitments in Trade in Services: Explanatory Note), para. 18, states (emphasis original): "The four modes of supply listed in the schedules correspond to the scope of the GATS as set out in Article I.2. The modes are essentially defined on the basis of the *origin* of the service supplier and consumer, and the degree and type of *territorial presence* which they have at the moment the service is delivered".

7.296 Therefore, with respect to situations of supply through commercial presence, Members' obligations under the GATS cover the treatment of services and service suppliers. We note that Article II requires a Member to extend to services and service suppliers of any other Member treatment no less favourable than that it accords to like services and service suppliers of any other country. And Article XVII requires a Member, subject to any limitations inscribed in its schedule, to accord services and service suppliers of any other Member treatment no less favourable than it accords to its own like services and service suppliers.

7.297 **Consequently, we find that the EC's obligations under Article II of GATS and commitments under Article XVII of GATS cover the treatment of suppliers of wholesale trade services within the jurisdiction of the EC.**

(iv) the scope of the Article II obligation

7.298 Article II:1 of GATS states:

> With respect to any measure covered by this Agreement, each Member shall accord immediately and unconditionally to services and service suppliers of any other Member treatment no less favourable than that it accords to like services and service suppliers of any other country.

We note that this provision refers to "any measures covered by this Agreement". This term could only be interpreted to mean all measures falling within the scope of the GATS. According to Article I:1 which defines the scope of the GATS, it applies to "measures by Members affecting trade in services". We also note that this provision constitutes a general obligation which is, in principle, applicable across the board by all Members to all services sectors, not only in sectors or sub-sectors where specific commitments have been undertaken. Any exception to this general obligation would have to be provided for explicitly in accordance with the terms of the GATS. Article II:2 provides for the possibility of exempting specific measures from this obligation where it states that

> A Member may maintain a measure inconsistent with paragraph 1 provided that such a measure is listed in, and meets the conditions of, the Annex on Article II Exemptions.

We note that the EC has not listed in that Annex any measures relating to "wholesale trade services" which are inconsistent with paragraph 1 of Article II. Therefore, the EC is fully bound by its obligations under Article II:1 in relation to "wholesale trade services".[473]

7.299 The Complainants submit that the term "treatment no less favourable" contained in paragraph 1 of Article II of GATS should be interpreted in the light of the language contained in paragraphs 2 and 3 of Article XVII of

[473] In the EC's understanding there are no MFN exemptions which would limit its obligation to provide MFN treatment in respect of the subsector of wholesale trade services, whereas in the Complainants' view there are no relevant MFN exemptions for the whole range of distribution services. By the terms of the GATS, the MFN treatment clause covers, subject to each Member's MFN exemption list, all services on a general basis. Accordingly, the range of the service transactions which are directly or indirectly related to trade in bananas is potentially wider than the sector of distribution services or the subsector of wholesale trade services. Likewise, a broader range of the exemptions which have been inscribed in the EC's MFN exemption list could be relevant to service transactions related to trade in bananas. However, in the light of the legal arguments advanced by the Complainants we proceed on the assumption that the scope of their claims under the GATS MFN clause is limited to the supply of wholesale trade services by commercial presence and that none of the MFN exemptions scheduled by the EC carves out components of the relevant CPC description.

GATS.[474] In their view although Article II does not contain the type of elaboration found in paragraphs 2 and 3 of Article XVII concerning formally identical and formally different treatment and modification of conditions of competition, the standard of treatment in Article II should be interpreted to be the same as that of paragraph 1 of Article XVII. They consider that paragraphs 2 and 3 of Article XVII do not set up any additional substantive rules but rather serve as guidance for the application of the national treatment rule articulated in the first paragraph. They also note that Article II of GATS deviated from the formulation used in Article I:1 of GATT[475] and refer to "treatment no less favourable" instead of "any advantage, favour, privilege or immunity". In their view that indicates a deliberate choice by the drafters to follow the same standard of treatment set in paragraph 1 of Article XVII.

7.300 The EC maintains that Article II:1 of GATS applies to "any measure covered by this Agreement" and Article I:1 defines the scope of the GATS by stating that it applies "to measures by Members affecting trade in services". The definition in Article XXVIII(c),[476] in particular under sub-paragraph (i), indicates that the measures concerned had to affect trade in services as such and could not be measures taken in other areas with repercussions on services such as measures in respect of the purchase of goods. Moreover, the EC considers that the use of the terms "in respect of" in the chapeau of Article XXVIII(c) demonstrates that the term "affecting" has to be interpreted in a narrow sense that did not include the reference to measures which modified the conditions of competition. Third, in the view of the EC, if the drafters had wished to make the "modification of competitive conditions" requirement an integral part of the "no less favourable treatment" test under the most-favoured-nation clause, they would have done so explicitly as it was done for the national treatment clause in Article XVII:3. Therefore, if it were to be established that certain EC measures violate the MFN obligation, it would have to be demonstrated that there was formally discriminatory treatment as between foreign services and service suppliers, which is not the case in this dispute.

7.301 With respect to the first two arguments of the EC, we recall our discussion above. In addressing the third argument, we note that the standard of "no less favourable treatment" in paragraph 1 of Article XVII is meant to provide for no less favourable conditions of competition regardless of whether that is achieved through the application of formally identical or formally different measures. Paragraphs 2 and 3 of Article XVII serve the purpose of codifying this interpretation, and in our view, do not impose new obligations on Members additional to those contained in paragraph 1. In essence, the "treatment no less favourable" standard of Article XVII:1 is clarified and reinforced in the language of paragraphs 2 and 3. The absence of similar language in Article II is not, in our view, a justification for giving a different ordinary meaning in terms of Article 31(1) of the Vienna Convention to the words "treatment no less favourable", which are identical in both Articles II:1 and XVII:1.

7.302 We also note that, while the object and purpose of paragraph 1 of Article XVII is to prohibit discrimination against foreign services and service suppliers to the advantage of like services and service suppliers

---

[474] Article XVII of GATS (National Treatment) provides:

1. In the sectors inscribed in its Schedule, and subject to any conditions and qualifications set out therein, each Member shall accord to services and service suppliers of any other Member, in respect of all measures affecting the supply of services, treatment no less favourable than that it accords to its own like services and service suppliers.[10]
2. A Member may meet the requirement of paragraph 1 by according to services and service suppliers of any other Member, either formally identical treatment or formally different treatment to that it accords to its own like services and service suppliers.
3. Formally identical or formally different treatment shall be considered to be less favourable if it modifies the conditions of competition in favour of services or service suppliers of the Member compared to like services or service suppliers of any other Member.

[10]Specific commitments assumed under this Article shall not be construed to require any Member to compensate for any inherent competitive disadvantages which result from the foreign character of the relevant services or service suppliers".

[475] Article I:1 of GATT provides: "... any advantage, favour, privilege or immunity granted by any Member to any product originating in or destined for any other country shall be accorded immediately and unconditionally...".

[476] Article XXVIII(c) is quoted in para. 7.0 supra.

of national origin, paragraph 1 of Article II has a similar objective of prohibiting discrimination against services and service suppliers of a Member in favour of like services or service suppliers of any other country. In addition, while the drafters of the GATS have been guided by GATT concepts, provisions and past practice, they have chosen to use identical operative language of "treatment no less favourable" in both Articles II and XVII, departing in the case of Article II from the formulation used in the GATT MFN clause in Article I which refers to "any advantage, favour, privilege or immunity ...". Thus, the formulation of both Articles II and XVII of GATS derives from the "treatment no less favourable" standard of the GATT national treatment provisions in Article III of GATT, which has been consistently interpreted by past panel reports to be concerned with conditions of competition between like domestic and imported products on internal markets.[477]

7.303 We also note that if the standard of "no less favourable treatment" in Article II were to be interpreted narrowly to require only formally identical treatment, that could lead in many situations to the frustration of the objective behind Article II which is to prohibit discrimination between like services and service suppliers of other Members. It would not be difficult for regulators to contemplate regulatory measures which are identical on their face while in effect provide less favourable competitive opportunities to a group of service suppliers to the advantage of others.

7.304 **Therefore, we find that the obligation contained in Article II:1 of GATS to extend "treatment no less favourable" should be interpreted *in casu* to require providing no less favourable conditions of competition.**

(v) the scope of the Article XVII commitment

7.305 Article XVII of the GATS is a specific commitment in the sense that it would be binding on a Member only in sectors or sub-sectors which that Member has inscribed in its schedule and to the extent specified therein. Article XVII:1 states:

> 1. In the sectors inscribed in its schedule, and subject to any conditions and qualifications set out therein, each Member shall accord to services and service suppliers of any other Member, in respect of all measures affecting the supply of services, treatment no less favourable than that it accords to its own like services and service suppliers.

We note that in its schedule of specific commitments[478] the EC has inscribed in the first column under the heading "Sector or Sub-sector" the sector of "Wholesale Trade Services". The related CPC classification number (CPC 622) has also been inscribed. As previously mentioned, this constitutes the basis on which the scope of the EC's national treatment commitment is to be determined. We also note that, with respect to the first mode (cross-border supply) and the third mode (supply through commercial presence) the EC has entered "none" in the third column of the schedule relating to limitations on national treatment. The EC, therefore, has undertaken a full commitment on national treatment in the sector of "Wholesale Trade Services" with respect of cross-border supply and supply through commercial presence.

7.306 **Thus, we find that the EC has undertaken a full commitment on national treatment in the sector of "Wholesale Trade Services" with respect to supply through commercial presence.**

---

[477] Panel Report on "Italian Discrimination of Imported Agricultural Machinery", adopted on 23 October 1958, BISD 7S/60, 63, para. 12. See also para. 7.0.

[478] European Communities and Their Member States - Schedule of Specific Commitments - April 1994.

(vi) effective date of GATS obligations

7.307 The EC argues that, given that the GATS entered into force on 1 January 1995, only the EC banana import regime as it existed in late 1994 and afterwards (rather than 1992 and before) should be examined in the light of Articles II and XVII of GATS.

7.308 We are not certain of the precise relevance of this argument. The EC does not argue that the introduction of the EC common market organization for bananas resulted in a single, non-recurring adjustment of the market which was completed by 31 December 1994. To the contrary, the EC banana regulations remained in force or were enacted or amended also after 1 January 1995 (e.g., Regulation 478/95 on the export certificate requirement) and, more importantly, they foresee a recurring and ongoing process of import licence allocations according to annually recalculated reference quantities on the basis of operator categories and activity functions. Consequently, the fact that the EC common market organization was introduced in 1993, prior to the entry into force of the GATS, is not relevant for our legal analysis. Thus, we examine the consistency of the EC banana regulations as they currently stand with the EC's obligations arising from the GATS. Therefore, the scope of our legal examination includes only actions which the EC took or continued to take, or measures that remained in force or continued to be applied by the EC, and thus did not cease to exist after the entry into force of the GATS.[479] Likewise, any finding of consistency or inconsistency with the requirements of Articles II and XVII of GATS would be made with respect to the period after the entry into force of the GATS. Moreover, in this connection we note that there is no grandfather clause in the WTO Agreement that would permit Members to maintain indefinitely national legislation that is inconsistent with WTO rules. Indeed, Article XVI:4 of the WTO Agreement provides that "[e]ach Member shall ensure the conformity of its laws, regulations and administrative procedures with its obligations as provided in the annexed Agreements".

(vii) claims by Mexico

[7.309-7.311 Used in the Mexico report.]
7.309 The EC argues that, in view of the brevity of its first submission, Mexico has failed to establish a *prima facie* case of nullification or impairment in the meaning of Article 3.8 of the DSU and that Mexico's complaint under the GATS should, therefore, not be sustained.

7.310 We agree that Mexico's first submission is not detailed. However, in its first submission, Mexico has raised claims under Article XVII of GATS with respect to operator category rules and under Article II of GATS with respect to the allocation of import licences on the basis of operator categories as well as activity functions, the export certificate requirement and the exemption of Category B operators thereof, and the issuance of hurricane licences to ACP producers. Moreover, Mexico has co-authored the Complainants' joint second submission and, further to that, endorsed all legal arguments concerning services which were advanced by Ecuador and the United States in these proceedings during the second substantive meeting of the Panel with the parties.

***7.311* Therefore, we examine Mexico's claims under the GATS along with those raised by Ecuador and the United States, except in the case of activity function rules, export certificates and hurricane licences, where we do not include Mexico in our discussion of the Article XVII claims.**

---

[479] Article 28 of the Vienna Convention embodies the general international law principle that "[u]nless a different intention appears from the treaty or is otherwise established, its provisions do not bind a party in relation to ... any situation which ceased to exist before the date of entry into force of the treaty ...". Under this rule, the EC measures at issue may be considered as continuing measures, which in some cases were enacted before the entry into force of GATS but which did *not* cease to exist after that date (the opposite of the situation envisaged in Article 28).

c) Operator categories
(i) Article XVII of GATS

7.312 The Complainants claim that the allocation of the third-country import licences on the basis of operator categories and the eligibility criteria for Category B operators discriminate against like third-country service suppliers. The EC is alleged to be in breach of Article XVII of GATS in respect of its commitments on wholesale service supply in that it accords more favourable treatment to wholesale service suppliers of EC origin because Category B operators are largely EC owned or controlled and Category A operators are largely in the Complainants' ownership or control.

7.313 The EC responds that the allocation of licences on the basis of operator categories does not automatically entail the transfer of market shares to Category B operators because licences are freely tradeable. Therefore, the allocation of licences to certain operators does not necessarily mean that these operators will actually carry out the physical importation. The EC emphasizes that the rules establishing operator categories do not classify companies as such but aim at distributing import licences according to past marketing of traditional ACP and EC or third-country and non-traditional ACP bananas. Consequently, the allocation of Category A and B licences is not mutually exclusive. Certain large operator companies are registered in both categories and hence receive both Category A and B licences. Therefore, the EC argues that the Complainants' insistence on equating Category A with firms of non-EC origin and Category B with firms of EC origin is misleading. Furthermore, the EC notes that the WTO agreements do not provide for rules governing the sharing of quota rents which are generated by a legitimate tariff quota and that, consequently, the EC retains its discretion to allocate quota rents among EC, ACP and third country producers and traders. In the EC's view, the Complainants fail to prove that quota rents and market shares have been reallocated at the expense of third-country firms, given that no evidence has been provided on how particular companies are linked through registration, ownership or control to the Complainants. In contrast, the EC notes that it submitted information on market shares of third-country firms, which in its view demonstrate that those firms have not lost market share in recent years.

7.314 In light of these arguments, we turn to an examination of the issues arising under this Article XVII claim. In order to establish a breach of the national treatment obligation of Article XVII, three elements need to be demonstrated: (i) the EC has undertaken a commitment in a relevant sector and mode of supply; (ii) the EC has adopted or applied a measure affecting the supply of services in that sector and/or mode of supply; and (iii) the measure accords to service suppliers of any other Member treatment less favourable than that it accords to the EC's own like service suppliers.

7.315 In respect of the first element, we recall that the EC has bound the wholesale trade service sub-sector as regards service supply across borders and through commercial presence without conditions and qualifications in the meaning of Article XVII:1 (*infra*).

7.316 As to the second element, i.e., whether the EC measures implementing the operator category rules constitute measures affecting the supply of services, we recall that we have found that the term "affecting" should be interpreted broadly. In this connection, we also note that supply of services through cross-border delivery or commercial presence is defined to include the production, distribution, marketing, sale and delivery of such services.[480] As a consequence, in our view, the EC measures, and more specifically the rules on operator categories, are measures affecting Complainants' trade in services in the meaning of the GATS.

7.317 We now turn to the third element that must be demonstrated to establish a breach of Article XVII, i.e., less favourable treatment of service suppliers of another Member than the treatment given to its own like service suppliers. There are four preliminary matters that should be addressed: (i) the definition of commercial presence

[480] Article XXVIII:(b) of GATS provides: "'Supply of a service' includes the production, distribution, marketing, sale and delivery of a service."

and service suppliers; (ii) whether operators in the meaning of the EC banana regulations are service suppliers under GATS, (iii) the definition of services covered by EC commitments; and (iv) to what extent services and service suppliers of different origin are like.

7.318 First, it is necessary to clarify what is meant by "commercial presence", as used in Article I:2, and "services and service suppliers of any other Member", as used in Article XVII:1. "Commercial presence" in general covers any type of business or professional establishment, including through (i) the constitution, acquisition or maintenance of a juridical person, or (ii) the creation or maintenance of a branch or representative office, within the EC territory for the purpose of supplying wholesale services.[481] Therefore, in the current dispute, we are concerned with the commercial presence of service suppliers that are "persons", or owned or controlled by such persons, of the Complainants. These include subsidiary companies owned[482] or controlled[483] by natural persons[484] of a Complainant and subsidiary companies owned or controlled by parent companies that are constituted or otherwise organized under the law of a Complainant[485] and are engaged in substantive business operations in the territory of any other Member.[486]

7.319 In this respect, we emphasize that in the following discussion, we will refer to service suppliers that are owned or controlled by persons of the Complainants as "suppliers of Complainants' origin", and service suppliers that are owned or controlled by persons of the EC will be referred to as "suppliers of EC origin".

7.320 Second, in the context of this case, operators in the meaning of Article 19 of Regulation 404/93 and operators performing the activities defined in Article 5 of Regulation 1442/93 are service suppliers in the meaning of Article I:2(c) of GATS provided that they are owned or controlled by natural persons or juridical persons of other Members and supply wholesale services. When operators provide wholesale services with respect to bananas which they have imported or acquired for marketing, cleared in customs or ripened, they are actual wholesale service suppliers. Where operators form part of vertically integrated companies, they have the capability and

---

[481] Article XXVIII(d) of GATS provides:

"'Commercial presence' means any type of business or professional establishment, including through

(i) the constitution, acquisition or maintenance of a juridical person, or

(ii) the creation or maintenance of a branch or a representative office,

within the territory of a Member for the purpose of supplying a service;

[482] Article XXVIII(n) provides: "A juridical person is (i) 'owned' by persons of a Member if more than 50 per cent of the equity interest in it is beneficially owned by persons of that Member".

[483] Article XXVIII(n) provides: " A juridical person is (ii) 'controlled' by persons of a Member if such persons have the power to name a majority of its directors or otherwise to legally direct its actions".

[484] Article XXVIII(k) provides: "'Natural person of another Member' means a natural person who resides in the territory of that other Member or any other Member, and who under the law of that other Member:

(i) is a national of that other Member; or

(ii) has the right of permanent residence in that other Member, in the case of a Member which:

1. does not have nationals; or

2. accords substantially the same treatment to its permanent residents as it does to its nationals in respect of measures affecting trade in services, as notified in its acceptance of or accession to the WTO Agreement, provided that no Member is obligated to accord to such permanent residents treatment more favourable than would be accorded by that other Member to such permanent residents. Such notification shall include the assurance to assume, in accordance with its laws and regulations, the same responsibilities that other Member bears with respect to its nationals".

[485] Article XXVIII(l) provides: "'[J]uridical person' means any legal entity duly constituted or otherwise organized under applicable laws, whether for profit or otherwise, and whether privately-owned or governmentally-owned, including any corporation, trust, partnership, joint venture, sole proprietorship or association. For the definition of "juridical person of another Member", see para. 7.295 supra.

[486] As a result, suppliers which are commercially present within the EC territory and owned or controlled by, for example, Del Monte Mexico would be entitled to benefit from GATS rights because it would not matter under Article XXVIII(m) of GATS whether Del Monte Mexico was owned or controlled by natural or juridical persons of Jordan, i.e. a WTO non-Member, as long as Del Monte Mexico was incorporated in Mexico and engaged in substantive business operations in the territory of Mexico or any other Member.

opportunity to enter the wholesale service market. They could at any time decide to re-sell bananas which they have imported or acquired from EC producers, or cleared in customs, or ripened instead of further transferring or processing bananas within an integrated company.[487] Since Article XVII of GATS is concerned with conditions of competition, it is appropriate for us to consider these vertically integrated companies as service suppliers for the purposes of analysing the claims made in this case.

7.321 Third, as discussed above (paragraphs *7.290 et seq.*), the services at issue in this case are wholesale trade services and the related subordinated services specified in headnote 6 to the CPC classification.

7.322 Fourth, in our view, the nature and the characteristics of wholesale transactions as such, as well as of each of the different subordinated services mentioned in the headnote to section 6 of the CPC, are "like" when supplied in connection with wholesale services, irrespective of whether these services are supplied with respect to bananas of EC and traditional ACP origin, on the one hand, or with respect to bananas of third-country or non-traditional ACP origin, on the other. Indeed, it seems that each of the different service activities taken individually is virtually the same and can only be distinguished by referring to the origin of the bananas in respect of which the service activity is being performed. Similarly, in our view, to the extent that entities provide these like services, they are like service suppliers.

7.323 We now have to ascertain whether, by applying operator category rules, the EC accords services supplied across borders or through commercial presence less favourable treatment than it accords its own like services or service suppliers in the meaning of Article XVII.

7.324 We note that the categorization of A and B operators is based on whether they have during a previous three-year period marketed EC and traditional ACP bananas or third-country and non-traditional ACP bananas. The operator category rules apply to service suppliers regardless of their nationality, ownership or control. In so far as the supply of wholesale trade services in respect of third-country and non-traditional ACP bananas is concerned, service suppliers of EC origin are equally subject to operator category rules as service suppliers of Complainants' origin. Likewise, with respect to the supply of wholesale trade services in respect of EC or traditional ACP bananas, service suppliers of EC origin are treated in the same way under the operator category rules as service suppliers of Complainants' origin. Thus, the EC rules establishing operator categories do not formally discriminate against Complainants' wholesale service suppliers on the basis of their origin.

7.325 We note, however, that service suppliers of Complainants' origin that provide wholesale services in respect of only third-country or non-traditional ACP bananas are subject to operator category rules, while service suppliers of EC origin that provide the same services in respect of EC or traditional ACP bananas are not. However, service suppliers of Complainants' origin that have in the past provided wholesale trade services in respect of only third-country or non-traditional ACP bananas are not legally prevented from supplying wholesale trade services with respect to EC and traditional ACP bananas.

7.326 By supplying wholesale trade services to the traditional ACP and EC market segment, suppliers of any origin can avoid, or reduce the extent to which they are subject to, operator category rules. In addition they will be eligible for the allocation of 30 per cent of the in-quota licences required for third-country and non-traditional ACP imports which are earmarked for Category B operators. Nothing in the operator category rules requires operators who are, on the basis of their previous marketing of EC and traditional ACP bananas, beneficiaries of the allocation of 30 per cent of the licences required for the in-quota importation of third-country and non-traditional ACP bananas regardless of whether they have previously dealt in that market segment, to be service suppliers in EC ownership or control. In other words, service suppliers of foreign as well as EC origin are arguably subject to formally identical treatment in the meaning of Article XVII:2 of GATS. Likewise, under the EC operator category

[487] Operators who always sell or resell bananas directly to consumers supply *retail* services which are not covered by the EC commitments on wholesale services under Article XVII.

rules services of foreign origin which are supplied across-borders are arguably subject to treatment that is formally identical to the treatment of domestic services.

7.327 We now turn to the question whether the application of formally identical operator category rules, nevertheless, modifies conditions of competition[488] in favour of service or service suppliers of EC origin, or at the expense of services or service suppliers of third-country origin, in the meaning of paragraphs 2 and 3 of Article XVII of GATS which provide as follows:

> 2. A Member may meet the requirement of paragraph 1 by according to services and service suppliers of any other Member, either *formally identical* treatment or *formally different* treatment to that it accords to its own like services and service suppliers.[489]
> 3. Formally identical or formally different treatment shall be considered to be less favourable if it *modifies the conditions of competition* in favour of services or service suppliers of the Member compared to like services or service suppliers of any other Member" (emphasis and footnotes added).[490]

Thus, according to Article XVII, formally identical treatment may, nevertheless, be considered to be less favourable treatment if it adversely modifies conditions of competition for foreign services or service suppliers. Therefore, we also have to examine whether the operator category (and activity function) rules have an impact on the conditions of competition for foreign-owned or controlled service suppliers. In order to do so, we must

---

[488] "The Panel, however, believes that an evaluation of the *trade effects* was not directly relevant to its findings because a breach of a GATT rules is presumed to have an adverse impact on other contracting parties ..." (emphasis added). Panel Report on "Canada - Administration of the Foreign Investment Review Act", adopted on 7 February 1984, BISD 30S/140, 167, para. 6.6.

"[Article III:2 of GATT] protects *expectations on the competitive relationship* between imported and domestic products. A change in the competitive relationship contrary to that provision must consequently be regarded *ipso facto* as a nullification or impairment of benefits accruing under the General Agreement". (emphasis added). Panel Report on "US - Taxes on Petroleum and Certain Imported Substances", adopted on 17 June 1987, BISD 34S/136, 158-159, para. 5.1.9.

"[T]he panel noted that previous panels had rejected arguments of de minimis trade consequences and had found that the size of the trade impact of a measure was not relevant to its consistency with Article III [GATT]". Panel Report on "US - Measures Affecting the Importation, Internal Sale and Use of Tobacco", adopted on 4 October 1994, DS 44/R, p.32, para. 99.

[489] The wording of paragraph 2 of Article XVII of GATS draws on the interpretation developed by a GATT panel with respect to Article III of GATT: "[T]he 'no less favourable' treatment requirement set out in Article III:4, is unqualified. These words are to be found throughout the General Agreement ... as an expression of the underlying principle of equality of treatment of imported products as compared to the treatment given either to other foreign products, under the most favoured nation treatment standard, or to domestic products, under the national treatment standard of Article III. The words 'treatment no less favourable' in paragraph 4 [of GATT Article III] call for *effective equality of opportunities* for imported products in respect of the application of laws, regulations and requirements affecting internal sale, offering for sale, purchase, transportation, distribution or use of products. This clearly sets a minimum permissible standard as a basis. On the one hand, contracting parties may apply to imported products different formal legal requirements if doing so would accord imported products more favourable treatment. On the other hand, it also has to be recognized that there may be cases where application of *formally identical legal provisions would in practice accord less favourable treatment to imported products* and a contracting party might thus have to apply different legal provisions to imported products to ensure that the treatment accorded to them is in fact no less favourable" (emphasis added). Panel Report on "US - Section 337 of the Tariff Act of 1930", adopted on 7 November 1989, BISD 36S/345, 386, para. *5.11*.

[490] The wording of paragraph 3 of Article XVII of GATS draws on the interpretation developed by a GATT panel with respect to Article III of GATT: "[T]he text of paragraph 4 [of GATT Article III] referred both in English and in French to laws and regulations and requirements *affecting* internal sale, purchase, etc., and to laws, regulations and requirements governing the conditions of sale or purchase. The selection of the word "*affecting*" would imply, in the opinion of the Panel, that the drafters of the Article intended to cover in paragraph 4 not only the laws and regulations which directly *governed* the conditions of sale or purchase but also any laws or regulations which might *adversely modify the conditions of competition* between the domestic and imported products on the internal markets" (emphasis added). Panel Report on "Italian Discrimination of Imported Agricultural Machinery", adopted on 23 October 1958, BISD 7S/60, 63, para. 12.

> "The Panel also noted that if the Italian contention were correct, and if the scope of Article III were limited in the way the Italian delegation suggested to a specific type of law and regulations, the value of the bindings under Article II of the Agreement and of the general rules of non-discrimination as between imported and domestic products could be easily evaded". Id., p.64, para. 15.

consider in the first instance whether there are non EC-owned or controlled service suppliers for GATS purposes that provide wholesale trade services in bananas in and to the EC.

7.328 The EC states that the European Commission does not have records of the actual ownership of companies registered to receive licences of whatever category. The EC submits that in the case of trans-national companies, the nationality of parent and subsidiary companies is usually not the same. Article XXVIII(m)(ii) of GATS defines the origin of a service supplier according to its ownership or control by a natural or juridical person of a Member. While the fact that subsidiaries in foreign ownership or control have a registered seat in their host country might matter in other legal contexts, this fact is not relevant for rights under Article XVII. If the parent company is registered in a Member and engages in substantive business operations there (or in another Member), the Member where the parent company is registered may invoke Article XVII in respect of any of the parent company's subsidiaries which are owned or controlled by the Member in the meaning of Article XXVIII(n).

7.329 In order for the Complainants to establish that there are non EC-owned or controlled service suppliers commercially present in the EC for GATS purposes that provide wholesale trade services in bananas in and to the EC, it would be sufficient for them to show that (i) entities of Complainants' origin (ii) control subsidiaries established in the EC that supply such services. In this case, we are of the opinion that the Complainants have submitted sufficient evidence to show that companies registered in the Complainants' countries provide wholesale trade services in respect of bananas to and in the EC through commercially present owned or controlled subsidiaries in the meaning of Article XXVIII(n).

7.330 As to the first point, the evidence presented and the statements by both parties indicate that there are entities of non EC-origin involved in the banana trade. In particular, both parties seem to accept that Chiquita and Dole are US companies, Del Monte is a Mexican company and Noboa is an Ecuadorian company, and no evidence suggesting the contrary has been presented by the EC.[491]

7.331 As to the second point, i.e., whether these non-EC companies control subsidiaries that supply wholesale trade services in bananas and are commercially present in the EC, the Complainants submitted a list entitled "Principal banana wholesaling companies established in the EC that were owned or controlled by the Complainants' services suppliers, 1992". The EC notes that no formal records of shareholders and company registrations were submitted by the Complainants. However, we recall that, according to Article IIIbis of GATS, "nothing in GATS requires any Member to provide confidential information, the disclosure of which ... would prejudice legitimate commercial interests of particular enterprises". According to the Complainants, their information was limited in part based on confidentiality concerns. Nonetheless, we believe that the Complainants' evidence is sufficient to establish that there are non-EC companies that control subsidiaries that supply wholesale trade services in bananas and that are commercially present in the EC. In this regard, we note that while the EC argued that more evidence should have been submitted by the Complainants, it did not present information that would cast doubt on the evidence presented by the Complainants. As a consequence, we must assess whether that evidence is sufficiently credible to be accepted by us. In making our objective assessment (Article 11 of the DSU), we are persuaded that the Complainants have sufficiently established that entities of Complainants' origin control subsidiaries established in the EC that provide wholesale trade services in bananas in and to the EC.

7.332 Recalling that under Article XVII of GATS, formally identical treatment may be considered to be less favourable treatment if it adversely modifies conditions of competition for foreign services or service suppliers, we now examine whether the rules establishing operator categories (and activity functions) have an impact on the conditions of competition for foreign-owned or controlled service suppliers. The EC notes that under the operator

---

[491] For example, the first submission of the EC, in referring to statistics in an Arthur D. Little study, refers to Chiquita and Dole as "US owned or controlled". A.D. Little, "Etude de l'evolution des effets de la remise en place de l'OCM bananes sur la filière dans l'Union européenne", 13 septembre 1995.

category rules companies may qualify as both Category A and B operators, thus making it difficult to categorize companies of any nationality as either A or B operators.

7.333 In this regard, the Complainants submit that before the introduction of the EC banana regime companies controlled or owned by natural or juridical persons of their nationalities held a market share of over 95 per cent of the imports of Latin American bananas to the EC. Accordingly, the Complainants argue, companies in EC and ACP ownership or control had a market share of less than 5 per cent of imports from Latin America. The EC questions the accuracy of these figures, but it does not submit comparable evidence of its own.[492] In our view, even if we accept the EC argument that the Complainants' 95 per cent figure may be somewhat too high, we believe that the Complainants have adequately demonstrated that companies of the Complainants' origin had by far the vast majority of the market for imports of Latin American bananas.

7.334 In respect of the EC market for EC and ACP bananas, the Complainants submit that prior to the introduction of the EC common market organization, the share of the three large banana companies (i.e., Chiquita, Dole and Del Monte) in the EC/ACP market segment was only 6 per cent and that the share for all non-ACP foreign-owned companies was less than 10 per cent. While the EC states that in 1994, 28 per cent of the EC/ACP production was controlled by three large banana companies, for our purposes what is important is the relative share of service suppliers of the Complainants' origin of the EC market for EC/ACP bananas.[493] On either view, we conclude that most of the suppliers of Complainants' origin are classified in Category A for the vast majority of their past marketing of bananas,[494] and that most of the suppliers of EC (or ACP) origin are classified in Category B for the vast majority of their past marketing of bananas.[495]

7.335 In light of the foregoing, we now consider whether the rules establishing operator categories (and activity functions) have an impact on the conditions of competition for foreign-owned or controlled service suppliers. Under the EC rules, based on their marketing during a preceding three-year period of EC and traditional ACP bananas, Category B operators are eligible for 30 per cent of the licences required for the importation of third-country (i.e., Latin American) and non-traditional ACP bananas at lower in-quota duty rates, regardless of whether they have previously traded in the latter market segment. Therefore, most beneficiaries of this allocation to Category B operators are service suppliers of EC origin. At the same time, most Category A operators, who historically traded third-country and non-traditional ACP bananas but who are eligible to receive only 66.5 per cent of the licences allowing in-quota imports of bananas from these sources, are service suppliers of third-country origin. Furthermore, we also note that there is no allocation of an EC/ACP market share for Category A operators equivalent to the allocation of 30 per cent of the third-country and non-traditional ACP import licences to Category B operators. Thus, at first sight it appears that the operator category rules would seem to modify conditions of competition in the EC wholesale services market for bananas in favour of service suppliers of EC origin.

7.336 Given that import licences are tradeable and transferable, the allocation of fixed percentages of licences according to operator categories does not automatically determine the new distribution of market shares between Category A and B operators. However, while Category B operators, on the basis of previous marketing of EC and traditional ACP bananas, obtain access to 30 per cent of the licences required for third-country imports regardless

---

[492] Pursuant to Regulations 404/93 and 1442/93, the EC Commission and competent member State authorities have to keep information concerning the reference quantities of past volumes of bananas marketed for which companies are registered in particularized form. We note that, according to the EC, these records do not include information on the ownership or control of the companies categorized or registered for reference quantities.

[493] As noted below, the difference in statistics may be a result of the EC rules. See para. 7.340.

[494] Operators classified in Category A for most of their past trade volume: Chiquita Brands (US), Dole Foods (US), Noboa (Ecuador), Del Monte (Mexico), Uniban (Colombia), Banacol (Colombia). (Information submitted by the Complainants).

[495] Operators classified in Category B for most of their past trade volume: e.g., Geest (UK), Fyffes (Ireland), Pomona (France), Compagnie Fruitière (France), CDB/Durand (France), Gipam (France), Coplaca (Spain), Bargoso SA (Spain). (Information submitted by the Complainants).

of whether they have previously marketed bananas in that market segment, at the same time, Category A operators, on the basis of their previous imports of third-country and non-traditional ACP bananas, obtain access to only 66.5 per cent of the licences required for the importation of third-country and non-traditional ACP bananas at in-quota tariff rates. Accordingly, when licences authorizing in-quota imports of third-country and non-traditional ACP bananas are traded, sellers of licences will usually be Category B operators and purchasers of licences will usually be Category A operators.[496] Indeed, both sides agree that large numbers of import licences are being traded on the market place. Thus, in general, Category A operators are able to purchase the licences they need in addition to their annual licence entitlement if they wish to maintain their previous market share.[497] However, initial licence holders who carry out the physical importation of bananas or sell the licences in any case reap tariff quota rents, whereas licence transferees have to purchase these licences for a price up to the amount of the tariff quota rent from initial licence holders.[498] Thus a licence transferee does not have the opportunity to benefit from tariff quota rents equivalent to that which accrues to an initial licence holder. Given that licence transferees are usually Category A operators who are most often service suppliers of foreign origin and since licence sellers are usually Category B operators who are most often service suppliers of EC (or ACP) origin, we conclude that service suppliers of Complainants' origin are subject to less favourable conditions of competition in their ability to compete in the wholesale services market for bananas than service suppliers of EC (or ACP) origin.

7.337 The EC notes that it presented evidence that in fact the EC market shares of the three major international banana traders do not reflect any adverse effect coming from the EC import licensing procedures. According to the EC, between 1991 and 1994 there was an increase in the EC market shares of Dole (11 per cent to 15 per cent) and Del Monte (7.5 per cent to 8 per cent), while that of Chiquita fell (25 per cent to 18.5 per cent) due to faulty business strategy. Thus, there was only a slight overall decline in the market share of the three companies from 43.5 per cent to 41.5 per cent. Moreover, the EC suggests that more recent data also indicates the lack of an effect on market shares. It notes that as of 1997 four of the biggest banana import companies have together claimed primary importer status for 64 per cent, 58 per cent and 63 per cent of the total primary importer reference quantity of bananas for the EC-15 for 1993, 1994 and 1995 respectively. In our view, this evidence does not counter the analysis outlined above. Because of the possibility (or even incentive) of purchasing licences or taking other action (such as entering into licence "pooling", investment or contractual arrangements with operators entitled to initial licence allocations) to preserve market share, a lack of significant change in market share does not demonstrate that there has not been a significant change in the conditions of competition.

7.338 For all these reasons, although operator category rules arguably apply on a formally identical basis regardless of the origin of the service or the service supplier concerned, service suppliers of Complainants' origin are subject to less favourable conditions of competition in the meaning of Article XVII:2-3 than service suppliers

---

[496] "The Council [of the European Communities] is ... correct in contending that the traditional dealers [in Latin American bananas] have the opportunity to buy 'market shares' back from those who have received a share of the 30 per cent quota. But again it must not be overlooked that that only confirms that the regulation, by means of the allocation of the quota, transfers the profit potential from the traditional dealers in third-country bananas to the traditional dealers in Community/ACP bananas ...". Opinion of Advocate General Gulman of the European Court of Justice, in Federal Republic of Germany v. Council, p.24.

> "The principal source of licences which are actually sold has been Community producer interests. Individual producers and producers' organizations which are not themselves necessarily 'importers' of bananas have been allocated Category B licences. Since in general they have no interest in importing dollar bananas, these licences are sold, providing a supplement to their income in addition to the support provided by the provisions on aid to compensate their loss of income. The main purchasers of licences appear to be the multinational companies themselves and certain German operators including newcomers." European Commission, Report on the EC Banana Regime, VI/5671/94, p.10f.

[497] "Transferability of licences is an essential feature of the regime so that operators who have not traditionally traded in EC or ACP fruit can have access to the Category B licence under partnership arrangements right from the start, before they have had the opportunity to develop their own trade in EC and ACP fruit." European Commission, Report on the EC Banana Regime, VI/5671/94, p.10.

[498] In the alternative, primary importers in the meaning of the activity function rules also have the option of "pooling" licences by entering into partnership arrangements with, or by investing in companies engaged in customs clearing or in ripening activities.

of EC origin, as a result of the allocation to Category B operators of 30 per cent of the licences required for in-quota imports of third-country and non-traditional ACP bananas.

7.339 While the foregoing analysis is sufficient for us to find that the operator category rules are inconsistent with the requirements of Article XVII of GATS, we consider that it is useful to note that our conclusions are confirmed by factual information submitted by the parties, such as considerations advanced by the EC in the context of the introduction of the licensing system for third-country and non-traditional ACP imports. According to EC sources,[499] the allocation of 30 per cent of the licences required for the importation of third-country and non-traditional ACP bananas at in-quota tariff rates to those operators who have previously marketed EC and traditional ACP bananas is intended to "cross-subsidize" the latter category of operators with tariff quota rents in order to offset the higher costs of production, to strengthen their competitive position and to encourage them to continue marketing bananas of EC and traditional ACP origin. In this regard, the EC Council noted that "... the [licensing] allocation formula is intended ... to strengthen the competitive position of operators who have previously marketed Community or ACP bananas, vis-à-vis their competitors who have previously marketed Latin American bananas ...".[500]

7.340 As noted above, the EC states that in 1994, 28 per cent of the EC/ACP production was controlled by three large integrated banana trading companies (i.e., Chiquita, Dole and Del Monte) which are ultimately in the Complainants' ownership or control. The Complainants submit that prior to the introduction of the EC common market organization, the share of the three large banana companies in the EC/ACP market segment was only 6 per cent and that it was less than 10 per cent for all non-ACP foreign-owned companies. If we assume, absent evidence to the contrary, that these figures are accurate, we believe that the significant increase in the market share of foreign-owned suppliers in the EC/ACP market segment may well be a result of the "cross-subsidization" between operator categories which creates an incentive for service suppliers to become Category B operators.[501]

7.341 **Consequently, we find that the allocation to Category B operators of 30 per cent of the licences allowing the importation of third-country and non-traditional ACP bananas at in-quota tariff rates creates less favourable conditions of competition for like service suppliers of Complainants' origin and is therefore inconsistent with the requirements of Article XVII of GATS.**

---

[499] "1 ... From the range of alternative methods which could be used to achieve this goal, the approach of cross-subsidization, through issuing licences to import 'dollar' bananas to those who traded in Community or ACP bananas was chosen because it not only provides some financial compensation for the higher production costs of these bananas, but also acts as an incentive for the market to become more integrated, and to encourage operators to trade in both 'dollar' and EU/ACP fruit. ...

2 ... Reserving a proportion of tariff quota licences for those operators who have marketed ACP and/or EU bananas is a means of transferring some of the quota rent to them, in order to offset the higher costs of production and therefore to make marketing fruit from these sources a viable commercial proposition. ...

3 ... From the producers' viewpoint, some of the larger dollar suppliers are building up interests in EU and ACP countries, either through establishing plantations, ... or through contractual arrangements with producer groups .... These links demonstrate the success of the cross-subsidization principle of encouraging integration of the different sources supplying the market". European Commission, Impact of cross-subsidization within the banana regime, Note for information, p.1.

[500] Written observation of the Council of the European Communities before the Court of Justice of the European Communities concerning the application for interim relief pursuant to Articles 185 and 186 of the EEC Treaty, 14 June 1993, in Case No. C-276/93R, Chiquita Banana Company B.V. and Others v. Council, p.15.

[501] "At the same time, bananas from EU and ACP sources are starting to penetrate markets outside those Member States which granted them preferential treatment, although these bananas are still primarily sold in their traditional markets. This latter observation might in part reflect the strategies of the multinational companies to become increasingly involved in the marketing of EU and ACP bananas. Since 1993, these companies have established joint ventures with or taken important stakes in organizations both producing and marketing from the Canary Islands, the French Antilles, Jamaica and Somalia. These new interests are in addition to those established in Cameroon and the Ivory Coast before 1993." European Commission, Report on the Operation of the Banana Regime, SEC(95) 1565 final, Brussels, 11 October 1995, p.7f.

(ii) Article II of GATS

7.342 The Complainants claim that the allocation of the third-country import licences on the basis of operator categories and the eligibility criteria for Category B operators discriminate against like service suppliers. As a result, the EC is alleged to be in violation of Article II of GATS because more favourable treatment is accorded to like service suppliers of ACP origin.

7.343 The EC responds with the same arguments that it raised in respect of the Complainants' claims concerning operator categories under Article XVII (see *infra*). In addition, the EC reiterates that, in the absence of a cross-reference to Article XVII, Article II cannot be interpreted using the "modification of competitive conditions" standard found in Article XVII:3.

7.344 In addressing the claim under Article II, we note that two elements need to be demonstrated in order to establish a violation of the GATS MFN clause: (i) the EC has adopted or applied a measure covered by GATS; (ii) the EC's measure accords to services or service suppliers of Complainants' origin treatment less favourable than that it accords to the like services or services suppliers of any other country.

7.345 As to the first element, we have already determined that the EC measures implementing the operator category rules constitute measures affecting trade in services (paragraphs 7.0 *et seq*.). We also recall our discussion on the absence of MFN exemptions in the EC list of Article II exemptions which would be relevant to the claims before us (paragraph *7.298*).

7.346 Turning to the second element, we must consider whether the EC, by applying operator category rules, accords services or service suppliers of any Member treatment less favourable than that it accords to like services or service suppliers of any other country, such as an ACP country.[502] In this connection, we recall that we have found that Category A, B and C operators who are engaged in the marketing of bananas are actual service suppliers and that operators that form part of vertically integrated companies have the capability and opportunity to become at any time service suppliers by entering the wholesale service supply market. Finally, we recall our findings that wholesale transactions as well as each of the different subordinated services mentioned in the headnote to section 6 of the CPC are "like" when supplied in connection with wholesale services, irrespective of whether these services are supplied in respect of bananas of EC and traditional ACP origin, on the one hand, or with respect to bananas of third-country or non-traditional ACP origin, on the other, and that, in our view, at least to the extent that entities provide these like services, they are like service suppliers.

7.347 In examining the Article II issues presented, we note that the categorization of operators and the allocation of licences to them is based on whether they have, during a previous three-year period, marketed EC and traditional ACP bananas or third-country and non-traditional ACP bananas. We recall our finding that operator category rules arguably apply on a formally identical basis to all services regardless of their origin and to all service suppliers regardless of their nationality, ownership or control. Thus, the EC rules establishing operator categories do not formally accord treatment less favourable to Complainants' services and service suppliers than to services and services suppliers of ACP countries on the basis of their origin.

7.348 As in the case of the Article XVII claim, we also note that it is true that service suppliers of Complainants' origin who provide wholesale trade services only with respect to third-country or non-traditional ACP bananas are subject to operator category rules, while service suppliers of ACP origin that market traditional ACP (or EC) bananas are not. However, operators who have supplied wholesale trade services only with respect to third-country and non-traditional ACP bananas are not legally prevented from supplying such services with respect

[502] Operators in ACP ownership or control: e.g. Jamaica Producers, Winban/Wibdeco. (Information submitted by the Complainants). According to the EC, at least one of the subsidiaries of Jamaica Producers is not in ACP ownership or control.

to EC and traditional ACP bananas. By supplying such services to the traditional ACP and EC market segment, suppliers can avoid, or reduce the extent to which they are affected by, operator category rules.

7.349 We then turn to the question whether the application of arguably formally identical operator category rules might nonetheless result in services or service suppliers of Complainants' origin being accorded less favourable treatment than like services or service suppliers of ACP origin in a manner inconsistent with Article II of GATS. In this context, we recall our finding that the obligations contained in Article II:1 of GATS to extend "treatment no less favourable" should be interpreted to require providing no less favourable conditions of competition. Thus, the same analysis used to evaluate the Article XVII claim in respect of operator category rules is applicable here as well.

7.350 Therefore, we recall our reasoning in the context of the parallel claim under Article XVII. Category B operators are eligible for the allocation of 30 per cent of the licences required for third-country or non-traditional ACP imports at in-quota tariff rates regardless of whether they have previously traded at all in third-country bananas. Based on their past import performance in third-country and non-traditional ACP bananas, Category A operators are eligible for only 66.5 per cent of the licences allowing third-country or non-traditional ACP imports at in-quota tariff rates. Accordingly, we found that, when third-country licences are traded, Category B operators will usually sell, and Category A operators will usually purchase, licences. Furthermore, we concluded that operators who are initial licence holders have a greater opportunity to benefit from tariff quota rents than operators who are licence transferees and that most licence transferees are Category A operators. We further found that most service suppliers of Complainants' origin are classified for most of their past marketing of bananas as Category A operators, while most service suppliers of ACP (and EC) origin are registered for most of their past marketing of bananas as Category B operators.[503]

7.351 For these reasons, although operator category rules apply regardless of the origin of the service or the service supplier concerned, service suppliers of Complainants' origin are subject to less favourable treatment than service suppliers of ACP origin as a result of the allocation to Category B operators of 30 per cent of the licences required for in-quota imports of third-country and non-traditional ACP bananas.

7.352 While the foregoing analysis is sufficient for us to find that the operator category rules are inconsistent with the requirements of Article II of GATS, we consider it useful to note that our conclusions are supported by the considerations advanced by the EC in the context of the introduction of the licensing system applicable to third-country and non-traditional ACP imports. According to EC sources,[504] the allocation of 30 per cent of the licences required for the importation of third-country and non-traditional ACP bananas at in-quota tariff rates to those operators who have previously marketed traditional ACP and EC bananas is intended to "cross-subsidize" the latter category of operators with tariff quota rents in order to offset the higher costs of production, to strengthen their competitive position and to encourage them to continue marketing bananas of traditional ACP (and EC) origin.

7.353 **Consequently, we find that the allocation to Category B operators of 30 per cent of the licences allowing the importation of third-country and non-traditional ACP bananas at in-quota tariff rates creates less favourable conditions of competition for like service suppliers of Complainants' origin and is therefore inconsistent with the requirements of Article II of GATS.**

d) Activity functions

7.354 Activity function rules apply to Category A operators as well as to Category B operators. Article 3 of Regulation 1442/93 defines three categories of economic activity, i.e., (1) "primary" importers, (2) "secondary"

---

[503] Operators classified for most of their past trade volume as Category B operators: e.g. Jamaica Producers (Jamaica), Winban/Wibdeco (Windward Islands). (Information submitted by the Complainants).

[504] The impact of cross-subsidization within the banana regime (cited in note Error! Bookmark not defined. supra).

importers (i.e., customs clearers) and (3) ripeners. Fixed percentages of the licences required for the importation originating in third countries or non-traditional ACP countries at in-quota tariff rates are allocated on the basis of these "activity functions": Article 5 of Regulation 1442/93 provides for a weighting coefficient of 57 per cent for primary importers, 15 per cent for secondary importers and 28 per cent for ripeners. In introducing activity functions the EC states that "the Commission is guided by the principle whereby the licences must be granted to natural or legal persons who have undertaken the commercial risk of marketing bananas and by the necessity of avoiding disturbing normal trading relations between persons occupying different points in the marketing chain".[505]

(i) Article XVII of GATS

[7.355-7.368 used in the Ecuador and United States report]

7.355 In the view of the Complainants, the allocation of third-country tariff quota licences based on activity functions-in particular the reservation of 15 per cent for secondary importers and of 28 per cent for ripeners, most of which they claim, are EC firms - serves the purpose of re-allocating market shares previously held by third-country firms and modifies the conditions of competition in favour of like services suppliers of EC origin. Therefore, the Complainants claim that the activity function rules violate Article XVII of GATS vis-à-vis like EC service suppliers of services covered by the EC commitments on national treatment.

7.356 The EC argues that the creation of activity functions aims at avoiding the concentration of economic bargaining power - which results from the allocation of import licences - in the hands of a few privileged recipients at a specific stage of the supply chain.

7.357 In light of these arguments we turn to an examination of the issues arising under this Article XVII claim. In order to establish a breach of the national treatment obligation of Article XVII, three elements need to be demonstrated: (i) the EC has undertaken a commitment in a relevant sector and mode of supply; (ii) the EC has adopted or applied a measure affecting the supply of services in that sector and/or mode of supply; and (iii) the EC's measure accords to service suppliers of any other Member treatment less favourable than that it accords to the EC's own like service suppliers.

7.358 As to the first two elements, we have already determined that the EC has made a commitment in respect of wholesale trade services with respect to service supply across borders and through commercial presence without conditions or qualifications in the meaning of Article XVII (*infra*). We find that the EC measures implementing the activity function rules constitute measures affecting trade in services for the same reasons that we found that the operator category rules constitute measures affecting trade in services.

7.359 Turning to the third element, we must consider whether the EC, by applying the activity function rules, accords service suppliers of any Complainant treatment less favourable than that it accords to like service suppliers of the EC. In this connection, we recall that we have found that Category A, B and C operators who are engaged in the marketing of bananas are actual service suppliers and that operators that form part of vertically integrated companies have the capability and opportunity to become at any time service suppliers by entering the wholesale service supply market (*infra*). Finally, we recall our findings (*infra*) that wholesale transactions as well as each of the different subordinated services mentioned in the headnote to section 6 of the CPC are "like" when supplied in connection with wholesale services, irrespective of whether these services are supplied in respect of bananas of EC and traditional ACP origin, on the one hand, or with respect to bananas of third-country or non-traditional ACP origin, on the other, and that, in our view, at least to the extent that entities provide these like services, they are like service suppliers.

---

[505] Recital 15 of Regulation No. 404/93.

7.360 In examining the issues presented by the Complainants, we recall that under the EC activity function rules, claims for reference quantities of EC and traditional ACP bananas marketed during a preceding three-year period by Category B operators as well as claims as to quantities of third-country and non-traditional ACP bananas imported during that period by Category A operators are weighted according to the activity functions performed by these operators. The weighting coefficient of 57 per cent for primary importers, 15 per cent for secondary importers and 28 per cent for ripeners relates to the importation, customs clearance and ripening activities performed by Category A and B operators during the previous three-year period. Activity function rules apply to all service suppliers regardless of their nationality, ownership or control. Suppliers of EC origin who supply wholesale services with respect to third-country and non-traditional ACP bananas are equally subject to activity function rules as suppliers of Complainants' origin who provide wholesale services with respect to third-country and non-traditional ACP bananas. Likewise, suppliers of EC origin are treated in the same way by activity function rules when they sell or market EC or traditional ACP bananas as suppliers of Complainants' origin that deal in EC or traditional ACP bananas. Accordingly, we conclude that the EC rules establishing activity functions do not discriminate against Complainants' like service suppliers on the basis of their origin and thus are arguably formally identical in the meaning of Article XVII:2 for service suppliers of domestic as well as foreign origin.

7.361 We then turn to the question whether the application of arguably formally identical activity function rules to service suppliers of Complainants' origin modifies, in the meaning of Article XVII, conditions of competition in favour of like service suppliers of EC origin. In this context, we note that service suppliers of Complainants' origin who sell third-country or non-traditional ACP bananas are subject to activity function rules, while like service suppliers of EC origin who sell EC bananas are not. However, operators who have supplied wholesale services exclusively or mainly with respect to third-country and non-traditional ACP bananas are not legally prevented from choosing to begin supplying or to supply more such services with respect to EC (and traditional ACP) bananas. By supplying wholesale services to the EC (and traditional ACP) banana market segment, suppliers can avoid, or reduce the extent to which they are, subject to activity function rules.[506]

7.362 However, we also have to examine the impact of the introduction of activity function rules on market conditions. As noted above, the EC states that the European Commission does not have a record of the actual ownership or control of companies registered to receive licences under whatever activity function. We note that a company may claim reference quantities for the calculation of their annual licence entitlement at the same time for primary importation, customs clearance as well as ripening activities. But we also have to consider the information submitted by the Complainants according to which in 1992 overall about 83 per cent of bananas imported or marketed in the EC - and between 57 and 100 per cent in individual EC Member States[507] - were ripened by EC

---

[506] Furthermore, these suppliers will become eligible for the allocation of 30 per cent of the in-quota licences required for third-country and non-traditional ACP imports which are allocated to Category B operators.

[507] Average estimated volume ripened by EC owned ripeners in 1992 (Information submitted by the Complainants):

[Austria:	100.0%]
Belgium/Luxembourg:	73.1%
Denmark:	100.0%
[Finland:	100.0%]
France:	87.5%
Germany:	57.0%
Greece:	100.0%
Ireland:	94.5%
Italy:	100.0%
Netherlands:	87.0%
Portugal:	100.0%
Spain:	94.9%
[Sweden:	100.0%]
United Kingdom:	100.0%
EC total:	83.7%

owned or controlled ripeners before the introduction of the common market organization. The EC challenges these statistics as exaggerated. But even the EC statistics[508] suggest that 74 to 80 per cent of ripeners are EC controlled. Thus, we conclude that the vast majority of the ripening capacity in the EC is owned or controlled by natural or juridical persons of the EC and that most of the bananas produced in or imported to the EC are ripened in EC owned or controlled ripening facilities. Indeed, as noted above by the EC itself, the activity function rules were put in place to prevent a concentration of economic bargaining power in the hands of the large multinational companies, which the EC elsewhere in its submission describes as Chiquita, Dole and Del Monte. Therefore, most of the claims as to ripening activities performed will be filed by ripeners of EC origin who are actual or potential wholesale service suppliers. Likewise, we are convinced that most of the service suppliers of Complainants' origin will usually be able to claim reference quantities only for primary importation and possibly for customs clearance, but not for the performance of ripening activities. We further note that we have not been presented with sufficient information to ascertain whether companies carrying out customs clearance activities are predominantly in EC or third-country ownership or control. Nor are we in a position to determine whether self-employed natural persons performing customs clearance activities are mainly EC or third-country nationals. Therefore, service suppliers of EC as well as third-country origin do have comparable opportunities to file claims as to primary and secondary importation activities performed with the EC authorities, whereas service suppliers of Complainants' origin do not enjoy equal competitive opportunities to make claims for the performance of ripening activities as service suppliers of EC origin.

7.363 Under the activity function rules, primary importers may obtain access to an amount of A and B licences equivalent to 57 per cent of their past import volumes unless they also perform customs clearance or ripening activities. At the same time, customs clearers are allocated 15 per cent, and ripeners are eligible for 28 per cent of the A and B licences required for the importation of third-country or non-traditional ACP bananas at in-quota tariff rates, regardless of whether they have imported bananas in the past. However, we also have to take into account that import licences are tradeable and transferable. Thus, the allocation of fixed percentages of licences through the application of weighting coefficients (to claims for reference quantities) to the performers of particular activity functions does not automatically determine the distribution of import shares between operators performing these different types of economic activity in the supply chain. In fact, both parties agree that large numbers of import licences are being traded on the market place. Consequently, primary importers are, in general, able to purchase the amount of the licences they need in addition to their annual licence entitlement if they wish to maintain their previous market share, e.g. from ripeners who have not imported bananas themselves. Thus we believe that, when licences are being traded, sellers of licences will usually be ripeners and purchasers of licences will usually be primary importers. Accordingly, most of the licence transferees will be primary importers, while most of those initial licence holders who do not carry out the physical importation themselves but sell the licences issued to them will be ripeners. However, while an initial licence holder who carries out the physical importation of bananas or sells the licence will in any case reap tariff quota rents, a licence transferee will have purchased the licence for an amount up to the tariff quota rent from the initial licence holder. Thus a licence transferee does not have the opportunity to benefit from tariff quota rents equivalent to those of an initial licence holder. Given that licence transferees are usually primary importers and that licence sellers are usually ripeners which, as noted above, are overwhelmingly EC owned or controlled, suppliers of EC origin, albeit being subject to formally identical treatment, enjoy more favourable conditions of competition in the meaning of Article XVII:3 of GATS than like wholesale service suppliers of Complainants' origin.

7.364 Primary importers who wish to maintain their previous market share also have the options of entering into contractual arrangements with, or investing in, companies performing customs clearing or ripening activities.

We note that Austria, Finland and Sweden did not become EC member States until 1995.

[508] In its second oral statement, the EC stated that "the ripening sector has always been ... penetrated by foreign suppliers of ripening services or of ripeners for the account of integrated firms (around 20%)". At the interim hearing, the EC stated that "[a]t present, our best indications are that the some 50 ripening companies owned or controlled by Chiquita and Dole and the 5 Del Monte companies count for 26 per cent of ripening declarations in the EC-15".

However, whatever option primary importers choose in order to obtain licences in addition to their initial entitlement, e.g., ad hoc purchases of licences from, or long-term investment or partnership arrangements with, secondary importers or ripeners, the fact that licence transferees are subject to less favourable conditions of competition than initial licence holders remains the same. Thus, the availability of alternative options to obtain access to additional licences does not detract from our conclusion in the preceding paragraph that the vast majority of ripeners are EC owned or controlled and enjoy more favourable conditions of competition than like wholesale service suppliers of foreign origin.

7.365 Under operator category rules, on the basis of their third-country and non-traditional ACP imports during a preceding three-year period, primary importers classified in operator Category A are eligible for licences for 66.5 per cent of the licences allowing imports of third-country and non-traditional ACP bananas at in-quota tariff rates. Under activity function rules, the entitlements of operators who are primary importers are reduced to 57 per cent of the bananas marketed during a preceding three-year period unless such operators also engage in customs clearance or ripening activities. While primary importers who are Category B operators are subject to the same weighting coefficients as Category A operators, these Category B operators have, on the basis of their marketing of EC and traditional ACP bananas during a preceding three-year period, access to 30 per cent of the licences allowing imports of third-country and non-traditional ACP bananas at in-quota tariff rates regardless of whether they have previously traded in the latter market segment. Therefore, the purchasers of licences will be more often primary importers who are Category A operators than primary importers who are Category B operators. Thus, the allocation of licences according to activity functions is capable of aggravating the adverse impact of the licence allocation to different operator categories for those service suppliers who are of Complainants' origin.

7.366 Therefore, we conclude that the allocation of fixed percentages of licences according to activity functions performed by operators arguably applies on a formally identical basis to all wholesale service suppliers regardless of their origin, nationality, ownership or control. However, the allocation of such licences according to activity functions modifies conditions of competition in favour of service suppliers of EC origin given that the vast majority of ripeners who are actually supplying, or capable of supplying, wholesale services are of EC origin.

7.367 The foregoing analysis is sufficient for us to find that the activity function rules are inconsistent with the requirements of Article XVII of GATS. Nevertheless, we consider it useful to note that our conclusions are supported by the fact that according to EC sources, the allocation of 28 per cent of the A and B licences allowing third-country and non-traditional ACP imports at in-quota tariff rates to ripeners regardless of whether they have previously imported bananas is intended to strengthen their bargaining position in the supply chain towards primary importers.[509]

7.368 **Consequently, we find that the allocation to ripeners of 28 per cent of the Category A and B licences allowing the importation of third-country and non-traditional ACP bananas at in-quota tariff rates creates less favourable conditions of competition for like service suppliers of Complainants' origin and is therefore inconsistent with the requirements of Article XVII of GATS.**

(ii) Article II of GATS

[7.369-7.372 Used in the Mexico report.]

7.369 In the view of Mexico, the allocation of third-country tariff quota licences based on activity functions serves the purpose of re-allocating market shares previously held by third-country firms and modifies the conditions of competition in favour of like services suppliers of EC origin. Therefore, Mexico claims that the activity function rules violate Article II of GATS vis-à-vis like ACP services and service suppliers.

[509] "At the ripener level, holders of Category B licences will use their licences to aid in their negotiations with their suppliers of bananas, be they dollar, ACP or EC". European Commission, Report on the EC Banana Regime, VI/5671/94, p.10f.

7.370 The EC argues that the creation of activity functions aims at avoiding the concentration of economic bargaining power - which results from the allocation of import licences - in the hands of a few privileged recipients at a specific stage of the supply chain.

7.371 We have not been presented with information on the nationality, origin, ownership or control of customs clearers, nor has Mexico submitted information on the extent to which ripening facilities are owned or controlled by countries which are traditional sources of ACP bananas. Therefore, we do not believe that the application of arguably formally identical activity function rules and the allocation of certain percentages of the licences allowing imports of third-country and non-traditional ACP bananas at in-quota tariff rates according to the activity functions performed by operators modify the conditions of conditions of competition in favour of ACP owned or controlled service suppliers.

7.372 **Accordingly, we make no finding on whether or not the allocation according to activity functions of fixed percentages of licences allowing the importation of third-country and non-traditional ACP bananas at in-quota tariff rates creates less favourable conditions of competition for service suppliers of Mexican origin.**

e) Export certificates

7.373 The Complainants claim that the exemption of Category B operators from the requirement imposed on other operators by Regulation 478/95 to match EC import licences with BFA export certificates with respect to imports from Colombia, Costa Rica and Nicaragua accords less favourable treatment to service suppliers of third country origin. As a result, the EC is alleged to be in violation of Article II of GATS with respect to like service suppliers of ACP origin, and Article XVII of GATS with respect to like service suppliers of EC origin.

7.374 The EC responds along the same lines that it has in respect of the other GATS claims. It points out that neither all Category A licence holders are in third-country ownership, nor are all Category B licences holders - that benefit from a BFA export certificate exemption - in EC/ACP control. It also argues that the GATS does not contain any rules governing the allocation or distribution of quota rents which are generated by trade instruments such as tariff quotas whose imposition is legitimate under WTO agreements.

(i) Article XVII of GATS

[7.375-7.380 Used in the Ecuador and United States report]

7.375 In order to establish a breach of the national treatment obligation of Article XVII, three elements need to be demonstrated: (i) the EC has undertaken a commitment in a relevant sector and mode of supply; (ii) the EC has adopted or applied a measure affecting the supply of services in that sector and/or mode of supply; and (iii) the EC's measure accords to service suppliers of any other Member treatment less favourable than that it accords to the EC's own like service suppliers.

7.376 In respect of the first element, we recall that the EC has bound the wholesale trade service sub-sector as regards service supply across borders and through commercial presence without conditions or qualifications limiting the scope of the commitments.

7.377 As to the second element, i.e., whether the EC measures implementing the export certificate requirement are measures affecting the supply of services, we recall that we have found that the term "affecting" should be interpreted broadly (paragraph *7.175 et seq*). In this connection, we also note that supply of services through cross-border supply or commercial presence is defined broadly to include the production, distribution, marketing, sale and delivery of such services.[510] As a consequence, in our view, the EC measures establishing export certificate

[510] GATS, Article XXVIII:(b).

requirements are "measures affecting trade in services" in the meaning of the GATS and are measures affecting Complainants' trade in services for the same reasons as are operator category and activity function rules.

7.378 We turn now to the third element of whether the export certificate requirement accords to service suppliers of the Complainants treatment less favourable than that it accords to the EC's own like service suppliers. We note that the parties do not disagree that the requirement to match EC import licences with BFA export certificates serves the purpose, or at least has the effect, of transferring part of the tariff quota rent which would normally accrue to initial EC import licence holders to the suppliers from Colombia, Costa Rica and Nicaragua who are initial holders of BFA export certificates. According to Article 3 of Regulation 478/95, Category A and C operators are subject to the EC's requirement to match import licences with BFA export certificates, whereas Category B operators are not subject to a similar requirement. Therefore, Category B operators who are initial holders of EC import licences do not have to share part of the tariff quota rent with initial holders of BFA export certificates. However, Category A and C operators must obtain export certificates from holders of BFA export certificates issued by the competent authorities of Colombia, Costa Rica or Nicaragua. When Category A and C operators are initial holders of EC import licences they share part of the tariff quota rent with initial holders of BFA export certificates. Consequently, the exemption of Category B operators from the BFA export certificate requirement ensures that tariff quota rent shares that would normally accrue to initial EC import licence holders are transferred exclusively from such holders who are Category A and C operators to initial holders of BFA export certificates.

7.379 In this context, we recall that operator category rules apply on an arguably formally identical basis to all service suppliers regardless of their nationality, ownership or control (*infra*). By the same token, we conclude that the exemption of Category B operators from the requirement to match EC import licences with BFA export certificates also arguably applies on a formally identical basis irrespective of the origin of the service suppliers concerned. However, we also recall that most service suppliers of Complainants' origin are classified as Category A operators for most of their previous trade volume and that most of the "like" service suppliers of EC origin are classified as Category B operators for most of the bananas they have marketed during a preceding three-year period. Accordingly, we conclude that the exemption of Category B operators from the requirement to match EC import licences with BFA export certificates constitutes less favourable treatment for suppliers of Complainants' origin because it modifies conditions of competition in the meaning of Article XVII:3 of GATS in favour of "like" service suppliers or EC origin.

7.380 **For these reasons, we find that the exemption of Category B operators of EC origin from the requirement to match EC import licences with BFA export certificates creates less favourable conditions of competition for like service suppliers of Complainants' origin and is therefore inconsistent with the requirements of Article XVII of GATS.**

(ii) Article II of GATS

7.381 In addressing the claim in respect of export certificates under Article II, we recall that two elements need to be demonstrated in order to establish a violation of the GATS MFN clause: (i) the EC has adopted or applied a measure covered by GATS; (ii) the EC's measure accords to service suppliers of the Complainants' origin treatment less favourable than that it accords to the like services suppliers of any other country.

7.382 As to the first element, i.e., whether the EC measures implementing the export certificate requirement are measures covered by GATS, we recall that we have found that the phrase "affecting trade in services" should be interpreted broadly (paragraph *7.175*). In this connection, we also note that supply of services through cross-border supply or commercial presence is defined broadly to include the production, distribution, marketing, sale and delivery of such services.[511] As a consequence, in our view, the EC measures are "measures affecting trade in

[511] GATS, Article XXVIII:(b).

services" in the meaning of the GATS. More specifically, the rules establishing export certificate requirements constitute measures affecting the Complainants' trade in services for the same reasons as do operator category and activity function rules and are therefore covered by GATS.

7.383 We turn now to the second element of whether the export certificate requirement accords to service suppliers of the Complainants treatment less favourable than that it accords to like service suppliers of ACP origin. We note that the parties do not disagree that the requirement to match EC import licences with BFA export certificates serves the purpose, or at least has the effect, of transferring part of the tariff quota rent which would normally accrue to initial EC import licence holders to the suppliers from Colombia, Costa Rica and Nicaragua who are initial holders of BFA export certificates. According to Article 3 of Regulation 478/95, Category A and C operators are subject to the EC's requirement to match import licences with BFA export certificates, whereas Category B operators are not subject to a similar requirement. Therefore, Category B operators who are initial holders of EC import licences do not have to share part of the tariff quota rent with initial holders of BFA export certificates. However, Category A and C operators must obtain export certificates from holders of BFA export certificates issued by the competent authorities of Colombia, Costa Rica or Nicaragua. When Category A and C operators are initial holders of EC import licences they share part of the tariff quota rent with initial holders of BFA export certificates. Consequently, the exemption of Category B operators from the BFA export certificate requirement ensures that tariff quota rent shares that would normally accrue to initial EC import licence holders are transferred exclusively from such holders who are Category A and C operators to initial holders of BFA export certificates.

7.384 In this context, we recall that operator category rules apply on an arguably formally identical basis to all service suppliers regardless of their nationality, ownership or control (*infra*). By the same token, we conclude that the exemption of Category B operators from the requirement to match EC import licences with BFA export certificates also arguably applies on a formally identical basis irrespective of the origin of the service suppliers concerned. However, we also recall that most service suppliers of Complainants' origin are classified as Category A operators for most of their previous trade volume and that most of the "like" service suppliers of ACP origin are classified as Category B operators for most of the bananas they have marketed during a preceding three-year period. Accordingly, we conclude that the exemption of Category B operators from the requirement to match EC import licences with BFA export certificates constitutes less favourable treatment for suppliers of Complainants' origin because it modifies conditions of competition in favour of "like" service suppliers or ACP origin.

***7.385* Accordingly, we find that the exemption of Category B operators of ACP origin from the requirement to match EC import licences with BFA export certificates creates less favourable conditions of competition for like service suppliers of Complainants' origin and is therefore inconsistent with the requirements of Article II of GATS.**

f) Hurricane licences

7.386 Hurricane licences[512] authorize operators who include or represent EC and ACP producers, or producer organizations "to import in compensation third-country bananas and non-traditional ACP bananas for the benefit of the operators who directly suffered damage as a result of the impossibility of supplying the Community market with bananas originating in affected producer regions" because of the impact of tropical storms. In the aftermath of the hurricanes Debbie, Iris, Luis and Marilyn, 281,605 tonnes of third-country or non-traditional ACP imports were authorized between 16 November 1994 and May 1996.

7.387 The Complainants claim that the award of large amounts of hurricane licences by the EC exclusively to Category B operators and EC producers accords less favourable treatment to third country service suppliers.

[512] See EC regulations cited in note 301, supra.

Therefore, the EC is alleged to be in violation of Article II of GATS because of its treatment of ACP suppliers, and in violation of Article XVII of GATS because of its treatment of EC suppliers.

7.388 The EC responds that the issuance of hurricane licences is required by the Lomé Convention. Further, the EC argues that the allocation of hurricane licences is directly linked to trade in goods. Therefore, inconsistencies with Article II or XVII of GATS cannot occur because the hurricane licences are not covered by the GATS in the EC's view.

(i) Article XVII of GATS

[7.389-7.393 Used in the Ecuador and United States report]

7.389 In order to establish a breach of the national treatment obligation of Article XVII, three elements need to be demonstrated: (i) the EC has undertaken a commitment in a relevant sector and mode of supply; (ii) the EC has adopted or applied a measure affecting the supply of services in that sector and/or mode of supply; and (iii) the EC's measure accords to service suppliers of any other Member treatment less favourable than that it accords to the EC's own like service suppliers.

7.390 In respect of the first element, we recall that the EC has bound the wholesale trade service sub-sector as regards service supply across borders and through commercial presence without conditions or qualifications limiting the scope of the commitments.

7.391 As to the second element, i.e., whether the EC measures implementing hurricane licences are measures affecting the supply of services, we recall that we have found that the term "affecting" should be interpreted broadly (paragraphs *7.175 et seq.*). In this connection, we also note that supply of services through cross-border supply or commercial presence is defined broadly to include the production, distribution, marketing, sale and delivery of such services. As a consequence, in our view, the EC banana regulations are "measures affecting trade in services" in the meaning of the GATS. More specifically, the rules establishing hurricane licences constitute measures affecting Complainants' trade in services.

7.392 We now turn to the third element of whether the issuance of hurricane licences accords to service suppliers of the Complainants treatment less favourable than that it accords to the EC's own like service suppliers. In addressing this issue, we note that while only operators who include or directly represent EC or ACP producers or producer organizations affected by a tropical storm are eligible for the allocation of hurricane licences,[513] the EC regulations authorizing the issuance of certain quantities of hurricane licences apply on an arguably formally identical basis to services and service suppliers regardless of their origin, nationality, ownership or control. However, like Category B operators in general, we find that the vast majority of operators who "include or directly represent" EC or ACP producers are service suppliers of EC (or ACP) origin. We further note that hurricane licences allow for the importation of third-country and non-traditional ACP bananas at in-quota tariff rates outside and additional to the tariff quota. Thus service suppliers of EC (or ACP) origin obtain access to an additional

---

513 "1.The quantities referred to in Article 1(2) shall be allocated to the operators who:

-include or directly represent banana producers affected by tropical storm Debbie.

-and who, during the last quarter of 1994, are unable to supply, on their own account, the Community market with bananas originating in the regions or countries referred to 1(2) on account of the damage caused by tropical storm Debbie.

2. The competent authorities in the Member States concerned shall determine the beneficiary operators who meet the requirements of paragraph 1 and shall make an allocation to each of them pursuant to this Regulation on the basis of:

-the quantities allocated to the producer regions or countries referred to in Article 1(2) and of

-the damage sustained as a result of tropical storm Debbie.

3. The competent authorities shall assess the damage sustained on the basis of all supporting documents and information collected from the operators concerned." Article 2 of Commission Regulation (EC) No. 2791/94 of 16 November 1994 on the exceptional allocation of a quantity additional to the tariff quota for imports of bananas in 1994 as a result of tropical storm Debbie." Id., Art. 4.

entitlement of licences allowing the importation of third-country and non-traditional ACP bananas at in-quota tariff rates beyond the existing allocation to Category B operators of 30 per cent of the licences allowing imports of such bananas within the tariff quota. To put it differently, the allocation of hurricane licences gives service suppliers of EC (and ACP) origin the opportunity to benefit from tariff quota rents in addition to the tariff quota rents generated by the allocation of 30 per cent of the in-quota import licences to them. Thus the fact that only operators who include or directly represent EC (or ACP) producers are eligible for such licences modifies conditions of competition in favour of wholesale services suppliers of EC (and ACP) origin, since like service suppliers of Complainants' origin, if and when affected by a hurricane, do not enjoy a similar rent-making opportunity. We further note that our findings are limited to the present factual situation where hurricane licences are issued to operators who exclusively include or represent EC (or ACP) producers. Our legal analysis would not necessarily apply to a situation where hurricane licences were issued directly and exclusively to EC (or ACP) producers.

7.393 **Consequently, we find that the allocation of hurricane licences exclusively to operators who include or directly represent EC producers creates less favourable conditions of competition for like service suppliers of Complainants' origin and is therefore inconsistent with the requirements of Article XVII of GATS.**

(ii) Article II of GATS

7.394 In addressing the claim in respect of hurricane licences under Article II, we recall that two elements need to be demonstrated in order to establish a violation of the GATS MFN clause: (i) the EC has adopted or applied a measure covered by GATS; (ii) the EC's measure accords to service suppliers of the Complainants' origin treatment less favourable than that it accords to the like services suppliers of any other country.

7.395 As to the first element, i.e., whether the EC has adopted or applied a measures covered by GATS, we recall that we have found that the phrase "affecting trade in services" should be interpreted broadly (paragraphs *7.175 et seq.*). In this connection, we also note that supply of services through cross-border supply or commercial presence is defined broadly to include the production, distribution, marketing, sale and delivery of such services. As a consequence, in our view, the EC banana regulations are "measures affecting trade in services" in the meaning of the GATS. More specifically, the rules establishing hurricane licences constitute measures affecting the Complainants' trade in services and are therefore covered by GATS.

7.396 We now turn to the second element of whether the issuance of hurricane licences accords to service suppliers of the Complainants treatment less favourable than that it accords to like service suppliers of ACP origin. In addressing this issue, we note that while only operators who include or directly represent EC or ACP producers or producer organizations affected by a tropical storm are eligible for the allocation of hurricane licences,[514] the EC regulations authorizing the issuance of certain quantities of hurricane licences apply on an arguably formally identical basis to services and service suppliers regardless of their origin, nationality, ownership or control. However, like Category B operators in general, we find that the vast majority of operators who "include or directly represent" EC or ACP producers are service suppliers of ACP (or EC) origin. We further note that hurricane licences allow for the importation of third-country and non-traditional ACP bananas at in-quota tariff rates outside and additional to the tariff quota. Thus service suppliers of ACP (or EC) origin obtain access to an additional entitlement of licences allowing the importation of third-country and non-traditional ACP bananas at in-quota tariff rates beyond the existing allocation to Category B operators of 30 per cent of the licences allowing imports of such bananas within the tariff quota. To put it differently, the allocation of hurricane licences gives service suppliers of ACP (and EC) origin the opportunity to benefit from tariff quota rents in addition to the tariff quota rents generated by the allocation of 30 per cent of the in-quota import licences to them. Thus the fact that only operators who include or directly represent ACP (or EC) producers are eligible for such licences modifies conditions of competition in favour of wholesale services suppliers of EC (and ACP) origin, since like service suppliers of

[514] Idem.

Complainants' origin, if and when affected by a hurricane, do not enjoy a similar rent-making opportunity. We further note that our findings are limited to the present factual situation where hurricane licences are issued to operators who exclusively include or represent ACP (or EC) producers.

7.397 **Consequently, we find that the allocation of hurricane licences exclusively to operators who include or directly represent ACP producers creates less favourable conditions of competition for like service suppliers of Complainants' origin and is therefore inconsistent with the requirements of Article II of GATS.**

5. *Nullification or impairment*

7.398 The measures taken by the EC affecting the importation of bananas from the Complainants, because of the infringement of obligations by the EC under a number of WTO agreements, are a *prima facie* case of nullification or impairment of benefits in the meaning of Article 3.8 of the DSU, which provides that "there is normally a presumption that a breach of the rules has an adverse impact on other Members parties to that covered agreement". To the extent that this presumption can be rebutted,[515] in our view the EC has not succeeded in rebutting the presumption that its breaches of GATT, GATS and Licensing Agreement rules have nullified or impaired benefits of the Complainants.

D. Summary of Findings

7.399 The complexity of this case, and the unprecedented number of claims, arguments and Agreements involved, has resulted in a long report with an unprecedented number of findings. To assist the reader, the findings on the various procedural and substantive issues are repeated here. In summary we find that

1. *Preliminary issues*

- the EC's claim that the Complainants' case should be dismissed because the consultations held concerning this dispute did not perform their minimum function of affording a possibility for arriving at a mutually satisfactory solution and a clear setting out of the different claims of which a dispute consists shall be rejected.

- the panel request made by the Complainants was sufficient to meet the requirements of Article 6.2 of the DSU to the extent that it alleged inconsistencies with the requirements of specific provisions of specific WTO agreements.

- under the DSU the United States has a right to advance the claims that it has raised in this case.

- the description of the Panel's proceedings, the factual aspects and the parties' arguments should be identical in the four reports. In the "Findings" section, however, the reports differ to the extent that the Complainants' initial written submissions to the Panel differ in respect of alleging inconsistencies with the requirements of specific provisions of specific agreements.

2. *The EC market for bananas: Article XIII of GATT*

- bananas are "like" products, for purposes of Article I, III, X and XIII of GATT, irrespective of whether they originate in the EC, in ACP countries, in BFA countries or in other third countries.

- the EC has only one regime for banana imports for purposes of analysing whether its allocation of tariff quota shares is consistent with the requirements of Article XIII.

[515] See Panel Report on "United States - Taxes on Petroleum and Certain Imported Substances", adopted on 17 June 1987, BISD 34S/136, 158, para. 5.1.9.

- it was not unreasonable for the EC to conclude that at the time the BFA was negotiated Colombia and Costa Rica were the only contracting parties that had a substantial interest in supplying the EC banana market in terms of Article XIII:2(d).

- it is not reasonable to conclude that at the time the BFA was negotiated Nicaragua and Venezuela had a substantial interest in supplying the EC banana market in the terms of Article XIII:2(d).

- the EC's allocation of tariff quota shares by agreement and by assignment to some Members not having a substantial interest in supplying bananas to the EC (including Nicaragua, Venezuela and certain ACP countries in respect of traditional and non-traditional exports) but not to other Members (such as Guatemala) and the tariff quota reallocation rules of the BFA, are inconsistent with the requirements of Article XIII:1.

- the failure of Ecuador's Protocol of Accession to address banana-related issues does not mean that Ecuador must accept the validity of the BFA as contained in the EC's Schedule or that it is precluded from invoking Article XIII:2 or XIII:4.

- it was not unreasonable for the EC to conclude that the Lomé Convention requires the EC to allocate country-specific tariff quota shares to traditional ACP banana supplying countries in an amount of their pre-1991 best-ever exports to the EC.

- the allocation of tariff quota shares to ACP countries in excess of their pre-1991 best-ever exports to the EC is not required by the Lomé Convention.

- to the extent that we have found that the EC has acted inconsistently with the requirements of Article XIII:1 (*infra*), we find that the Lomé waiver waives that inconsistency with Article XIII:1 to the extent necessary to permit the EC to allocate shares of its banana tariff quota to specific traditional ACP banana supplying countries in an amount not exceeding their pre-1991 best-ever exports to the EC.

- the inclusion of the BFA tariff quota shares in the EC's Schedule does not permit the EC to act inconsistently with the requirements of Article XIII of GATT.

- neither the negotiation of the BFA and its inclusion in the EC's Schedule nor the Agreement on Agriculture permit the EC to act inconsistently with the requirements of Article XIII of GATT.

3. *Tariff issues*

- to the extent that the EC's preferential tariff treatment of non-traditional ACP bananas is inconsistent with its obligations under Article I:1, those obligations have been waived by the Lomé waiver.

4. *The EC banana import licensing procedures*

- the Licensing Agreement applies to licensing procedures for tariff quotas.

- the provisions of GATT 1994, the Licensing Agreement and Article 2 of the TRIM'S Agreement all apply to the EC's import licensing procedures for bananas.

- the EC licensing procedures for traditional ACP bananas and third-country and non-traditional ACP bananas should be examined as one licensing regime.

- the allocation to Category B operators of 30 per cent of the licences allowing the importation of third-country and non-traditional ACP bananas at in-quota tariff rates is inconsistent with the requirements of Article III:4 of GATT.

- the application in general of operator category rules in respect of the importation of third-country and non-traditional ACP bananas at in-quota tariff rates, in the absence of the application of such rules to traditional ACP imports, and in particular the allocation to Category B operators of 30 per cent of the licences allowing the importation of third-country and non-traditional ACP bananas at in-quota tariff rates, are inconsistent with the requirements of Article I:1 of GATT.

- the Lomé waiver does not waive the EC's obligations under Article I:1 of GATT in respect of licensing procedures applied to third-country and non-traditional ACP imports, including those related to operator category rules.

- the application of activity function rules in respect of the importation of third-country and non-traditional ACP bananas at in-quota tariff rates, in the absence of the application of such rules to traditional ACP imports, is inconsistent with the requirements of Article I:1 of GATT.

- the EC import licensing procedures are subject to the requirements of Article X of GATT.

- the application of activity function rules in respect of the importation of third-country and non-traditional ACP bananas at in-quota tariff rates, in the absence of the application of such rules to traditional ACP imports, is inconsistent with the requirements of Article X:3(a) of GATT.

- the requirement to match EC import licences with BFA export certificates is inconsistent with the requirements of Article I:1 of GATT.

- to the extent that we find that specific aspects of the EC licensing procedures are not in conformity with Articles I, III or X of GATT, we necessarily also find an inconsistency with the requirements of Article 1.2 of the Licensing Agreement.

- we do not make a finding on whether the EC failed to take into account the needs of developing countries in a manner inconsistent with the requirements of Article 1.2 of the Licensing Agreement.

5. *The EC banana import licensing procedures and the GATS*

- there is no legal basis for an *a priori* exclusion of measures within the EC banana import licensing regime from the scope of the GATS.

- the distribution of bananas, regardless of whether they are green or ripened, falls within the scope of category CPC 622 "wholesale trade services" as inscribed in the EC's GATS Schedule of Commitments so long as it involves the sale of bananas to retailers, to industrial, commercial, institutional or other professional business users, or other wholesalers.

- the EC's obligations under Article II of GATS and commitments under Article XVII of GATS cover the treatment of suppliers of wholesale trade services within the jurisdiction of the EC.

- the obligation contained in Article II:1 of GATS to extend "treatment no less favourable" should be interpreted *in casu* to require providing no less favourable conditions of competition.

- the EC has undertaken a full commitment on national treatment in the sector of "Wholesale Trade Services" with respect to supply through commercial presence.

- the allocation to Category B operators of 30 per cent of the licences allowing the importation of third-country and non-traditional ACP bananas at in-quota tariff rates creates less favourable conditions of competition for like service suppliers of Complainants' origin and is therefore inconsistent with the requirements of Article XVII of GATS.

- the allocation to Category B operators of 30 per cent of the licences allowing the importation of third-country and non-traditional ACP bananas at in-quota tariff rates creates less favourable conditions of competition for like service suppliers of Complainants' origin and is therefore inconsistent with the requirements of Article II of GATS.

- the allocation to ripeners of 28 per cent of the Category A and B licences allowing the importation of third-country and non-traditional ACP bananas at in-quota tariff rates creates less favourable conditions of competition for like service suppliers of Complainants' origin and is therefore inconsistent with the requirements of Article XVII of GATS.

- the exemption of Category B operators of EC origin from the requirement to match EC import licences with BFA export certificates creates less favourable conditions of competition for like service suppliers of Complainants' origin and is therefore inconsistent with the requirements of Article XVII of GATS.

- the exemption of Category B operators of ACP origin from the requirement to match EC import licences with BFA export certificates creates less favourable conditions of competition for like service suppliers of Complainants' origin and is therefore inconsistent with the requirements of Article II of GATS.

- the allocation of hurricane licences exclusively to operators who include or directly represent EC producers creates less favourable conditions of competition for like service suppliers of Complainants' origin and is therefore inconsistent with the requirements of Article XVII of GATS.

- the allocation of hurricane licences exclusively to operators who include or directly represent ACP producers creates less favourable conditions of competition for like service suppliers of Complainants' origin and is therefore inconsistent with the requirements of Article II of GATS.

VIII. FINAL REMARKS

8.1 The procedures under the DSU serve to ensure the settlement of disputes among WTO Members in accordance with WTO obligations, not to add to or diminish these obligations. Accordingly, our terms of reference are to assist the DSB in reaching conclusions with regard to the legal consistency with WTO rules of the EC's common market organization for bananas.

8.2 Throughout our proceedings we were aware of the economic and social effects of the EC measures at issue in this case, particularly for the ACP and the Latin American banana exporting countries. In recognizing this, we decided to grant third parties participatory rights in our proceedings which were substantially broader than those normally afforded to them under the DSU.

8.3 From a substantive perspective, the fundamental principles of the WTO and WTO rules are designed to foster the development of countries, not impede it. Having heard the arguments of a large number of Members interested in this case and having worked through a complex set of claims under several WTO agreements, we conclude that the system is flexible enough to allow, through WTO-consistent trade and non-trade measures, appropriate policy responses in the wide variety of circumstances across countries, including countries that are currently heavily dependent on the production and commercialization of bananas.

IX. CONCLUSIONS

9.1 The Panel concludes that for the reasons outlined in this Report aspects of the European Communities' import regime for bananas are inconsistent with its obligations under Articles I:1, III:4, X:3 and XIII:1 of GATT, Article 1.2 of the Licensing Agreement and Articles II and XVII of the GATS. These conclusions are also described briefly in the summary of findings.

9.2 The Panel recommends that the Dispute Settlement Body request the European Communities to bring its import regime for bananas into conformity with its obligations under GATT, the Licensing Agreement and the GATS.

TABLES

TABLE I

OVERVIEW OF DISPUTE SETTLEMENT ACTIVITY

The following is a summary of dispute settlement activity from February 26, 1997 through May 31, 1997.

WT/DS13	European Communities – Duties on Imports of Grains Complainant: United States Action: Request for Panel withdrawn April 30, 1997
WT/DS16 WT/DS27	European Communities – Regime for the Importation, Sale and Distribution of Bananas Complainants: Ecuador, Guatemala, Honduras, Mexico, United States Action: Panel Report issued May 22, 1997
WT/DS18	Australia – Measures Affecting the Importation of Salmon Complainant: Canada Action: Panel established April 10, 1997
WT/DS22	Brazil – Measures Affecting Desiccated Coconut Complainant: Philippines Action: Appellate Body Report adopted March 20, 1997
WT/DS23	Venezuela – Anti-Dumping Investigation in Respect of Imports in Certain Oil Industry Tubular Goods Complainant: Mexico Action: Notification of terminated anti-dumping investigation received May 6, 1997
WT/DS27	See WT/DS16
WT/DS31	Canada – Certain Measures Concerning Periodicals Complainant: United States Action: Panel Report issued March 14, 1997 Canada notified appeal April 29, 1997
WT/DS33	United States – Measures Affecting Imports of Woven Wool Shirts and Blouses Complainant: India Action: Appellate Body Report adopted May 23, 1997
WT/DS38	United States – The Cuban Liberty and Democratic Solidarity Act Complainant: European Communities Action: Panel suspended upon request of European Communities April 21, 1997
WT/DS54	Indonesia – Certain Measures Affecting the Automobile Industry Complainant: European Communities Action: Panel requested May 12, 1997 * See WT/DS55, DS64

TABLE I – DISPUTE SETTLEMENT ACTIVITY

WT/DS55 Indonesia – Certain Measures Affecting the Automobile Industry
Complainant: Japan
Action: Panel requested May 12, 1997
* See WT/DS54, DS64

WT/DS58 United States – Import Prohibition of Certain Shrimp and Shrimp Products
Complainants: India, Malaysia, Pakistan, Thailand
Action: Panel request of India granted, included in panel established under DS58

WT/DS60 Guatemala – Anti-Dumping Investigation Regarding Imports of Portland Cement from Mexico
Complainant: Mexico
Action: Panel established March 20, 1997

WT/DS64 Indonesia – Certain Measures Affecting the Automobile Industry
Complainant: Japan
Action: Panel requested May 12, 1997
* See WT/DS54, DS55

WT/DS67 United Kingdom – Customs Classification of Certain Computer Equipment
Complainant: United States
Action: Incorporated into WT/DS62 Panel March 20, 1997
* See WT/DS68

WT/DS68 Ireland – Customs Classification of Certain Computer Equipment
Complainant: United States
Action: Incorporated into WT/DS62 Panel March 20, 1997
* See WT/DS67

WT/DS70 Canada – Measures Affecting the Export of Civilian Aircraft
WT/DS71 Complainant: Brazil
Action: Consultations requested March 10, 1997

WT/DS72 European Communities – Measures Affecting Butter Products
Complainant: New Zealand
Action: Consultations requested March 24, 1997

WT/DS73/1 Japan – Procurement of a Navigation Satellite
Complainant: European Communities
Action: Consultations requested March 26, 1997

WT/DS74/1 Philippines – Measures Affecting Pork and Poultry
Complainant: United States
Action: Consultations requested April 1, 1997

WT/DS75/1 Korea – Taxes on Alcoholic Beverages
Complainant: European Communities
Action: Consultations requested April 4, 1997
* See WT/DS84/1

WT/DS76/1 Japan – Measures Affecting Agricultural Products
Complainant: United States
Action: Consultations requested April 7, 1997

WT/DS77/1 Argentina – Measures Affecting Textiles and Clothing
Complainant: European Communities
Action: Consultations requested April 17, 1997

WT/DS78/1 United States – Safeguard Measure Against Imports of Broom Corn Brooms
Complainant: Columbia
Action: Consultations requested April 28, 1997

WT/DS79/1 India – Patent Protection for Pharmaceutical and Agricultural Chemical Products
Complainant: European Communities
Action: Consultations requested April 28, 1997

WT/DS80/1 Belgium – Measures Affecting Commercial Telephone Directory Services
Complainant: United States
Action: Consultations requested May 2, 1997

WT/DS82/1 Ireland – Measures Affecting the Grant of Copyright and Neighbouring Rights
Complainant: United States
Action: Consultations requested May 14, 1997

WT/DS83/1 Denmark – Measures Affecting the Enforcement of Intellectual Property Rights
Complainant: United States
Action: Consultations requested May 14, 1997

WT/DS84/1 Korea – Taxes on Alcoholic Beverages
Complainant: United States
Action: Consultations requested May 23, 1997
* See WT.DS75/1

WT/DS85/1 United States – Measures Affecting Textiles and Apparel Products
Complainant: European Communities
Action: Consultations requested May 23,1997

WT/DS86/1 Sweden – Measures Affecting the Enforcement of Intellectual Property Rights
Complainant: United States
Action: Consultations requested May 28, 1997

TABLE II

MEMBER COUNTRIES – INVOLVEMENT IN DISPUTES

As of May 31, 1997, the following Member Countries have been involved in the following disputes.

Argentina (3)	WT/DS35, WT/DS56, WT/DS77/1
Australia (3)	WT/DS18, WT/DS21, WT/DS35
Belgium	WT/DS80/1
Brazil (10)	WT/DS4, WT/DS22, WT/DS30, WT/DS46, WT/DS51, WT/DS52, WT/DS65, WT/DS69, WT/DS70, WT/DS71
Canada (11)	WT/DS7, WT/DS9, WT/DS10, WT/DS18, WT/DS20, WT/DS31, WT/DS35, WT/DS46, WT/DS48, WT/DS70, WT/DS71
Chile	WT/DS14
Columbia	WT/DS78/1
Costa Rica	WT/DS24
Denmark	WT/DS83/1
Ecuador	WT/DS27
European Communities (29)	WT/DS7, WT/DS8, WT/DS9, WT/DS12, WT/DS13, WT/DS14, WT/DS15, WT/DS16, WT/DS17, WT/DS25, WT/DS26, WT/DS27, WT/DS38, WT/DS39, WT/DS40, WT/DS42, WT/DS48, WT/DS53, WT/DS54, WT/DS62, WT/DS63, WT/DS66, WT/DS69, WT/DS72, WT/DS73/1, WT/DS75/1, WT/DS77/1, WT/DS79/1, WT/DS85/1
Guatemala (2)	WT/DS16, WT/DS60
Honduras	WT/DS16
Hong Kong	WT/DS29
Hungary	WT/DS35
India (6)	WT/DS19, WT/DS32, WT/DS33, WT/DS34, WT/DS50, WT/DS79/1
Indonesia (4)	WT/DS54, WT/DS55, WT/DS59, WT/DS64

TABLE II - COUNTRIES

Ireland (2)	WT/DS68, WT/DS82/1
Japan (15)	WT/DS6, WT/DS8, WT/DS10, WT/DS11, WT/DS15, WT/DS28, WT/DS42, WT/DS44, WT/DS45, WT/DS51, WT/DS55, WT/DS64, WT/DS66, WT/DS73/1, WT/DS76/1
Korea (7)	WT/DS3, WT/DS5, WT/DS20, WT/DS40, WT/DS41, WT/DS75/1, WT/DS84/1
Malaysia (2)	WT/DS1, WT/DS58
Mexico (5)	WT/DS16, WT/DS23, WT/DS49, WT/DS53, WT/DS60
New Zealand (2)	WT/DS35, WT/DS72
Pakistan	WT/DS36
Peru	WT/DS12
Philippines (3)	WT/DS22, WT/DS61, WT/DS74/1
Poland	WT/DS19
Portugal	WT/DS37
Singapore	WT/DS1
Sri Lanka	WT/DS30
Sweden	WT/DS86/1
Thailand (4)	WT/DS17, WT/DS35, WT/DS47, WT/DS58
Turkey (4)	WT/DS29, WT/DS34, WT/DS43, WT/DS47
United Kingdom	WT/DS67
United States (45)	WT/DS2, WT/DS3, WT/DS4, WT/DS5, WT/DS6, WT/DS11, WT/DS13, WT/DS16, WT/DS21, WT/DS24, WT/DS26, WT/DS28, WT/DS31, WT/DS32, WT/DS33, WT/DS35, WT/DS36, WT/DS37, WT/DS38, WT/DS39, WT/DS41, WT/DS43, WT/DS44, WT/DS45, WT/DS49, WT/DS50, WT/DS52, WT/DS56, WT/DS58, WT/DS59, WT/DS61, WT/DS62, WT/DS63, WT/DS65, WT/DS67, WT/DS68, WT/DS74/1, WT/DS76/1, WT/DS78/1, WT/DS80/1, WT/DS82/1, WT/DS83/1, WT/DS84/1, WT/DS85/1, WT/DS86/1
Uruguay	WT/DS25
Venezuela (2)	WT/DS2, WT/DS23

TABLE III

TREATY PROVISIONS INTERPRETED

The following is a table of treaty provisions interpreted by the Dispute Settlement Decisions included within this volume. Treatment of the particular provision of the agreement will be found starting at the paragraph number indicated adjacent to the case citation.

GENERAL AGREEMENT ON TARIFFS AND TRADE

Article I – General Most-Favoured-Nation Treatment
Paragraph 1: "Any advantage, favour, privilege or immunity"

European Communities – Bananas WT/DS27/R, 7.131-136, 7.188-204, 7.220-223, 7.235-241, 7.251-259

Article II – Schedules of Concessions
In General

European Communities – Bananas WT/DS27/R, 7.112-118

Article III – National Treatment on Internal Taxation and Regulation
Paragraph 2: "Like products"

Canada – Periodicals WT/DS31/R, 5.20-30

Paragraph 4: "Governmental"

Canada – Periodicals WT/DS31/R, 5.31-39

"Treatment no less favourable"

European Communities – Bananas WT/DS27/R, 7.171-182, 7.216-219, 7.244-250

Paragraph 8(d): "Subsidies to domestic producers"

Canada – Periodicals WT/DS31/R, 5.40-44

Article X – Publication and Administration of Trade Regulations
Paragraph 3(a): "A uniform, impartial and reasonable manner"

European Communities – Bananas WT/DS27/R, 7.205-212, 7.224-231

Article XI – General Elimination of Quantitative Restrictions

Paragraph 1: "Prohibitions or restrictions other than duties, taxes or other charges"

Canada – Periodicals WT/DS31/R, 5.5-5.8

Article XIII – Non-Discriminatory Administration of Quantitative Restrictions

In General

European Communities – Bananas WT/DS27/R, 7.64-118

Paragraph 1: "Similarly prohibited or restricted"

European Communities – Bananas WT/DS27/R, 7.73-82, 7.85-90

"All third countries"

European Communities – Bananas WT/DS27/R, 7.85-90

Paragraph 2(d): "Aim at distribution of trade"

European Communities – Bananas WT/DS27/R, 7.70-94

"Allocation of quotas"

European Communities – Bananas WT/DS27/R, 7.70-94

Paragraph 4

European Communities – Bananas WT/DS27/R, 7.91-93

Paragraph 5: "Tariff quota regimes"

European Communities – Bananas WT/DS27/R, 7.78-82

Article XX – General Exceptions

Paragraph (d): "Secure compliance"

Canada – Periodicals WT/DS31/R, 5.9-5.11

AGREEMENT ON AGRICULTURE

Article 4 – Market Access

European Communities – Bananas WT/DS27/R, 7.120-127

Article 21 – Final Provisions

European Communities – Bananas WT/DS27/R, 7.120-127

AGREEMENT ON IMPORT LICENSING PROCEDURES

In General

European Communities – Bananas WT/DS27/R, 7.145-156

Article 1 – General Provisions
Paragraph 2

European Communities – Bananas WT/DS27/R, 7.267-273

Paragraph 3

European Communities – Bananas WT/DS27/R, 7.260-264

Article 3 – Non-Automatic Import Licensing
Paragraph 2

European Communities – Bananas WT/DS27/R, 7.265-266

Paragraph 5

European Communities – Bananas WT/DS27/R, 7.265-266

AGREEMENT ON TEXTILES AND CLOTHING

Article 6

United States – Wool Shirts and Blouses WT/DS33/AB/R, 4.1-13

DISPUTE SETTLEMENT UNDERSTANDING

Article 3 – General Provisions

European Communities – Bananas WT/DS27/R, 7.47-52

Article 4 – Consultations

European Communities – Bananas WT/DS27/R, 7.17-21

Article 6 – Establishment of Panels
Paragraph 2

European Communities – Bananas WT/DS27/R, 7.22-46

Article 9 – Procedures for Multiple Complainants

European Communities – Bananas WT/DS27/R, 7-53-58

Article 10 – Third Parties

European Communities – Bananas WT/DS27/R, 7.4-7.9

Article 11 – Function of Panels

United States – Wool Shirts and Blouses WT/DS33/AB/R, 6.1-6.9

Article 15 – Interim Review Stage

European Communities – Bananas WT/DS27/R, 7.9

Appendix 3 – Working Procedures

Paragraphs 2 & 3

European Communities – Bananas WT/DS27/R, 7.10-12

GENERAL AGREEMENT ON TRADE IN SERVICES

In General

European Communities – Bananas WT/DS27/R, 7.274-293

Article II – Most-Favoured Nation Treatment

European Communities – Bananas WT/DS27/R, 7.294-304, 7.342-352, 7.369-372, 7.381-385, 7.394-397

Article XVII – National Treatment

European Communities – Bananas WT/DS27/R, 7.294-297, 7.305-341, 7.355-368, 7.375-380, 7.389-393

TABLE IV
BISD AND DISPUTE REFERENCES

The following table shows references to Basic Instruments and Selected Documents (BISD), and WTO and other disputes made by the Panels and Appellate Body in their opinion. On the right is the location of the reference (noted by paragraph number) in the report.

WT/DS33/AB/R

BISD II/188 *4.8*
The Australian Subsidy on Ammonium Sulphate

BISD 1S/53 *4.8*
Treatment by Germany of Imports of Sardines

BISD 25S/49 *4.9*
EEC - Measures on Animal Feed Proteins

BISD 27S/69 *4.9*
European Communities - Refunds on Exports of Sugar, Complaint by Brazil

BISD 30S/129 *6.3*
EEC - Quantitative Restrictions Against Imports of Certain Products from Hong Kong

BISD 30S/140 *4.9*
Canada, Administration of the Foreign Investment Review Act

BISD 31S/67 *6.3*
United States - Imports of Sugar from Nicaragua

BISD 31S/74 *6.3*
United States - Manufacturing Clause

BISD 31S/94 *6.3*
Japan - Measures on Imports of Leather

BISD 32S/245 *4.11*
United States - Customs User Fee

BISD 35S/116 *6.3*
Japan - Trade in Semi-Conductors

BISD 35S/163 *4.11*
Japan - Restriction on Certain Agricultural Products

BISD 36S/167 *4.9*
Japan - Tariff on Import of Spruce, Pine, Fir (SPF) Dimension Lumber

BISD	36S/68	*4.11*
EEC - Restrictions on Imports of Dessert Apples, Complaint by Chile		
BISD	36S/68	*4.11*
Canada - Import Restrictions on Ice Cream and Yoghurt		
BISD	37S/132	*6.3*
EEC - Regulations on Imports of Parts and Components		
BISD	39S/128	*6.3*
United States - Non-Rubber Footwear		
BISD	39S/206	*4.11*
United States - Measures Affecting Alcoholic and Malt Beverages		
BISD	39S/27	*4.10*
Canada - Import, Distribution and Sale of Certain Alcoholic Drinks by Provincial Marketing Agencies		
WTO DSD	WT/DS2/AB/R	*2.20*
United States - Standards for Reformulated and Conventional Gasoline		
WTO DSD	WT/DS8/AB/R	*2.25*
Japan - Taxes on Alcoholic Beverages		
WTO DSD	WT/DS24/R	*2.4*
United States - Restrictions on Imports of Cotton and Man-Made Fibre Underwear		
WTO DSD	WT/DS24/AB/R	*2.28*
Brazil - Measures Affecting Desiccated Coconut		
WTO DSD	WT/DS24/AB/R	*2.22*
United States - Restrictions on Imports of Cotton and Man-Made Fibre Underwear		
Unpublished	DS44/R	*4.10*
United States - Measures Affecting the Importation, Internal Sale and Use of Tobacco		

WT/DS31/R

BISD	II/181	*3.58*
Brazilian Internal Taxes		
BISD	7S/64	*3.148*
Italian Discrimination Against Agricultural Machinery		
BISD	18S/97	*3.77*
Border Tax Adjustments		
BISD	29S/91	*3.21*
United States - Probition on Imports of Tuna and Tuna Products from Canada		
BISD	30S/107	*3.21*
United States - Imports of Certain Automotice Spring Assemblies		
BISD	30S/140	*3.147*
Canada - Administration of the Foreign Investment Review Act		
BISD	34S/136	*3.58*
United States - Taxes on Petroleum and Certain Imported Substances		

WT/DS27/R

TABLE IV – BISD AND DISPUTE REFERENCES

TABLE IV – BISD AND DISPUTE REFERENCES

BISD 39S/206 — *4.54*
United States - Measures Affecting Alcoholic and Malt Beverages

WTO DSD WT/DS2/AB/R — *4.350*
United States - Standards for Reformulated and Conventional Gasoline

WTO DSD WT/DS8/R — *7.180*
Japan - Taxes on Alcoholic Beverages

WTO DSD WT/DS8/AB/R — *7.114*
Japan - Taxes on Alcoholic Beverages

WTO DSD WT/DS22/R — *7.40*
Brazil - Measures Affecting Desiccated Coconut

WTO DSD WT/DS22/AB/R — *7.26*
Brazil - Measures Affecting Desiccated Coconut

WTO DSD WT/DS33/AB/R — *7.32*
United States - Restrictions on Imports of Woven Wool Shirts and Blouses from India

WTO DSD WT/DS31/R — *7.283*
Canada - Certain Measures Concerning Periodicals

Unadopted DS29/R — *2.34*
United States - Restrictions on Imports of Tuna

Unadopted DS32/R — *4.97*
EEC - Production Aids Granted on Canned Peaches, Canned Pears, Canned Fruit Cocktail and Dried Grapes

Unadopted DS38/R
EEC - Import Regime for Bananas

Unadopted L/5776 — *7.5*
EEC - Tariff Treatment on Imports of Citrus Products from Certain Countries in the Mediterranean Region

Unpublished ADP/136 — *2.10*
United States - Imposition of Anti-Dumping Duties on Imports of Fresh and Chilled Atlantic Salmon from Norway

Unpublished ADP/137 — *7.42*
European Communities - Imposition of Anti-Dumping Duties on Imports of Cotton Yarn from Brazil

INDEX

INDEX

C

CANADA

CERTAIN MEASURES CONCERNING PERIODICALS

MEASURE AFFECTING IMPORTS OF WOVEN WOOL SHIRTS AND BLOUSES FROM INDIA

MEASURES CONCERNING PERIODICALS

MEXICO

MULTIPLE COMPLAINANTS

INDEX

REGULATIONS